THE LAND BEYOND THE MISTS

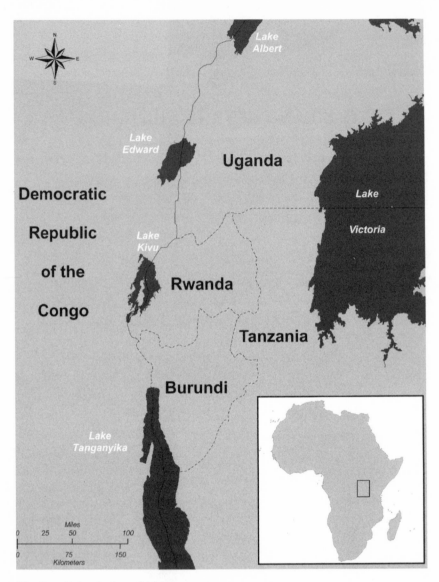

The Great Lakes Region of Africa

The Land beyond the Mists

ESSAYS ON IDENTITY AND AUTHORITY
IN PRECOLONIAL CONGO AND RWANDA

David Newbury

Foreword by Jan Vansina

OHIO UNIVERSITY PRESS

ATHENS

Ohio University Press, Athens, Ohio 45701
www.ohioswallow.com
© 2009 by Ohio University Press
All rights reserved

Printed in the United States of America
Ohio University Press books are printed on acid-free paper ⊗ ™

16 15 14 13 12 11 10 09   5 4 3 2 1

Library of Congress Cataloging-in-Publication Data

Newbury, David S.
  The land beyond the mists : essays on identity and authority in precolonial Congo and
Rwanda / David Newbury ; foreword by Jan Vansina.
     p. cm.
  Includes bibliographical references and index.
  ISBN 978-0-8214-1874-1 (cloth : alk. paper) — ISBN 978-0-8214-1875-8 (pbk. : alk. paper)
  1. Kivu, Lake, Region (Congo and Rwanda)—History. 2. Kivu, Lake, Region (Congo
and Rwanda)—Historiography. 3. Ethnology—Kivu, Lake, Region (Congo and Rwanda)
4. Congo (Democratic Republic)—History. 5. Congo (Democratic Republic)—
Historiography. 6. Ethnology—Congo (Democratic Republic) 7. Rwanda—History.
8. Rwanda—Historiography. 9. Ethnology—Rwanda. I. Title.
  DT665.K58N49 2009
  967.5'71—dc22

2009021935

For the people of Central Africa,
whose stories (and histories) these are.

And for Cathy,
who was always there.

CONTENTS

Contents

Part 4. Perceiving History through the Mists

ILLUSTRATIONS

Maps

Figures

Tables

FOREWORD

BETWEEN THE LOWLANDS of Central Africa, with their seemingly endless
equatorial forests, and the open landscapes on the seemingly endless undulating
plateaus of East Africa, there lies a dramatic seam, a huge valley filled with a few
big lakes, flanked by high mountain chains and marked by a few spectacular volcanoes. The history and cultures of the dense populations that lie athwart this
seam and provide the junction between two such different portions of Africa
have fascinated and preoccupied David Newbury for almost forty years now, especially those that lie on either side of Lake Kivu. The lake is bordered on its east
side by modern Rwanda and on the west by the two Kivu provinces of modern
Congo. Unfortunately, anyone with even the most superficial interest in Africa
knows that the lands around Lake Kivu have been the cockpit of violence in the
middle of Africa since 1994, when the genocide in Rwanda in 1994 began, followed by the continuing devastation in Kivu that began two years later. However,
this situation did not arise overnight. Rather, it was the outcome of several centuries of historical developments, and anyone who wants to understand the present situation in this region would do well to read this book, as it is the only overall
introduction to the history of that region.

It was Rwanda that first attracted the Newburys to this region in the 1960s,
Catharine as a political scientist and David as a historian, mainly because it had
just become painfully evident during the country's turbulent march to independence in 1962 that the relatively large and influential sociological and historical literature concerning the country was based on flawed colonial premises.[1] Yet
in colonial times, that same historiography and the conclusions of social anthropologists concerning Rwanda had been held up as the acme of scholarship—as
models to be followed anywhere else in the whole region. But before independence, very few scholarly studies had been carried out in the Kivu province, and
given the strength of the Rwanda model, many were practically worthless.

This was the context that David Newbury found as he started a quest he has
pursued ever since, as reflected in this book. His aim was (and still is) not merely
to uncover and understand the empirical evidence about what happened over
several past centuries, but to apply a rigorous analytic approach to this evidence in
order to lay the groundwork for a trustworthy history that is solidly grounded
in sociological reality and yields a sophisticated history of everyone's past, not just
that of political leaders. It is the equal of the most sophisticated studies elsewhere

in African history, not only because it is always informed by the existing social science theories but even more because history rests on fundamental concepts that have been carefully scrutinized and probed rather than merely assumed. Thus in his writings, for example, we will not find any thoughtless phrases about "atavistic tribal (ethnic) hatreds" still so beloved by passing journalists. Instead one finds carefully worked out analyses of the construction and the dynamics of social identities.

From his ceaseless grappling with the thorny issues so crucial to interpreting the social history of these regions, he has acquired the experience and the skills that have made him one of the best-known and most influential scholars on theory in African history generally. Thus, for example, his article "The Clans of Rwanda" (chapter 8) was a bombshell when it appeared in 1980 because it proved in an utterly convincing way that even such apparently perennial kinship groupings as clans were anything but static institutions. They were always changing and always reacting to larger political contexts.

The book now before you bundles a set of essays that trace Newbury's intellectual journey from the early days battling against colonial stereotypes to his recent vision of the overall outlines of the historical dynamics in the whole Kivu Rift area during the last few centuries. The chapters deal with a wide array of themes, ranging from surveys of the historical literature, to trade as a link and conduit between cultures, to parallel oral sources, to the politics of war, to the limitations of colonial power, to the mutations of kinship groups, to identities at court and the creation of a despised "other," to sacral kingship as cultural epitome, to the management of political memory and then to a conclusion that weaves all these themes and more together into a single tapestry showing us a multitude of actors shaping their ever-changing societies.

The great variety of the themes and their progression over time included in this book, as well as its emphasis on social history, are also representative of the trajectory followed by academic historiography in the whole region and beyond. Indeed, to a surprising extent the succession of essays in this work can stand as a faithful exemplar of the trajectory by which the professional literature about African history in the tropics has matured over half a century now, a maturity that could only be achieved by the slow accumulation of experience gained by persistent study over a lifetime of study. As readers of these essays will soon discover, there are no shortcuts to gaining the kind or depth of insights that are reached in this volume, and in the last instance those insights are the gems they will treasure.

Jan Vansina
Vilas Professor of History
University of Wisconsin

PREFACE

THE HIGHLAND AREAS at the center of Africa had long been neglected by the rest of the world. That changed from the 1990s. Drawn by the moral imperatives of multiple catastrophes, many outsiders have since then become aware of—indeed, deeply involved with—the peoples of this fascinating and beautiful region. However, because many such visitors were new to the field, they arrived with but minimal acquaintance with the social configurations and little understanding of the broader historical trends of this region.

These essays respond to that dilemma. They seek to remind us that there were indeed histories before the cataclysms of the late twentieth century, and that many aspects of these pasts have been explored. Indeed, since decolonization in the early 1960s, an enormous outpouring of work, by Congolese and Rwandan historians as well as by outside researchers, has radically reconfigured our understanding of the political, social, and cultural developments that marked the region.

As a minuscule sample of such work, this collection of essays has three main goals. One is to make available work often no longer accessible. A second is to illustrate the type of analysis necessary to understand historical dynamics in an area with limited archives. A third, more important goal is to explore the character of local agency that is the grounding of history in the region: even in the most neglected corners of this least-known of continents, careful work can illuminate the historical processes that characterized this area and the people who engaged in these processes—those who made history happen, and who continue to do so.

In a real sense, this is a work of salvage, for many of these essays originally appeared in journals now discontinued. More important, many of the issues explored here have been marginalized by more immediate preoccupations in a context where historical perspectives are sometimes seen as irrelevant. But if outsiders are unaware of these issues, local people are not: walking away from them—pretending that they don't exist, or that they don't matter—will not resolve the tensions that sometimes stem from such unresolved histories embedded in the collective memory of the people of the Rift. In fact, to some degree historical inquiry is just another way of grappling with unresolved issues from the past, in part by revealing the contexts within which people lived out their lives. Therefore, informed historical understanding can be seen as an integral part of addressing contemporary tensions. Furthermore, part of historical method is to recognize the integrity of multiple perspectives—and the consequences of

personal actions (one's own, as well as those of others). These are common parameters of historical method, but they also apply to the process of reconciliation.

Therefore, this is also salvage work on a method: a call for a rigorous analytic approach to our understanding of empirical representations, in part to provide historical perspective for contemporary concerns, and in part to confront the
continual promulgation of official truths—whether dynastic, colonial, or contemporary. For if historically informed work is essential to the foundations of enduring reconciliation, it must also be independent of the political process; intellectual
authority can coincide with political authority, but the two are not necessarily
synonymous. So even if their content may at first glance seem remote from current concerns, these essays can be seen as a reminder of critical methodological
foundations—and therefore directly relevant to contemporary concerns.

I am grateful to those who have encouraged the republication of these essays
—and who made such a project possible. But I am especially grateful to the hundreds of Central Africans who supported, guided, and assisted with this work: in
more ways than one, these are their histories.

I am grateful to the editors and publishers of the following journals and collections for permission to reprint work that first appeared therein:

    Africa, for "The Clans of Rwanda: An Historical Hypothesis," 50, no. 4 (1980):
        389–403;

    Africa-Tervuren, for "What Role Has Kingship? An Analysis of the *Umuganura* Rit-
        ual of Rwanda as Presented in M. d'Hertefelt and A. Coupez, *La royauté sacrée
        de l'ancien Rwanda,*" 27, no. 4 (1981): 89–101;

    Cahiers d'Études Africaines, for "Les campaigns de Rwabugiri: Chronologie et bibli-
        ographie," 14, no. 1 (1974): 181–91;

    Études d'Histoire Africaine, for "Rwabugiri and Ijwi," 7 (1975): 155–73;

    History in Africa, for "Bushi and the Historians: Historiographical Themes in East-
        ern Kivu," 5 (1978): 131–51;

      "Recent Historical Research in the Area of Lake Kivu," 7 (1980): 23–45; and

      "Trick Cyclists? Recontextualizing Rwandan Dynastic Chronology," 21 (1994):
        191–217;

    Indiana University Press, for "Bunyabungo: The Western Frontier in Rwanda," in
        The African Frontier: The Reproduction of Traditional African Societies, ed. Igor
        Kopytoff (Bloomington: 1987), 162–92;

    International Journal of African Historical Studies, for "King and Chief: Colonial Pol-
        itics on Ijwi Island," 15, no. 2 (1982): 221–46; and

      "Precolonial Burundi and Rwanda: Local Loyalties, Regional Royalties," 34, no. 2
        (2001): 255–314;

    Journal des Africanistes, for "Lake Kivu Regional Trade in the Nineteenth Century,"
        50, no. 2 (1980): 6–30;

    Les Cahiers du CEDAF, for "Kamo and Lubambo: Dual Genesis Traditions on Ijwi Is-
        land," 5 (1979): 1–47.

ACKNOWLEDGMENTS

FRIENDSHIP IS LIKE a river—fed by multiple springs, streams, and sluices that combine in ways that are always changing, always forming anew. In their growth and development, the original sources may seem indistinguishable, but they remain essential to the shape and power of the flow.

So, too, are the friendships that have gone into forty years of reflection on the people and patterns represented in these essays. What ultimately takes the form of print on a page is in fact simply a distillation of the inspiration and information I have received from many colleagues on three continents. I relish their engagement with the issues, I cherish their friendship, and I salute their patience with an errant colleague. I hope they know how grateful I am, and I ask their understanding—once more—if I cannot cite each individually here.

But a work is more than just collecting one's thoughts and honing one's understanding in conversation with others. It is also a production process, and I take pleasure in thanking—again—those who have helped with the process. Projet Ntaganda and his wife Léocadie first guided me to Ijwi Island, and over many years Projet's family has smoothed the way—as they continue to do today, providing crucial pathways of support to our ties to the island; Mirindi Bahali Janvier, Alphonsine, Poncelet, and Friand have all been very helpful. On Ijwi, Ntambuka Barhahakana and his son Pascal and grandson Roger made (and continue to make) the research possible and pleasurable. Members of two other families have been equally hospitable in many ways and over many years: the Balegamire family (Jean Marie and Gérance among them) and the Mudahama family (Zacharie and Césaire, among others). In Rwanda, Joseph Rwabukumba was crucial. He was not only a colleague but also an inspiration. His death in April 1994 was a deeply tragic loss; I miss him still today. Over many years, hundreds of colleagues in these beautiful if benighted lands have welcomed and guided and sustained Catharine and me—sometimes through difficult times—and we are acutely aware of their help.

Colleagues and teachers and friends in many institutions in Africa and North America have also shaped my work. Jan Vansina stands out as a friend over many years. I'm grateful to Smith College and to Barbara Olin Taylor for material support in preparing this collection—and to my students in several institutions for never failing to challenge me. Thanks also to Mollie Gabriel and Jon Caris for their expert help with the maps.

No one could ask for a better editor than Gillian Berchowitz at Ohio University Press. Gill is more than an editor; she has been a friend whose patience and good counsel made the process enjoyable. Rick Huard was a pleasure to work with and a pro in his own right.

But Catharine and Elizabeth have been the major influences in my life. Having walked farther than they bargained for, having slept in places they never imagined, and having consumed foods they hadn't expected—and done it all with good grace, and even (mostly) with gusto—they are proof that our friendships are really extensions of our selves. Their love sustains me and challenges me and humbles me.

THE LAND BEYOND THE MISTS

INTRODUCTION

Peering through the Mists

RWANDAN TRADITIONS SOMETIMES refer to the islands in Lake Kivu as "the land beyond the mists." Indeed, morning mists are common in this area, and when they arrive they affect our vision of the landforms in interesting ways. Through the mists we see those lands only dimly and in altered configurations: there is mystery in the mists, and intrigue in their changing artistry. But the phrase is not only a meteorological description of the lake at dawn: it is also a metaphor. It refers not just to a transitory moment but also to an understanding of culture and of history. For the past, too, is "a land beyond the mists," and the metaphor perfectly captures our vision of history in this area.

This collection refers to the lands contiguous to Lake Kivu, a beautiful highland lake in the western Rift Valley of Central Africa that today forms the boundary between Rwanda and the Democratic Republic of the Congo. On each side of the lake, the terrain rises sharply—in some places to five thousand feet or more above the lake surface. Across the summits to the west, the land descends into the vast Congo River basin, and the waters draining from the western slopes of these mountains eventually flow into the Atlantic. (By a more circuitous route, so too do the waters of Lake Kivu itself, first flowing south into Lake Tanganyika, then west into the Congo River, and eventually through the great arc of the Congo to the Atlantic.) To the east of Lake Kivu the mountains form the Congo-Nile watershed; beyond that divide the mountainous terrain first dissolves

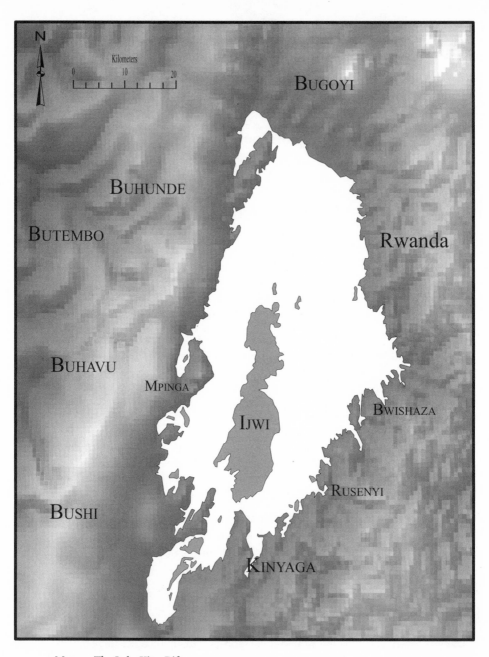

Map 1.1. The Lake Kivu Rift

into a plethora of rolling hills—the characteristic landform of central Rwanda —and then gradually opens onto the grasslands on both sides of the north-flowing arm of the Kagera River (see map I.1). From there the waters flow into Lake Victoria and eventually to the Mediterranean.

But in addition to serving as a hydrological divide, the Kivu Rift Valley also serves as a cultural divide distinguishing two vast culture zones: to the west are the forest cultures of the Congo basin; to the east, the highland states of the Great Lakes cultures. Yet this cultural divide is not definitive: historically, as still today, the islands in Lake Kivu and the lakeside communities on both sides of the lake saw much interaction with both forest cultures and highland states, and those interactions took place at many levels—political, economic, social, military, religious, and cultural. Indeed, before the nineteenth century the peoples of the Rift Valley formed an intensely interactive community of their own, and right through colonial rule the Rift's kaleidoscopic history vastly complicated the efforts by both African and European authorities to define precise political boundaries, where before there existed only ambiguous cultural frontiers. In short, around Lake Kivu the Rift Valley formed what some scholars refer to as a "middle ground"—a meeting place of many cultures, dynamic in themselves and fluid in their interaction.

The concept of a "middle ground" expands our vision and raises important questions of how we understand social process. Many states were involved in this region over the last two hundred years—but this book is not primarily about states. Human settlement here covers at least three thousand years—but this book is not about enduring social patterns. Distinct forms of political hierarchy marked this region—but this book does not adopt the vision of powerholders alone. Instead, these essays question assumptions of power, they dissolve the durability of social forms, and they temper ideologies with lived experience. While empirical data are essential to historical analysis (and we will engage with many individuals and events), this is not a simple narrative. Rather, these collected essays are about concepts—about decentering our vision of social dynamics in a region where in the past outsiders' focus on the "center" has been so important.

These essays provide diverse entry points to social formations where lived experiences took many forms. Their purpose is to place in historical context the protean character of the institutions and mental constructs that observers often assume to be fixed and permanent. We will explore the nature of frontiers, not boundaries; of personal experiences, not state histories; of multiple agency, not defining centers of historical legitimacy; and of local initiatives, not only central policies. While state power was important in this area, most people, most of the time, were not preoccupied with court politics or with state norms; their lives were lived outside of those familiar institutions that outsiders rely on to structure their knowledge. To understand their lives, therefore, we, too, need to venture beyond the conventional lines of inquiry to ask different questions, and to adopt different perspectives on conventional topics.

In fact, adopting the perspective of the middle ground accords more closely to the empirical record, for in this area, even with the arrival of competing colonial powers (Germany, Britain, and the agents of Leopold II of Belgium), the political boundaries were contested. And well they might have been, for in cultural terms, these heterogeneous societies were never bounded. Social networks and even political loyalties were never clearly distinct—and when such distinctions were defined by one party or another, it was not for very long: clear-cut political distinctions in this area were fleeting phenomena.

But that is not to say the inhabitants lived without cultures of their own; it is only to suggest that these were self-created and locally generated identities. Nestled between the Mitumba Mountains to the west (in what is now Congo) and the Congo-Nile divide to the east (in what is now Rwanda), the people of the Rift Valley had carved out ambiguous relationships to larger cultural units— and often found that there were benefits in cultural ambiguity. Nonetheless, there were drawbacks: such ambiguous relations at times implied contested relations. Well into the nineteenth century, for example, the royal court of Rwanda had an unsure presence in regions of this lacustrine littoral in what is now western Rwanda (including the areas of Kinyaga, Rusenyi, Bwishaza, Budaha, and Bugoyi). Whatever court presence existed remained superficial, and this condition persisted right up to the reign of Rwanda's powerful king Rwabugiri, in the late nineteenth century.

But from at least the late eighteenth century there were state overtures into these frontier regions. Indeed, the fertile lands on the eastern shores of Lake Kivu provided an area of intense interest for Rwandan expansion, and Rwabugiri was the military exemplar who most represented that expansionist vision: his presence—and his armies—dominated the region in the last half of the nineteenth century. He began his renowned military career by reinforcing a previously tenuous Rwandan political presence in Kinyaga—the area of extreme southwest Rwanda today (and still seen by some in the central areas of the country as not truly "Rwanda," being populated by "Banyabungu," a derogatory term for people from the west, from Congo). From Kinyaga some of Rwabugiri's first major campaigns were directed against the Shi kingdoms west of Lake Kivu and the Rusizi River. So were his last campaigns: almost thirty years later (after multiple military expeditions elsewhere), Rwabugiri was to die in his fourth assault on Bushi. In the interim he established army camps in the Rift region; he executed some sovereigns (and drove others away); he occupied land by force and extorted taxes and prestations (seizing cattle, small livestock, and food stocks); and he entered deeply into the local politics of the Rift (influencing succession disputes, among other effects). Despite this persistent presence, however, Rwabugiri was never to gain broad allegiance in these areas. Rwanda was always seen as an occupying force by the people of the islands in the lake and of the lands west of Lake Kivu, and with the withdrawal of Rwandan troops on Rwabugiri's death in 1895, nothing permanent was retained of Rwandan political power west of the Rwandan shores of Lake Kivu. Rwabugiri was seen as a scourge, not as a sovereign; his power was but an impermanent presence.

Even in areas east of the lake, the record was mixed: central court allegiance and local cultural affinities were seldom aligned. Indeed, the hegemonic views of an expansionist state only intensified the power holders' social distance from the people of the region: incorporation only transposed the axis of social distance from a horizontal scale (culturally defined) to a vertical scale (class-defined). In the southwest, Rwanda's firm control over Kinyaga was achieved only during the reign of Rwabugiri; from that time it became a prized administrative terrain of one of the most influential lineages in Rwandan court politics, the Abakagara lineage of the Abega clan—the lineage which, through various machinations, assassinations, and outright slaughter of its political opponents, effectively ruled Rwanda at the time of European arrival.

But outside Kinyaga the record was different. Large areas of Bugoyi in the northwest and Mulera in the north, and several smaller regions in the rugged mountains along the divide, all resisted rule by the Rwandan central court well into the period of colonial rule. Indeed, both before and after European arrival broad areas in what is now northwestern Rwanda actively resisted the imposition of court power. Associated with the intrusion of the court to this area, the first Christian martyr was murdered in Bugoyi in 1900, and a European priest representing the central court in a local dispute was killed in Mulera in 1907. Across this zone, mission diaries refer often to the attempts of armies of the court to raid and plunder such areas of resistance—in places like Bushiru, Bukunzi, and Kingogo—long into the 1920s. On the other side of the lake, the areas of Bushi,

Buhavu, and Bunyungu also resisted both Rwandan court penetration and European colonial imposition. Thus throughout this region during the nineteenth century (and well into the twentieth), territorial claims and political allegiance remained fluid. This was a zone autonomous of any enduring hegemonic power, one where formal structures and popular culture were only intersecting, but separate, domains of activity. This was a frontier zone—an area of poorly defined contours and quickly changing perceptions: a "land beyond the mists," politically as well as poetically.

Thus it is no wonder that this has been an area neglected by people who rely on a mental map defined by formal politics. In the Lake Kivu littoral, relying on formal state politics as a lens, and on fixed political affiliation as a defining feature, can distort one's understanding (at least until quite recently, when political and cultural identities became more closely aligned). Even during colonial rule the lines were blurred by the colonial imposition of fixed boundaries that had contradictory effects at several levels. Seeking to rigidify external differences and homogenize internal ambiguities, colonial policies bifurcated existing cultural identities. But these policies also introduced further political ambiguity, and the colonial power itself then abrogated those clear-cut boundaries. During colonial rule tens of thousands of people were affected by the forced displacement of Rwandans to the Congo, by the "recruitment" of Rwandans to work in the Congo, and by harsh policies that led others to flee to Uganda and Tanganyika to escape the requisitions of both Rwandan authorities and colonial administrators. In short, colonial power sought to resolve the ambiguities of the area by establishing fixed boundaries, intended to arrest social flow and harden a fluid cultural landscape. But even their own policies belied the fixed nature of those boundaries.

SUCH WAS the cultural context within which these essays are situated. From afar the Lake Kivu Rift would seem to articulate a clear geographical division. But clear geographical landmarks do not always translate easily into clearly defined administrative domains or political allegiances; in this area the transition from "frontier" to "boundary" was often an inconsistent and hesitant process, one poorly defined and capricious. Yet surely these so-called peripheral zones were important to the people who lived there; they were important to the colonial powers that argued over them (and that threatened to fight over them); they were important to Rwabugiri (and others from the Rwandan central court) who fought and died there; and, by the complex issues they raise and the competing conceptual frameworks they engender, they are important still today to those who seek a deeper understanding of social process—in this area and elsewhere, and in more recent times as well as in the past. Those realities—that historical complexity matters, and that peripheral zones can be important—define the vision behind this collection of essays.

Outsiders' struggles to define this area, and the local resistance to the imposition of such external definitions, suggest that this middle ground was important for more than its role as a divide. To be sure, the people of the Rift drew heavily on their strong opposition to court institutions encroaching from east of the lake. But there was also a strong legacy of interaction by Rwandans with the people in those same regions: people east and west of the lake were both linked and autonomous, and both those ties and that autonomy were important in the development of the identities and polities of the Rift Valley. Similarly, in developing their political and social constructs, the people on the mainland east of the lake had historically drawn on ideas and concepts from the western cultures, as well as on material items introduced through the vast commercial networks that worked their way through the region. The Rift Valley cultures were an integral part of the historical dynamics of this region of interlinked, but separate, cultures.

So frontier zones matter, not only as zones of separation and as zones of interaction but as interesting in themselves; areas disdained in the centers of political power sometimes emerge as zones of creativity. Indeed, in historical terms regional social innovations were derived as often from the perimeter—from the marginalized, those thinking and acting outside of prescribed conventional norms —as from the center. Yet it is a near-universal assumption of the powerful that power and knowledge are fused, that intellectual authority is the monopoly of the state, and that state actors are uniquely well placed to interpret events. And such claims are powerfully reflected in the historiography of the region. To the powerful, their superior status is nearly always presumed to derive from superior knowledge; for them (and their allies) there is no need to be informed of the history or culture of those outside the realm of power holders. However, by silencing other voices such assumptions reduce our awareness of the complexity of historical process and lead to misrepresentations of history. They also mark the earlier historiography of this area of Africa in a particularly dramatic fashion (as illustrated in the narratives of both colonial and local power holders).

The essays collected here explore the effects of such elitist assumptions on the historiography of the region. But they go beyond simply identifying the ideas that guide the presentation of history; they argue that familiarity with local testimony and analytic interpretations different from the state-centered models forces us to revisit, review, and rethink the subtle and complex histories of this area so deeply marked by ambiguity and flux. In short, they respond to what Feierman terms "the ethnographic impulse"—the attempt "to interpret ways of thinking . . . radically different from [our] own." Although these essays draw on neglected sources, relate to different locales, address various periods, and consider diverse issues, they do share a single vision: that to peer through those mists of past historiography—and to reconfigure our understanding—historical work must be empirically based, locally informed, and broadly inclusive; as Geertz phrases it, "the shapes of knowledge are always ineluctably local."

Some of these essays were published long ago (although the issues they address are often still in play). Some were published in outlets not easily accessible (sometimes outlets since discontinued). Some deal with episodes now largely neglected in the wake of more recent events demanding attention. But while compelling and important, events directly associated with the recent cataclysms are not the only issues to have marked the history of the area. It is for good reason that the genocide in Rwanda and the subsequent events in the Congo have become focal points for recent research, but such intense inquiry can also obscure other important issues, themes, and processes—issues that themselves are often essential in understanding contemporary events.

This selection of essays is presented in four interrelated sections. The first addresses historiographical issues, exploring some of the conceptual groundings that have molded the understanding of outsiders—and sometimes of insiders as well—in this intellectual arena. The second section consists of empirical work on the Rift Valley societies of Congo. These essays (augmented by the research of many colleagues working in the region) illustrate the expansion of historical interest in the region over the past decades. The third section poses questions specifically related to Rwandan history but directed at institutions and interactions outside the parameters of the central court. Building on the approaches and data explored in the earlier essays, the chapters in this section revisit established issues in Rwandan historiography to suggest new perspectives on material exchange, social identities, and political culture. The fourth section—a summary chapter—draws on these sources and methods to provide a new understanding of precolonial history based on the frameworks of inquiry explored here and on the empirical foundations to result from such research. The work of many people over the generation since colonial rule has made a monumental difference.

Part 1: Historiography

Historiography is an essential starting point for understanding "how it is we understand understandings not our own," as Geertz phrases it. The first section of this collection consists of two essays; one examines the intellectual foundations of earlier representations of history in the region, the other provides an overview of research carried out in the years immediately after decolonization.

"Bushi and the Historians" grapples with the distortions of the record introduced by colonial and missionary assumptions that "history" derives from state actors alone. Located southwest of Lake Kivu, and including seven distinct kingdoms, Bushi was home to by far the most populous cultural group in the area west of the lake. In addition to its demographic importance, it was also strategically located: encircling Bukavu (the colonial administrative center of the region), Bushi became a pole of attraction for administrators and missionaries. Drawing on the written sources on Rwanda, their early writings on Bushi often assumed that the history of the Rift area was derivative from (rather than interactive with) Rwandan central court actors. Yet from the perspective of the local level, it is clear that history takes shape from multiple interactions and conversations: the history of the Rift Valley region cannot be defined by Rwandan court initiatives alone, nor exclusively from the actions of people of western (Rift Valley) cultures; it can only be understood by accounting for the subtle webs of interaction among diverse arenas. To account for these changing interactive fields, we need to explore such activity where it has been neglected; we need to enter into and to look more closely at the "lands beyond the mists," in all their complexity.

To assess the lasting influence of these earlier paradigms, "Bushi and the Historians" examines the intellectual foundations of four influential colonial works. These drew essentially on racial assumptions of history and reified them through time: they identified culture with race, they assumed that broad cultural/racial groups acted as single (internally homogeneous) units of historical agency, and they took it for granted that racial/cultural groups were organized in a hierarchical fashion. There is an implicit assumption in these works that the structures of African societies observed during colonial rule could simply be extrapolated into the distant past, thus effacing the effects on African societies of both colonial influences and African agency within that colonial context. But in examining these works, what is most surprising is that these assumptions seemed to intensify over time, as researchers became further removed from local testimony: the early (missionary) researchers, working through the local language, were actually closer to their sources than those who came later. Each successive writer narrowed the vision, distilled the data, and condensed the arguments of his predecessors. Thus over time these works showed progressively simplified histories and increasingly narrow conceptual frameworks. In short, a rigid intellectual framework (which also increasingly reinforced colonial administrative thinking) became self-perpetuating.

Only after decolonization was this framework challenged by new research based on oral data derived from local sources. With decolonization, new approaches emerged. The second chapter in this section highlights the new historiographical issues to emerge in the wider arena over the period 1960–80. Jointly written with Bishikwabo Cubaka, a colleague at the Bukavu campus of the National University of Zaire, "Recent Research in the Area of Lake Kivu" surveys historical writing on Rwanda and eastern Congo produced by the first generation of postcolonial historical inquiry. It sets out the major themes of this research and highlights the enormous productivity of the period—and the prodigious effort that lay behind it. One conclusion to emerge is in sharp contrast to the period of colonial historiography. Then, writing on the history of the Congolese Rift societies had been largely derivative of Rwandan historiography—that is, the colonial writings on Congo societies showed a surfeit of interaction with earlier written work on Rwanda—to the point of intellectual dependence. After decolonization, however, the opposite problem emerged: there was perhaps too little interaction between historians working in the two arenas (Rwanda on the one hand, and the Lake Kivu Rift societies on the other), and the degree of separation between the two fields even intensified over time.

Though it is amply evident that historical influences did not respect political boundaries, the two fields increasingly represented discrete arenas of research, in part to respond to nationalist impulses, and in part because the technical demands of historical research were different on the two sides of the Rift. Historical research in Rwanda had to account for (and critique) a vast existing historiography, while research west of Lake Kivu had to account for historiographical neglect —researchers in the west needed to establish the empirical foundations of historical understanding. Thus, on both sides of the national boundary, historical interactions across the Rift Valley were downplayed. Historians in the Congo, west of the Rift, shunned regional contacts in the name of establishing the integrity of local agency, while those in Rwanda, to the east, essentially contradicted that approach, working from an impressive baseline of existing Rwandan historiography and privileging Rwandan court representations of neighboring societies. Consequently, in addition to paying tribute to the work accomplished in this extremely productive period (1960–80), one motivation for writing "Recent Historical Research" was to acquaint each set of historians with the work of the other.

Part 2: The Lake Kivu Arena

The second section consists of five essays that respond to some of the historiographical challenges outlined above. Drawing extensively on oral sources and incorporating local perspectives, they represent, in truncated form, the essential methodological turn away from colonial historiography. They also focus on societies almost entirely neglected in earlier writings. Though these analyses have regional implications, the central focus is on Ijwi Island, a densely populated island about twenty-five miles long located in Lake Kivu, with a royal dynasty dating from the early nineteenth century. Home to population segments deriving from (and maintaining continuing contacts with) many mainland areas, this kingdom became a nexus of Rift Valley interactions.

Illustrating the broad range of personal mobility and cultural interchange that marked this region before colonial arrival, the first of these essays examines the historical patterns associated with the production, transfer, and usage of but a single commodity, a bracelet-anklet fabricated of forest vines—a modest item in itself but one with important ramifications and associated with cultural interaction on a vast scale. These commercial networks connected Rwandan consumers with commodity production west of the Kivu Rift—in societies often disdained as "uncultured" by Rwandan court actors. The essay explores how these traders from west of the lake (and the social life of the commodities they traded) constructed networks of friendship, alliance, and reciprocity ramifying throughout this vast and varied region. (And the commercial networks highlighted here represented only one of several interrelated trade networks; two of the most important included salt from the northwest and iron implements from the southwest.)

In exploring this commercial history, the analysis introduces three features previously neglected in the historical literature on this region. First, it addresses an aspect of economic history (long-distance commerce) almost entirely ignored in earlier presentations. Material transfers within Rwanda were assumed to be entirely subsumed within the clientship system ultimately connected to the central court; those in other areas were deemed unimportant. Only by analyzing the system as a whole—as this essay tries to do—was a new vision possible. Second, the essay addresses the importance of commercial agency outside the control of powerful political centers. In Rwandan historiography such activity was rendered invisible (or unimportant) because beyond the reach of the central court; for areas outside Rwanda commercial activity was assumed to be unstructured, informal, and haphazard. (When considered at all, it was characterized as "exchange," not "commerce," therefore neglecting the scale and complexity of this commercial network and its significance as social text.) This analysis challenges such assumptions. Third, this essay underscores the importance of interaction across Rwanda's western cultural divide, where previous Rwandan historiographical interest focused almost exclusively on relations with areas to the east and north of Rwanda (areas of a common Interlacustrine culture zone with that of Rwanda). "Lake Kivu Regional Trade," by contrast, explores the initiatives of people from western cultures, the nature of their interaction with Rwandan commoners, and the transformation of trade patterns in response to attempts by court powers to control or channel such trade. Despite royal pretensions to the contrary, it is clear that such commercial interaction occurred mostly—and most effectively—outside the control of political power.

The second essay in this section is methodological in its focus: it addresses some of the paradoxes embedded in oral sources, particularly in what are referred to as "genesis traditions"—that is, traditions relating to dynastic origins. By providing detailed analysis of two contrasting traditions reporting on the same episode—the establishment of the royalty on Ijwi Island—it illustrates the depth of analysis necessary to derive historical understanding from such oral sources. Narrowing the broad vision of the first essay both geographically and chronologically, "Kamo and Lubambo" focuses on a single social community—and particularly on the conflict that eventually introduced a royal dynasty to the island. Unlike the two traditions, the essay does not present the installation of royalty in simple narrative form. Instead it compares competing oral traditions —sources that seem to disagree, to contradict, and to subvert each other, but that are today (somewhat surprisingly) almost entirely neglected on Ijwi itself. The import of the essay is found not in the dramatic content of the tale but rather in the competing forms of its presentation, illustrating an analytic approach to addressing conflicting voices and historical uncertainties.

Four levels of paradox characterized these particular sources. First, there was no generalized genesis tradition narrated on Ijwi—not even, surprisingly, among members of the royal family itself; only brief references to royal arrival existed among members of two social segments. But—and this is the second level of paradox—the two groups to recount such narratives are among the smallest, most geographically peripheral, and most socially marginalized of the clan units recognized on Ijwi today. Third, the traditions they recount are almost completely distinct from each other, both in substance and structure. Yet—and this is the fourth paradox—both appear to represent valid historical perceptions and relate to actual empirical events: rather than competing traditions, as their forms and content might suggest, they are complementary.

In short, knowledge of the arrival and establishment of royalty was not widespread on Ijwi, and even those who held such knowledge retained only fragmented references—just as they were socially segmented from the rest of the island's population. "Kamo and Lubambo" explores such paradoxes; it explains the historical use of divergent accounts; and it concludes that one can understand them only by careful attention to the specific social context of the social unit narrating them at the time the events occurred. Thus this essay illustrates the importance of the social contextualization of knowledge—or at least of narrative—relating to royal establishment on Ijwi in the second decade of the nineteenth century. It shows why peripheral voices and apparently contradictory testimony can be essential: these provide the only empirical sources we have on the establishment of kingship in this society—and through their analysis there emerges a process far different from that assumed in an ideology of divine origins: on Ijwi the origin of the royal family is portrayed in distinctly unheroic terms.

While "Kamo and Lubambo" addresses events at the very beginning of the nineteenth century, "The Campaigns of Rwabugiri" and "Rwabugiri and Ijwi" focus on the last three decades of the century. Though originally published separately, the two essays complement each other. Setting out a complete chronicle of the military expeditions of Kigeri Rwabugiri, a renowned warrior-king of late-nineteenth-century Rwanda, "The Campaigns of Rwabugiri" establishes the broad military context of his reign. By contrast, "Rwabugiri and Ijwi" provides a case study of his several campaigns directed specifically at Ijwi over a twenty-year interval. As the only case study available on Rwabugiri's wars that draws on data from the target population as well as from Rwandan sources, the essay both examines the tactics of Rwandan military units and explores the local effects of these campaigns. Some Ijwi authorities resisted Rwandan military initiatives, but others collaborated with the occupying forces, and these different relations to external power were to have enduring effects on the politics of the island (as explored in the next essay).

While numerous accounts of Rwabugiri's campaigns exist from the perspective of the Rwandan central court, we have only few (and fragmentary) accounts from the perspective of those attacked. "Rwabugiri and Ijwi" is based on a rich tapestry of detailed oral accounts; as such, it complements (and sometimes provides a counterweight to) accounts based exclusively on Rwandan court sources. Exploring the agency of the victims as well as of the invaders, the essay tries to illustrate the cunning and courage and perseverance of the actors, as well as the ambition, deceit, and brutality that marked the multiple conflicts sparked by Rwabugiri's invasion and occupation of the island. Illustrative of the contributions of narratives recounted by the victims of such attacks as well as of the victors, it testifies to the value of studying the local social parameters of political conflict.

The fifth chapter of this section examines the sequel to these events, extending the analysis to consider early colonial imposition on the island. Written jointly with Catharine Newbury, "King and Chief on Ijwi Island" explores the dramatic events of colonial establishment on Ijwi, examining the effects of colonial power among both political elites and commoners. It also demonstrates the significant internal restructuring to occur on the island at the time—restructuring brought about as much through the initiatives and ambitions of individuals on Ijwi as from outside policies and powerful colonial personalities. Within the island community, distinct political factions emerged within the royal family— reflecting those apparent during the Rwandan occupation of a generation earlier, with different political strategies apparent in the northern and southern portions of this domain.

In addition to tracing the legacy of Rwabugiri's occupation, however, the main focus of this essay is on Ijwi's internal political culture, showing the failed attempt by colonial agents to invest power with authority. The people of Ijwi understood the intimate interplay of power and authority as central to the political dialectic; they saw authority and power as distinct, but essential features defining the character of politics. However, colonial authorities made no attempt to understand that dialectic. For colonial agents, politics was power, expressed most efficiently through military might: it was sufficient to have delegates appointed by colonial power perform the rituals of enthronement; in their eyes, credulous subjects would blindly follow their "tribal" leader. By contrast, for the people of

Ijwi legitimate power derived only from ritual authority: no claimant to power was considered king except through the appropriate rituals of succession, performed by specific members of the recognized ritual corporations; the performance of these rituals was more important as a social statement—that effective power derived from cultural legitimation from below—than as a symbolic representation of high status or supernatural power. Thus the social consecration of kingship was essential to legitimate royal authority; indeed it was renewed each year in the annual First Fruits ceremony, which reflected the enthronement ceremony: in a sense, therefore, the king was reenthroned each year and the social contract was renewed annually at the time of the first harvest.

To understand the different political perceptions distinguishing colonial agents from Ijwi actors, this essay argues, one needs to understand, in some detail, the social experiences of the people on the island—not just the positions of the "leaders," but the broader social understanding that served as the foundation of collective identity. Individual leaders were respected only in so far as they recognized such social parameters. Thus the definition of political authority differed between Belgian agents and Congolese actors. But such different interpretations were also reflected in differences between the two major royal factions on the island. Therefore the objective of this chapter is not only to trace out the effects of Belgian impositions on the royal line but also to illustrate the divergent assumptions between two political factions on Ijwi, one in the south, the other in the north. In short, the analysis argues that it is important to account for the social parameters of political dynamics if we are to understand how it is we "understand understandings not our own," to draw again on Geertz's apt aphorism. Indeed, that is the continuing thread that knits these essays together.

Part 3: The Rwanda Arena

The third section draws on the analytic issues to emerge from such explorations among the Rift societies, and applies them to various elements of Rwandan historiography. Rwandan historical presentation is highly developed; indeed, Rwanda boasts one of the most extensive written historiographies of any society in Africa. Furthermore, this historiography has developed a distinct character: it often takes the form of fixed, known, and certain elements, closely linked to central court history. Official accounts present Rwandan history as exclusively the history of the kings (augmented by their central court allies and antagonists).

Where fundamental social institutions (such as clan identities) were discussed at all in these "official" accounts, they were presented as fixed and permanent—as social backdrop to the dynamism of the kings and court; where chronology was presented, it was done so in a mechanical fashion: thirty-three years per reign for thirty reigns (from 959 CE). The essays in this section revisit some of these issues, assessing such assumptions and institutions as fully historical constructions themselves and situating them within a historical matrix influenced by many factors.

The first essay in this set focuses on a narrowly defined issue but one with wide ramifications: the changing nature of social identities, in this case that of clan identities. "The Clans of Rwanda" wrestles with a set of paradoxes. In Western thinking, the term "clan" is clearly defined and often seen as marking primordial affiliation: at its most basic, it refers to a group of people united by belief in their common descent from a single ancestor and their shared responsibilities to each other. In Rwanda, however, the concept is much more ambiguous: *ubwoko,* the term that westerners translate as "clan," is used more broadly as a general term for "category" in Kinyarwanda (the language spoken by Rwandans); the same term refers to ethnic identity, as well as to many other types of categories—with both human and nonhuman referents. (One uses the same term for categories of trees, or animals, or beans, etc.) However, aside from the vague attributes associated with the term for "clan," this essay addresses a much more specific problem: how is it that in Rwanda clans are seen as determined by patrilineal descent (from a single common ancestor) yet they invariably included members of each of Rwanda's three major ethnic identities (Hutu, Tutsi, and Twa)—groups that themselves were assumed to be determined by separate lines of patrilineal descent (and therefore seen as biologically exclusive categories)? If clan and ethnic identities were each determined by biological descent, how could each of the multiple clans also incorporate significant numbers of each of the several ethnicities—and (in return) how could each of the ethnic groups incorporate members of each of the clans?

The answer lies in understanding these as historically constructed identities rather than as fixed, immutable categories. Drawing on data and analytic parameters derived from earlier work in the Kivu Rift societies, this essay proposes a resolution to this problem by viewing such identities as socially defined perceptions (in this case associated with the extension of royal power) rather than as individually defined perceptions (determined by descent). Because identity within Rwandan political culture was defined in part by membership in one of the eighteen predominant clan affiliations, the penetration of royal power into the social configuration of any given locale was marked by extension of such clan identities into those incorporated regions. Indeed, the reach of central court power correlated (in space and time) with the expansion of the eighteen "official" Rwandan clan categories to areas where they had not before been recognized. Thus the data here argue that clan identities are associated with a conceptual field related to the changing matrix of political power, rather than deriving from empirical realities at the individual level, such as descent.

The second chapter of this section, "Bunyabungo: The Western Frontier in Rwandan History," continues the focus on Rwanda's western areas, but shifts the point of reference: it explores how Rift Valley cultures were perceived by members of the royal court. Furthermore, it relates the introduction of these disdainful stereotypes of western peoples to a particular period of central court history in Rwanda: a time of the expansion of royal power toward the west, from the late eighteenth century (during the reign of the Rwandan king Cyilima Rujugira). Drawing on literary sources as well as on comparative social structures, this is an attempt to engage with the intellectual history of a segment of Rwandan society, the culture of the central court. But it relates also to a particular moment in the court's development—a time of growing self-awareness as an elite segment of society and increasingly self-conscious court etiquette, as social distinctions were taking on new importance.

Rwandan political expansion into the areas around Lake Kivu provoked an intensified awareness of cultural differences at the royal court, and the desire for dominance brought with it a desire to hierarchize those differences—to claim the Rwandan court as the superior culture, and therefore one fully justified in subordinating and dominating (as well as mocking) their neighbors. All these aspects are shown in court literary forms, and explored in this chapter. But they were not only illustrative of such changing norms; in the process of political expansion, these literary characterizations served as a tool of social separation; as geographical proximity with western peoples was narrowed, hierarchy increased. In other words, such literary representations were an integral part of the process of class formation; rather than serving as ethnographic descriptions of neighboring societies to the west, therefore, these literary accounts served as a mirror, reflecting the emerging values of the court itself more than the existing values of the people portrayed. Thus these accounts can be seen as an unintentional "auto-ethnography" of the Rwandan central court at that particular moment—more revealing of the speaker than of the object.

The third essay in this section extends the inquiry to the central feature of Rwandan royalty itself: the royal rituals of legitimation, the "esoteric code of kingship." Although the focus of "What Role Has Kingship?" is on but one aspect of a much broader ritual complex, it illustrates the multiple layers of interpretation involved. More importantly, it brings into question the autonomous nature of the king's power. It is no wonder that the message was carried in ritual form—and that large parts of it were in esoteric ritual and not open to the public—for defining the limitations of the king's powers (even in the name of respecting ritual authority) was politically dangerous.

From this theater, with its careful delineation of the multiple ritual requirements imposed on the sovereign, it is clear that the king was a captive of kingship. But in a broader context—and articulating that context is the burden of this essay—it was not only kingship that encapsulated the king, but also culture that encapsulated kingship. In short, by viewing political structures within their larger cultural context, this analysis suggests that the assumptions of divine kingship (prevalent in much early thinking on African kingship) were indeed but myth—although a myth convenient for both European suzerains and Rwandan sovereigns alike.

But the extension of this myth of divine kingship during colonial rule misrepresented the popular understanding of kingship, undermining its roots in social parameters meaningful to the people. During the colonial period the concept of kingship as a culturally consecrated mediating force was gradually replaced with the concept of kings as divine rulers. That process weakened popular support for kingship, for kingship was now seen as hegemonic power, not as a cultural point of reference. Such a shift in the concept of royal legitimacy held momentous implications for Rwanda's later history: in the 1950s, as European visions of political order began to change, this "power construct of kingship" (that is, as lacking foundations in popular legitimacy) left kingship (and therefore the kings) vulnerable to the political currents of the day.

The final essay in this section addresses chronology—one of the pillars of royal claims to legitimacy. Asserting antiquity was important, for the older kingship was claimed to be, the more solid, it was assumed, was the dynasty's claim to legitimacy. Postulating kingship as a permanent feature of Rwandan society (and seeing Rwandan royal forms as the fount of royalty in the wider region) was therefore a central element to the development of a sense of nationalist identity in Rwanda—at least at the central court. So the process of interpreting kingship as a venerable feature of Rwandan society became deeply embedded in court sources, with official sources situating the origin of the Rwandan dynasty in the tenth century (959, to be precise)—and subsequent kings supposedly succeeding in an unbroken line of father-to-son succession to 1959. Proponents of such antiquity claimed confirmation through comparative chronologies in neighboring societies.

But this returns us to the historiographical process noted above. "Bushi and the Historians" showed how the hegemony of Rwandan historical sources in the region brought into question the independence of such neighboring sources. In fact, as colonial interpreters sought to write the history of neighboring societies, they consciously aligned these histories (and their chronologies) with the history of Rwanda—and increasingly so as researchers progressively distanced themselves from local sources over the course of the colonial period. Rwandan sources then drew on those very external sources—themselves derivative of Rwandan chronological claims—to legitimate their own antiquity. And so by a complex tautological process Rwandan sources justified the antiquity of kingship though corroboration from their own claims reflected in the writings of others—and now presented as "independent" confirmation. But the manner of this distortion took different forms in each of the societies, which derived their own claims from tie-ins to Rwandan ideologies of antiquity. Therefore, in order to deconstruct the myth of antiquity, this analysis first had to reconstruct the ways in which the chronologies had been built in each of four contiguous societies. Once again, contextualizing knowledge—that is, historicizing the presentation of history—shows itself to be an essential tool in understanding the fundamental feature of Rwandan royalty.

So the structural parameters of kingship and chronology in Rwanda, like those of clanship and commerce, appear different when examined through the lens of rigorous historical analysis, based on careful attention to the interplay of precise local sources and broad regional influences. Although the simple "accumulation of facts" is not the objective of historical presentation, broader conceptual issues can hardly be advanced without solid evidence and careful analysis. It is hoped that the essays in this section, through both careful empirical data and enhanced analytic rigor, help raise questions about received historical understanding —and also that they help put to rest the accusations that "history" is nothing but the mindless accumulation of cold facts from the dead past. As others have noted, the past is not dead—except in the hands of those who kill it. In fact, it is not even past—for the issues related to these discussions are very much alive in the world of today, in very important ways. Once again, history may not determine our future—we are not entirely captives of our past—but our pathways to the future are illuminated by an improved grasp of history. And clearing away the mists of past assumptions—or understanding how those histories have been misrepresented, misused, neglected, and abused in the past—is an essential part of the process.

Many of these issues are considered—for a single society—in my earlier work, *Kings and Clans: A History of Ijwi Island and the Kivu Rift Valley.* Though focused on the evolution of Ijwi Island society, that monograph situated local dynamics explicitly within broader regional processes; in a sense it serves as a geographical counter balance to the final essay of this collection. But more precisely, it also shows how the process of political centralization on Ijwi—the creation of a new royal dynasty where none had existed before—was undertaken only within a field of developing ritual power and changing social identities in a complex trialectic where the evolution of each of the three factors (political centralization, ritual power, and the contours of social identities) both resulted from and created the others: the changing contours of each defined the vision of the others. Indeed, many of the themes explored in the current collection find application in that monograph.

Part 4: Perceiving History through the Mists

As noted above, the essays in the third section, on Rwandan history, seek to reassess some of the basic foundations of Rwandan social and political order; they question the permanence, durability, and autonomy of institutions of identity and authority in precolonial society east of Lake Kivu. But in themselves they have only served as the analytic building blocks to a new understanding. The concluding essay brings these insights together to provide a new vision of the precolonial history of the region east of Lake Kivu.

For those working in the period immediately after colonial rule, the process of explaining history east of the lake differed from similar processes west of the lake. West of the lake, little had been published, so the history of this area required familiarizing oneself with new data and establishing a new critical foundation. But east of the lake the situation was different: there, an extensive existing historiography meant that revisiting the history of Rwanda (or Burundi) required a different approach. New data (and new perspectives) were always valuable. But moving beyond the goal of simply extending the empirical record, to arrive instead at a coherent understanding of social process, meant moving from "additive history"—accumulating data—to "transformative history"—transforming our understanding of historical process in the region. In part that meant adopting an analytic approach privileging processes, not events alone. And it meant reassessing existing orthodoxies to arrive at new understandings—looking at interactions, not only individuals; at institutional dynamics, not fixed institutions alone; at multiple levels of analysis, not just simple narratives; and at new forms of understanding, rather than simply more knowledge.

The concluding section illustrates this approach through a single extended essay. Drawing on earlier analytic explorations, it proposes a new vision of the precolonial history east of the Rift Valley—a vision that accounts fully for the tensions between particular "local loyalties" and broader "regional royalties" (of which the two most prominent were the Baganwa dynasty of what became Burundi and the Abanyiginya dynasty of what became Rwanda). This essay seeks to move beyond three elements that characterized earlier works. Instead of a predominant focus on the royal court, this account explores regional influences and local loyalties. Instead of an overriding concern with ethnicity, the essay privileges ecological factors and local identities as formative influences on history. And instead of a focus on kings and courtiers, this analysis is interested in the interactions of royal power and rural power, of autonomy as well as incorporation. In seeking to transcend royalty and ethnicity as the principal explanatory features of history in this region, however, this presentation does not deny their importance as historical factors; they were still vitally important features on the political and cultural landscapes. Nonetheless, one can seek to contextualize royalty and ethnicity, to see them as historical constructions in themselves. For royal power was only one type of power—and not always the most important; ethnicity was only one level of identity—and not always the most salient. And each had its own history—histories that varied by region as well as evolving over time (and not always in linear fashion).

In short, this is a work of salvage: in part, recovering neglected histories and lost work, but also in part reintroducing the perspectives that animate those analyses. Whatever the intellectual or empirical limitations of these essays, they are premised on a call to move beyond histories defined by fixed categories and fixed assumptions. We need a vision that reaches beyond boundaries, a vision that is informed by multiple (and sometimes contradictory) voices and that celebrates diverse actions and identities. It is hoped that these essays provide examples of how to move in that direction. But even as we peer through the mists of an opaque past, it is also clear that new mists will appear. Unlike meteorological mists that evaporate with the sun's warmth, the mists that obscure the past never entirely dissipate. They may transform themselves—and the work we do moves that process—but they always return in new and intriguing patterns.

PART 1

X

Historiography

BUSHI AND THE HISTORIANS

Historiographical Themes in Eastern Kivu

1978

The form in which history is presented matters. Written historiographies in eastern Kivu were originally colonial historiographies: they drew on the cultural paradigms and intellectual assumptions of the colonial mindset, and they privileged themes important to colonial thinking—"race," migration, royal genealogies, and social hierarchy. Internal cultural change and local agency were often neglected. This chapter considers four influential examples of such literature in Bushi, a densely populated region (including seven kingdoms) southwest of Lake Kivu. In addition to tracing out the themes of colonial historiography, the essay illustrates two other aspects of historical writing in this region: its dependence on Rwandan historiography, and the tendency of such works to become increasingly condensed and more simplified over time, not more expansive, diverse, and open to new themes. More recently, research carried out since decolonization has transformed these images. Rather than reaffirming homogeneous ("tribal") histories, local research has demonstrated the broad diversity of historical perceptions that exist within cultural groups. Furthermore, the presentation of history in this region within Rwandan models has not been validated: kingship has been shown to have developed autonomously within Bushi, and the ritual foundations of states west of Lake Kivu have been shown to have been essential to the intellectual foundations of kingship in Rwanda—rather than the reverse. In short, the deep influences appear to have moved in the opposite direction from those assumed in colonial histories. Yet even with greater respect for autonomous local histories and more detailed empirical evidence in recent research, it is nonetheless important to note the characteristics of earlier historiographical presentations to account for their effects and to recognize the momentous changes to accrue in the generation since decolonization.

HISTORICAL STUDIES OF KIVU are still in their very infancy. Recent work has been carried out in Bufulero, Bushi, Buhavu, and Bunande, but, lacking the results of these studies, historians working from published materials have very few sources at their disposal. Existing sources include works by Colle, Moeller, Willame, and Cuypers, with the latter two based primarily on the former, at least in their historical dimensions. Because the sources are so few and are essentially similar, little critical attention has been given them; by constant citation and repetition they have become hallowed as truth and used as a basis for teaching and university theses. By this process such essentially colonial interpretations have become entrenched in the historical ontology of the region. This chapter proposes to review some of the written sources in light of current research in the region, by first presenting certain themes that appear to have guided earlier historical inquiry and then discussing the works of four influential authors in light of these themes.

The first attempts to record historical traditions in the Kivu area were influenced by earlier studies of Rwanda that emphasized the centralized and hierarchical nature of the Rwandan state. Many of the early missionaries and priests in Kivu, men to whom contemporary researchers owe much for their accumulated sources, had close contacts with the seminaries and published work in Rwanda. In most works, Rwanda was seen as the end development for other states in the region, and prominence was given to those historical factors that were assumed to have had a common impact throughout the area. Because early writings on Kivu focused on the similarities of the Kivu states with Rwanda, rather than on their differences, the Rwandan political and social system as described in these early sources became the model for later studies in Bushi, and especially in the most centralized of the Kivu states at the time of European arrival. Bushi, in turn, and for much the same reason, became a kind of prototype for other states in eastern Kivu.

Perhaps more important in guiding the sociological interests of the day was the nature of the colonial situation itself, based on the premises of race, class, and social stratification. The justification and success of the colonial policy of indirect rule required the identification of African "traditional" rulers with sufficient powers over the population to enforce colonial administrative policy. Where these powers were found to be insufficient, indeed where authorities suitable to the colonial purpose were found not to exist at all, these had to be created to conform to the exigencies of colonial policy—the effective administration of the area. On the model of Europe, it was believed that centralization and administrative efficiency were best assured through an aristocratic class to "guide" (*diriger*) the rest of the population.

Such pervasive assumptions—and the policies based on them—came to be increasingly reflected in many African colonial societies of eastern Kivu. Both European administrators and African beneficiaries of such reinforced powers justified them by recourse to indirect rule and appeal to concepts of a "traditional" system. As a result, from the 1930s works on Kivu presented a picture of the several societies as being each ruled by a "classe dirigeante" with close affinities to the corresponding class in the other societies throughout the region. As also in colonial society, class differences and consequently the whole system of social stratification in the lacustrine area (including eastern Kivu), were explained by racial factors: within any given society the different classes were seen to represent different racial groups, each endowed with certain inalienable cultural traits.

But while the presence of vertical strata may have been one of the most important characteristics noted in some sources, other early written works focused on discrete ethnic groups, each apparently geographically distinct from the other. As with the concepts applied to stratified class layers, these ethnic units were frequently seen as unchanging over time and without significant internal variation; such concepts of a static and homogeneous society are illustrated in the common phrases "traditional Shi society" and "the oral tradition of the Shi." Thus, while attempting to identify sociological differences for the various component groups, sources of this type nonetheless frequently accepted traditions of the current royal family (or a segment of it) as the only legitimate (and fixed) historical tradition for the group as a whole, thereby ignoring the composite sociological, regional, or occupational groups within a society, each of which may have different histories (or different interpretations of a common history).

One result of this reliance on a single body of presumably fixed tradition was that the social groups postulated in the models were often presented as having existed, more or less in a constant relationship to each other, and social change was thereby minimized. The underlying assumption was that a given group possessed a unique identifiable culture (or at least certain culture traits) that seldom changed and hence could always be associated with that group. Because culture was viewed as static, "history" considered only the initial formation of these societies; the study of history was therefore concerned almost exclusively with the geographic movements of the groups involved (i.e., the movement of certain culture traits) and their arrival in the area, and ultimately with the quest for the geographic origins of the culture traits and the people that carried them. Because the social dynamics of migrations were not considered to have altered social structure, a migrating people arrived with just about the same social structure as they had possessed on departing from their homeland.

Another problem associated with this form of historical "explanation" is the difficulty in most cases of attributing to any single group a given sociological input into a culture. Even where individual cultural elements can be identified with a particular people, these become part of a larger culture only by a process of adaptation and integration that affects both the absorbing culture and the trait absorbed. Rather than considering the transformations brought about by the organic nature of a culture and the interrelation of its elements, the early writings on Kivu frequently explained cultural complexity by the combination of discrete and clearly defined culture traits resulting from the simple superposition of diverse "racial" groups in a single area. Such analyses assumed that the presence of any particular trait can be (or rather must be) explained by the influx of a certain racial stock associated with that trait. By isolating the composite culture traits of the society and determining which characteristics were associated with which racial group, this form of analysis explained the formation of the composite society by the nature of the hierarchy of these different "racial" (i.e., cultural) stocks.

In addition to problems associated with theoretical assumptions, such an analysis also presents the more practical problem of arbitrarily defining a point of origin for the migrating people. According to this form of historical inquiry, every people must have originated from some previous "homeland"; every homeland in turn was itself a point of arrival for a previous migration. The historian, then, had to decide which point, of several possibilities throughout the history of these people, will be legitimately considered as their ultimate origin.

More recent thinking on the history of Africa, of course, has progressed far beyond such migration monomania, and even within migration studies there have been significant changes in approach. While migration theory has been frequently overemphasized and misused in the earlier works, population movements have nonetheless formed an important part of Africa's past, and their study at a more narrowly defined level still represents a legitimate field of historical inquiry. More recent study has focused on the form and nature of the population movements rather than on simple existence or geographic parameters. Because it is currently assumed that cultures as well as population placement were significantly altered by the process of such movement and subsequent sedentarization, the diverse forms of population movements and cultural interactions are seen to be as important as origins themselves in influencing the resulting social composition and organization of the mobile populations. In addition, historians have only recently begun asking questions such as which geographical landmarks are remembered and which time periods were involved in such movements. They have also started to grapple with the problem of identifying the composition of participating segments: how coherent as historical units are contemporary social units (e.g., "clans"), and how have identity concepts and symbols changed over time? The kind of highly intensive study necessary to account for the historical complexity of the more general pattern of slow movements and countercurrents, usually composed of very small (family) groups and moving for many different possible reasons, has been carried out only in very few areas of Africa.

Thus earlier historiographical works on Kivu portrayed a series of immigrant waves of coherent discrete populations, each one the "possessor" of unchanging culture traits, each one establishing in its turn a distinct class over the other, and with little social interaction between them. This form of analysis tended to emphasize cultural (and hence racial) hierarchies, and in doing so reflected the colonial situation itself. Because stratification was conveniently explained by a conquest theory of state formation and cultural evolution, this theory also served to justify the violence accompanying the establishment of colonial rule; hence the "rights" of colonial powers could be argued on the basis of the (colonially inspired) "traditional" history of the region. With these general observations in mind, we will consider some of the more influential studies on the history of eastern Kivu, in reverse chronological order.

PERHAPS THE most important of the recent works to serve as an introduction to the history and sociology of eastern Kivu is that of J.-B. Cuypers.[1] Because of its suitability for schools and universities, this publication had an important influence in postcolonial Zaire. As a whole, Cuypers provides a useful summary of the cultures of the area, especially on the material culture of Bushi. The present discussion will be limited to a consideration of the historical section of the work, which constitutes only a small portion of the total presentation.

Based primarily on Moeller, Cuypers's historical reconstruction postulates an autochthonous Twa (pygmy) group and subsequent waves of immigrants forming layers of stratified social classes that seem to apply to the region as a whole. The first two migrations are dated (without sources) to the sixteenth and seventeenth centuries. This dating probably derives from Moeller, although Cuypers offers no explanation as to how such dates were in fact arrived at.[2] According to Cuypers (and Moeller), the first of these immigrations was that of the Lega; the second, more composite, "comprenait surtout les Yira [Nande], les Hunde, les Nyanga, les Havu, les Shi, et les Furiiru, mais également les Hutu du Rwanda et du Burundi."[3] The "origins" of these migrations are inferred from Nyanga and Nande traditions (some apparently more recent than Moeller). While noting that other traditions do not refer specifically to identical origins, Cuypers's account implies that Nyanga- and Nande-cited origins are broadly valid for all the peoples of the area. Unfortunately, no consideration is given to the process of ethnic differentiation among the various defined segments of this postulated single, vast immigrant community.

Again, it is not clear in this presentation whether the ruling families arrived with the subordinate groups—thus performing a kind of "social transplant" from western Uganda to eastern Kivu—or after the establishment of other "racial" groups in the area—thus forming different strata based on different immigrant groups. However, the reference to "cette classe dirigeante" strengthens the notion of a single group whose members became rulers among the different peoples of the region, a group composed of "chefs d'origine hamite (ou galla, ou éthiopide)."[4] The apparent similarity among ruling classes of many of these states is explained in unequivocally historical terms: "Les traditions [which traditions?] donnent une origine commune aux familles regnantes des Shi, des Havu, des Furiiru, et des Rwanda."[5] Moreover, the claimed affinity among various royal families noted above explicitly excludes the Hunde, Nande, Nyanga, Tembo, and others whose political organizations differ from the Furiiru, Havu, Shi, and Rwanda. Because the extent of (or even possibility of) internal development is neglected and because of a postulated common migration, one is left with the supposition that the ruling families of the latter group, forming a discrete unit among themselves, immigrated separately from the rest of the population. However, appeal to common historical origins and the stereotyped use of "biological terminology" (e.g., that of brotherhood) to express shared social identity among royal families of neighboring states are common features in the historiography of the area. It is therefore of questionable validity to employ this reasoning to posit multiple migrations that serve in turn to explain social stratification in the area.

Cuypers's later work on the Shi of Katana places less emphasis on the origins of peoples and social classes, but his conception of "histoire" still seems closely synonymous to that of "origines." He includes a useful short summary of the relevant works of Colle and Moeller, noting the differences between these two presentations. According to Cuypers, Colle postulated a simple succession of migrations, each one composed of a different racial group and establishing a new social layer above the previous population, thus forming the social stratification found in the area today. Moeller, on the other hand, presented several immigrations, each of which included the three "associated" populations of "Hamites," "Bantu," and Twa. In this way, Moeller deferred the historical problem of the formation of social stratification to a period prior to the migrations themselves, and therefore outside the limits of his analysis.

Remarking that "les origines historiques des Shi ne sont encore connues que de façon imprécise et parfois contradictoire," Cuypers rightly mitigates the importance of racial characteristics in contemporary Shi society.[6] He implies, though, that this has resulted from a degeneration of an earlier situation: "Les Luzi [members of the royal family] ne forment qu'une infime partie de la population et il ne semble actuellement plus possible de les distinguer physiquement des Shi [commoners]."[7] Despite this, Cuypers cites works by Hiernaux, writing that Hiernaux distinguished between Luzi and Shi (or commoners), finding the Luzi closer to the Tutsi and the Shi closer to Hutu in physical characteristics: "J. Hiernaux, l'anthropologue physique qui a fait leur examen, rapproche les Shi proprement dits des Hutu du Rwanda et les Luzi des Tuutsi."[8]

In fact, Hiernaux rarely mentioned the Luzi at all, and while he did refer to them as "le même élément" as the Tutsi, he applied this more to sociological than to physical characteristics: "un aristocratie très limitée qui détient les hautes charges."[9] In places it is difficult to determine whether Hiernaux's statements were based on the scientific analysis of physical characteristics or on his preconceptions of the "history" of the region, as presented in the introductory comments to his work. For example, since Hiernaux accepted Moeller's conception of a "communauté d'origine" for both the "Shi" and "Hutu," his reference to Luzi as "apparentés aux Batuutsi" may be interpreted as referring to historical rather than biological affinities (also based on Moeller's hypothesis), though this is nowhere clearly stated.[10] Furthermore, despite reference to general "traits éthiopides," nowhere in his empirical presentation did Hiernaux discuss the physiological characteristics of the Luzi, and certainly not on pages 13–20 as cited by Cuypers. We are not even told if Luzi formed a part of his empirical sample, though his earlier narrow application of the term "Shi" to refer exclusively to non-Luzi (or nonroyal) elements of Shi society would imply that Luzi were excluded from his sample; no distinction is given in his results. Similarly, another reference to Hiernaux, cited by Cuypers in the same context, makes no mention at all of the Luzi as distinct from the Shi; there is only reference to the "Tuutsi."[11]

Without denying the potential utility of Hiernaux's work for historians, and leaving aside the problem of the Tutsi, it is clear that Cuypers's citations are faulty. It appears, for instance, that he interpreted the word "Tuutsi" to mean "Luzi" in every case; but this racial equation was the very premise he was attempting to prove in citing Hiernaux. Given the cited evidence, therefore, it is a misrepresentation to postulate a social stratification in Bushi that is "semblable" to that of Rwanda based on putative racial similarities, and consequently to postulate historical ties between the Luzi and Tutsi classes—"nous pouvons dire des castes—qui correspondent en partie à des coupures physico-anthropologiques."[12]

Cuypers recognizes that social stratification in Bushi has often been presented in terms that make it seem close to that in Rwanda. But there is no attempt to analyze just how the earlier and very prolific writings on Rwanda have influenced later analyses of Kivu states, especially the Shi and Havu states. He seems to accept the similarities entirely, and to portray Bushi as similar to Rwanda simply *because* Rwanda is better understood: "la comparaison avec le Rwanda s'impose car elle est fort bien connue."[13] Justification for doing so is based on two arguments: that both these societies are similarly structured into three different classes, and that in each society these classes are of unequal size. But it is not really sufficient to note that Rwanda and Bushi each have three numerically unequal classes, that they share geographical contiguity and supposed racial and historical affinities, and therefore to assert that "la stratification sociale qui existe chez les Shi est, dans son essence, la même que celle que l'on trouve au Rwanda."[14]

It appears, then, that in the absence of empirical historical data to establish common Hamitic, Galla, or Ethiopian origins (are these intended as synonymous or alternative terms?) for the several ruling classes in the lacustrine area, general cultural similarities (or at least common social rank) has been accepted as proof of common historical origins. This a priori acceptance of shared origins has led to an overemphasis on similarities of certain cultural features such as social stratification, especially as these developed during the colonial period. Such circular reasoning seems to derive from the belief that certain culture traits (such as "royalty" or "social stratification") belong uniquely to a particular group and therefore that the presence of this given element can be explained by the presence of, or direct contact with, the possessor group.

In fact, there are important differences in systems of social stratification between Bushi and Rwanda and between Bushi and other regions of Kivu—and the differences may well be greater than the similarities. The cultural differences, political prerogatives, and numerical size of the aristocratic class in Bushi are all much smaller than is the case for Rwanda; so small as to make artificial any arbitrary characterization of social stratification as such. In Bushi the Luzi form only a part of one clan, which is not a "ruling clan," but the clan to which the king belongs; in Rwanda, Tutsi are found as composite elements of nearly every clan. "Luzi" seems to be a term more determined by political characteristics (proximate agnatic descent from a king and legitimate exercise of power) than sociological classifications (clans), despite the fact that it is an inherited position. Furthermore, as presented by Cuypers, the Shi political system was organized in terms of territorial divisions only, with very broad political power delegated to subordinates within a given region.[15] In Rwanda the system included the delegation of restricted functions, overlapping powers, and interlocking domains. For such a brief treatment of social stratification in Bushi, the very fact that Cuypers was forced to rely on studies of Rwanda is itself witness to the poverty of primary empirical sources for Bushi.[16]

ANOTHER RECENT work, again one with wide influence within Zaire, is that by J.-C. Willame.[17] As applied to Bushi, the historical section of this study falls into some of the same difficulties we have seen above. The idea of conquest and of the Luzi as a conquering group in Bushi, apparently of different origins and race from the rest of the population, are presented more directly here than in Cuypers's works, but, alas, without references: "Au XVIIè siècle . . . les peuplades habitant le Bushi actuelle furent conquises par les clans Baluzi [*sic*] . . . Les Baluzi s'installèrent puis consolidèrent leur pourvoir sur les Bashi."[18] Here again are the elements of a necessary correlation between cultural elements and race. Here Tutsi influence is "proven" by the presence of clientship: "Les influences Tuutsi se révèlent notamment par le développement d'un système de clientèle."[19]

But Willame's historical presentation is intended only as a very short (one-page) background to political events in the region immediately following independence, and needs to be understood in this light.[20] His main theme is the juxtaposition of the new elite with the "authorités coutumières."[21] Willame's portrayal of internal Shi politics therefore seeks to illustrate, if not establish, the strong local political base controlled by the *mwami* (king), Kabare, during the early 1960s. In order to emphasize the important role of the mwami, to explain how "le mwami disposait d'un pouvoir populaire important à Bukavu, dans sa chefferie et chez les Bashi en générale," Willame portrays the Shi political system in these terms: "Une des charactéristiques les plus importantes du system socio-politique des Bashi réside en effet dans la souveraineté absolue et omni-présente du Mwami."[22]

As far as political relations with outsiders are concerned (including the colonial administration and the Kivu provincial authorities), it is clear that the overwhelming identification of the population was indeed with their mwami, as Willame states. But in terms of internal Shi politics and the domestic powers of the mwami, his argument is far from true. Willame recognizes as much when he refers to the "rivalités continuelles" and the "désagrégation politique de la classe conquérante" in reference to the internal politics of Bushi.[23] On the other hand, Willame skillfully explains Kabare's political ineffectiveness and total misunderstanding of the nature and processes of provincial politics by drawing on elements of Kabare's personal history: his unwillingness to enter into the new and wider political arena during colonial rule, and his exile during the greater part of the colonial period, especially during the important changes of the 1950s.

As with all works used as sources by the historian, Willame's essay must be understood and analyzed in light of the purposes for which it was written; it was not intended as a source for historical studies, nor is it suitable for this purpose. While I am in no way minimizing the contribution of this study to our understanding of politics in Zaire, it needs to be recognized that Willame's characterization of the political system of Bushi is applicable only to a small segment of political activity, and may not be a fair representation of Bushi as a whole. Furthermore, because Willame cites few references in his work, there is little possibility of evaluating the conclusions presented, and thus Willame's unsupported historical assertions can be accepted only with the greatest reserve and restraint.

FOR MANY of these arguments, the principal point of departure is the impressive work by Moeller. Basing his work on data collected by colonial administrators during the 1920s and 1930s, Moeller had access to a quantity of enormously valuable historical material, much of which cannot be recovered today. The later sections of the book, which consider the political institutions and ritual bases of several Kivu societies, attest to the enormous value of such data. The present discussion is concerned only with the historical presentation and particularly with some of the assumptions that guided the historical reconstruction advanced by Moeller; doing so reflects no intent to reflect on the value of the ethnographic sections of the work.

Unfortunately, in the collection of these data the testimonies and traditions were not preserved in their original form, thus impairing their value for later historians. In certain cases, however, Moeller did indicate the nature and quality of his data, a fact that is of great aid in evaluating his conclusions. Among others, he noted the sources and limitations of data for the Lega, the Hunde, and the Shi.[24] Furthermore, and perhaps even more important, Moeller occasionally made clear the multiplicity and variations of oral traditions, resulting in part from the composite nature of the societies involved: "Ces légendes donnent lieu à des variantes très appréciables lorsqu'on les recueille à la source.... Quant à la légende des origines, nous en avons des versions difficilement conciliables."[25]

While acknowledging the differences likely to arise in oral accounts, Moeller nonetheless viewed them as variants of a single original tradition that had degenerated over time. He consequently tended to combine different versions in order to reconcile the data to a single tradition valid for the entire ethnic group he is considering.[26] The same synthetic process was carried out at yet a higher level, where Moeller attempted to combine variant traditions from quite diverse ethnic groups over the entire region of Kivu, after having previously discounted specific variant traditions at the local level. Thus he selected traditions according to his a priori migration schema. For example, according to Moeller's account (based on royal traditions), most clans in Bushi arrived from Lwindi, southwest of Bushi; following this analysis, the postulated migration to Lwindi from an earlier dispersal center must have included the same social elements found in Bushi presently, that is, an association of "Hamite," "Bantu," and "Twa." Variants in the traditions may indeed represent a degeneration (either through simplification or elaboration) of a single original tradition. But they may also represent valid differences in historical experiences and interpretation. These differences may appear in similar forms either because expressed in a similar cultural and literary medium or because of interchange among traditions.

The enormous amount of local data in Moeller points to clear historical distinctions between the peoples whose kings claim historical associations to Lwindi (Shi, Havu, Fulero), those without such claims (Nyanga, Kumu, Hunde), and those to which Moeller assigns direct contact and origins in western Uganda (the Nande states). These historical differentiations, so apparent in Moeller's work, are associated with different cultural dispersal areas and reinforced by other cultural distinctions (in politics, kinship, and ritual structure, as well as in material culture) that historians interested in Kivu would do well to note. But Moeller tended to overlook the significance of these different dispersal areas by applying the same historical framework of migration from a few "models" to the entire Kivu region and by assuming that the various separate dispersal areas simply succeeded each other and therefore represented successive stages within a single migratory system. Thus, despite (or because of?) the paucity of direct historical data to this effect from areas other than Bunande, Moeller extended some unspecified Nande traditions of origin in Bunyoro to the entire region.[27] Such an extension was clearly a conscious assumption on his part, for he also specifically denied that the Hunde and Nyanga claimed origins in Bunyoro.[28] This is significant, for others have since claimed that Hunde/Nyanga traditions recount a Nyoro origin.[29] Given the lack of specific source citations in the written works, the possibility of direct feedback cannot be determined unequivocally.[30] However, it is likely, given Moeller's interests and position, that his account denying traditions of explicit Nyoro origins drew on "the ruling classes." (Certainly some members of the African elite later used Moeller's book to justify their position within the colonial context, since during my fieldwork I was shown mimeographed résumés of the work.) The contradictory accounts of Nyoro origin therefore probably represent a distinct change in the general corpus of the traditions, rather than simply regional or social variants. Moeller's influence among the Belgian administrators in the area, the pervasive quality of administrative hierarchy in this region, and the particular relationship of administrators and local elites all ensured that *Les grandes lignes* affected later dynastic traditions to some degree.[31] This is especially true in areas such as Buhunde and Bunyanga, where local political traditions tend to be of extremely shallow historical depth —genealogies of three or four generations being the norm.

It is also possible, of course, that earlier Hunde traditions did cite Nyoro origins and that these were not reported by Moeller, perhaps in deference to the boundary disputes between the British and Belgian administrations common early in the century; in general, the Africans near the border were keenly aware of such issues, and such assertions could be drawn on to aggravate colonial claims. But this possibility would itself indicate the sensitivity of "dynastic" traditions to contemporary political perceptions. Whether Moeller's account is accurate or not, it is clear that the independent character of the local source is compromised either by feedback or by political influences—or both. Consequently, more recent traditions on the distant dynastic past, especially the migratory past, can be used to confirm or revise earlier recorded sources only with due caution.

Moeller's quest for "origins," his preoccupation with long-distance migrations, and their predetermined general direction of movement raise certain problems concerning the interrelation of various levels of analysis. Moeller's methodology assumed that general regional trends in the movement of the Bantu-speaking peoples can be directly translated into local patterns of immigration and settlement of contemporary peoples. But in terms of influence on later historical reasoning, what is more serious is the use of an apparently automatic response mechanism within a preconceived general hypothesis, applied in a mechanistic fashion and in the absence of more empirical data. By this reasoning, it was necessary only to find a cause in order to postulate the migration that had already been established as effect: "La pouseée Shilluk-Dinka . . . mit en mouvement les Bantous de l'Entre-Albert-Victoria. . . . Plus tard, vers le milieu du XVIIè siècle, les Hamites Bashwezi, déthronés par las Babito et refoulés vers le sud, ont mis en mouvement les migrations consécutives Bahunde, Banande, Bahutu, etc."[32]

Furthermore, as portrayed by Moeller the migration process itself was not what one would expect based on known comparative examples. His migrations, composed of unchanging population elements, travel from one spot to another almost in a planned itinerary.

> De la sécheresse même de cette documentation se dégage une évocation, celle de ces hordes humaines en movement, qui n'est pas sans grandeur. Elles se sont mises en march à l'approche du danger. . . . Les clans cadets—c'est une règle invariable—sont parties les premiers chargés de vivres; les aînés s'arrachèrent les derniers de la terre où ils laissent les sepultures de leurs morts. Les cadets s'établissent en avant, préparent les cultures qui permettront au gros de la tribu de subsister en attendant que les uns et les autres soient à nouveau délogés de ces installations. . . . Les stations . . . ne durent pas toujours le temps d'une génération.[33]

It is all fiction. Migrations roughly similar to the type postulated by Moeller may be present in the history of Africa—witness the Ngoni—but they have been rare and have tended of necessity to be composed of very democratic elements, as a result of the rapid "turnover" of population caused by some groups (or families) dropping off, and new groups constantly being incorporated and assimilated during the migration. Furthermore, while the "migration" itself may continue, the actual individuals involved may change many times over, for the military basis and mobility of these long-distance migrations made it difficult to sustain a coherent system of social stratification during the long journey. In a few cases, such as the Bito in Kitara (in Uganda) and the Kololo among the Lozi (in western Zambia) and certain Ngoni states (in Malawi and Tanzania), the migration ended in a sedentary state showing important degrees of social stratification. But this was brought about by the superposition of the immigrating people over an earlier settled population and was not a situation maintained throughout the migration itself.

Moeller postulated the continuation of social stratification during the period of migration as a crucial element in his hypothesis, establishing the stratified societies of Kivu Province directly on the model of the former kingdom of Kitara. He therefore portrayed a migration "en formations qui associent Hamites, Bantous, et Batwa. Cette migration, qui laisse en cours de route les formations que nous trouvons échelonnées le long des Grands Lacs (notamment au Rwanda et en Urundi), atteint au Sud-Ouest du lac Kivu la région de la Lwindi (ou Ulindi)."[34] By arguing that the migrations were composed of socially distinct groups, Moeller did not need to account for the later emergence and development of the political units he was considering, or even the emergence of social classes. Implicitly, therefore, he viewed class structure simply as a continuation of previous stratification throughout the migration period, not as a result of migration.[35] By assuming that a fixed class formation preceded the migration, and that social institutions were rigid and unchanging, Moeller used the presence of the stratified class structure found "le long des Grands Lacs" as evidence for migrations. Under such conditions the search for such migrations is accepted as virtually the sole task of the historian: simply placing people and tracing migrations become substitutes for historical analysis.

THE EARLY and prolific writings of Fr. Pierre Colle have served as primary sources for many writers on Bushi; all the works cited in this chapter refer to at least one of his publications.[36] Colle's works represent an enormous and valuable compilation of numerous aspects of Shi life and culture. However, comparing his *Essai de monographie* with his own later work serves as a reminder to historians of their obligation always to consult the earliest available sources rather than being content to construct layer after layer of secondary and tertiary works. The quality of Colle's original work has not often been replicated in the subsequent brief summaries based on it. In fact, these summaries have all too often misrepresented Colle's work, both by simplifying and condensing it, and by extending his observations on the northern Shi to other regions that have been less well documented, notably the Havu.

Despite the highly generalized cultural similarities that Colle noted between the Shi and neighboring areas, his work cannot be applied to other areas of Kivu without careful corroborating studies.[37] The same stricture holds true even within Bushi itself, for, although the central Shi may form a coherent ethnic group, the Shi today (that is, in 1975) number well over five hundred thousand people, and included within that broad ethnic category are seven distinct political units of varying sizes and ecologies. Under these circumstances, one would indeed expect significant cultural and political variation. But Colle did not consider these in any systematic way, and others after him have tended to apply his studies of localized areas among the northern Shi indiscriminately to all of Bushi.[38]

One major problem in later works is the lack of any clear and agreed definition of the term "race" by writers on Bushi. Colle's work is interesting as an illustration of how inconsistent and ambivalent definitions have been interpreted and used by later writers in a manner generally determined by their preconceptions of Bushi (preconceptions based in part on Rwanda) more than by understanding the society. In his earlier work, Colle stated that "le Bushi est habité par deux populations bien différents; les Bashi qui forment le menu peuple, et les Baluzi, la classe dominante."[39] In his later work, however, this sentence was rendered as "Le Bushi est habité par deux races bien différents."[40] The substitution of "races" for "populations" is interesting and revealing in a sentence that was otherwise left unchanged.

The *Essai de monographie* was first published sixteen years after Colle's article. Between the appearance of these two publications, what Colle originally classified in social terms ("populations") became identified with, or rather transformed into, essentially a biological classification ("races"). This alteration in Colle's presentation is illustrative of the general trend in much European writing on Africa in the early years of this century—a trend toward increasing interest in racial identification and differentiation, and hence toward increasingly broad applications of racial terminology. At the time when it was written, the term "race," like "population," may indeed have contained a diffuse set of meanings covering social, historical, and cultural elements as well as physical characteristics (connotations that it sometimes maintains in popular French today). In later years, as the term has become more narrowly defined, groups that were not originally distinguished on biological criteria writings in Colle's writings came to be defined in terms of physical characteristics. This interpretation remains widespread in the more recent sources today, especially as reflected in the "common 'race' = common origins" hypothesis. Therefore, it seems that in the interests of claimed scientific "rigor," historical hypothesis has, over time and through frequent repetition, become elevated to historical "fact." At the same time, lexical transformations have replaced cultural identities ("populations") with biological categories ("races"). Combined with the absence of additional empirical data, this has significantly altered the understanding of "historical facts"; in short, these transformations have been treated as definitive.

However, as presented, Colle's data do not in fact seem to support the idea of racial differences between the Luzi and the rest of the population. While Colle did mention that certain physical characteristics are more evident among individuals of the royal line in Bushi, he expressly excluded collective references to the larger clan as a whole (the Banyamocha, of which the ruling aristocracy was but a part): "On trouve ... parmi ... les gens de clan Banyamwocha."[41] He noted that at the time of writing there had been no systematic identification and analysis of physical differences between the "Luzi" (the royal aristocracy) and other Shi. Nor, as noted above, have any other data since then established such physical distinctions. Nor are there apparent in Colle's works any references to cultural or social differences between the Luzi and the rest of the population, except those differences that might be attributed to distinctions in wealth and status determined by proximity to political power—and these differences are very minor in cultural terms. Such differentiation as exists in Bushi (in language, material culture, religion, etc.) appears to be more a question of regional variation than of "racial" or "migration-related" historical origins.

Another common confusion in the later works has been that of viewing Bushi as a conquest state. Cuypers refers to "invasion," and Willame refers explicitly to "la classe conquérante"; Moeller's position is ambiguous.[42] As we have seen above, Moeller believed that class differences preceded the migrations and arrived with the migrating peoples. But he also assumed that military conquest was inevitably closely associated with social stratification and racial differences ("sang watuzi"): "À l'origine des familles régnantes se trouvent des conquérants venus du Nord-Est du Lac Kivu, et sans doute de sang watuzi."[43]

This interpretation may in part result from the author's preoccupation with sources on Rwanda, where the early well-known accounts (Pagès, de Lacger) also portrayed the Tutsi as having conquered the previous inhabitants of the country. If the Luzi are identified as Tutsi, then the same historical processes are easily transposed from Rwanda to the later writers in Bushi. Colle, however, explicitly minimized the role of armed conquest in the formation of the Shi states: "Les deux autres [fils de Nyamuhoye] réussirent à supplanter les chefs du Bushi et du Rwanda par la ruse plus encore que par la force."[44] Here, as elsewhere in Africa, the establishment of a new social order and new dynasty is seen to be closely associated with the introduction of new food crops, possibly with important demographic results.[45]

The nonmilitary aspect of this process of state formation in Bushi is reinforced by constant reference in both legend and ritual to the role of the people, and by the importance to the ruling family of winning and keeping their support. In fact, the political system in Bushi appears to be much more fragile and flexible than that portrayed by Cuypers and Willame.[46] References to absolute power, to the "classe conquérante," and to power based on force, all result from a distortion of Colle's writings. Once the Luzi become identified as a "race," dominating politics and wielding "absolute" (instead of "ultimate") authority, it becomes perfectly acceptable to think of them in terms of a "conquering" people. But this is no more than a logical elaboration based on the later writers' own preconceptions: conquest, resulting from the meeting of the two distinct races, explains the presence of social stratification. Logic has replaced data; hypothesis has replaced research; confusion has replaced understanding. This is the fashion in which history has become transformed in the writings in question.

Part of the confusion in the later sources may result from the lack of precision in Colle's use of words. We have already seen that Colle apparently equated "population" with "race," although in current usage the two words have important differences in connotation. Colle also showed a preference for the same terms as those applied to Rwanda, a preference that makes the social categories appear more similar for the two areas than they may in fact be. In one case he equated the word "clan" with "caste."[47] He also applied the term "caste" to Shi political appointees of various strata, the *barhambo*. But the barhambo are not a hereditarily defined group (though in certain circumstances a *murhambo* may be succeeded by his son); they are not endogamous; and aside from the social distinctions associated with accessibility to power, there exist no important cultural distinctions between them and the rest of the population. They are not, in short, a "caste."

Yet a further semantic confusion adds to this effect of "transferring" the better-known social context of Rwanda to the lesser-known historical and sociological context of Bushi: the apparent similarity of the terms "Luzi" and "Tutsi." Although there has been no linguistic analysis of the relationship of these terms, they have often been accepted as simply minor variations of the same term, thus "proving" (in the eyes of some) the common origins of the two groups. Even aside from sociological differences in the two areas, and differences in their historical traditions, this does not seem a reliable transformation. In this area, it is true that the sounds represented by the letters "l" and "r" are difficult for outsiders to distinguish and apparently are virtually interchangeable; similarly with the sounds represented by the letters "rh" and "t." But there is no similar alteration current for "r" and "rh," despite the arbitrary choice of similar romanized letters to represent the sounds involved. And thus there is no interchangeability between the "l" sound and the "t" sound. Pending a proper linguistic analysis, those who assert the similarity of the two words as proof of the Luzi and Tutsi identity are arguing on doubtful evidence.[48]

In fact, Colle left the impression that one of the most important characteristics distinguishing the Luzi from the common people is to be found neither in their "race" nor in their culture, but rather in their historical traditions. Colle's historical presentation was brief. He was careful to point out both that these are *royal* traditions and that the genesis traditions consisted primarily of stories ("légendes") rather than constituting an analytical and complete historical study.[49] However, others who have followed him have neglected these observations, preferring to represent Luzi traditions as the only traditions valid for Bushi, and therefore applicable directly to the entire population. That is, they have tended to use Colle's selective "legends" as statements of historical fact without analysis.

References only to traditions of the Luzi have made it seem that the Luzi are the only dynamic and active elements in Shi society, and that the rest of the population is passive and static. In this way also the differences between the two groups are exaggerated. In fact, nonroyal family and local traditions refer equally to important movements, change, and the formation and alteration of local alliances, just as do the Luzi traditions; Colle himself referred to the movement and maneuvering of other groups.[50] Because later sources overlook the vigorous interactions between these social elements unaccounted for in Luzi traditions, the flexibility and dynamism of the political and social systems in this area are vastly underestimated in the more recent published condensations of Shi history.

Recent fieldwork has begun to correct some of these biases and misconceptions, and over the next several years our understanding of eastern Kivu societies, and Bushi in particular, may be transformed.[51] But until these works, based on fieldwork at the microlevel, are made accessible to the public, those working from written sources need to tread with care. It is hoped that this discussion has helped to identify some of the pitfalls that await the unwary. It is also hoped that by inquiring into the causes that have led others before us to tumble, we may be able to avoid some of the same pitfalls ourselves. At least we can hope that the failures of the next generation, if not also their achievements, will be original to them alone.

RECENT HISTORICAL RESEARCH
IN THE AREA OF LAKE KIVU

Rwanda and Zaire

1980

As in many areas of Africa, the first generation of historians to work in the Kivu Rift area after decolonization transformed our historical understanding of the region. They pioneered the incorporation of many types of sources into historical inquiry: archaeology, linguistics, ethnography—and, most importantly, oral sources. In the process, they also transformed the vision of history: African history was no longer exclusively the history of Europeans in Africa, but the history of Africans—indeed the history of many Africans, not just the elites and power holders. (However, only belatedly were women included as equal actors of history—and in this area more belatedly than elsewhere; that forms a major lacuna to the recent research in this area.)

Summarizing the work produced in the period 1960–80 for the areas east and west of Lake Kivu, this chapter discusses this recent historiography, exploring the new themes and focusing on new constituencies to be included in that new work. But this overview also points to a drawback: though these colleagues often collaborated, their writings were often individual contributions —this was parallel inquiry, not integrated inquiry. In some respects, research of the day simply "filled in the map"—driven by the huge task of

Cowritten with Bishikwabo Chubaka.

writing history anew, rather than formulating a new understanding of historical process. This essay illustrates both these trends: the enormous productivity of social research of this period, and the rather disparate nature of such contributions.

THE RWANDAN REVOLUTION of 1959–62 marked an important watershed not only for the history of the country but also for its historiography. Within Rwandan historical studies these political changes encouraged the development of a more broadly based analysis, one that went beyond the earlier tendency to focus on the Nyiginya royal court. The effects of this new historiography were not limited to Rwanda alone, however, since historical perceptions ultimately derived from Rwandan studies had dominated much of the earlier research on precolonial history both west and east of Lake Kivu. Combined with the emergence of new analytic assumptions elsewhere in Africa, the shift in Rwanda during the 1960s therefore freed studies west of the lake from the constraints of a particularly sterile historical model and opened the way for the initiatives of a new generation of Zairean historians conducting research there in the 1970s. The changing context of research initiatives and the continuing process of reassessment within Rwanda have also aligned perceptions of Rwandan history more closely with those of other areas. We can look forward in the future to more fruitful regional historical perspectives that transcend present political boundaries; it may well be that Rwandan research of the 1980s will draw increasingly on the concepts and conclusions of Zairean research of the 1970s.

Even while this new approach has perforated political boundaries on the ground, it has also dissolved the earlier rigid disciplinary boundaries of research. The major influence in this new approach came from the work of anthropologists (or historians with anthropological training). But this is not to say that historical studies per se became obsolete; on the contrary, they were immensely strengthened. Armed with such new perceptions, and with fieldwork techniques fully accounting for historical change, a new generation of researchers—including scholars of various disciplines—has brought about an important transformation in our historical understanding of the area.

Because of the cumulative contribution of these works in rethinking the history of this area, we feel that there is a clear need to share the initial findings with those lacking access to the research results. In this chapter, therefore, we shall try to summarize some of the more important work carried out over the last decade in both Rwanda and areas to the west of Lake Kivu.[1] Much of this work has not yet been published (and some is not fully available to us); consequently, rather than undertaking a full critical analysis of these works, we shall confine our comments to general indications of the topics considered and the analytic approaches pursued. Our intent here is to focus on lesser-known unpublished works; for the most part we shall omit considerations of readily available published work except for articles that are indicative of a much larger corpus of unpublished work and except for passing references to publications that have been particularly significant to the new historical work in the area.[2]

SEVERAL PUBLISHED works on Rwanda during the early 1960s were important precursors to this new genre of study. These served two functions: they provided a critical framework within which to assess the earlier work, which for the most part focused on central court politics and was drawn from normative idealist descriptions of the sociopolitical system; and they sketched out the new directions that subsequent work has since followed. Among the most valuable of these were Jan Vansina's *L'évolution du royaume Rwanda dès origins à 1900* (1962), Marcel d'Hertefelt's "Le Rwanda" (1962), and Alexis Kagame's *Les milices du Rwanda précolonial* (1963). Almost unnoticed, however, was a short article by Helen Codere, written from fieldwork conducted during the revolution itself, which cast a new perspective on the institutions of clientship, the keystone of previous anthropological work on Rwanda.[3] Together these works emphasized the importance of detailed empirical fieldwork on the institutions that so strongly characterized the Rwandan state. From such work there emerged fundamental questions concerning political differentiation, historical variability, and geographical diversity that could not be accounted for in colonially based work; the paradigms of the 1950s stressed political integration, historical durability, and geographical homogeneity—elements reflecting the administrative character of the colonial Rwandan state. Research of the 1960s thus stressed the importance of empirical studies over idealist constructions and local-level research over central court perceptions, and in this fashion laid the groundwork for subsequent important reappraisals of Rwandan history.

Most of the new works building on this legacy are the product of the 1970s. But the new interests of the turn of the decade had already been foreshadowed by a year, with the publication of Claudine Vidal's important analysis, "Le Rwanda des anthropologues ou le fétischisme de la vache" (1969). Like the works mentioned above, this article provided a cogent critique of earlier anthropological work—the staple of Rwandan social studies—but it also provided more suggestive leads to future work, and above all it demonstrated the value of detailed local-level anthropological studies as a corrective to the idealist assumptions that had guided earlier studies. Like Codere's article, Vidal's work focused on the portrayal of clientship institutions in earlier works. But where Codere attacked the ideology of class relations presented in these works, Vidal, using a broader range of empirical data, questioned the functional role of clientship, and indeed the central position of *ubuhake* clientship itself as portrayed in the earlier works. Drawing on empirical data from the level of the local community, Vidal suggested that "the fetishism of the cow" (as her article was subtitled) was more an anthropological model than a Rwandan reality. In previous works, cattle clientship had been portrayed as the exclusive mechanism of clientship; Vidal argued that ubuhake cattle clientship, far from serving as the only (or even the most important) such mechanism, was in fact only one among several kinds of clientship. Furthermore, she suggested that ubuhake was only a relatively recent form of clientship and not everywhere—perhaps not even in central Rwanda—was it historically the most important in terms of political power; other types, especially land clientship, seemed more significant as political mechanisms.[4]

Her conclusions were important and have been confirmed in many subsequent studies. But even more important was her methodology, based on a delimited "hill study,"[5] for it demonstrated definitively that an approach focusing on impact, not ideology, was feasible—indeed necessary—to provide a clear understanding of how the system actually worked on the ground. These results initiated a radical reassessment of Rwandan society; not only did they confirm earlier suggestions of variability in the client system, but more important, they raised questions as to the very applicability of the "patron-client" model for Rwandan studies.[6] It was clear that the idealist models of the Rwandan past were no longer acceptable.

Another early study utilized a similar technique. Pierre Gravel had worked on a single hill in Gisaka in eastern Rwanda during the revolution of 1959–62.[7] Despite (or because of) the upheaval, he was able to provide some new insights on the working of what he termed the "feudal manor" in Rwanda. In particular, he was able to catalogue the mobility of inhabitants of eastern Rwanda, considering especially their ties with Uganda—a topic that calls for much more work.[8] But perhaps his greatest contribution was to illustrate the process of lineage competition and the role of clientship as part of—but not as encapsulating—the political process of alliance-building at the local level: in this view clientship became a dynamic process in itself, and the specific political purpose of such alliances became manifest.

BUILDING ON these works as well as on the earlier historiography of Rwanda (an extraordinarily prolific outpouring for an African country of this size),[9] the new direction of Rwandan historiography was illustrated in a special issue of *Cahiers d'Études Africaines* in 1974, which included an important collection of local-level studies, many based on work still in progress at the time, others indicating the results of work already done. Although it is impossible to discuss all the articles of significance in this collection, three deserve mention in passing. The careful analytical work by Joseph Rwabukumba and Vincent Mudandagizi on "Les formes historiques de la dépendance personnelle dans l'état rwandais" provided substance to the historical dimension of clientship.[10] By tracing the implantation of ubuhake clientship in an area of south-central Rwanda from the early nineteenth century, the authors argued for a radical reassessment of the time span often attributed (without evidence) to Rwanda client institutions in general, and especially to certain specific forms often thought of as "traditional" and hence assumed to be ancient and enduring. Since then, as will be discussed below, work by various researchers working in different parts of Rwanda has corroborated their reassessment.

In the same issue of *Cahiers d'Études Africaines,* Lydia Meschi contributed a fascinating study on the evolution of land ownership on a single hill over a period of three generations. This work once again stressed the profound nature of changes over the last century—including important demographic changes—in almost completely transforming the earlier structures of land rights.[11] By tracing the development of land-settlement patterns, Meschi followed the lines of analysis first brilliantly set out in Gravel's chapter on the "Play for Power" in his *Remera.*[12]

A third article in this collection was less important for its direct application to earlier assumptions and ideologies than in plotting out a relatively new domain of inquiry for Rwandan studies.[13] Surprisingly, except for the role of cattle, the material basis to Rwandan political and social institutions was scarcely considered in the earlier works. (No doubt this is partly because Rwandan oral traditions, so rich in documenting personal ties, are almost completely devoid of economic transfers, even prestations to the central court.[14]) Claudine Vidal's "Économie de la société féodale rwandaise" traced out the nature of economic interrelations within precolonial Rwandan society and considered the ideologies associated with these economic strata. In particular, she showed the great discrepancies of wealth in precolonial Rwanda, the importance of control over labor (cautiously estimating that about one-half of the population were employed as "day laborers"), and the structural elements that reproduced this system.[15] The potential lines of inquiry sketched out in her article have not yet been followed up in any comprehensive way, although some work on economic transactions, if not structures, has been undertaken recently (as noted below). But the point is well taken: perhaps more thought need be given to both economic and conceptual structures in the analysis of Rwandan society. At the very least, Vidal's article suggests a possible analytic framework within which to assess this dimension of Rwandan life.

IN ADDITION to the material appearing in the special issue of *Cahiers d'Études Africaines,* other original fieldwork has resulted in the completion of several longer studies, as yet unpublished. As with the work already cited, these also provide a corpus of significantly different departures from earlier historiography (though foreshadowed, as mentioned above, by certain key earlier works). Some of these works are regional studies; so far, studies focusing on south-central, southwestern, and northern areas of Rwanda have been completed. (Other projects are currently underway in Bugoyi and Ruhengeri in the northwest of the country, and Bwishaza-Rusenyi, in western Rwanda.[16] The areas of eastern Rwanda, and especially those relating to areas farther east still—Bugufi and Bushubi—have been sadly neglected in this new approach.)

Although undertaken independently of each other, these projects tend to reinforce each other on certain key aspects, while still demonstrating the variety and variability that characterized precolonial Rwanda. The work of Jean-François Saucier, for example, extends considerably the empirical work on clientship mentioned in Rwabukumba and Mudandagizi's article, and it provides statistical evidence that forces a major revision in the earlier concepts of the age and extent of Rwandan client institutions.[17] From a careful inquiry carried out on four hills in the area south of Butare (south-central Rwanda) Saucier tested the postulates and hypotheses expounded by earlier writers on ubuhake clientship. Some significant conclusions emerge: only 16 percent of the fathers of present inhabitants, for example, experienced ubuhake ties—ties that had been portrayed by Maquet as the "social glue" linking all Rwandan society from top to bottom; and less than 9 percent of the grandfathers' generation did so, thus suggesting that the previous portrayal of ubuhake as the central social relationship of traditional (precolonial) Rwanda was erroneous. Furthermore, the figures for Tutsi participation in ubuhake were higher than those for Hutu, and "political" clientship was higher than "nonpolitical." This brings into question, yet again, Maquet's integrationist interpretation of ubuhake clientship, according to which all Hutu could—and had to—find some protection against the rulers by means of ubuhake clientship.[18] It is clear from Saucier's work that ubuhake was used as a political tool—and resulted from a direct power imbalance—rather than serving as a generalized social web of mutual protection pervading Rwandan society.

Saucier's statistical analysis finds independent confirmation on almost every point in the work of Catharine Newbury.[19] Based on fieldwork in Kinyaga in extreme southwest Rwanda, this study traced the changes in clientship structures from their imposition in the early nineteenth century through the period of colonial rule. By considering a range of clientship patterns (not just ubuhake) Newbury was able to account for changes in the relations of the various client forms both to each other and to the changing broader political context. The transformation of the different clientship forms, and the resultant formation of a "genealogy" of clientship types traced through time, related specifically to the changing political environment during the period from 1860 to 1960. These transformations also played an important role in spawning new social identities, based on access to different material and political resources, and giving new meaning to ethnic categories within Kinyaga.[20] Thus the form and significance of both clientship and ethnicity (often seen as "primordial" features of Rwandan society) can be seen as varying with the changing political patterns of which they formed a part.

Jim Freedman's work on northern Rwanda (Byumba Prefecture) extended the general reassessment of Rwandan society in two ways.[21] First, it reemphasized the differences of this region from the central Rwandan model portrayed as universal in the earlier sources.[22] At the same time, it advanced the conceptual framework applied to Rwandan studies in its most comprehensive form by de Heusch.[23] Using the concepts derived from de Heusch's structural analysis of interlacustrine history, Freedman went on to provide a theoretical contribution to the concept of "joking relations"—a contribution summarized in a later article.[24] His thesis also provided many interesting insights in to the history of Ndorwa-Mpororo, along the northern border of Rwanda.[25]

Other recent works have contributed to areas of study neglected in the historiography. Alison Des Forges's dissertation was perhaps the first to provide an in-depth analysis of court-oriented politics under colonial rule—a period surprisingly neglected in Rwanda compared to other areas of Africa.[26] Relying on meticulous research, she demonstrated convergence of European and Rwandan elite goals, the ways in which European administrations became Rwandanized, and the crucial changes in the patterns of kingship in the period before 1931. She also provided much fascinating material on the political cleavages that occurred in Rwanda during this time of major social alterations. Finally, her study served to deepen the contribution of her own earlier articles on the period of the imposition of colonial rule and the new religious and economic structures that went with it.[27]

Work presently underway in Rwanda will also serve to fill important gaps in the historical picture of Rwanda. Ferdinand Nahimana of the Department of History at the National University of Rwanda has undertaken research on the pre-Nyiginya Hutu polities of northern and western Rwanda.[28] Oral traditions from those areas where Nyiginya expansion was relatively recent, for example, will help to provide a new perspective to the political history of this region and add to the intriguing but sketchy sources presently available.

The research of Bernard Lugan will help fill another gap in the literature, concerning economic activity in the early colonial period—a field almost totally absent from the formal court traditions and hence from the public record. Using a questionnaire research technique and interviewing in many different parts of Rwanda, Lugan has been able to establish the existence—and to plot the locations —of early markets in Rwanda.[29] He has also contributed to the related field of famine history.[30] Though the historical depth of his studies has been hampered for lack of adequate data, and these economic aspects still need to be related to the currents of historical change in the larger Rwandan society (as Vidal has suggested), such studies have provided a welcome contribution to Rwandan studies at the empirical level.

In sum, Rwandan historiography has made some important strides in the last decade or so, and is poised at an exciting point of departure for future work. The general direction of this new trend is clear. Much more remains to be done, however, both in regional studies and in further conceptual refinements, working toward a global, comprehensive interpretation of Rwandan history. In addition, the histories of famine, disease, and ecological change have not yet been broached; colonial history has been relatively neglected; and religious and economic histories leave room for considerable interesting work.[31] Finally, more needs to be done in considering Rwandan history within a wider regional framework, one transcending the present political boundaries, rather than focusing on the Rwandan state as a historical and historiographical enclave.[32]

TO THE west of Lake Kivu, similar strides have been made over the course of the last decade, and the basic precolonial historical outline based on a solid groundwork of local and historical monographs has now taken shape, although much remains to be done. This work is perhaps all the more important, as this is an area where little scholarly research into the precolonial period had been carried out before the 1970s.[33] Nonetheless, this corpus is more difficult to summarize because it is spread over a greater diversity of geographical areas and historical contexts, and it includes a wide variety of different topics and conceptual approaches.

The publication of the 1975 issue of *Études d'Histoire Africaine*, devoted entirely to the lacustrine area, was an important turning point in the historiography of this region. Just as the 1974 edition of *Cahiers d'Études Africaines* provided a forum for Rwandan scholars, this collection of essays included numerous Zairean and Rundi nationals among the contributors.[34] This was both a tribute to the dynamism of the History Department at UNAZA (the National University of Zaire) and the quality of their research programs, and a testimony to the work of many competent Zaireans—the first generation of Zairean historians trained in Zaire.[35]

A second noteworthy aspect of this issue was that it included some preliminary results of recent fieldwork undertaken in the region itself, and thus introduced an international audience to an area of Africa long neglected in historical scholarship. These articles were based on both local archives and oral interviews, precisely the kind of material needed to assess the value of the earlier secondary sources of the region. Thirdly, it provided an indication of the variety of themes being explored in the area, including demographic history, social history, church history, and the history of resistance, of land rights, and of regional contacts. The breadth of the thematic treatment was also reflected in the wide geographical scope covered, thus providing the hope that a broader regional history based on solid local-level empirical investigations would eventually be possible.

From about the same time a series of important earlier research projects began to come to fruition. The area of Bushi southwest of Lake Kivu has been the most important (though not the only) focus of these studies, and over the last few years at least four full-length studies have been undertaken that relate to the historical study of this region. Of these, only one has as yet been published. J.-B. Cuypers's *Alimentation chez les Shi* brings together a wealth of detail on the material culture of the Shi based on his own research, for the most part in northern Bushi (Irhambi).[36] Most of these data relate to food preparation and storage, but there is much of a general ethnographic interest in this book as well.

The second of these works is the doctoral thesis on Shi rituals by Dikonda wa Lumanyisha, one of the first full-scale works on Bushi by a Zairean scholar.[37]

It includes many valuable texts, which in themselves make the work of interest to students of Shi society. The rituals analyzed include those relating to marriage and succession, as well as royal rituals. There is, however, a tendency to generalize a local pattern (often drawn from northern Bushi) to all regions of Bushi, a culture area that today probably includes close to one million people and that in the past included at least six kingdoms. Historians using this work will need to take account of the significant regional differences in the area; nonetheless, Dikonda's work contains a wealth of data for historians and others.

Two other works are more directly related to the precolonial history of the area. One of these is based on an anthropological study of a community in Ngweshe, one of the Shi kingdoms. Elinor Sosne's "Kinship and Contract in Bushi" provides the first comprehensive analysis of a Shi social system as it actually functions over time and as it affects individual members of Shi society.[38] This study focuses on the processes of inheritance (or kinship ideology) and contract, the twin foundations of Shi society. The importance of the former is reflected in the institution of "positional succession," whereby a man's heir adopts the total social role of his predecessor, including most of the predecessor's material wealth and virtually all of his social status within the larger kinship structure. This means that others (nonheirs) must eventually move to new land and establish roles within the politico-jural complex through contractual mechanisms to other individuals. By focusing on the constant "play for power" at all levels of Shi society and showing how these institutions function within a given empirical context, Sosne has provided a major advance over earlier descriptions of isolated "structures" within Shi society: "society" is no longer seen as simply the sum of a series of discrete independent institutions. "Kinship and Contract" thus once again illustrates the value of the technique employed by Vidal and others in getting beyond the framework of how society "ought" to work, and into the realm of empirical behavior.

Another of the important new works is more directly historical in that it seeks to document fundamental transformations in Shi society dating from the establishment of the Banyamocha dynasty in Bushi. Paradoxically, however, it does not provide an empirical history of individuals and events. Instead, Richard Sigwalt's "The Early History of Bushi" is concerned with the transformations in the underlying conceptions of kingship.[39] From a careful analysis of nine genesis traditions, Sigwalt traces the provenance and diffusion of *ubwami*—the concept of kingship—from the areas west of present-day Bushi, areas in which there exist no centralized political structures on the model of the lacustrine states today. By considering how Shi concepts of ubwami originally derived from the southwest and developed within Shi society, this work rebuts earlier suggestions that royal institutions were introduced from the north and east.[40] The study also provides an important methodological contribution; through comparison of the different variants of traditions, it shows how the sources themselves have altered over time. In proposing a history of conceptualizations and institutions rather than one focusing on individuals and events, this work has shifted analysis a long way from the rigid concern with migration, settlement, and "origins" as ends of historical studies in themselves, an approach that strongly characterized earlier studies on precolonial history of this region. Instead we are entering a realm in which we can hope to account for adaptation, incorporation, and structural change.

But despite these contributions, there is much work left to be done in the field of precolonial Shi history. We lack even a brief outline of a political history for the eighteenth and nineteenth centuries that is based on anything more than uninformed speculation and bland hypothesis. The most likely remedy to this is to be found in the careful recording, transcription, and annotation of oral texts, a research program now being undertaken by Zairean researchers—teachers, priests, and students among them. It is impossible to overestimate the value and importance of their work along these lines. The work of Bishikwabo Chubaka, presently researching the history of the smaller Shi kingdoms on the southern perimeter of Bushi, represents one aspect of this work. Focusing on areas previously neglected in most sources, Bishikwabo's work will provide a new perspective, not only on Bushi as a whole, but on the internal working of one Shi polity.[41] This will serve as an important contribution, for often in the larger, more centralized states the subtleties of the state-level dynamics are obscured by the hierarchized administrative framework; until now, our understanding of Shi central court politics has been based largely on generalizations and idealizations, rather than on empirical analysis. Secondly, the kingdom of Kaziba, the focus of Bishikwabo's studies, was a major iron-working center during the late nineteenth century; hoes from Kaziba were known throughout the region and far into Rwanda. As a commercial center, Kaziba benefited from its position between the Lake Tanganyika–Lake Kivu network and the Rwandan trade with the forest areas to the west. Thus this study could eventually alter our understanding of the fundamental material basis of kingship in this area, as well as provide many new insights on commercial interaction in the wider region.

Yet another important initiative into precolonial historical studies is the careful collection of the rich oral sources now being done by various Shi priests; the work of Abbé Cenyange Lubula is particularly outstanding. Carefully collected, transcribed, translated, and annotated, this type of work can provide an essential building block for future historical inquiry; it is also an impressive testimony to the Shi past, for which the oral data are presently much more extensive than for neighboring regions.[42]

Although the present overview is concerned primarily with work in precolonial history, three research projects now underway that deal with the early colonial period in Bushi deserve mention, for they will require research into various aspects of precolonial social structures. At the same time, they are representative of a much larger body of recent research carried out in Bushi by Zairean scholars. These three deal with the questions of resistance to the imposition of early colonial rule, labor mobilization, and urbanization.

Bushi and the neighboring areas of eastern Kivu provide a particularly interesting and complex field for the study of early colonial resistance. First, the area was first brought into contact with European administration relatively late, around 1900, and the civilian colonial administrative structures were often not established until after World War I (and only toward 1930 in some areas). As a result, patterns of resistance against colonial rule in these areas are relatively recent; in some cases they relate directly to earlier resistance against structures in the area, or more recent politics. Secondly, since this area was on the frontier of German-Belgian rivalry before World War I, "resistance" was often tied to the capacity of African authorities to draw on the support of one European power against the other, and was therefore often directly or indirectly related to the hostilities between these European powers. Finally, political centralization and social differences in the area were such that often European activities became directly involved in the internal politics and conflicts—and often resistance and collaboration can best be explained by reference to these internal factions, rather than by reference to European institutions alone. These and other aspects of Shi resistance (including the religious aspects) have been explored in several articles by Njangu Canda-Ciri.[43] Njangu distinguishes between European and Shi accounts, and between the perceptions of various Shi participants, and shows that the initial struggle against, or collaboration with, colonialism can be seen as an extension of earlier political conflicts with Bushi.

The subjects of land and labor are also central to the colonial history of eastern Kivu. But as we have seen above for the institutions of land, labor and clientship in Rwanda, these aspects of colonial Shi society can best be understood within the context of their evolution from the precolonial period. The work now being undertaken by Bashizi Cirhagarhula on agriculture and rural development in colonial Bushi, including both European plantations and African production, will provide an important contribution to precolonial as well as to colonial studies on Bushi. In fact, the subjects of labor mobilization and land accessibility would themselves make suitable topics for a precolonial historical study along lines similar to those which Bashizi or Sosne have outlined for the later period.

Finally, the study of residential agglomerations and urbanization, and the factors behind such patterns of social change in Bushi, is another field where colonial history cannot be clearly separated from precolonial history. In this regard, Pilipili's work on the establishment of Bukavu provides another new departure in Kivu studies.[44] Building particularly on two relevant earlier works, Pilipili focuses on the early communities serving as intermediaries between Bushi and Kinyaga to the east of the Rusizi River and highlights the initiatives of Africans—especially of the "communauté extra-coutumière"—in the establishment and evolution of Bukavu, especially in the years before 1935.[45] Although based on both oral and archival accounts, this work could be extended both by a comprehensive project of consulting Africans in Bukavu and by more detailed studies on the evolution of the wider colonial context within Kivu. Taken together, these three initiatives—the forms of resistance to and collaboration with early colonial structures; the economic aspects of labor and land (including both plantation agriculture and African cash-crop cultivation); and the establishment of a new cultural milieu around the administrative-economic center of Bukavu —represent important new directions for Kivu (and specifically Shi) studies.[46]

THE HEAVY concentration of work on Bushi, however, presents the danger of imbalance. Where Shi studies dominate the work on other areas in the region, there will be a strong temptation to extrapolate from a relatively well-known area such as Bushi to other areas that present apparent similarities. But it is a particularly hazardous task to do so, for while the general forces influencing historical change and perceptions may have been regional in scope (especially during the colonial period), the reactions, as well as the local initiatives, naturally varied significantly from one locale to another. In many respects, despite superficial similarities, social structures and political organization differed significantly from region to region. Until recently it has been the similarities that have been stressed; the differences—perhaps more significant in accounting for (and testifying to) local dynamics—have for the most part been neglected. Consequently the studies undertaken outside Bushi, though less numerous, are no less important.

The problem of generalizing from Bushi has been most evident for the history of the Havu. Many earlier studies simply assumed that the Havu societies, located just north of Bushi, were similar if not identical to Shi society. This assumption was based partly on the apparent linguistic and political similarities between the mainland Havu and the Shi, but it also resulted, at least in part, from the fact that many of the earlier historical inquiries were apparently carried out by missionaries with the help of Shi interpreters or guides. This appears to have resulted in a tendency to favor those informants who concurred with Shi perceptions of Havu history.[47]

However, recent research among the Havu makes it possible to present a new perspective on Havu history. The linguistic work of Aramazani Birusha will provide a valuable foundation for such work, in a field for which there have as yet been no studies at all because Kihavu has simply been assumed to be similar, both lexically and morphologically, to Mashi, the language of the Shi. His preliminary findings indicate that the differences between the two languages are more significant than previously assumed, but for the exact nature and degree of these differences we must await the completion of Aramazani's meticulous research. In addition, students from both UNAZA-Bukavu (ISP) and UNAZA-Lubumbashi have completed theses on the precolonial histories of Ijwi Island and mainland Havu areas on the western lakeshore; unfortunately, these are not available at present.[48]

The early history of the Ijwi kingdom is also the focus of research that examines Ijwi history both within the wider regional context and in terms of the local-level interaction between the royal family and other groups on Ijwi.[49] On the wider plan this work ties Ijwi history to processes of historical change occurring in the forest regions west of the Mitumba Mountains, in areas east of Lake Kivu (now western Rwanda), and in the Rusizi River valley and northern Burundi, by the shared influences and changing historical contexts within which these societies evolved, as well as by more direct interactions. Within Ijwi history this work suggests that increasingly strong clan identities emerged with increasing political centralization. It therefore questions the "primordial" association of clan structures, arguing instead that the present clan structure on Ijwi resulted in part from recent changes in the wider political context.

FARTHER NORTH, another important locus of recent research is the area of Bunande (including the administrative zones of Beni and Lubero), just west of Lake Edward and the Semliki Valley.[50] For this area the same general historiographical influences are apparent that have been noted for other areas west of the Kivu Rift Valley. There is less concentration on a *problèmatique* structured around "origins and migrations." Increasingly, interest is turning toward internal processes of change, based more on local-level research. Once again, however, our discussion of this work can only be selective; most of these studies at present consist of unpublished theses found in Bukavu or Lubumbashi, presently unavailable to us.[51]

One precolonial study from this area, however, is particularly important, not only for its analysis of the history of the Bashu (one of several Nande groups) but also because of the conceptual frameworks explored.[52] Using an analytical approach drawn from F. G. Bailey and A. W. Southall, R. Packard analyzes in detail the processes of alliance-building and confrontation among rivals for power.[53] In both these domains the assertion of ritual power was an important tactic; competition over political power was expressed in competing claims to ritual authority. In Bunande this ritual authority was most directly illustrated by control over rain, and beyond that over the productivity and security of the people, for the centralization of ritual power to overcome or prevent ecological disaster was the essential quality of *obwami*—legitimate political authority. The fragmentation of such ritual authority—that is, all situations that threatened political centralization, such as succession disputes—opened the way to ecological disaster and thus were often associated with periods of famine. The essential characteristic (and necessary proof) of legitimate kingship was therefore the successful centralization of ritual and the bountiful harvests resulting from this.

But Packard's study is not simply an inventory of ritual practices. It is a history of ritual concepts in action, one that relates their use to specific political contexts. In particular, the political significance of ritual and religious concepts is closely tied to both ecological history and changing disease environments. This of course opens the way to an analysis of the historicity of ritual concepts, as the ecological context is progressively transformed and ritual practices alter accordingly.[54]

"The Politics of Ritual Control" also provides an example of a structural analysis of Shu genesis traditions. Drawing on similar work done elsewhere, Packard shows how structural analyses can be applied to historical studies by relating the analysis of these "myths of origin" to three levels of Shu thought and action. He analyzes them successively as instruments of political action, as indications of historical processes, and as testaments of fundamental cultural values, illustrating another important methodological tool for this area, where the time depth of oral traditions is generally very shallow and where no written records are available from before the early years of this century.[55]

THE SOUTHERN end of the region considered here, the area of the Rusizi River valley between lakes Tanganyika and Kivu, is the focus for yet another unpublished thesis, Jacques Depelchin's "From Precapitalism to Imperialism."[56] This is less a chronological study of a history of events than an essay on Marxist perspectives on the history of the Rusizi River valley; the major contribution of this work is to the conceptualization of the African past, the mode of thought within which new questions are generated.

Rather than tracing migrations or dynastic history, Depelchin focuses on the changing interpersonal relations within which people lived out their lives. Though he sees the economic basis as important, it is not the exclusive determinant in this historical framework. He also gives consideration to ideologies and modes of perception among the Vira, Furiiru, and Rundi peoples themselves; Depelchin emphasizes that his approach derived from the nature of the data and reflects the way these people themselves portray their own past.

The essential characteristic of this approach is the attempt at a more holistic analysis, one less divided into separate institutions and discrete events. Within the economic sphere, for example, the focus is not on production as an activity, but on relations of production. It includes an analysis of which group performed a given activity and the group's relations to other groups through this activity, as well as a description of the activity itself. For instance, Depelchin notes that while certain aspects of agricultural activity (such as clearing the brush before planting, weeding, or harvesting) may be technically similar now to these processes as performed in 1894, the social groups involved in these tasks clearly have different relations to other groups than was the case in 1894, and the harvest is used for different purposes. Thus the meaning and quality of the work of clearing the land is transformed by the nature of the changing political environment within which such an activity takes place. Within this perspective, it is the change in the relations of production—the social and political significance of productive activities—that is the significant dimension of the history of this area. According to Depelchin, these changing relations of production, not changing powers in the hands of local authorities or changing institutions looked at in isolation, were the significant alterations that occurred during the sixty years of colonial rule in the area. One aspect of this process that interests Depelchin is how these alterations are related to other changing perceptions—how ideologies account for (or obscure, as the case may be) these long-term perspectives on the changing material bases of social processes and the inequalities reproduced in social institutions.

IT IS therefore the diversity of approaches that distinguishes the historiography of the Zairean regions from recent Rwandan historiography. Despite its clear break with the past, the latter still operates within a well-established historiographical tradition and a clearly defined geographical and cultural domain. This aspect of Rwandan historiography may be salutary in relating the various strands of work to each other and thus providing a more detailed picture of the wider whole. But there are drawbacks to this approach as well. Where the essential historical issues are defined by the previous works, the scope for new approaches is reduced. The very dynamism of recent Rwandan research has resulted at least in part from the tension of breaking through the dominant framework that existed before 1960, while still relating to it. There is still the danger, however, of establishing a new orthodoxy, and thus there is a constant need to break into new conceptual fields of analysis.

West of Lake Kivu, on the other hand, where there are fewer constraints imposed by earlier paradigms, less thought has tended to be devoted to the conceptual underpinnings and perspectives of recent research, except insofar as these are related to more general historical issues being addressed elsewhere in African history. The result of this lack of imposed historiographical structure has been that studies of different locales for the period before 1900 in this area at present represent a variety of conceptual approaches. Until now, little has been done to try to relate these studies to each other or to a common intellectual framework, or to develop a regional concept of historical change. Indeed, until very recently we lacked the detailed understanding of the area that would make such an attempt feasible. But in a sense the existence of different conceptual approaches—the focus of ritual/ecological factors among the Banande, the role of structural oppositions in the social history of Ijwi, the analysis of genesis traditions for what they mean as well as for what they say in Bushi, and the materialist conception of history proposed in the study of the Rusizi River valley—is for the moment a strength. The lack of any dominant single paradigm may yet force a more systematic examination of the conceptual frameworks required to achieve an understanding of the significant patterns of historical change, not only in this area but elsewhere in Africa as well.

The historiographical development of this area over the last decade has shown some important breakthroughs that are all the more remarkable considering that they have been concentrated in a relatively small area, and considering the relative paucity of previous studies relating directly to the region. Much, of course, remains to be done: it is clear that "tribal" or "institutional" studies will not take us very far.[57] Obvious frontiers for future research in this area include specific elements of social identities, of conceptualizations of history and society, of medical and religious conceptualizations, and of material bases of historical activity(including ecological as well as economic factors).[58] Nor has any study yet focused on the role of women.[59] We need texts; we need religious concepts; we need material on production and the flow of goods (within as well as between societies); and we need a better understanding of the impact of the changing broader political contexts.

But it is at least as important to consider and to consider fully what we need to do with the material. What do we seek to understand? Do we have the historical questions to guide our analyses? Do we have coherent concepts of history that give rise to questions—not in a rigid fashion, but in an open-ended fashion, one that leads continually to new frontiers rather than which closes frontiers by simply filling in the gaps in an outmoded historical problèmatique. It is toward an answer to this fundamental question that research in Kivu has been groping its way forward. The past decade has seen progress, but we need now to consider historiographical progress on at least two levels. This essay is intended, therefore, to place the local studies in a wider framework, in an attempt to avoid the possibility of turning the historiographical development of the 1970s into the historiographical underdevelopment of the 1980s.

PART 2

X

The Lake Kivu Arena

LAKE KIVU REGIONAL TRADE IN
THE NINETEENTH CENTURY

1980

*Early histories on this region focused on royalty and on clientship—
specifically clientship as a hierarchical institution that included political
patronage from above and economic tribute from below. Material transfer
was assumed to occur only within the contours of social affiliations and political dependence. It was also assumed that only through the security of the
state could long-distance trade develop; only the state, it was presumed, could
organize and protect such commerce.*

*This chapter challenges such assumptions. It focuses on the ways socie-
ties without centralized state structures (such as those west of Lake Kivu)
actually encouraged mobility and exchange between complementary economic zones, and it argues that, by seeking to control such commerce and to
benefit from it, state power actually impeded such mobility and reduced long-
distance trade. This essay focuses on the commerce associated with a humble
bracelet-anklet, fabricated of forest vines west of Lake Kivu and traded as a
luxury item in the aristocratic milieux east of the lake. It explores the range
and depth of the cultural contacts to emerge from such commercial networks. And it traces changes in the system—from north of Lake Kivu in the
early part of the nineteenth century to the southern reaches of the lake in*

the last quarter of the century. It shows that for all the apparent differences in this region, these diverse cultures were woven together into tight networks of exchange.

The analysis points out what is lost from history by focusing on states alone: adventure, friendship, profit, culture—in addition to power—are also important as motivating human action. Furthermore, it analyzes the development of a commercial network on a vast scale, showing intense interaction between a highly centralized, highly stratified society on the one hand (Rwanda), and societies lacking centralization and stratification on the other (those west of Lake Kivu). As an example of only one of several such interlocking trade networks in this region, this case study illustrates the vitality and initiatives present at the local level in these "lands beyond the mists."

THE DEBATE ON THE RELATION of trade and markets in West Africa has only belatedly been taken up in East African historiography.[1] For the most part this debate has focused on the origin of markets; the two most extreme positions attribute them either to a "propensity to trade" at the local level or to contacts with long-distance trade routes linked directly to the global economy.[2] Aside from the question of origins, however, there are other important aspects of this discussion, dealing more broadly with trade than with markets. Three such themes are addressed here: the role of trade between markedly different cultural regions; the relation of trade and markets; and the relation of trade networks to political centralization. It will be argued that in the area of Lake Kivu, environmental and cultural differences encouraged rather than impeded commercial interaction, that trade was carried out on a significant scale without organized markets, and that the Lake Kivu trade networks flourished independently of direct political control by local state structures.

This chapter focuses on the precolonial trade system around Lake Kivu, today the boundary between Zaire and Rwanda. Because this area was not directly tied to the coastal trade until late in the nineteenth century, the trade in bracelets, livestock, and food products discussed here remained largely autonomous of extra-African ties. Nevertheless, the Lake Kivu network was sensitive to alterations in the larger commercial environment, and commercial influences from neighboring systems north and south of the lake had important repercussions on the evolution of the Lake Kivu trade network; the effects of this will provide the fourth theme traced out below. Before exploring the historical evolution of the regional trade, however, I will first consider the general characteristics of the trade system, the commodities included in it, and the relation of this regional trade network to more local trade patterns.

The Peoples of the Lake Kivu Trade

Running north and south, and bordered by mountain ranges with peaks of three thousand meters and more in altitude, the Lake Kivu Rift has served as a major cultural as well as geographical divide, separating the Interlacustrine societies to the east (of which Rwanda is the best-known example) from the "forest cultures" to the west (including the Lega, Tembo, and Nyanga societies).[3] The sharp social and political distinctions between these areas, however, have tended to obscure the strong historical interactions across the Kivu Rift, linking societies east and west of the lake. Combined with environmental and cultural differences distinguishing these areas, such enduring interactions served as a basis for the strong commercial ties that developed between Rwanda and areas west of the lake during the nineteenth century (see map 3.1).

The regional trade system that emerged from these factors—one transcending political and cultural differences—was distinguished from more locally determined economic networks on several grounds. Producer and ultimate consumer in this system seldom interacted directly, as the goods passed through many hands, sometimes over long distances. Transactions of the principal goods in this regional trade were not characterized by processes of reciprocity or redistribution; although traders often returned to earlier trading partners, each transfer was seen as a discrete transaction in itself. Blood brotherhood and clan identities sometimes facilitated trade patterns, but kinship and social roles were not the determinant factors in the regional commercial patterns. All these factors distinguished this trade from more local forms of exchange.

The regional trade discussed here involved the present Havu, Hunde, and Shi peoples, but the major poles of trade, for which environmental and cultural differences were the most pronounced, were the Tembo and Nyanga areas (in the west) and Rwanda (in the east). Living just west of the Mitumba Mountains marking the western edge of the Rift Valley, the Tembo and Nyanga peoples form the eastern flank of the vast culture zone associated with the equatorial forest of the Zaire basin. Sparsely settled in precolonial times, they were organized politically into small-scale, ritually based units with a minimum of specialized

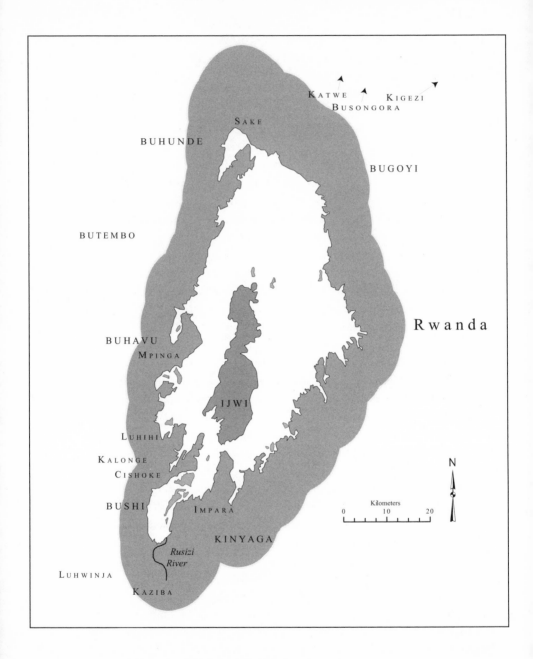

Map 3.1. Regions of the Lake Kivu regional trade

political institutions. Their economy today is essentially agricultural (manioc, groundnuts, maize, legumes) but supplemented with game, fish, and vegetable products from the forest. As attested by ritual, myth, and cosmology, these hunting activities and forest products seem to have been more important in the past than they are today.[4]

To the east, the Rwandan state was characterized by a strongly centralized polity, a markedly hierarchical administrative apparatus, and a highly stratified social structure.[5] These aspects of the Rwandan state became increasingly marked during the course of the nineteenth century, and were especially important during the second half of the century.[6] The mixed pastoralist-agricultural economy, relatively productive environment, and high population density of Rwanda were associated with a complex sociopolitical network that also served as the mechanism for considerable internal material transfer. Geographical expansion accompanied the increasing social stratification of the nineteenth century. The Rwandan state was much smaller in extent at the beginning of the century than at present; much of its effective expansion into the western regions took place in the last third of the century, a fact of considerable importance to the regional trade.

Between these two poles of the trade were the Havu, essentially associated with the shores and islands of Lake Kivu, and the Shi, on the plateau to the southwest of the lake. Although the Havu and Shi were primarily agriculturalist, their kingdoms included people of diverse cultural backgrounds, and thus pastoralism, hunting, and fishing activities were each important among some segments of the population.[7] Of the two, the Shi were the more populous and their states the more centralized. They shared many features of Interlacustrine culture, but (except for the immediate royal family) they lacked the institutionalized social stratification and the degree of pastoral specialization that characterized Rwanda in the late nineteenth century. However, the Shi were incorporated into the Lake Kivu regional trade only late in the nineteenth century; their role in the trade became increasingly important as some Shi areas came to serve as contact points for the expanding trade network on Lake Tanganyika to the south of Lake Kivu. As essentially a lacustrine people, the Havu were important intermediaries within the Lake Kivu system itself (though some of their products also entered the trade). Indeed on Ijwi Island they maintained important social, commercial, and historical ties with the populations of what is today western Rwanda, while the mainland Havu (west of Lake Kivu) shared many cultural ties with the Tembo. But, as with the Shi participation in the trade, strong Havu ties with Tembo populations were forged only later in the century, as the Havu political centers moved north along the western shores of the lake.

Thus the Havu and Shi people were important to this particular trade network primarily in the second half of the century. Before that time, the most important participants in the trade were the Hunde and the Nyanga, at the northern end of the lake. Although the pattern of social and political organization introduced to Buhunde during colonial rule has caused them to be identified as part of the Interlacustrine area in recent scholarship,[8] historically the people of Buhunde shared many similarities with Bunyanga and Butembo to the west, as well as with Bugoyi to the east. These historical ties enabled them to play a major role in facilitating east-west interchange in the early nineteenth century.[9]

The Commodities of the Regional Trade Network

Many commodities traded in the Lake Kivu area were important primarily within localized patterns of material transfer resulting from seasonal or local variations in production or from the presence of such specialized skills as smithing, boat-making, and fishing. Iron goods, agricultural goods, livestock, and fish formed the most important commodities of this trade. Because they were transferred primarily through social mechanisms, such items did not travel far. Nonetheless, they formed an important part of the larger network of material exchange in the region, for these transactions provided the mechanisms and personal contacts for the regional trade items.

Trade in iron products was especially important within Rwanda. During the early nineteenth century, one major source for hoes used in Rwanda was the small state of Kayonza, north of Rwanda.[10] Over time, however, a new center for the Rwandan trade in iron hoes emerged in the southwest, focusing especially on Kaziba, south of Bushi.[11] The timing of this shift in the Rwandan trade suggests that it was related to new sources of trade goods, including iron, arriving in the area from the Lake Tanganyika trade network to the south.

West of the lake, however, neither the sources of iron ore nor the skills of ironworking were sufficiently restricted to promote a regional trade in iron products such as occurred in Rwanda. Instead, iron products tended to radiate out from many local centers, wherever families or villages engaged in smelting and forging. These tasks were not occupations exclusive to single clans (though the skills tended to be hereditary), nor was ironworking an exclusive occupation; most smiths were also cultivators. Although in this area hoes were important socially as well as economically (as part of bridewealth, for example), only toward the end of the nineteenth century, when the expanding trade networks brought higher-quality iron into more widespread circulation, did hoes truly achieve a regional trade status and serve as regional standards of value west of the lake.

While the regionally based trade in iron goods showed important alterations during the nineteenth century, the localized trade in agricultural goods was more stable and less sensitive to new products and political changes. This trade resulted as much from cultural and occupational differentiation in the area—the presence of predominantly hunting, fishing, cultivating, or pastoral communities —as from environmental differences. From the later eighteenth century, a specialized aspect of this form of trade emerged with the establishment on Ijwi Island of small agricultural "colonies" from the mainland in what is today western Rwanda. Benefiting from fertile land and a superior climate for agriculture (as well as slightly different cropping periods from the mainland areas), these island communities sent food, including beans, beer, bananas, and fish, to Rwanda in exchange for cattle, goats, and sheep.[12] Although originally restricted to their home communities east of the lake, these transfer patterns outlasted the historical ties between communities; with the political changes east of the lake (associated with Rwanda's expansion into the western areas), the Ijwi communities were increasingly separated from their parent communities east of the lake; the trade patterns were continued but extended more generally to include other communities as well, in a pattern well adapted to the larger regional trade discussed below.

In addition to the localized transfer of iron goods and food, other commodities were traded on a wider scale and tied to commercial links outside the region. Ivory was exploited locally, and probably some ivory from the Lake Kivu area reached the important trade centers of Maniema, west of the Rift, by the late nineteenth century.[13] Slaves, too, were exported from Rwanda toward the end of the nineteenth century.[14] But the quantities were small, and the impact of the trade in slaves and ivory in the immediate area of Lake Kivu was negligible during most of the nineteenth century.

However, despite the wide range of materials exchanged in the region, two commodities most strongly characterized the regional trade: livestock (goats and especially cattle) and fiber bracelets. Despite the prominence given to the former in most accounts of this region, it was the latter that most distinguished this trade network. The culturally determined demand for goods of a purely prestige nature was a commercial characteristic strongly developed in Rwanda, where social stratification encouraged a demand for such items. Furthermore, the hierarchical nature of the centralized Rwandan state structure meant that a small group of people accumulated locally produced resources that could be used to buy such imports. And what Rwandans at the central court sought most from the west were *butega* (Kitembo: *bute'a*),[15] a bracelet-anklet made of raffia fibers woven into a highly distinctive pattern. Because these were small, light, and relatively easy to transport, and because of their assured demand throughout the year in Rwanda, butega bracelets were used as a form of currency, at least insofar as they provided standards of value (and to a lesser degree as a medium of exchange, as well). In return, the major market demand among the Tembo was for livestock, not for social or political purposes as in Rwanda, but rather for meat, supplementing game in the Tembo diet.[16]

Butega were fabricated by both sexes of all ages, though female domestic activities meant that in fact butega fabrication was predominantly the enterprise of men. The primary limitation of butega production (and hence the condition that ensured favorable market terms in the trade with Rwanda) was the size of the producing population relative to the market demand.[17] Butega therefore were not a wasting asset, whose production was affected by a limited or slowly diminishing resource base over time, as were many other long-distance trade commodities elsewhere in Africa.[18] But the Rwandan market was not the only source of demand for butega. Within Tembo society, butega assumed important roles in both social transactions (primarily for bridewealth) and local commerce (for hoes and salt); butega were also used in commerce to the west (to Bukano and Bulega).[19] Therefore, it was possible to accumulate butega in several ways, in addition to direct production. Yet there is no indication either of specialized production (to the exclusion of other economic activities) or of a developing class system whereby some people produced butega directly for the use and profit of others outside of the accepted social and commercial channels noted above.[20]

Tembo traders traded butega not solely for meat but for profit to acquire yet more butega which could be converted into a whole range of products and services: iron hoes, salt, hats, beads, wives, fish traps, nets, and other implements, or divining or medical services. And high profit margins, exceeding 100 percent (and often much more), characterized regional commerce in butega: cattle or goats bought in Rwanda fetched at least double their original cost when sold in

Butembo for butega.[21] In the early twentieth century, cattle were obtained in Rwanda for butega amounting to 280–300 man-days of work; bulls, for 180–200 man-days. Goats, the most commonly traded livestock in this system, were usually bought in Rwanda for about 1,000 butega, or forty to fifty man-days of work. But since making butega was a relatively simple skill, not requiring high levels of specialization (though speed and quality of workmanship varied), production was normally extended to an entire kin—or residence—group, and therefore the time for group production was reduced to a fifth and perhaps even a tenth of that for an individual working alone.[22]

The Mechanisms of the Trade

As with production, the commercial aspect of the butega trade did not involve specialized knowledge or technology, nor were large capital or social resources necessary (to organize caravans, for example). There were, of course, individual differences among traders in terms of physical stamina, friendship ties, language skills, and business acumen, but these were relative differences and did not serve as exclusive barriers to participation in the trade. In short, the trade in butega was never as important an institution in Butembo as was regional trade or travel abroad in other African societies; therefore, this trade did not develop the specialized characteristics found elsewhere in the nineteenth century.[23]

In addition to personal hardships of the trade, there were also social costs associated with prolonged absence from home. Hence trade, like production, was usually conducted in such a way as not to interfere with agricultural functions. This imported a seasonal bias to the Tembo side of the trade, though it was not a necessity brought about by resource availability or demand patterns. In consequence, much of the trade was conducted through intermediary populations; this reduced the social and economic costs of extended absence, and ensured that some trade, indeed, continued throughout the year.

The Tembo apparently traveled in small groups (usually less than ten). But they did not pool their resources; they traded as individuals or pairs, and hence these groups cannot be said to have formed caravans with a corporate commercial interest. In such groups individuals lodged separately, often staying several days at each stop before rejoining others (not always the same colleagues) for the march during the day. Especially among the intermediary populations, mobility was based on alliance, sometimes resulting from social ties such as marriage or cattle contracts, more frequently from friendship ties formalized by blood pacts. Within Rwanda, however, Tembo traders seldom contracted formal blood pacts; they would usually be lodged by their trade partner, but would pay for their food with butega.[24] Though a Tembo would tend to return to the same trading partner, this did not establish formalized social ties or enduring obligations; there is no indication of a commercial contract form based on butega that was reflective of Rwanda social contracts based on cattle.

The distribution network of butega was therefore informal and very diffuse. Distribution was often undertaken by intermediaries—Hunde, Havu, Goyi, and, within Rwanda, through the hands of many Rwandans—and at least in the earlier period there was apparently no control over the trade by political authorities. These aspects are reflected in the Rwandan literature, which contains no indication of an organized butega commerce; in fact, precolonial trade contacts to the west tend to be overlooked.[25] Such omissions attest to the informality and diffuse nature of economic exchange in Rwanda, the lack of political control over the trade, and the greater importance of political mechanisms (such as army organization or clientship) than commercial exchange for material transfer within Rwanda.

Despite the absence of court references to this exchange, recent research outside the court milieu indicates that trade with the west was carried out on a significant scale, independent of the social and political types of transfer. Though precolonial markets in Rwanda may have been infrequent and irregular, they were not totally absent; their omission from the official sources becomes all the more interesting in this light.[26] In Kinyaga they were used by traders to obtain hoes of good quality as well as goats and cattle; within the society at large they became an expected marriage gift from groom to bride for both Hutu and Tutsi. By the late nineteenth century, butega were circulating widely in western Rwanda and were eagerly sought west of the lake, bringing traders from Kinyaga (in southwestern Rwanda) as far west as Kaziba and Kalonge (in Bushi).[27] The expansion of the trade to new areas and the increasing participation of Rwandan traders moving west for butega indicate (in the absence of quantitative figures) an overall increase in the trade. Thus the western trade—especially in butega, but in other goods (mentioned above) as well—was much more important than commonly recognized in the official central court sources, not only in terms of the quantity of goods traded but also in terms of the institutional mechanisms that emerged along with the trade.

The Historical Evolution of the Trade

Although the major axis of trade was oriented east and west, within the larger trade system important subpatterns developed, where the butega network was influenced by products such as salt, iron goods, copper, and (later) beads from other regional trade networks. These variants appear to be associated with distinct stages in the evolution of the larger Kivu network, and therefore they will be examined as indicative of the dynamics of the system.

Important historical contacts east and west across Lake Kivu have endured for several centuries.[28] Although it is likely that the transfer of livestock was included in those ties, it is impossible to determine when these assumed a commercial character.[29] However, the emergence of butega as trade commodities may provide some indication of this; the available evidence indicates that the trade in butega was specifically tied to the growth of the Rwandan court culture, and we are presently able to trace its early evolution only through oral traditions relating to the Rwandan royal court.[30]

The earliest references to butega in these court traditions apply to the regions of Bugoyi (now the northwestern portion of Rwanda) and to Kinyaga (in the southwest).[31] Although the region of Bugoyi was incorporated within the Rwandan polity only late in the nineteenth century, it is clear that the people of Bugoyi maintained commercial contacts with central Rwanda much earlier; they also shared intensive historical and cultural ties with Buhunde, and hence with Butembo to the west.[32] Because the Tembo did not generally speak Kinyarwanda (the language of Rwanda), and Kiswahili seems to have been employed as a widespread vehicular language in the area only recently, the Goyi were well suited and well situated to serve as primary intermediaries in the emergent butega-livestock trade patterns. This earlier trade with the west seems in fact to have served as a major prop in their later reputation as traders within Rwanda: "On every road in Rwanda and even far beyond, one meets the [trader from Bugoyi] . . . carrying a valuable load [of tobacco] on his head. . . . [The Bagoyi] have also become merchants of bracelets and anklets for women. These ornaments, much sought after by women, are woven from vegetable fibers and are made northwest of Lake Kivu among the Bahunde, who trade them to the Bagoyi. These latter take them to the interior [of Rwanda] and exchange them there for goats and young bulls."[33]

It is significant that one of the armies mentioned by Kagame as paying butega prestations to the Rwandan central court was stationed in Bugoyi.[34] Although this particular army was established only during the reign of Rwogera in the mid-nineteenth century, Bugoyi was subjected to nominal central court influence much earlier, perhaps from the reign of Mwami Cyilima Rujugira near the middle of the eighteenth century.[35] It is probable that rather than representing new material items for Bugoyi, army prestations were composed of items long established as important and valuable trade commodities with the central court.

Thus Tembo cultural ties with Buhunde and Bugoyi, and the commercial ties of Bugoyi with Rwanda, all indicate an early trade directed around the northern end of Lake Kivu. Because these conditions apparently predated the early nineteenth century, the emergence of butega commerce in the region may have preceded direct central control in Bugoyi. This conclusion provides not only a *terminus post quem* for dating the emergence of the trade with Rwanda, but also an explanation for the character of the butega trade as independent of political control, given that it preceded direct Rwandan control in Bugoyi. Nevertheless, it is also likely that later direct royal involvement in the region, correlated with a general expansion of Rwandan power (increasing both the degree of social stratification and the size of the elite), significantly increased the demand for butega.

Although earlier Rwandan-Tembo contacts were probably directed around the northern end of Lake Kivu, the major trade axis appears to have shifted south during the second half of the nineteenth century. Three factors seem to have influenced such a shift: the extension of Rwandan political influence toward the southwest; the movement of Shi and Havu political centers northward, more directly into the butega commercial zone; and the increasing influence of the Lake Tanganyika trade system in the Kivu area together with a decline in influence of the Katwe commercial system in the north. Each of these factors will be discussed in turn.

In the region of Kinyaga in southwestern Rwanda, the introduction of Rwandan central court institutions occurred relatively recently; it is therefore possible to trace the historical process involved with some precision.[36] Here, the demand for items such as butega was clearly related to the extension of social army prestations and land prestations, and therefore also to the degree of central court presence. Although central court sources date the installation of social armies in Kinyaga to the eighteenth century,[37] recent research suggests that butega became army prestations to the court only toward the end of the nineteenth century, when Hutu families (who were responsible for western commerce) were incorporated within a central Rwandan network.[38]

Paradoxically, then, one can postulate an earlier presence of butega in Bugoyi, where there was a relatively late army establishment, and a later butega presence in Kinyaga, despite earlier army presence. This is explained by Bugoyi's long tradition of commercial links to central Rwanda and its apparently long-standing cultural ties to butega-producing areas. Kinyaga shared no such direct and extensive ties to butega areas in the west, and there are few indications that Kinyaga (separated from central Rwanda by rugged mountainous forest) maintained early commercial ties with central Rwanda on a scale commensurate with that of Bugoyi until the late nineteenth century.[39]

Aside from the references to army prestations in butega, there is little mention of Kinyaga participation in the butega trade in the Rwandan sources; Pagès and d'Hertefelt cite butega only with regard to the northwest of Rwanda, attributing an origin in Buhunde. The absence of butega references to Kinyaga indicates that by the time the Tembo trade nexus shifted south to Kaziba and Kinyaga, new products (hoes of high-quality iron, cloth, and other prestige items) were viewed as the significant trade elements, obscuring the continuing active role of butega underpinning the trade in other products.[40] This would confirm a late-nineteenth-century shift in the trade patterns and suggest that the presence of other goods served as a possible cause of such a shift.

Geopolitical factors were of some importance in this shift from northern to southern routes. Throughout the later eighteenth and nineteenth centuries, long-term changes were occurring in Shi political institutions, resulting in an augmentation of power and alterations in the loci of power. In general, Shi populations and political centers west of the lake shifted progressively north over the eighteenth and nineteenth centuries. This shift brought about closer interaction of Shi and Tembo, and undoubtedly facilitated commercial ties between them. At the same time, Havu political centers were moving north along the western shore and onto the islands in the lake, which previously had been only sparsely populated; these moves facilitated commercial contacts by introducing potential intermediary population in the trade.[41] While kingship on Ijwi Island did not directly participate in the trade, the establishment of kingship on Ijwi was associated with immigration from the west. Together with ties of other Ijwi communities east of the lake, this demographic shift brought the Havu directly into the mainstream of east-west trade patterns; such changes on the southwestern shores of Lake Kivu coincided with growing Rwandan central court influence in Kinyaga, southeast of the lake.

Alterations in the Neighboring Trade Networks

Because the subpatterns within the regional trade network were associated with products introduced from outside, the indirect influences of other trade networks were even more important than local political considerations in the evolution of the trade. Mineral salt, much preferred to the local salt produced from vegetable sources, was particularly important in this regard. During the early years of the nineteenth century, the regional trade around the northern end of Lake Kivu had combined with the trade in salt from Lake Katwe (north of Lake Edward), itself the center of an extensive salt trade from at least the early nineteenth century.[42]

From the mid-nineteenth century, however, and especially during the final quarter of the century, the Lake Edward trade may have been frequently interrupted, as Busongora, the state most closely associated with the Katwe salt trade, suffered a series of political catastrophes and military occupations. By an important marriage alliance, the royal family of Busongora was drawn into factional disputes in Nkore,[43] and thus the region around Lake Katwe became enmeshed in the "big-power" politics of its neighbors. Subsequently, salt production and trade were also affected by the long series of wars associated with the secession of Toro from Bunyoro.[44] Although political motivations were undoubtedly preeminent, the strategy of Bunyoro's King Kabarega may have extended beyond the mere conquest of Toro to include control over the economic resources of the Lake Katwe area as well; the kingdom of Buganda, Bunyoro's major competitor for hegemony in the region, had also shown an interest in the Katwe salt trade.[45] Kabarega already controlled the Kibero salt center on Lake Albert (to the north of Lake Katwe), but apparently found the Katwe salt both superior in quality and more plentiful—and the more attractive because control of Katwe would give Bunyoro a monopoly over the mineral salt trade in the region.[46] His occupation of Busongora therefore may have been intended to complete his domination of the salt-production centers in the western Rift Valley.

Thus, while political rivalries between the powerful states affected trade patterns in the region, European military presence also affected Busongora and disrupted salt production and distribution from Lake Katwe.[47] Disease factors, associated both with Belgian administrative presence in areas bordering on Busongora and with the salt trade itself, also had an important impact on the area during the early twentieth century and perhaps before.[48] All these influences undoubtedly affected the salt trade connections around the north end of Lake Kivu, and the frequent disruption of these supplies may well have made the northern route less attractive for butega traders.

In the latter part of the nineteenth century, the salt trade around Lake Kivu seems to have been diverted south to Kaziba, where it benefited also from other supplies of salt, perhaps originating in Uvinza, east of Lake Tanganyika (south of Ujiji).[49] This shift occured as closer contacts were developing between the Havu-Shi populations and the Tembo, and was also associated with the influx of new goods from the Lake Tanganyika network. The salt trade from Uvinza increased during the nineteenth century, and this expansion may well have reached the northern reaches of Lake Tanganyika later in the century.[50] Salt was, however, only one of several commodities in the Tanganyika trade system that had an impact on the Kivu regional trade network late in the nineteenth century.[51] The convergence of several such commodities, all focusing on Bushi (especially Kaziba), was apparently an important factor bringing Bushi into the butega commercial network.

During much of the nineteenth century, Shi trade remained tied to the Tanganyika network and had very little influence in the Lake Kivu area before the arrival of new goods in the 1860s and after. In the earlier stages, therefore, the butega trade system seems to have touched the Shi states only peripherally.[52] Although earlier east-west contacts may have occurred through the Havu-associated populations located on both sides of the narrow throat near the southern end of the lake (Cishoke-Luhihi in the west and Impara in the east),[53] no intensive contacts with the Tanganyika system emerged in this region until the northward movement of Shi political centers in the mid-nineteenth century.[54] This northward movement occurred at roughly the same time that Lake Tanganyika entered into direct contact with the coastal trading network, and the combination of these factors had a major impact on the evolution of the southern axis of the Tembo-Rwanda trade.[55]

The alterations in trade patterns around Lake Kivu may also have been associated with Rwanda's evolving trade policy. Until then the Rwandan court had remained independent of formal commercial contacts with the outside, and particularly with long-distance trade.[56] But several references in the central court traditions refer to the development of such contacts late in the nineteenth century, both through Kinyaga to the Lake Tanganyika trade and through Rusubi to the southeast.[57] It is significant that this change in official policy seems roughly to have coincided with other transformations in the regional trade and the extension of Rwandan power in Kinyaga.

Another alteration during the nineteenth century was the emergence of middlemen from Buhavu and Ijwi, men who often had important social ties in Butembo and in Rwanda. The intermediary status of the people on Ijwi in this trade is underscored by the goods involved. On the one hand, butega did not have the social role on Ijwi that they did in Butembo; they were fabricated on Ijwi specifically for the trade; most were obtained in Butembo and destined for the trade in Rwanda. On the other hand, cattle obtained through the butega trade frequently had commercial value only; those obtained in other ways (marriage, inheritance, gift, or cattle contract) were seldom a part of the commercial network. Because most cattle contracts associated with political alliance involved fertile cows and heifers, sterile cows and bulls were freed from social demands, and therefore available for trade; only under the most extreme conditions would one part with a productive cow in a strictly commercial transaction. Therefore, even by the nature of the goods involved, the trade was a separate sphere of activity from other forms of material transfer.[58]

THE REGIONAL trade in butega was distinct both from more locally determined economic networks and from wider patterns of trade, and these differences would seem to have been significant in the development and evolution of the network described here. Within the regional network, the producer and ultimate consumer seldom interacted directly. This meant that others, not primarily producers or ultimate consumers, participated in the trade, and hence the trade served as one mechanism of interaction between markedly different societies within the region. Although related to other forms of transfer, the butega network was of a largely commercial nature and was not absorbed within social institutions of transfer in the immediate lake area; it did not result in the creation of enduring social ties or in the establishment of obligations resulting from the politicization of such ties. Goods in the regional trade were neither gift nor prestation. The butega trade system was not primarily characterized by reciprocity (deferred payments to meet social obligations) or redistribution (from accumulated goods obtained through social ties).

What most distinguished the regional trade from the local trade was that the former occurred in a predominantly transcultural commercial context; the dynamism of the trade network was determined by economic criteria and market considerations.[59] Yet, while market considerations were important, the network described here also seems to indicate the presence of highly developed trade prior to formalized marketplaces, and indeed this may have been a pattern of trade widespread in eastern and central Africa.[60] Even where some precolonial markets existed in the Kivu area, the presence of markets and currency was not a necessary prerequisite to trade based on market principles. In fact, the opposite correlation would be more exact: the presence of a regional trade, attracting new goods from other systems, seemed to encourage the emergence of markets, even where they had not existed before (e.g., for local commerce).

The most important of the factors distinguishing the regional trade from long-distance trade was the lack of direct linkage to—and ultimately dependence on—global economic networks. To be sure, the regional trade did not exist in absolute isolation, and this essay has stressed the important role of neighboring systems on the evolution of the Lake Kivu system. It is nonetheless true that regional butega trade was independent of outside factors for its motivation, origin, organization, production, and realization. Both producers and traders were native to the region; they were in no way supported or organized by capital from outside the region. Both the commercial network and the commodities traded were ultimately to be overtaken by such outside forces, but the very fact that such an intrusion resulted in the nearly total demise of the specifically regional trade of the Lake Kivu system only underscores the independent viability and integrity of this earlier system in its own right.

It would seem, then, that both markets and trade can emerge within a restricted regional context, and the present study has explored the conditions that favor such developments. The trade system considered here embraced markedly different cultures that corresponded with different ecological regions and zones of production. While distance or commodity alone does not seem to have been a defining characteristic of the regional trade, the transfer of goods between different cultures does seem to have met this criterion, for it removed transfer from the pervasive influence of social mechanisms. This factor corroborates the conclusions of Meillassoux[61] and Vansina[62] regarding markets among the Guro and the Kuba. M. G. Smith also identifies early market activity emerging from foreign contact,[63] and he extends this analysis to include earlier (noncommercial) exchanges among occupationally specialized groups within Hausaland, groups that correspond with our criteria of cultural differentiation.[64] Trade as a commercial phenomenon, therefore, emerged from the interchange of complementary goods, grouping complementary cultures, rather than through the simple extension or expansion in scale of local transfers.

The hypothesis that the early signs of commercial activity are more likely to be found in the contact zones between different cultures (and productive areas) seems borne out by this case. Early markets do in fact seem to have first appeared near lines of cultural differentiation; markets oriented to regional trade preceded markets for local trade.[65] The sharpness of cultural differentiation and the intensity of commercial interaction relative to social interaction would seem also to influence this development. Markets are more likely to form where cultural differences are clear and immediate and where there is either intense commercial interaction (measured by the number and variety of goods exchanged and their diversity of origins) or fewer social and political mechanisms (such as clientship).[66] Thus a large intermediary population may inhibit the emergence of markets, whether by providing transfer mechanisms through dispersed social channels or by diffusing commercial transfer through many channels.

Perhaps partly because markets were likely to form (and indeed trade likely to be more intense) in sharply transitional and in peripheral areas, regional trade in the Kivu area was also characterized by autonomy from direct control by political powers. It is significant that all of the major centers of this trade seem to have emerged in areas of minimal political control and centralization.[67] It would seem that the Kivu regional trade gravitated to those areas that provided both security and autonomy, and that the latter was at least as important as the former.[68] This may in part reflect the relative violence of the process of political centralization in the region, at least during the late nineteenth century.[69]

The data presented here suggest a refinement of the argument that the growth of market trade occurs primarily in areas of strong political power. This view is most notably argued by B. W. Hodder, whose work was done in an area where well-established long-distance trade was closely associated with powerful state structures.[70] Because the development of new markets there correlated with long-distance trade routes, market development therefore ultimately appeared to be associated with centralized structures. In the Lake Kivu area, too, there were important interactions of commercial development and political factors associated with centralized political units.[71] However, the regional trade most flourished on the periphery of these units and may well have developed along lines of pre-existing cultural ties (as in Bugoyi), which seem to have been largely independent of direct political control by the major states. Consequently, it is possible that political centralization does not function as a necessary causal factor of market development. Instead, both centralization and market development may emerge from similar conditions also suggested by Hodder: cultural heterogeneity and a relatively dense population. In Kivu, as within Rwanda, these two concurrent factors served as a necessary, if not sufficient, condition for commercial development.

Finally, the Lake Kivu regional trade consisted primarily of elements that had a long history of production and exchange in the region in other contexts and that performed other noneconomic functions in their respective societies.

Hence there emerged neither a specialization of production for purely market demands nor the economic and social transformations often associated with "growth." Such transformations, often associated with the process of increasing centralized control, ensured the greater accumulation of productive or distributive resources in the hands of a few. In this case, however, production and distribution were not exclusive to or controlled by a small group; trade west of Lake Kivu did not encourage the emergence of a class system, nor did it result in the domination of some groups by others. In Rwanda, the commerce did provide symbols representing, and hence perhaps reinforcing, internal class domination, but this process within Rwanda was a phenomenon whose origins and objectives were independent of the butega trade.

The importance of the Lake Kivu regional trade is not to be measured exclusively in economic terms, nor in terms of social transformation, nor in its interaction with political developments. Perhaps its most significant role was its contribution to cross-cultural ties as one of several mechanisms of cultural interchange within an ethnically heterogeneous region in the precolonial period.

KAMO AND LUBAMBO

Dual Genesis Traditions on Ijwi Island

1979

Oral sources are as diverse as they are important. They are also complex; they are not self-evident history. As much as any other source, oral testimony needs to be subjected to analysis and critique. With this awareness, from the 1960s there has developed a complex subfield of the critique of oral sources in Africa. While addressing many issues, the fundamental line of debate has revolved around two approaches: the concept of a single "chain of transmission," on the one hand, or the free flow of information, on the other. Do oral sources represent a lineage of knowledge handed down a chain of transmission with little alteration: do they derive from some pure "original testimony"? Or do such narratives flow in society, changing with the context and with every retelling, as individuals and groups use them as entertainment in the present as well as affidavits of the past? In short, to what degree is the "documentary analogy" valid?

This chapter provides a critique of two versions of the origins of kingship on Ijwi Island. The accounts are very different in form: one is composed of fragmentary references; the other is a much more coherent narrative, full and flowing. One deals with metaphor and "mythical themes," the other with individuals and actions. Yet while they both consider the same events, neither relates directly to the other: they seem as autonomous in the histories they recount as in their literary tropes. And other paradoxes emerge around this issue. Why does the royal family have no tradition of its own arrival on Ijwi? Why were these royal origins retained only by members of two small (and politically insignificant) social identity groups today? Why do they present such different perspectives? And which is "true"? By examining each in context and placing each set of commentaries in its larger historical relationships, this essay tries to show how they are complementary, not competing, versions of a larger, more complex political episode.

GENESIS TRADITIONS HAVE LONG been important to historians of Africa, but recently interest in these forms of oral data has intensified with the development of analytic tools ultimately derived from structural anthropology.[1] Where historians have applied these techniques, they have usually referred to a "tradition" (obtained from a single source or reconstructed from several sources to form a single tradition).[2] Hence writers often refer to "the oral tradition" of a society in the singular. Even where two such traditions have been noted for a single people, these refer to the arrival of separate dynasties, composed of different peoples, located in different areas, and arriving at different times.[3]

But oral sources even within a single society are multiple; they not only relate to different groups but also are recounted by different—specific—individuals. This essay considers two separate genesis traditions that both refer to the arrival of a single dynasty on Ijwi Island in Lake Kivu (Zaire). The traditions appear to be distinct in three ways: they are recounted by members of different groups; they refer to different events within the larger episode of royal arrival; and they exist today in very different forms.[4] Each tradition is associated with a particular social group (in one case a "clan," in the other a "subclan"); both groups, the Baloho and the Babambo, identify with the principal nonroyal figure in the tradition that each recounts.[5] Despite their small size on Ijwi today, both of these groups claim a historical importance greater than their present status on Ijwi would otherwise indicate.

What is most remarkable about these two traditions is that they are exclusive of each other, and each is, with very few exceptions, known only by informants from within one of the two clans in question. Members of one clan do not know the traditions held by the other; when asked to identify a person mentioned in the other tradition, for example, an informant might be able to associate the character with the proper clan, but could provide no other information about his ties to royalty—the principal subject of the tradition. Even those with close contacts at the central court—including those from within the royal family itself—do not recount a full version of the royal arrival and do not combine elements from the two traditions examined here. It is clear, therefore, that the primary social function of these traditions is not simply that of justifying kingship or explaining royal presence to the Ijwi population as a whole. The traditions are much more localized than such an interpretation would allow; each is important only to the social group that holds it.

In addition to the distinct distribution patterns of the two traditions, there are differences in the traditions themselves, both in terms of content and in terms of the form in which they are narrated today. Aside from common reference to Mwendanga, the first king of the Basibula dynasty on Ijwi, events that figure prominently in one tradition have no reflection in the other, nor could people who know one tradition identify episodes in the other tradition. The two traditions also differ in form—in the kinds of events included and in the way in which they are recounted. One is a longer narrative recounted in greater detail with references to precise events and individual names. The other contains few direct references to individual names and discrete events; instead, it is characterized by vague references to broad cultural themes that are not today an important part of Ijwi society. Each version consists of elements that relate primarily to the "possessor" group; this specificity of the traditions, as also their localization to two small social groups, speaks to the lack of political socialization and cultural integration directly associated with royalty in the Ijwi kingdom.

In summary, then, on Ijwi there are two traditions relating to royal arrival that appear mutually exclusive: the individuals who know one do not know the other, the elements and events in one never appear in the other, and the two traditions are very different in form. This chapter inquires into how it is that two such different traditions can relate to the same episode (the royal establishment on Ijwi) and why they have remained so distinct from each other and of such a narrow distribution on Ijwi over a considerable period of time. What follows will discuss the traditions in light of the sociological characteristics of the two clans that recount them; it will relate the traditions to the historical role of each "possessor" clan; and it will consider how the two traditions evolved over time, indicating some of the historical factors acting on these changes.

THE TRADITIONS discussed here refer to the relations of two clans with a single segment of the Basibula dynasty, the ruling family of the Havu peoples, who live on the western shores of Lake Kivu and on the islands in the lake (see map 4.1). Though the senior line of the dynasty is today located in Mpinga, on the Zairian mainland, the junior line is located on Iwji Island, an island about 25 miles long and including an area of approximately 150 square miles. The separation of these two dynastic segments took place in the aftermath of a succession dispute to the Havu throne, a dispute that occurred at the southern end of Lake Kivu late in the eighteenth century. Following this dispute, the descendant of the unsuccessful claimant traveled to Ijwi, where he established the present dynasty on the island. How this occurred is the subject of the traditions discussed here.

The population of Ijwi, numbering today (i.e., 1975) about fifty thousand and forming a dozen major clans, is neither culturally nor historically homogeneous, for even within certain clans there are important differences in the time of their arrival on Ijwi and their immediate points of origin. Although many families came with or after the establishment of the present dynasty on Ijwi, an important proportion of the population arrived prior to that time. Many came from east of the lake, from areas that are today part of Rwanda; others came from west and north of the lake, while the royal family itself arrived on Ijwi from the south. Furthermore, the different populations on Ijwi (referred to collectively as the Bany'Iju) have experienced different influences from mainland areas over the nineteenth and twentieth centuries, and these influences have affected the nature and type of cultural change each has undergone. The cultural heterogeneity associated with such diverse influences is an important element in understanding the nature of the distinctions between the two traditions, as will be discussed below.[6]

Conversely, differences in the content of the traditions testify to the strength of the cultural differences on Ijwi in the past (and to their continuity through time), as well as to the specific events associated with the arrival of the Basibula dynasty about 150 years ago. The events of royal arrival are privileged in one tradition. The other emphasizes those features that differentiate current conceptions of a former way of life from the mainstream of present Ijwi culture; in the process, it also vividly associates the presence of royalty on Ijwi with a given (nonroyal) clan. These two different levels of historical data (that of specific events on the one hand, and that of tracing broad trends of cultural change on the other) are also reflected in the different narrative forms of the traditions; together with their differences in content, these markedly different literary forms would seem to argue for their independence as historical testimony and hence also for the historical validity of their essential convergence on events: that Mwendanga, as

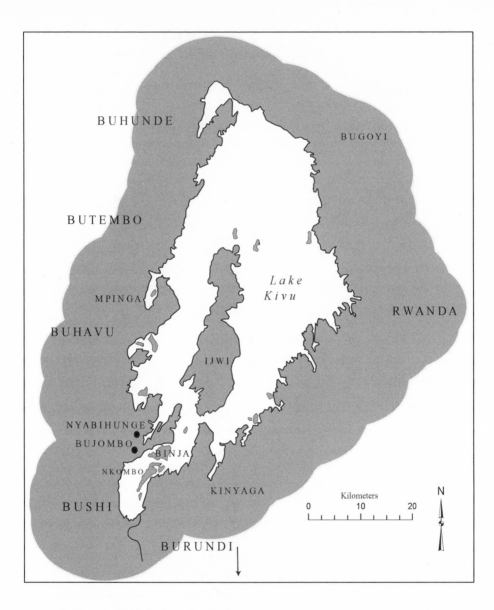

BUHUNDE

BUGOYI

BUTEMBO

MPINGA

Lake Kivu

RWANDA

BUHAVU

IJWI

NYABIHUNGE

BUJOMBO

BINJA

NKOMBO

KINYAGA

BUSHI

BURUNDI

Kilometers

0   10   20

N

Map 4.1. Ijwi Island and neighboring islands

a "royal orphan" (i.e., without the support of his own agnatic kin), sought alliances and arrived on Ijwi from the south. The two traditions relate in various ways to the same events and tend to confirm each other both in the nature of Mwendanga's arrival and in the rough dating of these events (from genealogies and tie-ins). This not to say that all elements of the narratives are "true" as historical events, not even those elements shared (or implied) by the two traditions—that is, that the first monarch on Ijwi arrived as an orphan. It means only that he accomplished his ends independently of his agnates and therefore the story is to be told more in terms of other clans and Mwendanga's relations to them than in any definitive narrative of the royal family—a Basibula narrative.

The Two Traditions

This section will briefly present the two traditions and discuss certain aspects of them that relate to their historical validity.[7] Later sections will consider how the traditions reflect various sociological characteristics of their possessor clans and how the more recent history of the island may have affected the evolution of the traditions (and their importance to royal culture) on Ijwi.

The more complete, comprehensive, and geographically widespread tradition is that recounted primarily by informants of the Babambo clan.[8] This tradition relates that at a hill called Nyabihunge, near the southern end of Lake Kivu, there occurred a succession struggle within the Havu royal family, the Basibula. According to this account, the losing contender for the throne, a certain Kabwiika, fled east of the lake to Kinyaga, which, although today a part of Rwanda, had not at that time been integrated into Rwandan central court administration. There, in Kinyaga, continue the sources, Kabwiika received a sympathetic welcome from a man named Lubambo, the eponymous ancestor of his (Ba)bambo descendants.[9] Lubambo appears to have been an important local authority: Babambo informants state that although not himself of Rwandan origin, Lubambo had achieved considerable acclaim at the Rwandan court for having healed members of the royal family (including the king of Rwanda, Gahindiro, some versions add) of smallpox.

The tradition continues that while staying with Lubambo in Kinyaga, Kabwiika fathered a son named Mwendanga, by Nkobwa, an unmarried daughter of Lubambo. Preparing to celebrate the birth with the customary feast, Kabwiika went to seek fish at the lakeshore, where he was accidentally speared and killed by one of his own associates; this on the very day of Mwendanga's birth.[10] Mwendanga, illegitimate as well as a paternal orphan, was then raised by the family of Lubambo. Here the tradition reflects a theme common to royal genesis traditions —that of the orphan, brought up by an "outside" clan, who later succeeds in obtaining the royal throne.[11]

Certain variants, the most vivid being those by Babambo informants on the mainland, recount that the Babambo fought Kamerogosa, the successful contender to the Sibula throne (and Mwendanga's paternal uncle—half-brother to Kabwiika), in an attempt to "regain" the Havu drums (a synonym for "throne") for Mwendanga. They succeeded in killing Kamerogosa, but Mwendanga, saddened and chagrined at the death of his uncle, according to these accounts, refused to claim the throne. Instead, with the encouragement of the Babambo, Mwendanga established himself on Ijwi, while retaining his ties to the lands on the mainland shores southwest of the lake.[12]

The emphases of this tradition are on conflict and alliance associated with royalty and the retention or recovery of royal status; all the people in the tradition except the fishermen are explicitly tied in some way to royalty, and these ties are emphasized throughout. Stress is placed on political success and on the role of the Babambo, both in their ascribed status as maternal uncles to Mwendanga (and hence ritually as "maternal uncles" to all Ijwi kings) and in their own ambitions for royal status and power. The essential elements of these traditions, then, are:

a. Kabwiika, potential heir to the Havu throne, was driven out of "Buhavu" in a succession dispute;

b. Nkobwa, the mother of Mwendanga and daughter of Lubambo, was not married to Kabwiika;

c. Kabwiika, seeking fish from fishermen at the lakeshore, was accidentally killed by one of his own men;

d. Mwendanga was raised by Lubambo, who perhaps had ties to the royal court of Rwanda;

e. Mwendanga's maternal uncles sought to regain the throne for him, and eventually were responsible for helping to establish Mwendanga as *mwami* on Ijwi.

In element "a," the different versions vary as to whether Kabwiika was the designated successor. Those informants close to the Ijwi royal court today imply that he was; others omit this point. This, of course, leaves open the question of how and by whom the Havu successor was designated. Current norms differ in the two royal segments (at Mpinga and on Ijwi), as they both do from the ideological explanations current in Bushi. There is thus no historically established "Havu" or regional norm, and in such a historically fluid situation, it would appear that Kabwiika simply failed to mobilize support for his cause. It is also interesting that, despite the few informants who claim that Kabwiika was the rightful heir (without explaining on what grounds), no one claims that the Ijwi line is actually the rightful senior Havu line. The Ijwi dynasty is always accepted as junior to its Mpinga collaterals, and this fact would surely weaken the case for Kabwiika's claim as sole legitimate heir implied in the term "designated successor."

In element "b," only a few sources close to the Ijwi royal court state that Nkobwa was married to Kabwiika (or even that at least the formalities had been initiated). Such a claim would clearly help to establish Mwendanga and his descendants as of legitimate royal (Basibula) status. But most informants state quite clearly that Nkobwa was not married to Kabwiika at the time of his death; most agree that she was a single woman, as implied in the name "Nkobwa," which means "unmarried woman" or "girl" in the Rwandan language. It is possible that the narrators are taking the personal name to be an indication of her civil status. However, most women in this area are referred to not by their proper names, but only by the names of their father ("the daughter of . . .") or sometimes that of their husband ("the wife of . . ."). It is therefore more likely that the name "Nkobwa" has been retained in the tradition because it refers to her civil status, rather than the reverse (that is, that it was retained independently and her civil status mistakenly inferred from it).

Nkobwa's single status does not conform to Mwendanga's accepted membership in the Basibula family, however, and this presents an unresolved paradox: that of Mwendanga's royal heritage but without social descent within the Basibula clan. Given the important emphasis on royal legitimacy, a tendency to deny Nkobwa's single status would seem probable, both for literary and for social reasons (as in fact some informants do). Yet because the most commonly accepted versions of this story describe her as single, some other reason needs to be advanced to account for this. Broad structural reasons inherent in the nature of this type of "lost hero" tradition will not serve to explain this factor, because most other forms of this stereotypical tradition drawn from elsewhere do not question the legitimacy of the ruler's claims to rule; in fact, they sometimes go to elaborate lengths to establish just this. Hence the illegitimacy of Mwendanga cannot be seen as the result of a purely structural device embedded within the tradition itself.

There are, however, two ways in which this tradition reflects themes and conceptions apparent in other traditions in the area. At the local level, it is often said (by non-Bany'Iju) that unmarried Rwandan women who became pregnant were sent to Ijwi—this reflects both the low status of the Ijwi population in the eyes of the Rwandans and the transfer of women west from Rwanda to Ijwi, often through accepted marriage institutions. (The people on Ijwi know of the same story, but apply it to a smaller island, Cihaya, south of Nkombo, saying that Rwandans sent pregnant unmarried women there.) Thus the tale of a pregnant unmarried woman is widespread in the popular tales of the region; Nkobwa's story fits into a widespread trope.

At a higher level, the story of Mwendanga's illegitimate heritage can be seen to reflect the common conception in the area that royalty divorces the king from his own patrilineage. In Rwanda this takes the form that the king was above class and people and hence a member of no particular lineage.[13] The queen mother was also an important person in the kingdom, reigning jointly with the king (but sometimes also she "ruled," in competition with him), thus also removing royalty from too close a tie with a given patrilineage. The case of Buganda, however, may be even more instructive than that of Rwanda in this context.[14] There the royal family, the king and his children, did not share a common totem, nor did they rely on support from their agnates. Instead, they looked to support from their maternal kin, and in fact they adopted the totems of their mothers and hence tended to be associated with that clan. The Babambo tradition related here would seem to refer precisely to such a situation—relating Mwendanga, as an illegitimate child, to his mother's family.

Yet socially the king on Ijwi is definitely not associated with the same Babambo clan in any way. Instead, he is very strongly associated with the Basibula clan and accepted by all to be of the same (patrilineal) descent as the kings of Mpinga (the senior Havu kingdom on the mainland). Furthermore, the concepts of royal identity on Ijwi today do not approach those reported for Rwanda, where the king was considered to be above class and clan. Nor was the class situation on Ijwi ever such as to indicate that this was different in the past: the king never needed to be elevated above society to mediate between different classes. Similarly, he does not seem to have been elevated above his patriclan, because on Ijwi the Basibula are a very small clan: by their numbers they were never a threat to the status of other clans. On the contrary, the presence of the royal clan seems to have augmented the status of certain other of the most important clans—and hence it was never necessary to dissociate the king from his own clan in order to keep inviolate the concept of royalty: legitimacy through Sibula membership seems to have been more important than the political role of remaining neutral by dissociation from Basibula status.

Therefore, although the story of Nkobwa may in certain aspects reflect concepts common to royalty elsewhere in the area, it does not seem to have emerged as a result of these concepts. Although the tradition stresses the manner of the birth and contains within it certain unresolved paradoxes, such as exist in the concept of royalty itself and especially in the relation of Ijwi royalty to Mpinga royalty, this does not itself mean that the tradition is not also of historical validity, at least in its major tenets. As pointed out above, it seems entirely plausible that Nkowba was not married at the time of Kabwiika's death.

Of the essential elements noted above, only "c" is accepted in all the variants, even in identifying the fishermen involved—the Bene Shando, the sons (or lineage) of Shando. Kabwiika's death is the major element of the Babambo tradition, for it simultaneously explains Mwendanga's royal status and justifies the Babambo role as Sibula benefactors; the detail of how Kabwiika died is only incidental to this point. Still, despite the unanimity among the narrative variants on this point, even this incidental detail is open to various interpretations; possibly this very interpretive ambiguity allows for the unanimity among the variants. First, the tradition implies a conflict of the land-based royal family with the fishermen, associated with water and with fish, one of the essential foods consumed in the First Fruits ceremony on Ijwi.[15] This potential ritual association, as well as the mobility of the fishermen, casts them into a role analogous to that of the hunter in genesis traditions elsewhere.[16] In addition, there is a potential conflict situation portrayed here between Kabwiika and his own men, and this tradition could be interpreted as rebellion on the part of Kabwiika's own (unspecified) followers. The narration of some versions emphasizes this possibility in its telling: by drawing out the full dramatic implications of Kabwiika's death, by interjections of amazement reflecting that of Kabwiika's men at having speared Kabwiika, and by dwelling on their subsequent fear and consternation, which led to the formation of a joint blood pact among them designed to conceal their role in Kabwiika's death, thus shifting the blame to the fishermen instead.[17]

For element "d" above, some informants deny that Lubambo had ties to the Rwandan royal court. But this claim can be seen as an affirmation of contemporary distinctions between Ijwi and Rwanda. Lubambo's ties with the Rwandan court are mentioned in Rwanda and on the Zaire mainland as well as on Ijwi; the Rwandan Babambo today note that there is a major segment of their family living in "Nyanza" near the former (colonial) royal capital of Rwanda, and they claim that this stems from a continuing close tie to the royal court since the time of Gahindiro.[18] In support of this, it seems clear (though our only sources of this are oral traditions from the area) that Lubambo was a man of some ambition, building his alliances both east and west of the lake.[19] In addition, Rwandan traditions, apparently independent of the Babambo traditions because the Babambo do not appear in them, cite an (unspecified) epidemic at the time of Gahindiro[20] and note that Mibambwe Sentabyo, the father of Gahindiro, died of smallpox, apparently introduced to Rwanda from Burundi.[21]

Despite the possible tie-ins, the significance of Lubambo's ties to the court for the Basibula and the nature of the relationship of Mwendanga to the Rwandan court remain obscure. Some informants state that the ties were very close and that Gahindiro "gave" Mwendanga wives and cattle (an inversion of conventional marriage transfer). Others deny that there were any formal ties between the Rwandan and Ijwi royal courts. As reported by Kagame, Rwandan traditions emphasize the fact of Ijwi's subordination to Rwanda, though the explanation is clearly fallacious.[22] The lack of any evidence on Ijwi to confirm these assertions, even when the Bany'Iju accept with perfect equanimity their subordination under the Rwandan king Rwabugiri (two generations later), and the total absence of any indications of ties between the Ijwi elite and other members of the Rwandan elite, would argue against the likelihood of this, whatever the normative views of the Rwandan court toward their neighbors.

The fact of important economic and social ties between Rwanda and Ijwi, with both women and cattle moving west, is indisputable; but to read these in purely political terms as inevitably "gifts" of the Rwandan king and hence symbols of accepted subordination on the part of the recipients (Basibula/Babambo) is not supported in the Ijwi data. Those accounts that mention Mwendanga's ties to the Rwandan court seem to extrapolate from Lubambo's claimed ties (or later Ijwi subordinate status) rather than deriving support from the traditions of other sources. In short, the sources are inconclusive on this point, and the silence on the part of Ijwi sources seems weightier than the somewhat facile assertions of the Rwandan sources.

How instrumental were the Babambo in helping to establish Mwendanga on Ijwi (element "e" above) is also a point in dispute among the different versions of this tradition. There can be no doubt that the Babambo initially benefited in status from Mwendanga's accession to "royal" status—or at least preeminent political status—on Ijwi. Also, the Babambo claims to have raised Mwendanga and to have served as his principal allies on the mainland seem justified; all testimonies—from diverse areas, from Ijwi ritual practices, and from the later history of the royal family—support this conclusion. But the related question on the nature of Mwendanga's position in the political structure in the mainland areas, and in the processes of forming a kingdom on Ijwi, are not at all illuminated in these traditions. Indeed the internal history of Ijwi shows that, whatever their role elsewhere, the Babambo played a minor role in politics on Ijwi; there was apparently no direct transfer to Ijwi of the relations between Mwendanga and the Babambo as these existed on the mainland, if the Babambo traditions are to be accepted on this point.

But in addition, there is no indication, either from Ijwi or from mainland traditions, of the exact status and power of Mwendanga on the mainland. It appears that his primary residence was on the mainland at Bujombo, a hill rising high above the narrow straits of the lake, overlooking Binja and Nkombo islands, and neighboring Nyabihunge, the hill of Kamerogosa's court. Many informants on Ijwi, when questioned on the historical aspects of kingship on Ijwi, replied that Mwendanga was king at Bujombo and arrived on Ijwi with the entire panoply of fully developed and functioning royal institutions. Other data, drawn from local traditions on Ijwi, indicate that this was not the case. Certain basic features of Havu kingship were retained (or reconstructed) on Ijwi; but evidence of a functioning kingdom under Mwendanga at Bujombo is lacking.[23] The assertions to this effect would seem to be a result of reading the present into the past; it is from such anachronisms that emerge hypotheses of the "state created whole" through the importation of royalty in toto to Ijwi.

Reference to Bujombo in the Babambo tradition is either incidental to the main narrative (sometimes mentioned in the context of the Babambo attack on Kamerogosa) or omitted entirely. But Ijwi royal sources (and others) refer explicitly to Bujombo as Mwendanga's principal mainland residence and point of departure for Ijwi, and there is enough support for this from other mainland sources to confirm that Mwendanga's primary residence on the mainland as an adult was west of the lake, at Bujombo, not east of the lake, in Kinyaga. Thus there appears to have been a stage in the life of Mwendanga that is omitted in most Babambo traditions, traditions that in general prefer to portray a direct move from Kinyaga to Ijwi, under continuous Babambo tutelage and guidance.

The evidence of a Bujombo residence for Mwendanga (west of the lake) does not invalidate the role of the Babambo, however, because it seems that their dominance of the area extended on both sides of the lake in this area at this time.

But such differences between the Ijwi and the Babambo traditions do illustrate the emphasis in the latter toward the privileged role of the Babambo in all of the significant events—birth and upbringing, revenge (and hence a continuing claim to the throne, as if the succession struggle between Kabwiika and Kamerogosa had never been resolved), and arrival on Ijwi. However, other Ijwi accounts of Mwendanga's arrival on the island (notably those of the Banyakabwa, the predominant clan on Ijwi at the time) do not include the Babambo in any prominent role in Mwendanga's arrival, if at all, and there is no other evidence to support this aspect of the Babambo claim.[24] Furthermore, the Babambo traditions are entirely silent about specific events and people on Ijwi at Mwendanga's arrival.

Still, evidence of various types lends support to the major thrust of the Babambo tradition: that during much of his youth Mwendanga was dependent on the Babambo and much of his early political training was at their hands. Traditions from other sources refer to the Babambo drive for power in the area of the Nkombo-Binja straits at this time.[25] Ijwi ritual also recognizes the Babambo as maternal uncles to the king and hence enshrines the Babambo relationship to Ijwi royalty. Finally, the role of the Babambo as major participants in the succession struggles following Mwendanga's death is also explained in terms of their relationship to Mwendanga, and as maternal uncles, cousins, and brothers-in-law to one of Mwendanga's sons, who was apparently a prime contender as a successor to Mwendanga.

All of these independent data are explained historically by the Babambo traditions relating their early ties to Kabwiika and Mwendanga; such a convergence would add weight to the essential validity of the historical relationship portrayed in the tradition, if not to each narrative element within the tradition individually. It is difficult to account for the convergence of three such separate forms of data (traditions on the later succession struggle, present royal ritual, and direct testimony) if the Lubambo-Kabwiika tradition is read simply as an ex post facto explanation of one or the other. The difference among the various alternative sources for the history of this period (e.g., the traditions of other clans) does not touch on the fact of the Babambo relationship to the Ijwi royal line during the early years, but it does help define the limitations of this relationship and its significance. The Babambo traditions imply that Mwendanga was under their tutelage and that they were instrumental in all of the major stages of Mwendanga's arrival and establishment on Ijwi. Others disagree: the Banyakabwa on the latter point; the Baloho on the former.

All the data available on the royal court on Ijwi indicate that Babambo influence at the royal court has been limited to their role as ritual maternal uncles to the king (not a very influential role at that), rather than to any historical role as advisors and power wielders. Even where Babambo are important today in their own communities, they do not hold influence at the court commensurate with this prestige. Nor do they associate with any particular regional political role on Ijwi as is found associated with Baloho, a role that will be discussed below; the succession struggle following Mwendanga's death can be interpreted to be as much a regional struggle to determine the major center of royal power (on the mainland or on the island) as it was simply a struggle among contenders or clans, with the Babambo supporting the mainland contender. It would thus appear that, whatever their role in Mwendanga's arrival on Ijwi, the role of the Babambo in Mwendanga's royal establishment on the island and in the formation of the structures and character of royalty was minimal. Therefore, the traditions of other clans—the Baloho, the Banyakabwa, the Bashaho, and others—may be a better guide on this aspect of royal history than the Babambo "traditions of genesis" considered here.

To the historian, one of the most notable aspects of the Babambo tradition (and one that distinguishes it from the Baloho tradition) is its potential in providing approximate chronological references. It has been shown above how the Babambo narratives, because they name particular individuals and identify discrete historical events, can be cross-referenced to other oral sources, both Havu and Rwandan. For chronological purposes, the primary synchronism is the reference to Gahindiro, the king of Rwanda, who appears as a contemporary of Lubambo (and hence of Kabwiika). Lubambo is said to have gained favor at the court by his ability to heal a smallpox epidemic, which had affected even the royal family. As noted above, the Rwandan traditions reported by Kagame mention smallpox as the cause of the death of Sentabyo, the predecessor of Gahindiro; the epidemic proportions noted in the Babambo tradition may well be hyperbole, as it was sufficient for the king himself to be threatened for "all of Rwanda" to be threatened. Such a dating would locate Lubambo's ties to the court early in the reign of Gahindiro or near the turn of the nineteenth century (or even slightly before, because the smallpox epidemic occurred in the reign of Sentabyo, Gahindiro's predecessor).

There is no precise way of relating this event to Mwendanga's arrival on Ijwi, but there is likely to have been a considerable lapse of time between the two events. Mwendanga's accession to power on Ijwi seems based more on the process of alliance formation than on claims to ascribed royal status. To achieve such alliances he needed to reach outside his cognatic links, because it is unlikely, as we have seen, that the Babambo themselves were the key instruments of royal establishment on Ijwi. Thus (to allow for the creation of alliance formations), one can roughly estimate a period exceeding thirty years from his birth for Mwendanga's arrival on Ijwi. Despite the lack of precision relating Mwendanga's birth to Lubambo's ties to the royal court, one can estimate that Mwendanga arrived on Ijwi during the first quarter of the nineteenth century.[26]

Independently derived genealogies, as well as other traditions on Ijwi, provide some check on this rough chronology. The royal king list at Mpinga shows eight names (putatively father-to-son succession) to Kamerogosa (the brother of Kabwiika), but of those, five lived in the period of two Ijwi kings. The sixth name back is a contemporary of the son of Mwendanga, and thus the two most remote generations parallel those of Mwendanga and his son. Furthermore, the Babambo genealogies are roughly in agreement with this chronology of Mwendanga, counting back six generations to Lubambo (Mwendanga's maternal grandfather). Finally, the traditions of some clans to have arrived on Ijwi prior to Mwendanga make it seem likely that they arrived only during the reign of Gahindiro in Rwanda. Yet their presence clearly predated that of Mwendanga; hence Mwendanga could only have arrived late in the reign of Gahindiro or in the reign of his successor, Rwogera, if these traditions are to be taken as valid.[27] All of these data, then, converge at roughly the same time for Mwendanga's arrival on Ijwi, but none provide the means for a more precise chronological reconstruction.

IN CONTRAST to the Babambo tradition, the Baloho tradition is very short. Rather than forming a narrative referring to particular individuals and events, this "tradition" consists of fragmentary components reconstructed from the testimony of several Baloho informants—a process of synthesis that treats these separate testimonies as belonging to the clan as a whole, which their distribution (and convergence) would indicate.[28]

The references that make up this tradition, unlike those of the (more unitary) Babambo tradition, include very little circumstantial evidence or secondary information concerning other persons, events, places, or timing. Despite the many cultural allusions contained in it, the Baloho tradition refers to only three named individuals (Kabwiika, Mwendanga, and Kamo) without mentioning their social identification (except that vaguely tied to royalty) or any relation to a precise or geographical context. At first glance this would seem to be a result of the present fragmentary form of the tradition. But this absence of empirical detail (or reference to discrete events and individuals) also conforms to the nature of the

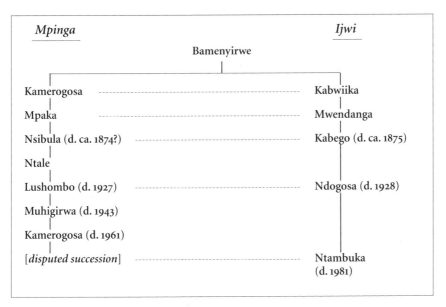

Figure 4.1. Havu royal genealogies

tradition itself and to the social and historical characteristics of the clan. These latter aspects will be discussed at greater length below. Here it only need be pointed out that the tradition itself refers to travel in the forest. The principal themes (to be discussed below) also relate to cultures associated with the forest, and the historical and sociological characteristics of the Baloho on Ijwi, even today, in some ways indicate similar ties to the forest cultures west of Lake Kivu. In these areas west of the mountains, oral testimonies today characteristically lack chronological depth and historical detail, in just the same manner as the Baloho traditions on Ijwi concerning Kamo and Mwendanga.[29] Thus the present fragmentary form of the Baloho tradition today may be more a reflection of the social and historical context from which the Baloho derive than a definitive statement on the validity of the content. To understand the validity of the content, we need to understand the history of the Baloho on Ijwi, as told in independent sources.

The Baloho genesis tradition is actually formed of bits of references held by different individuals. Despite their fragmentary nature, these data can be viewed as forming a single tradition, for they are recounted exclusively by members of a single small descent group, and the narrative elements held by one individual often overlap with those of another testimony. Furthermore, even though this tradition is usually found in fragmentary form today, there are two examples of longer and more complete recitations of this tradition that include several of the separate elements. Thus, irrespective of whether the tradition ever formed a single whole, it is seen as such today; at least some informants regard the various fragments as part of a coherent whole.

Regardless of the historical processes at work that created such a fragmentary form today (whether a breakdown of an earlier coherent tradition or simply a series of ideas or observations seized on by members of this single descent group), and regardless of the historical validity of the various elements, they can be seen as a single tradition in their complementary content, in their shared form, and in their combination by a few informants themselves. Even if the tradition is seen as an artificial reconstruction formed of disparate narrative elements drawn from members of this clan, the Baloho, such a reconstruction is achieved without incorporating elements from the other tradition, that told by the Babambo. Fragmentary as they may be in their narration, therefore, the Baloho accounts form a single tradition in opposition to the Babambo narratives.

Finally, other elements define these fragmentary accounts as part of a continuous narrative tradition. Where they include cultural items not a part of Ijwi's mainstream culture today, these references can be identified as retentions from pre-Ijwi referents. For example, utility bags (used for carrying pipes, tobacco, snuff, medicines, twine, or small game) are rare on Ijwi today but still common west of the mountains on the mainland, in areas that have not maintained long-term contacts with the Baloho on Ijwi. (The "sack" could be seen as a magnified reference to this.) Such references therefore—the more remarkable for their rarity and isolation on Ijwi today—probably retain earlier Baloho cultural traits and serve as testimony to internal Baloho clan history. Thus, despite the present fragmentary form of these accounts, they may indeed contain historical features that provide an interpretation of past events.

As reconstructed from these sources, the Baloho tradition recounts how a certain Kamo, a diviner, himself apparently fleeing from the west,[30] befriended Kabwiika, the father of the first Basibula king on Ijwi. On the death of Kabwiika, Kamo protected Mwendanga from unspecified enemies who sought him out because of his royal descent and status. Finally, on the divinatory advice of Kamo, Mwendanga moved to Ijwi and began to rule with Kamo's counsel and support. Thus the essential narrative elements in this tradition are:

a. Kamo befriends Kabwiika;

b. On Kabwiika's death, Kamo travels widely, usually within a forest context, carrying Mwendanga in a sack;

c. As a diviner, Kamo counsels Mwendanga to establish himself on Ijwi.

What is important in this context is the prominence given to literary images and allusions to objects and tasks today associated with the forest cultures to the west of Lake Kivu. Among these themes are the sack motif, the travel theme, the role of divination, and the achieved status associated with "friendship." So, too, of course, is the legitimizing role of the descendants of Kamo, the Baloho, as advisors and friends of the king, a general social function that it shares, of course, with the Babambo tradition.

Thus the major present function of these traditions is that of explaining past royal favor toward the two possessor clans, in a period when neither clan holds positions of power and respect through proximity to royalty. Yet the fact that the traditions serve such a generalized contemporary function does not automatically exclude the possibility of some historical foundation for them. We have already noted that in terms of specific royal history the traditions serve only as a very general guide, and in their details they can be misleading. But certainly there is no evidence that contradicts the major assertion of past association with the Basibula dynasty. In fact, what other evidence exists—as well as that drawn from many other areas—concurs. It would be surprising, for example, if a mainland tradition emerged among non-Babambo informants, on the basis of the current Babambo status as ritual maternal uncles on Ijwi.

THIS SECTION has considered not the structure of the traditions but their content—the internal elements that may have some bearing on their use as historical sources. Because the two traditions are very different in form and content, this exercise has not been equally productive for both traditions; more precise details and greater historical understanding can be derived from the internal attributes of the Babambo tradition than from the Baloho tradition. The following sections focus on similar questions, but differently, by comparing the two traditions on the basis of their external attributes—their distribution, the forms in which they are retained and recounted, the historical and social characteristics of the possessor groups, and the way in which events more recent than those accounted for in the traditions may have influenced their evolution and present form and content.

The Social and Historical Characteristics of the Two Clans on Ijwi

The previous section examined the content of each of the two traditions for its consistency and historical plausibility. Their differences can be explained in part by the fact that the two traditions are so localized on the island today; each tradition is associated only with a single, rather small clan. This section considers the characteristics of each of those clans that relate to the content or form of the tradition as it is held today.

Understanding the historical roles of the two clans, particularly their relationships with the royal family, contributes to our understanding of the traditions, just as the traditions in some ways provide an explanation for those historical roles. Yet it is not a common sociological device for clans on Ijwi to relate present situations or past glories to an earlier history of ties with the royal family. Indeed, the Babambo and Baloho—the two clans involved with these genesis traditions—are the only clans on Ijwi that have such traditions; it is a rare narrator from another clan who offers any account of royal arrival beyond the most succinct (and often etiological) statement of the fact of arrival itself.[31] Consequently, genesis traditions of this sort on Ijwi cannot be seen as a common structural device to explain or justify present status or subsequent events.

The different forms of the two traditions can be accounted for by three factors: the different milieux within which these two groups functioned, their pre-Ijwi cultural heritage, and their subsequent history on Ijwi. Many of the dominant literary elements in each tradition reflect or reinforce the social characteristics predominating in the areas of settlement of each group. The Babambo, for example, lived in an area of more intense social interaction and political conflict over the past 150 years than did the Baloho; they also live today in an area more heavily influenced by Rwandan cultural values (as since the mid-nineteenth century, Kinyaga has become increasingly integrated into the Rwandan state). Consequently it is not surprising that intense social interaction and conflict, and frequent Rwandan contacts and literary style (e.g., the "orphan-king" theme), are two characteristics prominent in the Babambo tradition. On the other hand, the Baloho today live in an area of relatively high clan autonomy. Therefore, it is not surprising that in narrating their relations with Mwendanga, these narratives do not identify any other specific clans (or other individuals aside from Kabwiika, Mwendanga, and Kamo). Furthermore, the Baloho settlement area is more compatible with the preservation of forest-type cultural values and literary traditions, of which the "sack theme" is one.

As emphasized in the traditions, Baloho and Babambo collectively associate their own arrival and presence on Ijwi with the arrival of the royal heir. But the Baloho have no local power base independent of the Basibula dynasty; their status and significance stem exclusively from their asserted ties to Mwendanga and his successors. The primary areas of Babambo residence, on the other hand, are located on the mainland, on both eastern and western shores at the southern end of the lake. On Ijwi, the Babambo are concentrated in the lakeshore areas in the southwest of the island, facing the areas of Babambo strength on the mainland (map 4.2). Indeed, this part of the lake is intersected by numerous interlocking peninsulas and small islands, a geographical fact reflected socially in intensive interaction, interchange, and communication between the lakeshore areas. Because they share in this general mobility, the Babambo on Ijwi have maintained relatively close ties with their mainland relatives.

Babambo political strength in the mainland areas seems to have considerable historical depth, as the tradition implies by their role in Kabwiika's succession struggle and the subsequent war against Kamerogosa. In addition, other Ijwi and mainland traditions refer to a later succession dispute on Ijwi that is better understood when the Babambo locus of power on the mainland is accounted for. At the time of Mwendanga's death, one of the claimants to the throne was Vuningoma, Mwendanga's son by a Babambo wife; some say Vuningoma was Mwendanga's first-born son, *nfula.* The term *nfula,* however, has an ambiguous meaning in this patrilineal society, since in addition to "first-born son" it also carries the meaning of "successor," and in fact, this is often its primary meaning; a man who succeeds his father is referred to as his nfula, regardless of the position of his birth. Therefore, some informants also imply that Vuningoma was designated (or at least favored) as heir to Mwendanga's throne—just as his grandfather, Kabwiika, had been before him, according to some accounts.[32] However, in part because of the arrogance of the Babambo on Ijwi,[33] continue these narratives, Vuningoma was rejected by the "population" on Ijwi. (While it is not clear which segments of the population this refers to, it is significant that internal popular pressure is presented as having played such an important role in the Ijwi succession disputes.)

The succession finally went to Kabego, a son of Mwendanga by a different mainland wife. Kabego, however, had lived on Ijwi, while Vuningoma had

Map 4.2. Ijwi Island, showing the distribution of Babambo and Baloho settlements

remained on the mainland, at a peninsula called Rambira, near Ishungu (map 4.2). The succession dispute, apparently of long duration, seems to have been essentially a struggle between the mainland areas of Mwendanga's domain and Ijwi, with Vuningoma and the mainland areas represented primarily by the Babambo. Finally, the traditions state, the Bany'Iju under Kabego rounded up all the Babambo on Ijwi and placed them on a tiny island located between Ijwi and the mainland. Those who could not escape were slaughtered to a man. Since then, only a few Babambo have remained on Ijwi, in their capacity as ritual maternal uncles to the king; they have not been seriously involved in the power equation of Ijwi Island.

The minimal social status of the Babambo on Ijwi today, therefore, is very different from the glory portrayed in the Kabwiika-Mwendanga tradition; the genesis tradition that relates the Babambo to royal status certainly does not serve the role of a "social charter" explaining or justifying their current (limited) presence and status on Ijwi. In fact, the two aspects of the tradition relating to the Babambo (that of Mwendanga's youth and that of the succession struggle following Mwendanga's death) are quite distinct: they are never run together into one continuous narrative, and while other clans know almost nothing of the Babambo genesis tradition, the tradition of Kabego's "pogrom" against the Babambo is more widely known and recounted. It could be said that the Babambo tradition—with all its detail—is no more than an attempt to assert distant glories in the face of more recent disaster. However, this interpretation does not account for its presence on the mainland, among people who are concerned with the intricacies of nineteenth-century internal Ijwi succession struggles.

The interpretation of the Babambo tradition as "social charter," simply an attempt to augment their status, would not also explain their ritual role as maternal uncles, a role widely accepted on Ijwi even by those unfamiliar with the Babambo tradition. Furthermore, it would not seem necessary for the Babambo to assert a totally fictive tradition to claim their ritual role—other clans do not, and they suffer no more status deprivation than the Babambo. In fact, as mentioned above, neither the Babambo nor Baloho enjoy a particularly high status on Ijwi today. In short while low status may account for the retention of a tradition, it seems hardly to have been responsible for having created it. Nor would it seem plausible that Babambo strength off Ijwi was responsible for the emergence of a tradition to explain that (former) status: Ijwi kingship is of little importance to those off the island, and mainlanders are not generally informed on

Ijwi history or politics. It seems incongruous that a tradition concerning an area of little importance (if not also one subject to some disdain)—Ijwi Island—evolved in order to justify status in an area supposedly of greater importance to the Babambo (their mainland strongholds).

The Baloho, on the other hand, are concentrated in a very different part of the island—the eastern highlands (referred to here simply as "the east" for convenience; see map 4.2).[34] This mountainous forest area has served to make them much more isolated from formal contacts outside Ijwi than were the Babambo. Curiously, it was also an area relatively isolated from royal presence until recently. Furthermore, the ecology of their area of settlement on Ijwi is notably similar to that of their immediate origin among the Tembo peoples west of the Mitumba Mountains,[35] and in certain cultural aspects the highland areas on Ijwi differ from other areas on the island, even while they approach forest-culture norms.[36] As discussed below in more detail, the form of the Baloho tradition as well as the imagery contained within it are similar to traditions in other areas of Tembo influence but are not common in other Ijwi traditions today; elements in this category include the "sack" theme, the prominent significance of individual mobility, and the achieved "friendship" status between Kamo and Kabwiika. It is possible therefore that this cultural microenvironment that distinguishes the eastern highland areas from other areas of Ijwi has also helped preserve forms of oral literature that would not have been retained.

It is political factors, however, that explain Baloho settlement in the east, if the general orientation of the story is to be believed. In an informal manner, the Baloho appear to have represented the Ijwi royal line in this area during most of the nineteenth century, tied to royalty through Kamo's original "friendship" with Mwendanga and reinforced by frequent marriages between the Baloho and the royal family.[37] The east in general represented a difficult area in the process of political integration to the new kingdom; it was in this region that groups from east of the lake (from areas today included as part of Rwanda) had settled in several autonomous communities prior to Basibula arrival. Some of these settlements appear to have maintained strong social and economic ties with their home areas east of the lake, and their oral accounts indicate that on Ijwi they initially had relatively few contacts with each other (or at least that these were not seen as socially significant).[38] Although for the most part these settlements preceded the Basibula, many of them were formed by relatively recent immigrants at the time of Mwendanga's arrival; this fact, along with their continuing ties off Ijwi, provided them with a ready alternative to direct submission to the new dynasty. In fact, the east was one of the few areas on the island where there appears to have been any overt resistance to Basibula arrival; Mwendanga is said to have driven a segment of the Banyakabwa clan from this area off Ijwi, to the eastern shore of the lake.

There was an added ambiguity to relations between the royal family and the eastern highlands, however. In addition to this being an area of prior settlement by relatively well-defined social units, several of these groups claimed historical ties to ritual groups associated with royalty in Rwanda, related both to the First Fruits ceremonies and to an identification with the royal drum.[39] This fact probably provided these clans (and by extension the area of their settlement) with an added appeal—and potential danger—in the eyes of a new dynastic line such as the Basibula on Ijwi. The east, therefore, was a part of the island that the Basibula treated with some caution—and some distance: members of the royal family did not settle in the east until after colonial rule had been established one hundred years later.[40]

In this context, the Baloho appear to have served as intermediaries between the east and the royal court; even today they are spread among several villages of the east, where they have in the past served as designated village headmen, named by the court in numbers disproportionate to their population size.[41] Some Baloho from this area (such as Camukenge Bitaha) became the most trusted partisans to the kings in the late nineteenth and early twentieth centuries.[42] Indeed, some reports go even further, to imply that the early Baloho held certain royal rituals of their own and that they may have functioned as a sort of counter-dynasty in this region.[43]

But the brilliant history of precolonial ties between the Baloho and the royal family did not survive the new context of colonial rule. The eastern part of the island suffered heavy losses from devastating cattle raids and labor demands that accompanied the imposition of colonial rule on the island, and Baloho prestige declined accordingly. Some Baloho apparently fled; cut off from more recent immigration, the Baloho remain today a relatively small group on Ijwi. Their former sociopolitical status is much eroded, retained only in a few peripheral villages of the area; the more important central villages have been lost to them in the recent administrative reshuffles associated with colonial rule.[44]

Despite their small numbers and diminished status, the Baloho historical role as royal intermediaries to a remote but important region is significant, for the Baloho are apparently the only clan on Ijwi to have served in this role. Certainly other clans were close to the royal family, and other individuals served in the same eminent capacity as men such as Camukenge and Shankulu (both Baloho), but no other early clan on Ijwi maintained such a politically significant role for so long or developed such a strong collective identification from their relationship to the kings. Baloho coherence and autonomy deriving from this is apparent even today in their sense of a strong corporate feeling: virtually all Baloho on Ijwi claim descent from Kamo, Kabwiika's friend, who (may have) arrived on Ijwi with Mwendanga. Indicative of this, Baloho informants are able to cite genealogical ties wider and deeper than members of most other clans on Ijwi.

THUS, DESPITE their differences in form and content, the two distinct genesis traditions share the common attribute of explaining subsequent roles played by the two groups in Ijwi history. In turn, these later historical roles help explain the presence or retention of the two traditions; but this fact does not explain their content, and especially not their clear limitations. The Babambo tradition helps clarify the events of the struggle between Vuningoma and Kabego to succeed Mwendanga. A knowledge of the depth and nature of Babambo relations with Kabwiika (and especially with Mwendanga) helps cast the nature of subsequent Babambo ties with Vuningoma into more satisfying perspective. Similarly, their political involvement and willingness to fight for political ends, characteristics that appear so strongly in the Babambo genesis tradition, are additional factors in understanding the succession struggle. But the genesis tradition is not merely a prologue to the succession disputes, as we have seen; the two traditions are quite different in their distribution on Ijwi. Finally, Babambo strength on the mainland, something so apparent in the genesis tradition, adds an important dimension to the tradition of the succession struggle that is not otherwise apparent; supplementing the theme of personal competition, it explains the succession struggle as a regional struggle between the two domains of Mwendanga's influence—Ijwi Island and the mainland.[45]

Similarly, the Baloho genesis tradition serves as a justification of later Baloho influence and authority, and therefore approaches more closely the form and function of the conventional "social charter." For although the Babambo tradition does justify the Babambo role as maternal uncles to the king, it does less to "justify" the succession dispute than explain it, since the arrival trope and the succession trope (the Kabwiika-Mwendanga episode, a father-son narrative) are not directly linked to the Mwendanga-Vuningoma episode (a father-son narrative of the next generation). Nonetheless, the Baloho tradition—as far as it goes—does explain as well as justify, and the two functions cannot be said to be mutually exclusive in this case. If justifying the current order is the main function of a social charter, then this applies more fully to the Baloho tradition than to the Babambo tradition.

The different structures of the two traditions can be largely accounted for by the different milieux in which these two groups lived and in which their traditions functioned, by their pre-Ijwi cultural heritage (the Babambo within the Rwandan cultural orbit, the Baloho within a forest-culture environment), and by their subsequent histories on Ijwi. Many of the dominant elements in each tradition can be seen to reflect or reinforce the social characteristics predominating in each group's principal area of settlement. The Babambo lived in an area of much greater social interaction and much more intense political conflict than did the Baloho; they have also intensified their ties with Rwandan cultural values as their ancestral area has been increasingly integrated into the Rwandan state. And indeed, both conflict and Rwandan contacts are prominent features in the Babambo tradition. The Baloho, on the other hand, lived in an area of relatively high clan autonomy on Ijwi, one also compatible with the preservation of forest-type cultural values and traditions. Their tradition makes mention of but few other clans, and the themes appearing in them are those of forest cultures, as noted above.

Thus it seems that the traditions are retained and narrated in their present form in part because they are compatible with both the present and earlier cultural contexts of the people who narrate them. In this sense their historicity—as traditions referring to a specific series of unique historical events, and as handed down from the time of those events—is open to question. Their different forms and their differing (and mutually exclusive) versions of the events of Sibula arrival can be ascribed to their function as independent "social charters" attempting to recoup some of the disastrous decline in status that the two clans have experienced over the past century.

But there are limits to the degree to which such a monolithic functionalist interpretation can be pressed. Other aspects of these traditions may indicate that they are more than simply literary expressions of cultural values or products of contemporary social and political factors, although their retained forms can be viewed in such terms. The very differences in the traditions, differences that some would say negate any potentiality for their use as historical sources, offer the possibility for others to penetrate beyond form and structure and seek out content. In fact, the traditions need not be identical to refer to a single set of events. Rather than factoring out what is similar, we shall try to analyze events from what is different in these two traditions. In fact, the variant narrative elements of the two traditions can be seen—within their limitations—to provide acceptable historical accounts of the particular events associated with royal arrival on Ijwi.

While not denying the influence of present or past factors on the form of the traditions, as noted in here, the next section will attempt to go beyond this. For the essential question—whether they reflect history (i.e., the interpretation of past events significant for the present) or whether they reflect present cultural and social conditions and perceptions—need not be answered in exclusive terms: the traditions can serve both functions. We saw above how they conform to the latter possibility; the succeeding section will attempt to determine if, and how, they fulfill the former.

The Traditions as Historical Documents

The previous two sections have stressed the considerable differences in these two traditions. They appear mutually exclusive in content and narrative form, as well as in their distribution: those who know one tradition do not know the other. They therefore do not draw on a common stock of cliché or metaphor (though each shows a formidable arsenal in these domains), nor are they simply two distinct versions told by the same people with a common objective. In fact, given this presence among a relatively small island population forming a single political unit, the two traditions appear to be close to independent testimony. And yet these two clans relate traditions whose essential cores converge; they appear to agree on a common set of events, a single (very important) episode in Ijwi's past. Thus, for the historian, these traditions are more than simply literary expressions of cultural values or of contemporary social factors, though their form of expression can be viewed in these terms.

Partial confirmation for the general corpus of clan histories of the Babambo and Baloho is available from the traditions of other clans. Although few people outside the Babambo and Baloho clans know of the genesis traditions discussed here, the patterns of conflict and alliance that the Babambo and Baloho have experienced with the royal family since their arrival on Ijwi are indeed known to others. Even the names of individuals involved in these interaction patterns (though not the names of the central nonroyal figures in the genesis traditions, Kamo and Lubambo) are known to some other informants, despite the fact that the names of historical members of other clans are generally not retained in local traditions on Ijwi. Still, where the Babambo and Baloho histories take place on Ijwi, other Bany'Iju today know enough of these histories to be able to serve as confirmation, though they do not know the genesis traditions in any precise manner.

This conclusion is important in considering the "social charter" hypothesis, whereby the traditions serve the unique function of justifying sociopolitical status (or refuting a relative lack of status) at a given moment in the flow of time. If the present genesis traditions do serve that function, then that moment does not seem to belong to the postcolonial or even the colonial "present." But various traditions agree on the outlines of Babambo and Baloho relations with the royal family over the nineteenth century, and, as pointed out above, the genesis traditions discussed here provide a plausible explanation for these nineteenth-century interactions of the Babambo and Baloho with the royal family.[46] It would therefore seem that the genesis traditions relate more directly to these nineteenth-century alliance and conflict patterns, partially known to others on Ijwi, than they do to more recent conditions. Consequently, if their primary function was originally etiological, then they seem to have been stopped in time, and if this is so, then it seems that their function is to justify these nineteenth-century patterns of interaction more than to attempt to refute present "status deflation."

Moreover, if the genesis traditions were somehow generated in two different idioms to account for nineteenth-century events, then one can conclude that they have been handed down over that period of time at least. Therefore, they would show the essential characteristic of a historical tradition, that of transmission over time, and would in fact be no longer etiological but historical. Were they originally etiological explanations relating to nineteenth-century Ijwi relationships with the royal family, one would expect these traditions to refer directly to the events they are trying to explain. In fact, they do not: the lived histories discussed in the preceding section do not appear at all in the genesis traditions, which appear quite distinct.

Furthermore, the genre of etiological tradition, by its use as a popular explanation and its immersion in contemporary society, would seem to be highly sensitive to the evolving social norms. If these two traditions were originally primarily etiological, referring to nineteenth-century royal history, it is therefore probable that they would have been superseded by more recent traditions that explain their current status. In fact, traditions relating to the earlier events are retained, not simply forgotten; present events are explained by additional traditions.

Finally, etiological traditions usually relate to a single cultural item (e.g., the introduction of cattle, iron, or certain food crops) or a single complex of related royal rites (which are only implicitly dealt with in these traditions), rather than a whole series of discrete but interlocking sociological elements that are apparent in independent forms of data and in different domains of activities: etiologies are usually simplified and reductive rather than complex and potentially applicable to a wide range of patterns and sources. Therefore, the presence on Ijwi of continuing ritual roles (such as for the Babambo), present-day residential patterns historically validated through independent local traditions, and other historical and cultural indications (noted in the preceding section and including patterns of joking relations) all appear to confirm the historical traditions at an analytical level of convergent confirmations above that at which an etiological argument could be upheld.[47]

Etiological tales, by their simplified nature and appeal to present concerns, are usually widespread in a culture. This characteristic does not conform at all to the distinctive and highly defined distribution patterns of the two genesis traditions discussed here. It is clear that they are not intended as general explanations whose function is to reinforce common values and provide social cohesion as well as entertainment. It would therefore seem that these traditions are not etiological in their function (that of explaining the present), their origin (that of explaining events that were once "present" events, but doing so in etiological forms with reference to contemporary values alone), their present form (as simplified representations of a particular social element), or their distribution.

The possibility that the two genesis traditions are simply recent variants of what was originally a single tradition of origin legitimizing the royal line need also be considered. In that case, there is no assurance that the events happened as portrayed because there would be no independent confirmation of the different sources. Indeed, the relatively recent immigration of a social group from outside, but claiming royal status and associated with aspects of royalty foreign to the Ijwi experience, would seem to provide suitable conditions for the generation of a single tradition of origin legitimizing the royal line.[48] But under such conditions it is more plausible that the resultant explanation would represent the Basibula ties to the kingdom as a whole and would be shared by many of the constituent groups of the kingdom. Certainly, one would expect a tradition of this sort to be found among the royal family—which it is not! And certainly also there would be some common ground in the form of the two traditions. But because these two traditions differ in both thematic and narrative content, as well as in form, they do not appear to be simply variants of a single generalized social charter of the Ijwi kingdom.

Nor does it appear that the tradition of Sibula arrival has been built up by a gradual process of convergence of several competing traditions focusing on royal ties with different independent clans. In such a process one would expect a synthesis or amalgamation to appear that would weld the variants into one "official tradition," but there is no indication that this has taken place. Nor do other clans (some of whose sections may well have arrived contemporaneously with the Basibula) claim ties in the same form as do the Baloho and Babambo in their royal genesis traditions, despite whatever prestige the Babambo and Baloho may have derived from their historical claims. Certain clans on Ijwi can boast greater ritual importance to royalty than either the Babambo or Baloho, yet they do not attempt to validate their role though legitimizing traditions of the type narrated by the Babambo and Baloho.

All the indications are, therefore, that the two genesis traditions are not only independent in origin (as discussed above), but that they independently arrive at their general conclusions; there is no apparent cultural bias on Ijwi for clan identity to coalesce around concepts of ties with the royal family. Consequently, there appears neither interchange through direct interaction among the traditions nor indirect common influences acting on them from the wider cultural environment. Thus, while one can account for the differences between the present forms of the traditions as the previous section attempted to do, the similarities within such differences still need to be accounted for.

The traditions are not divergent from a single original tradition: how, then, does one reconcile the fact of their differences with the claim that they refer to a single historical episode? Since the differences in content are so great, they are not simply conflicting accounts of similar events resulting from different social perspectives. Instead they seem more complementary than contradictory, referring to different aspects within the same larger episode of royal advent to Ijwi. Thus, though the traditions are mutually exclusive in content and distribution, the validity of one need not exclude the validity of the other: in this case historians are not faced with an either/or choice, failing which they must choose neither.

The two traditions seem plausible as historical reconstructions when judged against independent historical data related either to the royal family or to the Babambo and Baloho alone. The same can be said when the two traditions are judged against each other. All traditions, as well as indirect evidence,[49] indicate that Mwendanga arrived on Ijwi as a full adult. Prior to his arrival, he had his own domain on the mainland (at Bujombo), which seems to have always been an area important to him: several of his sons and wives apparently remained there even after his arrival on Ijwi, and it was there that he eventually died and was buried. It is clear, therefore, that there was a certain lapse of time between the attack on Kamerogosa by the Babambo (possibly the cause of Mwendanga's schism with the Babambo) and Mwendanga's arrival on Ijwi. Consequently, it is likely that this tradition deals only with a very small and highly selective portion of Mwendanga's life before his arrival on Ijwi; the same is clearly true for the Baloho tradition. In other words, it is likely that the two traditions are accounts of different periods in Mwendanga's life, and there is no incompatibility in what some people may object to as their contradictory character.

The Babambo tradition concentrates particularly on the earlier phases of Mwendanga's life: Kabwiika's relationship with Lubambo's family and his death, and the early Babambo attempts to regain the Havu drums for Mwendanga. The later aspects are downplayed, and in fact presented in a style very different from the bulk of the traditions—almost as an epilogue. Indeed, given the importance of Babambo claims to have sent Mwendanga to Ijwi, this particular part of the traditions can be seen as an epilogue, strongly influenced by the perceived need to establish the tie of the Babambo family on Ijwi (and royal presence on Ijwi) directly with the Babambo community on the mainland. At any rate, because this section of the tradition is so sparse, it is very difficult to compare it with other data or to provide a check on its historical probability, which therefore must remain less certain than the earlier part of the tradition that speaks to Mwendanga's matrilateral ties to the Babambo.

Furthermore, there may have been more or less continuous tension between the Babambo and the Basibula (the royal family) during the later part of Mwendanga's life. Various traditions mention conflict (or at least tensions) between Mwendanga and his maternal uncles and matrilateral cousins at the time of the attack on Kamerogosa, before the royal arrival on Ijwi. The succession dispute on Mwendanga's death is also presented as a case of Babambo ambitions against Basibula status; even Babambo traditions imply that it was at least in part Babambo pretensions to power that provoked the split. It therefore seems likely that this tension between the two groups continued throughout the greater part of Mwendanga's later life, and that where the Babambo claim to have sent Mwendanga to Ijwi, in fact they more likely only accompanied him.[50] Finally, the Babambo seem never to have exercised political power on Ijwi itself; the later succession dispute indicates that their main area of strength was always on the mainland. This, too, would lend a certain aura of disbelief to the Babambo claim to have been the primary influence in Mwendanga's arrival. Thus the principal historical value of this tradition appears to be found in the earlier sections, describing the Sibula succession dispute and Kabwiika's refuge among the Babambo.

The Babambo tradition, therefore, seems most valid for the earlier periods of Mwendanga's life: Kabwiika's exile and death, Mwendanga's birth to Nkobwa, and the early Babambo attempts to place Mwendanga on the Havu throne. Each of these segments is confirmed from other oral sources; and each conforms to several other types of supporting data. But the later part of the Babambo tradition lacks support of this kind. Furthermore, it seems likely that, more than other parts, the later section of the narrative has been influenced by the functional need to tie the Babambo community on Ijwi to the early history of Mwendanga's royal claims, by linking royalty on Ijwi with Lubambo's hospitality toward Kabwiika. In short, Mwendanga's early dependence on the Babambo as a child seems carried over—without supporting evidence—to his later career and arrival on Ijwi.

It is this aspect of the tradition that most directly conflicts with the Baloho version, and in this case the Baloho version seems to carry more authority. The Babambo held no important political positions on Ijwi during the first two reigns (those of Mwendanga and Kabego); it is only during the early twentieth century, as clients and colleagues of Ndogosa's eldest son, that they appear in positions of delegated, political authority, and none of the major military leaders from Ijwi's past have been Babambo. Therefore, the evidence does not support Babambo claims as influential in Mwendanga's establishment or early reign on Ijwi; the Babambo claim to having sent Mwendanga to Ijwi seems largely to serve as a post facto explanation to account for the Basibula move to Ijwi—and to connect that to the Babambo relation to Kabwiika (through Nkobwa).

BALOHO TRADITIONS, however, deal with exactly those time periods where the Babambo appear weakest as historical sources. If the Babambo had little influence in the early Ijwi kingdom, it is clear that the Baloho had influence all out of proportion to their numbers—regionally defined, but no less real for that. They state that Kamo tutored Mwendanga, and it is clear, through marriage ties and their privileged position at the court, that Baloho at least had access to the king in an advisory capacity. Thus it is the Baloho tradition that provides the continuity from Mwendanga's original status as mainland exile to his later status as king on Ijwi.

On the other hand, just as Babambo traditions are weak on Mwendanga's later life, the Baloho variants omit all reference to Mwendanga's ancestry, birth, and contacts with other groups—just the areas of strength (and external confirmation) in the Babambo tradition. The only reference to royal descent in the Baloho tradition is implicit: that Mwendanga was sought by his enemies (and hence the sack) "because he was [to be] a king." Kabwiika does appear in some versions of the Baloho traditions, but all we know from these references is that Kabwiika died leaving behind the infant Mwendanga, who was cared for by Kabwiika's friend Kamo. The Baloho accounts make no mention of the succession dispute at Nyabihunge, or of how Kabwiika died, or of royalty, or of the Babambo —as indeed, these are all secondary to the Baloho interest in Mwendanga's arrival on Ijwi with Kamo.

In such ways, therefore, the two traditions appear to be consecutive commentaries on Mwendanga's life, rather than contradictory statements; with few exceptions, the narrative elements of these two traditions complement each other well. While we can never know with absolute certainty the details of Mwendanga's life, we can learn much about the Babambo and Baloho by the way they portray his life, and the way they see themselves relating to it. Through their common concern with Mwendanga, the two traditions can be used as a form of evaluation on each other, even when they are not directly interrelated.

THIS SECTION has tried to look at the potential use of these two traditions for historians. In the absence of acceptable data from historical sources other than oral tradition, the argument has necessarily been based on negative analysis: refuting potential obstacles to viewing the traditions as proper historical guides. Having presented the differences of the two traditions within their essential convergence (their agreement on Mwendanga's historicity and his arrival on Ijwi to found a new royal line), we have tried to account for all the possible alternative explanations for the presence of the traditions being studied. While this technique may not establish the traditions as "straight history," it will, by defining their limitations as historical sources, help to identify those aspects of the traditions that are more plausible historical data than others. In the process, I have tried to bring into account many of the historical and sociological aspects of Ijwi that may bear on this problem; though certainly a part of contemporary Ijwi society, they do not seem rooted in contemporary concepts and symbolism. There is therefore no obstacle, either in form or in content, to viewing these traditions as properly historical accounts, though they provide different data from each other.

The Two Traditions in Time Perspective

The first section discussed the differences in the forms of the two genesis traditions. The second discussed differences in the areas of residence, the histories, and the contacts with others sustained by the Baloho and Babambo, and speculated on the influence these factors may have had on the different forms of the traditions. But of course, the local cultural systems from which the two narratives are drawn have themselves undergone significant change during the past 150 years, and these changes may well have been reflected in changes in the forms of the traditions. This section explores how such changes in the traditions have influenced our understanding of the past. To do so, it will compare Ijwi variants of the traditions with those elsewhere. The similarities and differences between these narratives may provide some clues to the nature of change that each tradition has undergone.

The cultural milieu of the Baloho has evolved in two ways: at the level of specific politics—in terms of their relation to the royal family and how that affects their status on the island; and simultaneously at a more general level, in their changing relation to more general cultural norms on Ijwi over the last century. The change in their political status has already been examined above. It was noted that while this may have encouraged the retention of an earlier tradition, such alterations were not likely to have served as the stimulus for the etiological creation of the genesis tradition in the form in which they tell it today. The second aspect, however, concerning the broader cultural changes on Ijwi, has not been considered.

It was pointed out that certain features of the east, where the Baloho live, indicate a former way of life similar to that of the Batembo peoples now living west of the mountains, in exactly those areas from which the Baloho claim to have emigrated. The cultural norms portrayed in the Baloho tradition—the fragmentary nature of the tradition itself, the forest motif, the sack theme—are associated both with regional differences and historical differences on Ijwi. It appears that the cultural norms for most of the island's population, including many Baloho, have gradually shifted away from the norms portrayed in the Baloho tradition. The traditions may therefore be expected to retain certain forms and emphases that reflect this early period, and hence to bear witness to the changes. In fact, in a free-form tradition such as this, it is possible that there are elements of every period in the life of the tradition; the problem is to determine which periods are retained in which elements.[51] (In fact, it is possible that a tradition retains cultural elements from a period prior to the events to which it appears to relate.)

There are two distinct types of Baloho tradition on Ijwi, the one fragmentary, the other (less common) a longer version. As noted above, because they overlap, the fragmentary forms appear to be part of a larger tradition: recounted by members of the same clan—and only that clan—their synthesis is reflected in the longer traditions. But though they are rare and show signs of more elaboration, the longer versions are nonetheless similar to a tradition now found in Mpinga, the area near Kalehe on the western mainland where the senior Basibula line (the descendants of Kamerogosa) is now centered (see map 4.1).[52] The Mpinga tradition, however, though similar in form to the Ijwi tradition, applies to a different historical episode than that of the Ijwi tradition, an episode distinct in time, place, and actors. Precisely because their forms are so similar but the historical referents in the traditions are so distinct, the Mpinga and Ijwi versions of the tradition must have drawn either on each other or on a source common to them both to have attained such structural homogeneity.

To account for their similarity in structure, it will be necessary to outline briefly the Mpinga tradition, which relates to the last quarter of the nineteenth century, when Ntale, the Havu king, fled the attacks of the Rwandan king Rwabugiri, who had earlier killed Ntale's father (Nsibula).[53] As recounted in the Mpinga tradition, Ntale's closest advisors placed him in a sack and traveled with him widely, feeding him in the sack as they traveled, even to the court of Rwabugiri, without Ntale being discovered. In its presentation, this episode is obviously very close to the Kamo-Mwendanga tale, except that the historical context (Rwabugiri's attacks on Mpinga) is explicitly noted, whereas the enemies seeking Mwendanga are not specified. The parallel between the Mpinga and Ijwi episodes is strengthened by the fact that the threatened king (in the sack) in each of the traditions (Ntale in one, Mwendanga in the other) is referred to by the sobriquet of "Kalimumvumba."[54] Several themes are repeated in the two traditions: the sack (notably), the mobility, and the context of protecting the king from his enemies.

In determining the exact relation of the two traditions, we are left with two alternatives: either one derives directly from the other, or they both derive from a common prior source. (For reasons to be discussed below, I exclude the possibility of independent invention in such a restricted area of such pervasive cultural interaction.) Though the data do not bear directly on this problem, certain historical considerations make it unlikely that elements of one of these traditions were drawn on directly in the formation of the other. Because the Mpinga tale refers to events that occurred well over half a century after those associated with the dynastic schism at Nyabihunge,[55] and because, as discussed above, it is most unlikely that the Ijwi version is of recent provenance, it is therefore also unlikely that the Ijwi tradition is derived from that told in Mpinga. This conclusion is reinforced by the localization of the Baloho in the far eastern portions of Ijwi—a single small group with no apparent recent contacts to Kalehe.[56]

The Baloho tradition on Ijwi relates exclusively to the Ijwi branch of the Basibula family. In most variants, it ignores even Kabwiika's relation to the senior branch of the Basibula line: Kabwiika's ancestry, for example, is nowhere mentioned in the Baloho traditions on Ijwi. In addition, the Ijwi and mainland dynasties have had little interaction with each other since the schism, and even so, the royal line on Ijwi has no knowledge of the Baloho tradition at all—except that Basibula narratives do recognize "Kalimumvumba" as associated with Mwendanga. But Mwendanga is little known in Mpinga, and Kamo is unheard of. It therefore seems improbable that the Mpinga line selected the formal elements of the Baloho-Ijwi tradition and applied them to their own history, just as the converse is also highly unlikely.

What seems more plausible, given the distribution of this element, is that both the Ijwi and Mpinga versions derive their common form from an earlier stereotype present in the area. In one form or another, the sack theme, for example, is found over a wide area to the northeast, south, and west of Ijwi. To the south, the Rundi speak of a regent wrapped in a "mat" and transported thus.[57] Another variant on the theme is found in Bugoyi, northeast of Lake Kivu.[58] This region shares certain sociological, linguistic, and historical ties with areas west of Lake Kivu, and these elements help to distinguish this area from other areas of Rwanda.[59] (In Bugoyi, however, the sack theme is incorporated into a popular tale, or *umugani*, rather than one that is supposed to relate to empirical events of the human past.[60]) Therefore, the Basibula areas seem to be well within the domain of the recorded presence of this tale across a wide region. Nonetheless, it remains true also that in such areas this form of narrative is not connected with court culture or with political (or at least royal) themes.

At first glance the presence of this stereotype among the Havu seems associated with Basibula royalty, because both the Mpinga and Ijwi traditions refer primarily to members of the royal family. But simply associating it with Basibula royalty does not account for the timing of its appearance, given that the Basibula dynasty preceded the emergence of the traditions now extant; nor would such an explanation conform to the distribution of the tradition on Ijwi, which is restricted to the Baloho in the east and apparently unknown to the royal family or the royal court.

But both traditions also indicate ties to the forest culture similar to that of the Tembo peoples today, societies located west of the Mitumba Mountains.[61] Formerly, it appears, certain elements of Tembo culture were more widespread in the region, both on Ijwi and on the mainland areas west and north of Lake Kivu.[62] Therefore, despite the presence of this tradition among the two branches of the Sibula royal family, the sociological associations common to both the Baloho and Mpinga traditions relate more to Tembo contacts than to a narrowly defined concept of Basibula history. The Baloho on Ijwi have already been discussed in the context of their probable origins in the west, from an area today inhabited by the Tembo. On the mainland, the Basibula dynasty arrived in Mpinga only in the generation prior to Ntale;[63] before their arrival the area was inhabited by Hunde and Tembo peoples—two categories closely related culturally—who in fact remained in the area of Mpinga after the arrival of the Basibula dynasty. Indeed, Mpinga today retains intensive contacts with peoples identified as Tembo, those who live west of the Mitumba Mountains.

Thus these two traditions—the Kamo-Mwendanga tradition on Ijwi and the Ntale-Rwabugiri tradition in Mpinga—both apply to periods when analogous historical circumstances occurred within similar sociological contexts: when Basibula royal flight from an enemy coincided with important Basibula contacts with Tembo-type peoples. The thematic features emphasized in the traditions are compatible with Tembo-type cultural values (at least as they exist today). Therefore, it can fairly be postulated that the present forms of these traditions have resulted from grafting elements of specific Basibula dynastic history to the tropes of a common Tembo-type tradition. Such a Tembo connection helps explain the restriction of the Kamo tradition on Ijwi so narrowly to the Baloho because, like the royal family, other groups in the east did not share the cultural orientation of the Baloho.

In traditions such as these, each narrative element is, of course, a part of both the form and content of the tradition. But where there exists a common episode that recurs in different historical contexts (as with the Kamo tradition on Ijwi and the Ntale tradition on Mpinga), it is possible to distinguish the common form from the more local content of each tradition. In this case, clearly the sack theme, the mobility, and the theme of royal protection by a commoner are common to the two. Assuming the traditions have remained independent of each other, as these two seem to have done, it is possible to account for such common factors either by the structural requirements of the traditions themselves or by historical additions; where they are structurally required, the probability of their historicity at a literal level is diminished. Obviously this is true in reference to the sack, which is clearly a literary device.

On the other hand, as noted above, the presence of that common theme may well apply to a historical situation at a more general level: while not literally true, the sack theme does indicate a common theme of protection of the king from his enemies; and this aspect of the episode, as shown above, is confirmed by supporting evidence in each case. Thus the structural elements of the common episode may well be metaphorical references to a specific perceived historical situation.

Other aspects of the tradition, those not required by the common structure, relate differently to the historicity of a tradition and hence need be evaluated differently. Here it is what is specific to one context, not what is common to several variants, that is important. Although no definitive categorization is possible distinguishing specific historical referents from common cultural themes, individual elements may tend toward one end or the other of the spectrum between these two poles. Those elements that refer primarily to a specific situation rather than a common cultural theme will most likely refer either to some specific historical referent or to contemporary perceptions and situations for that particular place. Where the latter can be ruled out as a possibility and where there are supporting data for the historical situation, this element can be used as historical evidence.

However, this can best be done when two conditions apply: where the element in question can be dissociated from the broader structural requirements of the tradition, and where it finds specific support from independent data. For example, the Kamo tradition highlights the relation of the king to his benefactors as an important theme, emphasizing the friendship of Kamo and Mwendanga and the services rendered by the Baloho to the king. In contrast, the Ntale version almost entirely neglects these aspects. Because this particular element cannot be ascribed to the structure of the tradition, it may have been generated by more local considerations; whether or not these considerations are historical in origin, or generated from contemporary concerns, need be demonstrated from an analysis of the corpus of local data. The preceding presentation has shown that it is unlikely that this particular Baloho element developed out of present considerations, and that other evidence supports Kamo's historicity. Therefore, it seems probable that Kamo existed as a historical character and that he did develop some kind of affective tie with Mwendanga.

Although the structure of a tradition may provide valuable clues for histori-cal analysis, it cannot be taken itself as a guide to the historicity of a tradition. Just as great elaboration in detail need not guarantee historicity, so relative frag-mentation in form need not in itself deny historicity. One might conclude, for example, that there is little of historical value in a tradition as fragmentary as that of the Baloho on Ijwi. But virtually the same structural elements are found in two apparently independent historical contexts (that of Kamo on Ijwi and Ntale at Mpinga), with no apparent interaction of the two lines of transmission. The geographical spread of these two versions and the regularity of their struc-tural elements indicate that the prototypical form of the tradition is likely to be considerably older than either version discussed here. Because of this age factor, and given their present fragmentary forms, it seems likely that most extant vari-ants on Ijwi are condensed forms of an earlier (and broader) narrative. Yet we have seen above that Kamo's historicity is generally upheld by other evidence. The structure of the data alone, therefore, is not a reliable guide to the validity of its content.

The condensation of the Baloho tradition seems to have been more a result of the changing cultural context within which it is narrated than of the changing political fortunes of the Baloho (though these factors, too, may well have played a lesser role). The few items that remain in the narrative today emphasize the struc-tural over the historical, thus reinforcing the distinctive Baloho cultural identifica-tion (which sets them slightly apart from Ijwi society today). The Babambo tradi-tion, on the other hand, is structurally less unified; it is not so clearly a part of a single encompassing structural formula, which itself exists independently of the content in question, as the Baloho tradition appears to be. While the Baloho tra-dition in its present form seems to have been the result of compression, the Babambo tradition today appears to have resulted more from a process of elabo-ration, as seems apparent from the number of different and poorly integrated episodes—Kabwiika's death, the Babambo attack on Kamerogosa, Gahindiro's court, and Mwendanga's arrival on Ijwi. The Baloho tradition avoids this type of additive, synthetic presentation. Mwendanga's royal status, for example, is sim-ply inferred from the present situation (his descendants being of "royal" Basi-bula status); the tradition does not go out of its way to assert the fact.

The form of the Babambo tradition is determined more by the linking of successive discrete episodes than from a single overarching and consistent sym-bolic form that includes everything—as among the Baloho, where the sack repre-sents, or refers to, flight (hence conflict), mobility, and protection (by the Baloho).

This additive aspect of the Babambo tradition may help explain its current spread, its more comprehensive content, and its detail relative to the Baloho tradition, for the process of synthesis that seems to characterize the Babambo structure allows it to be expressed in norms more in harmony with contemporary social norms. The Babambo tradition portrays events and political struggles in terms closer to more common narrative forms today on Ijwi and the mainland. It has also permitted the tradition to remain consistent with contemporary social structure and values.

It is not only the different structural flexibility found in the two traditions that has favored the preservation of a more elaborate tradition among the Babambo. The recent development of Ijwi society has also done much to provide an environment in which one tradition could flourish while the other languished. One important factor of this changing history would have been the Rwandan occupation of Ijwi during the late nineteenth century and the simultaneous intensification of Rwandan central court control in Kinyaga, the mainland area south of Ijwi and east of the southern extension of Lake Kivu (see map 4.1). During the Rwandan occupation of Ijwi, important segments of the Ijwi population may well have adopted certain affinities with Rwandan culture, of which one element is a richly elaborated oral literature of many types.[64] The form and length of the full Babambo tradition make it possible, even easy, to accentuate, embellish, or add selective elements to conform to different sociopolitical and historical contexts.

The intense population interaction with Kinyaga that occurred for some segments during this period, especially in the southern part of Ijwi (the area of greatest Babambo strength), undoubtedly contributed to a general Rwandan orientation of cultural evolution in this period just prior to colonial rule. In some respects this orientation may have extended into the colonial period itself, because "chiefs" were favored on the model of Rwandan chiefs; strong Rwandan cultural and political influences among the local Ijwi colonial elite[65] would also have reinforced Rwandan elements in the traditions during the early twentieth century. The colonially imposed chief on Ijwi, for example, had lived his youth in central Rwanda, and certain Belgian administrators (including the one with the greatest impact on Ijwi) had had previous experience in Rwanda and hence encouraged a Rwandan mode of "colonial comportment." In general during this period, Rwanda was used as the administrative standard, if not norm, by colonial authorities, and the values subscribed to in this particular administrative context may well have filtered through to influence other social contexts. Consequently, there was a favorable climate to augment, elaborate, and extend the Babambo tradition; at the same time, such changes may have undermined the appeal and significance of the Baloho form of tradition.

THE OBJECT of this essay has been to present two traditions current on Ijwi Island relating to the arrival of the present-day dynasty, and to analyze these traditions for their historical contributions. These two traditions, held by independent possessor groups, are apparently mutually exclusive in content. While referring to roughly the same events and individuals, the content of these traditions appears otherwise nonintersecting and their forms are clearly distinct. However, it has been shown that their apparently independent historical data are complementary rather than contradictory. Viewed in time perspective, the traditions take on new light as portraying successive episodes within a larger historical transformation, even while they also reflect the differing perspectives of two social groups each tied to royalty through very different historical processes.

The distinct forms of the two traditions have been examined by reference to a tradition parallel to one of those found on Ijwi, and associated with another segment of the same royal dynastic complex. While diverging historically from the Ijwi royal family, this segment is found today at Mpinga, on the mainland west of Lake Kivu, in an area with very few contacts to Ijwi Island; from the time of the dynastic split there have been no continuing contacts of the mainland group with the Baloho, the social group that preserves the tradition on Ijwi. Comparison of the Ijwi and mainland versions has shown that a similar stereotype has been employed both on Ijwi and at Mpinga. From the histories of the two areas, it has been determined that these two traditions relate to events associated with the Sibula interaction with Tembo peoples, peoples who today live west of the Mitumba Mountains but whose culture formerly was probably more widespread in the area of Lake Kivu.

In addition, some attention has been given to the possible evolutions of each of the Ijwi traditions in light of the subsequent known historical events. From this, it was shown to be probable that the eclectic structure of the Babambo tradition helped it to adapt to various regions. But the more important reason for its spread—and indeed for its very eclectic nature—may have been the expansion of Rwandan cultural norms in the area from the late nineteenth century and continuing, perhaps with increasing intensity, into the colonial period. Despite the political influence of individual Baloho on Ijwi during most of the periods, the Baloho genesis tradition apparently was confined to a few Baloho informants by its form and content.

Finally, the problem of the localization and specificity of the traditions can be seen in perspective. Their regional localization and their very clear separation from each other despite their common focus on the same person reemphasize their character as documents rooted in their specific social group by their very form. They are clearly part of the social group that holds them, not only because of this content but because of the way they are told—by their relation to a specific cultural area.

At the same time, they can be seen to belong to a given clan by their content. It is this that accounts for the specificity of these traditions: their exclusive nature, which ties them to one clan; they document the unique claim of one clan to the royal establishment. The dramatic cultural differences in the two narrative forms prevent the two traditions from contaminating each other. Because each tradition refers to one clan only, and each details a specific interaction with the kings, they do not spread more widely through the region. In itself this limited extent of such traditions testifies to the imperfect political integration of royalty on Ijwi and to the continuing strength of particular regional and social identities on Ijwi.

Yet even these differences help to prove the unity of the island. Both traditions, so different and so separate, refer to the same dynasty, the same king, and roughly the same episode surrounding his arrival. There is no division into different dynasties or disagreement on events. As noted above, these accounts are completely complementary. In the narratives, as in social relations, the kingdom provides a single focus transcending the cultural differences of the clans: kingship brings them together without necessarily diminishing their status. To the contrary, as in the traditions, kingship on Ijwi can be said to have augmented the role of clan identities, formerly restricted and regional. Not every clan shares the traditions explicitly, but no clan or region stands outside the meaning of kingship. Even the Babambo, after their expulsion, and the Baloho, in their relative isolation of the east, retain this focus.

GENESIS TRADITIONS, especially those for which there are several variants of a single tradition, are increasingly suspect on several grounds.[66] From the point of view of the historian, the conclusion of many of these analyses is pessimistic. In some cases historians relate the widespread variants uniquely to general cosmological values in the area, interpreting these traditions as magnificently elaborate statements on belief systems and values. Alternatively, they tend to view the tradition as widespread core clichés to which all manner of extraneous data can be (and are) affixed, thereby making it impossible to decipher the historical elements from the structural, and complicating, if not negating, the historian's efforts.

This essay has tried to show how some of these problems can be approached by the analysis of two traditions found within the same local context and pertaining to the same series of events. The approach consists of several strategies. By carefully examining the similarities and differences of the traditions, one hopes to distinguish the convergent episodes, and to isolate conflicting elements. By analyzing their distribution and the historical role of the possessor clan, one can arrive at a fuller understanding of the form and how the narratives may have been altered. By examining the traditions in relation to the larger corpus of oral literature—not simply historical traditions—one hopes to identify those elements that may have been incorporated within the traditions and presented as history. By looking at the presence of certain clichés and sociological patterns, one hopes to arrive at a better understanding of metaphorical elements within the traditions. By looking at the wider geographical spread of similar narrative structures to those in the traditions, one hopes to gain insight into the manner, and perhaps also the processes, of how such general themes became embedded in particular social contexts. Finally, by looking at the historical evolution of the society within which these traditions function (and an evolution that the traditions themselves may influence), one can arrive at a better understanding of the specific historical referents contained within these narratives.

Much more, of course, is possible when multiple sources are accessible, whether these be written, ethnographic, or archaeological. Material items, residence patterns, rituals, linguistic analysis, and the study of the general literary culture in the broader area, as well as within the specific society, all lend potential value to the historian's search for the how's and the why's of the past that have led to the present. But for many areas of Africa, there is little possibility of multiple sources converging on a single problem, without the geographical field of inquiry being so expanded as to alter the nature of the historical phenomenon under study. For more limited areas, with more precise historical problems to be considered, one is all too often left with only one or two sources from which to draw the data.

The principal sources employed here are the oral traditions themselves. I have attempted to determine what, if any, historical value can be derived from a careful analysis of the traditions. Because independent sources are few in this region, historical analysis is largely limited at present to oral sources. Therefore, my guiding approach here has been to treat oral narratives as functionally part of their society and culture, and influenced by changes in these domains; but at the same time, oral traditions need not be considered exclusively in this light— in short, the cultural context is not determinant. Although these contemporary functions are real and important, the traditions are not perfectly integrated to the society: even as they are products of an evolving social milieu, they also bear witness to that evolution. In both senses, they are historical traditions.

One analytical aspect that becomes important in such an analysis is the interdependence of all historical sources and aspects of cultural change. So close is this that historians are faced with the dilemma that in order to understand how oral sources change and function, they need to understand how the society altered and how social perceptions have changed. But in order to understand societal change in an area such as this, one is dependent primarily on the traditions themselves. This dilemma is partially circumvented by employing many different —and independent—types of data. While these may not always provide precise historical knowledge, they can often help define the limits of what can be safely asserted.

In this perspective, what is of crucial importance in an analysis such as this is to explain the differences in the various traditions, rather than to seek the similarities among them. For the fact is that an episode or event is never perceived in exactly the same way by different groups or individuals, either initially or (especially) through the perspective of time. That there be differences, then, need not in itself be surprising, or reason to cast out all as invalid. Nor is it enough simply to accept the common core of variants, because this is potentially most clearly the result of structural influences.[67]

Instead, the initial observations of similarities and differences need be viewed as the point of departure for the application of the historian's craft: both similarities and differences need be explained. To do this may require reading into a variety of domains sometimes ignored—often because the data are insufficient or totally lacking—by one school of analysis or another. It is essential to know how society changed; it is essential to know how the individual traditions changed; it is essential to explain the differences in the different interpretations, if we are to understand their historical meaning. In other words, historians are engaged in—as are the sources themselves—a continual and multidirectional dialogue. All this is evident and often recognized; but it is less often practiced.

What appears in the preceding sections is only an initial attempt to come to grips with the problem, but I have tried to show one way that this kind of inquiry might be undertaken, in this particular area for these particular traditions. Unfortunately, the number of variables is so great, as is the potential importance of any one variable in understanding a tradition and its historical meaning, that at this stage it would seem impossible to draw up any guidelines of analysis but the most general canons. Until more is known of social change in many parts of Africa, and especially until we understand better how oral literature of all types functions in a changing society, there are no specific methodological rules to follow—there are only standards by which to evaluate whatever techniques are applied. The most that can be done, from the point of view of historians, is to keep in mind the complexity of the materials they are handling, as well as the delicacy and finesse of these invaluable and intriguing sources.

THE CAMPAIGNS OF RWABUGIRI

1974

Kigeri Rwabugiri, king of Rwanda from 1865 to 1895, transformed Rwan-
dan kingship. As the last independent king of Rwanda before European in-
trusion, he is remembered in monumental terms. Within the royal domains,
he reconfigured internal power relations by appointing delegates to posi-
tions of power dependent on him alone, thus confronting the entrenched
power of the aristocratic lineages of the court. But Rwabugiri was most
renowned for his foreign military expeditions: his reign was marked by al-
most continuous campaigns directed against virtually every neighboring
society. Military success became one of the most assured pathways to court
status and power in Rwandan politics. The booty from such expeditions
provided resources in the hands of the king with which he rewarded his po-
litical favorites; under Rwabugiri internal politics was closely linked to ex-
ternal warfare. This chapter presents an overview of Rwabugiri's military
campaigns: it establishes the chronology of these expeditions and examines
the evolution of Rwabugiri's military objectives, organization, and strate-
gies. This overview of his military career also sets the broader context of his
wars, providing historical perspective on the series of campaigns waged
against the people of Ijwi Island over a twenty-five-year period. (The next
chapter provides a case study of his campaigns against Ijwi.)

KING KIGERI RWABUGIRI DOMINATED the history of Rwanda in the late nineteenth century. Renowned as the quintessential military monarch of Rwandan history, Rwabugiri embarked on military expeditions virtually every year of his long reign (1865–95). The effect of this within Rwanda was momentous, for through his army commands he sought to circumvent the intricate politics of the dominant factions at the court, and by his constant movement he introduced the court and its power into many regions of Rwanda. However, these expeditions were no less significant in their effects on neighboring societies, particularly those contiguous to Lake Kivu. In both political and military terms, Rwabugiri's armies refashioned the Lake Kivu Rift Valley in the late nineteenth century; any history of the region has to take account of Rwabugiri—and his strategies, his tactics, and his objectives.

The Rift Valley societies were the areas of his most enduring and most intense attention: his first and his final campaigns were directed there, and he returned to attack the various kingdoms of the western Rift Valley consistently during the intervening years of his long reign. Yet these Kivu expeditions were but a portion of his broader military career. Continuous military expeditions were his mark; accompanying his armies, Rwabugiri traveled through every region of Rwanda and attacked all the neighboring countries except Karagwe to the east, across the Kagera River. (Karagwe had a special status in Rwandan myth as the place claimed from which Ruganzu, another royal hero, returned to establish the Nyiginya dynasty.[1])

Such mobility was to have enormous repercussions internally, within Rwanda, as well as externally, on the societies attacked.[2] Army structures were the principal framework of his political formation as well as of his military success, and army expeditions were to have a dramatic impact on the internal population of Rwanda as well as on those attacked; for the consolidation of army organizations, and the demand for a wide range of material support for these armies, brought about a dramatic shift in the internal character of political power in the kingdom. Powers formerly retained by local authorities became increasingly concentrated in the hands of the king and his court (as indeed was happening in other states of the Interlacustrine area during the same period).[3] The expeditions, therefore, were significant not only for their expansionist goals or external ramifications; through recruitment, through demands for food, through the requisition of materials and labor for constructing and provisioning the royal court, and through the reconfiguration of local social hierarchies, many common people were drawn into the vortex of Rwabugiri's constant military preoccupations. While Rwandans at the central court benefited from the campaigns abroad, the growth of the glory of the court had its internal costs. Outside the country his expeditions affected the politics of the states, and certainly the lives of the people attacked. Yet in these regions the effects were not enduring; indeed, one could argue that the internal ramifications were greater than the external effects.

Given the importance of the military activities for his reign as a whole, an analysis of these campaigns serves as a valuable foundation for understanding this period of Rwandan history. Such an analysis suggests a distinct evolution to Rwabugiri's military objectives and strategies over the thirty years of his reign; his involvement in the area of Lake Kivu provides a microcosm of these larger trends.

Although at present no detailed analysis exists on the entirety of his reign and the military activities for which he was so well known, there are numerous references to aspects of his career in a variety of sources. Among these, the collection of dynastic poems (*ibisigo*) by Abbé Alexis Kagame is particularly useful.[4] But references abound in many other secondary sources—often including that of Europeans to arrive in the next generation.[5] Together these sources lend themselves to an assessment of the relative sequence of his expeditions and the broader trends of the military components of his reign as a whole.

A Typology of the Military Campaigns of Rwabugiri

His campaigns began early in his long reign. Nonetheless, it was only in later years that these campaigns appear to have sought the annexation of the conquered territories. Earlier attacks seem motivated more by more limited goals than by outright conquest. While expeditions to Gisaka, Kinyaga, and the western regions of current Rwanda suggest that the incorporation of Kinyarwanda-speaking people within a single political entity seems to have driven the sovereign in the early years, in other cases, Rwabugiri apparently attempted no administrative incorporation in the first two decades of his rule (to about 1885). For example, the attacks against Ijwi, Buhunde, and Buhavu seem to have been motivated more by personal vengeance against the kings of these countries than by any definitive political incorporation of the populations to Rwanda. While Ijwi Island was eventually brought under Rwandan administration, this occurred only several years after the initial conquest of the island, through the actions of

Nkundiye, who betrayed his father, the king Kabego. With the original conquest of the island (about 1880), Rwabugiri was content to rule through Nkundiye himself rather than placing his own chiefs on the island. It was only after Nkundiye directly challenged Rwabugiri's authority that Rwabugiri placed his own chiefs on the island.[6] Overall, many of these multiple expeditions had as their primary objective the extraction of booty and the weakening of the states neighboring Rwanda—as an expression of Rwanda's power and the accumulation of cattle and other goods.

A typology of Rwabugiri's expeditions might include the following criteria:

Table 5.1			
Classification of Rwabugiri's external military campaigns			
Criteria of classification	*Group I*	*Group II*	*Group III*
Size:	small	moderate or large	large
Preparation:	weak	modest	considerable
Direction:	without precise orientation	small states to the west	concentrated against Bushi
Motivation:	often internal to Rwanda	personal affront; a rupture of a perceived client status	desire of conquest or submission
Objective:	simple booty	personal vengeance against a ruler	occupation of the country
Strategy:	no overall strategy	utilizing internal dissent within the states attacked	utilizing internal dissent within the states attacked
Result:	without effect beyond booty	normally successful	overall, without success

These three categories (groups I–III) generally (but not always) correspond to the chronological succession of the campaigns: over the course of Rwabugiri's reign his expeditions were increasingly characterized by longer campaigns, by a greater concentration of force, by broader objectives, and by more refined tactics (such as the use of espionage and the manipulation of internal divisions within the countries attacked). Such criteria help define a chronology of the expeditions classified according to the typology above. This is followed by a commentary on individual campaigns where the data permit.

Commentary on the Military Campaigns

In the first period (group I—roughly to 1880), Rwabugiri launched many raids in diverse directions. Dispersed to the north, west, and south, these attacks give the impression of being closely tied to the internal politics of the Rwandan central court, notably to the problems relative to Rwabugiri's accession to the throne.[7] Aside from the acquisition of booty, however, these early incursions seem to have had no long-term objectives and produced no enduring results; they were raids.

The first two expeditions of Rwabugiri were directed against Mpororo, just northeast of Rwanda (in a campaign referred to as Mirambo), and against Ijwi Island, in Lake Kivu, west of Rwanda (about 1870).[8] Although the chronology of these attacks is not given in the sources, they could only have succeeded in this order, because the commander of the expedition of Mirambo was dismissed during the expedition against Ijwi. The Rwandan sources tell us nothing more on the results of the battles in Mpororo, although the subsequent dismissal of the Rwandan leader would suggest it was not successful. On the results of the Ijwi campaign the Rwandan sources are misleading; either they gratuitously assert a Rwandan victory, or they confuse the results of this first expedition against the island with the results of the second expedition, ten years later and launched from a different site, with vastly different resources and benefiting from local internal dissension within the Ijwi royal family. Here is a case where the local sources from Ijwi Island are explicit; in their detail they raise serious doubts about the Rwandan assertions.[9] We can only conclude that these attacks were unsuccessful, or else that the objectives and scale of these undertakings were insignificant. (See the following chapter for a presentation of these wars from the perspective of accounts on Ijwi Island.)

Another expedition was directed against Burundi.[10] Although difficult to date with precision, we know that it occurred early in his reign, before the death of the queen mother, who organized it,[11] and perhaps also before the expedition to Bumpaka. A separate source situates it after the expeditions toward Mirambo and Ijwi (noted above).[12] The goals and details of this raid are nowhere explained, and although "significant booty" is mentioned, the sources give the impression that this was only a minor raid, probably undertaken by a single regiment of a single army and directed by a nephew of the queen mother.[13] However, Kagame notes that this campaign included the loss of a "Libérateur-Offensif" (a common Rwandan idiom noting the death of an important warrior, whose sacrifice was considered necessary to ensure the victory), a detail that might just as well

Table 5.2
Chronology of Rwabugiri's external military campaigns

Group I	Group II	Group III
[accession to the throne—about 1867 by Vansina's chronology]	—	—
Mirambo (Mpororo—to the northeast)	—	—
Ijwi—the first expedition [the blinding of Nwamwesa, the eldest son of Rwogera]	—	—
incursion into Burundi	—	—
—	expedition to **Bumpaka**, east of Lake Edward [massive booty acquired]	—
raid to **Ndorwa**	—	—
mu Lito (Burundi): attempted assassination of Nkoronko	—	—
—	expedition to **Butembo** [on return, the construction of Rubengera capital and the arrest of Nkoronko]	—
—	second campaign against **Ijwi Island** [the death of Kabego]	—
raid to **Gikore** (Uganda)	—	—
—	—	**ku Buntubuzindu** (Bushi): first expedition to Bushi [a disastrous defeat for Rwabugiri; death of Rwanyonga]
—	—	**Kanywilili** (Bushi): second expedition to Bushi [a second disastrous defeat for Rwabugiri; deaths of Nyirimigabo and Nyamushanja]
—	third expedition against **Ijwi Island** [death of Nkundiye, a son of Kabego]	—

Table 5.2 *(continued)*
Chronology of Rwabugiri's external military campaigns

Group I	Group II	Group III
—	attack against **Mpinga**?	—
—	attack against **Irhambi**?	—
—	—	ku **Kidogoro** (Bushi): third expedition to Bushi [Rwandan victory]
raid on **Nkore** (Uganda)	—	—
raid on **Bushubi** (Tanzania) [Nsoro executed by Rwabugiri]	—	—
—	—	ku **Mira** (Bushi): fourth attack on Bushi [desertion of a Rwandan military post]
—	—	??expedition to **Nkore** [battle of Shongi against Banyankore armed with guns]
—	—	fifth attack on **Bushi** [death of Rwabugiri]

indicate a defeat of the Rwandan forces (especially because "victory" here seems to have been minimal in scope).[14]

The first of Rwabugiri's campaigns to cover any great distance and to bring significant results for Rwanda was directed against Bumpaka (or Bunyampaka),[15] to the east of Lake Edward.[16] This large expedition, often noted in the sources,[17] returned with considerable booty: at least five "military herds"[18] were formed with the cattle seized from this campaign alone.[19] Because of its scope and its results— the first on this scale—this campaign belongs to the second group of within the typology noted above.

This significant undertaking was followed by another, smaller campaign directed toward the north: to Ndorwa,[20] already "conquered" by Rwanda but often in revolt against the Nyiginya court. The sources on this campaign, however, are ambiguous: could this have been, perhaps, a supplementary reference to the expedition against Bumpaka, or perhaps a raid associated with this larger expedition? In fact, the only firm detail known to us on this campaign is that the army departed during the rains.

The expedition known as mu Lito, directed again against Burundi, took place quite early in the reign of Rwabugiri. Because its effect on Burundi seems to have been minimal, the decision to launch this campaign seems more likely to have resulted from factors internal to the politics of Rwanda than from any broader objective of conquest.[21] It seems to have revolved around court intrigue over Nkoronko, the brother (by the same father and same mother) of Rwogera, the king who preceded Rwabugiri; therefore Nkoronko was the paternal uncle of Rwabugiri. He was accused of being implicated in the assassination of the queen mother,[22] but his political position, and especially his popularity with his army, made him too powerful to allow Rwabugiri to attack him directly. Moreover, it was proscribed for a prince of the royal line to die a violent death on Rwandan territory. Therefore, it is entirely likely, suggest the sources, that the expedition of mu Lito was organized to draw Nkoronko to Burundi, far from the court, where he would die in foreign territory, either killed by enemy forces or assassinated by Rwandan troops. For Rwabugiri, Nkoronko's demise in this fashion would have been an opportune ending, simultaneously eliminating a powerful political rival and avenging the death of his mother. This immediate goal of the campaign of mu Lito was not achieved, however, because Nkoronko, informed of the plot, separated his troops from the principal regiments of the Rwandan army and, surrounded by his own loyal regiment, returned to Rwanda without difficulty.[23]

From this point in the chronology of Rwabugiri's campaigns, however, a new type of external attack emerged, as expeditions were increasingly directed against the small states situated to the west of Rwanda. The objectives of these attacks became more clearly defined and often sought the death of a ruler or of other members of the royal family. In these attacks, strategic considerations were no longer concerned exclusively with the internal politics of Rwanda; instead, attention shifted to focus dramatically on the lines of cleavage, actual or potential, within the royal families of the targeted states. During this period, Rwabugiri was personally involved in both the preparations for and the conduct of these expeditions.

The campaign against Butembo,[24] northwest of Lake Kivu, illustrates these characteristics: it showed a broad conception, it was of relatively long duration, and its targeted region was situated far from Rwanda.[25] In short, it represented a new (and larger) scale of organization from previous campaigns. Like that against Ijwi, this attack was motivated by questions concerning tribute and accusations of cattle theft (always a convenient pretext in this area); for these transgressions the expedition sought to punish the king and the royal family. The campaign was enormously destructive. But this devastation seems to have resulted not from planned policy but from logistical problems: the need to provide for a sizable army in a sparsely populated region distant from Rwanda. Furthermore, the permanent conquest and the incorporation of the country into Rwanda do not seem to have been the goals of this campaign, and its principal objective— that of disciplining a recalcitrant king—was not achieved in spite of the deaths of several members of the royal family, including one of the sons of the king.

The following year, some of the same characteristics were apparent in the second attack against Ijwi. Better prepared than the first attack, this campaign was carried out with a more experienced army, with more clearly defined strategies, and with more comprehensive objectives. Again, Rwabugiri personally oversaw the preparations, and he himself directed the attacks against Kabego, the king of Ijwi. The campaign was launched from a new royal enclosure, situated at Rubengera (near the present-day Kibuye); this royal establishment would become Rwabugiri's principal capital in the west throughout the rest of his reign. As in Butembo, Rwabugiri took advantage of the divisions within the Ijwi royal family concerning disputes among competing parties as to who would succeed the already aged king, Kabego. But this second attack on Ijwi also represented a larger strategic reorientation of Rwabugiri's campaigns because it initiated an entire series of wars directed against the areas west of Lake Kivu. Over the next decade these included, in addition to the expedition against Kabego on Ijwi, an attack against Nkundiye, Kabego's son, and other campaigns against the king of Buhavu at Mpinga (Kalehe) on the western mainland, against Irhambi (Katana) on the lakeshore south of Mpinga, and against other Shi states southwest of the lake.

Nkundiye was the son of Kabego, the king of Ijwi killed by Rwabugiri during the second attack against the island. After the failure of his first attack, Rwabugiri had formed an alliance with Nkundiye; because his father was already aged, Nkundiye sought Rwabugiri's support to succeed to power at the expense of Kabego's other sons. And so, on the death of Kabego, Rwabugiri named Nkundiye as chief of Ijwi under Rwabugiri's suzerainty; Nkundiye, in return, assisted Rwabugiri in his wars against Bushi, southwest of the lake. After the expedition of Kanywilili in Bushi, where Nkundiye was shown to be one of the most courageous among Rwabugiri's warriors, the other Rwandan chiefs, jealous of Nkundiye (according to the Bahavu on Ijwi), accused him of having betrayed Rwabugiri. But it also appears that, with his new military standing and seeking his own independence from Rwabugiri, Nkundiye refused his obligation to pay court to the Rwandan king. And therefore, five years after his second attack Rwabugiri returned to discipline his former ally; his troops killed Nkundiye on an island near Mpinga. Rwabugiri replaced him on Ijwi with Rwandan chiefs loyal to him alone and thus submitted Ijwi to direct Rwandan occupation for the first time.

But several years passed between the death of Kabego and the death of Nkundiye, and in the intervening years Rwabugiri's military passions did not diminish. Although we lack a precise chronology for the following attack against the Havu kingdom of Mpinga on the mainland just west of Ijwi, this would seem to have been associated either with the death of Kabego or with the death of Nkundiye, several years later. (Some local testimonies on the mainland suggest that the king of Mpinga had been killed even before the death of Kabego, but these historical events are not clear from the data available at the moment.)

Some years after his victory against Kabego, Rwabugiri sent an expedition to Gikore (near present-day Kabale, in Uganda).[26] Unfortunately, the sources note only the existence and approximate chronology of this expedition; the existing sources provide no other details on it. Following the attack on Gikore, but before the attack against Nkundiye (the third attack against Ijwi), Rwabugiri launched the first of numerous campaigns directed against the Shi states to the southwest of Lake Kivu; these wars in Bushi were to absorb much of Rwabugiri's energy and attention over the last decades of his life. While the results of these wars might be similar to those of earlier attacks to the west of the lake, the intensity of the attacks against the Shi, the scale of human resources mobilized, as well as the strategies employed and objectives adopted (such as those shown by the near permanent occupation of the countries conquered by the Rwandan armies) distinguished these campaigns from the preceding attacks directed against the royal families of the other states of the west.

For Bushi, the struggle was not limited to the royal families, however; these states had their own internal political preoccupations, as the kings of the two most important Shi states had died only shortly after the first attacks. At the same time, the size and complexity of these Shi states (as well as their considerable distance from central Rwanda) allowed them to mount vigorous resistance to the Rwandan intruders. The combination of Rwabugiri's persistent ambitions in the area with Shi intransigence led to a long series of major campaigns. All these factors suggest that the objective of these final wars of Rwabugiri was outright conquest. Nonetheless, these campaigns were the least successful of all of Rwabugiri's wars: in Bushi, Rwabugiri suffered defeat after defeat, his "victories" were few and ephemeral, and they were costly. These expeditions imposed much greater challenges than earlier campaigns, for the internal structures of Shi politics, so fluid at this particular moment, required the continual occupation of the country: it was not possible simply to kill the king and claim conquest of the state. That was why the Rwandan tactics relied so intensely on espionage and required a much more complicated involvement in the internal politics of the Shi states.

Yet despite their magnitude, Rwabugiri's wars in Bushi are not portrayed with any clarity in the Rwandan sources. We await Kagame's promised publication of a poem described as a summary of the expeditions undertaken in Kivu, and of another cited as "a valuable testimony on the wars in Bunyabungo."[27] But we also await the results of current research in Bushi, because the events associated with these wars are intimately intertwined with the internal politics of these individual states.

Among this series of campaigns, the first two major battles in Bushi found in the sources were disastrous defeats for the Rwandans. The first expedition, shortly after that of Gikore, led to the battle known as ku Buntubuzindu, near the residence of Byaterana, the king of Buhaya, the largest of the Shi states.[28] Among the numerous losses on both sides, this battle saw the death of Rwanyonga, one of Rwabugiri's most celebrated warriors, as well as many young Rwandan warriors: "le roi [Rwabugiri] fut consterné."[29] This heavy setback was followed with a second, still more serious for Rwabugiri.[30] Taking place in southern Bushi, in a place called Buzimu ye Bunge (near Nyangezi, south of Bukavu), this battle of Kanywilili saw the near total destruction of his most valued regiments, as well as the loss of several of his most trusted and bravest leaders, including Nyamushanja and Nyirimigabo. This latter, who died at Kanywilili with many other important members of his army, was more than a simple soldier; he was also closely involved with many of the activities of the Rwandan court. Even influential in the events that brought Rwabugiri to power, he was among the most favored of the court.[31] As for Nyamushanja, he belonged to one of the most well-known families during Rwabugiri's reign, one that was allied by marriage to the royal family many times over.[32] He had been named head of his army, after his half-brother, in early battles, was accused of embezzling the booty due the court and retaining the provisions for himself.[33] However, Nyamushanja was also one of the only important warriors of his army to perish in the battle of Kanywilili; as a result, Rwabugiri considered that Nyamushanja's soldiers had abandoned him, leaving him and Nyirimigabo's regiment isolated.[34] Rwabugiri grieved their loss deeply, and he fined every member of that army a cow.[35]

After the battle of Kanywilili, the series of Shi campaigns was interrupted by Rwabugiri's attack against Nkundiye on Ijwi, perhaps associated with the loss at Kanywilili (and the accusations against him by Rwandan court actors), perhaps also tied to the broader attacks on Mpinga and Irhambi, although at this stage the chronology of these battles is not well established.[36] Following this episode, Rwabugiri increasingly turned his attention to the Shi states. Toward 1890 he initiated a long expedition during which occurred the Rwandan victory of ku Kidogoro, at the time of a massive famine in Bushi.[37] (This expedition might have also included a victory over a group of slavers coming from the west and armed with guns; few other details on this expedition, however, exist in the published Rwandan sources.[38])

After ku Kidogoro, Rwabugiri launched several other attacks, on which, once again, we are ill-informed from the sources. There is reference to an expedition against Nkore (in the southwest of present-day Uganda) during which many cows were captured.[39] And there is mention of another raid against Bushubi, a small state southeast of Rwanda. In this raid, Nsoro, the king of Bushubi and a former ally, was taken prisoner and later executed by Rwabugiri in Kinyaga (in the southwest of Rwanda). We have no information on the reasons for this raid, although the timing and location would appear to link it to Rwabugiri's emerging commercial strategies.[40]

Once again Rwabugiri's attention was drawn to Bushi, this time apparently by the desertion of a regiment from their military camp in Bushi; this was the famous ku Mira affair.[41] As recounted in the Rwandan sources, the soldiers, lacking food, tired of the routines of a military occupation so vigorously resisted by the local population, and believing that Rwabugiri could not effectively discipline an entire army if they acted collectively—especially an army so large and so important—abandoned their camp and returned home. Those implicated in this incident were removed from their commands and lost all prerogatives.[42]

The last expedition of Rwabugiri's reign was that directed against Nkore.[43] This campaign was memorable because it is noted that Rwandan troops fought against an Nkore force armed with guns at the battle of Shangi, near Butake. Yet Rwandan sources state that although this battle was an "important victory," it resulted only in a large booty of cows. The nature of these sources implies that this was simply a successful raid, a distraction from the more prolonged and difficult incursions in Bushi, which were at best only partially successful.[44] These sources note only that the enclosure of Rutaraka was assaulted by the Banyankore, but we do not know if this was a cause or effect of Rwabugiri's campaigns in the area.[45] A short time later, Rwabugiri returned to focus his attention once again on his campaigns to the west, against Bushi, where he died.

Other sources suggest that the campaign against Nkore was a major expedition, perhaps the most important and most ambitious of Rwabugiri's entire reign.[46] Such an interpretation of the war against Nkore would agree with the fundamental changes in Rwabugiri's policies toward the countries attacked. Such changes in his general foreign policy, then, would have followed the same evolution as those already observed for the area west of Lake Kivu, and especially in Bushi.

Thus throughout his rule Rwabugiri was absorbed with multiple expeditions —of increasing size and ambition over the course of his reign. Many led to the acquisition of status and booty distributed within Rwanda, thus consolidating structures of power and hierarchy within the state. Some led to the conquest of other countries. And certainly the constant warfare also affected Rwandan internal organization: army organizations became a major preoccupation of the court, army positions were avidly sought as a pathway to power at the court, and the larger structures associated with army organization (food supply, portage, cattle herders, construction) became the sinews that extended the ties of the state to the people. In the end the penetration of army organization and the demands of constant military campaigns affected vast numbers of the population within Rwanda—just as the effects of these campaigns affected many abroad.

Nonetheless, despite the destruction wrought on the neighboring countries, there were few true conquests to result, and few permanent political annexations. Burundi was unaffected. Nkore and other areas north of Rwanda were devastated but otherwise remained outside of Rwandan political influence. Bushubi to the east and Bushi to the west retained their independence, as did mainland Buhavu. After the death of Nkundiye, Rwandan military chiefs settled on the island for a decade. But that was all, and even that situation did not endure after Rwabugiri's death in 1895. Militarily, then, Rwabugiri's state appeared formidable, and within Rwanda the internal changes were significant. But in the end the militarism of Rwabugiri's state was to turn inward; on his demise the internal factions at the court fought over positions and power. The lasting external effects were few and ephemeral, while the short-term internal effects were monumental. European power arrived at just this moment of intense competition at the court, set off by the militaristic legacy of its powerful ruler of the late nineteenth century, Rwabugiri.

RWABUGIRI AND IJWI

1975

Rwandan sources dominate the history of the region: they are voluminous, detailed, and accessible. Therefore, most accounts of Rwanda's interrelations with other societies are seen only through the perspective of the Rwandan royal court. That vision is particularly telling in the case of military encounters, where official Rwandan court traditions often claim that any Rwandan battle was a victory, any victory a conquest, and any conquest a permanent annexation; royal sources often present Rwandan history as a history of inexorable expansion. But seen from other perspectives, this history appears more complex; progress is less linear and victories less inevitable. Multiple sources—in particular, testimonies from those targeted by Rwandan military campaigns, not just from their architects—help round out our understanding, illustrating the strategies, perseverance, and sometimes frustrations on both sides of the battle. We learn a lot about Rwanda by listening to other voices, as indeed we learn about other societies through these detailed local testimonies.

This chapter presents a case study of a series of Rwandan campaigns directed against the kings of Ijwi Island from about 1870 to 1895 (the year of Rwabugiri's death and the withdrawal of Rwanda's occupation forces). But the essay is not only a military history; entering into the political history of Ijwi Island, it also explores the diverse local political responses to these external challenges. It shows that even small societies were not simple—and that understanding the nature of the responses is instructive in itself, far beyond the history or politics of the island alone. This chapter provides a sequel to the larger political history of Ijwi shown in Kings and Clans, *and a prelude to the political history explored in the next chapter, which deals with the effects and aftermath of the next external attack on the island, associated with colonial conquest.*

THE HEROIC FIGURE OF Mwami Kigeri Rwabugiri, king of Rwanda, dominates the history of the later nineteenth century in the Lake Kivu region, not only for Rwanda but for virtually all the neighboring countries to which he turned his attention.[1] His prominence can be accounted for as much by his almost mythical association with other events as by his own heroic exploits. In the broadest terms, the arrival of Rwabugiri on Ijwi shattered the relative peace and stability of the sixty years previous; it was also the culmination of a succession struggle already under way. At the same time, it was a harbinger of the turmoil that was to accompany the introduction of colonial rule not long afterward. While the Rwandan sources on Rwabugiri are very rich, sources from neighboring regions often provide the historian with much additional detail as well as corroborative evidence to add to the Rwandan sources. For example, through their close contact with him, the people of Ijwi vividly recall Rwabugiri's exploits in the area, even a century later. This chapter, intended as a case study in Rwabugiri's military and administrative techniques, reconstructs the historical process of Rwabugiri's conquest and administration of Ijwi through oral accounts narrated on the island.

Rwabugiri's interest in Ijwi spanned his reign; his first attack on Ijwi was one of his earliest military expeditions, and twenty-five years later he died not far from Ijwi during a campaign to the west. Rwabugiri himself arrived on the island during the 1870s, and he was to return often until his death in 1895. For the Bany'Iju (the people of Ijwi), the Rwabugiri period is best remembered through the personalities involved in the dynastic struggles on Ijwi associated with Rwabugiri's invasion. In the present discussion, however, these internal factions and their social effects will be covered only insofar as they affected Rwabugiri's aims, military tactics, and administrative organization.

Ijwi: The Geographical and Historical Situation

Ijwi is an island of some forty kilometers in length, located in Lake Kivu on the eastern boundary of Zaire, just to the west of Rwanda. Currently numbering about fifty thousand [1975], its population is today divided into two political and administrative units, along the lines of a long-standing cleavage whose origins were adroitly used by Rwabugiri in his conquest of the island. Although politically, geographically, and historically distinct from the peoples on the mainland, the Bany'Iju comprise a part of the Havu-speaking peoples living in several different kingdoms on the islands and peninsulas in Lake Kivu as well as on the mainland west of the lake. The present ruling dynasty established itself on the island in the early nineteenth century, bringing a short-lived political unity to the whole of Ijwi for the first time. Throughout the nineteenth century, Ijwi Island, under independent Havu rulers, served as a buffer and intermediary between an increasingly powerful Rwanda and her neighbors to the west of Lake Kivu.

Strategically, Ijwi was of great importance to Rwabugiri. It bordered on several states to the west, including the Shi states. In addition, to the east it faced the shoreline of Kinyaga, a rich province of Rwanda speakers that at that time had been only nominally integrated into the Rwandan polity. The kings of Ijwi also controlled the smaller islands and some of the peninsulas to the west, which may well have been used as staging areas for Rwabugiri's attacks against Mpinga and Irhambi.[2] Historically, there were many close ties between Ijwi and Rwanda, derived from population movements, commercial bonds, and political relations. Many of the clans on Ijwi, particularly those on the eastern shore, originally immigrated from western Rwanda during the eighteenth century. Sometimes they sought political refuge; more often they were driven out of Rwanda by famine or localized land shortages and drawn to Ijwi by the relative security of dependable rains and a long growing season. Once established on Ijwi, these early settler groups kept close contact with their homelands in Rwanda through personal ties, and especially through marriage ties.

Commercial ties were also strong. Before the arrival of the Havu kings, these contacts resembled those between a commercial colony and metropolitan power, not with the Rwandan court, but with the various population centers in western Rwanda. While Ijwi did not offer complementary goods for trade, the favorable agricultural climate (and the slightly different agrarian calendar) provided agricultural surpluses sufficient for a limited but socially important external commerce with neighboring areas. Growing out of personal and social contacts in

BUHUNDE

KAMURONZA

BUZI

BUHAVU

RWANDA

RUBENGERA

MALAMBO

KISHUSHU

KIBUYE

MPINGA

TSHOVU   IJWI

IRHAMBI

KARHONGO

NYAMSHEKE

BUSHI

NYAMURUNDI

KINYAGA

Kilometers

0   5   10   20

N

Map 6.1. Ijwi at the end of the nineteenth century

Rwanda—but by no means confined to these—commerce often took place through institutionalized channels of "friendship" formalized by rituals of blood brotherhood.

It was primarily through such friends in Rwanda that the Bany'Iju obtained cattle in a *bugabire* relationship, the principal mechanism of cattle transfer between Rwanda and Ijwi. In return for animals (cattle and goats), the Bany'Iju sent agricultural goods on a continuing (but not very regular) basis to their friends in Rwanda. The donor of the animal had the right to claim about one out of every four offspring of the livestock given. There were apparently few other obligations placed on the Muny'Iju recipient of livestock; in any case, it was virtually impossible to enforce agricultural gifts to Rwanda. Although the Bany'Iju usually found it expedient to continue such gifts, enabling them to obtain more cows later, they unanimously refer to such gifts as voluntary expressions of friendship, like the hospitality they receive from friends in Rwanda. In addition to serving as the major social mechanism of commerce, these cattle relationships between Ijwi and Rwanda also contained important (but imperfectly defined) political overtones. Engaged in by Bany'Iju of all social levels, they served as the major political ties between the two countries. With the establishment of the present dynasty on the island, the Ijwi settlements became increasingly independent of their Rwandan homelands. Meanwhile from its historical centers to the east, the Rwandan court was extending its influence and administration westward toward the lake, altering the nature and significance of cattle contracts in the area—for court clientship differed from the friendship alliances of Ijwi client patterns. With these two developments the political nature of the bugabire relations between the two areas assumed greater significance, at least in the eyes of the Rwandans. So did the ambiguity of this relationship.

On Ijwi, though expressed in many different forms (through cattle, goats, or land), bugabire was and is viewed primarily as an alliance: the two parties referred to each other as "friends." Aside from the sharing of the increase, there were no formalized obligations, although sometimes food and beer were exchanged; moreover, it was a relationship often associated with blood brotherhood.[3] Even today, between Bany'Iju and most Rwandans there is little confusion over the significance of this form of cattle transfer contracted between close personal friends. Rwandans from Kinyaga understand the bugabire relationship, describe it in the same terms as the Bany'Iju, and distinguish between that relation and the relations undertaken within Rwanda. But in central Rwanda, particularly at the Rwandan court, the cattle contract seems to have been understood differently. Although sometimes engaged in between equals or for reasons of personal friendship, the cattle transfer was more often undertaken in a hierarchical relationship, motivated by political considerations and symbolizing (or recording) the social inequality between the two parties.[4] Under such an agreement (most commonly called *ubuhake*), different terms of reference were employed for the two parties involved, and the obligations of the recipient were formally defined and strictly enforced. In areas such as Kinyaga, such a transfer of cows also became an important instrument of political domination,[5] and Rwandans no doubt looked on it as such with regard to Ijwi.

Thus a significant conceptual difference appears between the Rwandan court and Ijwi over the interpretation of the political element involved in cattle transfer. On Ijwi it was looked on as alliance; in Rwanda, most probably as subordination. From the point of view of the Rwandan court, subordination of the Ijwi kings was ensured by gifts of cattle, while the agricultural goods from Ijwi were looked on as a confirmation of the suzerainty of Rwanda over Ijwi.[6] Thus for the Rwandan court the right to expect agricultural goods from Ijwi became a demand of tribute payments coupled with the eventual duty to enforce them in case of any "insurrection" (i.e., nonpayment). Such external ties (with Rwanda) were instrumental in the establishment of Ijwi's present dynasty following its secession from the parent line on the (Zaire) mainland. During his youth, Mwendanga, the first king of Ijwi, had frequent access to the Rwandan court through his maternal grandfather, a favorite of Mwami Yuhi Gahindiro, the grandfather of Rwabugiri. Mwendanga probably established bugabire ties with important men in Rwanda, influential at the court. He married at least two wives given him by Gahindiro, and had many ties and friends in Rwanda. In addition, certain sons of the Ijwi king may also have lived some of their youth with important Rwandans.[7] Kabego, Mwendanga's successor, sent at least two of his sons to Rwanda, where both were eventually killed. At about this time, Kabego ceased sending gifts to the Rwandan court, though it is unclear whether this cessation was the cause or the effect of the deaths of his sons at the Rwandan court.[8]

This rupture of a historical relationship appears to have been the determining factor in Rwabugiri's decision to attack Ijwi. His original aims were limited: to gain revenge on Kabego and to reestablish the clientship status that, in the eyes of the Rwandan court, had previously characterized Ijwi's relationship with Rwanda.

The Resources Available to Rwabugiri

Rwabugiri did not lack resources to effect these aims. First, within Rwanda itself, he had at his disposal an effective military organization, including herds to feed the men, heavy forced logistical support by the Hutu class, the material and political means to reward the valorous in battle, and a cosmology of social values, often expressed through lyric poetry, praising individual soldiers as well as glorifying Rwanda the warrior state and its invincible king, Rwabugiri. Secondly, there were on Ijwi a substantial number of Rwandan immigrants, some of them recent arrivals. Not all of these would come to the support of a Rwandan invader —many were undoubtedly political refugees—but probably some would have been sympathetic to Rwabugiri's designs toward Ijwi. The information they could provide was a potential resource of great value to Rwabugiri, whose tactics depended so heavily on the internal cleavages of the island.

But Rwabugiri did not depend entirely or even mainly on the force of a superior military organization or on underground intelligence. He was also a gifted tactician, well able to employ feints and the knowledge of terrain, although in the case of Ijwi (as in other campaigns in Bushi and Buhunde) he did commit some major blunders, and the primary explanation for his eventual success must be sought in other factors. Above all, his mastery at encouraging and exploiting political cleavages on the island provided him with his most important resource—the mounting succession struggle among the sons of Kabego, in anticipation of the aged king's imminent death. It is to this decisive internal conflict that we must now turn in order to understand the subsequent events of Rwabugiri's invasion of the island.

Internal Divisions on Ijwi

Each of the first three kings of the present dynasty on Ijwi witnessed a succession struggle of severe proportions near the end of his reign. In each case the weaker party sought assistance from outside, usually from his maternal uncles; in each case they looked to a different source of support: to Irhambi, to Rwanda, or to the colonial power. The central figure in the succession struggle during Kabego's reign was Nkundiye, a son of one of the later of Kabego's many wives.

Nkundiye's ambitions had been earlier reflected in his continuing poor relations with his brothers. He had driven one of them from a hill neighboring his own, thus consolidating his hold on an important political center in the southern part of the island. He may also have instigated or encouraged the death of another brother, Rugina, who lived on an island west of Ijwi. Rugina's full brother, Ndogosa, had injured another half-brother in a quarrel. The maternal uncles of the injured party, who lived on the mainland west of Ijwi, then took vengeance by attacking and killing Rugina, the eldest son of Kabego. Some informants imply that it was Nkundiye who guided them to Rugina; both Rugina and Ndogosa could have been viewed as threats to Nkundiye's succession bid, although Rugina was at that time the more vulnerable. Nkundiye's actual involvement in the death of Rugina is not yet clearly established from the data, but the strong implications to this effect testify to the popular assessment of Nkundiye's ambitions and the means he was capable of using to achieve them.

Nkundiye's mother was from a family in Kinyaga, Rwanda, and he was without close maternal relatives on Ijwi. Furthermore, his ruthlessness had lost him popular support as well as the support of his brothers and the royal family. He had few political resources with which to fuel his succession bid, except outside assistance. He therefore appears to have settled on a policy of overthrowing Kabego rather than taking part in a struggle among brothers after Kabego's death. In the event, he was attracted to the acknowledged power of Rwabugiri in Rwanda, who had by that time already launched his first attack against Kabego.

By ignoring the historical relationship of the kings of Ijwi to those of Rwanda, Kabego had incurred the wrath of Rwabugiri, resulting in the first unsuccessful attack against the island kingdom early in Rwabugiri's reign. The enmity between the two kings played into Nkundiye's hands, and he sought to turn it to his own advantage. Kabego's act gave Rwabugiri the will to attack Ijwi, to reestablish the clientship relation of Ijwi to Rwanda; Nkundiye's search for political and military support gave Rwabugiri an important means for carrying out this will to revenge. Their ambitions dovetailed nicely. Although both Nkundiye's mother and his wife were from Rwanda, there is at present no evidence that either woman or their families acted as intermediary between Rwabugiri and Nkundiye. Nevertheless, it was known that Rwabugiri sought to launch another attack against Kabego, and it seems that, seeking a means to his own ends, Nkundiye offered Rwabugiri tactical assistance. More important, he apparently offered to reestablish the client relationship with Rwanda once Rwabugiri had helped him to power.

But Nkundiye was not the only member of the royal line seeking to usurp power. There was another rift in the royal family, of which Rwabugiri also took advantage. This rift was based on both genealogical distance from the throne and

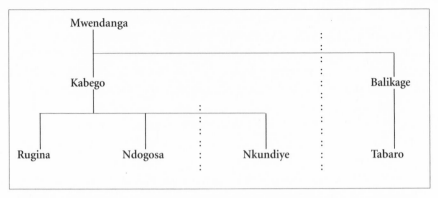

Figure 6.1. Political cleavages within the royal family of Ijwi at the time of Rwabugiri's attack

on geographical divisions of the island. Mwendanga, the first king, had delegated his son, Balikage, as his representative to the northern part of the island, referred to as Malambo. The successor to Mwendanga, Kabego, maintained authority as king over the entire island but left considerable power in the hands of Balikage's son, Tabaro, rather than redistributing the power among his own sons. By the end of Kabego's reign, Tabaro had effectively consolidated his power in the north while still nominally recognizing Kabego as the ultimate authority; Tabaro made no move toward independence until after the death of Kabego. These then were the major lines of cleavage within the royal family that were important to Rwabugiri's attack on Ijwi (see figure 6.1).

The First Attack on Ijwi

Rwabugiri's first attack on Ijwi was launched from Nyamasheke and from Nyamirundi, the long finger of land reaching out from Kinyaga almost to touch the southern tip of Ijwi (see map 6.1).[9] As pointed out above, the peninsulas of western Rwanda had had long-standing demographic, marital, and commercial contacts with Ijwi. This social interchange between the two countries was dramatically demonstrated at the time of Rwabugiri's attacks.

Mugogo lived near the northern tip of Nyamirundi. Women from his family had married for two successive generations with a family on Ijwi, and his sons had received fields on Ijwi near their "brothers" of the same clan. As Rwabugiri prepared for the attack, several men from Nyamirundi, including Mugogo, came to Ijwi to ask their daughters to return temporarily to Nyamirundi and thus to escape the imminent battle. Mugogo's daughter refused to return to Nyamirundi but promised to flee to a secure place on Ijwi if she were given warning of the attack; and thus a system of signals was set up. Mugogo built a house on the northern tip of Nyamirundi (clearly within sight of Ijwi across one kilometer of water), which he burned shortly before Rwabugiri launched his attack, to warn the Bany'Iju. Mugogo and a neighbor who had helped him build the house were later killed by Rwabugiri for their treasonous demonstration of family solidarity.

But the Havu had at any rate been warned several weeks in advance and had massed several armies from the south (armies from the north did not take part) along the southern rim of Ijwi. Men from the extreme south were able to continue cultivation in their fields during the day while descending to sleep on the lakeshore at night. Those from farther away had their families bring them food or were fed by brothers or friends closer to the scene of the impending battle.

When the attack came, it was launched in a dual thrust. The main body of Rwandans set out before dawn from the eastern shore of Nyamirundi and directed their attacks to the southeastern shore of Ijwi, above the eastern angle of the island. Slightly later a smaller, faster thrust was made across the narrowest straits, apparently in an attempt to gain a foothold on the island and circle behind the defending troops. But with their advance warning, and aided by the terrain in the east (which offered only a few suitable landing areas on the steep lakeshore), the Bany'Iju were able to prevent the Rwandans from consolidating any firm position on the island. The fiercest fighting, however, raged on the lake, near the second, faster, thrust from the south. Here, too, advance warning was important for massing the necessary canoes. But the deciding factor, and one apparently overlooked or discounted by Rwabugiri, was the superior seamanship of the Havu, by which they were able to disperse the main body, preventing any concentrated attack by the first group and completely overwhelming the second group, inflicting many casualties on the Rwandans. With their mastery over the lake and daring courage, as the battle is described on Ijwi, the Bany'Iju were able to overcome the force of Rwandan numbers and repulse the attack from Rwanda.

Following this first attack on Ijwi, a considerable amount of time—perhaps more than a decade—lapsed before Rwabugiri sent a second expedition against Ijwi. During that time Rwabugiri's armies had seasoned considerably with much experience, and his strategies and objectives had been refined. He was now also better able to capitalize on the internal divisions of the island. Fresh from his expedition in Buhunde (the "Butembo" expedition[10]), he constructed a new capital at Rubengera (near present-day Kibuye), which was to remain his major residence in western Rwanda. Rubengera was far from Ijwi, and Rwabugiri thus deprived the Bany'Iju of the rapid advance warning they had received from Nyamirundi in the earlier contest.

The second Rwandan attack, launched near Rubengera, crossed a wide expanse of water to arrive at Malambo, the vulnerable back door to Ijwi. Because this northern part of the island was not fully under Kabego's control, Rwabugiri profited from Tabaro's considerable autonomy and his neutrality, or even partiality toward, the Rwandans.[11] Also, this time Rwabugiri was able to use the canoes to his advantage, giving himself greater mobility and latitude of choice for the attack against the less maneuverable land armies of the Bany'Iju. It was here, say the Bany'Iju of the south, that Nkundiye advised Rwabugiri to attack. And it was here that Rwabugiri this time made good his attack.

The Death of Kabego

At the time of the Rwandan attacks, Kabego was an old man whose long reign had been peaceful until the outbreak of the succession struggle. It does not appear that Kabego himself took any active role in these struggles; he was above the battle for the kingship. At the time of the second Rwandan attack, he had retired, with certain members of the royal family and a few chosen subjects, to the small island of Kishushu just off the western shore of Ijwi.

The Rwandan armies drove south from Malambo along the western shore of the island, always on the advice of Nkundiye, reports from Ijwi have it. At Mitsimbwe, near the thin waist of the island dividing north from south, the armies of the south made their defensive stand. There are many differing accounts of the battle at Mitsimbwe: some have Nkundiye providing canoes for the Rwandan troops to outflank the Havu defensive positions; others refer to the Rwandans' deceit in sending the Havu troops poisoned cattle, or cattle as a false sign of friendship. Still others say that houses were burned behind the Havu forces and the Bany'Iju, thinking they were surrounded and defeated, lost heart and fled. Those who stayed were routed by the Rwandan forces.

The primary and immediate objective of the Rwandan victory was achieved with the death of Kabego and his small entourage on Kishushu. Led to Kabego's refuge by Nkundiye (or by a disgruntled servant), Rwandan troops under the leadership of Rwanyonga (one of Rwabugiri's most celebrated military leaders) surrounded the island in canoes at dawn. They attacked and easily overwhelmed the small force protecting the king, who was killed at the door of his hut by Rwanyonga himself. The head and testicles of the old king were taken to be added to the ritual regalia of the Rwandan court. The body of Kabego never did receive a ritual burial on Ijwi, and today on the island it is not known how the body was disposed of. Just prior to the Rwandan attack, according to most sources, Kabego had sent off his son Ndogosa with the royal ivory bracelets and probably other elements of the Ijwi regalia. But the principal symbol of kingship—the drum named "Kalinga"—and other royal regalia were hidden in a cave on the eastern side of Ijwi, and were never seized during Rwabugiri's time on the island. Ndogosa fled to Bushi (to Lwindi—considered the source of kingship in the region) and stayed there for the duration of Rwandan rule on Ijwi. Rwabugiri's initial objective had been achieved—personal revenge on Kabego, the king who had flouted Rwabugiri's hegemony over Ijwi.

The initial effect of the Rwandan victory was almost a scorched-earth policy in the south. Many houses were burned; cattle were taken by individual groups of Rwandan soldiers and never found their way to Rwabugiri; goods were taken, crops were destroyed, and women were seized and sometimes taken back to Rwanda. The initial reaction of the island people, defenseless before such powerful and arbitrary force, was to flee. Those who had close relatives on the western mainland fled there; most, however, went to the forest. Large groups often fled together, camping in the rugged mountainous forest stretching east-west across the island just south of the waist, and in other forested areas. Some of them stayed there for the duration of Rwabugiri's administration of Ijwi, and the traditions of such groups do not include accounts of his attacks and subsequent events. However, it was more indicative of Rwabugiri's objectives that the Bany'Iju were encouraged to return to their homes after a few months and that most of them did. Rwabugiri's amnesty was an honorable one; there are only scattered reports of victimization found on Ijwi.

In a sense the anarchic period following the death of Kabego and the order accompanying Rwabugiri's arrival only confirm the fundamental ideology on Ijwi toward kingship: anarchy necessarily exists in a kingless situation, but inevitably a king will be attracted into the political vacuum and calm will be restored. The arrival of Rwabugiri into the political vacuum is consequently described in the same terms as the process of expansion of kingship throughout the area. And in fact it seems true that calm was restored and continued throughout the rule of Rwabugiri on Ijwi.

The Death of Nkundiye

The limited aims of Rwabugiri's attack on Ijwi are best demonstrated in the initial results. Nkundiye was placed as chief over the south by the Rwandans, politically assuming his father's mantle but without Kabego's ritual position. Tabaro retained power in the north, and apparently over some hills in the south as well. Very few Rwandan chiefs were on the island during this initial stage. Those who were held only minimal effective power. They commanded only small numbers of Rwandan soldiers, while Nkundiye and Tabaro and their appointed representatives retained important judicial authority. Once the initial shock and looting were over, the Rwandan victory had few lasting social effects on Ijwi. Rwabugiri had effected a decapitation of the state, but had left the corpus quite intact.

Nkundiye more than restored the client relationship, in Rwandan eyes. Whereas Mwendanga and Kabego had sent gifts symbolizing (to Rwandans) the subordination of Ijwi to Rwanda, Nkundiye became the personal client of Rwabugiri, going himself to visit the court of Rwabugiri and fighting with great distinction in Rwabugiri's wars in Bushi. But the real relation of this "king without drums" on Ijwi to his patron Rwabugiri is shown in the fact that he is said to have received command of several hills on Nyamirundi. This is not to say that he was more powerful than his father Kabego because of this extension of territory. To the contrary, it rather served to underscore Nkundiye's position as a subordinate of Rwabugiri, dependent on him in the same way as Rwabugiri's other chiefs. This was clearly not an extension of Ijwi power to Nyamirundi (in fact, it is little remembered on Ijwi); it reflected unequivocally an expansion of Rwandan influence to Ijwi.

The difference in Nkundiye's position from that of his father is well illustrated in his relation to Tabaro. For the "king" of the south, the loss of independent status ended even his nominal authority in the north. What apparently most hurt Nkundiye's pride was the retention by Tabaro of several hills in the south, including Muhyahya, just south of the forest belt accepted as the division of north and south, and on which Tabaro had an important residence. It was here, several years later, that Nkundiye and Tabaro were to clash. The events leading up to their battle are not remembered well on Ijwi; beyond the establishment of the residence itself, there seems to have been no overt provocative act to open hostilities. But the end result is quite clear: Nkundiye attacked Tabaro at Muhyahya and took him prisoner. Eventually he killed him at Bihembe, a hill in the far south, and the sons of Tabaro fled to Rwanda. Nkundiye was momentarily master of the entire island, at least in his control of force if not in the loyalty of the people.

THIS VICTORY was the culmination of a conscious policy on the part of Nkundiye to establish himself as the supreme political authority for the whole island. But in Rwabugiri's wars in Bushi, Nkundiye had fought with such distinction as to arouse the jealousy of his comrades in arms, who, it is said, plotted and whispered against him at the court. As if to confirm the calumny, Nkundiye was also engaged in a double-bladed policy of seizing the cattle brought back from Rwabugiri's wars by those on the island who fought for Rwabugiri, and confiscating the cattle of those Rwandans on Ijwi who died in Rwabugiri's wars, whether booty cattle or not. Some even assert that Nkundiye had killed other Rwandan soldiers in battle so as to claim their cattle.[12]

Thus, within several years of the death of Kabego, Nkundiye had fallen out of favor at the Rwandan court, and the death of Tabaro only further removed him from favor. In fact, the attack on Tabaro seems likely to have been interpreted by Rwabugiri and a court already disposed against Nkundiye as a direct affront to the Rwandan king's authority; after all, Tabaro could only have held his position through the grace of Rwabugiri, and there is no evidence that Rwabugiri authorized Nkundiye's offensive against Tabaro.

Having eliminated Tabaro, Nkundiye busily attempted to consolidate his position on the island. Expropriating the cows of others to augment his own herds, Nkundiye distributed "a whole hill of cattle" among influential men on the island in his quest for popular support. This speaks as much to the perceived weakness of his political position as it does to his political acumen. Finally, Rwabugiri sent messengers to command Nkundiye's presence at the court: all but one were killed by Nkundiye. The sole survivor was mutilated and sent back to Rwabugiri as testimony to Nkundiye's regard for Rwabugiri's word. Nkundiye then ordered his drums beaten (but not the ritual drums of the kingdom, which he never possessed) on one of the tall bluffs on the east of the island, looking across to Rwanda and within hearing distance of the Rwandan shore (and of Rubengera, Rwabugiri's capital): it represented a defiant act by Nkundiye—a deliberate challenge to Rwabugiri.

With all these deliberate preparations on Nkundiye's part to declare himself independent, it is surprising there was so little response to Rwabugiri's inevitable attack. Indeed, there was almost no response at all: Nkundiye fled with a few friends, including his son, Katobera, to Tshofu, an island just off the western shore of the lake, near present-day Kalehe. His installation and rule on Tshofu were apparently very harsh, driving off many people during his stay of several years. Finally, his son Katobera fell out with him over a question of land, and, for the second successive generation over the span of perhaps a decade, the plaintiff took his case to Rwabugiri, this time located on Ijwi.

Informants on Ijwi portray this as a virtual duplication of Nkundiye's earlier appeal for assistance to Rwabugiri: Katobera offered his aid in capturing or killing Nkundiye; in return, Katobera would serve as client of Rwabugiri on Tshofu. Obviously such a plan appealed to Rwabugiri: he would at once gain his revenge against the insubordinate Nkundiye and extend his influence to islands over which he had never established his power—islands which moreover were separated from another Havu kingdom on the mainland by only several hundred yards of water. And so the attack against Nkundiye was launched.

The end was swift. With Rwabugiri's canoes in sight of Tshofu, Nkundiye realized that there was little point in further flight, and no chance in open battle. Breaking his spear over his knee, he vowed never to be killed by Rwabugiri, and, with a trusted servant, threw himself into the lake and drowned. By spreading roasted sorghum on the water, so these accounts continue, the attacking Rwandans quickly recovered the body, which miraculously surfaced almost immediately. Again, as with Nkundiye's father, they took the head and testicles and returned to Rwabugiri. Once again Rwabugiri had achieved personal vengeance against a single insubordinate "client"; at the same time, he had positioned himself strategically for new attacks on the mainland. Katobera left for Rwanda with his wife and never returned to Ijwi, leaving no descendants on the island.

There are many on Ijwi who say that in Rwanda Rwabugiri killed Katobera because "if you could betray your father, you could yet betray me."[13] On Ijwi this serves as an indication of the brutality of the political game in Rwanda.

The Administration of Rwabugiri on Ijwi

Ijwi under its Havu king had always been independent of Rwanda ritually, politically and militarily. However, both ritually and politically there were indeed royal elements similar to those in Rwanda—perhaps introduced by immigrants to Ijwi but more likely drawn (both on Ijwi and in Rwanda) from a deeper, common cultural source.[14] To the Bany'Iju, this was a fact of their royal heritage, but it was considered a symbolic representation of their historical past rather than subordination. They viewed their king as a "brother" to the Rwandan king, as to them all kings were brothers, not clients. To Rwandans, the relationship between the Ijwi and Rwandan kings was manifested in the payments, which the Rwandan court saw as tribute and which they interpreted as the expression of a clientship status. In the eyes of the Rwandan king, at least of Rwabugiri, it was clearly an important statement of the preeminence of Rwanda.

The restitution of this status of subordination, as Rwabugiri obviously chose to interpret it, became the major objective of his administration on Ijwi. But aside from that, what is remarkable is the continuity in patterns of administration on Ijwi. Before his death, Nkundiye wielded ultimate authority in the south, and Rwabugiri seems willingly to have let him do so. Administration remained largely in the hands of the Bany'Iju at all levels, and those who had served as close advisors to Kabego were often retained under Nkundiye. There do not appear to have been any reprisals against the local leaders and second-tier political leadership. With the exception of members of the royal family and their close friends who had fled, the authority structure remained intact and the authorities remained unchanged. This pattern indicates that political identification with the institutions of the political structure was stronger than was personal allegiance. It suggests that many positions of authority, even those delegated from above, were seen less as administrative than as representative—to pay court and to petition the king on behalf of the people. A change in the king thus did not affect their position.

During the second period, following the death of Nkundiye, the character of Rwandan rule changed. Rwandan chiefs were placed on the island,[15] and the highest levels of political and administrative authority were removed from Havu control, though Rwabugiri did retain important Havu advisors on the island. During this period there seemed to be a more conscious attempt to tie Ijwi closer politically and symbolically to the Rwandan king. Rwabugiri himself spent some time on the island. He built at least three residences and had at least two wives there (at different times). He also brought one of his royal bulls, Fizi,[16] to Ijwi. A small number of Bany'Iju were recruited as rowers, and a few important warriors fought in his ranks in Bushi. That there were some individuals who sought to identify with Rwandan court culture is illustrated in the work by A. Kashamura,[17] but Ijwi accounts make it clear that this was nowhere near as generalized—nor as enduring—as he implies.

The population seemed but slightly affected by this loss of independence. Their obligations remained largely the same toward the new chiefs; some served in wars and as rowers for Rwabugiri. The demand on them for material goods does not seem to have been greatly increased, although there was a heavier demand for labor to construct the new residences. There was no attempt to introduce clientship on the Rwandan pattern here or to settle Rwandans on the island; the number of Rwandan chiefs was always very small. In short, Rwabugiri's presence brought little change in the people's lives that is remembered today, and few demographic changes, certainly much less than what occurred with the arrival of the Europeans.

The forms of Rwabugiri's administration on Ijwi are in some ways reminiscent of his policy in Gisaka, Ndorwa, and Kinyaga in similar circumstances. Yet there remained important differences from the Gisaka model: the limited numbers, powers, and influence (at least as this is today remembered in the traditions) of the Rwandan chiefs on Ijwi; the cultural differences of Ijwi from Rwanda; and (at least today) the clear lack of identification of the population as a whole with Rwandan culture. Rwandan chiefs on Ijwi were not at all influential before the death of Nkundiye; in other words, there was no immediate attempt at direct rule. The superficiality of Rwandan rule is illustrated by the immediate departure of Rwandan chiefs on the death of Rwabugiri, not a sign of successful cultural assimilation after perhaps twenty years of Rwandan political domination. Furthermore, the Rwandan period (for it cannot properly be called an occupation) left no widespread legacy of Rwandan cultural institutions (as, for example, Rwandan forms of clientship).

What is most notable is Rwabugiri's failure to integrate Ijwi into Rwanda. In fact, this conclusion can be validly applied to other areas west of Rwanda, which were not in the cultural sense already substantially integrated into Rwanda: Bushi, Ijwi, Kalehe, and Buhunde were all defeated by Rwabugiri in battle without being incorporated into Rwanda, though among the western states, Ijwi most closely approached this. These differences (in achievement, if not in goals) between the incorporation of areas of broadly Rwandan culture (Gisaka, Kinyaga, Bwishaza, Ndorwa) and areas of distinct differences from Rwandan culture (Kalehe, Bushi, Buhunde) leads to the conclusion that the lasting effects of Rwabugiri's military exploits were less pronounced than is generally accepted—more irredentist than imperialist.[18]

On Ijwi there were interesting variants to the basic Rwandan administrative pattern of coopting the local leadership and replacing the ruling elite with a thin overlay of Rwandan chiefs. In one village in the east, Rwabugiri was met by a second-generation Rwandan immigrant: though he himself had been born on Ijwi, his father had immigrated to the island from Rwanda for unstated reasons. On Rwabugiri's arrival, this man presented himself to Rwabugiri's court, not far from his village, and was appointed as village headman. Two other unrelated examples demonstrate a similar pattern. Both concern men who had left Ijwi for Rwanda over some social dispute, probably during the period between Rwabugiri's second and third attacks (i.e., during Nkundiye's "reign"). Each of them returned with Rwabugiri, after Nkundiye's death, and was delegated authority in their villages; one of them reemigrated to Rwanda after Rwabugiri's death. These are the only cases that do not conform to the pattern of cooptation of Bany'Iju at the local level and the appointment of Rwandans as political chiefs at higher levels. The only men directly delegated by Rwabugiri at the lower levels of administration were those who, while depending entirely on the Rwandan king for their position, were not strangers to the Bany'Iju.

The relative immunity of the population to these changes was mirrored in their detachment from events at higher levels. While they had been willing to fight for Kabego, they did not respond similarly in the case of Nkundiye, whom they viewed as an illegitimate king: a "king without drums." He was a chief with political power, but one lacking the ritual power of kingship. Nkundiye's attempt to attract public support with which to assert his independence against Rwabugiri was clearly a failure. Yet the idea of responsibility to the kingship, even if not personal loyalty to an individual, was not absent. Military leaders who had fought against Rwabugiri later fought with him in his wars outside; others served as rowers for Rwabugiri's expeditions to Bushi. There is no contradiction in the eyes of the Havu today that their grandfathers should have fought for Kabego, Nkundiye, and Rwabugiri at different times. Nor was there any question that the important advisors of Kabego would later perform the same functions for Rwabugiri. The Bany'Iju honor the king in power; Rwabugiri surely was more powerful than Nkundiye.

But the Bany'Iju add that Nkundiye was not their king; on the death of Kabego, "Rwabugiri became our king." Thus they view the question as one of legitimacy as well as one of power. This suggests a pattern of loyalty to the institution of kingship, to the system, rather than to the individual king. Although a Muny'Iju and the son of Kabego, Nkundiye was not the king of Ijwi; Rwabugiri was the true and legitimate king *on* (if not *of*) Ijwi. Legitimacy in this case seems not to have been determined by nationality or by descent. Rather, it seems an aspect of the nonexclusive nature of political loyalty: political loyalties were determined not by who was excluded by certain characteristics, but rather by who met certain criteria, regardless of other aspects. In this case, Rwabugiri was not excluded from the legitimacy of kingship on Ijwi because he was not a Muny'Iju; rather, he was accepted because he had political authority on the island *and* he had drums—the ritual power—of kingship.

The Death of Rwabugiri

The thin veneer of Rwandan administrative occupation is again evident from the events following Rwabugiri's death, about a decade after the death of Nkundiye. Rwabugiri died in a canoe off Nyamisi, one of the islands near the western shore of Ijwi. The explanation given on Ijwi is that he carried with him a whistle (*ngisha*) with very strong magical properties. The Bany'Iju rowers in the canoe suggested that he blow the whistle against anyone in the boat who did not row with sufficient energy. Because Rwabugiri was the only one in the canoe who was not rowing, it was he who became the victim of his own magic. Other informants add that he suffered from dysentery at the time. The Bany'Iju deposited the body with the Rwandans at the royal residence at Nyamasheke (near Nyamirundi); they then returned to Ijwi to inform the population and to send a delegation immediately to find their own king, Ndogosa, then still in Bushi.

Ndogosa returned and was immediately enthroned. Thereafter he conducted a campaign of reconciliation and rapprochement with the Rwandans. He returned the wife of Rwabugiri and the royal bull, Fizi, to Rwanda with a royal escort, so that they would not only return safely but in a manner befitting their status. This action earned him the respect of the Rwandans, report the Bany'Iju, who thenceforth treated Ndogosa with the honor due to a king. Meanwhile, the Rwandan overlords on the island at the time of Rwabugiri's death were allowed to return to Rwanda.

Otherwise, there is no memory on Ijwi of dislocations or other major changes effected by the return of Ndogosa. There is no reference to general recriminations against the Rwandans, just as there is no reference on Ijwi to resistance to Rwandan rule after Rwabugiri's conquest. There seems little antagonism held either against the Rwandan king or against Rwandans who chose to stay on the island after the death of Rwabugiri. Ndogosa cooperated closely with Musinga on occasion for common objectives; several Rwandans who stayed were not only given land but also served Ndogosa as herdsmen for his personal herds. The positions held by the Rwandan chiefs were assumed once again by members of the royal family and friends of Ndogosa. Ndogosa appears to have had an initially untroubled reign, until, he too faced his own succession dispute, and until he met with a series of unprecedented misfortunes to the kingdom that accompanied the arrival of the Europeans in the Kivu area and on Ijwi.

KING AND CHIEF ON IJWI ISLAND

1982

All politics is local. But all political activity occurs within larger contexts. For this area of Africa there are few case studies available on local responses to the process of colonial conquest—and on the deeper effects that such a process initiated. This essay shows that even with overwhelming military power, neither the European conquest nor the colonial administration of the small community on Ijwi Island was easy. On the other side of the ledger, resistance, so often portrayed in ideological terms as heroic, was accompanied by political complexity and by material hardship: flight, taxes, epidemics, exile, and dislocation were all part of the experience. This chapter, however, is not only about conquest and resistance; it is also concerned with the more subtle effects of new political strategies and the presence of new resources in molding politics in the community. Drawing on a variety of sources (particularly oral testimony), it considers the differences between two political cultures—one based on local legitimacy and one based on external power—and the mediations between the two models. (These differences were manifest both in the modernizing agenda of the delegated "chief"—as distinct from traditional "king"—and in the resistance of the population in the different

Cowritten with Catharine Newbury.

administrative regions of the island.) Both locally derived "legitimate" authority and externally derived delegated power needed to address the questions of loyalty and power, but each did so in different ways. In a sense, Ijwi's history provides a historical laboratory for studying such differences in political structure. It also traces the effects on the people of a system that responded primarily to an externally driven rationale—in this case the irony of the "civilizing mission" that drove colonial rule. By attending to local dimensions of colonial imposition, even in this small locale, the analysis shows that the effects of colonial establishment were momentous and the lessons important.

O NE EARLY LEGACY OF colonial rule in Africa was an academic focus on the process of elite formation in African societies. A product of the perceived political needs of the early independence period, this perspective generally emphasized manpower development as the critical element of bureaucratic stability and political modernization. It was postulated that individual leaders were progressive nation builders, in contrast to the backward and conservative masses, and therefore studies on the early postcolonial period devoted little attention to the specific interactions between members of the elite and the masses.[1]

Still less attention was given to the significance of these relationships for the rural people involved. By the very fact of their powerlessness, these people were not considered part of the political nexus. However, as Joan Vincent has recently indicated, the character of a political system may best be understood by examining the nature of its impact on the powerless, rather than by describing its structure or stated objectives and focusing on the incorporation of elites into the hierarchical political framework.[2] Indeed, the very existence of a large relatively powerless sector of society is itself an important indicator of the quality and conception of politics within that society.

Emphasis on the process of elite formation has also focused attention on the role of "traditional elites." Wherever possible, Belgian colonial policy combined the two categories of precolonial authority and colonially imposed authority within the single concept of traditional elite, in an attempt to cloak colonial administrative personnel in the garb of legitimacy. Despite such attempts to forge a sense of continuity, the transformation from a precolonial to a colonial context was significant. It affected local authorities in two ways: in their loss of status (particularly in the loss of sovereignty) and in the extension of new powers applicable to the local context. The loss of sovereignty was felt most directly by the elites themselves, while the new powers placed in the hands of the elites were realized at the expense of the population in general. But there is a sense in which these two aspects of the transition to colonial rule were intimately related, for the issues of sovereignty and legitimacy affected the quality of administration, and especially the nature of relations between elites and others, in ways that reinforced each other. These two themes—the different types of "traditional" authority in the colonial context on the one hand, and the relationship between local administrative authorities and the population on the other—will provide the focus for this essay.

Ijwi is a large island, some forty kilometers north to south, its width varying from two to ten kilometers east and west, located in Lake Kivu on Zaire's eastern border. Prior to colonial rule, Ijwi formed a single kingdom, but colonial administrative divisions permitted two types of chiefly rule to coexist, one in the north of the island, one in the south. In the 1970s, the two men who headed the administration in each sector were members of the same family of precolonial rulers; though of different descent lines within the dynasty, they shared a common ancestor four and five generations distant (see figure 7.1). Nonetheless, despite their common family ties and their common position within the present administrative structures, there were important differences in the character of their rule on Ijwi. The two men were regarded differently by their populations, they exercised their powers differently, and they entertained markedly different relations with the political hierarchy of the state. Indeed, the latter factor is important in understanding the former two; it is the significance of this relationship of the elites to the wider administrative context that will be explored below. We shall first trace the careers of the two segments of the royal family during the colonial period, and then examine certain political changes affecting the status and powers of the political authorities, and their effect on political life on Ijwi.

Ijwi in the Precolonial Period: The Competing Lines of Royal Division

The schism of the royal family into two segments had roots that long preceded the European arrival on Lake Kivu. So also did the tactics that members of each segment employed in their competition with each other. Members of the dynasty arrived on the island in the early nineteenth century, and over the next decades the senior descent line—those who possessed kingship—progressively reinforced

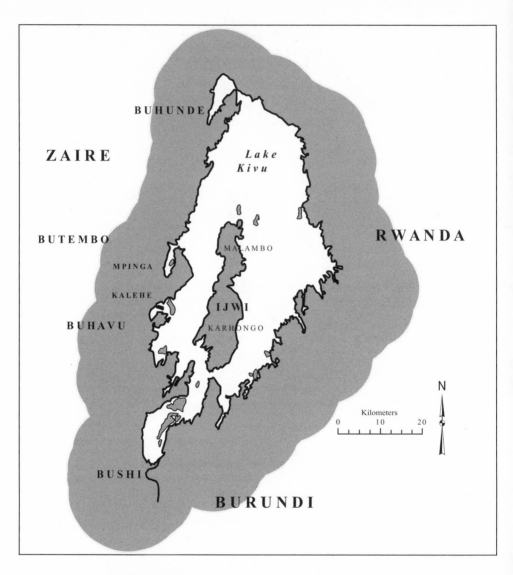

Map 7.1. Ijwi Island and surrounding areas

their political penetration within Ijwi society. During this period their major concerns focused on the issue of sovereignty: independence from external political control. From the late nineteenth century, however, members of the junior line, attempting to consolidate their power in the north of the island, seized on foreign support whenever this opportunity presented itself. Historically less concerned with sovereignty, they were more concerned with forging external alliances to assure their less-than-secure position. These different political concerns, reflected in markedly different tactics, reinforced the lines of cleavage and thus subsequently had an enduring influence on Ijwi politics.[3]

Despite the common political focus shared by the people of Ijwi in the late nineteenth century, they were internally distinguished on historical and cultural grounds, particularly in terms of their identification with royalty. The political differences were also reflected in geographical features. Ijwi was divided into two roughly equal parts by a rugged, heavily forested mountain belt stretching east and west across the middle of the island. This area was virtually unpopulated even late into the twentieth century, and so defined the population into two geographical segments, the northern and southern parts of the island.

A high proportion of the present population descends from immigrants who came to Ijwi in the late eighteenth and early nineteenth centuries, about the same time as the royal dynasty, the Basibula. The nonroyal groups, however, did not arrive on Ijwi with the royal family, nor did they come from the same areas. The development of royal authority on Ijwi was a slow process; throughout the nineteenth century, the central court was only partially integrated into the heterogeneous Ijwi population.[4] Although the first king, Mwendanga, and his successor Kabego (died 1875) established residences in both the north and south of Ijwi, the political focus for each king was in the southern portion of the island.

The kings did, however, send sons and brothers to various areas of Ijwi. Over a period of three generations, one of those families, located in the north of the island, began to develop its own identity as a segment of the royal dynasty opposed to the senior line in the south. It is important that the early political status of this group rested on their role as representatives of a nominally superior political power. Their perceived functions and priorities derived from higher authority, and their status and primary political identity were associated essentially with "outside" networks; they did not seek to be accepted within the new society by marriage ties or ritual as did their cousins in the south. Indeed, their adeptness in adapting to such external power networks would later provide an excellent platform from which to launch their successful colonial careers.

During the last quarter of the nineteenth century, Ijwi was subjected to a series of attacks by the troops of the Rwandan king Rwabugiri.[5] At one level the struggle to retain sovereignty against the Rwandan incursion served to unify the Ijwi population. But it also crystallized internal conflicts associated with a developing succession struggle among the sons of Kabego, the Ijwi king. By adroitly exploiting these cleavages within the Ijwi royal family, Rwabugiri was able to mount a successful attack on the island, during which Kabego was killed. Although the Ijwi royal family was subsequently dispersed, two of its members remained on the island as Rwabugiri's representatives, one in the south and one in the north.

The preeminent member of the royal family in the north at this time was a man named Tabaro, a grandson of the first Ijwi king. After the death of Kabego, the competition between the descent lines of the royal family intensified as each sought control of the entire island. Eventually Tabaro was killed by his primary adversary in the south, Nkundiye; Tabaro's son Bera, then but a child, escaped to Rwanda. Later, following the death of Rwabugiri and the reestablishment of the Sibula dynasty on the island toward the very end of the nineteenth century, Bera returned to Ijwi, where he, in his turn, became involved in conflicts with other members of the royal family more proximate to royal power than he. Once again he fled to Rwanda, where he was to stay for many years. He learned much during this self-imposed exile, and he was later to turn to his advantage the political lessons acquired in Rwanda.

The Changing of the Guard under Colonial Rule

The death of Rwabugiri, the Rwandan conqueror, led to the withdrawal of direct Rwandan power from Ijwi. But the reestablishment of the royal Sibula line in the southern part of Ijwi after the death of Rwabugiri did not signal a new era of sovereignty unimpeded by external influences. Ijwi was soon to find itself a part of the disputes between Germany and Belgium over the location of colonial territorial boundaries (1899–1910).[6] Belgian officers established a military post on Ijwi in 1912,[7] and about a year later Kabego's successor Ndogosa was officially recognized by the Belgian authorities as "Chief of Kwidjwi."[8]

Throughout the island the population found their early experience of Belgian occupation burdensome, but the initial impact was especially severe in the south. Ijwi oral traditions still reflect these tensions today.[9] Belgian officers and

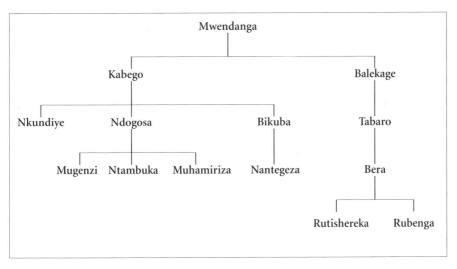

Figure 7.1. Partial genealogy of the Ijwi royal family

their Congolese soldiers requisitioned large quantities of food; it is recounted that they demanded 350 fish daily, a bull each week, and numerous chickens and eggs. They also introduced the population to *corvée* (forced labor) and the *chicotte* (whip). Cattle raids were a frequent occurrence.[10] A misunderstanding soon arose between the Belgians and Mugenzi, Ndogosa's oldest son and local delegate in the far south; at issue was a shortage one day in the number of fish delivered to the post. During the course of this dispute, Mugenzi and Ndogosa and many among the population went into hiding, and the Belgian forces set fire to Ndogosa's residence.[11]

During World War I, Ijwi again became the focus of German-Belgian rivalries. In September 1914, a German force from Rwanda attacked and defeated the Belgian installation on Ijwi; the Belgian officers were taken prisoner, and the Germans occupied the island.[12] The Belgians suspected that Ijwi authorities had cooperated with, if not actively aided, the German offensive.[13] Therefore, despite the fact that the German presence on the island was only nominal and ephemeral, on the retreat of the Germans and the Belgian reoccupation of Ijwi in 1916, the Belgians looked with great suspicion at the Ijwi royal family and viewed them as former German sympathizers. This suspicion was reflected in Belgian administrative policy and was to color the relationship between the Belgians and Ndogosa, the king of Ijwi, for the next decade.

Belgian exactions on the island were viewed as onerous by both the population and the royal family, but the latter, of course, also saw the demands as a direct threat to their sovereignty. In neighboring Rwanda, the Belgians took over from the Germans a minimal but nonetheless functioning administrative structure, built in part on the earlier structures of the Rwandan kingdom.[14] On Ijwi, however, the Germans had established nothing even remotely comparable, nor were there effective preexisting structures of the type found in Rwanda. Nonetheless, the Belgians pushed ahead as if similar administrative structures were fully in place, and they considered Ndogosa's lack of cooperation to be "rebellion." In fact, it was much more than that: it was a fully committed effort to preserve sovereignty in the face of yet another external threat. It was not Ndogosa's intransigence alone, for to comply with Belgian demands would have violated indigenous constraints on kingship and compromised Ndogosa's position as king on Ijwi. Furthermore, the Ijwi kingdom lacked sufficiently strong administrative structures to extract such demands from an unwilling population even had the king so wished. It would have been almost impossible for him to comply with Belgian demands without relying on European force and thus forfeiting both internal support and external independence—important constituents of legitimate claims to kingship on Ijwi.[15] Consequently, the goods and services demanded of the Ijwi king were slow in forthcoming, and it was not long before the Belgians sought to exile Ndogosa and replace him with a man of their own choosing.

Ndogosa had not regained his throne from the Rwandans simply to hand it over to the Belgians, however. At that time the island included substantial areas of heavy forest, and Ndogosa faded from Belgian contact.[16] It is a commentary on the unity of general population on this issue that Ndogosa was able to maintain his authority with the people of Ijwi (at least those in the south) while hidden from the Europeans for more than seven years (1913–14 and 1916–23). Even though not all of the population was privy to his hiding places, he could not have maintained his tactics without the support of most Bany'Iju (the people of Ijwi), especially in the face of constant attempts by the Belgians and their soldiers to locate him.[17]

In their search for the elusive Ndogosa, the Belgian administration imposed additional burdens besides the "normal" requirements of taxation, prestations in food, and, most onerous, cutting timber in the forests of the island. Now the population had to support, as well as to endure, the presence of a quasi-permanent military occupation. Certain individuals, those thought to be close the king, suffered especially under this regime; some were killed in the most barbaric fashion.[18] All this, of course, took place in the name of imposing peace and tranquility.[19] Further disruption occurred from the indiscriminate and widespread expropriation of cattle by colonial authorities both on and off Ijwi (from Rwanda and the Congolese mainland).[20] It was also a time of cattle epidemics and human diseases, with spinal meningitis taking a particularly grim toll.[21] The herds on Ijwi diminished greatly, never to revive, and human mobility increased as islanders sought to escape the exactions.[22] Bany'Iju today recount that many people, including many members of the royal family, were jailed or sent into exile for refusing either to divulge Ndogosa's hiding place or to carry out European demands with the proper zeal. According to the Belgian colonial reports, many fled to neighboring areas and had to be searched out and returned to the island during this period.[23] Both sources were probably right. Either one alone would testify to the turmoil of the times, but taken together they demonstrate the depth of disruption of Ijwi society. One Belgian observer described the situation in the following terms: "During all this period the most complete anarchy reigned in the region. The occupation ruined the country, the natives left the island to take refuge in the chiefdoms on the mainland, in Buhavu, as well as in Unya-Bongo [the Shi states southwest of Lake Kivu] and in Rwanda, where many settled without the intention of returning."[24]

From 1920, the Belgian administration initiated a series of new policies designed to terminate the resistance on Ijwi and reinforce administrative control. First, Ijwi lost its status as a territorial headquarters; in 1920 the administrative center of what had been the "Territoire de Kwidjwi" was moved from Ijwi to the Congo mainland at Kalehe. Second, the administration moved to reinforce and extend the power of Lushombo, the Havu king of Mpinga (the area around Kalehe). By a decree (*arrêté*) of August 13, 1921, the Buhavu Chiefdom was created, with Lushombo as "Grand Chef." In addition to Mpinga, therefore, Lushombo's domain now included Ijwi and several other chiefdoms, most of which, like Ijwi, had formerly been autonomous of this Havu chief.[25] By 1928, those chiefdoms had all been officially demoted to the status of "sub-chiefdoms" (later termed "groupements").[26] These policies marked a definitive shift in the locus of power in the region. The political arena was enlarged, both in area and in the scope of powers available to the authorities within the hierarchical network. Formerly independent areas now became subordinated not only to the colonial authority, but (and symbolically equally significant) also to other mainland areas. It now became essential for political authorities such as those on Ijwi to develop alliance networks on the mainland, both with the Belgian administration and with Lushombo's following; the Ijwi royal family had always resisted both.

During this period the Belgians considered the southern part of Ijwi to be the major problem area of the island because of their difficulty with Ndogosa. Thus they were delighted when, in 1921, Ndogosa's oldest son, Mugenzi, presented himself to the administration and assured them that if they would recognize him as chief, he would locate his father and brothers and turn them over to the Belgian authorities within six months.[27] But though he exiled several of his brothers, he failed to locate Ndogosa, and finally was exiled himself, two years later, to South Kivu. Shortly thereafter, Ndogosa emerged from hiding. Faced with the realization that the Belgians were there to stay, discouraged with the purposelessness of continued resistance, and apparently upset by the conduct of his son Mugenzi and the sufferings of his other sons in exile, Ndogosa surrendered to the Europeans in 1923.

For the first time in more than seven years, Ndogosa was allowed to govern in public. The results, however, were exceedingly disappointing to the Belgian administration. The Europeans had hoped that the restoration of Ndogosa would bring about a change in attitude of the Ijwi population; they wanted people to return to their villages, to pay taxes, and to participate in corvée, and they wanted the king to act in a respectful and helpful manner toward the Belgian authorities. None of these expectations was fulfilled. In March 1926, the Belgian *commissaire de district assistant*, Monsieur Dargent, went to Ijwi to look into the situation personally. The following conversation between Dargent and Ndogosa gives an idea of the immense gap between Belgian views and Ijwi attitudes on the king's status.[28]

> Q: Have you received all my notes? Why did you remain eight days without coming to greet me, while I summoned you each day?
>
> R: If I did not come to you when I received all your notes, it was because I was sick and I have not been able to walk [far].
>
> Q: Why did your people flee from me, instead of remaining in their homes for my arrival?
>
> R: If they fled, that is their business; I can't do anything about it.
>
> Q: If you had sent someone to warn the people that I was coming, and to tell them to stay around, they would have stayed, isn't that so?
>
> R: If you are the master, take care of such palavers yourself.
>
> Q: Have your sons killed someone, or do they want to make war? [Is this why they aren't able to appear before the administration?]

R: You will see my children only on condition that you return to me all my country that I had in the past.[29]

Q: You have come alone, without any of your children, and none of your notables—why?

R: What do you bring to me here? I will not show anyone to you and no one will come, as long as I have not received what I am asking from you.

Q: Which one of your sons is going to succeed you?

R: Could you tell me as well which one from among your sons will be commissaire?

Q: You answer me as if I were your equal or your inferior. I repeat, I want to see your sons, among others Rutwaza, the one designated by custom to succeed you.

R: You will not see him.

Within the week, Ijwi was again subjected to a "regime of military occupation," which was to last until 1929. The justification given for this extreme measure was as follows: "The natives of the subchiefdom Mihigo Ndogosa on Ijwi Island are in a state of collective non-submission characterized by the systematic disappearance of people upon the approach of agents of the government and the population opposes the normal execution of our laws. Despite different exhortations and solemn summons we have not managed to overcome the resistance of these people. . . . It is necessary to take measures to influence the attitudes of these populations."[30]

Only a few weeks after this decree was issued, Ndogosa was sent into exile at Rutshuru, never to return.[31] During the following months, those sons of Ndogosa who had not already been exiled were deported from the island. After almost two years in exile, Ndogosa died on February 9, 1928. He was buried in Rutshuru (in North Kivu), and the people of Ijwi observed the customary rites of mourning to honor their proud king.[32] In October of the same year, the "Chefferie Mihigo" was officially abolished by Belgian decree.[33]

With the death of Ndogosa and the exile of Rutwaza, the last of his sons remaining on the island, Ijwi administration was thereafter in the hands of the Belgians. But still they lacked a convenient instrument through which to extend their newly achieved domination.[34] Their policy of using traditional chiefs was obviously unworkable, because they themselves had deported the entire family of the legitimate king. They reached more widely, therefore, calling on Bera, who had since been returned from his self-imposed refuge in Rwanda by an earlier call from the Europeans. During the turmoil and uncertainties in the south of the island after 1916, the Belgians had delegated authority in the north to two men: Nantegeza, the son of Bikuba, Ndogosa's full brother; and Bera, the son of Tabaro (see figure 7.1). Bera turned out to be a willing, even eager, colonial factotum, and his long residence in Rwanda had fully acquainted him with the techniques and rewards (at least for those within the political hierarchy) of a class-based administrative system. But Nantegeza experienced the same difficulties relating to the imposition of externally based power as other members of the royal family; he was soon also assured of exile when he offended Lushombo, the newly appointed *grand chef* of the Havu kingdoms, by failing to produce the requisite number of cattle demanded, and his domain fell to Bera.[35] Having consolidated his power in the north, Bera did well; the colonial reports on him during the early 1930s are filled with glowing praise: "very dedicated," producing "much good work . . . and very satisfying results from native tax collection and various assignments."[36] On Ndogosa's surrender and exile, Bera was named to rule over the entire island. Here was the colonial creation of a "traditional" authority.

The Changing Political Game:
New Goals, New Rules, New Strategies

During his long retreat and flight, Ndogosa had acted to avoid relinquishing sovereignty. For him, the question of sovereignty had been more important than preserving and extending his internal power by manipulating or negotiating with the colonial overlords. Indeed, since his power was based on the Ijwi conception of legitimate authority, he stood to lose much in relinquishing sovereignty. Ndogosa had always worked in a political system where the ideal was a series of competing but independent units within the larger regional framework. Within this context, political competition between members of the royal family focused on succession or secession (a course of action that had led to the foundation of the Ijwi kingdom itself). But there did not exist the will—nor indeed the capacity—to maximize administrative powers over the population for some ulterior political purpose. As noted above, Ndogosa's legitimacy arose from his ritual authority requiring the regular participation of many different Ijwi groups in performing the royal rituals.

Bera's rise to power represented a major break with this pattern. For Bera, sovereignty was not at issue. He could accommodate himself to the colonial situation because he had continually worked within a larger framework defined by external parameters. From his position in the administrative hierarchy, European rule did not pose significant obstacles—in fact, the greater political resources and regional influence of the colonial administrative apparatus provided greater potential for him, after the changing of the guard at the higher levels and especially after the eclipse of the entire senior line of the Ijwi royal family. While Bera achieved his new status at the expense of Ndogosa and his sons, therefore, his accession to power did not represent the simple replacement of one descent line of the royal lineage by another within a roughly similar political context. The nature of political resources had altered dramatically, and with this transformation, the goals and techniques of the exercise of power also changed.

Legitimacy in the new system was less important than the accumulation of these new power resources. The use of these powers was directed not primarily toward other members of the elite (from formerly competing royal families or segments of a single royal family) but toward the population as a whole, to acquire control of their productivity and behavior. Previously, popular support had been looked on as a tool in the struggle against competing adversaries for the prestige of royalty. But during Bera's administration there emerged among the Ijwi elite a new concept of cohesion with other members of royalty (both within the Ijwi kingdom and with royalty in other kingdoms on the mainland) who shared a common interest in maximizing leverage over the population— ostensibly to satisfy the demands and meet the goals of a colonial administration. And not incidentally, these efforts brought satisfying results also to the new elites themselves.

New Authority Patterns of Colonial Rule and Local Response

One of the resources that Bera employed in this process of administering the population was his discretion in the delegation of power. Previously there had developed two formal types of contact between court and people on Ijwi. Delegated authority, usually through members of the royal family, was distinct from other lines of representation between local groups and the court. The functions of the royal family were largely confined to judicial cases; representatives of local groups, on the other hand, usually had more direct influence both on the court and with the local social groups. This was particularly true in the south, where a tradition existed of more clearly defined clan identities than in the north. Such clan distinctions on Ijwi, in fact, had jelled around the presence of the royal court in the south. In the north, clan identity was not such a consistent determinant of political action, nor, with the exception of the extreme north (Kirhanga), were there leaders in the north with a strong local power base, as was true in the south. Hence Bera's experience, both by his position within the political hierarchy and by the nature of local level political behavior in the north, was that of exercising authority derived from elsewhere.

With the expansion of Bera's power to the whole of Ijwi, the same administrative characteristics were applied to the south. Local representatives were suppressed, and new authorities were named directly by Bera. Obviously, these were neither local men nor members of the royal family (except for Bera's sons), since all claimants to legitimate royal status—that is, those who had direct links with kingship—had been exiled. These new men were Bera's favorites, and they shared two traits: they often had had experience with Europeans, either through education in mission schools (and so were literate) or as plantation workers (or workers in other enterprises); and they were, in the eyes of the governed, outsiders. Their lines of responsibility, and the measure of their capacity to rule, were determined from above, as was true for Bera himself. This was a major break with previous patterns of authority, and the difference was most strongly felt in the south. In general, the former centers of royalty in the south held the peoples in the north in no particularly high regard, and they resented the colonial impositions all the more because they were administered by Bera's appointees from the north—men trusted by him, perhaps, but lacking local ties.

It is instructive to follow the colonial reports on this period. During the period of Ndogosa's flight from the Belgians, it was noted that various "acts of insubordination on the part of Mihigo [Ndogosa] and his partisans occur with increasing frequency."[37] In 1926, the year of exile of Ndogosa and the military occupation of the island, the reports deplore the exodus of the population "en masse" to Rwanda and Bushi, and note that those leaving were the "former subjects" of Ndogosa.[38] The report for 1928, only a year after Bera assumed rule over the whole island, notes considerable opposition to the new authorities; a "band" of fifty men that had "perpetrated certain attempts against personnel and property in the south of the island" was arrested. The report continues by noting the large numbers of people from Ijwi fleeing to Rwanda and Bushi.[39] Strong measures were taken against these population movements, which were in fact simply a continuation of earlier historical patterns; the administration was correct in noting the political nature of such emigration. This connection between administrative demands and population mobility is brought home in the report on the following year: "The military occupation continues in the south of Ijwi. A considerable improvement has occurred during the last months of the year: Activities [against the regime] have ended or diminished greatly. It is [also] true that all types of corvée have been diminished there as much as possible."[40]

The reports of the middle 1930s saw the population as "calm and docile." But after the death of Bera in July 1936, there was renewed resistance against the administration when Bera's son took power. In 1937, the people of one section of the south, an area in the eastern highlands that had suffered heavily under colonial rule, refused to pay taxes in protest against their treatment at the hands of the tax collectors. In the report for the same year, a summary of the administration over the earlier years gives a dreary picture: "In sum, the political situation produced a general malaise; tax collection was atrocious, villages were deserted at the approach of any European, and the population opposed the weight of inertia to all orders and all [colonial] authorities."[41] These conditions produced a remarkable response on the part of the colonial administration: "A territorial agent was sent on the spot with an escort of eighteen soldiers, in order to intimidate the natives and to ensure the return of calm among the population in the shortest possible delay." The result was that "corvée was was reimposed, but the number of those fleeing did not diminish in the least." Finally, the report notes that the great majority of the population desired the return of Ntambuka, the exiled son of Ndogosa.[42] Altogether, therefore, the report represented a curious blend of insightful diagnosis and blundering prescriptive action.

After the death of Bera, his designated heir, Rutishereka, was installed as chief of Ijwi on July 8, 1936. Rutishereka did not last for even one year. In February 1937, just one month after the widespread refusal to pay taxes had been manifested in the eastern areas of south Ijwi, he was deported. The reasons given for Rutishereka's removal were vague; he allegedly had committed a number of faults, including illegal exactions from the population. What was not officially stated (but what everyone recognized, especially the Bany'Iju) was that he had not cemented the external alliances to powerful actors that were now necessary to maintain his position.[43] "Illegal exactions," after all, were not uncommon; what was different in this case was the coherence of the Ijwi response and the fact that the authorities on the mainland chose to remove Rutishereka.

The forced exile of Rutishereka provided the opportunity for the return of Ntambuka. The Belgian decision to bring back Ntambuka was clearly a response to the Ijwi resistance movement, specifically to the tax revolt in the eastern areas.[44] Concerned about the continuing "state of anarchy" on the island, and the depopulation resulting from substantial out-migration, the Belgians looked to Ntambuka to restore order.[45] Ntambuka was therefore recalled from exile in Lubero and installed as chief, but with control over only the southern portion of the island. The north was placed under the control of Rubenga, another son of Bera and the younger half-brother of Rutishereka.[46]

Ntambuka's return to the island did bring calm. Unlike Bera, Rutishereka, or Rubenga, Ntambuka was the legitimate *mwami* of Ijwi, properly enthroned by the ritual specialists, and holding in his possession the ritual objects (regalia) associated with the kingship. The population knew this, and recognized him as their king. Yet in part because he was indeed a king, proud like his father, and assured of a base of support among the population, he did not curry the favor of the Belgian administration and other powerful decision makers. Unlike some of his rivals, Ntambuka did not scramble to gain the approval of the Belgian officials, the Catholic missionaries, and the "Grand Chef" of the colonially defined "Buhavu Chiefdom." He viewed himself as a sovereign in his own right, and he acted accordingly.[47]

Ntambuka was deported from Ijwi for the second time in 1943, eventually to be exiled to Kalembelembe.[48] It would be seventeen years before he would return again to Ijwi. Meanwhile, the position of chief of the southern part of Ijwi was filled by another son of Ndogosa, Ntambuka's younger half-brother Muhamiriza. Muhamiriza had close ties to Rubenga in the north, where he had spent some time as a youth. He was linked by marriage ties to Kamerogosa, the son of Bahole (and grandson of Lushombo), who had succeeded to the position of chief of Buhavu in 1942.[49] Moreover, Muhamiriza was accustomed to working with Europeans. He had attended school while in exile in Uvira, and later he had worked for the administration at the headquarters of the Territory of Kalehe. Thus Muhamiriza had alliances that permitted him to operate successfully in the broader colonial arena beyond Ijwi. He was not a mwami, however, and he never possessed the regalia of kingship. The regalia remained with Ntambuka throughout his exile.[50]

The Social Impact of the New Game

One of the blinders on colonial perceptions resulted from the perpetuation of the myth of indirect rule. Because he was local to Ijwi and a member of the royal family, Bera was anointed by the colonial regime as a "traditional" authority. However, neither he nor the authority which he administered were part of traditional Ijwi political life. Indeed, as implied above, it would have been difficult for a truly traditional authority to have fit into the new political framework, and it was in fact Bera's status as nontraditional authority (and indeed as a non-authority) to the Bany'Iju that perhaps best suited him to participate so effectively in the new arena. Similar observations could be made about Rubenga and Muhamiriza. On the other hand, while as a member of the royal family he may have been seen as legitimate, to the Belgians, he was a catalyst for strenuous opposition for much of the population on Ijwi because his northern origins represented the major opposition to the royal line in the south, and a principal symbol of internal insubordination. His appointments and policies only confirmed this view and intensified the bitterness.

The most important changes, however, were not in personnel, but in institutions—in administrative demands and in the exercise of power. The new authorities made zealous demands of tax collections and labor recruitment. Men were sent to work on plantations, to cut and saw lumber in the forest, to build roads. They were also expected to provide food, including cattle, for the colonially imposed elite. In addition, the population had direct responsibilities to Bera and his successors: working in the chief's personal fields (*busane*), producing food crops that were later sold, was only one form of nontraditional tribute.[51] Men in the north frequently mentioned that it was only under Bera that they first paid for the right to settle on the land; some, however, also noted that their family had provided the payment earlier, but had had to pay again under Bera, a miscarriage of justice in their eyes. Others mentioned the constant harassment of the work they were called on to perform—constructing canoes, providing services such as chopping wood, fetching water, porterage, maintaining the buildings in Bera's enclosure, or rowing Bera and his soldiers on frequent trips to meet the colonial authorities at Kalehe. Men called for such service were expected provide their own food for the trip. Still others speak of greatly increased demands for food provisions and an augmentation in the required acreage of obligatory crops (*maendeleo* fields). Most of these demands were new—if not in nature, at least in the quantities required.[52]

The New Pattern of "Legitimate" Status among the Elites

Much of Bera's new-found power resulted from the colonial situation. Yet his behavior reflects the alacrity with which he sought to use these powers at the expense of what might formerly have been seen as his constituency. For all the powers that Bera exercised, his single-minded dedication to achieving political goals determined by outside demands appears to have made him less accepted by the population. Many stress the fact that Bera was not a true mwami. He was never enthroned, never endowed with the rituals and responsibilities of royalty. The new structures required of him something different.

Bera's colonial orientation can be seen in the friendship patterns that he forged with other chiefs. Although he did not entirely neglect Ijwi's social networks, Bera's principal network of institutionalized links (measured through the exchange of cattle and marriage ties) was with chiefs outside the island. In particular, he had ties to chiefs of a status similar to his own, had come to prominence under colonial rule; the major characteristic of these authorities was administrative efficiency and apparent loyalty within the colonial framework. Bera's closest marriage ties were with Bigilimani, the exemplary colonial chief of the Lake Kivu region, who administered the peninsula of Buzi at the northwest corner of the lake, an area that had historically maintained many social ties with the population of northern Ijwi. Bera was Bigilimani's maternal uncle, a position of very close affinity within the Havu kinship network. Bigilimani had also married both a daughter and a granddaughter of Bera's. The ties of the two families were strengthened in the next generation as at least one of Bigilimani's sons took wives from Ijwi and lived on the island. In addition, Bera and his sons had cattle ties with several chiefs around the Kivu area: in Kalonge, in Mpinga Nord (a subsidiary chiefdom of Kalehe), and in Luhihi. Finally, Bera had contact with Rwanda, forged during his long exile there. Several of his older children had been born to a Rwandan wife, and his ties to the east were continued through cattle exchanges and marriage ties of some of his sons.[53]

Because the mwami and his sons were all exiled for such long periods of time, it is impossible to characterize the social network of the royal line within a comparable context. It is nonetheless significant that (at least until the death of Ntambuka in 1981) the king in the south had placed much less importance on external ties of this nature than had his counterpart in the north. Still, it was notable that the family of the king claimed "friendship" (that is, social identity) with other fully enthroned *bami* of the region rather than with the colonially emergent elite. The closest marriage ties were with the kingdom of Ngweshe, in southern Bushi, but this is more a historical product of Ndogosa's exile during the Rwandan occupation of Ijwi than of any planned strategy of social alliance during the colonial period. Otherwise, claims were made of ties with the kings of Buhunde, Bushi (Buhaya), and even (despite the strained political relations) with Kalehe as well as Karhana, an ambiguous state whose ritual independence of the parent Shi kingdom (Buhaya) seems to have occurred largely during the colonial period; Karhana is a lakeshore kingdom, however, one of the closest to Ijwi, and the two are united in their antipathy toward the Kalehe line.[54]

Secondary Social Change under Colonial Rule

Other social alterations occurring during this period had a less direct impact on the population than did the administrative impositions discussed above, but they were of no less long-term importance. One such factor was the constraint placed on population mobility during colonial rule. Historically, demographic mobility in the lakeshore regions had been fostered by general cultural similarities that transcended political and ethnic divisions. By its very location, Ijwi had become a geographical focus for this movement. Mobility and interchange had always served as an important countercheck to the abuse—or even consolidation—of royal power on the island. The several political units of the lakeshore areas were largely independent of each other and in fact competed among themselves for prestige and power, translated into population numbers.

During the initial stages of colonial imposition, mobility from some parts of the island and lakeshore areas apparently greatly increased. Kinyaga (in southwestern Rwanda) and the eastern parts of Ijwi were especially affected. This was reflected in the preoccupation with these movements apparent in the colonial documents, as noted above; it is even more apparent in the oral data derived from some parts of Ijwi (the eastern shore in particular).[55] But whereas in earlier times such flight and migration could have had an important impact on political balance within the region, during the colonial period it did not markedly affect the character of political rule and oppression, because political power was no longer based ultimately on internal support and population acquiescence. Increasingly, mobility became more a question of individual flight than the movement of families or whole groups. As colonial administrative efficiency increased throughout the region through the services of men like Bera, colonial exactions became more difficult to avoid by moving to new areas, and the general mobility of the population substantially declined during and after the 1930s.

Important changes in the nature of social ties were also evident during this period. The cattle epidemics of the late nineteenth century and the devastating cattle raids conducted against Ijwi by early Europeans both from Rwanda and from the Zairean mainland had greatly reduced the cattle on Ijwi. This had also reduced the need for pasture, and much of the land that had formerly served as pasturage lay vacant during the later years of European establishment on Ijwi. Eventually much of this land was incorporated into the Belgian-owned plantation, Linea, which came to include approximately one-sixth of the island. Other areas, those in the highland watershed of the island, were set aside as forest reserve. Thus, not only through population growth but also through colonial policy, land came to be an increasingly scarce resource, and hence increasingly valuable. Control over access to land, consequently, became one of the major tools (and weapons) in the chief's administrative arsenal, and the new discretionary administrative powers and police force facilitated the imposition of such control. These measures provided direct benefits the ruling group in two ways: from those willing to pay for land, and from the productive resources of those "clients" who worked the chief's fields.

Marriage patterns were also affected. Formerly, matrilateral cross-cousin marriages (*ubuzala*) had increased lineage solidarity by reinforcing the moral obligations of reciprocity between mother's brother and sister's son. They also minimized the expected bridewealth (beyond ritually prescribed exchanges), since the groom's mother's brother was principal donor of bridewealth to his sister's son, and a recipient of the same bridewealth as father-in-law. But under colonial rule, individual accumulation of wealth became more important while reciprocal work obligations and lineage solidarity became less important. It was no longer so incumbent on the father to provide for the son's marriage; indeed, since much of the bridewealth had formerly been drawn from other sources, with the constriction of lineage responsibilities the father alone was often unable to provide it all. As reciprocity and lineage solidarity declined, the maternal uncles no longer found it advantageous to contribute to their sororal nephews' bridewealth; indeed, since bridewealth was no longer distributed so widely among the members of the recipient lineage, participation in ubuzala marriage meant forgoing the potential wealth to be derived from forging marriage bonds outside the family. Younger men were increasingly expected to find their own bridewealth; to be sure, with new employment possibilities in the colonial sphere, they often preferred to do so, thus freeing themselves from their fathers' influence in marriage. Consequently, what had formerly been a predominant marriage pattern became increasingly rare, restricted to the very young and very poor and increasingly seen as a sign of poverty on the part of the bridegroom. Instead, young men became dependent on the generosity of the wealthy, men like Bera, to provide them with bridewealth, and thus the perpetuation of the family became related to retaining Bera's goodwill.

Finally, social repercussions were apparent in the changing relationships with royalty experienced by the northern and southern parts of the island. In pre-colonial times, areas in the south had enjoyed proximity to the central court, and both institutionalized and informal ties had developed between the kingship and certain segments of the population. Though by no means did all people had access to the king, influences from many directions were brought to bear on the king's decisions, and the court therefore did remain intimately tied to important strains of popular sentiment. The north, however, had been historically distant from kingship. Although all the kings had residences and/or marriage ties in the north, that region never became a focal point of royal interest. Thus in compari-son to the south, the northern areas of the island were much less involved in court affairs and decisions.

In their relations to kingship, people in the north generally showed two characteristics that distinguished them from people in the south. Those groups in the north that had preceded the arrival of the royal family on Ijwi and main-tained a strong corporate sentiment tended to remain aloof from kingship; they never fully participated in the social, political, or ritual aspects of royalty in nineteenth-century Ijwi.[56] On the other hand, a significant proportion of the population of the north appear to have settled there after the establishment of royalty in the south. These groups do not reflect a strong corporate tradition in political matters, especially in dealing with kingship; often their strongest links are with communities in the south rather than in their own locale.

By contrast, in the south, early corporate groups were more effectively inte-grated into the network of kingship on Ijwi through ritual and social ties. Never-theless, in dealing with kingship, many of these groups maintained their own strong corporate identity. On certain occasions this manifested itself in overt opposition to the king—a tradition which has continued in the south even into postcolonial times. In the north, opposition at the level of corporate identity was never expressed so openly, nor were enduring ties with kingship developed at the group level. Thus in the south, for example, many people would share in the prestige of the king's marriage to a member of their lineage; in the north, only the immediate family would identify with such a marriage.[57]

It is interesting that the nature of colonial resistance differed between north and south. The north was Bera's own region; the new colonial demands were most directly imposed there, and that part of the island seems to have experi-enced more effective political penetration in terms of work obligations for the local authorities. In the north, the people were more dependent on Bera's regime and less willing to act collectively to oppose administrative exactions. In the south, there were demands too, equally as heavy and with the added burden of two military occupations. The techniques of administration, in fact, may well have been more harsh, to judge from a comparison of oral reminiscences today. But in the south Bera was an outsider, facing more coherent group identity. Given this context, it is possible that the south was administered with less zealous surveillance by Bera. Certainly it was administered with less assurance: it appears that administrative demands were less effective there than in the north. Resistance was more marked in the south, therefore, both because a tradition of social cohesion there had made the population better able to oppose exactions and because people especially resented the impositions by northerners—by Bera and his appointed village *capitas*. In this area today, people frequently remark on the illegitimacy of these colonial officials; it is likely also that this feeling includes a sense of diminished status and resentment at having almost none of the influence or maneuvering capability that they had held previously through positions of influence, or at least through their presence, at the royal court. The older men on Ijwi today imply that group cohesion (of clans, subclans, or regional groups) diminished during the colonial period because these groups no longer functioned as instruments of corporate political influence. Thus the historical identification of people in the south with the network of royalty may well have made them more willing to resist Bera's demands (and colonial demands in general) as illegitimate exactions. Their social traditions, including their group cohesion and intensive interaction with areas outside the island, may have rendered their resistance more effective.[58]

The Colonial Legacy in the Postcolonial Period

Following a second exile of seventeen years, Ntambuka, Ndogosa's son and successor, returned to Ijwi just before independence in 1960.[59] Yet the territorial division of the island remained as it had been since Bera's death in 1936. Ndogosa's son retained only the southern part, and Bera's son, Rubenga, the northern.

There was, however, more continuity between the postcolonial regime and the colonial structure than in the territorial divisions alone. The chief in the north followed a pattern similar to that of his father. He was a "modernizer" who faithfully (and rather ostentatiously) transmitted hierarchical commands; he entertained his superiors lavishly when they visited him; he encouraged his population, in various ways, to work outside the island; and he implemented general commands with considerable zeal. (The attempts to implement the Zairean poli-cies of *salongo,* a new form of corvée labor, and of *regroupement de villages* dur-ing the 1970s provide examples of this.[60]) Before the separation of Ijwi from the Zone of Kalehe (formerly the "Territoire," the foundational administrative unit) in 1974, he was also a frequent visitor to the administrative headquarters of the Zone at Kalehe. He obeyed orders with alacrity; in December 1971, for example, when President Mobutu gave a speech in Bukavu, the provincial capital of Kivu, in which he implied that a forthcoming administrative reorganization would remove the bami from positions within the administrative hierarchy, Rubenga submitted his resignation. This he quietly withdrew several weeks later when it be-came clear that the proposed administrative reforms would be delayed. Ntambuka in the south did not even think of resigning. He was willing to accept a reduction of power (in fact, he had already ceded most administrative powers to his son). But he simply could not resign from the bwami—this was a status outside his administrative competence to change. Again, the comparison shows the willing flexibility of the northern segment of the royal family acting to protect their in-terest by conforming to administrative proposals from above.

Another parallel of Rubenga's rule with that of his father was in his ap-pointment of authorities. While capitas at the village level in general have tended to come more from the local population, Rubenga also assigned certain villages to members of the modern elite—to teachers and administrators. These men per-formed functions within the new system analogous to those formerly assumed by members of the royal family—sons and brothers (occasionally wives and sis-ters) of the king. In the south these functions were carried out by local residents of the area concerned or members of the king's family, as was done historically.

Yet the social dynamics in the postcolonial period changed the focus of power for people from Ijwi. Whereas before, the Westernized elite looked to Bera as a patron and colleague, the bitterest complaints about his son Rubenga often em-anated from the elite. In the south, however, where Ntambuka worked primarily through local capitas who were representatives from the areas where they lived, there was less overt conflict between the modern elite and the administration. Outlets for the elite were found off the island in their occupational, commercial, or social contexts, and with Ntambuka's interests focused primarily on the local level of village affairs, there was little confrontation. Ntambuka in the south, like his father before him, based his authority primarily on his internal position: it was, after all, the support of his followers (in the "tax revolt") that returned him from his first exile, and the results of a popular referendum that did so from his second period of exile.[61] His long absence from Ijwi and hence removal from the political game during the 1940s and 1950s made him less adept at and less willing to engage in regional politics than his counterpart in the north. He was less zealous in carrying out the demands of authorities above him and in following the short-term fluctuations and alterations in administrative policy and innuendo. But he was also perhaps more sensitive to, if not actually involved in, the local affairs of his domain.

This pattern of differences can be traced back for several decades, to the period following death and the recall of Ntambuka from his first period of exile. The colonial summary of the political situation on Ijwi for 1939 provides an example of such differences in its assessment of the two rulers, Rubenga in the north and Ntambuka in the south.

> On Ijwi the two chiefs [Rubenga, son of Bera, and Ntambuka, son of Ndogosa] rival each other in zeal. Rubenga shows a sincere desire to do well [by the administrative norms]. However, he is sometimes lazy [in his relations with the population] and still lacks experience. . . . Ntambuka is less eager to please before the Europeans. He finds himself in a difficult position. He has to provide simultaneously for the population which he found on his return [from exile] on the southern part of the island, and those who, having formerly left the island with members of the family of the former mwami Mihigo Ndogosa, have since returned with Ntambuka and now make demands on him. . . . He is totally uninterested in the colonial functions demanded of him.[62]

Thus the more aggressive style of the chief in the north led to greater demands on the population; but there was less overt opposition to the system as a whole at the village level in the north than in the south, where the tradition of resistance was encouraged by the intensity of colonial imposition and the greater sense of corporate action. The difference between the two areas in this regard was a constant feature of Ijwi politics since early colonial rule was imposed. Among the population of the south, a manifest capacity for conflict with higher administrative authorities surfaced at times in the postcolonial period. But such activity was more a question of groups acting to oppose administrative encroachment in local affairs (especially in the opposition to the abuse of tax collectors, police, or census takers) than outright rebellion to the court and its functions; in fact, the sense of continuing loyalty to the court by the population in the south included a clear concept of the limits to the court's power and of its responsibilities to protect the population from colonial exactions. And this difference, which has historically distinguished the two regions, is explained in part by how both the political authorities and people approached the question of political legitimacy. Ntambuka derived his power from local factors; Rubenga derived his from external sources. These two political bases made a significant difference in the types of power each chief employed and in their application of power.

The litany of imposed colonial burdens is frequently encountered in the African context. But the history of colonial rule is not simply the product of short-term political decisions of the moment. It is rather the product of the conjunction of the accumulated traditions of social and political behavior with newly imposed demands. The longer-term historical rhythms and social patterns are important because they affect, even if they do not determine, the manner of application and the nature of the impact of policy decisions. This chapter has explored the relations of such local traditions to the imposed colonial superstructure. Although society changed, often drastically, during the period of early colonial rule, such changes as occurred were often implicitly within the social structures and the character of political behavior of earlier periods. It is these internal mechanisms that colonial rule seized on and adapted—even distorted—in pursuing the goals of colonial administration.

In this case, alternative leadership was ready at the crucial moments of colonial history to step into new positions posing as traditional authorities; these leaders thus made it possible to preserve intact the mirage of indirect rule where the actual image had been shattered by the resistance of legitimate rulers to the surrender of their sovereignty. Faced with conflicting conceptions of political authority, Ndogosa and Ntambuka chose to conform to popular local notions of kingship, and their behavior then appeared uncooperative in the eyes of the Belgian administrators, who wanted the power of chiefs to be clothed with the authority of kings. Furthermore, as colonial administrative power increasingly affected the population, the people in turn responded to the changing political context in ways that were also derived from their earlier traditions of political behavior and perceptions. Not all initiative had left them; at the very least, they retained the potential of the "politics of inertia," and often where they retained the possibility of corporate action and the recognition of legitimacy in political behavior, they preserved an ability to affect policy directly. After all, they twice brought back Ntambuka. But the essential components of power had dramatically shifted from earlier times, and such change as was possible was increasingly circumscribed within the hardening colonial matrix.

This abrupt alteration in fundamental power relations created tensions within the structures of colonial rule that were never fully resolved. The most important manifestations of this contradiction between colonial power and its uses and local concepts of legitimacy with its limitations were products of colonial attempts to manipulate the concept of legitimacy in order to justify the imposition of purely administrative norms in government. The attempt to subordinate political issues to questions of bureaucratic effectiveness in this manner, to elevate technical efficiency above perceptions of social values, continued well into the postcolonial period, and many of the tensions that accompanied the introduction of these policies remain as an enduring legacy of colonial rule in Zaire today. For although kingship may no longer pose any political threat to the present political system, the system of values that underlay concepts of legitimacy of kingship remains largely intact. For the people of Ijwi still today, it is these norms that provide the basis for judging the legitimacy of political action.

PART 3

X

The Rwanda Arena

THE CLANS OF RWANDA

A Historical Hypothesis

1980

Colonial historiography assumed that African societies were static, permanent, and primordial. The presence of "clans" in African societies was taken to prove to the case, for clans were seen as atavistic features that represented the legacy of a political order that preceded kingship. But in Rwanda there was a paradox associated with the concept of descent-based clans, for these supposedly kin-based units each included members of different ethnic identities, themselves also supposed to be based on descent: how could such unchanging descent groups each include members of different descent groups? (The paradox went further, for each of the ethnic categories included members of all clans.) This essay proposes a way out of this conundrum. But it goes further and addresses a methodological approach as well, illustrating how questions that arise in one society can be illuminated by data (and conceptual approaches) drawn from neighboring societies—even those presumed to be inferior and less important. Drawing on this approach, the essay suggests that that clan identities in Rwanda were themselves the product of a historical process—even deep social institutions have histories—and that the process of this historical construction becomes most apparent in an area of relatively recent incorporation to the political culture of Rwandan kingship (such as western Rwanda). In making this argument, the analysis relies on a concept of clan seen not as a biological descent group (though that was the ideology of clan membership), but as a social identity constructed as part of a broader cultural dynamic, associated with the extension of royal power into this region. With clan identities seen as tools of incorporation into a new political domain, it became beneficial—even expected—that lineage groups would be included in one of the eighteen major clan groups associated with Rwandan political culture. In the process, however, individuals did not abandon earlier identities; these simply became subordinate identities—"subclans" or "major lineages," in the language of outside observers. Like ethnic identity, clan identity became one of several levels of individual identity, with each level of identity drawn on in its own particular contexts. Furthermore, tracing the process of restructuring clan identities to conform to royal culture also helps date such transformations in this area to roughly the late eighteenth century, a time of royal expansion to the west. In short, as it explores the complex local effects of Rwanda's expanding political culture, this essay raises fundamental questions on the permanence of Rwandan social institutions and suggests a methodological approach transcending Rwandan state ideologies.

> If anthropologists come to look upon kinship as a parameter which can be studied in isolation, they will always be led . . . to think of human society as composed of equilibrium systems structured according to ideal legal rules. . . . The study of social adaptations to changing circumstances is made impossible. . . . My protest is not directed against the study of kinship . . . but against attempts to isolate kinship behavior as a distinct category explainable by jural rules without reference to context.
>
> —Edmund R. Leach, *Rethinking Anthropology*

ONLY RECENTLY HAVE PRECOLONIAL African historical studies broken away from their fixation on dynastic histories and trade. In reassessing the dynastic traditions, historians of the African past have increasingly drawn on oral traditions from nonroyal sources. In particular, they have placed a great deal of emphasis on clan traditions, and the clan group has consequently served as an important building block in reconstructing the African past.[1] But in Rwandan studies this process has often been undertaken in a rather uncritical manner; in fact, historians may have been building on a foundation that is less enduring than they realize, for their new construct is often based on the assumption of "primordial" clan units reaching far back into the past, antedating the dynastic political units of which they came to form a part. It is usually argued that these enduring clan units could absorb individuals from other clans or experience geographical expansion through migration; but the basic structure of clan identities is seen as unchanging.

THIS CONCEPTION of the past has presented certain severe problems of explanation. On the one hand, Rwanda has been seen as a society divided into distinct, exclusive clan units. Membership in these units, it has been assumed, was determined by descent from a putative common ancestor, so that all members of a single clan were held to be ultimately related by descent, even if the exact genealogical ties had long since been forgotten. On the other hand, it was early realized that each of these clans contained members of different ethnic groups—Hutu, Tutsi, and Twa—groups that were also (theoretically) mutually exclusive and determined predominantly by descent.[2] How, then, could members of a single clan be considered also members of different ethnic groups? How, if clans were originally subsections of a single ethnic group, could they have come to contain large proportions of members of other ethnic groups?

For a while this paradox was explained essentially by recourse to another Rwandan characteristic: the "caste" nature of the society, and the role of clientship in integrating the castes (or ethnic categories).[3] By this reasoning it was the institution of clientship (notably *ubuhake* clientship) that united members of different ethnic groups. Therefore, by adopting the clan identity of a patron, clients could be adopted into a new clan while retaining their former ethnic identities. This explanation presupposed that a strong clientship system and a caste structure characterized by hierarchical ethnic identities existed before the multiethnic character of present clan structure emerged.

Recently, however, these assumptions have been questioned on several fronts. The work of Claudine Vidal has been important in initiating a general reassessment of the historical developments of the structures of clientship.[4] Subsequently, several other empirical studies in various regions of Rwanda have shown that the "caste" aspects of Rwandan society have been more flexible over time and more variable from region to region than had previously been thought. More important, the clientship structure (at least in the form it assumed under colonial rule) is now seen as a relatively recent phenomenon.[5]

In addition to the caste perception of Rwandan society, the rigid ethnic categories (Tutsi, Hutu, Twa), so characteristic of most portrayals of Rwandan society, have also been reconsidered. Recent studies have confirmed the flexibility of the categories remarked on in the earlier accounts; they have even questioned the duration of the hierarchical nature of the present ethnic categories in some contexts.[6] Thus important reassessments are underway on several grounds once thought clearly defined for Rwandan society.

This essay raises similar questions about the concept of clan as a historical category in the Rwandan context. It suggests that to explain the apparent contradictions in the empirical data we need to reexamine the concepts of clan status in Rwanda, and particularly to account for changes over time in these concepts. More precisely, it will argue that clan changes were not simply a result of individuals moving from one clan to another, or members of one clan dispersing over the land, but also a result of changes in the very conceptual categories from which clan identities derived.

But a word of caution is also called for. To question the concepts of clientship, ethnicity, or clanship in historical perspective is not immediately to imply that no ethnic differences, clientship forms, or clan categories formerly existed in Rwanda at all. The reassessments noted above demonstrate the variability in form and significance of these institutions, the qualitative differences in conception and meaning. They do not address the simplistic question of presence or absence of these structures. Rather, we are interested here in the condition under which these institutions assumed certain forms, and how these relationships came to be what they are: it is context, not institutions, that is the ultimate focus of our inquiry.

DESPITE RECONSIDERATIONS of clientship and caste as primordial to Rwandan society, the present clan structure in Rwanda has been assumed to be of great historical time depth. One reason for this assumption is the presumed lack of clan function within the present Rwandan system, or at least their lack of function as exogamous corporate groups.[7] By this reasoning the present clans must therefore necessarily be survivals of an earlier period. The universality of clan structures throughout the area—and throughout Africa—was taken as another indication of the enormous time depth that the clans were assumed to represent. Looked at in terms of geographical spread (not internal institutional structures), clans were thought to be very old institutions indeed; the historical problem of "clans" then became that of tracing their spread through migration, and their relations to political structures, especially to particular dynasties.

Despite this neat schema, there remained certain anomalies related to the internal structures of clan organization. One of these was that of accounting for the differences in clan systems, in particular differences between the Rwandan system and that of nearby areas. In Rwanda and Nkore, for example, clans tended to be much larger units, but at the same time much less numerous than clans in other Interlacustrine areas such as Bunyoro, Karagwe (Buhaya), and Burundi.[8] This was generally accounted for by the migration and consequent fragmentation of earlier units into secondary units.[9] The migration hypothesis both resolved the problem and reinforced the concept of a single origin of a given clan group.

Another problem for historians working with these assumptions in areas marked by multiethnic clans was that of determining the "origin" of a given clan within the ethnic categories and the consequent identification of each clan as (in the Rwanda case) either "Tutsi" or "Hutu." This problem, of course, was based on the descent model of clanship, according to which clans derived from an individual of one or another ethnic group; therefore the multiethnic character of clans could be explained only by postulating mechanisms of integration and absorption of members of other groups.[10] In all these models the prevailing concept of clans is that of discrete boxes into which individuals are born and between which they can sometimes be transferred. Most works accept the possibility of personal interchange, but despite such individual mobility the boxes, the clan categories, remained unchanged.

Rather than viewing clans primarily as descent groups, I propose to look at the larger structure of clan identities—the arrangement and size of the boxes—as products of certain perceptions of society. Clan identities then are seen not to result from the individual relationship alone (as implied by descent theory concepts of clan); clan structure itself results from the classification of groups within the larger structure of society, and therefore clan identity reflects the relationship of the individual to that larger structure. From this perspective, the clan structure within society is not seen as the sum of various local-level elements (such as lineage structures) writ large, but as the pattern formed by the conception of society itself. To account adequately for the anomalies of clan organization mentioned above, therefore, means to account for these changing historical perceptions of society. Over the long term, it is this changing pattern of perceptions that determines, as well as results from, clan identities. Clientship, caste, and clans were not randomly changing, to be sure, but neither were they static, enduring primordial features of Rwandan social structures.

THE MOST important recent discussion of this topic is found in Marcel d'Hertefelt's *Les clans du Rwanda ancien*. While providing valuable statistical data on clan membership in Rwanda, this work also summarizes material on contemporary clan concepts in Rwanda and the earlier works of others on this topic. From d'Hertefelt's analysis it is apparent that most students of Rwandan society view clans within a conceptual model of the lineage—a corporate group with membership ascribed by descent. Because individuals are ascribed their clan identities at birth, clans are also seen as descent groups, and clan concepts tend to become simply the extension of the lineage concept. The false understanding of clan thus derives from a transposition of the conceptual framework from a focus on individual recruitment to lineages (by birth) to an understanding of the clan as a descent group.

D'Hertefelt is quick to dispose of this concept in terms of its present significance. In addition to drawing on empirical studies to make this point, he also notes that the Rwandan term used for clan (*ubwoko*) is applicable only to the classification of items (a herd of cattle, or a species) but never for a corporate group—a concept expressed by *umuryango,* the Rwandan term for "lineage" (and other types of groups with internal corporate responsibilities).[11] The model by which clans are portrayed in most writings, then, differs from both the empirical reality and linguistic indications that the clan concept is essentially an identity, not a corporate group. It is the incompatibility of empirical realities with the conceptual framework used in most analyses that gives rise to the problems of clan analysis.

These problems are not seen as problems of conceptualization, however, because it is assumed that the descent model of clans is shared by both Rwandans and Western anthropologists. And so it is; at the level of the conception of clan structures, the lineage analogy is used by Rwandans as well as outsiders.[12] But the normative ideal differs from the behavioral norm, and it is the former that is applied to the historical characterization of clans. Thus, while d'Hertefelt skillfully demonstrates the fallacy in viewing present clans as exogamous descent groups, he appears to accept the opinion of others that clans were formerly exogamous.[13] He thus curiously reaffirms for an earlier period ("une époque plus ou moins lointaine") the conception of clan that he rejects in contemporary terms; such an analysis implies that the present is merely a deviation from a past that functioned according to the very model he so effectively brings into question.[14]

One way to avoid the tautological reasoning implicit in working through the same conceptual models we are trying to explain is to draw on data from historically related areas outside the immediate field of study and to compare these with the internal model.[15] In Rwanda this is particularly important because of the strength of the central court paradigms and the enormous influence that central court traditions have exerted on our past understanding of Rwanda.[16] Furthermore, historically significant geographical units may differ from those defined by present political boundaries; therefore, to limit our analytic perspectives to present-day geographic Rwanda is to limit ourselves to an artificial social unit in terms of the historical problem addressed. In other words, a historical analysis of Rwandan social categories need not be confined to a Rwandan context alone, but may best be extended to other areas with close historical ties to Rwanda.

ONE OF those areas is Ijwi Island, located in Lake Kivu, to the west of Rwanda. Although the clan system of Ijwi is different from that of Rwanda today, many of the people of Ijwi have experienced close ties in the past with areas east of the lake. Of the dozen or so clans now recognized on Ijwi (the number varies according to the definition of "clan" one chooses to employ, and therefore with context), several claim an origin east of the lake; today these areas are included as part of Rwanda, but at the time these people migrated to Ijwi in the late eighteenth century the areas immediately east of the lake were not yet fully incorporated into Rwanda (see map 8.1).

In what follows, I will consider two of these clans on Ijwi, the Mbiriri and the Ishaza. Members of both these clans claim to have come from east of the lake, from areas now part of Rwanda but formerly autonomous from central court control.[17] Their immigration to Ijwi took place before the present (Havu) dynasty arrived on the island from the south. Since then, despite continued ties across the lake and despite twenty years of Rwandan occupation of Ijwi at the end of the nineteenth century, these clans have remained largely autonomous of direct Rwandan political penetration.[18]

Members of the Mbiriri clan of Ijwi claim origin from an area called Bunyambiriri in Rwanda. They arrived in very small numbers, and all claim association with Singa clan status in Rwanda today.[19] Indeed, Bunyambiriri is today an area of predominantly Singa clan affiliation.[20] Why then do the Mbiriri on Ijwi not call themselves "Singa"? While it is common practice for people to be identified by their place of origin—though that is often selected from several options—it is not clear why this form of social identification should be favored over clan names from the area of origin, particularly in the early stages of Ijwi history and particularly when dealing with such small groups of immigrants who most likely shared a common clan identity. Nor is there any indication that these Ijwi clan

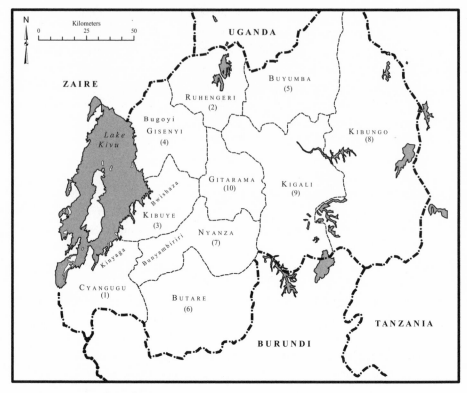

Map 8.1. Rwanda prefectures

names have since been altered: from the Ijwi data it is clear that these people arrived on Ijwi as "Banyambiriri," not as "Basinga." What is more, despite the importance of Rwandan immigration to Ijwi, no group on Ijwi—nor anywhere else west of Lake Kivu—retains a clan identity presently found among the eighteen largest clans of Rwanda (though many can cite these names, and even identify a "sister clan").

What emerges from these considerations is that present Rwandan clan identities were not important to these people on Ijwi two hundred years ago. It is therefore likely that the Mbiriri arrived on Ijwi before (or roughly contemporaneously with) the extension of current Rwandan clan appellations into areas such as Bunyambiriri. Consequently, current discrepancies between Ijwi and Rwanda can be explained by subsequent transformations on the mainland, changes that

Figure 8.1. Banyambiriri ties (Ijwi) to Abeshaza (Rwanda)

progressively increased the cultural differences between Ijwi and the areas east of the lake from the time of their first establishment on the island.

The areas just east of Lake Kivu are also prominent in Rwandan historical traditions. It is said that Gihanga, the first Nyiginya king of Rwanda, received the royal drums from a man named Jeni, whom the Rwandan traditions associate with Singa clan status.[21] But on Ijwi another clan, the Ishaza (Beshaza), claims a strong identity as composed of the common putative descendants from a man named Jeni, himself of royal status. Because in Rwanda Jeni is assumed to be a Singa, and the Ishaza on Ijwi are said to descend from Jeni, the implication is that the Ishaza on Ijwi are therefore to be associated with the Singa clan in Rwanda.

Although not presently recognized as an autonomous clan within Rwanda, the Ishaza on Ijwi claim the area of Bwishaza as their homeland. Located in the Kibuye Prefecture of Rwanda, Bwishaza is an area of strong Singa presence: among Hutu the Singa constitute over 21 percent of the population in Kibuye Prefecture, by far the largest component of the population there. This figure also represents the second-highest concentration of Hutu Singa in all prefectures of Rwanda, surpassed only by the figure of Kinyaga, just to the southwest of Kibuye (see map 8.1).[22] Taken together, these clan figures confirm the inference noted above that the Ishaza on Ijwi are to be identified with the Singa in Rwanda, through their common claims to association with the person of Jeni. Therefore, the Mbiriri would seem to be associated with the Ishaza on Ijwi through the Mbiriri claims to Singa affiliation and the Rwandan traditions that claim Singa status for Jeni (an ancestor of the Ishaza). Figure 8.1 illustrates this arrangement.

But juxtaposing data from Rwanda and from Ijwi in this fashion produces a paradox: the Ishaza on Ijwi explicitly and universally deny Singa status, and people from all clans on Ijwi distinguish sharply between Mbiriri and Ishaza.[23] Furthermore, the Ishaza have a joking relationship with the Mbiriri that differentiates them and maintains the differences between them.[24] Moreover, on Ijwi Jeni does not appear in the historical affiliations of the Mbiriri.

The most plausible argument to explain this series of traditions is that Jeni, the putative ancestor of the Ishaza, was a member of a localized group that only later became absorbed within the more all-inclusive Singa identity to conform to Rwandan categories of social identity. This absorption apparently occurred after the Ishaza and Mbiriri emigrations from Rwanda in the late eighteenth century, and thus corresponds with the period when Rwandan cultural norms spread through the area: it is primarily in the Rwandan traditions associated with the central court milieu that the descendants of Jeni are considered Singa.

The apparent contradictions in these data then raise the questions of why, despite these apparent indications of common origins, the Mbiriri and Ishaza on Ijwi claim different status from each other and why neither calls itself Singa. This discrepancy between the Ijwi data, which are clear and consistent, and the Rwandan claims can be explained by looking at the assertions of Rwandan associations as separate elements within an evolving process of clan identity formation. While the Mbiriri on Ijwi identify specifically as Singa in Rwanda, the Ishaza deny they are Singa; but they, in turn, admit to being descendants of Jeni, a figure apparently since absorbed into the Singa clan category in Rwandan conceptions. From a historical perspective, therefore, the present differences between the Mbiriri and Ishaza traditions on Ijwi attest to localized identities of an earlier period in the area directly east of Lake Kivu—what is today western Rwanda. Consequently, in figure 8.1 the vertical ties represent the primary linkages in historical terms, while the tie between Jeni and the Singa in Rwanda (a tie-in paralleling but contradicting the Ishaza-Mbiriri interrelation on Ijwi) can be seen as a later phenomenon. Thus the separate identities of these two clans on Ijwi apparently preserve the earlier differentiation of the two groups east of the lake, while the Rwandan situation represents their more recent amalgamation as Singa.

In this case, the effect of the joking relationship between the Mbiriri and Ishaza on Ijwi has been to resist any accommodation of the two groups on Ijwi such as that which occurred in Rwanda and by which Jeni's group has been associated with the Singa. By identifying the Mbiriri as different from the Ishaza, this relationship between the two clans on Ijwi serves to maintain social distinctions that may well have existed east of the lake in the late nineteenth century and before. It is also significant that in Rwanda the link noted between Jeni and Singa derives from a source external to the clans in question: it appears only in the Nyiginya traditions of the royal court. It is therefore not internal data, deriving from the participants directly involved, but a statement of royal perceptions.

We are dependent exclusively on the Nyiginya court interpretations for these social classifications, and these interpretations most likely refer to a time only after court influence had penetrated the area and after the diffusion of the central court classifications into western Rwanda.

Though no evidence on this point is presently available from Bwishaza itself, data from neighboring Kinyaga provide some confirmation that the diffusion of the Singa identity within this area is a more recent phenomenon—that the area was earlier characterized by smaller localized group identities. Located in the extreme southwest of present Rwanda, Kinyaga is an area where Rwandan central court political norms and perceptions penetrated only relatively recently; before the mid- or late nineteenth century, Rwandan penetration affected only a tiny proportion of the population, mostly immigrants who had come from outside Kinyaga during the previous two generations.[25] Perhaps as a consequence of this recent political penetration and the social transformations that went with it, the pattern of social identities in Kinyaga today differs from that in other areas of Rwanda. Whereas in central Rwanda there are essentially two levels of classificatory identities (ubwoko and umuryango, or "clan" and "lineage"), for certain groups in Kinyaga there are three such levels. It is interesting that both Mbiriri and Ishaza identities are represented as intermediary identities in Kinyaga and both are considered to be subgroups of the Singa clan. This too reflects the conjunction of these two identities within a larger Singa classificatory identity remarked on above.

Taken alone, the Kinyaga data simply show an association of these two groups with Singa identity. It remains possible that the Ishaza and Mbiriri identities are subcategories formed by the segmentation of an earlier clan identity into subgroups, rather than formerly autonomous identities now combined within a Singa "supra-clan" concept. But it seems more likely that such intermediate identities in Kinyaga resulted from the diffusion of the larger Singa classificatory identity and the subsequent incorporation of localized identities within this larger category. For in most other areas, especially those long a part of the Rwandan culture zone, clans have not segmented into subgroups in this fashion, and on Ijwi a common Singa identity is emphatically denied—rather than sublimated—despite the fact that there is no stigma attached to such identity. Therefore, rather than breaking down clan groups, centralized state penetration in the Rwandan case appears to have encouraged, maintained, and perhaps extended broader identities. Such a process would help explain the presence of both Tutsi and Hutu within a single clan (although other factors probably also played a part in this phenomenon).[26] Likewise, it would explain the separate identities on Ijwi of two clans joined in the Rwandan context, since what appears as an anomaly in the Rwandan data may well relate to a period prior to the Singa expansion (or consolidation) into the far reaches of the west. Indeed, there may still be areas in the west of Rwanda (such as the lacustrine peninsulas) where Rwandan norms have not fully penetrated and where people still identify as Ishaza or as members of other small clans.

The distribution of clan identities in Rwanda lends some support to this view. If Rwandan state norms helped consolidate clan identities, it would be expected that a higher proportion of members of the eighteen principal Rwandan classificatory units would be found in those areas of longest and most intensive assimilation to Rwandan cultural norms. According to d'Hertefelt's figures, this is precisely the case.[27] Despite the difficulties of defining and identifying appropriate clan units,[28] d'Hertefelt's data classify the population by prefecture in terms of these eighteen principal units, with a residual category to include minute representations of various other identities claimed.[29] Since the total number of individuals associated with "other" clans in the sample surpasses forty-three hundred, and since the number of any given segment includes less than one hundred individuals (otherwise we assume it would have been included in the tabulation under its own separate clan heading), we can estimate that there are well over fifty such groups (since some will probably be very small indeed). By the same reasoning, we can estimate that there are at least ten such different groups for Kibuye Prefecture alone.

The distribution of individuals excluded from the eighteen named clans on d'Hertefelt's list conforms exactly to the hypothesis discussed above: in the areas of most recent and least intensive Rwandan central court penetration, these very small clans claim a much higher proportion of the population than is true for the areas of the country with the greatest assimilation to court norms. In percentage terms, clan membership in this category (outside the principal eighteen named clans) for the four western- and northwesternmost prefectures averages more than thirteen times as much as for the four central and east-central prefectures where Rwandan cultural norms were most in evidence (see table 8.1).[30] Consequently, there is clearly a process at work by which the population in such areas of strong central court influence is progressively consolidated into these eighteen basic social categories. Rather than resulting from the fragmentation of large clan units, therefore, these smaller units seem to be precursors to such formations. At the very least, it can be concluded that the presence of Rwandan

Table 8.1
Hutu membership in Rwandan clans other than the largest eighteen (1960)

Prefecture	Sample population	"Others" in sample	Percentage
1. Cyangugu	5,823	794	13.64
2. Ruhengeri	11,214	1,071	9.55
3. Kibuye	5,022	420	8.36
4. Gisenyi	7,324	571	7.80
5. Byumba	7,600	243	3.20
6. Butare	11,460	204	1.78
7. Nyanza	7,469	84	1.12
8. Kibungo	6,260	56	0.89
9. Kigali	7,888	42	0.53
10. Gitarama	7,314	32	0.44

Averages: For Cyangugu, Ruhengeri, Kibuye, Gisenyi, 9.72 %; for Nyanza, Kibungo, Kigali, Gitarama, 0.74 %. The numbers for the prefectures correspond to their location on map 8.1.

Source: D'Hertefelt, *Les clans*, table II.

state forms inhibited the fragmentation process that occurred in areas outside strong state influence. Nor do the largest clans concentrate in those areas of greatest representation of smaller groups ("others"), a correlation that might confirm the fragmentation hypothesis. Three of the oldest clans of Rwanda (to judge from their ritual status as "owners of the soil") are included among the four largest clans, but only one is concentrated in the west and north (the areas of greatest number of small units); another is concentrated in the more assimilated areas, and the third is more evenly spread throughout the country.[31]

The argument advanced here, therefore, suggests that in relatively recent times the Singa clan category has absorbed certain groups that were previously autonomous. This process of amalgamating localized identities within the wider "supra-clan" identities, those associated with the Rwandan political context, may have been relatively common in the area.[32]

One such instance from Rwanda is the elusive identity of the Renge, a group that is mentioned in the Rwandan traditions as a former dynastic group associated with the Singa clan, or as simply an early population of Rwanda.[33] This is sometimes seen as a contradiction: that the Renge identity signifies either a subgroup of a larger unit or a general name for an earlier population. Either one or the other—but not both—must be true, according to this logic.[34]

But in historical perspective, both identities may have existed at different times. It is quite possible that "Renge" was a general term applied to formerly autonomous populations that were later incorporated within a system of state (in this case Rwandan central court) identities. This is exactly the way in which the term (in a slightly different form—"Binyalenge," not "Barenge") is used on Ijwi; moreover, in areas both northeast and southwest of Lake Kivu the Renge are seen as an autonomous clan, sometimes as the clan associated with royal status.[35] This suggests that the Renge identity in western Rwanda has become submerged within the Singa supra-clan identity with earlier Renge autonomy represented only by their claim to former royal status.

The approach suggested here also relates to the discussion on the ethnic origin of the Renge. The most complete text available on the subject notes that the Renge were neither Tutsi nor Hutu.[36] Such an apparent contradiction can be explained if it is assumed that the Renge were at one time autonomous from the Singa (and from all clan identities associated with the Rwandan royal court paradigms). Thus they were outside the Hutu-Tutsi dichotomy associated with these clan identities; the fact that they were not Singa (or some other Rwandan clan identity) meant in itself that they were neither Tutsi nor Hutu, but simply Renge.

The perspective suggested above helps explain one other apparent paradox. Alexis Kagame asserts that all Rwandan clans are Tutsi in origin, a claim discussed at length by d'Hertefelt.[37] Within the conceptual framework proposed here, however, Kagame's claim assumes a new significance. Some Rwandan clan identities have expanded with the extension of Rwandan culture norms associated with the royal court. If this is true of all the *-ooko* identity classifications, then they can be said to form a conceptual framework associated with Tutsi (read "dynastic") paradigms in Rwanda. Therefore, the present clan structures can be said to emanate from this Tutsi context, even though such a Tutsi origin would obviously not apply to the individual members within the clans, as d'Hertefelt has demonstrated. It is in this sense (that of "individual" origins) that d'Hertefelt interprets Kagame's statement. But in quite another sense, by focusing on perceptions and identities associated with the royal court (Kagame's "clan purement politique"), the statement can be seen to carry considerable weight, at least for western Rwanda.[38]

This perspective would also lend some support to the authors who seek to explain the multiclass character of Rwandan clans by recourse to the extension of Tutsi (or at least hierarchical) norms, in this case associated with various types of land and cattle clientship.[39] If the present clan structures are a result of the extension of central court influence (and power), indeed, if the extension (or reinforcement) of ethnic identities has occurred in part from the extension of central court power, then the multiethnic character of clans is also a product of this new context.[40] There remains, however, a significant difference: the hypothesis proposed here does not depend on ubuhake client ties, nor directly on client ties between Tutsi and Hutu—a constant preoccupation of the earlier writers.[41] Instead, it is seen as linking a political context identified with Rwanda's central court to people formerly outside the system. Rather than concentrating on individual mechanisms (which link a Hutu client to a Tutsi patron, or which link children from a Hutu-Tutsi union to the clan of one parent and the ethnic group of the other), we need to explore the structural changes and changes in conceptualizations at the levels of social classifications.

This difference in the personal element is crucial to the perspective proposed here. From the point of view of the individual involved, there is little difference between this perspective and the mechanisms so clearly delimited by d'Hertefelt, for it was, after all, individuals who adopted new identities. But looked at from the point of view of clan structures, the two perspectives have significant differences. Former identities became submerged—but not abandoned—in the new Rwandan identity paradigms explored above. These classifications became predominant not by the movement and spread of individuals but by alterations in the essential conception of clan structures. It was not always necessary that such transformations result from contact with individual clan members; they could result instead from contact with a new political or social context. It is this larger context—with its various levels of historical change—that needs to be explored in our efforts to gain that fuller understanding of social change implicit in the concept of "histoire globale."

In short, a different set of social identities existed in the western areas of what is now Rwanda before the extension of royal power into these regions. Therefore, the current eighteen "official" clans are not primordial to Rwandan society (at least not as they exist today). Instead, their current composition and diffusion result from the expanding reach of the Nyiginya court: Rwandan identity meant belonging to one of these "official" clans. The current clan configuration in this area, in short, has a history. Furthermore, because it is tied to royal expansion, the present set of clan structures can be dated to the mid- or late eighteenth century. And that, in turn, can be used to date the movement of certain groups into neighboring areas, outside the reach of Rwandan court power—areas where clan identities do not replicate Rwandan appellations. How this process of cultural hegemonic expansion took place will be the focus of the next chapter.

BUNYABUNGO

The Western Frontier in Rwanda, ca. 1750–1850

1986

Social hierarchy is manifested in many ways: politically, economically, and culturally. And asserting superiority occurs in many forms, including literary narratives, where assumptions of social superiority can be expressed in entertaining ways, even as the narrative carries a powerful didactic lesson. This chapter draws on one of the many literary tropes of Rwandan court culture directed toward people not of Rwandan culture (and considered distinctly less worthy by Rwandan elite culture). But such blatant representations are sometimes more a reflection of the speaker than of the object: they illustrate the speaker's own sense of superiority by mocking the differences of others from them—"they don't do these things as [well as] we do." Moreover, such alterity (attributing lesser status to "others") also becomes an important tool of internal group cohesion: to belong to a group, one has to accept the denigration of an agreed target group—the "other." This chapter illustrates this process at work in Rwanda at a time of the emergence of strong elitist tendencies in Rwanda, associated with the consolidation of a distinct court culture where etiquette, dress, dance forms, style, values—and expressed superiority—all became critical to one's acceptance. Distinguishing oneself from others—and distinguishing between royal cultures and commoner culture—became imperative to one's social advancement. Far from

*showing precolonial Rwanda as a land of egalitarian harmony, these sources
illustrate the deeply hierarchical nature of Rwandan court culture. However,
there was an irony here, since the western frontier zones that were the object
of court disdain were also in fact areas of enormous creativity and productivity: the differences were worthy of disdain only in the eye of the beholder.*

T HE CONCEPT OF THE FRONTIER is paradoxical: distinct from the metropolitan society, a frontier society can only be defined and perceived in
relation to the cultural heartland of which it is an extension. This relationship
between frontier and metropole is critical, differentiating the frontier from other
types of "peripheral" areas, such as the "bush" or the "outback." From the perspective of the metropole, the bush and the outback are seen negatively, as truly
peripheral areas; the frontier, on the other hand, is usually seen positively, as geographically peripheral but not unimportant. Bush and outback are not seen as
areas of external expansion for the metropole, while the frontier often is; nor are
they seen as crucial to the cultural identity of the heartland, while the frontier
often is.

But while identified by reference to the metropole, the frontier is a zone where
the cultural values of the metropole are very much at issue. By providing alternatives to metropolitan culture—in the form of different cultural values or even
a perceived lack of culture—the presence of the frontier may well threaten the
harmony and hegemony of metropolitan values. Consequently, the frontier zone
is a region on which the essential values of the metropolitan society are projected with great intensity, creating an identity for the frontier in relation to the
metropole that reinforces or justifies the metropole's claims to the frontier. Yet
these projected values need only focus on the core ties to the frontier, but not
replicate those of the core area itself. The values used to shape this identity are
therefore selective values, determined by conditions within the metropole and
not by the realities of the frontier. They are therefore often idealized values that
may be declining or even absent in the cultural heartland. By thus reinforcing
the ideological underpinnings seen as constant and enduring within the heartland, the created identity link between frontier and metropole may obscure the
tensions of a society in rapid change.

The idealization of the western American frontier, for example, became important approximately with the closing of the frontier and the late-nineteenth-
century transformation of the eastern cities. In the "land of the free" on the

western frontier, it was argued, individual initiative was rewarded with wealth and status, even while in fact the lives of those on the frontier were often marked by physical hardship and violence. But the myth of the West grew in the East; in ideological terms, the characterization of "freedom" on the western frontier came to be reflected back onto the metropolitan areas, and eventually applied to the polity as a whole. In this case, therefore, the metropolitan areas adopted the perceived values of the frontier zone as their own, even though these may in fact have been as far removed from the reality of life in the metropole as they were from that of the frontier.

These are the images of the frontiersmen, who are seen as an extension of the metropole into the frontier zone. But there is also another aspect of the frontier, represented most directly by its indigenous population. For societies expanding through conquest, the concept of the frontier also lends itself to ideologies that justify state expansion and rationalize the incorporation of new groups. The most common form of this ideological construction is found in the opposition between the metropolitan values and the cultural stereotypes of those to whom the frontier zone is their homeland. Juxtaposing two cultural ideals in a polarized form invariably emphasizes the humanity of the metropolitan culture in opposition to the inhumanity—or anarchic culture—of the "barbarians." As illustrated below, the choice may be posed in stark terms: culture or chaos. Such an attitude often justifies the inhumane treatment of the "barbarians" by the representatives of "civilized" society—by incorporation, elimination, or extirpation. The conceptual paradigm of the frontier, then, is as much a product of the perceptions of other cultures (generated by political conditions within the metropole) as it is a product of the ethnographic realities on the ground.

The history of the Central African kingdom of Rwanda provides an example of the association between the growth of the frontier concept, the development of metropolitan ideology, and the westward expansion of Rwandan social and political structures. It illustrates how certain values, initially strongly anchored in the military expeditions to the west (conquest and hierarchy), came to be incorporated as essential elements of the political ideology of the Rwandan central court, and applied even within (perhaps most strongly within) the central regions. Historical traditions provide abundant evidence of the strength of the oppositions between Rwandan culture and non-Rwandan culture: regardless of their origins, emigrants to the west from the Rwandan culture area were seen (both by the central court and by the original inhabitants of the region) as "Rwandan" relative to those who lived in the western highlands. Furthermore,

the culture of the inhabitants of these regions is portrayed in the Rwandan literature in monolithic terms, as a single atavistic culture associated with the stereotypes applied today to peoples living farther west still, west of Lake Kivu.

To the Rwandans, the inhabitants of these areas were collectively known as
"Banyabungo" (or "Bashi"), though in fact several distinct ethnic groups were
represented in these lands. Therefore, although today applied to areas west of Lake
Kivu, the term "Bunyabungo" (the locative form of the personal plural nominal
"Banyabungo") can be taken as historically representative of non-Rwandan societies of the western areas in general, including the regions now of western Rwanda
but west of the Nile-Congo divide; even today the people of central Rwanda often
refer to the inhabitants of western Rwanda as "Banyabungo." Therefore, rather
than referring to a precise cultural entity, the term is used in the classificatory
sense of a relative category, in opposition to the concept of "Rwandan-ness."
And it is almost invariably used in a derogatory manner, to mean "non-cultured"
as well as "non-Rwandan"—in the political lexicon, the two were synonyms. The
term "Bunyabungo" therefore encodes the basic opposition inherent in the Rwandan conception of the western frontier.

But the significance of these concepts was not limited to the frontier zone.
Most analyses of the Rwandan state emphasize the expansion of state institutions, stressing the impact of Rwandan structures on conquered areas. Less attention has been given to the transformations that occurred within the Rwandan heartland; it is assumed that, except for changes in scale, central Rwandan
institutions remained largely unaltered as a result of the western frontier experience. In fact, the expansion of the western frontier had significant repercussions
on the internal development of Rwandan political culture: the hierarchical administrative forms and the cultural distancing so apparent on the western frontier appear to have developed roughly at the same time in central Rwanda, as the
values associated with the Rwandan expansion became more deeply embedded
within Rwandan central court institutions in metropolitan areas. In this way the
western frontier in Rwanda had a profound impact on the internal development
of Rwanda, not only through expansion itself but in terms of wider political and
cultural changes, as the inclusion of large numbers of culturally distinct populations provided a model for social interaction throughout the areas where Rwandan state structures were found. These changes therefore were a product not of
a unidirectional cause-effect relationship (following the political hierarchy),
but of mutual reinforcement between center and periphery—with effects in
both domains.

In pursuing these themes, the discussion will first focus on the westward expansion of the Rwandan state, based on published historical traditions. Doing so will provide the political context within which to examine the development of Rwandan cultural stereotypes applied to the west. The second section illustrates the nature of the cultural stereotypes by drawing on examples from Rwandan Court literature. I will argue that the use of non-Rwandan cultural traits in ways that portray non-Rwandans as "acultural" beings reinforces a particular concept of Rwandan-ness. Thus the frontier becomes not simply a geographical place, but also a conceptual field for a set of attitudes affecting identity and culture— but attitudes generated in a particular political context. The third section examines the types of interaction that occurred across the cultural divide delineated in the literary productions of the court. The same people who (in some social contexts) stress the barbarous nature of their western neighbors also trade with them, marry with them, and move to settle among them. These forms of interaction bring into question the set of conceptual oppositions portrayed in the court literature and emphasize the contingent nature of such characterizations. The significance of the discursive (and class) contexts in generating these stereotypes reinforces the conclusion that such portrayals speak more to the nature and conditions of the central areas that generated them than they do to the nature of the people they purportedly described.

THE STATE of Rwanda emerged in its earliest forms near Lake Mohazi, on the open savannah areas between Lake Victoria and Lake Kivu. This was pastoral country par excellence, and the various states that gradually took shape there were originally built on the alliance of pastoralist groups. Rwanda was, in the beginning, one state among many in this region, and through several centuries of turbulent political history, the nucleus of this state was gradually displaced westward until it was located in the area near the Nile-Congo divide—a forested highland area, geographically quite different from its original homeland in the east. Although there had been some contact between the Rwandan Court and the areas farther west (even as far as Lake Kivu) in earlier periods, it was not until the reign of Cyilima Rujugira in the mid-eighteenth century that there appears to have been a permanent Rwandan presence in the area between the divide and Lake Kivu.[1]

As the Rwandan state grew and as its center gradually shifted westward, its state structures also came to encompass a greater variety of ethnic groups, distinguished as much by their relative social positions and access to power in the

Rwandan state as by cultural or geographical factors. In later years, as the state structures took stronger form, these multiple ethnicities were categorized essentially in bipolar terms, as "Tutsi" and "Hutu" (though there were important differences within each group, and individual family status could sometimes shift, gradually, from one category to another). The Tutsi shared essentially pastoralist cultural values, and virtually all positions of political authority within the Rwandan state were held by Tutsi. The Hutu were, in general, associated with agriculturalist values (though many Hutu owned cattle as well); as the state structures expanded and rigidified, Hutu were increasingly excluded from positions of effective power.[2]

During the reign of Rujugira, Rwanda faced the combined military threat of three of its most powerful competitors in the region, Burundi to the south, Gisaka to the east, and Ndorwa to the northeast.[3] Eventually, Rwanda was able to prevail over its rivals, although in various forms the struggle with Ndorwa and Gisaka was to extend over several reigns and even into the period of colonial rule. But the history of these wars is not in itself important to this discussion. What is important are the internal administrative reorganization, the new conception of the state, and the inclusion of different cultures within the state that resulted, for the changes brought about by these wars had significant repercussions on Rwanda's later expansion to the west.[4]

Two of these alterations proved particularly important: in military reorganization, and in internal administrative restructuring. More armies were formed during the reign of Rujugira than under all the kings before or (with one exception) since: together, the armies formed by Rujugira represent about one-third of all the armies for which historical records remain today.[5] Associated with this growth in army formations was a new policy of posting armies permanently to certain areas, thus making these units suitable for occupying a conquered area as well as for raiding. At the same time, this policy provided a more enduring continuity to the *umuheto* group, the corporate groups performing military/administrative functions within the Rwandan state structures.[6] Although drawn from geographically diverse areas—another policy that became increasingly prevalent under Rujugira—army members (assigned by the court) joined together for several years of common service in areas outside their home regions; the lack of geographical concentration to recruitment enhanced the armies' common focus on the court.[7] In addition, the very expansion of the army organizations provided positions of leadership and recognition for the court to bestow upon its favorites. In a period of increasing status consciousness, control over the distribution of prestige in this manner was one of the most valuable resources in the hands of the court.

Originally, this change in policy toward permanent army postings was dictated by military necessity, but over time other functions served by the new policy became more important. Chief among these was socialization to the Rwandan state norms and the development of embryo administrative structures channeling family prestations to the court—and thus also providing a means of accumulating material goods in the hands of the court elite. As the educational and administrative functions of these hereditary "social armies" became increasingly important from the time of Rujugira, the armies themselves became the principal mechanism for incorporating new populations into the administrative structure of the state. Formerly, booty seized during raids was sent to the court, while individual families were required to send provisions to their members in the army; but over time these differences between booty seized from raids and resources accumulated from individual army members blurred. Increasingly (and especially from the mid-nineteenth century) the armies included some lineage groups that supplied prestations on a regular basis, regardless of the state of military mobilization, and thus these transfers gradually took on more of the characteristics of tribute. In addition to provisions for warriors, these included prestige goods—bracelets, mats, artifacts—that were sent to the court; over time, the army leader (appointed by the court) became increasingly an administrative official responsible for prestations rather than a military leader renowned for the spoils of war delivered to the court. Administrative prestations from within the umuheto group therefore came to replace the earlier spoils of military raiding outside the territorial domain of Rwanda, and the administrative functions of these umuheto groups came to predominate over the military functions.

At the same time, army organization itself became more hierarchical as army membership came to include virtually all social groups. It is from the time of Rujugira, for example, that the first Hutu sections of armies are noted in the sources.[8] Not all were warriors, however; many (and this applied especially to Hutu groups) were simply associated with army administrative structures and thus required to provide prestations. Thus the army played a paradoxical role: it served as a means of assimilation to Rwandan forms for some, but it also served to keep others from full assimilation (by the hierarchical structures of its internal organization), and these groups continued to provide prestations on a permanent basis. Such forms of army organization created and reinforced social distance from inhabitants of new areas even while spreading Rwandan norms to

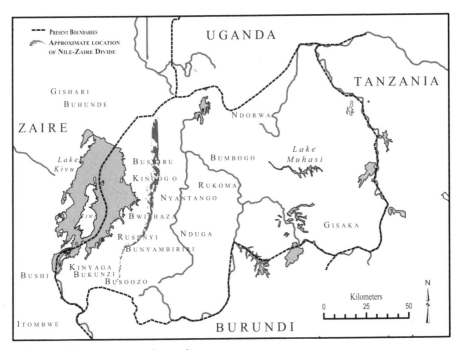

Map 9.1. Western regions of Rwanda

these areas. In this way, the army came to serve as an ideal administrative structure for the expansion of the Rwandan state, combining military, administrative, and educative functions, while being closely controlled, politically and ideologically, by the royal court. With this consolidation of power, the state was no longer dependent on alliances with various groups, each of which drew its political strength from resources essentially outside the control of the central court. Instead, the court became the dominant political actor, having a preponderant role in the distribution of political resources among the various factions in the country. This concentration of power meant that the court was increasingly able to demand services and goods from the various social groups of the country, and to punish those that did not comply with these demands. Equally important, it was able to withhold rewards from those (often Hutu) whom it defined as outside the immediate political system and whose former autonomy had previously made it possible for them to accumulate goods independently of their status at the central court. What was important in this process was the relationship that emerged between military expansion and administrative consolidation: through such internal reorganization, the augmentation of power at the center resulted from, as well as facilitated, Rwandan expansion to the west.

Growing Rwandan military capacity and the increasingly exclusive character of the central political arena also had important repercussions in the frontier areas that are today western Rwanda. In the wake of expanding Rwandan hegemony in the east, those who fled Ndorwa and Gisaka to search for refuge from Rwandan state power often moved west, into (and beyond) the highland areas of the Nile-Congo divide. Despite occasional military forays, these areas had, for the most part, remained until then outside of Rwandan control. The arrival of refugees with cultural characteristics similar to those of the Rwandan central court changed this relationship. Since most refugees were apparently from the military war zones of Ndorwa and Gisaka, they were not, strictly speaking, Rwandans. But they nonetheless shared attributes that made them appear Rwandan to the peoples of the highland areas. Their very presence may have attracted more direct Rwandan military thrusts into the area; often, indeed, they did develop later ties to the central court of Rwanda, serving as the vanguard in establishing Rwandan administrative structures in the area. Consequently, in retrospect, they were often seen as Rwandan from the beginning, politically as well as culturally. In addition, within the context of Rwandan westward expansion, these refugees from central court power were often retroactively claimed as Rwandan colonizers by the central court, especially where they later came to serve as the nucleus for the growth of new army organizations.[9]

The expansion of this western frontier is difficult to trace with precision because the Tutsi "colonists" (originally "refugees") did not move into the area in any regular pattern. Instead, their slow penetration over several generations created a loose series of intersecting ties that eventually became incorporated within the political network of the central court. But these ties did not form a continuous web; many areas remained independent of this network, and in some cases Tutsi refugees continued to move farther west still, to Itombwe and Gishari in the mountainous highlands west of Lake Kivu.[10] In other cases, small polities along the Nile-Congo divide remained autonomous of the central court until well into the period of colonial rule.[11]

The general pattern of the penetration of central court norms into the western areas can be followed through the court traditions relating to army expeditions (sometimes only raids) and through the settlement patterns of Tutsi families. Tutsi movements were first directed west from Nyantango, near the bend in the Nyabarongo River and the ritual centers of the kingdom at Rukoma and

Bumbogo. From Nyantango, the armies pushed westward through the lower areas across the divide toward Lake Kivu, reaching the lake in the area of Bwishaza and Rusenyi, in present Kibuye Prefecture.[12] Initial Rwandan presence in these areas may date to long before Rujugira's time,[13] but it seems clear that the patterns of continuous settlement and continuous claims of the court in these areas date only from the reign of Rujugira. Traditions from the areas themselves (which differ from central court claims) and army locations also indicate the recent of this expansion of central court power.[14] Subsequent military expeditions were made south to Kinyaga (the provinces of Impara and Biru) and north to Bugoyi.[15]

The history of the Abagwabiro lineage illustrates the gradual nature of Tutsi penetration into the western areas. Originally from Ndorwa, this family moved first to the area of Bunyambiriri along the Nile-Congo divide, just west and southwest of the Rwandan heartland in Nduga, probably during the reign of Rujugira. From there, they moved north into what is today Gisenyi Prefecture (the area of Bugoyi) in northwestern Rwanda.[16] This pattern of movement suggests that here was a family seeking autonomy from the Rwandan central court, rather than serving as its agent (as the court sources imply). Furthermore, in most sources, Macumu, the lineage head, is described as Hutu (i.e., not a direct participant in central court politics), while central court traditions describe him as Tutsi (or one of their own). But whatever their early status, in later generations the Abagwabiro were to forge ties to the central court. Perhaps their tenuous position as eastern refugees without a foothold in local political networks, in an area of strong interaction with areas farther west, made them willing as well as likely candidates for this role. Their orientation toward Rwandan cultural values provided a basis for later claims by the Rwandan court that they had always been "official representatives" in the area.

Similar patterns of incorporation are found in Kinyaga, in the extreme southwest of the country, where a significant proportion of the present population claims to have arrived from farther east, especially from Ndorwa and Gisaka, during the reign of Rujugira or his successor Ndabarasa.[17] Although the precise war leading to their exodus is not cited in these traditions, the process conforms to that above, and the timing of these wars would confirm the general agreement noted in the sources that many groups arrived during, or just after, Rujugira's reign. Subsequently, many of these immigrants were instrumental in forging ties between this remote region (Kinyaga) and the central court political arena.

The very intensity of the military struggles to the east, with Gisaka and Ndorwa, has obscured the historical record of Rwanda's military ties with the west. But even the murkiness of this record has its lesson to convey: military records, army postings, the nature of later central court alliances with "Tutsi" refugees (from the defeated states),[18] and even the nature of the terrain and the structure of earlier political groups—all these lead to a common conclusion that this area was not one where a clear military front was in evidence, as had occurred in wars to the east. This area became part of Rwanda not by a once-for-all campaign and the subsequent redrawing of political boundaries. Conquest in the west occurred piecemeal, gradually. Rwandan penetration here was discontinuous, both geographically and temporally. This was an area of the slow absorption of varying degrees of Rwandan (i.e., central court) penetration, often an area of refuge for those seeking autonomy from central court power but carrying with them Rwandan norms of language, dress, and consumption. Most of all, this Rwandan character was conveyed in a quality of social behavior: in the turn of a phrase, in the type of poetry recited over the evening fire, in the nature and mechanism of social alliance (cattle contracts often, rather than blood pacts or marriage ties), perhaps also in religious concepts. The spread of central court power was especially evident in the aloof social bearing of the elite, a bearing bred in court etiquette, nurtured in army training, and matured in contacts with the west.

Thus, while we lack the military details, the cultural implications of this move west are clear. And they were as important to the central court arena as to the incorporated western areas themselves, for complementing the growth of administrative structures was the growth of increasingly rigid categories of social classification; in fact, the concepts of social distancing appear to have intensified with the expansion of the Rwandan state into areas which did not share its basic cultural norms. It was a period in which Rwandan society was becoming strongly hierarchical. And just as the material spoils from western raiding strengthened the court, it seems very likely that the norms and classifications developed in the western conquest areas—where cultural differences were more marked, political structures more rigid, and social differences hence more accentuated—were carried back into the central areas to serve as a model for the general structural development occurring in the central arena of the Rwandan kingdom.

THE LITERATURE of the Rwandan Court articulates these concepts of social distancing and demonstrates the norms inculcated by Rwandan army training: the glorification of military prowess, of personal heroism, and of the invincibility of the state. These values appear vividly in the individual praise poems by which a warrior celebrated his own virtues before his army colleagues or before the court. Such *ibyivugo* (singular, *icyivugo*) are recited rapidly and at full voice, with great formality, often with the speaker brandishing a spear.[19] The artistry is evidenced by the number of syllables pronounced in a single breath, the complexity of the poetic allusions, and the audacity of the deeds claimed, as well as by the presence and bearing of the speaker.[20]

The features so apparent in these poems—the militaristic ethic, the training in court etiquette, the glorification of the power of the state, and the stress on individual achievement in the conception of heroism so characteristic of court culture—are even more apparent in the dynastic poetry (*ibisigo*; singular, *igisigo*) glorifying the kings and especially their military deeds, and in so doing denigrating the conquered peoples.[21] These poems, too long to include here, detail the reigns of each of the last sixteen kings to figure in the royal genealogy. They form an important body of warrior literature, asserting Rwandan values at the official level of the court in the same way that the individual praise poems do for the armies and their members.[22]

In other types of literature, such as the *ibiteekerezo* historical narratives, the contrast in Rwandan perceptions between their own cultural values and those of the western peoples is similarly marked. This opposition is apparent both in the political distinctions made between western kings and those of Rwanda (as they are portrayed in the Rwandan narratives) and in the cultural features that the traditions commonly attribute to the western peoples. Among such traditions, the best known relate to Ruganzu Ndoori, a Rwandan king who appears as the quintessential epic hero of Rwanda.[23] One of the most widespread traditions dealing with his reign concerns his rivalry with a courtier named Muvunyi, son of Karema. It is an exciting tale of intense competition between friends, a story filled with espionage, temptations, and daring. It is told through a text replete with hyperbole, cultural allusions, references to magical power, and humor. Of particular interest here is the way in which these stylistic elements relate to Rwandan perceptions of the western cultural frontier. Before discussing these textual elements, however, it will be necessary first to sketch out the main lines of the story.[24]

(1) The story tells of a western king, Gatabirora, son of Kabibi, son of Kabirogosa, "the Mushi" with his teeth filed to a point; Gatabirora, son of Kabibi, son of Kabirogosa who was tied by a string to a chicken, and thence to his mother so that she might know when her son had died.

(2) One day Gatabirora sent a message to Ruganzu, the Rwandan king, summoning him to build for him an enclosure of the same dimensions as his

own (that of Ruganzu) and requiring him to send enough butter to make a drinking trough for his cows, as they were tired of always drinking from a trough made of sand. All this because, according to Gatabirora, Ruganzu lives in the country of his father, Kabibi.

(3) On their arrival at court, the messengers are stupefied with awe at the size and fine construction of the enclosure and at the numbers and bearing of the courtiers. Realizing the danger they would be in were they to relate the message as given, they simply say they have come to pay their respects on behalf of Gatabirora. Ruganzu thanks them initially, but by a clever ruse—aided by generous quantities of the court's best honey beer—he tricks them into conveying the message in its entirety.

(4) Ruganzu responds to their true message with a long praise poem (icyivugo). He then mutilates the messengers and sends them back to Gatabirora.

(5) Ruganzu then publicly offers his wager—a challenge to anyone at the court to kill Gatabirora before he does. Muvunyi accepts the challenge by placing his spear next to that of Ruganzu and drinking from the same urn as Ruganzu—drinking it dry, in fact. (These are actions that in most contexts would be considered acts of lèse-majesté; indeed, they can be considered as such here.) Muvunyi then leaves the court, and his father sets him obstacles to overcome to prepare him for his coming ordeal.

(6) On Muvunyi's departure from the court, Ruganzu makes plans to distract Muvunyi by providing him with beer, dancing, and women. Ruganzu then leaves immediately for his confrontation with Gatabirora, though the agreement was that they would set out only on the eighth day.

(7) Ruganzu meets Gatabirora and they begin by sparring. Finally, Gatabirora hurls his spear. It misses Ruganzu, but the force from it as it flies by knocks Ruganzu unconscious and sets the forest ablaze.

(8) Muvunyi learns of Ruganzu's departure and sets out in all haste towards Gatabirora's. After many adventures en route, he arrives just as Ruganzu falls unconscious. After reciting his own icyivugo, Muvunyi kills Gatabirora and leaves, having cut off the head and testicles of the western king.

(9) On awakening, Ruganzu finds that Muvunyi has killed Gatabirora. He is at first angered at having lost the wager. But in the end Ruganzu is placated by Muvunyi's father, and the two are reconciled, the one achieving status and fortune, the other retaining his kingdom against the insolence of "Gatabirora, son of Kabibi, son of Kabirogosa, the Mushi with the filed teeth."

The story is of interest not only because it is one of the best known of Rwandan stories of this kind,[25] but also because it deals with the problem of the conceptual differences by which Rwandans set themselves apart from western cultures. (It also includes certain thematic and stylistic elements that reappear in other traditions, as will be discussed below.) The story as a whole is interesting because it talks of a western king seeking to alter—even to invert—the structure of relationships between himself and Ruganzu by demanding prestations from the Rwandan king. Significantly, this attempt is expressed through a contest in a domain in which the Rwandan court prides itself as clearly superior to its western neighbors, that of material culture. The western king seeks to build a thatched house and cattle troughs equal to those of the Rwandans.

(1) But the tenor of the narrative is set even before the story begins to unfold, with the announcement of the names "Gatabirora, son of Kabibi, son of Kabirogosa." "Gatabirora" and "Kabibi" are representative of common names found in the west.[26] "Kabirogosa," however, is even more explicitly tied to the west, as a Rwandan deformation of the (more recent) Havu dynastic name "Kamerogosa." He is identified as a "Mushi," one of the names applied to mean "those of the west" and carrying very strong pejorative connotations in Rwandan usage. He is characterized as having filed and pointed teeth, a custom disdained by Rwandans, whose cultural norms do not allow for bodily mutilation for ornamentation or for ritual purposes. In fact, filed teeth are not common among the Havu or Shi; they are most closely associated with the forest cultures west of the Mitumba Mountains, west of Lake Kivu. Thus this portrayal combines elements from many cultural groups—some even beyond the immediate frontier—to create a single general category in opposition to Rwandan norms.

Finally, Gatabirora's own masculinity and independence are questioned by the use of a metaphor common in this type of story: his genitals are tied by a string leading to a chicken that would inform his mother of his death.[27] (Other versions of this tale—even more scandalous—note that the string was held directly by Gatabirora's mother without any intermediary.) Aside from the obvious suggestion of dependence on the mother (an allusion, perhaps, to the tendency to matrilateral succession in royal practices in the west[28]), the metaphor also carries the implication that Gatabirora will die alone in the forest, with no one to bring news of his death but a chicken. There is also an allusion here (which is in fact the basis of the metaphor in question) to the form of dress of the "uncouth" forest peoples of the west, who formerly dressed only in a loincloth tied between the legs and around the waist.

Nor does Gatabirora's mother escape the caustic tone of the Rwandan narrative: she is portrayed as hiding monkeys and cockroaches between her legs. The characterization ends with a phrase of gibberish Kihavu, a language used in areas west of Lake Kivu, repeated at intervals throughout the narrative. In many respects, then, the initial portions of this tale establish the tone by which the western cultures will be characterized throughout.

(2) The parody of western character continues as Gatabirora assembles his messengers. There are seven of them, as we find out later. This is a deformation of the conventional numerical scheme applying to royalty, which is associated with multiples of four (most frequently eight). Seven, then, represents nonroyalty, or perhaps pretentious and gauche attempts to claim royal status on the part of the hopelessly inept Gatabirora.[29] This image is reinforced by the nature of the meal offered them on their arrival at home. The meal consists of taro, a root plant closely associated with forest cultures but disdained as food by the Rwandans. To serve this food to others, especially as part of a formal presentation to his own men, would be, in the eyes of most Rwandans, either a bad joke or a most pointed insult.

Following the meal, Gatabirora informs the messengers of their mission: to demand of Ruganzu a new house and a new drinking trough for cattle. All this is phrased in mock Kinyarwanda, the language of Rwanda, filled with mispronunciations: "Ruganzu, king of Rwanda," for example, becomes "Rugamvu ga Gwanda."[30] Gatabirora offers a long recitation of his own self-characterization, similar in form to the praise poetry of Rwanda but including elements that would be anything but heroic to Rwandan audiences and with a hilarious transformation of the conventional icyivugo form: "Go and tell Rugamvu ga Gwanda that it is Katabirora [who speaks], Katabirora son of Kabibi, son of Kabirogosa, the Mushi with the pointed teeth, who comes drawing with him the string [tied to his genitals], who brings with him the chickens cackling in the forest. . . . [then there is more gibberish in Kihavu]. It is he, Katabirora, who sends you these messengers. You will say to him 'Leta seke, leta seke' [a deformation of the Ki-Havu imperative "leta soko," bring tribute or offer prestations]." The command is explicit, as is the threat of punishment for disobedience: for failing to pay court in this manner, Rugamvu ga Gwanda will be chewed up and spit out like so much tobacco (a northern commodity, but also associated in Rwanda with western trade networks). All this is based on the assertion that "Rugamvu ga Gwanda" lives on the land of Gatabirora's father, Kabibi.

(3) The next episode describes the reaction of the messengers from the forest to the court of Ruganzu. It illustrates the simple naiveté of these men, overawed by the splendor of the Rwandan court. They are stupefied and see that the simple home of Gatabirora could not begin to compare with the grandeur of the court of Ruganzu. And so they decide to change their message; in fact, they invert it, by saying that they bring the greetings of Gatabirora, that Gatabirora seeks to come to Ruganzu bearing prestations of the forest (mats, *ubutega* fiber bracelets,

and hoes), and that the land that Gatabirora inhabits is not the land of his father, Kabibi, but that of Ruganzu's father, Ndahiro. Such an inversion illustrates the lack of character of these forest bumpkins; but Ruganzu's reaction to it and his careful distrust of such flattery also show the celebrated cunning intelligence of the court milieu.

In other versions of the story, this theme is drawn out at greater length.[31] The messengers arrive, and no one understands them when they speak their own language; they are portrayed as walking up to various courtiers and addressing them as Ruganzu, mistaking the noble bearing of person after person at the court (never having seen such splendor before) for that of the king himself.[32] These forward, uncultured visitors, lacking all finesse and social grace, then eat rotten food offered them and drink the dregs of others—food and drink no one at court would deign to touch. Having filled themselves like gluttons, they fall asleep and in their sleep break wind in such volume that Ruganzu himself is awakened by the noise. Flatulence is, in fact, a common pejorative theme applied to westerners within the Rwandan court context—the epitome of the uncultured barbarian (it thus serves as another core cliché, as discussed in note 27). One version of the narrative continues with the men awakening and speaking, again, in gibberish or pidgin Kinyarwanda. In both versions discussed here, there is reference to Gatabirora, the son of Kabibi of Kabirogosa, the Mushi who lived in the forest of Nzira, a reference to yet another narrative tale dealing with westerners.[33] Once again, as with the theme of flatulence, the manner in which this theme is intertwined with the main story forms an important element in the meaning conveyed. By thus relating this narrative to other traditions dealing with westerners (or, in the case of Nzira, to unsuccessful Hutu opposition to Tutsi expansion), the superiority of the Tutsi court culture is further emphasized by allusion to the larger corpus of traditions on the common theme.

Ruganzu then shows his pleasure (and his sarcastic turn of mind) by summoning each of his warrior courtiers separately and reciting in turn their praise poems, recounting their military exploits and heroic deeds. He ends each recitation with "Have you heard how this Mushi has sent me a good message!" Finally, after Ruganzu has finished showing his gratitude to the messengers and extended a formal invitation to Gatabirora to visit his court, one of the messengers breaks down and reveals the true message. He begins with gibberish and continues by noting that since Gatabirora had provided them with such a sumptuous feast of delicious taro before sending them off, the messengers cannot betray him by hiding the truth. He then tells Ruganzu what Gatabirora had asked for: "Leta seke [give tribute]!" In the second version considered here, the messengers add that if Ruganzu does not obey, Gatabirora will take off the clothes of his mother, the one who chases monkeys and hides cockroaches between her legs. Such a statement of course is an unimaginable, unthinkable blasphemy in the form of a barbaric oath, and underscores once again the disgusting, crude nature of these western "Banyabungo."

(4) Ruganzu then responds with a long praise poem of his own, by implication contrasting the glories of the Rwandan regime and the refinement of the Rwandan language with the blunt straightforwardness of the uncultured "Bashi." Included in this response are many references to the western areas and themes shared with other ibiteekerezo. One such fragment, drawn from a story well known to Rwandan audiences, tells of the formation of Lake Kivu from an indiscretion on the part of Nyiransibula (a reference to "the mother of Nsibula," the eponymous founder of the Basibula dynasty), portrayed a woman from the western areas (i.e., "Bunyabungo") serving at the Rwandan court. One day, while sweeping the courtyard, she created a scandal by breaking wind—loud and clear —before the assembled courtiers pondering the affairs of state. (As in the story of Gatabirora's messengers, there is ample latitude here for a graphic performance in the telling of this tale.) Exiled from the court, she threw out her chamber pot; where it broke, a gigantic flow of water issued forth, flooding the entire surrounding area and eventually creating Lake Kivu. By magical means, Ruganzu was able to halt the rising waters and thus save Rwanda.[34] Finally, to return to the story of Gatabirora, Ruganzu terminates his response to the western messengers— but in reality addressing his own warriors—with "Have you heard the dog of a Mushi come to insult us here!" (In Kinyarwanda, there is a play on words between this phrase and the phrase he repeated earlier: "Have you heard the good news," thus dramatizing the contrast between the two responses all the more.)

In the account given here, Ruganzu then kills all but one messenger (again a common theme in these stories), whom he mutilates and sends home to Gatabirora. After limping home—falling, crying out, and lamenting on the long road back to his king—the surviving messenger finally enters Gatabirora's compound, where he begins once again with his gibberish Kihavu and goes on to tell Gatabirora how Ruganzu responded. "He is here, he is here, and you will burn, you will die, you will die." He faints, and to revive him the courtiers bring bells to ring in his ears. Although bells are used in some court ceremonies in Rwanda, they are most frequently associated with the anticourt Ryangombe rituals; they are also, of course, used on hunting dogs, perhaps the strongest connotation (associated with western cultures) drawn to mind in this context. After hearing his laconic story, Gatabirora looks up in fright and asks, "Where are they coming from? Where will they pass amongst my nettles, amongst my reeds, amongst my taro plants?" This final reference, of course, serves as yet another reminder of the forest milieu and the inferior staple food attributed to these simple and hopelessly uncultured "Bashi" of Gatabirora. In another version, Ruganzu mutilates each messenger in a different way, cutting off a leg of one, an arm of another, an ear of a third. He then hands each the severed part, saying: "Here, these are your provisions for the return trip. Go and tell Gatabirora I shall be there."

The remainder of the narrative (sections 6 to 9 in the synopsis above) deals with the competition between Muvunyi and Ruganzu—the drama of the wager, the cunning of Ruganzu's tactics, the excitement of the race to Gatabirora's, and the heroics of Muvunyi in assuring Gatabirora's death. It is entertainment at its most intense. But these later sections concern us less here, for though intriguing in themselves, they do not directly offer the parody of western cultures that is so effectively portrayed in the earlier sections—and that is the subject of our focus.

The important point of such comparisons between western cultures and Rwanda is not just that these stories portray western peoples as uncouth, but that they relate to elements deemed central to Rwandan culture. The references to such uncultured behavior, such unrefined language, and such unthinkable foods are all framed as deformations of accepted Rwandan etiquette rather than as valid characterizations of western peoples. In reality, then, the parody also serves as a commentary on exquisite Rwandan norms, reinforcing Rwandan identity by stressing the non-Rwandan quality of the western cultures. To be sure, there are allusions to western traits in the names, the literary themes, the foods; but these are taken out of context and thus can only be judged in the context of the Rwandan cultural norms of the listener. It is this perspective that makes them seem so ridiculous, not the inherent quality of the traits alone (though allusions such as those to the cockroaches or the flatulence are clearly derogatory on their own account). The portrayal of western cultures in the narratives therefore need not be valid in itself to have its maximum effect; it need only provide unthinkable oppositions to Rwandan culture. The major role of the allusions to the west is to make the story plausible (and entertaining), to provide some kind of narrative line to hold together the images offered. Although ostensibly a cultural commentary on western peoples, the terms employed are not always terms of ethnographic ascription; instead, they are generated by a particular context of oppositions and used to enhance those oppositions. It is thus the nature of the relationships that defined the "frontier," not the presence of some "objective" frontier that defined the relationships among groups.[35]

THE LITERARY sources, however, reflect only one aspect of the frontier concept: they speak for the ideology of the Rwandan central court alone. The influence of these norms was of course very strong; even the local nonroyal traditions tend to pick up the stereotypes of social categories as defined by these court perceptions. But such a view of the frontier—stressing idealized norms and polarized oppositions—tends to overlook, or even to contradict, the day-to-day behavior of westerners, which reflected the strong linkages at work both within the area (which today forms part of western Rwanda) and with areas farther west still. Looked at from the point of view of interaction networks, there was no clear hiatus dividing Rwandan and western norms; in fact, the evidence at hand suggests that until quite recently noncourt Rwandan people had closer ties with the west than with the east, the area of most intensive court culture. The most significant forms of social distancing were those that separated the court milieu from noncourt milieu within Rwanda itself. To illustrate this important difference in court perceptions and local perceptions, three forms of linkages between western Rwanda and areas farther west will be discussed briefly here: commerce, marriage ties, and mobility.

Recent research has altered our understanding of the intensive commercial networks that existed in this region, at least in the late nineteenth century and probably from well before.[36] What is particularly pertinent to the present discussion—and the feature that apparently obscured this commercial activity from earlier researchers—is that it was conducted outside the court milieu. But even before these studies were undertaken, there were suggestions of significant levels of commercial contacts that included a wide network of ties throughout the western region of Rwanda. Though markets were present (indicating the intensity of the trade in some areas), commercial interaction mainly occurred through many individual traders, dealing with trade partners linked to them by kin ties, blood-pact ties, or other, more informal social ties. Typical of the testimony from the western areas are these descriptions from Ijwi Island (in Lake Kivu, just west of Rwanda) by participants in the trade from more recent periods.[37]

[The people of Ijwi] took beans and sorghum to Rwanda for goats and bulls. They [the Rwandans] then took them to Nduga to buy livestock, [to] Nduga and Nyanza. [Nduga is the general area of central Rwanda; Nyanza was the location of the royal capital during colonial rule but is used in a metonymi-cal sense to refer to the royal court.] The food we grew here—in great quantities. . . . The beads we bought in Karhana, Kabare, Ngweshe, [all to the west and southwest of Lake Kivu]. The *burhega* [fiber bracelets] we made ourselves, here on Ijwi. We made them from vines in the forest called *ndamba-gizi* and *ntunda*. After cutting them and drying them we wove them, wove them, wove them . . . like this . . . in patterns so they look nice—so! Then we took goats to Butembo, to the land of Ndalemwa [to Mubugu, west of the Mitumba Mountains in Congo] to look for *burhega*. We took sorghum and bought *burhega* [in Butembo]. . . .

The Batembo brought *burhega* made of vines [*ishuli*] and we carried them to Rwanda. That was before the *amafranga* [European money] arrived; there were no amafranga then. They brought *burhega* and we took them to Rwanda to buy goats. On returning from Rwanda we took the goats to Irhambi [on the western shore] to sell them there. But this was done with friends. In those days whosoever did not have a friend was not able to buy anything. [Commerce was carried out through networks of blood brothers ("friends").]

There were no markets but one could go [to Rwanda] to look for a friend. Then you could ask for a cow or a goat. One had to have a friend to trade.

[Summary:] Migamba, a man of the Ishaza clan came from Rwanda [to Ijwi] to buy things here. Rubenga [the interviewee] was looking for goats and goatskins for his wife [or for "his marriage"]. So Migamba told Rubenga to come to Rwanda to look for skins there. When he [Rubenga] went there, they made a blood pact in Rwanda. He took beer and beans and went to look for goats in Rwanda. There in Rwanda he traded cultivated crops and food and "harvests" and hoes for goats. When he made friendship he did not actually make a blood pact but only exchanged things like beans [except for the blood pact with Migamba].

Thus the trade passed through many hands, and included many families in informal networks. To be sure, these testimonies refer to the early years of the colonial period, that is, to the early years of the twentieth century. But because there were no barriers to earlier involvement in this type of network, it seems reasonable to see in these descriptions a model of commercial ties in the area for as long as the demand conditions held. Given the mobility found in this subregion (a matter discussed below), local trade was undoubtedly a part of this regional interaction, even though trade directly with the court milieu may have developed only more recently.[38]

The most important items mentioned in the sources (both oral and written) are the ornamental *ubutega* bracelet-anklets that elite Rwandan women wore by the hundreds on their legs.[39] Traded in the thousands in Rwanda, these delicate items of raffia or other fiber, woven into a distinctive design, were fabricated in the areas west of Lake Kivu. Because the trade in ubutega was strongly influenced by central court demand, trade patterns for these commodities are not representative of the overall network of local trade patterns within the region. Nevertheless, because they are so distinctive and hence are so often mentioned in both oral and written sources, ubutega trade patterns are useful in tracing the extent of this broader commercial network; included were regions stretching from far to the west of Lake Kivu to the area of the Rwandan Court east of the Nile-Congo divide.[40] People in most areas in between were also participants in the trade, as producers, intermediaries, or consumers. Although ubutega are the most frequently cited commodity in this commercial network, many other products were traded as well. Important among these were tobacco, salt, hoes, and foodstuffs from the north and northwest, and mats, hoes, and foodstuffs from the southwest. Livestock—goats and, more rarely, cattle—were the most frequent Rwandan return item traded for ubutega and other goods from the west.

Essentially similar commercial mechanisms prevailed for all such items. Although hoes (and sometimes ubutega) traveled with specialized traders—and traveled greater distances—most of this localized trade appears to have involved short distances between each transaction, moving from hand to hand within the commercial web. Mutual dependence, even trust, was essential in such a commercial network, one that included many participants and into which entry was easy. Commercial relations in this area, therefore, convey no sense of the clear-cut oppositions, posed in terms of culture/barbarism so prevalent in the court traditions applying to this region. In fact, they underscore the importance of linkages, not oppositions—linkages demonstrated both by the fact of widespread commercial interaction and by the nature of such interaction, characterized by face-to-face transactions where friendship networks were important in facilitating material transfer.

Marriage ties also seem to cut across the cultural barrier posited by Rwandan literary sources. Precise data on this are scanty, but the message is clear. While marriage ties on a hierarchical axis—between court families and local residents —appear to have become more and more rare,[41] marriage ties both between different regions of present-day western Rwanda and between those regions and areas farther west still, around and beyond Lake Kivu, were neither difficult to arrange nor infrequent.

One social sector for which data on such ties are preserved (although incompletely) is that of the local ruling families among the many small autonomous polities that existed in the area before Rwandan penetration and incorporation. Numbering well over a score, these political units expressed their autonomy through the ritual authority of their rulers, or *abami;* singular, *umwami.*[42] Though the data on marriage ties are very incomplete, it is clear that these abami sometimes married among themselves. Rugaba, the umwami of Mpembe, for example, is said to have married women from Bugoyi in northwestern Rwanda and Bukunzi in southwestern Rwanda.[43] Other sources mention the marriages between people from Bukunzi and Bumbogo[44] and between Mashira, the umwami of Nduga in central Rwanda, and a woman from an unnamed polity on Buzi, a peninsula in the northwest of Lake Kivu.[45] Bukunzi data add that the kings there maintained marriage ties with the Shi kingdoms to the west (especially Ngweshe). Mobility patterns would also indicate that there were few barriers to marrying within the region, as new immigrants to an area apparently had little difficulty in establishing themselves.

If there were few obstacles to marriage among the different regions of what is now western Rwanda, the same is true for marriages between people in this area and regions farther west. This was especially true for women marrying "out," from areas of what is now western Rwanda toward areas farther west; it was a general characteristic of these social networks that women moved west. (It is not uncommon to find Rwandan-born women married on Ijwi, but rare to find Ijwi-born women married in Rwanda.) The same general trend is found west of Ijwi, where Ijwi women are married to partners on the Congolese mainland, but few women from the west marry men on Ijwi.

Without data on the massive scale required to establish this point, such an observation can only be suggestive. Nonetheless, these observed tendencies mesh with both marriage institutions and ideological explanations. Bridewealth is greater in the west, and hence it is financially beneficial to the bride's family, generally speaking, to marry women west; conversely, it is disadvantageous to marry women east. Ijwi ideology explains this tendency to marry women west in another way: there is not enough food in Rwanda, say the people of Ijwi; Ijwi women who marry in Rwanda will starve, and eventually they will return home.[46] At the least, such an explanation obviously agrees with the Ijwi practice of constantly sending food to family members living east of Lake Kivu; at the same time, it serves as an Ijwi commentary on how stingy Rwandans are in terms of food exchange.[47]

The general movement of women toward the west is a phenomenon that blends with the third element considered here, the mobility of people within the region. Both trade and marriage presuppose some forms of mobility, but these were probably less indicative of the linkages within the region than were movements that led to permanent settlement in new areas. Indeed, trade and marriage ties were in part a result of the movement of people, both eastward and westward. There is a great deal of evidence suggesting movements into northwestern Rwanda (Bugoyi) and southwestern Rwanda (Kinyaga) from regions farther west. For Bugoyi, Pagès notes that "les Bagoyi . . . sont presque tous originaires du ouest du Lac Kivu."[48] In the list he gives of "clans et sous-clans" of Bugoyi, almost one-half (twenty-seven of fifty-seven) claim a western origin,[49] and elsewhere he provides numerous examples of this immigration to Bugoyi from the west.[50]

In more recent periods, however, the overall trend of this movement seems to have been reversed, and it is now generally toward the west. It is possible that this shift was associated with the political pressures connected with the expansion of the royal court structures into this area. Many people moved from present-day western Rwanda onto highland areas known as Gishari, northwest of Lake Kivu, from at least the nineteenth century (and probably considerably earlier), and this movement continued well into the twentieth century, both as part of colonial policy and for less formal reasons.[51] Similarly, the immigration of families from western Rwanda onto Ijwi Island is noticeable from about the middle or late eighteenth century, and intense communication between Ijwi and areas east of Lake Kivu through family ties, blood-pact ties, and commercial channels has continued in some instances into the present.[52] Such an enduring historical pattern apparently met with few obstacles—a testimony to the strength of cultural continuities in the region. Even during the wars directed against Ijwi in the late nineteenth century by the Rwandan king Rwabugiri, these local-level contacts across the lake continued virtually uninterrupted—indeed, they flourished. They were to play a part in the war itself and in the subsequent administration, as recent immigrants who could claim ties to Rwanda were often favored as appointed administrative authorities during the Rwandan occupation.[53]

The reality of such linkages east and west of the lake therefore challenges the categorical polarization and regional differentiation portrayed in the traditions of the Rwandan Court. This again illustrates the contextual nature of the concept of the frontier: both in terms of geographical distance (held mostly in the central court milieu, well removed from contact with the west) and, perhaps more significantly, in terms of the social class in which such perceptions originated. It was predominantly those tied to the court milieu (as soldiers, narrators, or even servants) who articulated this set of frontier perceptions. But frontier concepts were important not only as they were applied to the frontier zones themselves; they also had significant internal applications, for the hierarchical categories applied to the frontier were also applied within Rwandan society, a society marked by a high degree of social stratification. Indeed, as noted earlier, when drawn in such stark terms, the concept of the frontier could be used to reinforce and extend the internal structures social hierarchy.

The dual implication of these perceptions went further still. As the populations of the west gradually adopted Rwandan cultural norms, they also adopted the form of expression and hence the mode of characterization of others implicit within court perceptions.[54] Thus the literary genres of the court—which included such core images as we have noted above in the Gatabirora tale—came to be adopted, recounted, and enjoyed by the people of these western regions even while they continued with the activities that belied such superficial stereotypical characterizations. The literary models provided a good tale, whose hilarity to the listeners may have partly resided in the shocking frivolity of such a portrayal. In these areas, in fact, such stereotypes may have acted to discredit or to parody the Rwandan heroes themselves, serving as local versions of *Don Quixote*. As court perceptions gradually penetrated the area, however, these people west of the Nile-Congo divide—who were themselves included among the original referents of the tale—increasingly accepted such portrayals as "true," but they applied the stereotypes to others farther west still. In so doing, of course, they reinforced their own identity as Rwandans, in this increasingly polarized (but evolving) context opposing "us" to "them." For each people, therefore, the "barbarians" always lived farther west.[55]

However the relativity of such a frontier concept lies not only in geographical or social parameters but in situational parameters as well. The "frontier" is not defined by the intrinsic elements of a given situation alone, but in a concept—generated by political perceptions of the day and phrased in terms of clear cultural oppositions, even polarization. The arbitrary aspect of the frontier concept applies even where the frontier zone is located in an area perceived as "empty" (though often such a categorization simply neglects—or denies—the presence of other inhabitants, as illustrated in the western frontier of the United States, the Canadian far north, or the Australian outback). For just as there is always continuity in interaction between cultures, so there is always an evolving interaction between culture and nature, and to oppose "empty" areas to "inhabited" areas is to deny this continuity. The oppositions implied in the frontier discourse, then, are a product of perceptions generated outside the frontier area itself, not emerging from within it: we choose where to define ruptures within complicated continuities. Thus the frontier metaphor speaks more to the metropolitan area than to the apparent locus of reference, the frontier zone itself. This may in part explain the problems involved in defining the American frontier, and the long debate that has followed from such definitional problems.

Literary genres such as those discussed above have an important place in the shaping of the frontier image. Often the action portrayed in such tales takes place on the boundaries of the real and the fictive, on the frontiers of culture.[56] By continually exploring the cultural boundaries that define the social group and the limits of acceptable cultural features and behavior, such stories are constantly redefining "us" by defining "them." The frontier concept itself differed little by social and geographical context—after all, in this case the people in the west had stereotypes of other people farther west still. But the political significance which these images acquired and to which these clichés applied did vary, for these images were embedded in political activity and the clichés justified political action. And they did more than that. The power that made such clichés effective came in part from the metropolitan elite's sense of internal cohesion and cultural arrogance, themselves a product of the contrasting cultural universes portrayed by the images of the frontier. In Rwanda, as elsewhere, the concept of the frontier was thus both effect and cause of specific kinds of political interaction.

WHAT ROLE HAS KINGSHIP?

An Analysis of the *Umuganura* Ritual of Rwanda
as presented in M. d'Hertefelt and A. Coupez,
La royauté sacrée de l'ancien Rwanda

1981

*Divine kingship is one of the hoary tropes of precolonial Africa as seen by
outside observers. Associated with myths of heroic (or mystical) origins and
surrounded with exotic rituals of legitimation, African kings often seemed
autocratic and autonomous from local control. But internal theories of kingship present a different view. Even in Rwanda, one of the most powerful and
centralized kingdoms of precolonial Africa, the king was subject to an elaborate "code of kingship": the published version includes 4,766 lines in seventeen separate rituals, all supposedly committed to memory by a powerful
corporation of specialized ritual authorities. The ritual code makes it clear
that, far from being omnipotent, the king was deeply embedded within a
larger domain of kingship, and surrounded with intensely structured ritual
prescriptions. This essay provides an example: an analysis of one segment
of a much larger published ritual corpus, the annual First Fruits ceremony,*
umuganura. *A structural analysis of the ritual shows the practices of kingship to be much more complex and the concepts behind this protocol much
more coherent and sophisticated than earlier outside assumptions imagined:
the role of the king was to mediate between the essential values of culture,
society, and ecology. Kingship was defined by culture, and the king's sacrality*

—his ritual power—derived from his status as mediator between broader conceptual categories, rather than from any source autonomous from the world at large. (Confirmation for such a vision is found in a separate analysis of a cognate ritual on Ijwi Island—muganuro—discussed in my larger work, Kings and Clans.*)*

MANY SOURCES ON AFRICAN kingdoms portray the king as the dominant central figure of royal rituals of precolonial African states. This essay reevaluates the role of kingship as expressed in the rituals of *umuganura,* the First Fruits ceremony of Rwanda. By accounting for the ritual as a whole rather than focusing on the role of a single person, the analysis shows the monarch as having played a relatively passive role; rather than the source of power, he serves as an intermediary among the conceptual categories that defined the nature of kingship. The king's "sacred" nature derived from his liminal status as mediating between larger conceptual categories that serve as the ultimate preoccupation of the ritual, much of which is concerned with people and places away from the central court. Ritual power emerges from the conjunction of these various enduring forces at work in the world rather than resulting from a person, or even from sources autonomous from the world at large. Thus "sacral kingship" was not always associated with a "divine king," in the sense of a king drawing his power and legitimacy from supernatural forces outside society. Instead, he drew his sacrality from the representation of a set of internal relationships central to the concepts of the culture itself.

LÉVI-STRAUSS tells us that "the unconscious meaning of a myth [is revealed in] the problem it is trying to solve."[1] According to him, this problem is more reliably illustrated in the structure of the myth than in the plot, or the apparent "content" of the myth. This analysis addresses the "problem" at the core of a royal ritual of signal importance in the precolonial kingdom of Rwanda. In doing so, it will first identify elements fundamental to the ritual and to the problem of kingship—indeed to all of human society. It will then examine in detail the successive episodes of the ritual in order to explore the way in which these elements are structured (and restructured) to show their meaning in relation to each other (in relations that are at once ambiguous and interdependent). But first, some consideration must be given to the application to the ritual domain of an analytic technique most frequently used and elaborately developed in the study of myth.

Ritual as Communication: Structuralists and the Analysis of Drama

Rituals are essentially formalized social drama. They are performed by people; therefore (where not esoteric) they invariably focus attention on the social aspects of the ritual, because in the performance there is no way of ignoring the question of *who* is carrying out a certain action. In myth, on the other hand, the sociological meaning is not an element essential to the genre: it may be important, but it need not be so. In myth, actions can be portrayed without direct relevance to a given social situation.

The immediate relevance of ritual is also apparent in temporal considerations. The performance of ritual—or at least of rites—requires a certain organization; at the very least, people (and props) must meet together. As illustrated below, rituals directed to a conscious social goal often demand a precise temporal organization, performed at an externally defined moment (planting, harvest, birth, marriage, death, or succession). To be effective, they must adhere to prescribed timing, determined either by regular intervals (calendrical time) or by social, biological, or cultural rhythms that may occur at irregular intervals on a calendrical scale. Thus, by the very context of this type of ritual performance, there is a required immediacy or temporal orientation, placing the performance in a time frame relative to the present. The immediate relevance of ritual in two domains, the temporal and the social, tends to reinforce their conceptual interrelation, thus providing temporal significance to the social patterns portrayed and reflecting the social significance of the timing of the performance.

Myth, on the other hand, often refers to the extremities of conventional time scales; it is seen as portraying events "outside of time," speaking to the universal and eternal preoccupations of people. The timing of narration can also be more flexible than is the usual performance of a ritual: though external stimuli—seasonal, cultural, or particular (e.g., illness or misfortune)—may serve as catalysts to the recitation of a myth, such stimuli are not required as a condition of narration; myths (or mythical characters) can be alluded to at any time. Finally, myth can be more flexible in its use of actors, at times only alluding to human characterization, or employing other literary devices to free itself from the question of direct social relevance. Removed from both social and temporal immediacy, the mythical form thus most frequently addresses questions of the "beyond."

Hence both by their nature and purpose, rituals are related to time and society in a way that myth need not be. Both these factors derive directly from the performance of the art: the power of social roles in ritual performances, on the one hand, and the very context of immediacy, on the other, may well mean that rituals will be seen in the context of present social structures more than myth. When a person of a certain status performs in a ritual, the conjunction of person and role carries a meaning for contemporary society that is more compelling than what is often present in the recital of a myth. A ritual happens; the same is not always true (or not true in the same way) for a myth.

The social aspect inherent in ritual performance highlights a particular problem of interpretation for structural analysis: as is illustrated in Lévi-Strauss's interpretation of ritual among the Coma of Panama, a structural approach to analysis is essentially based on textual data.[2] For Lévi-Strauss, the analytical referent is the "song"—that is, the *text* that describes (or directs) the ritual—rather than the ritual itself. Similarly, the analysis of Rwandan ritual presented here is based on a ritual "code"—a text that amounts virtually to a series of stage directions. Such a text is almost totally devoid of the emotions, the "sense" of the performance, and the drama of performance; for all the precision and detail found in the text, we are denied the sense of creativity—or re-creation—of the moment. Only after having thus torn out the heart of the performing art, the structuralist technique seems to say, can one proceed beyond the immediate sociological concerns to seek the ultimate (structural) meaning of the performance.

Thus the nature of the analysis depends to a large extent on the type of sources employed. The significance of the sources of analysis can be illustrated with reference to the ritual discussed below, for which there are available both a formal text and secondary descriptions (by others) based on personal observation and discussion with participants in the ritual (though the authors of such descriptions did not have access to the exotic ritual Code on which this analysis is based).[3] The latter provide a remarkable degree of detail and a general fidelity to the ritual as an event (in its syntagmatic unfolding). But lacking access to the entire esoteric Code (and thus relying on description and observation), these observers were faced with a dilemma as they tried to portray the structure of the ritual. Because of the vast spatial and temporal dimensions included in the ritual in its entirety, such a description had to be either based on a compilation of diverse sources dealing with different aspects of the ritual or presented from a single perspective that could encompass only part of the ritual. In either case, the structure of the ritual presented in these observer accounts differs significantly from what appears in the official Code; this leads to interpretations in the published accounts that differ in important ways from that which will emerge from the structural analysis presented below.

Most of these (colonial) observer accounts privilege the role of court and king: the former as the most prominent locus of the ritual drama (at least to the nonparticipant); the latter as the central presence in any social interaction, whether or not of a ritual nature. Because these sources are based on the perspectives of a single observer viewing only selected segments of the ritual, a selection based on contemporary (e.g., colonial) sociological concerns, and because this ritual is interpreted as a ritual of the court, these accounts stress the overriding political preoccupation of colonial Rwanda—relations between Tutsi, Hutu, and Twa, the three most broadly based social identities within Rwandan society. In certain respects, such an interpretation differs markedly from an interpretation derived from the perspective of the ritual as an integrated whole used as a device for understanding the wider world around kingship. In this analysis, we intend to look through the prism of ritual to the overriding questions of human concern rather than looking at the ritual through the lenses of particular questions of the day.

Thus the textual form of the Code—a form that seems at first glance to deny the essential sense of involvement and drama of any ritual presentation— ultimately succeeds in providing the tools for (or at least the hope of) penetrating beyond drama to the structural components of what is being communicated. Drama, like lexicon, then, is a form of communication: but structure, like syntax, is what carries the meaning—at least at one level. And it is at this level that, after briefly looking at the Rwandan context, we shall attempt our analysis.

The Rwandan Context of the Royal Rituals

Following a period of important military expansion and internal political consolidation, the kingdom of Rwanda included close to two million people within a highly centralized polity and hierarchized society at the time of European arrival in the early twentieth century.[4] Accompanying the institutional developments in the social and political domains of Rwandan culture over the previous century was a remarkable elaboration of court culture in general, including royal ritual forms of considerable complexity. The central focus of the latter was the esoteric ritual Code, the *Ubwiiru,* composed of eighteen separate but interrelated rituals. Seventeen of these (amounting to some 4,766 lines) are included in a most extraordinary publication, *La royauté sacrée de l'ancien Rwanda,* edited by Marcel d'Hertefelt and André Coupez, on which the present analysis is based.[5]

The specific ritual considered here is the annual First Fruits ceremony (Ritual VIII in the Code: *Inzira y'Umuganura*). Though culminating at the time of the sorghum harvest (February–March), the full ritual was composed of four temporal segments spaced throughout the year: at the appearance of the moons of *kaanama* (August–September), *uzeri* (September–October), *mutarema* (January–February), and *gashantare* (February–March).[6] This umuganura ceremony was selected for analysis here for three reasons. It was one of the major social and ritual events of the kingdom, an annual festivity culminating (normatively) at a time of plenty and rejoicing, and it touches on very broad questions pertaining to the nature of society in general and the role of kingship within it. Furthermore, it is also a type of ritual widespread among neighboring peoples; the umuganura ritual of Rwanda includes prominent features shared among several kingdoms within the region, thus opening the possibility of ethnographic (if not also structural) comparisons. Finally, though complex—and this presentation omits or only barely touches on the complexity and significance of color symbolism, social interactions, the items used and their materials of fabrication (sometimes rigorously prescribed), the relations of ritual to other art forms (especially myth), and other similar aspects—the umuganura text is still of manageable length for these purposes. (It is 386 lines long; the enthronization ritual, by contrast, includes 1,249 lines, and that itself is neither the longest nor the most complex of the seventeen rituals included in the published Code.)

The most important methodological point to make here is that umuganura comprised only part of the integrated Code of royal ritual. There are many indications within the Code itself—including aspects of one ritual repeated in another —that establish that the separate rituals are conceived of as an integral whole; each one, then, is only part of the ritual physiology of the living kingdom. In extracting only one ritual for analysis here, I have consequently done violence to the integrity of the whole as well as to the subtlety and savor of the part. But the attempt to explore these aspects more fully would have exceeded the resources available to me and placed unfair demands on the patience of the reader. Within the limitations of time and space, however, I have tried to be fair to the concept of the Code as a whole.

The Umuganura Ritual of Rwanda: An Overview

In Rwanda of the late nineteenth century, the centralized political structure and hierarchialized administrative structures meant that in most areas of the country the influence of the central court was able to penetrate directly to the lowest level of society. Kingship was thus the preeminent factor in the political and social life of the country. As such, it was a constant preoccupation, philosophically as well as socially: needless to say, this focus on kingship was all the more intense at those levels of society that maintained direct contact with the court and with royalty. Within this context, the royal rituals in particular were oriented to the question of "What role has kingship?" But in addressing this question the rituals did not focus on kingship; instead, they examined the wider context within which kingship was located and sought to clarify the relationship of kingship with other aspects of ultimate concern: Ecology (in this sense of "Nature" or fertility, and hence also including food crops), Society, and Technology (or "Culture" within the Lévi-Straussian paradigm).

The terms "Society," "Culture," and "Ecology" are used here in ways that sometimes appear ambiguous. Thus within the umuganura ritual, food crops are sometimes seen to represent Nature and sometimes Culture. They are ambiguous in fact as well as in their symbolic roles, and their classification as symbols within the rites depends on the context and the oppositions in effect at any given time. Hence there is no consistent definition to the terms: since categorization can only be relative, the boundaries of these classifications can only be determined by context. In short, the categories are not determined by their content but by the nature of their interrelation with other structurally equivalent categories. Because of this, in what follows the terms should always be read not as universally accepted concepts but rather as "What is meant by 'Culture' (or 'Ecology') in this context."

The tripartite cosmological division (Ecology, Technology, Society) is present in each separate episode of the umuganura ritual, though within the different episodes the three may be structured differently in relation to each other. Kingship, according to the interpretation presented here, mediates between them. In this role kingship is analogous to Culture, which, both by definition and within the ritual, also mediates between Society and Ecology, between the human and natural domains. In certain respects, culture and kingship are therefore identified

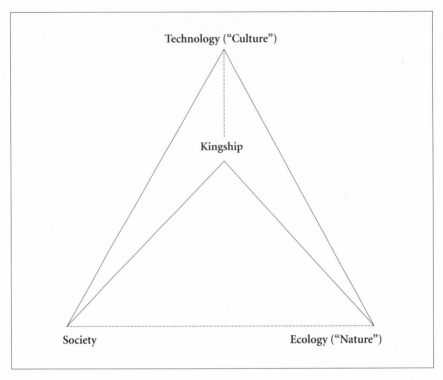

Figure 10.1. Structural representation of the concepts embedded in the *umuganura* ritual. The dotted lines indicate reduced opposition: kingship had a stronger identity with Culture (through kings' structurally analogous positions as mediators) than with either of the other two concepts; Society and Ecology were sometimes identified with each other in common classificatory opposition to Culture and/or kingship. The triangle could not be inverted because, by the logic of the ritual, Culture always must be located at the apex.

with—or reinforce—each other in the ritual. At the same time, however, there remains an ambiguous relationship of kingship with the wider concept of "culture."

The oppositions presented in the ritual are usually binary in form: thus two elements of the triad are combined in opposition to the third. But these binary oppositions themselves alter, so that sometimes Culture and Ecology are seen as opposed to Society, while at other times Culture and Society are opposed to Ecology. Most frequently, however, Society and Ecology are (usually separately, occasionally jointly) opposed to Culture—and to each other as well. A schematic representation appears in figure 10.1.

This structural paradigm is also reflected in other spheres (aside from action within the ritual itself). Geographically there appear (from the ritual itself and from other sources as well—in myth, historical traditions, and cultural differences between the two areas) two ritual domains of the kingdom, separated by the Nyabarongo River. North of the river, the region of Bumbogo—home of the primary ritualists of the umuganura ritual and also the location of the ritual planting and cultivation—represents the domain of Nature. All of the natural materials whose origin is prescribed in the ritual come from north of the Nyabarongo. Nduga, the area south of the river (which makes a large semicircular bend, thus partially defining the limits of Nduga) was the principal focus of the kingdom (and most common area for the localization of the royal court, despite the court's frequent displacement). Finally, the Nyabarongo River was also an object of considerable ritual importance in its own right within the context of other rituals. For example, certain kings were (partially or totally) proscribed from crossing the river, and the ritual Code often prescribes an exact locality when it cites a passage across the Nyaborongo—as in traversing all ritual boundaries, this must be accomplished in the prescribed manner.

It will be seen that early in the ritual the passage of hoes and baskets (two material elements representing the domain of Culture in our schema) mediates between the two geographical domains: Bumbogo, the domain of fertility and Nature, and Nduga, the focus of the kingdom and Society. In the later stages of the ritual, the sorghum harvest is transported in a specified type of basket (representing the work of man—Culture) by an unidentified "Hutu" (i.e., a nonroyal, in this context, and hence a generalized representation of Society at large), thus combining Ecology, Culture, and Society in traversing the two ritual/geographical domains and hence making them one. In the earlier stages of the ritual, therefore, Culture mediates between the two domains (representing Society and Nature); in the later stages all three elements of the triad join in unifying the two regions.

The balance of the two areas portrayed in the ritual goes beyond this, since there is also a ritual court in Bumbogo with all the trappings of the royal court in Nduga, thus helping also to tie the two domains by their common possession of a similar culture element, "kingship." But while reflecting the royal court, the court in Bumbogo is in some ways also the inversion of the royal court in Nduga. The Bumbogo court, for example, is very small, and its size is emphasized in the ritual cultivation of the sorghum, where a tiny plot (of only one square meter) is first hoed; wider areas are cultivated later. In addition, this ritual cultivation is accomplished at night—an inversion of the normal pattern of work.[7] Thus the two regions are both joined and differentiated by the common cultural element of kingship, and the transformations occurring in Bumbogo only serve to emphasize and reinforce the "proper" patterns of kingship in Nduga.

In myth, too, it is possible to discern the same tripartite categorization (with the same sliding of categories). First, several common myths relate the introduction of sorghum to Rwanda, to the travels of a famous royal culture hero, through the region of Bumbogo. According to different versions, either this king, while passing through Bumbogo, saw an ant carrying a grain of sorghum and brought it back to his people, or the king of Bumbogo sent sorghum to mediate a local dispute; in either case, the sorghum of Bumbogo was thereafter distributed to the people of Nduga. In both cases the Rwandan king is the intermediary between Bumbogo (Nature), sorghum (in this case, as a food crop, representing Culture), and the people of Rwanda (Society). Secondly, other widespread myths relate how the royal ancestors descended from the sky bringing with them iron, fire, and food crops to the people living in a "wild" state below; hence kingship is explicitly identified with important cultural items as mediators between the human and natural domains.

Therefore, the interpretation advanced here differs from the conventional interpretation, which emphasizes the ritual as reinforcing the linkages between the Tutsi rulers and the "peasant masses." While the analysis presented here does not deny the existence nor importance of such class differences in Rwandan society, it looks at the significance of the ritual within a wider cultural perspective, in which the linkage problem seems only part of the concern of the ritual as a whole: broader questions were being addressed in the ritual as indicated both by the relatively passive roles of the ruling elite in the ritual and by the infrequent references to specific social groups (i.e., to class divisions within society). In fact, as will be discussed below in greater detail, within the ritual the role of the rulers is portrayed as that of intermediaries within a wider cultural domain, while the focus of the ritual is on the polar extremes—the things to be related—rather than on the mechanism of this linkage (kingship), the significance of which remains implicit rather than directly declared.

What follows will analyze the ritual of umuganura—the annual First Fruits ceremony as it is portrayed in the esoteric Code of Rwandan royal ritual—in light of this structural paradigm. It will not be an exhaustive examination of the ethnographic data by any means, but what emerges will be sufficient, I hope, to articulate the nature and meaning of the ritual itself. To do this, I divide the ritual into six episodes; for each, the analysis describes the action and discusses the significance of the relations expressed in the episode.

The Umuganura Ritual of Rwanda:
An Analysis

Episode I (*La royauté sacrée*, VIII, lines 1–33). The ritual begins in the moon of *kaanama* (corresponding to the month of August–September in the Gregorian calendar) with the transfer of hoes that are ritually pure; they must be without blemish, they must never have touched the ground, and they must have handles of a prescribed type, fashioned from the wood of a tree whose name is derived from a cognate of the verb "to desire."[8] (Bourgeois notes that they number eight —an observation of some significance given the number symbolism discussed below.) These are hoes newly forged in Buberuka, north of the Nyabarongo; they are brought to the king by the Tsoobe ritualist, the principal ritualist of the kingdom, a man with a role especially prominent in the umuganura ceremony. His principal residence is in Bumbogo, the area where the sorghum is ritually cultivated, and he himself is considered a "ritual king" with a "royal" court. He, in his turn, also has a ritualist—the guardian of the ritual purity of the Tsoobe king. These ritualists of the Swere lineage (Ega clan) succeed under a series of three dynastic names (the significance of number symbolism will be discussed below); to simplify the presentation, they will here be referred to simply as "Muswere," following their lineage identity.[9]

The king and court therefore play a notably passive role in this episode; the initial phases of the ritual are concentrated on the area north of the Nyabarongo —the ritual area associated with Ecology. The hoes come from there (Buberuka) and return to there (Bumbogo), only passing through the hands of the king: he receives them from the Tsoobe and returns them to the same man with the words "Go cultivate that you may have productive harvests!" Tsoobe then gives them to Muswere, who in turn gives them to "anyone"—an unspecified person but not a member of the royal family or a ritualist. Thus the ritual begins with the mediating role of the king: it is the king who consecrates the hoes—a cultural element par excellence—and, having received them from Buberuka, proceeds to give them to a member of the society at large; they then return to the land north of the Nyabarongo for the cultivation of food crops. It will be noted that the mediating role of the king reflects—and is identified with—that of the hoes; it is also reinforced by the double repetition of mediation (by Tsoobe and again by Muswere). The king's role also provides an analogue to that of Society in this episode, for the hoes, having come from Buberuka, are returned to Bumbogo by the intermediary of an unidentified person, just as the king, having received them from Tsoobe, returns them to him.

But the analogy is stronger for the king's classificatory role with technology, both by his direct contact with the hoes and by the reinforcement through the repetitive acts of Tsoobe and Muswere. The hoes and the king provide meaning to each other's unique ritual status; the king would not be ritually consecrated without the hoes to consecrate, and the hoes would not be ritually significant (and hence would be unnoticed among the universe of profane items) without being consecrated by the king. In this ritual, therefore, the king's role is more closely identified with the abstract aspects of Culture than with Society of which he is physically a part.[10] Thus the structural features emphasize the classificatory roles being acted out in this ritual rather than specific material relationships.

Therefore, from the beginning, the king has been established as an intermediary between technology and society, on the one hand, and technology and ecology, on the other; intermediary, in other words, between Culture and the two pillars on which culture is based: human social groups and nature. Thus the primary axis of differentiation is that portrayed as the vertical dimension on the triangular schema in figure 10.1, that between culture and its schematic opposites; the secondary differentiation is that portrayed by the two extremes of the horizontal axis, that between nature and society. The king also mediates, as do the hoes themselves (in both their production and their productive uses), between Nature and Society. (It might also be noted that there is less chance of ambiguity between the latter two than between culture and either society or nature; where there is less ambiguity, the schematic classifications need be less pronounced in order to preserve the triadic conceptual framework.)

The common schematic position shared by ecology and society relative to culture is illustrated in another conceptual dimension, expressed in a different medium, the creation myths. Here the kingship is seen as mediating between the "above" and the "below," and between cultural elements on the one hand and society/nature on the other. Rwandan cosmology provides for the celestial origin of such things as fire and iron (and, illustrating the classificatory ambiguity between culture and nature, certain food crops); the creation myths explicitly state that it was through the royal ancestors (or ancestors incorporated into the royal genealogy) that these cultural elements came to be known in Rwanda.

Once in Bumbogo, the hoes are greeted with the acclamations usually reserved for the king, thus once again reinforcing the identity—earlier reflected in their analogous mediating roles—of the king and the hoes. There are drums and acclamations and more: at the arrival of the hoes a new fire is kindled. This both recalls the association of fire with the arrival of the kings as portrayed in the creation myths, and reflects the specific ritual within the Code dedicated to the rekindling of the sacred fire of kingship at the beginning of each new dynastic cycle.[11] Firemaking also appears in other rituals and is specifically associated with the king —notably in the enthronization ritual. It is then left to the family of Muswere (during the moon of *nzeri,* September–October) to sow the sorghum two days in succession, after which cultivation takes place normally, by the whole population in Bumbogo. From then until the harvest, this area is virtually in quarantine —no one not resident of the area can enter Bumbogo, and the greatest precautions are taken to prevent any grain from leaving the area before the completion of the umuganura rituals. (Bourgeois adds that the initial cultivation takes place on a tiny plot of land, no more than one meter square, and is done at night, by Muswere and his own ritualist, of the Zigaaba clan.[12] The former point, as an inversion of normal activities, has already been discussed above; the latter point reflects a later episode in the umuganura ritual, to be discussed below.)

In this case, then, the ritual Code introduces a tie of a specific social group, the Swere ritualists, as mediating between ecology and technology: the application of the hoes to the soil, or the transformation from sorghum seed to (eventually) food crops. In other words, the relationship that makes productive the application of technology to ecology is specific, not diffuse: it has to be applied action; it does not "just happen."

Episode II (*La royauté sacrée*, VIII, 34–72). The second episode is essentially concerned with the mediation between fertility and society: it follows the First Fruits of the sorghum from the ripening ear through presentation at the court to consumption by an unidentified Hutu member of society at large. Throughout this process of "plant becoming food," the sorghum (and millet) represent fertility, reproduction, and well-being: they are placed in contexts that reinforce these connotations. The intermediary role of the court and king is evident, but there is a secondary intermediary role of an interesting sort. As before, this is the role of technological elements—tools made by man. But in this case it is manifested in the number of containers (and huts) through which the sorghum passes on its journey toward becoming food. This aspect of Culture continues throughout the ritual sequence, where the movement through the sequential stages of a given episode is given ritual confirmation by the movement from container to container, containers sometimes fabricated of specified materials.

In the moon of *mutarama* (roughly corresponding to January–February), the first sorghum is mature. A sample is taken to the court, along with four grains of millet, in a basket made of bamboo with a pointed cover (*ikangara*). The four grains of millet represent the belief that historically sorghum was preceded by millet as the staple cereal crop of the kingdom. In some neighboring areas, millet is the sole ritual food cultivated specifically for these ceremonies, as apparently it was earlier in Rwanda.[13] At the arrival of the sorghum/millet in *Kambere* (the principal quarters of the king for public audiences), the king leaves, as do all others not associated directly with the ritual. The king then returns and is seated —but not on the ritual stool, as specified in other contexts of the ritual. He touches the basket of sorghum, as does the queen mother, and the basket is then taken to another (unspecified) house, where the sorghum/millet mixture is ground. The meal from this—great precautions are taken to avoid dropping on the ground or profaning a single morsel—is placed in two baskets (*icyibo*) made of plaited reeds. Milk from a given herd is brought in two wooden milk pots made of the wood of an erythrene tree, a tree with very strong ritual connotations because of its brilliant red flowers and because its vegetation passes through four (a powerful ritual number) very distinct stages during the year. The sorghum and milk are then brought back to Kambere, where only the ritualists are permitted. The king looks at the sorghum meal four times (in this case, the verb used in the Code for "to look at" could also possibly mean "to taste," a cognate verb); a specified wife (of the same clan, Ega, as the principal ritualist responsible for the cultivation of the sorghum) also looks at it four times.

The icyibo baskets are then placed in a large wooden pot of several quarts capacity (*igicuba*, usually used for drawing water), and this in turn is placed on a shelf over the royal bed, behind *nyarushara*, the principal iron regalium of the kingship and source of exceedingly strong ritual power. That night the king and his Ega wife have intercourse "in the presence" of the sorghum/millet mixture and the nyarushara insignia. This has been interpreted as an act intended to ensure a productive sorghum harvest.[14] It would seem to me, instead, that this is not intended as a one-way influence (either way) between human sexual fertility and agricultural productivity, but rather that the juxtaposition of the three acts/objects—the sorghum, the act of intercourse, and the nyarushara—all represent a single classificatory category: they all reflect, and their mutual presence reinforces, the fertility and power of reproduction—of the land, of the people, of the kingdom; ecology, society, culture. Just before the drums signaling the new day are sounded, an unidentified member of society (but specified as "Hutu") removes the sorghum meal from the igicuba pot and takes it out of the house, where he eats it at his ease.

Thus the new harvest, after passing through many intermediary stages involving baskets and pots, contacts with certain people, and juxtaposition with objects/acts of a similar classificatory nature, is finally fit to serve as food for society: the significance of a lack of any specific identification of the Hutu beneficiary is clear; it also recalls the creation myths wherein the royal ancestors brought down food crops (sorghum among them) for the people below. This then consecrates the new harvest, reflects its fertility and power in other domains, reinforces the dietary staple of the kingdom (juxtaposing it with milk during part of the ceremony), and reconfirms the role of the king as intermediary and benefactor of society.

Episode III (*La royauté sacrée*, VIII, 73–137). The principal themes then are clearly established before the beginning of the rituals most evident to the public. Those themes include the role of Culture mediating between Ecology and Society; the king mediating between both Ecology and Society; and the king mediating between both Ecology and Society at one level of involvement and between Culture and both Ecology and Society at another level (see figure 10.1). The next section develops these themes, and in so doing adds some new dimensions. The most important is that of movement: in this portion of the ritual, food and people are moved from place to place frequently and with powerful meaning. Furthermore, this displacement occurs at various levels: within Kambere, between houses and areas within the court, and through the wider ritual domain representing the larger kingdom. In addition, the intermediary roles of cultural elements are emphasized by the fact of their being more precisely defined, both in their use and their construction: certain containers are to be made of materials drawn from specific areas. (However, this aspect of the Code is less pronounced in this particular ritual than in certain other rituals, such as VI, *Izira y'Umuriro*, "La Voie du Feu.")

At the new moon of *gashantare* (February–March), the ritualist of the Swere lineage arrives at the court to ask for the *igitenga*, a basket of enormous dimensions (roughly ten feet wide by five feet high), so that in spite of the implications of the Code, it seems impossible for one man to have carried it alone on his head; more likely it was carried in a litter.[15]

An unmarried woman of the Ega clan smears the inside of the igitenga basket with butter, a symbol of fertility in this and in other contexts throughout the royal rituals and more local rituals (e.g., marriage).[16] This takes place at a specified section of the royal enclosure set aside for ritual performances; it is a locale especially associated with drums. The basket (with butter inside) is then given to an unspecified Hutu, who takes it to the king, seated on the stool—the principal seat—with a sheepskin attached to it. The king then takes the basket by the top rim only and hands it to the Tsoobe ritualist, who "looks into it" (*akakibanza mu mutwe:* he places his head into it); the Swere ritualist does the same. The basket is then taken away by an unspecified Hutu.

The significant aspect of this episode, it seems to me, is the social anonymity of most actors, especially noticeable with regard to the king. This is reinforced by the king's absence from the succeeding ritual episode; it is only much later in the course of the ritual that the king reappears. It is of particular significance that the king is seated on a sheepskin, which is a form of clothing prohibited to the monarch (except when he is ritually forging: see Ritual XVII, 882, for example). Similarly, mutton or lamb is a disdained, almost tabooed, meat by Rwandan court norms. This aspect of the ritual is emphasized in the Code itself: a full six lines is devoted to the fact that it is a sheepskin, not a cow's hide or leopard skin, on which the king is seated, despite the fact (continues the Code) that sheepskin has been prohibited him since the time "he was still a Tuutsi" (e.g., before he was enthroned king: royal status elevates him above any particular social group identity). Thus the king is placed in almost an aroyal role (or at least minimized royal role); his liminal status in this portion of the ritual emphasizes again his purely intermediary status throughout the ritual as a whole. The emphasis is on the basket, as the propitious recipient for the harvest, and as consecrated as such by the ritualists—the only specified actors aside from the king. Thus the basket could be seen as intermediary between nature and society in this episode. But from what follows, and from the reduced social emphasis in what precedes, it may be more useful to see this as a "marriage," a union of the basket and the harvest, and thus as a statement of the complementarity of culture and nature.

Immediately on leaving the king's house, the igitenga basket departs on its journey across the Nyabarongo—always carried by an unspecified Hutu—to Bumbogo, the area where the sorghum was cultivated.[17] It thus mediates between the two sacral domains of the kingdom (with the Nyabarongo dividing essentially the royal domain from the agricultural domain—and it achieves this differentiation, it might be noted, without actually defining the extent, or the limits, of either domain). Along the route the basket even travels by night—Bourgeois says that it travels only at night;[18] the people line the path to greet the basket with great applause. Drums greet it in Bumbogo—there were no drums at the central court ritual, and in fact they were explicitly proscribed—amid un-restrained joy and acclamations of the most enthusiastic nature.[19] On arrival in Bumbogo, the basket is filled with new sorghum and the return trip is under-taken immediately, the same day, this time in the form of a conquest. As before, great acclamations accompany the progress of the igitenga, but this time there is more: the inhabitants of Bumbogo who accompany the igitenga/sorghum enter a period of institutionalized license (apparently for them alone?): the Code vir-tually requires of them to rob and beat those whom they meet en route, and steal—or expropriate, since they are acting in the capacity of "antiroyalty"—at will, and without reprisals.

They lodge at homes of ritually prescribed clans (two of the *abasangwabu-taka* clans taken to be the original "owners of the land," whose members fulfill a variety of ritual roles relative to the population as a whole); every night they are expected to receive "gifts of hospitality" (-*zimaana*; but in this case the term is used almost in the sense of "tribute"). They can even seize prestations destined for the chiefs or royal court without recourse on the part of those so despoiled. Again, on arrival at the court the basket/sorghum is greeted by drums—not the royal drums, but the ritual drums of the Tsoobe ritualist. The next morning the inhabitants of Bumbogo are presented with an ox—the quintessential "gift of hospitality"—and from there the emphasis of the ritual is on the introduction of the sorghum to the royal court.

One other aspect of this episode is worth mentioning as relevant to the pre-ceding analysis. The igitenga basket is said in the text to have been carried by a Hutu (singular). But given its dimensions, this is impossible; it is virtually in-conceivable that the basket when filled with grain could have been carried even on a litter. Hence, despite the note in *La royauté sacrée,* it seems more likely that the basket was transported empty to and from Bumbogo.[20] This would certainly reinforce the idea of the symbolic role of the basket as intermediary between the two domains on either side of the Nyabarongo.

Episode IV (*La royauté sacrée,* VIII, 138–200). What follows is a very brief condensation of the procession from the Tsoobe enclosure to Kambere, the king's house. In itself this section takes almost one-sixth of the ritual (sixty-two lines) and is clearly of considerable importance. The cortège includes the royal drums of the kingdom, butter placed in a clay pot of a prescribed type, with the pot placed on a support of special uncut grass (i.e., the grass is pulled out by hand); on arrival at the court, the butter is taken to the sacral portion of the enclosure and transferred to wooden pots of a prescribed type (igicuba). Included in the procession are two unmarried women, carried on hammocks, who play a role in the ritual and later become wives to the king.

As the drums arrive at the Tsoobe enclosure, where they meet the igitenga/ sorghum, the handles of the principal drum (*Karinga*) are intertwined with those of the igitenga basket, thus uniting the two domains: drums-igitenga/ sorghum; southern and northern ritual domains of the kingdom; power and authority; court and commoner. In addition, there are included two clay jars from Buhanga, the area of Rwanda associated with the memory of Gihanga, the culture hero and mythical founder of Rwanda (and putatively the ultimate ancestor of the kings): the sacral fire of the kingdom was supposed to be kept in a jar of this type. (Otherwise there is no other mention of this aspect in this particular ritual, though it does relate to other rituals.) Two grinding stones also accompany the procession.

As the procession arrives at the court, the Code gives rather explicit attention to the role of king as king in this instance, rather in contrast to the preceding section, even specifying at some length what he should have with him. Among these are a red necklace received at his enthronization and a ring made of fibers of a certain plant of prolific foliage that bears a white flower: it was a plant used as a charm to ensure the fertility of seeds as reflected in its role in this ceremony.[21] The king also wears a cloth made of banana fibers and a hare's tail—also white, but more directly recalling the king's solidarity with his generals, as also in the enthronization and burial ceremonies.

As the drums arrive, the king goes to them and beats out a special rhythm associated with the royal drums exclusively (*igihubi*). In this way he announces his active role in the ceremony—a role he has not assumed in previous episodes. It is at this point, therefore, that the royal focus of the ritual becomes dominant. The prominent role of the royal drums and of the king, the prescribed apparel recalling enthronization and other rituals where the king as a person is the central focus, the pots recalling Gihanga, the "dismissal" of the people of Bumbogo and the diminished role of Tsoobe/Muswere henceforth: all these serve to reinstate the royalty as the focus of the final stages of the ritual. But it is worth noting that such was not the case throughout the preceding aspects of the ritual. Though the emotional pitch may be highest in the succeeding episodes, the symbolic and structural significance is not limited to the drama at the court, nor confined to those episodes in which the king predominates.

Episode V (*La royauté sacrée*, VIII, 200–322). The next section of the ritual is concerned with two complementary processes: that of integrating the sorghum into the royal court—in a sense the ritual emphasizes the change of focus from the Tsoobe (who himself has taken over from Muswere as the central actor) to the king; and that of the transformation of sorghum into food. There is thus evoked both a social and a cultural transformation (in the very restrictive senses in which these terms are used in this chapter)—the movement from Bumbogo to "central" Rwanda ("central" from the perspective of the court), and the transformation from plant to food. In both processes Ecology (Nature) becomes subordinated or transformed, or integrated into other domains, and hence in this instance the two aspects that we have (roughly) designated as Society and Technology/Culture become identified, in a classificatory sense, by their common opposition to what we have termed Ecology. Though color symbolism is still present, numerical symbolism seems to become more important a symbolic form than color, or at least more apparent; it is possible that this shift relates to the focus on integration to the court, since numerical symbolism, as used here, has a more direct relationship to (or separation from) the royal court than color symbolism, which is more generalized.

As the igitenga/sorghum is introduced, the Tsoobe ritualist kneels on one side while the king is seated on the other; the Code refers to the former as "behind" the basket, the latter as "in front of" the basket. They "comb" the sorghum, a gesture involving four stalks of sorghum (with heads?), which they then place "upright" in the basket.[22] The king and Tsoobe ritualist together transfer sorghum by hand to fill four small baskets (icyibo); the igitenga basket is then placed in the house, on a shelf (no regalia are supposed to touch the soil except in prescribed circumstances) just "in front of" the shelf with two grinding stones: in other words, once again the igitenga is in an intermediary position between the sorghum and the symbols of royalty (the kingdom); it is also a mediator since it here assumes an aspect of regalia (by its position and sacral aspect, having been smeared with butter) and yet is still a container of sorghum—it is literally "through the basket" that the sorghum arrives at the court. Sorghum-honey beer (explicitly of a reddish tint, as also recalled by its name, *rugina*, derived from the reddish earth of a termite hill, as will be noted below) is then presented to the king and Tsoobe. In addition to its color (reflecting the reddish color of sorghum grain, with which it is presented to the court), the identification of this beer with the sorghum First Fruits is demonstrated in two ways. It is made by the

Swere ritualist and brought (or "tasted") in a similar fashion to that in which the sorghum is consumed (including the presence of similar personnel, in the performance of similar gestures, and a prescription that the king be dressed in similar ritual regalia).[23] The king and the Tsoobe ritualist each go through the ritual gesture of drinking beer four times; then the king (he alone) tastes it. The beer is then placed on the shelf before the bed, along with the iron regalium noted above.

The next scenes of the ritual have a slightly different character from the preceding: the numeration system changes from four-based to three-based, and the king again appears in a ritual role of slight eclipse. The ceremony continues as an unidentified Hutu brings three blocks of clay, formed of the red earth from a termite hill, and places them as three supports for a cooking pot. The king then "arrives" (although there was no mention of his having left) carrying two types of "soft" plants used in funerary rites; the explicit interpretation of their softness is that they represent the desire that the newly departed shades (in the funerary rites) will be "soft" in dealing with the profane.[24] From the calabash containing these plants the king then pours water nine times before the jar resting on the clay supports; the same gesture is made by the queen mother, the wife of the king, the Tsoobe ritualist, and the Muswere. The number nine is associated in Rwanda as a sign of fertility, especially in nonroyal contexts (in the Ryangombe ceremony, the veneration of a spirit explicitly opposed to royalty, for example, or in marriage ceremonies); it also appears in certain royal rituals, but I would interpret these cases as eight-plus-one, not nine as such. It is always associated with the beginning of a new cycle in these rites, but the completed preceding cycle (in royal rituals) is still a multiple of four: in these contexts the "nine" indicates a break with the past, not the completion of a cycle.

A fire fed by a special kind of very hard wood (*umurama*) is then lit to the right (the ritually propitious side) of the jar, and the water is brought to a boil. The king then comes before the pot and kneels and claps his hands before it, exactly as one would show respect to a superior—exactly as one would greet the king. He is followed in this gesture, again, by the queen mother, the king's wife, the Tsoobe ritualist, and the Swere ritualist: at this point, the Code says, the jar has become "favorable."

The four baskets of ground sorghum flour are then brought in, and the king with his wife and the Tsoobe ritualist all add some of the flour to the water (four times, in a ritual gesture): the wife adds the rest alone. The king, his wife, and the

Tsoobe ritualist all place the spatula in the pot together. When cooked, the gruel is placed again in the four icyibo baskets. While the gruel is cooking, however, the king, Tsoobe ritualist, and Muswere ritualist all go out and cultivate "solemnly." They are subsequently joined by the inhabitants of Bumbogo who arrived with the sorghum. This cultivation reflects the earlier planting ceremony, performed at night and without the king, in Bumbogo. When the gruel has finished cooking, all cultivation stops, thus making a clear temporal identification with the initial and final stages of the process of transforming "nature" into "culture," or plant into food. Also, by this action the king appears to have regained his ritual initiative—he participates first in all subsequent ritual acts, and the number system has returned to a four-based symbolism rather than a three-based system, which was associated (temporally at least) with the king's apparent eclipse and subordination to the sorghum and ritual.

Milk is then brought from a given herd, carried in two milk pots fashioned from the wood of the erythrene tree, as had been done in the earlier ceremony of the moon of *munanira*. The king again adorns himself in the banana-fiber "pagnes des prémices" and the *igihanda* ring, made of a plant with white flowers, and is seated on the royal stool. Butter is brought, in a specified type of pot. The Tsoobe then comes in with gruel and kneels before the king; all this again emphasizes the newly regained preeminent role of the king. After having drunk twice of the milk, the king takes the gruel (in an icyibo basket) and touches it to the interior of the *ididokombwa* pot four times; he then drinks again of the milk. The queen mother does the same (with her own icyibo basket of gruel). The king's wife does the same, but she uses the icyibo basket of the king. The Tsoobe and Muswere ritualists repeat the same gestures, each using his own icyibo basket. They then take out all the gruel.

The king and his wife then retire to the bed, where they have intercourse. One of the unmarried women participants in the ritual, a woman of the Tsoobe clan, stands in the doorway to acclaim them; no other Tsoobe can be present in the enclosure at this time, and in fact no other Tsoobe appears further in the ritual, which is, for all practical purposes, ended. The rest of the Code for this particular ritual is concerned with placing the pots and baskets in the sacral area of the enclosure and the tribute required of the chiefs—both for the court and for (as well as from) Bumbogo. It ends with a statement that calls to mind the joy (the celebrations continue day and night), the satisfaction (they drink in "long drafts"), and the reminder that this is, in fact, a public as well as an esoteric ceremony.

ONE STRIKING aspect of this ceremony to emerge from such an analysis concerns the role of the king. He appears explicitly in the Muganuro text less often than one would expect (given that this is a royal ritual central to the kingship), and his role through most of the ritual is not dominant: he is usually very explicitly a mediator (e.g., he touches the basket or looks at the sorghum). Finally, he often acts with others, not in sequence but simultaneously (usually with Tsoobe). This aspect might well, of course, be emphasized differently in the actual observation of the ritual performed, simply because of the dominant social role of the king in any gathering. But the Code as a text is clearly focused on the sorghum. The court is the place where much of the action occurs (and significant for that), but it is not the central focus of the ritual, in the wider sense, of which the king is only part. This would cast some question on the rather bold statement by Bourgeois: "It is therefore natural that the court should hold the preeminent role in the festivities surrounding the prémices of sorghum and millet for which the guardians of the tradition were located at Bumbogo."[25]

In conclusion, this ceremony can be seen as quite different from the conventional portrayal, whereby the king plays the central role of initiator and unique source of power, both ritual and political, for the kingdom. Nor is the king elevated above others. Instead, umuganura in Rwanda demonstrates the degree of participation in kingship shared by the ritualists drawn from commoner clans. In fact, it is their participation that creates kingship and strengthens the king. The ritual implies that the Rwandan *mwami* was far from being a "divine king," if this term is understood as referring to a ruler above and beyond society, deriving his powers from an extraterrestrial divine source and therefore owing no allegiance to the society over which he ruled. In fact, kingship seems more the creation of the conjunction, or the interrelationship, of forces of the world here below. The king's role was the product of social participation. He was a relatively passive, relatively immobile personage in these rituals. His position outside society derived from the ambivalence of his role, which provided him a liminal status; he was an intermediary between several classificatory categories, and therefore unequivocally a member of none. In this sense he could not be seen in the ritual context of kingship as a full participant in society, but a liminal figure. He was a sacral figure, perhaps, but not a "divine king."

It has been observed for other areas of Africa that the basic conception behind installation ceremonies of this type is summed up in the phrase "the kingship captures the king."[26] But kingship itself is not autonomous of the conceptual framework of a culture any more than it is autonomous of the social ligaments of a culture. If kingship captures the king, then it is also clear that culture captures the kingship. As I have tried to demonstrate for these rituals, kingship is embedded within the conceptual universe shared by all elements of society. More than responding to questions of seizing kingship or exercising power, these rituals of kingship speak to more profound dimensions of social thought, for within this conceptual framework the meaning of kingship touched on—as kingship was indeed a product of—the conjunction of important categories of the universe. Kingship mediated between them, but in so doing it reemphasized their separation, their differentiation. Consequently, the rites reaffirming the power of kingship also reaffirmed the essential nature of the universe itself. It was in this sense, not in the narrower Durkheimian sense, that society continually redefined kingship.

TRICK CYCLISTS?

Recontextualizing Rwandan Dynastic Chronology

1994

The ideology of kingship asserted that kingship was legitimated by its an-
tiquity: the dynasty was at the heart of Rwandan culture, so the founding of
the dynasty must (logically) correspond to the origin of the culture. By one
official source, that meant that kingship in Rwanda was formed in 1091 and
followed invariable father-to-son succession to 1959. Court sources claimed
to substantiate that chronology by drawing on tie-ins linking the Rwandan
genealogy to the chronologies of royal lines in neighboring states. But inter-
nal evidence casts doubt both on the depth of such a proposed chronology
and even on the sovereign status of some of those individuals named in the
official Rwandan king list. Analysis of the dynastic histories of four neigh-
boring states only confirms such skepticism; both internal and external
evidence suggest quite a different (and much shorter) royal chronology for
Rwanda than that presented in the official sources. Based on detailed analy-
sis of the comparative data, this chapter proposes a reassessment of both the
chronology and the content of the "official" king list of Rwanda, showing
again how historical analysis can apply even to fundamental elements of
society—in this case the chronology of kingship.

The Conundrum of Chronology

CHRONOLOGY USED TO BE an object of great interest among African historians because it was seen as essential to history, it provided exactitude where so much else was interpretive, and it was such a challenging feature to determine from oral accounts. More recently, historical analysis has been concerned more with processes and periods than with defined events and dates.[1] Although deemed to be useful when available, precise chronology is now seen as less essential to historical reconstruction; it is accepted that chronologies are subject to interpretation and debate, and that these debates themselves illuminate the way in which local communities reconstruct—and historians understand—history.

This chapter addresses such issues of debate, contestation, and negotiation —that is, it explores the nature of intellectual hegemony—but it does so across cultural boundaries. It thus illustrates a fundamental contradiction in the manner by which historians have treated cultural units defined as distinct: while as independent polities they have been assumed to be culturally autonomous, yet source material from one is often drawn on to fill in the gaps of others. This procedure was especially common where there were powerful kingdoms whose political boundaries were assumed to be rigid and inviolate. The states of the western Interlacustrine area, each believed to be ruled by an established dynastic line whose origins reached far back into antiquity, provide an exemplary illustration of this process.

By the early twentieth century, at the time of European conquest, Rwanda was one of the most powerful of these states, having either conquered and absorbed, or at least dominated, many of the distinct kingdoms with which it formerly competed. The political ascendancy of Rwanda was also reflected in its historical luster, for the power that ensured its regional political hegemony also legitimated its historical claims, at least in the eyes of many. Rwandan power also attracted the interest of Europeans; it is not surprising that many of the first written works on the dynastic history of the region focused on Rwandan court traditions. Over time these early attempts were elaborated, consolidated, and standardized, a process culminating in the massive corpus produced from the 1940s by Alexis Kagame, a Rwandan priest. Others studying in this region often came to refer to this work as the validating text, the central historical core to which other histories were compared; among neighboring dynastic histories, each individual chronicle taken in isolation was proven correct only if it conformed to—and thus implicitly confirmed—the official Rwandan texts.

However, a new pattern emerges when these different dynastic histories are viewed not in isolation, each in its own terms relative to Rwanda, but in regional perspective. Within this framework, certain patterns emerge: in every case we know of, the dynastic genealogies of states outside Rwanda are shorter than the official Rwandan chronology and by approximately the same amount. Furthermore, where these are known to have been revised, in every case they were lengthened—with the Rwandan dynastic history as the validating factor for its extension. In other words, when looked at within a regional perspective, the Rwandan line becomes itself an exception to the general pattern, rather than its exemplar. To explore this issue, therefore, is to inquire into the transfer of knowledge, to reflect on intellectual authority in a contested field, and to seek out the forces that serve to create knowledge by validating our understanding of a given historical "fact." In this case, it is specifically to inquire into the authority of the official Rwandan dynastic list over competing interpretations. It reflects the fact that struggle for political autonomy is also a struggle over defining historical legitimacy.

Without engaging in a full examination of the development, elaboration, and legitimation of the Rwandan royal chronicle, I seek simply to open up new questions by looking at elements of the regional patterns of dynastic histories common to the region, and to indicate aspects of the Rwandan dynastic history that are suggestive of how this process of elaboration and legitimation took place. This inquiry builds on the work of others who have engaged with these questions before.[2] But rather than suggesting slight adjustments to the official texts, refining the currently accepted dynastic history (and chronology) as currently accepted, I focus on larger issues based on regional perspectives, not isolated chronologies. I do not arrive at assured conclusions; this inquiry thus reflects the nature of oral knowledge and oral discourse. We may have to be satisfied with articulating the debates rather than resolving them, with identifying the issues of contention rather than arriving at a single consolidated, definitive account.

The argument suggests that looking carefully at materials drawn from outside the confines of the central court of Rwanda will lead to a reexamination of the published sources on the Rwandan king list. I will first examine four cases of states neighboring Rwanda: Gisaka to the southeast, Ndorwa to the northeast, Burundi to the south, and Buhavu to the west. In each of these instances, the written chronicle of the dynastic line appears to have been altered to correspond to the imputed chronology of Rwanda. But I am not interested simply in reconstructing the chronologies. Instead, the common pattern to emerge from such a survey suggests that the Rwandan king list and its associated chronology need to be radically rethought. Doing so in turn leads me to examine elements in the Rwandan dynastic chronicles that bear on this revisualized chronology. In particular, I will focus on a single cycle of four king names, the cycle immediately following Ruganzu Ndori and preceding Cyilima Rujugira. (For reference, the Rwandan king list appears as table 11.5 in the appendix to this chapter.)

Gisaka and Rwanda: The Dynastic Tie-Ins

Early writings on Rwanda noted only a few kings, without fixed order.[3] It was not until the work of Alexis Kagame in the 1940s and 1950s that the published dynastic chronicles assumed their grandest forms.[4] Since that time, the Rwandan royal history has been celebrated for its precision, its comprehensive character, and its antiquity; and in the eyes of many commentators, greater precision and greater antiquity ipso facto implied greater legitimacy. Because the comprehensive nature of the Rwandan chronicles included many references to the dynastic lines of neighboring kingdoms, the greater antiquity and greater perceived validity of the Rwandan line resulted in a lengthening of the royal histories of neighboring states.

The most explicit example of this process is that of the king list of Gisaka, a region in southeast Rwanda incorporated into the Rwandan state at intervals over the course of the later nineteenth and early twentieth centuries (and in the end, with German and Belgian assistance). The major chronicler for this kingdom is A. d'Arianoff, whose *Histoire des Bagesera* serves as the principal precolonial source for this area. Early king lists counted eight or nine names back from Kimenyi Getura, who reigned early in the nineteenth century.[5] (Table 11.1 gives four examples.) But of those names, only six were consistent among the three extant king lists. D'Arianoff explained such divergence not in terms of differential perspectives (the process of uneven regional expansion, or differential class incorporation to Gisaka royal structures), but by the tendency of informants to alter their testimony to please—or deceive—the listener. Rwandan court sources, he averred, were more reliable because they contained formal checks assuring the validity of the information transmitted.[6] And so d'Arianoff sought recourse to Kagame.

Although he had never set foot in Gisaka, Kagame not only confirmed d'Arianoff's list, but extended it.[7] He claimed that the name of Kimenyi recurred several times within the Gisaka king list, but that local sources (or those who

Table 11.1
Comparative king lists of Gisaka

Pagès	Kibungu archives	D'Arianoff	Kagame/D'Arianoff
—	Kagesera	Kagesera	Kagesera
Kimenyi	*Kimenyi* Rwahashya	*Kimenyi* Rwahashya	*Kimenyi* I Musaya
Mukanya	—	—	—
—	Kavuma Kabishatse	—	—
—	—	Kabunda	Kabunda
Mutwa	—	—	—
—	—	—	Kimenyi II
Mutuminka	*Mutuminka*	*Mutuminka*	*Mutuminka*
—	—	Ntaho	Ntaho
—	—	—	Kimenyi III Rwahashya
Kwezi	*Kwezi* kw'Irusagwe	*Kwezi* kw'iRusagwe	*Kwezi* kw'iRusagwe
Luregeya	*Lulegeya*	*Ruregeya*	*Ruregeya*
Muhoza	—	—	—
Bazimya	*Bazimya* Shumbusho	*Bazimya* Shumbusho	*Bazimya* Shumbuso
Kimenyi Getura	*Kimenyi* i Kimenya	*Kimenyi* i Kimenyi	*Kimenyi* IV Getura

Italicized names are those shared on all lists.
Source: D'Arianoff, *L'histoire des Bagesera*, 38, 43.

recorded them) had omitted the replications. In essence, then, Kagame retained d'Arianoff's list, the longest of the three available, but inserted two more kings named Kimenyi, so that this dynastic name not only appeared as the first and last names on the list, but at quasi-regular intervals as well. As a result of Kagame's intervention, d'Arianoff felt able to assert: "Rwandan sources establish *with certainty* the existence of four kings with the name of Kimenyi, although Kisaka elders account for only two."[8] Such was the authority of Kagame.

Justification for this assurance was found in four tie-ins between the Rwanda and Gisaka ruling lines. Two consisted of marriage alliances—one very early, the other very late in the Gisaka list. In the first case, Robwa, the sister of Ruganzu Bwimba (the first "historically validated" Rwandan king; r. 1312–45 by Kagame's chronology) is said to have married Kimenyi, king of Gisaka. She is remembered in Rwandan traditions because, on hearing that her brother had been killed on the field of battle against Gisaka, she killed herself. Her unborn child, the prospective heir to the Gisaka throne, died with her; according to the Rwandan augurs at the time, this child, had he grown to maturity, would eventually have overthrown the Rwandan dynasty. Thus, according to this interpretation, her action saved the Rwandan state at the moment when her own brother had died in battle against Gisaka.[9] The second case occurred in the penultimate reign of the Gisaka dynastic list, when the cousin of Bazimya is said to have married Cyilima Rujugira (r. 1740–60 by Kagame's chronology).

Between these two marriage ties, for over two centuries, the Gisaka traditions presented by d'Arianoff add little: the two added kings named Kimenyi are known only by recourse to Kagame's Rwandan chronicles, where each is noted with a tie-in to a Rwandan king, the first to Mibambwe Mutabazi, the second to Kigeri Nyamuheshera.[10] It is almost as if the Gisaka list has been extended to fit the tie-ins . . . Such an appearance is even stronger when it is noted that this revised list for the Gisaka kings, validated only by the Rwandan tie-ins, is said to include eleven kings over four centuries—that is to say, almost a forty-year average maintained over four hundred years.

Yet, skepticism aside, the authority of the Rwandan priest who was also privy to Rwandan esoteric traditions—the historian who was also a member of one of the elite families of late nineteenth-century Rwanda—was immense.[11] D'Arianoff notes that "the remarkable work of classifying, unifying, and interpreting the diverse data undertaken by Abbé Kagame has spared me much laborious research, and made it possible to compare easily the results of our fieldwork with the indications—few but sure—on the early history of Gisaka accounted for in Rwandan sources."[12] And he goes on to add, apparently without irony, "May we express here our heartfelt thanks to Abbé Kagame for his disinterested support offered in both information and advice."[13] d'Arianoff is thus explicit both about his debts and about the way in which he "rectified" the deficient Bagesera king list—by placing the Bagesera line in conformity with the Rwandan line and adding the requisite kings to the list.

Ndorwa and Rwanda: Cyclic Traditions

A similar, though more sophisticated, process of alignment occurred for Ndorwa, a kingdom associated with a Bashambo dynasty northeast of the Rwandan heartland. Here Freedman presents a most interesting example of recycling king names.

But they are once again premised on the assumption that they must coincide with the Rwandan king list and that the Rwandan line as given by Kagame is correct.

For this area Freedman notes diverse and incompatible local traditions associated with the names Gahaya and Murari; he suggests that these incompatibilities result from references to different individuals bearing the same name. As support he notes that one Gahaya was a contemporary of Rujugira in Rwanda, and he cites Kagame. But Gahaya was also the name of the ruler at the time of Ndorwa's grandeur, which apparently occurred four Rwandan reigns earlier, at the time of Kigeri Nyamuheshera; the source—Alexis Kagame. Accepting these references to two different—and widely separated—Rwandan kings, Freedman postulates that these references actually refer to two distinct individuals sharing a common dynastic name. Noting that the pattern of recurring dynastic names appears frequently in the region (and citing the examples of Nkore, Gisaka, and Rwanda, the last two based on Kagame), Freedman concludes that "it is only reasonable that the Bashambo of Ndorwa should also have designated their kings according to a repeating cycle of names. . . . With this in mind, many of the anomalies of the history of Ndorwa begin to dissolve."[14]

His analysis builds on these premises, stated as established facts: "Assuming that as in the other Interlacustrine kingdoms, the names in the dynasty of the Bashambo-ruled kingdom recurred, one may begin to inquire how the cycles of kingship merge with the historical facts available."[15] But two aspects to this argument are worthy of note. First, dynastic names are assumed to recur in all ("the," not "some") Interlacustrine kingdoms. In addition, this feature of repeating dynastic names becomes transformed to a "cycle" (or a recurring pattern) of kingship names; in fact, very few kingdoms adhered to such a cyclical pattern. But even with these arguments, not all the anomalies dissolve. Freedman notes that "there are considerable gaps in the [newly constructed] chronology, periods when no kings at all are mentioned."[16] Yet these gaps appear only "in comparison to the ruling genealogy of Rwanda."[17]

It is an elegant and sophisticated analysis, based on intimate familiarity with the sources, both local and published. Indeed, I am not arguing here against the appearance of common names in a king list, or even against repeating cycles of names, as a principle in itself. These characteristics can, and do, occur, although not in all states. Nor am I arguing against the utility of comparative analysis in historical reconstruction. Nonetheless, such analytic techniques need to conform to the canons of historical analysis, which include attention to the sources and especially to the independent provenance of data to be compared. To prove one set of data by reference to another set derived from the first is to engage in tautological thinking: if one draws on Rwandan data to reconstruct the Ndorwa king list, one cannot prove its validity by reference to the Rwandan king list. The events in question could well have occurred, but such reasoning does not establish that they did.

What is striking in this case is the recurring pattern of such a process: in Ndorwa as in Gisaka, in Burundi as in Buhavu (as we shall see below), the same pattern appears to hold. In each case the chronology is established—and the king list lengthened—by reference to Rwanda; the gaps are filled in with recurring names (or recurring cycles); and the Rwandan chronology is then implicitly validated by the convergence of neighboring dynastic genealogies which then appear to correspond to—and thus to confirm—the Rwandan core chronology.

Burundi and Rwanda: The Recurring Ntare

In Burundi, south of Rwanda, there occurred a similar process of reconstructing the royal line, a process that assumed the cyclic succession of a given set of dynastic names and the correspondence of Rundi dynastic generation lengths with those of Rwanda. Vansina notes the presence of two schools of thought on the Rundi king list.[18] One postulates four cycles of four names each (hence sixteen kings) in the genealogy of the most recent dynasty. The other accounts for only two cycles, or eight kings. Two characteristics of this debate are worth noting. First, it is argued not in terms of kings but of cycles: dynastic cycles are assumed to be inviolate, immutable, and complete. Second, this dispute cannot be settled on the basis of external logic alone; it is as reasonable that events from the distant past have been telescoped, combined into more recent reigns (hence yielding a shorter chronology), as it is that names and events have been projected back into the distant past and accepted as part of antiquity because of the legitimacy that adheres to longevity. In fact, in any given list both processes (telescoping and projection) may well have occurred over time; they are not mutually exclusive.

In Burundi, as elsewhere, earlier testimonies (often presented in European accounts) tend toward the shorter option. In Rwanda, analogous presentations were dismissed by Kagame because, he implies, these authors lacked access to the "true," esoteric sources on dynastic history. In Burundi, however, such esoteric sources were less important, less formalized, less commanding as authoritative texts. Furthermore, in Rwanda the official chronology appears to be in part supported by internal evidence—by multiple references and the circumstantial evidence of deeds attributed to successive Rwandan kings.[19] In Burundi, such circumstantial references are largely absent; claims to the longer chronology of four (rather than two) cycles rest largely on external tie-ins—tie-ins with Rwanda.[20] There is thus an appearance of a set of a priori assumptions: that the Rwandan historical depth is correct; that the Rundi chronology must correspond to that; and that therefore, there *must have* existed four cycles (sixteen reigns) in the most recent Rundi dynasty, not two cycles (eight reigns) as the earlier sources maintain. From what we have seen above, this conforms to a common pattern of chronological reconstruction.

It is not irrelevant, perhaps, that several of the more recent sources on Burundi, those arguing for four cycles, have a direct relation to Kagame and his work; Pierre Baranyanka played an especially important role in this process of establishing an extended chronology.[21] At the least, it is clear that these are not independent traditions and that there was a certain flow and flux to orality in Burundi (as elsewhere) that differs from the classic Rwandan model of lineal transmission unchanged through time. Instead of such linearity, there was wide horizontal diffusion across space, with multiple variants and contested perspectives on the past.[22] Most oral sources, Vansina notes, indicate two cycles.[23] There are differences in the sources, to be sure, but these can be accounted for by the geographical expansion of the state, by differences in social class, or by differing individual interests in the affairs of state. But the concordance among those traditions is nonetheless remarkable: they all agree on two cycles, eight kings—something that would appear to argue against spatial, social, or individual explanation of the different sets.[24]

In presenting his specific analyses, Kagame notes that the Rwandan chronicles pertaining to Cyilima Rugwe (r. 1345–78 by Kagame's chronology) mention a king of Burundi named Mwezi—one of the Rundi dynastic names. From that he concludes—by the logic of the inviolate dynastic cycle—that "after this Mwezi there undoubtedly must have reigned a Mutaga and a Mwambutsa," even if later accounts no longer remember them.[25] But in fact, these accounts only mention the establishment of a new dynasty by Ntare Rushatsi, associating him with the reign of the Rwandan king Mibambwe Mutabazi (r. 1411–44 by Kagame's chronology). The Rwandan traditions next mention (yet again) Ntare, this time associated with the reign of the great Rwandan hero Ruganzu Ndori. The Rwandan chronicles thus appear to omit several successors to Ntare Rushatsi;

Table 11.2
Comparative king lists of Burundi and Rwanda

Rwanda	Burundi
Mibambwe I Mutabazi	*Ntare I Rushatsi*
Yuhi II Gahima	Mwezi I Barindamunka
Ndahiro II Cyamatare	Mutaga I
Ruganzu II Ndoli	Mwambutsa I Nkomati
Mutara I Semugeshi	*Ntare II Kibogora*
Kigeri II Nyamuheshera	Mwezi II Nyaburunga
Mibambwe II Gisanura	Mutaga II Nyamubi
Yuhi III Mazimpaka	Mwambutsa II Nyarushumba
Cyilima II Rujugira	Ntare III Kivimira
Kigeri III Ndabarasa	*Mwezi III Kavuyimbo*
Mibambwe III Sentabyo	*Mutaga III Sebitungwa*
Yuhi IV Gahindiro	Mwambutsa III Mbonuburundi
Mutara II Rwogera	Ntare IV Rugamba
Kigeri IV Rwabugiri	Mwezi IV Gisabo
Yuhi V Musinga	Mutage IV Mikije
Mutara III Rudahigwa	Mwambutsa IV Bangiricenge

The tie-ins for the reigns through the Rwandan king Rujugira are italicized; later tie-ins are not noted here.

Source: Kagame, "Chronologie," 22.

by his dynastic logic, Kagame suggests that there were three: Mwezi, Mutaga, and Mwambutsa. While Kagame refers to a Mwezi as the successor to this Ntare (but provides no commentary on his reign), there are apparently no extant references to two subsequent successors, who (by this same logic) would have completed the second cycle: Mutaga and Mwambutsa. Once again we are told that the Rwandan traditions pick up with Ntare, of the "third cycle." Thus Rwandan traditions, which provide Kagame the sole evidence for the first two cycles of the four-cycle king list of Burundi, apparently retain only three of eight names for the first two cycles —and give circumstantial details on only two kings, both named Ntare.[26]

From these two tie-ins Kagame constructed his king list for Burundi, carefully aligning it with that of Rwanda, as shown in table 11.2. From Kagame's account,

Cyilima Rujugira was the contemporary of Mwezi Kavuyimbo and Mutaga Sebitungwa, and Ruganzu the contemporary of Ntare Kibogora. Kagame fills in the intermediary names from the inexorable logic of his schema; nothing is known of them from either Rwandan or Rundi sources. However, the chronology of the Rwandan cycle after Ruganzu is also less than certain—as we shall suggest below. If this cycle were very short (or incomplete), then the Ntare whom Kagame identifies as the contemporary of Ruganzu ("Ntare II") would correspond with the predecessor of Mwezi Kavuyimbo ("Ntare III"), contemporary of Rujugira. This would explain the absence of data on Kagame's Rundi cycle between these two Ntares; indeed, there are significant lacunae on the Rwanda list at the identical cycle, as we shall see.

In other sources Kagame clarifies his logic on this point. He begins by noting that there are four dynastic names for Burundi: Ntare, Mwezi, Mutaga, and Mwambutsa. "It follows that if one dynastic name reappears so many times, one must conclude, *without fear of error,* that the three other dynastic names were held the same number of times. And Rwandan traditions recall four kings named Ntare. . . . Based only on this fact and recognizing that the present king is Mwambutsa [the "last" name of the cycle], we arrive at 16 kings of the dynasty."[27]

So this dispute (of two cycles versus four cycles) is not over empirical evidence alone but over deeper differences, relating to the concept of history and the techniques of reconstructing and understanding social process. Thus those who hold to a four-cycle schema generally start from an external tie-in; that is, they accept that internal historical understanding is legitimated by reference to an external authority. And this in turn depends to a large degree on establishing a regional consensus, a framework to which component histories will conform.[28] They then assume the inviolate nature of cyclic succession, as if it were invariably accepted in historical practice.[29]

Such deductive reasoning starts with a generalization, a law of social process, and *infers* that individual events occurred to conform to the general principle. It also assumes a corporate history of the unified kingdom, a history that encompassed all regions, classes, and factions within the same chronological framework. From these guiding assumptions it seeks to fill in the events. Furthermore, it is assumed that there is only one king per generation and that generations are always of equal length; hence, commoner generations correspond to royal generations, and royal generations neatly align across cultures—for example, Rwanda and Burundi. Indeed, such may be the case, but it needs to be proved, not assumed, nor (still less) used to support other arguments ex post facto.

Finally, in this conceptual universe the search for origins becomes the object of historical inquiry: legitimate royalty can refer only to a single dynasty; there can be no "true" kings before the establishment of the most recent dynasty; the entire panoply of kingship, including name cycles, succession practices, an "esoteric code," and ritual procedures and personnel, must have existed unchanged from this founding, without dispute, contestation, or elaboration. Such a system in perfect stasis of course is at odds with most concepts of history.

But such a conceptual framework for Rundi history has its own history, one that has been traced out in some detail by others.[30] Pierre Baranyanka, one of the most influential of the colonial chiefs, was central to this process. Of an elite family himself, Baranyanka took an interest in the royal history of Burundi (in his later years his administrative domain included the region of the Rundi royal tombs), and he collaborated with European researchers from early on. And so he became familiar with the written accounts of Rundi history—and with the power of the written word. His interest in history led him to an awareness of Kagame's work; Baranyanka's later work showed the effects of both formal correspondence and direct personal interaction—some would say collaboration—with Kagame.[31] Given these influences, it is not surprising that over time Baranyanka's vision of Rundi dynastic history shifted from two cycles to three, and eventually to four, cycles of Rundi kings. Only from the 1930s did the king of the day become known as Mwambutsa IV, and thus considered the sixteenth king of the dynasty; from that time a chronology based on four cycles became more or less official under the colonial administration; it was taught in the schools, referred to in public documents, and widely diffused among the population.[32]

Such analysis could be continued. But our purpose here is only to note the common patterns relative to the Rwandan king list, not to enter into the internal dynamics of each state. It is striking that each of the three cases examined shows similar parameters: a short genealogy, found to be wanting by reference to the Rwandan king list and subsequently altered to correspond to the "more legitimate" Rwandan line. The assumption here is that twentieth-century political hegemony serves to establish the cultural authority of Rwanda over competing interpretations and to legitimate primacy in historical debates.[33] In some instances, that may hold true; in other situations (such as Gisaka and Buhavu), we can be sure that is not the case. Taken alone, perhaps, each case can be argued (to varying degrees) plausibly; it is possible that, independently, all the dynastic histories surrounding Rwanda were incorrect in an identical fashion. But such a recurring pattern is nonetheless sufficient to arouse one's interest.

From Interest to Suspicion: The Havu Case

The royal genealogy of the senior Havu kingdom, along the western shores of Lake Kivu, repeats the general pattern noted above. But it does more, transforming "interest" to "suspicion" by deepening the parallels. Most written materials on Havu royal history give prominence to the tie-in between Nsibula, said to be the first king of this dynasty, and the Rwandan king Ruganzu Ndori.[34] In addition, various other genealogies from west of the lake trace back firmly to Ruganzu: these appear independent both of each other and (except for the Havu royal genealogy) of the Rwandan sources. With multiple testimonies a parallax effect emerges, whereby genealogies of the royal family, of ritual groups, and of other commoner groups all converge on the figure of Ruganzu. Because of the renown of the name of Ruganzu, it is possible that these genealogies have been telescoped, retaining the name of Ruganzu while ignoring more recent events, or that events undertaken by other kings have been attributed to the reign of Ruganzu.[35] But they are too closely parallel to other corroborative evidence available for Rwanda, they are too strongly and consistently convergent on a new dating for Ruganzu, and there are simply too many of them from different groups to be brushed aside complacently. The implications are intriguing.

On Ijwi Island, one of the genealogies to Ruganzu is that of the most important ritual group, the Abeeru—the men who make and guard the royal drum. The Beeru on Ijwi say that they came directly from Kabagali (in Rwanda) to Ijwi.[36] The Rwandan sources confirm that the Ijwi Beeru came from Kabagali, and they elaborate on this story by noting that an early Rwandan ritualist left Rwanda as prisoner of Nsibula (a Havu king and a contemporary of Ruganzu and his predecessor, Ndahiro Cyamatare) and was established on Ijwi.[37] However, there is no evidence on Ijwi to point to Nsibula's presence there; in fact, there was no kingdom even established on Ijwi at that time. Nonetheless, although the Rwandan traditions add circumstantial detail to the Ijwi accounts, the two traditions concur on the essential tie-in: the historical connections of the Ijwi ritualist family with Kabagali in Rwanda seem plausible. It is on the genealogical lengths that the sources most notably differ.

Although Ijwi genealogical reconstructions are problematic, the Beeru sources generally go back some eight to ten generations—very long genealogies by Ijwi standards. They claim to have come directly from Rwanda to Ijwi and not to have been associated with the senior line of the Havu dynasty, on the mainland west of Lake Kivu, before arriving on Ijwi. Furthermore, the Ijwi rituals differ from those of the senior Havu kingdom, as do oral histories pertaining to these subjects. In these aspects the Ijwi rituals conform more closely to the Rwandan ritual traditions. However, despite these ethnographic tie-ins, the oral traditions differ significantly. The traditions of the Beeru on Ijwi have no mention of Nyamutege, whom the Rwandan sources claim was seized in Rwanda by Nsibula and established by him on Ijwi—nor even of Nsibula, whom the Rwandan sources claim was instrumental in the Beeru placement on Ijwi. Given their later association with the Basibula royal dynasty on Ijwi, the omission of any reference to Nsibula is curious indeed.

Other discrepancies abound. Despite the lack of precise agreement on individual genealogical entries, there is general agreement among the Beeru on Ijwi that their departure from Kabagali occurred around eight generations ago. Rwandan sources note fourteen generations—almost double the Ijwi length—back to Nyamutege (from whom there is no continuous transmission to the Ijwi Beeru). Furthermore, we are referring to a Rwandan king list of sixteen names from 1959 (if one includes Rwaaka) back to Ndahiro II Cyamataare. It is not plausible to attribute these discrepancies to differences in generation lengths, because Rwandan patrilateral generations are generally taken to be quite long (at least for the more recent periods) and those on Ijwi, with the notable exception of the royal genealogy, much shorter. At the moment, then, the puzzle is this: what happened to the missing six to eight names from the Ijwi list? As noted above, the presence of such a recurring pattern was sufficient to arouse interest; what aroused suspicion was that, when looked at in closer detail, each case led to the same result, one that placed Ruganzu likely near the beginning of the eighteenth century.

Comparative Explorations from West of Lake Kivu

First, the Abozi on Ijwi, who are said to be a part of the Balega clan, take their name from Mwoozi, an ancestor who is said to have helped Ruganzu escape by canoe from some (unspecified) enemies. The Abozi trace their genealogies of about eight names back to Mwoozi. Rwandan commoner genealogies suggest a similar time frame to Ruganzu. In Rwandan traditions the Abanyabyinshi are said to have descended from a man named Byinshi, a cousin of Ruganzu, accused of having plotted against the Rwandan king. In the pogrom that followed against his family, the Abanyabyinshi were scattered to the west. Drawing on

Table 11.3 Comparative king lists of Buhavu and Rwanda	
Buhavu	*Rwanda (per Kagame)*
Nsibula I Nyebunga	Ruganzu Ndori (1510–1543)
Nsibula Nyabitatire	Mutare Semugeshi (1543–1576)
Mpaka, Bamenyirwe I	Kigeri Nyamuheshera (1576–1609)
Nyamushanja	Mibambwe Gisanura (1609–1642)
Mpalampala	Yuhi Mazimpaka (1642–1675)
Mukulu Orhabona	Karemera Rwaka (pretender)
Kamerokosa I	Cyilima Rujugira (1675–1708)
Bamenyirwe II	Kigeri Ndabarasa (1708–1741)
Ntale I	Mibambwe Sentabyo (1741–1746)
Mpaka ya Lushasha	Yuhi Gahindiro (1746–?)
Nsibula III (Bahole I)	Mutara Rwogera (?–1853)
Ntale II	Kigeri Rwabugiri (1853–1895)
Bamenyirwe III (Lushombo) (d. 1928)	Mibambwe Rutarindwa (pretender)
Muhirwa (Bahole II) (d. 1942)	Yuhi Musinga (1896–1931)
Kamerokosa II (d. 1960)	Mutara Rudahigwa (1931–1959)

Sources: Feys, "Histoire des Bahavu"; Kagame, *La notion de génération,* 87.

extensive Rwandan sources, Delmas situates the origin of Abanyabyinshi identity at seven to eight generations back from 1950.[38]

Aside from the ritual and commoner genealogies from Ijwi, the royal genealogies from Bunyungu (a Hunde state located at the northwest corner of Lake Kivu) and of the Havu parent kingdom on the mainland west of Lake Kivu also contain relevant data. The Hunde list cites a contemporary of Ruganzu and Nsibula; it places him seven generations (from the 1950s), five generations before the Rwandan king Rwabugiri (r. 1865–95), and four generations before a Hunde king killed by Gahindiro (or possibly Rwogera, successor to Gahindiro).[39] Again, this chronological framework points to a time depth to Ruganzu (in Rwanda) and Nsibula (in Buhavu) significantly shallower than we are led to believe from the Rwandan sources cited by Kagame.[40]

The Kalehe list presents a slightly different problem. One version was recorded by a priest of the White Fathers missionary order, a person with access to the Rwandan king list, because the White Fathers had been intimately involved in the early historical studies in Rwanda, and those in Kivu had frequent contact with the Rwandan Fathers.[41] This Havu king list, set beside the official Rwanda list, is given in table 11.3. As it turns out, on this list Nsibula is exactly fifteen names back from 1960; on the Rwandan list, Ruganzu is fifteen names back from 1959. (Nsibula is also given as the contemporary of Ruganzu and of his father Ndahiro II Cyamutaare.) There is a striking concordance of the two king lists, again drawn up by someone with intimate knowledge of the writings on the Rwanda domain but only passing knowledge of Buhavu.[42]

But there are two small quirks to account for in this Kalehe list. First, it must be noted that the correspondence is not exact in each generation; for example, the Kalehe list has five names since Rwabugiri (late nineteenth century) and nine names encompassing the time of only four Ijwi kings. Granted the Ijwi kings had exceedingly long reigns; that leaves six names before ca. 1820 on the Kalehe list, to cover about three hundred years by Kagame's chronology.[43]

The other quirk that needs to be explained is that Kabwiika, the father of the first Ijwi king, is said to have been the son of Bamenyirwe I and the brother of Kamerogosa; Kamerogosa had to fight a succession dispute with Kabwiika in order to retain the throne.[44] On this Kalehe genealogy, however, three names appear between Bamenyirwe I and Kamerogosa I (though Kamerogosa's son is also given as Bamenyirwe). These three names (Nyamushanja, Mpalampala, and Mukulu Orhabona) attract attention, for three reasons. First, they do not correspond to the Ijwi version of Kabwiika's succession. Second, none of these three names appear in the Kalehe genealogy drawn up by the Belgian administrators of the 1930s; nor does that of Bamenyirwe II, son of Kamerogosa. Third, in the short histories of the kings given in Feys's list, there are no histories given of these three kings—those between Bamenyirwe I and Kamerogosa I—except the fact that each was enthroned in Kinyaga (a region that now forms the southwestern portion of Rwanda). There is no mention of the hill, or the exact location. Both Kamerogosa and Bamenyirwe, however, were cited as having been enthroned at "Luvumu chez Rwabika" on the western shore of the lake.

No explanation is given for this sudden shift to Kinyaga and the sudden return west of the lake to the same hill that had been the site of the capital four generations previously. There is no mention of these Havu kings in the data available from Kinyaga, despite intensive local-level historical study recently carried out in this region.[45] My own work on Ijwi indicates that, although significant elements of the population arrived on Ijwi from Kinyaga, the Havu kings did not control Kinyaga at that time. Other variants indicate that Mpalampala was in fact a son of Bamenyirwe and brother of Kamerogosa—but not a king. Mukulu Orhabona is not a dynastic name. Most probably this is an apocryphal sobriquet; it means "the elder who does not see." It is doubtful that any king carried this name. It is, however, possible that these names were in fact historical personages, though not kings; a Nyamushanja does appear in the Rwandan documents as having been killed by Ruganzu. It is also possible (if unlikely) that some of them were kings who succeeded rapidly one after another, so as to have left few traces in the historical traditions.[46] But even in this case, it is likely the three combined did not rule more than a generation.

On balance, the evidence suggests that it is unlikely that these three were historical Havu sovereigns. No oral data that I am aware of confirm their names; nor is there any commentary on how Père Feys constructed this king list. If the suspicion cast on the validity of these three names as kings proves valid, the effect will be to shorten the Kalehe king list to some twelve names total; but, it is important to note, it would then contain only four names before the first quarter of the nineteenth century.

On Kigeri Nyamuheshera, One of Rwanda's Great Warrior Kings

Thus the external evidence relating to Ruganzu suggests that Ruganzu may have lived sometime near, and maybe shortly after, 1700. Of course the search for such chronological precision may be, as Henige suggests, but a chimera. Nonetheless, inquiry of this type is still worthwhile, since it can direct attention to new issues and lead to greater understanding of the internal processes of historical social change. In this case the questions on chronology, which derive from an examination of the external sources, suggest the need to look closely at the Rwandan sources for internal inconsistencies as well.

Such a query elicits many questions on the cycle of the three Rwandan kings to follow Ruganzu Ndori. In the principal historical sources associated with the Rwandan central court, very few historical details are provided for these kings over the course of a century (by Kagame's chronological reckoning), and those observations that are mentioned are suspect; furthermore, such vagueness contrasts with the quality of historical knowledge for the periods both preceding and following this cycle of kings between Ruganzu and Rujugira.[47] The section of the official king list we are interested in is given in table 11.4.

Table 11.4
Comparative chronologies of the Rwandan king list, Ruganzu to Rwabugiri

	Kagame	Vansina	Rennie
Ruganzu Ndori	1510–1543	1600–1624	1603–1630
Mutara Semugeshi	1543–1576	1624–1648	1630–1657
Kigeri Nyamuheshera	1576–1609	1648–1672	1657–1684
Mibambwe Gisanura	1609–1642	1672–1696	1684–1711
Yuhi Mazimpaka	1642–1675	1696–1720	1711–1738
Karemera Rwaka	—	1720–1744	1738–1756
Cyilima Rujugira	1675–1708	1744–1768	1756–1765
Kigeri Ndabarasa	1708–1741	1768–1792	1765–1792
Mibambwe Sentabyo	1741–1746	1792–1797	1792–1797
Yuhi Gahindiro	1746–	1797–1830	1797–1830
Mutara Rwogera	–1853	1830–1860	1830–1860
Kigeri Rwabugiri	1853–1895	1860–1895	1860–1895

Sources: Kagame, La notion de génération, 87; Rennie, "Precolonial Kingdom of Rwanda," 25–26; Vansina, L'évolution du royaume Rwanda, 56.

The reign of Kigeri Nyamuheshera serves well by way of illustration, partly because there is more concrete historical data (as opposed to attributed ethnographical innovations) for Nyamuheshera than for the kings either before or after. This should make him less suspect as a later addition to the list. Kagame notes that Kigeri Nyamuheshera was a renowned warrior king, and the claims advanced for Nyamuheshera's conquests are indeed extensive: Busozo and Bukunzi in the mountainous areas of what is today southwestern Rwanda; Ngweshi, a Shi state west of the Rusizi River, in what is now eastern Zaire; Buzi and Buhunde, northwest of Lake Kivu; the area around Lake Edward (Lake Idi Amin) in the north; and Ndorwa, in the mountainous region northeast of central Rwanda.[48]

Vansina seems to have sensed the vulnerability of the traditions on this point—grandiose claims without much corroboration; he mentions that many of the attacks associated with Ruganzu in the official traditions may actually have been undertaken by Nyamuheshera.[49] But it is also possible that many of the claims advanced for Nyamuheshera in fact are attributable to other kings. From current knowledge, it is impossible to give credence to traditions citing Nyamuheshera's exploits in Busozo and Bukunzi. Ruganzu is said to have raided there, and Rwabugiri remained in Kinyaga for an extended period of time, but there is no evidence of any conquest of Bukunzi, nor is there local evidence of Nyamuheshera's presence there—despite extensive fieldwork in that region; as far as can reasonably be ascertained, these areas were autonomous of the Rwandan state until the 1920s.[50] In addition, while de Lacger attributes to Nyamuheshera the death of Balishake, king of Bukunzi, Kagame refers to Balishake as "of Itahire" (north of Rusenyi).[51] There is no mention of Balishake in the available genealogies of the Bukunzi royal family.

As for Ngweshe, the indications are that it was Gahindiro who first submitted the ruling line of Ngweshe (i.e., Bishugi) to tributary status to the Rwandan kings, in protecting them from the senior Shi line in Buhaya (Kabare)—Gahindiro, who lived in the early nineteenth century, not Nyamuheshera, who lived in the late sixteenth century (by Kagame's chronology).[52] Furthermore, the exploits attributed to Nyamuheshera on Ijwi are almost certainly misattributed. "Il dirigea . . . une expédition punitive contre l'île d'Idjwi, qui refusait de payer tribute."[53] In fact there was no kingdom on Ijwi for the period Kagame identifies with Nyamuheshera.[54] Aside from these references in the Rwandan sources, there is virtually no mention of Nyamuheshera in the poetry; Kagame mentions him in three fragments of poems totaling less than a hundred lines, and without a trace of his military exploits.[55] From the Ijwi sources there is no question that what Kagame describes for Kigeri Nyamuheshera is attributable only to his homonym Kigeri Rwabugiri in the late nineteenth century.[56]

The attack attributed to Nyamuheshera on Buzi and Buhunde was probably in fact carried out by Gahindiro or Rwogera—Hunde tradition says that Rwogera killed Kalinda; Rwandan records attribute this to Gahindiro. The attack on Masisi, far into the mountains northwest of Lake Kivu—a long march not to have more of an account than appears in the sources—is more likely that of Kigeri Rwabugiri (who did pursue a Buhunde king to Masisi). Rwabugiri was the homonym of Nyamuheshera—they shared the same dynastic name (Kigeri), and hence, in theory, the same ideological/historical attributes, and it is not unusual to find the historical events associated with one repeated for the other.[57] The same is true of the Rwandan penetration toward Lake Edward, attributed to Kigeri Nyamuheshera. In the east, despite claims of a glorious victory over Ndorwa, there were neither major territorial gains nor traditions on the war left as a legacy to such exploits.[58] In sum, there is no evidence in the western "conquered" regions for the vaunted military exploits claimed for Nyamuheshera, and little evidence in the Rwandan traditions to support the claims put forth on Nyamuheshera's behalf elsewhere.

Nyamuheshera is cited always as a warrior king of immense stature, but we still find from the army histories that there was only a single army created under his reign, a single army that "disappeared without explanation" leaving no military organization to his credit, and no names of the leaders of the army to posterity.[59] One of the companies of his army appears to have been the Ingangurarugo; that name reappears as the name of the personal royal guard under Kigeri Rwabugiri. (While it is plausible that each of the two kings had an important military company of same name, it needs to be seen also as part of a wider pattern of intellectual appropriation and shifting attribution.) In addition, in the histories of the armies formed *preceding* Kigeri Nyamuheshera, there is no mention, or even trace, of any of the immense campaigns that Nyamuheshera is said to have launched against his neighbors.

Thus the man whom the court histories claim as one of Rwanda's grand warrior kings has left no trace in the countries he is said to have conquered, though they remember Ruganzu, of greater antiquity. Kigeri Nyamuheshera recruited only a single army (which disappeared mysteriously), and he receives no mention in the military histories of armies formed before his time (although such histories typically include references to subsequent campaigns under later kings). In short, "the renowned monarch added not a single army to the military institutions of the country."[60] And even Kagame, never one to underplay the glorification of the kings of Rwanda, concludes that "Kigeli [Kigeri] II left no other institutional legacy that we know of."[61] In addition, Kigeri Nyamuheshera was not at first buried in the cemetery reserved for sepulchres of kings of the dynastic name of Kigeri; we are told that at the time of Nyamuheshera's death this cemetery was included in land conquered by Ndorwa. His body was interred there only later, during the time of Cyilima Rujugira, some four reigns later.[62]

Furthermore, Delmas states that for three successive generations (Ruganzu, Mutara Semugeshi, and Kigeri Nyamuheshera) the king left only a single son, his heir; and that the successor to Nyamuheshera, Mibambwe Gisanura, left only a single son in addition to the heir.[63] Thus four generations of kings from Ruganzu left a total of only five male offspring. (It is nonetheless notable that Delmas does note another son of Semugeshi, Nzuki, eight to ten generations back from 1950, whose descendants are called, interestingly enough, the Abaganzu, thus indicating descent from Ruganzu).[64] Such an eventuality is curious, given the status of descent from the king and the reign lengths which Kagame attributes to these kings. At the very least it raises questions about the veracity of the claim that they were indeed successive kings.

Mutara Semugeshi and Mibambwe Gisanura:
Innovative Kings or Imaginary Kings?

Such questions can be extended. Many of the uncertainties in the traditions attributable to Nyamuheshera appear also in the traditions of his immediate predecessor and successor. To Mutara Semugeshi are attributed few historical traditions, over a reign that Kagame estimates at the standard thirty-three years.[65] The great bulk of the traditions on Semugeshi are limited to the attribution of cultural features introduced during his reign. While ethnographic data are valuable for historical analysis, questions arise on the validity of attributing the introduction of complex phenomena to a single moment of time by a single person. Oral sources frequently telescope complex processes, associating their invention with a single individual. Therefore the presence of any given cultural element can hardly be used as proof of the historicity of any given king. In addition, we have already mentioned that the sons of Nzuki, said to be himself the son of Mutara Semugeshi and the grandson of Ruganzu, are called the Abaganzu; they are said to count six to eight generations from Nzuki to 1950.[66]

By far the most significant event that Kagame attributed to the reign of Semugeshi was the introduction of the position of "king of the Immandwa" to the royal court of Rwanda.[67] One of the reasons that Kagame attributes this event to Mutara Semugeshi is that his reign followed that of Ruganzu, who is associated with the first arrival of Ryangombe into the country.[68] In addition, the names of the first officeholders of this position are not known, despite its importance for Rwandan ritual and despite the political influence wielded by any individual designated as head of the initiates to the cult: "Le nouveau dignitaire, comme bien l'on pense, devint brusquement un gros personnage, grace à son autorité morale sur tous les initiés du pays. Nous ignorons cependant, les tout premiers titulaires de cette dignité."[69]

A similar absence of data is apparent for the reign of Mibambwe Selarongoro Gisanura (reign twelve back from 1959), given as the successor to Nyamuheshera. From the fact that during his reign a certain Rwambali is said to have died as liberator-hero in a war against Gisaka, Kagame deduces that Gisanura fought a war against Gisaka.[70] But Delmas cites Rwambali as about nine generations back from 1950 (with a spread among different sources of seven to eleven generations); the Rwandan king list includes twelve reigns over that span.[71] In addition, Kagame uses Poem No. 49 as a source to establish the historicity of Gisanura, but he tells us too that the poem was composed under Cyilima Rujugira, a much later ruler (and one who ruled at a time of the elaboration of court culture). If this is the case, Kagame's conclusion is not based on contemporary evidence, only reinforcing the suspicion of an ex post facto assertion of Gisanura as king.[72]

Because some of the most complete royal traditions deal with army organizations for each of the kings, it might be useful to summarize the information on relevant armies cited in Kagame's *Les milices,* a valuable collection of official army histories for the kingdom of Rwanda.[73] Of the armies of Ruganzu, we have already noted the case of the Ibisumizi, of which Semugeshi was a member. After Ruganzu, this army is not heard of again in the sources until the reign of Rujugira. The son and successor of the army leader at the time of Rujugira died during the reign of Rwogera, it is said. For the Abaruhije, another army recruited under Ruganzu, there are no data appearing under the three successors to Ruganzu: Semugeshi, Nyaruheshera, and Gisanura. For Nyakara, a third army formed under Ruganzu, there is no subsequent mention until the time of Rujugira, when it was led by a certain Nkoko. Bashana, the son of Nkoko (seven generations from 1950) was killed under Gahindiro (early nineteenth century), as was the grandson of Bashana.[74] The same pattern holds for the Nyantango, a fourth army formed under Ruganzu: no subsequent leaders are known until the time of Rujugira—despite the many campaigns said to have been undertaken by Nyamuheshera in other sources.[75]

The armies of Semugeshi (the Abaganda) and Nyamuheshera have been mentioned above. It need only be remarked here that it is characteristic of the sources on all these armies that no details are retained before Cyilima Rujugira; from the time of his reign (or occasionally from the reign of Gahindiro three reigns later), all army leaders are traced precisely reign by reign. Of the five armies cited for Mibambwe Gisanura, four were, in Kagame's own words, "insignificant." (Two of them, in fact, were not truly milices but local neighborhood units to which a chief was assigned.) For none of them does a chief list go back beyond Gahindiro with the exception of one, which in turn is portrayed by Kagame as simply a land fief. The chief list for this group includes twelve names (generations and royal tie-ins are not given), to Mibambwe Gisanura (who is also twelve royal generations back from 1960).

In many cases, therefore, in a consistent pattern the traditions of institutions associated to the kingship omit reference to the four kings who follow Ruganzu in Kagame's king list, and pick up again only with Rujugira or Gahindiro. For the first three successors to Ruganzu, there is room to wonder if the men now called "kings" were not in fact army leaders of some kind; in the fourth case, if he wasn't a judge or other royal counselor. In other words, the entire cycle of kings to follow Ruganzu seems suspect; given the predilection for the integrity of dynastic cycles, it is likely that the entire cycle has been elaborated, along the lines of what appears to have been the case for the Burundi chronology. Questioning the integrity of the entire cycle after Ruganzu, of course, would force a significant revision of the official chronology of the kingdom. But the same analytic calculus can be applied to the reign of Ndabarasa—the successor to Rujugira on the official king list and (like Nyamuheshera) another dynastic "Kigeri"—for data on his reign are equally scanty and suggest that Ndabarasa was a military hero (especially prominent for his wars in Ndorwa) only later ascribed royal status, with a twenty- to thirty-year reign, according to the diverse royal chronologies. (Even were he enthroned as king, it is plausible that the reign length attributed to him was extended to include both his career as military leader and as royal sovereign.) Such revision suggests that the period of Rwaaka/Rujugira occurred in the second half of the eighteenth century, and that Ruganzu's reign was closer to the mid-eighteenth century—a significant condensation of the official royal chronology (Kagame places Ruganzu at 1510–43).

I am not arguing that all the names in the "suspect cycle" are simple historical fabrications. Oral testimony does not often invent items out of thin air; instead it reclassifies—and reinterprets—historical actors. Indeed, it is entirely possible that some were kings, who perhaps had only short reigns, not the standard thirty-three-year reign assigned to them in the formalized king list. However, it is also possible that they (or some among them) were not legitimate kings at all, but functionaries associated with the institution of kingship who, over time, have come to be accepted as having royal status. At any rate, the indications are that as presented in the official histories, the chronological depth ascribed to the royal genealogy before Rujugira is suspect, and this opens questions as to other aspects of the king list, a list that, as we have seen, has been widely used to provide the chronological foundation for the region as a whole.

Collectively, these data suggest that a period of turmoil followed the reign of Ruganzu in the interval leading up to Rujugira's accession. In fact, both Vansina and Rennie argue that effective power was held for many years before Rujugira by his brother Rwaaka; indeed, the official accounts acknowledge his "rule," if not his "reign." Yet Rwaaka has been expunged from the official chronicle. Two reasons (and they could be the same) are advanced for this: it is said he was not properly invested as king according to the requisite rituals, and dynastic ideology proscribes two rulers in any given generation.[76] Regardless of the specific details, however, the fact remains that this period was one of considerable irregularities; out of this complexity the concept of kingship came to have much tighter ritual codification and ideological consistency. Under Rujugira, for example, the Ryangombe religious authorities—hitherto outside the purview of the court, perhaps in outright opposition to it—were brought under court control; army organization was given greater coherence, including the extension of army units to include Hutu formations; the corporation of ritualists was reorganized; royal traditions on army histories were reinforced and standardized; tribute forms were extended to new segments of the population; the ideology of family genealogies was established; and the poetic forms praising the king and court were elaborated and systematized.

The absence of firm data from earlier periods, of course, does not prove that the cycle before Rujugira did not exist, or even that it existed in diminished stature; it is, after all, no easy task to prove a negative. Nonetheless, it is suggestive, for many other elements from Rwandan sources support such a revision of the royal chronology. Furthermore, such internal indications need be seen in the context of the clear elaborations of multiple royal chronicles outside Rwanda, as explored earlier. And between the internal indications and the independent external data there is a clear convergence.

It is fair to ask, however, if we are not ignoring internal development within these institutions. It might well be that in criticizing the traditions in this manner, we are postulating the presence of a static state as in the time of Rwabugiri by assuming that armies always had a standing organization headed by a recognized leader delegated by the king. When we find no cattle army associated with the milices until after Rwogera, for example, might this not be associated with the institutional developments taking place at the time? To be too rigid in our demands on traditions is to ignore the characteristic of traditions, which obviously retain more and become fuller and more complete as the temporal distance from the present narrows. It is also to ignore the very historical development we seek, and which might exist right before our very eyes. Nonetheless, three facts militate against such a simple dismissal of this inquiry. First, the pattern set out here is consistent and suggestive: there is very little evidence to assert the historicity of the kings in the cycle between Ruganzu and Rujugira on the official king list. Second, there do exist data of much superior quality from previous reigns, so the difference cannot be attributed to temporal distance alone. And finally, the external data from neighboring slates—independent data, both from each other and from Rwanda (at least until the recent interventions traced out above)—converge to raise the specter of "systematic doubt."[77]

To be sure, the critique of oral sources alone is not equivalent to writing history. Nonetheless, before we can rely on such sources for historical reconstruction with any confidence, we must be clear on the type of sources we are dealing with. The remarkable characteristic here is that traditions from outside the Rwandan dynastic arena have always been dismissed because they did not conform to the official Rwandan traditions. As we have seen, one by one each was invalidated and reconstructed, until only the Rwandan chronology remained. Yet when looked at as a whole, it is clear that those sources—even those independent of one another—all concur: the Rwandan line as reported is longer than the others. There is no necessary reason why the Rwandan line should be considered as more valid than the others, especially when, collectively and independently, all others point in the same direction.[78]

This essay has not tried to reconstruct the royal history even at this schematic level. But it has pointed to certain parameters in the process of understanding Rwandan history, even if that understanding leads to agnosticism rather than certainty. It questions our faith in those elements formerly taken as essential to historical understanding and as capable of exactitude: the Rwandan dynastic chronology is certainly not the latter, capable of exactitude; and perhaps it is not quite the former, the essential characteristic of history. Precisely because such inquiry cannot respond to these concerns, it forces us to look to other forms of conceiving history. Pursuing such questions still opens up valuable insights, not of historical "fact" but of historical process. If in some fields of study the message is the medium, in this field the essential fact is in the formulation of the concept of fact; the meaning of the fact is in its imagining. For many people in this area, the fantasy of the Rwandan chronology may have become part of their own historical reality.

Appendix

Table 11.5
Rwandan royal chronology per various authorities

	Kagame	*Vansina*	*Rennie*	*Nkurikiyimfura*
Ruganzu Bwimba	1312–1345	1458–1482	1532–1559	1468–1470
Cyilima Rugwe	1345–1378	1482–1506	1559–1586	1470–1520
Kigeri Mukobanya	1378–1411	1506–1528	1586–1588	1520–1543
Mibambwe Mutabazi	1411–1444	1528–1552	1588–1593	1543–1566
Yuhi Gahima	1444–1477	1552–1576	1593–1603	1566–1589
Ndahiro Cyamatare	1477–1510	1576–1600	1603	1589–1600
Ruganzu Ndori	1510–1543	1600–1624	1603–1630	1600–1623
Mutara Semugeshi	1543–1576	1624–1648	1630–1657	1623–1646
Kigeri Nyamuheshera	1576–1609	1648–1672	1657–1684	1646–1669
Mibambwe Gisanura	1609–1642	1672–1696	1684–1711	1669–1692
Yuhi Mazimpaka.	1642–1675	1696–1720	1711–1738	1692–1715
Karemera Rwaka	—	1720–1744	1738–1756	1715–1731
Cyilima Rujugira	1675–1708	1744–1768	1756–1765	1731–1769
Kigeri Ndabarasa	1708–1741	1768–1792	1765–1792	1769–1792
Mibambwe Sentabyo	1741–1746	1792–1797	1792–1797	1792–1797
Yuhi Gahindiro	1746–	1797–1830	1797–1830	1797–1830
Mutara Rwogera	–1853	1830–1860	1830–1860	1830–1860
Kigeri Rwabugiri	1853–1895	1860–1895	1860–1895	1860–1895
Mibambwe Rutarindwa	—	1896	1895–1896	—
Yuhi Musinga	1897–1931	1897–1931	1896–1931	—
Mutara Rudahigwa	1931–1959	1931–1959	1931–1959	—

Sources: Kagame, *La notion de génération,* 87; Rennie, "Precolonial Kingdom of Rwanda," 25–26; Vansina, *L'évolution du royaume Rwanda,* 56; Nkurikiyimfura, "La révision d'une chronologie," 166.

PART 4

Perceiving History through the Mists

PRECOLONIAL BURUNDI
AND RWANDA

Local Loyalties, Regional Royalties

2001

This chapter brings together a critique of earlier assumptions with more recent sources on the history of the region to propose a new overview of history for precolonial Burundi and Rwanda. It discusses the depth of settlement in the area (including the evidence for the duration of cattle in the region), and it reconsiders earlier paradigms based on migration theory. In doing so, it discusses the importance of ecological diversity and local identity, the emergence of diverse political cultures (including several dynastic centers of power), and the transformations of royal power in two regional royalties—the Ganwa dynasty of Burundi and the Nyiginya dynasty of Rwanda. In presenting these data, the analysis questions the assumptions of fixed and unchanging political institutions and social structures, tracing the internal influences (and influential actors) on the broader social formations that marked this region over time. Accounting for regional history as well as royal history, ecology as well as ethnicity, and commoners as well as courtesans, this essay seeks to provide a broad overview of precolonial dynamics and developments in the regions east of Lake Kivu and northern Lake Tanganyika, the areas now known as Rwanda and Burundi.

I T H A S L O N G B E E N recognized that African history has its own history. In many areas of the world, historians first focused on national units. But one of the characteristics of the relatively young field of African history is that in many instances historians' concerns moved rapidly beyond any "nationalistic" phase to address thematic issues.[1] To do so often meant moving beyond political history, history hemmed in by colonially defined boundaries, or history in a narrative vein. It meant moving beyond elites to include the actions of many constituencies. It meant that comparative frameworks could be addressed in thematic symposia—on slavery, on labor, on gender, on peasants, and on many other issues. But moving beyond political history to explore either the broader historical contexts that set the contours to human agency or the local implications of these themes also meant that in many cases the underlying political processes were neglected.[2]

In the past, this was perhaps but a minor inconvenience; thematic or local studies were fully conceived within the ongoing development of historical understanding taking place in the field as a whole. More recently, however, historians' work has become relevant to a growing number of interested parties— diplomats, journalists, aid workers, and others. Therefore, it may be useful to lay out some of the broad contours to emerge from the past forty years of sustained historical inquiry and to integrate the political orientations (focusing often on dynastic actors) with broader thematic issues. Without such a process, those seeking historical context—including historians themselves—have little recourse but to refer back to the materials produced at the end of the colonial rule, writings that often incorporated colonial assumptions on the nature of African history.

This chapter attempts to take stock of our historical understanding of precolonial Central Africa, an area where history is particularly contested, contorted, and misconstrued, an area where debates over history have been a central feature of the recent cataclysms that have wracked the region.[3] While this will be a condensed presentation, the need for such a survey is particularly acute, because of the complexity of the history in this region, because of the power and broad diffusion of misleading earlier stereotypes applied to the history, because of the intensity and urgency of contemporary social tensions, and because of the numbers of outside observers new to the field. Scholarly work has deepened our understanding on many crucial issues often by addressing thematic concerns, or by focusing on narrowly defined arenas, but work in the field has been less attentive to broader political contexts.[4] The objective here is not to place different levels of historical inquiry in adversarial opposition to each other. Instead, it is to ex-

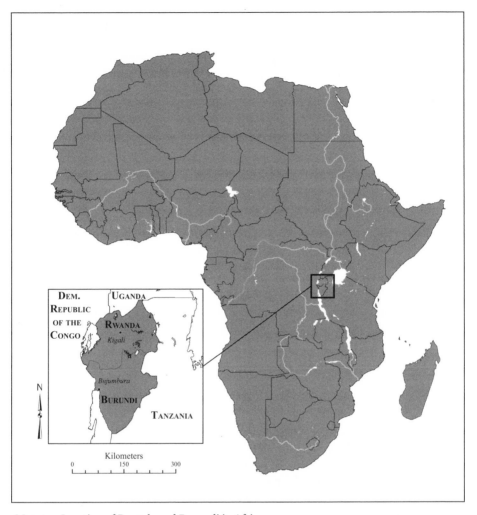

Map 12.1. Location of Rwanda and Burundi in Africa

plore the complementary nature of such forms of historical inquiry. Indeed, the amount and quality of this detailed work make it possible to work on a larger canvas without resorting to superficial banalities or stale stereotypes.

The historical sketch proposed here is but a first step in the search to understand the precolonial history of the areas now included in the states of Burundi and Rwanda. It does not pretend to be comprehensive, but it does seek to set out the contours to revising received stereotypes. It omits many themes and many sources,[5] but it does so in the interest of working toward a comprehensive vision of the regional trends, especially those dealing with the construction of formal political structures. This overview focuses on two processes of statebuilding in these highlands between the Western Rift Valley (marked by Lakes Kivu and Tanganyika) in the west and the Kagera and Malagarasi rivers in the east. By the time of European arrival in the late nineteenth century, two dynasties appeared dominant in this region, and the kingdoms associated with them, Rwanda and Burundi, became identified as paradigmatic of the social organization in Africa's Great Lakes region. Recent events have only solidified these assumptions on the dominance of state power in these two societies and reinforced the tendency to project current social parameters (such as the broad-based nature of recent ethnic confrontation) back into the past; taken as a whole, the historical evidence suggests that the lived reality was much more complicated than such frequent assumptions account for.

It was not simply a focus on the state, however, that captured the imaginations of the outside observers from the late nineteenth century; the relationship of state structures to human cultural characteristics also intrigued them. The European image of Rwanda and Burundi emphasized extraordinary political centralization, marked social hierarchy, and prominent mixed economies based on both pastoralism and agricultural production. To European observers, each of these forms of differentiation—political, social, and economic—was related to presumed ethnic attributes: "Tutsi" ethnicity was associated with power, pastoralism, and a distinctive physique—tall, thin, and often light-skinned; "Hutu" were assumed to be linked to servitude, horticulture, and stockier build; and "Twa" were seen as hunters or potters, living on the margins of the political order, and with their own physical characteristics—short of stature, with stocky legs, round heads, broad noses. In this vision, race, culture, and power were all interlocked.

But the historical reality was quite different, for in fact this region included a variety of local ecologies, a range of physical stocks, and a multitude of political units, ranging from centralized polities to small-scale kin-based units. Amidst such diversity, the emergence, development, and meaning of the two dominant state structures of Rwanda and Burundi form the essential historical puzzle of this region: a "puzzle" because these histories deal with so many complex interlocking explanatory factors, and because in some cases precise explanations escape us even today. Their intense focus on the two major kingdoms (and on the internal dynastic sources associated with them) has led historians to assume that culture was fixed and politics was the only evolving factor. They have often failed to look at the history of these states as fundamental to the formation of ethnic identities, of social relations, and of differential economic activity. In short, they have failed to conceptualize state power as one of the causes of social differentiation, not the product of unchanging social differences. This chapter seeks to unravel the elements of this puzzle of state formation, to identify the multiple factors involved, and to distinguish between outside ideologies and other approaches to understanding internal social dynamics.

Ecologies and Cultures

Located just south of the equator in the center of Africa, these two countries appear diminutive compared to the continental land mass around them, where the lakes are inland seas, the mountains are perfectly symmetrical cones reaching over 4000 meters, and the plains seem to go on forever (see map 12.1).[6] But in fact the family of Kinyarwanda- and Kirundi-speakers (the two languages are over 80 percent cognate) forms the largest Bantu language group next to Kiswahili speakers, and the attraction of these societies has been far greater than their size would indicate: their histories and cultures have been the objects of powerful fascination leading to endless conjecture by both outsiders and people within.[7] As a result of such a focus, the power attributed to these state structures and the political boundaries implying isolation from other areas can be misleading: historically these populations were fully part of the cultures and societies of a vast region astride the Congo-Nile watershed separating the two great African culture zones of the Congo River basin and the Great Lakes region; the societies that came to be included in Rwanda and Burundi drew in important ways from both culture zones. Simultaneously, they drew on local ecological realities; the state units are internally differentiated as well as regionally integrated.

Although we—like the historical actors that molded these societies—draw ultimately on a broad canvas, our interest is on the area immediately east of Lake Kivu and the northern shores of Lake Tanganyika, an area whose northern limits are marked roughly by the spectacular chain of volcanoes north of Lake Kivu, and whose southern limits are defined by the northern reaches of the Malagarasi River (see map 12.2). Within those contours, the area of our concern is marked by three broad geographical zones, distinguished by altitude, topography, and precipitation. The eastern and southern areas formed part of the broad open

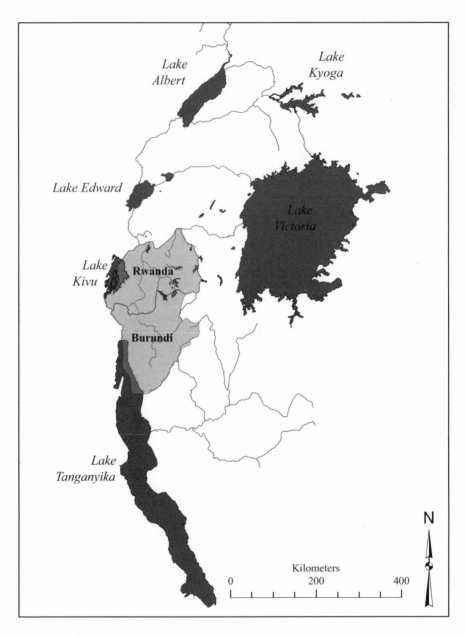

N

Kilometers

0   200   400

Map 12.2. Rwanda and Burundi in regional perspective

grasslands stretching through northern Uganda, a wide corridor west of Lake Victoria, and the vast plateau of western Tanzania, becoming more dry-woodland as one moves south. These plains formed pastoral land par excellence; as open grassland with few topographical obstacles, they offered an area of unrestricted mobility. Having somewhat less (and much less reliable) rainfall than other areas in the region, this vegetation band, covering the eastern half of what is now Rwanda and Burundi, showed markedly lower population densities than either the well-watered areas to the east, around Lake Victoria, or the fertile highland areas to the west.[8]

The mountainous regions west of these savanna plateaus constitute the massive Congo-Nile divide and form the dramatic backdrop to this region, reaching over 2,000 meters in most places and over 4,500 meters among the volcanoes of northwest Rwanda. These highland areas are well suited to agricultural pursuits: rainfall is reliable, averaging over 2,000 mm annually in some locales; the soils are rich and deep; and the temperatures are moderate, even by European standards. A wide range of both cultivated crops and natural vegetation thrives there. But large areas of this zone remained forested until recently, and the very presence of this forest contributed to the conditions of its own preservation, ensuring the ranges of temperature, humidity, precipitation, and soil nutrients for a productive agricultural milieu and dense settlement; in some areas today population densities reach over 1,000 people/km^2 (400/mi^2) (see map 12.3).

The third major geographical zone of this larger region is formed by the dry lowland areas, called the Imbo, along the eastern Lake Tanganyika shore and stretching north into the Rusizi River Valley. The ecology, the economy, and the epidemiological characteristics of the Imbo all differed from those of the highland or grasslands areas. Consequently, the people of this lakeside zone developed productive rhythms, economic relationships, and social contacts with the larger Lake Tanganyika cultural community, distinct from the highland areas; from the mid-nineteenth century, they had important commercial ties to the Lake Tanganyika Muslim trade networks associated ultimately with the East African coast. But these differences, and different resource bases, meant that the royal dynasty of Burundi had trouble asserting any consistent control in much of this area. Instead, to the royal court the Imbo often appeared as the cradle of resistance and the refuge for pretenders to power, as indeed did the northern mountainous areas of Rwanda to the Rwandan dynasty, but for opposite reasons: the Imbo was too lightly populated, the mountainous areas of northern

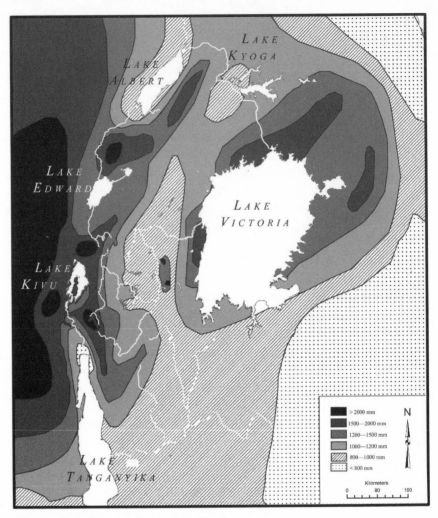

Map 12.3. Rainfall in the Great Lakes region

Rwanda too densely populated for royal control to be asserted easily; and as we shall see, the mountainous regions were areas of strong local solidarities, while the Imbo was an area that accumulated resources from outside state control.

But interspersed within this general pattern of three distinct geographical/cultural zones were many smaller microenvironments. One of the most prominent of these was the Kanyaru/Kagera River basin, marked by a series of swamps and a particular riverain culture distinct from the agriculturalist or pastoralist economies around it. In this culture, people came to live both on the banks of the lakes and the marshes that define the area and on floating islands of papyrus and vegetation; they exploited the aquatic resources of the river and its littoral; and they came to identify not as Rwandans but as Banyambo (also the name of the dynastic clan of Karagwe, the kingdom immediately east of the Kagera River).

There were many other such microenvironments in the region, such as the Rugezi swamp cultures around Lake Bulera in northern Rwanda, where the cold morning rains and deep mists marked much of the rainy season; or the pastoralist culture of the Bagogwe, high on the mountainous slopes of northwestern Rwanda, representative of many others on the high pastures along the crests of the mountain ranges west of Lake Kivu; or the Twa hunting traditions of the Nyungwe forest; or the escarpment pattern of Buragane in southern Burundi, where the hilltops on the escarpment look out over the vast lowlands stretching to the southeast, and where the people of the area can easily exploit complementary production and commercial zones. Such small but significant variations to the general ecological patterns form an ecological kaleidoscope; for the areas now included within Burundi and Rwanda they not only added rich texture to the concept of these cultures and extended the range of productive zones, but they also changed the cultures and influenced the histories of these states in important ways.

While such microenvironments were often self-enclosed, confined within the region, the broader patterns noted above, including that of the Imbo, all extended well beyond the region of our focus and hence served as cultural conduits as well as geographical corridors tying this multifarious area to many broader regional patterns. So both the diversity of microenvironments within, and the diverse continuities with areas outside the region, belie the homogeneity assumed in most accounts of social structure in this area. In short, the units we know as Burundi and Rwanda were each formed of internal interlocking cultures, related as much through their activities outside state control as through the internal state structures themselves. Such factors have been misportrayed because of outsiders' and nationalists' shared focus on state power—dynastic integrity and colonial boundaries have exerted a powerful focus for many recent analysts, and blinded outside observers to both the broader continuities and internal diversity. We think of these countries as homogeneous units at the risk of compromising our understanding of their histories and their identities.

The three major geographical categories in this region—the eastern grasslands, the western highlands, and the Tanganyika shoreline—have tied this region to broader cultural universes, different in each case. The grasslands brought

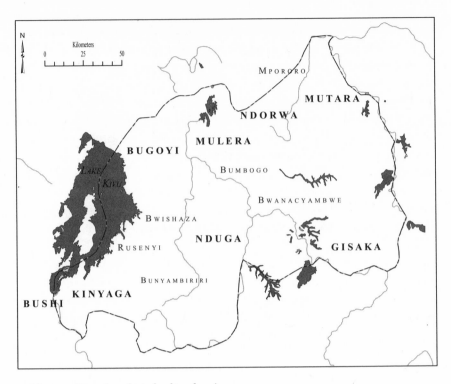

Map 12.4. Rwanda: selected cultural regions

this area into contact with the Interlacustrine cultural traditions to the east; the highlands shared many elements also found in the Congo River basin to the west; and the Lake Tanganyika littoral provided close contacts across the lake, serving more recently as the northern extension of a vast commercial zone ultimately linked to the trade networks of the East Coast of Africa. Nonetheless, of these three, the highland forest cultures played the most significant role in laying the foundations to the cultures of this region, and hence also to its histories; in both states it was the highland core that served as the center of both the recent demographic growth and the dynastic structures associated with the modern states.

Even within these broad patterns, there were significant commercial and social differences, as smaller regions developed their own outside fields of action and forged individual identities in opposition to each other as well as to the dynastic core. For example, at least nine such zones are clearly identifiable for Rwanda. Each brought separate characteristics to the region and maintained separate ties to outside areas; most were not fully incorporated into the Rwandan state structures until colonial rule (see map 12.4). From at least the eighteenth century, the center of the kingdom was located in Nduga, cradled on three sides by the broad arc of the Nyabarongo and Kanyaru Rivers in the south-central portions of what became the colonially defined state. To the southwest, across the mountainous forests of the divide, Kinyaga was a region with close social and commercial ties to the west, trading livestock to the Shi states for iron products and fiber bracelets. Rusenyi/Bwishaza, farther north along the western shores of Lake Kivu, had its own contacts across Lake Kivu in both material items and social relations (defined by marriage, clientship, and land ties). In the far northwest of what became the colonial state of Rwanda, Bugoyi was settled by people with close cultural, social, and economic ties to Hunde, Tembo, and Nande populations in the corridor between Lakes Kivu and Rweru (Edward); these mobile populations maintained a thriving trade in tobacco, fiber bracelets, and livestock, and their religious practices remained somewhat distinct from those of other Rwandans.

Similarly, those living in Mulera, north of Nduga, maintained their own distinctive social organization, part of a cultural zone stretching north into what is today Kigezi (southwestern Uganda); they too participated in widely ramifying commercial networks, this time stretching as far as the Lake Rweru salt plains to the north. Ndorwa and Mpororo shared in this general northward orientation, but they differed from Mulera in their legacy of greater political cohesion, and they had closer ties to the cultural field of Nkore and other kingdoms in southern Uganda (including shared religious traditions).

Mutara, on the other hand, in the grasslands of the extreme northeast, had strong political and social relationships to Karagwe east of the Kagera River, including frequent cattle ties; within this region Mubale, along the Kagera River, formed a distinct region of its own in ecological and cultural terms. In the southeast, the people of Gisaka—a region itself divided into four distinct culture zones—also showed a strong sense of their own identity and developed an enduring tradition of cultural autonomy from central Rwanda, even in recent times. Finally, Bugesera, a region of sparsely populated woodlands, was part of a larger social and political unit of its own, stretching south across the current border into what became northern Burundi; with the growth of its two powerful neighbors, Bugesera was divided and absorbed into the expanding states of Burundi and Rwanda during the late eighteenth and early nineteenth centuries, but has in some ways remained a distinctive region.[9]

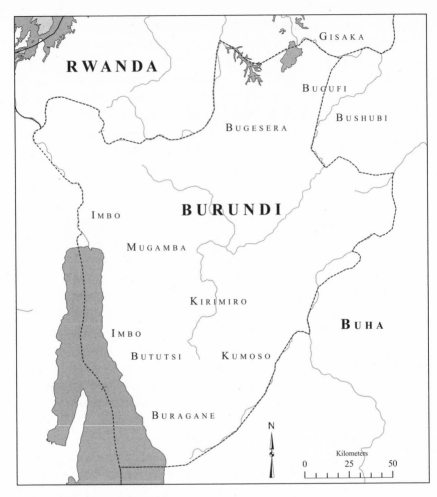

Map 12.5. **Burundi: selected cultural regions**

Cultural configurations in Burundi showed greater local diversity and fewer, but more highly pronounced autonomous regions; most were incorporated into the Burundi state only in the early nineteenth century during the reign of Ntare Rugamba (see map 12.5). The dynastic center along the central highlands included Kirimiro and parts of southern Mugamba and northern Bututsi. To the north, the region of Bugesera had its own social and political identities across the Rwandan border. Farther to the northeast, the population had strong political, social, and economic ties east to Bugufi; while Buyogoma, formed of the broad grasslands east of the central highlands, was formerly part of the northern Buha culture zone and retained strong economic and social ties with the grazing areas farther east still. The southern zones of Buragane and Buvugarimwe-Kumoso had their own external connections, more involved with southern Buha than with the highlands of Bututsi to the north. And finally, the Imbo, stretching along the Lake Tanganyika littoral and north through the Rusizi River plain, covering the entire northwest of the colonially defined state, was a region distinct in many ways from the culture of dynastic Burundi.[10]

These regions were not simply ethnographic curiosities but important features of the historical landscape, for each had its own history to tell, and their separate historical and cultural characteristics continue to affect politics and identity even today. From the early nineteenth century, successive central authorities (dynastic, colonial, and postcolonial) did more than cobble these regions together; they tried to forge a new identity from the individual regional units—though they also sought to subordinate these regional identities to a national logic. But the process of forging a common identity occurred in an uneven fashion; "national" cultural identity coexisted, sometimes rather uneasily, with the legacy of regional awareness, an awareness that often remained relevant even within highly centralized state structures. This means that broad classificatory labels of "Hutu," "Tutsi," and "Twa" carry little explanatory value for historical understanding. Instead, the histories of these states can more effectively be told in terms of regional histories—including their individual relations to the central dynasty—than through ethnic histories.

Early Settlement

Archaeological findings reach back well beyond twenty-five hundred years ago in central Rwanda and nearly as far in Burundi. These dates correspond well with work done on the shores of Lake Victoria; in fact, they precede them slightly.[11] The earlier dates of the Rwanda sites, and the presence of iron-working techniques in Rwanda that are slightly different from those along the shores of Lake Victoria, suggest the possibility of an independent evolution (if not also the independent invention) of metallurgy in this region. But irrespective of temporal priority, the basic material elements to iron-working cultures on the plateaus, just to the east of the mountains forming the divide, were in place for the period between about 700 BCE and 700 CE.[12]

The archaeological remains are too sparse to permit drawing definitive conclusions over this vast region and time span. Nonetheless, despite the differences among Old Iron Age cultures, Van Noten's work strongly suggests a distinct pattern. Regional differentiation in pottery styles, roughly corresponding to the north-south axis along the divide, is more marked than are the differences among the several local communities. This suggests that significant cultural differences between western and eastern regions long preceded any putative immigration from the north, and that these differences corresponded with ecological zones, not racial groups, at this distant time remove.[13] Earlier accounts postulated that culture was rigidly tied to migrating population groups, the latest (and dominant) group having arrived around 1500. However, these recent archaeological findings tend to undercut the assumptions of the migration theorists on which much of the state-centered history of Rwanda and Burundi has been premised.[14]

Linguistic data also lend support to such an interpretation. By two thousand years ago, the early forest had been largely removed from the plateau areas of Rwanda and Burundi east of the divide. The period 500 BCE to 500 CE also shows a changing configuration of linguistic zones in the region, as demography, climate, crops, cattle, and ecology altered. But there is one consistent element through this period: in the area east of Lakes Kivu and Tanganyika, the linguistic divide corresponds to the ecological zones: the language groups on the plateaus east of the divide, and on both sides of the Kagera River, differed from those in the highlands of the Continental divide and west of the Rift Valley. Nonetheless, linguistic as well as other evidence shows that the people throughout these regions, even those west of the divide, had cattle and used milk from them, once again calling into question the assumption that pastoral skills were associated with only one culture in the region and that cattle were introduced to the region only with a more recent particular immigrant group.[15]

In the past, cultural differences in the region have been linked with productive forms, highlighting especially the opposition of cattle culture and agricultural economies. In this conceptual framework, each mode of production was taken to be associated exclusively with a particular ethnic group, and ultimately with particular races—Tutsi with cattle, Hutu with agriculture, and Twa with trapping and hunting. In short, in the past the history of cattle has been linked to the history of the ruling elite. But in fact cattle were in the area long before the current dynasties took shape: in western Uganda, cattle remains appear in the archaeological findings no later than 30 CE, and in Rwanda even the long-horned varieties of cattle common in this area today were present no later than 1100 CE.[16] In short, as Schoenbrun suggests, we need to disaggregate the history of cattle from the histories of specific population groups.

Instead of ethnic associations or social groups as our entry to the history at this time remove, one might better turn to ecological processes for historical understanding, noting particularly the effects of early Iron Age production techniques on the ecology of the region. Iron production on a massive scale, and the destructive land use associated with the collection of huge quantities of firewood required for such smelting, led to the removal of the forest cover and the deterioration of the soils. To accommodate this development, two processes occurred. One was a shorter fallow period on the richer agricultural soils, accompanied by the development and cultivation of new crops on a wide scale, including new varieties of bananas and plantains. The second consisted of the expansion of pastoralism into the depleted lands and the elaboration of an entirely new culture of pastoralism, shown by the efflorescence of a new lexicon relating to cattle aesthetics (colors and horn shapes), reproduction (age and sex of cattle), and pastoral production techniques.[17]

Linguistic evidence on the time depth within which such processes occurred suggests that this was largely an internally generated process, not the result primarily of cultural infusion from outside (though influences and skills from outside could well have expedited the processes involved). By 800 CE, these communities (including the people settled between Lake Victoria and the north-flowing leg of the Kagera, speaking variants of Kinyambo and Kihaya) had a word for "large cow with horns," probably referring to the Sanga cattle so common in the grassland areas today. But this was not the only, or even the earliest, type of cattle in the area; cattle and herding skills were widespread there long before the arrival of Sanga cattle. Furthermore, between 100 and 1400 CE many new terms appeared in this area pertaining to specialized cattle practitioners, and these terms appeared among a vast range of language communities within the Great Lakes Bantu family. In fact, linguistic models suggest that an interest in cattle types appears to have developed earlier in languages belonging to the Forest Group (Kihunde, Kitembo, Mashi, et al.) and only later in languages of the West Highlands group (Kinyarwanda and Kirundi). Therefore, neither the presence of cattle—not even of particular breeds of cattle—nor the emergence of specialized cattle cultures can historically be associated with any particular cultural or social group immigrating from the north or east. This conclusion, of course, does not deny the immigration of pastoralist groups; it only raises questions on the claims to the exclusive association of such groups with the introduction of cattle to this region.

In agricultural change, too, the history is much more complex than previously accounted for in the region around the western Rift Valley. For example, the forest cultures west of Lakes Kivu and Tanganyika developed banana cultivation independently of the societies along the northern shores of Lake Victoria. But the antecedent linguistic groups, from which Kinyarwanda and Kirundi derive, borrowed widely. Sharing much linguistically with forest cultures to the west, they also adopted cultigens (and the vocabularies associated with them) from areas to the east—from the ancestors of people who came to speak Kihaya and through them from the ancestors of Luganda- and Lusoga-speakers, north of Lake Victoria. While crop knowledge was ancient, modern cultivation methods appear to be quite recent, developing between 1400 and 1700.[18] This dating corresponds with the general historical understanding derived from a variety of sources, that the areas now included in Burundi and Rwanda absorbed influences from both east and west, but those from the west were earlier.

Agricultural history remains one of those domains that reflects such influences. Because of the importance of agricultural production both in maintaining population densities in the region and in prestations to the court, it is not surprising that agricultural symbols form the foundation of royal rituals throughout the region. The rites at the center of the rituals of royalty exclude New World crops (such as maize, certain types of beans, manioc, and tobacco), and even bananas (introduced from the east), in favor of millet and sorghum; by their content, therefore, these agricultural rituals suggest the chronological depth within which the transition from tubers to cereals took place. Equally significant is that the essential actors were distinct from the royal lines: these rituals were validated through the participation of families not associated with the dynastic power elite —in fact, the indications are that these court ritualists were sometimes descendants of authorities replaced by the more recent dynastic elites.[19] As the forest became cleared, there followed a shift from tubers to cereals, a process already well advanced by the first years of the Christian era.[20] However, the social significance of this transition cannot be dated precisely, for it was not a unilineal one-time shift; instead, the process consisted of a complex pattern of oscillating shifts and regional differences. Grain-producing communities could revert to tuber production, and this pattern of diverse production techniques occurred differently in different locales.

But still more important, in view of later African ideologies and European myths, is the association of cattle with early cereals from the distant past without reference to specific "ethnic" groups, let alone racial groups. In fact, their association seems likely to have been essential to the development of agriculture—and especially with the shift to banana cultivation. Having cattle graze in the pastures but drop dung in the enclosure close to the home provided manure used to fertilize banana groves near the homestead. This in effect served as a mechanism of transferring energy from the grasslands to the enclosure. Consequently, the decline in cattle over the past forty years has been accompanied by a decline in soil fertility.[21] So agricultural history developed in much more complex ways than any simplistic ethnic interpretation would allow for.

Ethnicities and Histories

These are broad historical sketches, to be sure, and accounting for particular regional variations in language and culture complicates this general image, as we shall see. Nonetheless, it is important to note that these historical processes relate to broad categories, widely spread; they cannot be associated specifically with a given, fixed (and often racially defined) population segment. (This is not to say that later groups did not enter the area, bringing with them new cultural items, skills, and values; it is only to stress that such movement must be seen not as directed migration of discrete groups, but as complex patterns of mobility building on enduring historical foundations of considerable geographical breadth.) The histories of this region are told in terms of cultural processes of invention, interchange, and adaptation all occurring in different patterns and in different regions over long periods: multiple interactions and complex cultural processes, not simple physical migration or simplistic cultural diffusion, form the principal explanatory framework of the early history of this region.

Such complex patterns of cultural development undercut models of discrete ethnic groups as the foundations of social action. Ethnicity was important to social process in these two societies, but it was important in ways very different from the popular image. Ethnic identities were not primordial; they were contextually created, they altered over time, and they evolved differently in different places and contexts.[22] Therefore, ethnic groups cannot be seen as internally homogeneous, externally distinct, and constantly in confrontation with other such groups. Like many other social categories, ethnicity was not an institution but an identity, and hence ethnic categories were contextually defined. In some instances, ethnic identity and class identity overlapped, perhaps indicative of the process by which these broad identities emerged. By one interpretation, for example, in Rwanda "*ingabo*" was a term that applied to the descendants of former warriors; they held their own land and paid taxes to the army chief, but had no other obligations, and they were treated as neither "Tutsi" nor "Hutu." Their presence only in the outlying areas of the kingdom, where former armies were posted, suggests that this class identity emerged only with the extension of state power to an area and that such "intermediate" identities seem to be part of that process of state expansion. Other data that show that a shared "Hutu" identity emerged in some areas only with the imposition of state norms suggest that such ingabo formed an example of an intermediary group, both structurally and chronologically—an example of the contextual nature of identities that varied over time and locale.[23]

Much of the popular history of these two countries has treated ethnic groups as if they were racial groups, biologically distinct, each with its own history separate from the others. But despite the presence of different physical stocks in this area, two points are worth noting: these ethnic groups are not clearly distinct and internally homogeneous racial categories, as many mental models assume; and, even if they were, such racial categories provide a poor guide to historical understanding. Because of the power of such assumptions by outsiders, some of the relevant issues need be addressed briefly here.

First, while there are individual type-cases of Hutu and Tutsi, there are wide physical variations within each ethnic category and significant physical overlap between the two. So it is impossible to draw any reliable conclusions based on the "internal characteristics" of a specific group: there are tall Hutu and short Tutsi, just as color and physiognomy vary as well.[24] Second, the internal cultural variations in such broad categories are so great as to render any facile generalizations specious: the deviations from the statistical norms are as important as the differences in the norms. For example, "Hutu" today number over thirteen million people of diverse backgrounds who live in diverse ecologies; and while Tutsi are assumed to be pastoralist, the majority of Tutsi in recent times were cultivators, and many Hutu had their own cattle. And in many regions—outside the dominance of the central court—and especially in Burundi, the very terms were in question in precolonial times. Nonetheless, the tendency has been to extrapolate to an entire cultural category the characteristics of an unrepresentative sample—if the ruling lineage was Tutsi, then all Tutsi are presumed to have been powerful; if some Hutu were landless, then all were said to have lived on the edge of poverty.[25] Such generalizations deny logic and belie the empirical record.

In addition, social categorization judged by unilineal descent through the male line does not adequately account for biological reality. For example, a child of a Hutu father and Tutsi mother is classified as Hutu, while one with a Hutu mother and Tutsi father is seen as Tutsi; though they may both draw from similar gene pools, the external logic that equates ethnicity with race will classify them as "racially" different. Similarly, a person is of the same category as his or her paternal grandfather, even if the other three grandparents belonged to another social category. Over many generations and many permutations, it becomes clear that even if there were such a thing as a "pure" race with a single point of origin—as these approaches assume—race and ethnicity cannot be seen as equivalent.

Furthermore, though they easily attract the attention of many outside observers, such physical traits as height, skin color, and physiognomy vary at different rates relative to other genetic markers, and vary individually from each other, showing high internal standard deviations from the norm; thus they are inappropriate as historical markers. But more reliable physical markers, such as blood groups, lactose tolerance, and sickle cell averages, change so slowly as to carry questionable historical significance. Some researchers argue that such slow rates of change in fact justify their use as historical data, for they situate populations historically; but this tells us little of historical process unless one combines these data with other assumptions: that culture traits are associated invariably with physical origins, that conflict is inevitable between groups of different origins, that mobility equals conquest, and so on. In other words, identifying different geographical origins within a population raises historical questions more than it provides historical answers.

In fact, we lack meaningful historical data on the origins and migrations of these groups; current popular perceptions derive from the 1862 observations of one of the earliest European travelers to the region, J. H. Speke, who admitted to hypothesizing on the history of the kingdoms he visited.[26] Such was the authority of the written word that his admitted conjecture became accepted as truth, and over the next century subsequent further research was conducted fully within Speke's intellectual framework, accepting the same intellectual premises—that historical inquiry consists of searching for origins, that race and culture were closely related, that cultural groups were associated with particular traits unchanging over long periods of time, that external influences were more important for historical change than internal dynamics, and that interaction among such different groups inevitably implied conflict.

But even if we did possess data on such "migrations," it would not tell us much, since current ethnic identity is misleading as a guide to ancestral culture —people in this area today share largely the same culture traits, irrespective of ethnicity. Furthermore, the terms used for ethnic identities themselves change. If we assume that "Tutsi" immigrated as a group to this region, why are no Tutsi groups found outside this area? Then how did the term arise, and under what circumstances? We know more about the term "Hutu": its development as a meaningful social category can be associated in some areas with a political context in which such a broad social identity became salient. It was context, not content, that generated this ethnic identity. For example, a century ago in some areas of western Rwanda, people identified by local kin-group and residence. In other areas there were political identities reaching beyond the kin group, but there was no broad social category uniting all as Hutu; in fact, the very term "Hutu" was meaningless. Only with the slow infiltration of state power, and in a complex process of mutual agency, did people come to see themselves as part of a collective Hutu identity that transcended lineage and hill.[27]

Not only did these ethnic identities change over time (and differently for different regions), in more fundamental ways they also varied between the two societies discussed here, for social stratification and ethnic identity in Burundi differed in important ways from the Rwanda models.[28] While regional identities were strong in both states, they were even more coherent and enduring in Burundi than in Rwanda, and this meant that in Burundi there emerged significant fragmentation even within the tripartite social model of Hutu, Tutsi, and Twa. Among Tutsi, for example, there were at least four clear internal distinctions, which were often more salient than their categorical opposition to Hutu. The Baganwa were the descendants of the kings, up to four generations; they were often said to be of no other category—that is, they were distinct from Tutsi. Yet although many saw the origin of the dynasty (and hence of the Ganwa) as Hutu, nonetheless, socially and politically the Baganwa were clearly associated with Tutsi, and when demoted from an aristocratic classification (after four subsequent reigns), Baganwa were accepted as of "Tutsi" status. Hima, too, was a category with ambiguous claims to Tutsi status. While clearly classified as part of a general social class of Tutsi, Hima were seen as culturally distinct; they were often assumed to be cattle herders and regionally associated with the eastern regions, the areas with better grazing. (In fact, in more recent times Hima has served as a particularly powerful political identity.) Finally, the term "Tutsi Banyaruguru" technically referred to all Tutsi other than those in these special groups, but when the term "Banyaruguru" was used, it usually referred to a special class of powerful Tutsi, distinct from common Tutsi. (In addition, region and class conveyed powerful social distinctions among Tutsi, sometimes overriding the cohesion of ethnic affiliation alone.)

Among Hutu in Burundi, too, there were important distinctions beyond the regional particularities. Two examples will suffice. The ritualists—guardians of the royal tombs, those responsible for royal rituals, court diviners, healers, religious personnel, and many others—often had separate status. Such roles, of course also existed in Rwanda, but in Burundi these were more numerous and more diverse (and included more women) than in Rwanda, attesting to the less complete consolidation of centralized authority—or more coherent regional integrity—in Burundi than in Rwanda.[29] A second example is found in the role of *abashingantahe* in Burundi, elders who served as intermediaries to central power. Part judge, part ombudsman, part moral interpreter, abashingantahe held their status by their respect in the local community, and they often served to articulate local concerns.[30] Although commonly (though not exclusively) Hutu, they were fully recognized within the Burundi political system in a way unknown— even adamantly opposed—in Rwanda under the Nyiginya dynasty. In short, these two states were not simply reflections of each other, but different in organization and rationale—and even in their perception of ethnic identities, despite the shared ethnic labels on which outsiders place so much weight. Social categories within the two states may both have drawn on the same ethnic labels, and in roughly the same proportions, but the meaning of these terms differed between them in fundamental ways.

In short, ethnic labels did not apply to internally homogeneous corporate groups, but to broad collective identities that emerged in a given context, and that were based on concepts drawing on descent, occupation, class, and personal characteristics in various combinations. So while ethnicity serves as a powerful construct in these societies, it is powerful in ways different from what is portrayed in most popular assumptions, premised on purely biological models. If in historical terms ethnicity is not a reliable guide to social characteristics, still less is ethnicity meaningful as a guide to historical actions based on a static model of colonial relationships.[31] Regional diversities, ecological transformations, and political particularities are much more important than ethnic determinism in understanding the histories of these areas.

The Genesis Traditions

Popular understanding of early history in this region is rooted in what is referred to as the Hamitic Hypothesis, founded on four assumptions: that ethnic categories are defined by biological criteria (that is, that they represent distinct racial groups); that each group has a unique point of origin; that each has a corporate history (that is, without meaningful internal cultural or historical variations within the group); and that the history of this region is explained by the migration of these corporate groups and the conquest of one by another. In this instance (following Speke), "Tutsi" are said to have migrated from Ethiopia (or Somalia) and to have conquered the "Hutu," previously settled in the region; the Tutsi immigrants are said to have brought with them all the accoutrements of royalty and so introduced kingship to the region (as well as cattle, the mechanism of their domination). But if this were the case—if there were a single origin for all "Tutsi" and a single historical pattern for the imposition of kingship—we would expect to find traditions of origin that are roughly comparable in Burundi and Rwanda, since the ethnic groups—and therefore their histories—are presumed to be equivalent in the two countries.

Yet Rwanda and Burundi each have distinctive genesis traditions—in fact, they each have more than one, and there are important differences between these internal variants. For Rwanda, there are two hegemonic traditions, which appear to be chronologically distinct. Nonetheless, both versions are closely linked to the central court; they refer to issues important exclusively to the dynastic elite rather than referring to perspectives that privilege local history. The Rundi traditions, by contrast, derive from a wide range of local sources. Although they are less standardized and less formalized than those from Rwanda, the Rundi traditions also fit into two different categories of genesis traditions; by comparing the different versions one can determine with some precision the regional differences and changes over time in this founding narrative.

Rwanda

The first of the Rwandan traditions on the founding of the royal dynasty deals primarily with pastoralist interests and was explicitly located on the grasslands of eastern Rwanda.[32] It notes that the Tutsi arrived in corporate "clan" groups, entirely distinct from each other, and it postulates the relations among the various "Tutsi" clans that settled in this area.[33] In short, this genesis tradition— clearly etiological ideology—is intensely concerned with ethnic issues, and with the monopoly of royalty by Tutsi, to the virtual exclusion of others.[34]

The second genesis tradition is quite different. It reflects cultural features associated with the mountainous western regions of the country, rather than the eastern grasslands. It focuses on Gihanga ("the founder") and portrays him as a great hunter who traveled widely in the area west of the divide, marrying women from local groups with whom Gihanga is said to have forged especially close ties and which were to play important roles in the later elaboration of the royal rituals. In addition, Gihanga is said to have introduced such elements as fire, iron-working, certain essential crops, and cattle, and to have inaugurated the royal drum (the symbol of royalty); it was he, according to this myth-charter, who appointed particular families to serve as ritualists for the Rwandan state. In short, though it focuses on relations with non-Tutsi, this tradition claims that the Abanyiginya introduced all the essential elements of Rwandan culture, including kingship itself.[35] Hence the genesis traditions in Rwanda portray royal history as a "Tutsi"-imported tradition rather than as the interaction of many locally derived cultural traditions.

Taken in all their variants, these narratives obviously go far beyond the retention of discrete historical events.[36] Nonetheless there is a remarkable conjunction of the Gihanga narratives with accounts relating to the period of court penetration into the forest areas along the divide.[37] Most prominently, these deal with the reign of Ruganzu Ndori, portrayed as the archetype of the warrior-king; his campaigns are recounted in epic proportions, and they directly recall the accounts of Gihanga's exploits in the western areas, so much so that the Gihanga narrative appears in part to argue that Ruganzu was simply reasserting Nyiginya rule over all those areas formerly ruled by Gihanga; therefore, these traditions seem simply to serve as justification for Ruganzu's wars. Furthermore, like Gihanga, Ruganzu is said to have introduced a new royal drum, to replace that lost under his predecessor Cyamatare Ndahiro. And since drums serve as the essential dynastic symbols, the introduction of a new drum can be understood as the inauguration of a new dynasty, especially as the traditions on the loss of Ndahiro's drum are clearly apocryphal.[38]

But while many of Gihanga's exploits reappear in Ruganzu's reign, these traditions do not serve simply as an etiological prelude to Ruganzu's reign; they clearly relate to a whole epoch. The initial contacts with areas from which the principal ritualists were to be drawn, for example, apparently occurred four reigns previous, under Mukobanya,[39] a time when these western cultural influences on Rwandan royalty seemed most intense. Mukobanya and his son Mibambwe were said to have been driven west by foreign invaders; Mukobanya is then said to have reconquered the kingdom from the west. Indeed, since he brought with him much of the panoply of western royal culture, it is likely that this reconquest represents the introduction of a new dynastic tradition from the west. In short, the indications are that here, as elsewhere in the official chronicle, the continuity of the royal line is fabricated—and that the essential features of Rwandan kingship were derived at least as much from western cultural traditions as from imported features from the east, represented in the first genesis tradition.[40]

Burundi

The genesis traditions of Burundi differ from those of Rwanda; they are much less formalized and much more diverse,[41] but they too can be divided into two categories. At first sight, these appear distinguished by geographical domain, but the differences correlate with other features as well. One cycle, referred to as the Nkoma cycle, is associated particularly with the south and central portions of the country; by reference to the ritual locales important to more recent kingship in Burundi, it traces the moves of Ntare Rushatsi, the founder of the Ganwa dynasty, from Buha in the south to Kirimiro and parts of Mugamba, highlands that became the historical center of the kingdom.

The Kanyaru traditions, by contrast, focus on the extreme north of present Burundi (see map 12.6). These variants refer to the descent of the Ganwa dynasty from Gihanga, the putative ancestor of the Nyiginya dynasty in Rwanda. Three conclusions emerge from these traditions that differentiate the Kanyaru claims from the Nkoma cycle: that Ganwa origins in Burundi are tied to the Rwandan dynasty, and beyond that to the "Hamitic" scenario of the wider region; that the Ganwa dynasty was Tutsi, not Hutu as earlier (Nkoma-cycle) traditions aver;

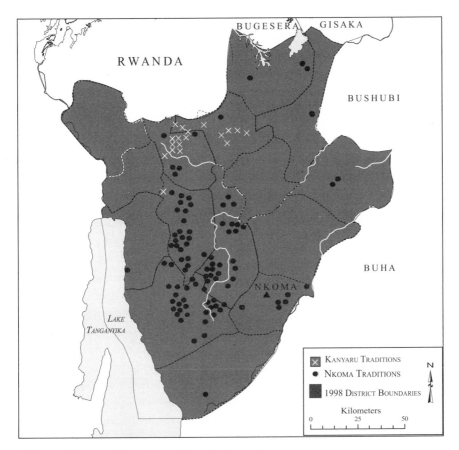

Map 12.6. Patterns of genesis traditions in Burundi

and that the chronology of Ganwa kings consisted of four cycles (of four kings each) rather than two cycles of kings, as suggested by internal data.

Through a careful analysis, Chrétien concludes that the Nkoma cycle, consisting of sixty-four testimonies drawn from all regions of the country, is more deeply rooted in Rundi culture and in the culture of kingship (including the ritual ideology of kingship) than the Kanyaru traditions. The Kanyaru cycle, on the other hand, derives from eleven traditions from a localized region, and from sources tightly linked with each other (and linked to Rwandan historians as well).[42] Tracing both the European influences on (and the particular colonial interests of) the narrators of the Kanyaru tales, Chrétien shows that the traditions associated with this cycle clearly evolved with deepening colonial rule. Nonetheless, these traditions were not invented whole: this area was formerly incorporated into Bugesera, an earlier kingdom, and these traditions appear to derive from pre-Ganwa polities that emerged between the collapse of Bugesera royalty and the eventual incorporation of this region into the expanding states of Rwanda and Burundi at the turn of the nineteenth century.[43]

So the indications are that this set of genesis traditions was based on earlier idioms, but by the 1930s these were recast in the forms we know them today, to address essentially three problems raised by colonial historiography. One was to integrate Rundi traditions into wider regional historical hypotheses, and especially to align this vision with the Hamitic Hypothesis—the notion that a single corporate group of "Tutsi" pastoralist invaders from the north conquered the local people and imposed kingship on them. This assumption represented the racialized "migration and conquest" model of kingship favored by the early colonial power holders. A second problem to be addressed in these accounts was the relation of the Ganwa dynasty in Burundi to the Nyiginya dynasty in Rwanda, at a time when European administrators saw these as "twin" kingdoms, each with centralized power, similar ethnic representation and social stratification, and mixed pastoral-agricultural economies. There were problems with each of these assumptions, but the "obvious" similarities of the two states—still a pervasive (if facile) assumption for outside observers today—served as a foundation for colonial powers to establish a unified administration over Rwanda and Burundi: given the assumptions of indirect rule, postulating a common dynastic origin served as a useful rationale for this administrative objective.[44] Third, and more prosaically, privileging the Kanyaru cycle also served to tie the Rundi authorities in the north of the country to claims of dynastic ancestry, bolstering their regional claims to greater status within the colonial construct.[45]

In fact, Chrétien and others now see the Nkoma (southern) cycle as the more likely guide to the early dynastic history of Burundi. That would date the consolidation of Ganwa hegemony probably to the early eighteenth century (though the figure of Ntare Rushatsi himself may well be a composite image of a process that spanned a much longer period). By the late eighteenth century, the ideological claims of Rundi kingship encompassed much of the central and southern areas of the current state. During the reign of Ntare Rugamba, in the early nineteenth century, the size of the kingdom doubled, expanding to the north (with the collapse of Bugesera), to the Imbo regions north of Lake Tanganyika, and to the northeast (Bushubi).

Precolonial Dynastic Histories

The precolonial political and social traditions of Burundi and Rwanda each showed complex patterns of internal cultural variations, but three coherent distinctions emerged in these geographic domains, different in each case. In Burundi the areas of the south and east—linked to the drier open plains of the cultural regions farther east still—differed markedly from the central areas. To the northwest, the Imbo also developed its own political forms, distinct from the patterns of centralization and hierarchy on the central plateau and interacting with the political field of highland eastern Congo.[46] Nonetheless, for Burundi our knowledge is sparse before about 1800, and the nineteenth century was dominated by two very long reigns, that of Ntare Rugamba (ca. 1796–ca. 1850) and that of Mwezi Gisabo (ca. 1850–1908).[47]

By contrast, the data on Rwanda are much more dense and accessible than those for Burundi. Here, too, three distinct political traditions emerged, each with ties to different cultural fields beyond, but also interacting with each other from the early eighteenth century as well, in ways that are more clearly defined than for Burundi. In the northwest, kinship structures served as the connecting tissue of political discussion. In the western regions, small polities emerged, based on concepts of ritual power. In the east, more clearly articulated and hierarchical dynastic traditions were based on the political use of force.

Because of the different data sets and different forms of interaction, this section will have slightly different organization for the two country units. The discussion on Burundi will be dominated by the two long reigns of Ntare Rugamba and Mwezi Gisabo; that on Rwanda will first survey alternative social paradigms to that of the Nyiginya dynastic model, and then provide a dynastic narrative focusing on four selected reigns spanning the eighteenth and nineteenth centuries.

Burundi

Our detailed knowledge of Burundi dynastic history is limited before about 1800.[48] But it is clear that regional autonomy was very marked. In the eastern and southern areas in particular, widespread personal interaction encouraged both the flow of religious ideas and ritual practices, on the one hand, and the exchange of material goods, on the other; livestock, agricultural produce, salt, and iron, were among the more important commodities.[49] Indeed, the movement of people in the open plains differed distinctly from the pattern of social interaction in the highlands areas, where politically recognizable groups are discernible in the record by the late seventeenth century. Prominent in these traditions are the figures of Jabwe and Nsoro, said to have been Hutu, with ties to the northwest, across Lake Tanganyika. But such references can be taken as a personification of cultural continuities rather than as literal testimony to the personal mobility of given individuals; furthermore, they are likely representative of many other political nuclei.[50] It is also clear that these regions had longstanding commercial and cultural ties with lakeshore areas; these may have been intensified during the nineteenth century with the extension of the East Coast networks, but they existed long before.[51] What is significant is that although the exact process is not clear from the sparse traditions available, these small polities along the crest of the mountains, which appear to reflect cultural forms today familiar west of Lake Tanganyika, were incorporated into an emergent political domain from the later seventeenth or early eighteenth century.

Thus a new political pattern associated with the figure of Ntare Rushatsi emerged in southern Burundi; this process of restructuring political space combined areas formerly distinct into a shared historical field. (The western regions along the lakeshore, the Imbo, where people had strong commercial and cultural ties with the Lake Tanganyika culture zone, were not included in this political transformation; these regions retained considerable autonomy even in recent times.) The focal point for this new political tradition was in south-central Burundi, along the eastern slopes of the divide, with strong influences reaching along the highlands to the north and onto the plains of the south and southeast portions of what we now know as Burundi (see map 12.7). The extent of political coalescence occurred on an entirely new scale. But more important, this new political culture was not imposed from the outside. Rather, it was forged through a synthesis of many local cultural fields into a single ritual space, through shared responsibilities in the celebration of *umuganuro*, the annual First Fruits ceremony, which remained critical to kingship in Burundi.[52] In short, although it is significant that many traditions speak of Ntare Rushatsi as Hutu, this process seems to speak to the political amalgamation of eastern populations from the plains with areas having strong "western" cultural traditions in the highlands. Two points are of interest in this process. First, despite political conflict between Ntare and Jabwe, there does not seem to be an overt ethnic component to this process; state-building here was not part of some "age old ethnic animosity," nor did it adopt the pattern of "tribal warfare." (Indeed, it is unlikely that the recent attribution of Hutu status to these actors had any meaning at this historical remove.) Second, the consolidation of power in the western highlands appears to have oc-

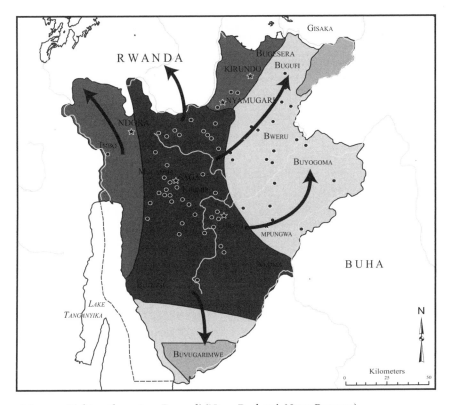

Map 12.7. Eighteenth-century Burundi (Ntare Rushatsi–Ntare Rugama)

curred here at roughly the same time that similar processes were occurring in Rwanda. Such indications over a broad region suggest not a calculated political movement, as would underlie assumptions of migration and conquest by corporate groups, but more likely a common response by separate groups to broad ecological influences, perhaps a period of prolonged drought, as people from the east sought access to grazing or cultivation rights in the hills.

In addition to linking the accumulation of royal rituals to the expansion of political space, these traditions also refer to the emergence of new religious practices associated with a spirit named Kiranga: Ntare is said to have included at his court the celebration of Kiranga, a spirit figure associated with a broad field of *emmandwa* religious belief patterns stretching across the Great Lakes region of Africa; it was particularly associated with the Ryangombe spirit in Rwanda.[53] But the cultural meaning of Kiranga in this context was more precise. Defined by an elaborate series of initiation rituals, this new religious community transcended separate family ritual practices and combined many independent spirits and mediums into a coherent religious family, backed by traditions explaining the relationships among the diverse emmandwa spirits. The association of Ntare with Kiranga in the traditions is therefore clearly an attempt to assert court authority over what was potentially an autonomous religious field; the range of these practices suggests that Kiranga was introduced to Burundi long before, but incorporated to the royal field only with Ntare I in the early eighteenth century. Once again, the independent correspondence with Rwandan history is remarkable, for Ryangombe, the Rwandan analogue to Kiranga, was incorporated to the central court of Rwanda during the reign of Rujugira in the mid-eighteenth century, only slightly later than Rundi traditions suggest this happened for Kiranga in Burundi.

The chronology associated with this dynastic history has a history of its own (though kingship may indeed have preceded the Ganwa dynasty). The dates are disputed between those who argue for two cycles of four kings each (succeeding each other under the dynastic names of Ntare, Mwezi, Mutaga, and Mwambutsa), and those who argue for four such cycles. But the evidence today suggests strongly that the four-cycle assertion is a recent extension, in part to find a closer fit to the official Rwandan chronology.[54] We know almost nothing about the reigns of the three monarchs who followed Ntare Rushatsi and completed the first cycle of kings, covering the eighteenth century; these fragmented traditions may well reflect the weak, fluid, and regionally circumscribed character of central court power in Burundi.

The first king for whom we have detailed information after Ntare Rushatsi was Ntare Rugamba, whose reign covered the first half of the nineteenth century (ca. 1796–1850). This Ntare set the geographical contours to modern Burundi by extending royal power in many directions. He conquered parts of Bugesera to the north and Bugufi in the northeast; he incorporated Buyogoma in the east, and occupied the Rusizi Valley to the northwest. However, not all of Ntare's campaigns led to permanent expansion. He invaded Kinyaga (in what is now southwest Rwanda) and briefly occupied the eastern shore of Lake Kivu, though the Burundi court never successfully administered these areas; and in other areas, too, it is not clear that court claims to conquest were valid.[55]

Though Ntare Rugamba is said to have doubled the area of the country, the administrative legacy of Ntare's rule was at least as important to Burundi political history as were his military exploits. With such rapid expansion, Ntare relied on his sons as administrators: he was strong enough to set up his sons, but not strong enough to incorporate these regions fully within central control. His successor, Mwezi Gisabo, acceded to power in 1852. But he was one of the younger sons of Ntare—in fact, he came to power under the regency of his older brother, and there is some question of his own parentage—so Mwezi had to struggle against his older brothers to retain his claim to kingship. This pattern of succession struggle was not unusual in the area. But in this case, two long reigns, just preceding European arrival, fostered protracted conflict between different descent lines among the Baganwa, opposing the Batare (the sons of Ntare) to the Bezi (the sons of Mwezi). This pattern of conflict within the dynastic family was to continue as the central administrative characteristic of the Rundi state, and it became the single greatest impediment to the consolidation of central rule.[56] While indicative of personal struggles, these conflicts also suggest that competitors to Mwezi's rule—itself based on rather tenuous claims—sought to establish themselves in precisely those regions resistant to court control. Although the traditions tend to personalize these struggles, such durable resistance probably reflects as much the political diversity and cultural autonomy of various regions of the Rundi culture zone—and the precarious nature of court rule over these regions—as it does the personal ambitions of those who sought court power.

During the late nineteenth century, under the reign of Mwezi Gisabo, a four-tiered system of administration emerged: a central area around Muramvya under the control of the king; an area under the administration of his sons or brothers most closely allied to the king; a broad swath farther east and south administered by Batare chiefs, the descendants of Ntare; and another zone, covering the western and northwestern areas of the country, under the administration of others, not Baganwa (in fact, they were mostly Hutu authorities; see map 12.8). From this pattern, three types of political relations emerged. Administrative authorities in the east and southeast, often Batare (descendants of Ntare Rugamba), simply retained their administrative autonomy while acknowledging nominal central court ritual hegemony. Those in the northeast more characteristically undertook open revolt, often by those who sought to overthrow Mwezi. Paradoxically, the principal actors in these revolts were often the sons and grandsons of Ndivyariye, an older brother of Mwezi, one of his strongest early supporters in the succession struggle on Ntare's death, and the principal regent in the early years of Mwezi's reign. But Ndivyariye was accused of plotting to retain administrative regions for himself and was driven out of the court and later assassinated; it was his descendants who revolted against the king. In the northwest, by

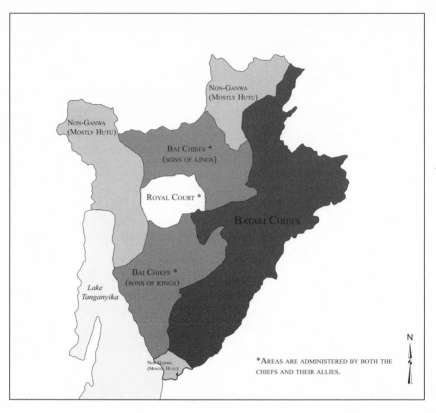

Map 12.8. Burundi: administrative chiefs (early 1900s)

contrast, pretenders to royal power had more tenuous claims to Ganwa identity; they drew on local traditions of resistance and benefited from the resources of the Lake Tanganyika trade network (as well as support from other states such as the Shi kingdoms west of Lake Kivu).

Such conflicts—and indeed the precarious nature of central court power—marked Mwezi's entire reign, spanning more than fifty years. These were broad political struggles which represented not only conflict among Baganwa personalities, but true popular movements asserting limits to court penetration; they represented complex combinations of individual ambition on the part of the Ganwa, with a sense of class awareness and regional autonomy on the part of the cultivators. Despite such pervasive political segmentation and the fragmented appearance resulting from the local diversity of such movements, however, this was political struggle, not anarchy: Baganwa often fought over recognized positions, including that of kingship itself—and the control of royal rituals. Without standing army organizations, conflict in Burundi was short-lived, often lasting only a few days; the court itself frequently mediated between competing Baganwa, and ritual and religious authorities often asserted a common set of cultural values in mediating or restraining competitors. In other words, kingship in Burundi was in many cases not strong enough to suppress political conflict; nonetheless, it was often central to political struggle in Burundi and influential in the forms those struggles assumed.

Such competition was generic to elite political culture in Burundi; these were not simply succession disputes, nor did the competition diminish over time. The late nineteenth century saw three types of challenges to Mwezi's rule: an increase in popular resistance to the court; a series of unremitting ecological and epidemiological calamities from the 1880s, which undermined both the material resources and the moral authority of the court; and new forms of political intrusion, which included attacks by African actors (such as Mirambo) from the east, threats from the commercial power associated with the East Coast Swahili networks, and direct European intervention. In fact, viewed from the perspective of royal centralization, so great was the disarray in the area we now call Burundi that Europeans themselves doubted Mwezi's existence until the turn of the century—even though the first European contacts dated from 1858, their durable presence from the 1870s, and permanent residence from 1896. Again, this was a reflection of the regional autonomy within the country, since European contacts with Burundi were first made through the northeast and northwest, areas that did not recognize the authority of Mwezi's rule; European intrusion was seen by the court as simply another form of resistance, in a country marked by a variety of challenges to the central court aspirations for authority.

But if Mwezi was a phantom to Europeans, he was very real to Barundi pretenders to power, who often allied themselves with these new external forces. Of many cases, two are illustrative.[57] Kilima was an adventurer from Bushi to the northwest, though some accounts say he claimed—or was ascribed—Ganwa parentage. But whatever his biological origins, he obtained arms from the Lake Tanganyika Swahili commercial contacts, and he managed to draw successfully on the traditions of local autonomy and strong opposition to the central court that characterized the societies of the Rusizi River Valley. Eventually he allied with the Germans in their attempt to seize Mwezi, and with the rout of the king, the Germans rewarded Kilima with an important administrative position. But

German favor shifted as the colonial power sought to bolster the authority of the central court, and Kilima was later deposed and exiled from Burundi.[58]

Maconco's story is even more dramatic.[59] As an early ally of Mwezi, he married one of Mwezi's daughters. But the alliance fell apart, say the oral sources, because of a dispute over a hunting dog (a frequent cliché for conflict in the western areas, and especially symbolic in the context of royal rituals) and with the death of his wife, the daughter of the king. Maconco then allied himself with the Germans as they sought to capture Mwezi, and he, too, assumed a prominent administrative position. But eventually he was accused of stealing a gun (again, symbolic in the context of German power), arrested, and hanged. So the Maconco tale is indicative of Ganwa power struggles and shifting alliances: it tells the story of alliance with the king and eventual treason; alliance with European power and eventual revolt; and finally European execution of one of the great of the land.

Following their military exploits along the Indian Ocean coast, the Germans turned their attention to Burundi after the turn of the century.[60] Allied with Kilima and Maconco and others, they drove Mwezi from his compound and finally forced an agreement on him: Mwezi would recognize German authority, respect the presence of missionaries, and accept the administrative authority of German allies (such as Kilima and Maconco) in certain areas; in return, the Germans would support Mwezi as king of Burundi. So Mwezi traded Rundi sovereignty for German support in consolidating the power of the central court throughout Burundi—ceding external integrity for increased local power. With the assistance of German forces, central court rule was extended over numerous recalcitrant areas: Kilima was exiled, Maconco was executed, and many other political opponents were either killed or arrested. German beliefs in the despotic power of African kings led them to exaggerate the power of the state, and administrative expedience led them to extend court power throughout the territory of the Barundi; rather than diminishing the extent or the power of the central court, European rule (first German, then Belgian) vastly extended both the domain and the internal power of the court. And in the process of legitimizing kingly authority, colonialism created the context for a new understanding of dynastic historical traditions as well (in the form of the Kanyaru cycle).[61]

But colonial policy affected not only the central court. To be sure, it undermined both the external sovereignty and the local legitimacy of the central court, primarily though a campaign waged against umuganuro and other royal rituals of legitimacy—a campaign carried out with the strong support of the Catholic missionary community.[62] However, at the (redefined) "national" level, German rule also built up the administrative capacity of court officials to impose policy from above. So the state gained precedence over society: one of the most important internal effects of German policies in Burundi was to move power away from the ritualist community, whose members often served as representatives of local integrity and whose authority implicitly set limits on state power. Instead, with the slow dissolution of the influence of the community of ritualists at the court, more power was invested in the administrative elites, who came to exercise greater powers from above over the local population.[63] Thus the character of colonial rule reconfigured the political culture to enhance the political power of the second tier of delegated chiefs, authorities whose rule would impinge directly on the lives of the population. Over time the chiefly cadre became increasingly Ganwa and (within the Ganwa) increasingly Bezi: between 1929 and 1945, the total number of chiefs was reduced from 133 to 35, while Hutu chiefs went from 27 to 0.[64] The rise of Pierre Baranyanka is illustrative of the colonial alliance of chiefs and European administrators: through the protection of several highly placed European administrators, Baranyanka became the most eminent colonial chief of Burundi, even a rival to the power of the king himself.[65] In time, such newly reconfigured, "neotraditional" functionaries became strong advocates of the mystique of a dynastic power that extended far back into the past, in a colonial context where longevity was equated with legitimacy.[66]

Three general points are worth retaining from this sketch of late-nineteenth century Burundi dynastic history. First, the challenge to royalty did not come predominantly in the form of ethnic confrontation, and conflict in precolonial Burundi was not primarily along ethnic lines. Most frequently, conflict occurred among the Baganwa themselves, and even those not Baganwa (such as Kilima) drew on support from the masses resisting the potential power of the central elites. Second, throughout the precolonial period in Burundi the power of the state was very circumscribed; that was true even for the expansion of Ntare Rugamba, where the record is clear that military conquest proved easier than the exercise of administrative power. And finally, while it is salient to note the limits on the power of the Rundi central court, it is also essential to note the differences between Burundi and Rwanda on this point. The nature of territorial identities differed; the nature of ethnic identities differed; the nature of clientship forms differed; and the nature of army organization differed. (Burundi had no standing armies.) Therefore, these were not "twin states," as outsiders often label them, whose histories can simply be melded into one another or substituted for one another: Burundi and Rwanda were autonomous polities and separate societies;

they did not have identical histories any more than they shared common cultural constructs or similar social processes.[67]

Rwanda

Our knowledge of precolonial Rwanda is more complete, in part because of the more structured and standardized traditions associated with the court. But as more formalized statements, they were also more controlled to serve court purposes and to glorify court power, to the neglect of examining the relations of court and commoners.[68] Yet three institutions central to court power in Rwanda suggest that such relationships were a constant theme in Rwandan dynastic history: the evolution of ritual and religious claims to legitimize kingship; the development of army corporations; and the transformation of client institutions. All were central to the development of kingship, and all turned on the relation of court and commoner. After examining the early dynastic establishment through the reign of Ruganzu Ndoori, we will trace these factors through three important subsequent reigns: Cyilima Rujugira, during the late eighteenth century; Yuhi Gahindiro, during the early nineteenth century; and Kigeri Rwabugiri, during the late nineteenth century.[69]

What little we know of the early history of these regions suggests that on the open plateaus west of the Kagera River there emerged a number of small political units. One of these was associated with a descent line within the Nyiginya clan affiliation, and over several centuries this was eventually to become the dynastic line to the state known as Rwanda. But it is important to note that the small and localized unit of Rwanda was only one of many such conglomerations. The early history of this area is told in the interactions among these similar but distinct units, and the relations between this emergent dynastic line and other populations that did not always see themselves as subjected to the Nyiginya court.

In fact, before the mid-eighteenth century or so, the cluster of dynastic cores in the east was only one of three different larger models of political organization in this territory that was to become Rwanda. In the northern and northwestern areas, people lived in small-scale political sectors within densely populated agricultural societies. In these areas political identities combined *umuryango* ("lineage") and *ishanja* ("subclan") units. As corporate units, important lineages controlled land, often known as *ubukonde*, or land said to have been cleared of forest by an early lineage; ubukonde land was held independently of court control. The dominant lineage (*abakonde*) allowed others to reside on this land in a client relationship called *ubugererwa*. So political organization was defined by a combination of descent and residence.[70]

Along the crest of the Congo-Nile divide and to the west of the divide, by contrast, political organization focused on ritual polities, not broadly ramifying kin ties.[71] The organizing factor in these polities was not kinship, but ritual claims to the productivity of the land and the well-being of the population: several of these ritual heads, for example, were renowned rainmakers, even at the Nyiginya court of Rwanda through the nineteenth century.[72] This political format existed throughout the area, but was especially associated with the forest ecology of the Congo-Nile divide, and west into the Rift Valley and beyond.[73] In the area that became Rwanda there may have been twenty or so such entities, but only four retained their autonomy into colonial rule: Bukunzi and Busozo in the southwest and Kingogo and Bushiru in the northwest.[74] Despite significant diversity, they were all characterized by strong ritual prescriptions, a high degree of population mobility (because of an economy based in part on trapping, gathering, and hunting), the importance of certain grain crops such as eleusine millet, and a tendency for succession to pass through a system that (in practice if not in ideology) resembled matrilateral descent—the role of women in succession was critical, and a deceased *mwami* was often succeeded by his sororal nephew, though there were many variations and much fluidity in such institutions.[75]

The ritual justification of kingship and the tendency toward matrilateral succession seem to be prominent features of these polities. Military organization was less important: we have very few cases of such royalties fighting each other.[76] But in most cases these political units flourished or foundered on their ability to attract followers and settlement—in a culture where mobility was frequent, highly valued, and indeed essential; trapping, gathering, and hunting all placed high value on mobility, and such cultures benefited from low population densities. But over the course of the eighteenth and early nineteenth centuries, increasing population densities brought a shift to agricultural production, fishing, and animal husbandry. In these situations land claims and territorial recognition became more important. Therefore, the development of social institutions to establish such claims increasingly defined lines of descent and inheritance.

These small polities formed the second model of political organization in the region east of Lake Kivu in the eighteenth century; they were important to the political history of this cultural zone, for they defined the contours of kingship, establishing a tie between ritual recognition and political power. This led to a form of political incorporation independent of conquest. Historically the

Nyiginya court intruded into this area by incorporation as well as by conquest, by adopting the rituals of preexisting polities and including them in the central rituals of the Nyiginya dynastic structures of the eighteenth century and after. It was these local rituals that in essence defined the power of kingship.[77] So one of the contradictions that faced the Nyiginya state as it extended its power to the west was its attempt to claim exclusive moral legitimacy, while drawing on those very elements that implicitly undermined such claims to exclusive authority.

While there developed a complex set of interlocking royal rituals in both Rwanda and Burundi, one of the most important of these rituals was the annual First Fruits ceremony, central to the restatement—and renewal—of kingship.[78] Despite some differences between the two countries, this ceremony (*umuganura* in Kinyarwanda; *umuganuro* in Kirundi) was structurally quite similar in the two kingdoms and represented certain fundamental features of kingship. At the harvest of sorghum and eleusine millet, the ritualists—mostly Hutu from historically significant areas of the kingdom—came together to present the First Fruits to the king. In Rwanda these harvests derived from grain planted in carefully prescribed ritual patterns—in tiny plots, at night, and by specific ritualists who themselves were referred to as *bami* (kings); their domains were themselves ritually and politically inviolate from the central court. Other subjects could not consume (or in Burundi, plant) their crop before the royal ritual had been accomplished.

Structurally, however, the royal rituals in Rwanda did not deal with a drama of Tutsi/Hutu interaction, nor were they intended to celebrate the king, for within this central ritual the king played a relatively restrained role. Instead, this ritual addressed more fundamental issues of culture and kingship, defining their roles in mediating between nature and society, transforming grain into food, and joining two symbolic regions of the country, Nduga (the home of the central court from before the time of Rujugira) and Bumbogo (one of the small pre-Nyiginya dynasties in the region). So this ritual placed royalty in a clear cultural context that juxtaposed society, culture, and ecology and that justified kingship by its relationship to both social constructs and ecological particularities.[79]

The earlier local ritual cultures were therefore central to the integrity of the court; if kingship was validated by its ritual expression, then this ritual universe served as the basis to the Nyiginya state. The importance of this legacy of the western cultures to Nyiginya (and Ganwa) rule is also shown in royal terminology and in the solemn expressions of kingship: succession rituals and the annual First Fruits ceremonies were central to such expressions.[80] Yet it is important to note that despite the importance of ritual propriety in the definition of kingship, this was sacral kingship, not divine kingship; the king was in no way a god. Far from it. In some ways he was a prisoner of ritual norms of kingship; the rituals assert unequivocally that kingship captured the king, but they also show unequivocally how wider cultural norms defined kingship. Despite the misguided claims of outside observers, the concept of divine kingship does not apply to these polities, regardless of the power of the state.[81]

Given the importance of the local culture in defining kingship, the power holders in Rwanda sought to free themselves from the prison house of cultural norms in two ways: through the exercise of military power, and through the development of class distinctions. While they could not dispense with the rituals of kingship, they sought to subordinate the ritualists to court power and incorporate them within a centralized court culture—a process much more successful in Rwanda than in Burundi. As we shall see, the mid- or late eighteenth century was the critical period for this process, for it seems to be during the reign of Rujugira (ca. 1770–86, by Vansina's dating) that the rituals were firmly codified (though the process of incorporating rituals from the western highlands probably dates from Ruganzu and Semugeshi, a century before). At the same time Rujugira's reign saw the elaboration of a clearly defined culture of the court, one very distinct— and consciously so—from the "commoner" culture of the population and the ritualists (the most important of whom did not live at the court).

Thus the dynastic political structures found in the east were only one of several political forms in this area. It is important to keep in perspective the growth and expansion of the Nyiginya court, for these different models were embedded in important ways in the political development of Rwanda,[82] and were even to reassert themselves in the postcolonial political struggles.[83] Consequently, the history of the region now included in Rwanda cannot be reduced to the history of one dynastic family alone. The very identity of Rwanda, and of the Nyiginya ruling line, was forged in the course of interaction with many dynastic units as well as with commoner groups outside the dynastic framework.[84] Furthermore, state formation in the region did not occur in a linear progression or through the continuous expansion of state power; these processes were discontinuous, contested from within, and challenged from outside. Nonetheless while Rwandan history cannot be understood through dynastic history alone, it also cannot be understood without dynastic history, for the Nyiginya dynasty was to become the core institution of colonial rule, and the nemesis of the postcolonial state.

The Early History. There are in essence two distinct origin traditions of the Nyiginya dynastic line. One situates the early dynasty in the Buganza region, just south of Lake Mohasi. It consists of dynastic names that are fictive, symbolic, or etiological; consequently, the traditions which associate the origins of the Nyiginya dynastic line to Buganza are most likely apochryphal.[85] The second makes little mention of the "eastern areas" so prominent in the first origin traditions. Vansina is clear on this point: the Nyiginya dynasty emerged from the mid- or late seventeenth century with the reign of Ruganzu Ndori, one of the epic heroes of Nyiginya dynastic history.[86] Stories of Ruganzu pervade a wide range of literary genres (stories, tales, poetry, proverbs), and his figure dominates accounts on early history.[87] It is said that as a young child he was sent out of the country during the wars that his predecessor waged in the regions west of the divide. This king, Ndahiro Cyamatare, was killed by "westerners," and after a twelve-year interregnum, Ruganzu is said to have reentered the country from the east, waging campaigns in the highland areas and taking from there a new royal drum for the Nyiginya court.[88] His claims to reestablishing the royal line, and therefore to the continuity of that unbroken descent line, may in fact cover the fact that he was a usurper: since royal drums were the essential symbol of royalty, this reference may well serve as a metaphor for the inauguration of a new dynasty. In any event, Ruganzu represents a tenuous line of descent from earlier kings; Vansina notes that the return of a king formerly sent out of the country is a common cliché in the region, one often employed to mask the introduction of a new dynasty, and usually used to legitimate conquest by allowing the usurper to claim descent from earlier kings.[89]

Ruganzu is portrayed as the prototypical military hero: he is said to have engaged in many military campaigns, and the expansion of the state is seen as his principal political legacy. But in addition, his reign established the ideological underpinnings to the dynastic state in two ways: he inaugurated a new royal drum, rooted in the representation of royalty found in the west; and many traditions note a close association of his reign with Ryangombe, a mythic religious figure, as both colleague and competitor. Yet many aspects of the traditions on Ruganzu are either ideological (claiming the exercise of Nyiginya state power in all areas of Rwanda speakers) or etiological (telescoping material from many eras into a single reign).[90] In short, Ruganzu's reign clearly represents a turning point in Rwandan dynastic history from the late seventeenth or early eighteenth century. His reign marks the definitive establishment of Nyiginya power in areas west of Buganza and Bwanacyambwe (the plains south and west of Lake Mohasi) and the early hegemony of an "eastern" dynastic tradition over the western areas.

(And, as noted above, it is remarkable that this roughly coincides with the movement of Ntare Rushatsi into the western highlands of Burundi, also from the eastern plains areas—a region long known for periodic drought and famine.[91]) Ideologically, through Ruganzu's stated alliances with ritualists in Rukoma and Bumbogo, his reign represents the early synthesis of power from the plains with western concepts of kingship, a response to the moves of Mukobanya from the west and the defeat of Ndahiro in the highlands. And Ruganzu's association with Ryangombe suggests a tension between kingship and a religious movement, likely to have served as a vehicle for popular protest (the celebration of Ryangombe), which would be expected with such expansion.

Cyilima Rujugira. Despite the cluster of etiological narratives that focus on the figure of Ruganzu Ndori, it is the reign of Rujugira for which we first have data associated with modern kingship.[92] Rujugira, whose reign included much of the last quarter of the eighteenth century, was most likely a usurper, again from the east. The person whom he replaced, Rwaka Karemera, has been removed from the official king list; the official sources portray Rwaka as an illegitimate pretender. But many other indications, even in the official sources themselves, suggest that Rujugira was the usurper. Rwaka was designated as co-ruler before the death of his predecessor; the retention of this information itself suggests legitimacy. The sources recall the exact length of Rwaka's reign (twelve years: eight years as co-ruler with Mazimpaka, four years on his own; however, both these figures—multiples of four—are ritually pure figures in Rwandan culture), while the reign length of Rujugira is not known with certainty. This suggests that Rwaka celebrated the annual First Fruits ceremonies twelve times, for that is how reign lengths are calculated; yet only a king who is legitimate in the eyes of the ritualists can celebrate the First Fruits ceremonies.[93]

Furthermore, on the accession of Rujugira, Rwaka was not killed, as one would expect if Rwaka had been a usurper. Rujugira, on the other hand, is said to have sojourned in Gisaka and married a Gisaka wife.[94] On many occasions he was supported by a Gisaka army, and indeed, on both his death and the death of his successor, Gisaka forces were again involved in the succession disputes. Furthermore, Rujugira substantially revised both the military structures (on which he depended) and the ritual bases of the kingdom, discontinuities more in line with a usurper than a legitimate heir.

Two elements characterize Rujugira's reign. The first was the development of the ideology of kingship in Rwanda, in various forms, most prominently (in the sources available today) in the efflorescence of verbal art forms extolling court culture and reinforcing the exclusive nature of the central court. For example, under Rujugira a particular type of verbal art (*icyivugo*) was elaborated that celebrated the heroic deeds of earlier kings, glorified Nyiginya kingship, and asserted Nyiginya moral superiority as justification for the conquest of other communities. Another literary form distinctive to the court is illustrated in the vast and impressive collection of dynastic poetry, for many of the early dynastic poems can be traced to Rujugira's reign: before Rujugira, for example, there was an average of four such poems composed for each reign; after Rujugira, the average jumped to twenty-three per reign. Thirty were attributed to Rujugira's reign alone, a number surpassed only in Rwabugiri's reign—the last before colonial conquest.[95] And not least important, during this reign there was a significant move to incorporate the Ryangombe religious cult at the court virtually as the state religion; in so doing, the court sought to establish control over a set of practices—expressed in the form of popular religion—which implicitly challenged the premise of social stratification as it was emerging so dramatically in this new expanding and militaristic order under Rujugira.[96]

A second major distinction of Rujugira's reign was the strong centralization of military power in the hands of the Nyiginya dynasty. This was apparently a time of intense competition among rival dynasties, and we hear of many wars against similarly constructed political units during this period. Two significant elements characterize these conflicts. First, they were fought in the east, apparently over the control of scarce resources common to all parties—cattle and pasture. Three powerful adversaries were especially involved: Ndorwa to the northeast, Gisaka to the southeast, and Burundi to the south. Second, these wars were most often fought against other dynasties associated with Tutsi status. Military consolidation therefore occurred primarily through conflict among similar ("Tutsi") dynasties, not in interethnic conflict; in fact, though military power was important, the later incorporation of western agricultural ("Hutu") regions often took a form different from and more complex than outright military conquest.[97]

Therefore, in many ways the use of military power in the east was an essential element to the consolidation of the state. In response to these threats from the east and south, the Nyiginya court reorganized the military institutions of Rwanda; military operations provided both booty to be redistributed by the court and the core of an emergent administrative framework. The number of armies and the number of sections within any given army grew substantially. Army corporations came to be associated with a given cattle herd and, through that, with a defined territorial land grant. While their coherence fluctuated with the changing fortunes of their patron at the court, and while some existed only a short time (such as Ndabarasa's armies in Ndorwa, which were withdrawn at his death), in general these army units were made more permanent and the official histories of these armies were formalized through a type of corporate genealogy. Armies came to be posted permanently in the frontier regions—which of course did not remain frontier regions as Rwanda expanded—to the south (Muyaga and Buhonga), to the east (around Lake Mohasi) and northeast (Ndorwa), and to the west (Rukoma and Budaha), regions particularly important in the developing ritual protocol of the Nyiginya state.[98]

For the Nyiginya dynasty itself, therefore, the external military actions coincided with a shift in the political center of gravity of the kingdom, westward toward the foothills of the Congo-Nile divide (in the south-central portions of the colonial state). This shift coincided with the development of a coherent military organization, through recruitment, training, and the strategic placement of army units.[99] Under Rujugira, two strata emerged within the army organizations—*intore* (elite warriors) and *ingabo* (commoner warriors). From the time of Gahindiro, in the early nineteenth century, another stratum was added. Formerly, *ingabo* members had to provide their own supplies, and those who had retired as active warriors continued to be responsible for sustaining the remaining army members. With the evolution of the army organizations under Gahindiro, people or lineages were recruited for that function, and some men were associated with an army as producers, not warriors.

This change coincided with dynastic moves toward the southwest and northwest, areas with agricultural (and commercial) cultures without formal state organization and therefore without permanent army posts. Instead, individuals and important kin groups from these regions were recruited as the army representatives in the region; they provided material goods and received political and military support in their relations with others.[100] So central court moves into these regions were marked by a slow process of incorporation, through the co-optation of local elites.

These social corporations acted as both army organizations and early administrative structures, but they also served as alliance mechanisms, as intermediaries between the local population and the court. For example, rather than directly contesting the power of local elites, they often validated the cession of land usufruct by lineage heads to non-kin. Similarly, land grants from the court, in the form of *ibikingi* grants, had taken on heightened importance with the influx of many immigrants seeking refuge from the wars in the east, but coincidentally acting as cultural emissaries, bringing more hierarchical state-legitimated values from the east into these western areas. While often not subjects of the Rwandan state—in fact, they were often refugees from state power—the immigrants were seen as "Rwandan" in culture by the outsiders, and many of these new arrivals (formerly fleeing Nyiginya power) came to draw on the power of the Rwandan armies to validate claims to land holdings. By legitimating the ibikingi relations of local elites, the army organizations were also validating the claims of the new arrivals. In return, some of these refugee-immigrants came to serve as representatives of the state to these regions during the nineteenth century, from the reign of Gahindiro and after.[101]

The case of the Abagwabiro lineage under the leadership of a man named Macumu illustrates this process.[102] At the time of Rujugira—the period that coincided with the wars of the Nyiginya dynastic formation (Rwanda) against the Abashamo and Abagesera dynasties (in Ndorwa and Gisaka, respectively)—Macumu left Ndorwa to move west to Bunyambiriri, far back on the crest of the Congo-Nile divide. But Bunyambiriri was also an area of subsequent Nyiginya court expansion, and so from Bunyambiriri the Abagwabiro moved again, to Bugoyi, in the northwest. There they drove off the local Bagoyi lineages from their settled lands and resettled these with poor immigrants; by the nineteenth century more than one-third of the people on their lands were dependents (or clients) from other lineages. Over time, in the eyes of the court, the political status of the Abagwabiro had clearly changed—and so had their function, for during the reigns of Rwogera and Rwabugiri (in the mid- and late nineteenth century), some of the descendants of Macumu came to be claimed as "emissaries" of the Rwandan court: "The Abagwabiro set themselves up as the direct clients of the king and collected taxes among other clans of the Bagoyi, keeping some of the taxes for themselves and sending some along to the court." [103]

The figures on the retention of the formalized army histories in the official traditions testify both to the development of the social corporations and to the efflorescence of court etiquette and court histories under Rujugira. For example, in an official king list of twenty-six names, one-third of all the armies noted for Rwanda attribute their founding to the reign of Rujugira or his immediate predecessor or successor, and of the twenty-nine armies that are said to have been formed before Rujugira's time, only two have continuous histories that reach back before Rujugira's reign.[104] Furthermore, this period saw the ascendance of army formations over provincial chiefs in those areas of the army postings. This gave the court the means and the precedents for subordinating regional authori-

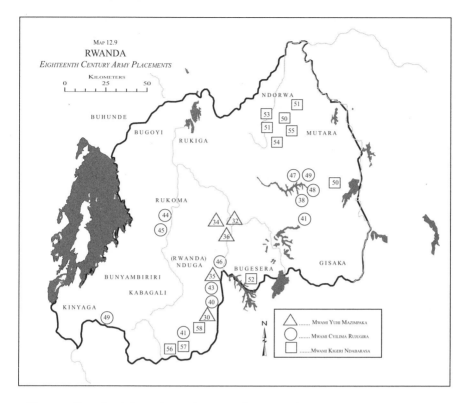

Map 12.9. Rwanda: eighteenth-century army placements

ties to court authority, a policy in distinct contrast to developments in Burundi, where regional authority was generally much less susceptible to central court influence.

But for the Rwandan people there were further repercussions no less important, for these armies were not only royal ornaments, they were also instruments of projecting state power; their actions directly affected the wider population, either by incorporating them into the hierarchical army structure or by making them victims of army campaigns. In turn, Rujugira's wars produced many refugees, who often fled west, beyond the mountains on the Congo-Nile divide. As refugees, they traveled with little loyalty to the Nyiginya court; nonetheless, in the eyes of the local populations, culturally and politically autonomous from the court, such new arrivals brought with them many elements of Rwandan culture.

Over time, these immigrants to the west came to serve the interests of dynastic expansion in two ways: since they often maintained relations with their home areas, they provided the social sinews that traversed the area that became Rwanda; and they provided the opportunity for the court to establish claims to these western areas by claiming that these immigrants of Rwandan culture had been sent by the court and therefore that the Nyiginya dynasty had claims to the regions where these immigrants settled.[105] In fact, although originally these were people fleeing from the power and exactions and extractions of the Nyiginya court, over time they often found it expedient and beneficial to become instruments of that power and agents of that extractive process. So in the western areas there came to be a conjunction of interest of former opponents turned allies.

In short, three elements—each with a history of its own—characterized Rujugira's reign: the consolidation of a class culture at the court, including the development of a distinctive court etiquette; the restructuring of army organizations; and the attempt to incorporate popular religious forms at the court, and therefore to strengthen court claims on the moral legitimacy to rule in these western areas and to co-opt the religious forms of popular resistance to the growing power of the court itself.

Yuhi Gahindiro. The reign of Gahindiro (from 1801) was also a time of internal conflict, associated with serious epidemics for the population and no less serious internal competition at the court. Gahindiro's predecessor, Sentabyo, had faced a long struggle at the time of his own accession to power. But Sentabyo's challenger, Gatarabuhura, sought assistance from the king of Gisaka (a neighboring kingdom to the east) at a time, as it turned out, of a smallpox epidemic in Gisaka.[106] Consequently, Rwanda sealed the border with the east, hoping to stop the spread of smallpox. Gatarabuhura, however, managed to send to Sentabyo a barkcloth gift that contained infected lice, and when Sentabyo's brother kept the gift he contracted smallpox. When Sentabyo came to console his brother, he too came down with the disease, and died after a reign of only five years; his only son died with him. So Sentabyo's death is attributed to a ruse by Gatarabuhura; and on Sentabyo's death (together with the death of his brother and only son) Gatarabuhura renewed his campaign to seize power. But—so we are told— Sentabyo had fortuitously fathered another son with Nyiratunga, the widow of Sentabyo's paternal uncle, a military hero who had died early in Rujugira's reign; despite her advanced age, Nyiratunga is said to have given birth to a son by Sentabyo just before the king's death.[107] With the military support of the most powerful *ngabo* at the time (as it happens, an army commanded by the son of Nyiratunga's own sister), this child, named Gahindiro, was submitted to the rituals of kingship—and Nyiratunga to the rituals of queen mother—with extraordinary haste. Such a process illustrates a key characteristic to succession struggles in nineteenth-century Rwanda: in important ways these represented struggles among the wives of the former king, or the families of these women, for it was the relative strength among the competing matrilateral kin that often determined the successor.[108]

Gahindiro's reign saw significant internal change both for Rwanda at large and within the dynasty. Outside sources confirm that this was a time of serious epidemics, with substantial population mobility and demographic growth in the aftermath, probably a legacy of Rujugira's wars to the east.[109] Many local traditions note it as a time of significant movement from the east toward the western areas; the dynastic genealogies of small Hutu polities in the west, for example, often date from this time. Whether these families established themselves as important social units—for a good number of these genealogies mention origins in Ndorwa or in Gisaka—or whether the influx of these groups provoked greater consciousness of the ritual claims of earlier groups, we do not know. But clearly the political contours of western Rwanda were deeply affected in this period.

In addition to these changes, new forms of state power were explored. For example, this was, again, a time of significant transformations in the ritual foundation of Nyiginya royal authority. In the fear that another epidemic would remove those responsible for preserving the ritual protocol of the dynasty, the number of ritual specialists performing the legitimizing functions of the esoteric code was augmented tenfold.[110] More important than the numbers alone, these changes introduced to the corporation of ritualists (*abiiru*) new members, not previously associated with ritual functions but drawn instead from the court allies of the king and from the Tutsi aristocracy.

The effect was to dilute the power of Hutu ritualist families as well as to provide influential status and power to friends of the court. Furthermore (with the same exceptions), the new positions added were not hereditary; the king was unwilling to create political autonomy among the powerful families of the kingdom, a stance also adopted by Rwabugiri in the late nineteenth century.[111] It is notable that the ritual development of kingship under Gahindiro and the limitations placed on the accumulation of power by aristocratic families coincided with a decrease in army formations. Fearing the challenge that the army units posed to royal control—and even despite the threat of military attack by the armies of Ntare Rugamba of Burundi at the time—Nyiratunga organized only three army corporations; she placed one under the command of her brother, another under an adult son, and the third under the court favorite and *éminence grise,* Rugaju. Even then, tight control was maintained: when armies returned from battle to parade at the court, the executioner's axe was prominently displayed—and occasionally put to use against those who tried to keep battle booty or who were suspected of any lapse in loyalty. "We were never so loyal as just after an execution," noted one participant in the armies of a later period, undoubtedly reflecting a point of view of earlier times as well.[112]

In addition, this appears to have been a time of significant population growth; multiple traditions in the west comment on famine conditions in such places as Bunyambiriri in these periods, and refer to the lack of food rather than to warfare as the principal reason for mobility. And perhaps associated with that growth, this was a time of significant institutional change, most notably in the changes in client forms that emerged from a conjunction of army policy and population movements. Armies posted to a frontier region proceeded to reorganize relations with the local population; in return for providing food for the army members, the rights of these groups over vast forest areas were recognized and backed by court power. In earlier times, where land was plentiful, this recognition of legitimate claims was meaningless—a legal fiction—or symbolic at best. But with the arrival of new groups, these legal claims backed by Rwandan court power became important, as immigrants sought permission to settle from these recognized landholders. And so, as noted above, tied to the extension of army power emerged a type of land clientship (*ubukingi*) that became institutionalized under Gahindiro and intensified and extended in the two reigns to follow; sometimes this came to mean expelling local inhabitants and settling dependent clients on those lands.[113]

The evolution of these client forms is as important as it is misunderstood. In fact, cattle clientship has been one of the most prominent features of anthropological writing on Rwanda; Maquet's influential work saw *ubuhake* clientship as the key element of social cohesion in a social organization characterized by the "premise of inequality."[114] For Maquet, this highly stratified society was held together by an intense network of patron-client relations that ramified throughout society, from top to bottom: in that image the gift of a cow, and the consequent responsibilities incumbent on the recipient, tied people to their patron and included virtually every male throughout the realm. In fact, however, more recent studies have brought this model into question.

First, the conventional model omitted political factors. What Maquet saw as a psychological dependence of the peasants for the usufruct of a cow was in fact a relationship established and maintained through power; the transfer of a cow was not the cause of the social relationship, but a symbol of a relationship based on other grounds. Second, several works based on empirical inquiry rather than elitist ideology have established that there were many forms of clientship and that the social significance of the different forms of clientship varied by region and over time. In some instances this was more a loose alliance structure among "friends"; in others, this was more an exploitative relationship, although before colonial rule even this form was not a codified, incontrovertible law so much as a negotiated relationship. Third, just as the psychological model of "the premise of inequality" omitted politics and neglected variant forms, it also overlooked the history of ubuhake itself, which varied from the ideological model, as two works in particular make clear.

The most careful statistical survey of ubuhake (carried out in south-central Rwanda near the dynastic heartland, where the institution would be of longest duration and would be found in its most elaborated form) showed that only 15 percent of the respondents' fathers' generation were involved in ubuhake relationships. But that percentage dropped to 8 percent in the grandfathers' generation (in the last years before colonial rule).[115] Three salient conclusions emerge from this work. First, ubuhake was hardly the pervasive cultural institution of precolonial Rwanda portrayed in elite models, as expressed in Maquet's work. Second, cattle clientship seems to have increased in the colonial period, not decreased; therefore, these data do not conform to the model of an authentic "primordial" institution that was then eroded during colonial rule by the forces of "modernization." Third, in this particular sample, this institution occurred more often among Tutsi—indeed, among aristocratic Tutsi—than between Tutsi and Hutu, thus suggesting that, in this area at least, ubuhake served primarily as an alliance among the politically powerful. So on various criteria, Maquet's image of ubuhake—as universal, primordial, and exclusively hierarchical—does not conform to the empirical data.

Furthermore, the rigidity of the institution has been drawn into question. For one region of Rwanda, the history of multiple clientship forms shows the importance of the political and economic contexts that created, transformed, and distinguished different forms of clientship—and demonstrates their effects on clients. In particular, qualitative work on the evolution of clientship forms makes it clear how changing clientship patterns served to control land access, mobilize labor, or enforce hierarchy; in other words, it establishes these varying forms of clientship as significant to the consolidation of ethnicities and of state power.[116] For central Rwanda, other studies demonstrate the significance of the diversity of clientship forms and the particular importance of land clientship over cattle clientship as a tool of political power; in many areas land clientship was much more frequent—and politically more important—than cattle clientship.[117]

Once again, an analysis of clientship patterns illustrates how social structure in Burundi differed from that in Rwanda. While in Rwanda cattle clientship often was transformed, because of the power of the state, from an alliance to an exploitative relationship, in Burundi clientship was most often expressed through *ubugabire* ties, with greater reciprocity, greater independence among the two parties, and a greater exchange component.[118] This indeed was closer to an expression of alliance than a subterfuge for covert aggression, more institutionalized friendship than political "protection." Furthermore, the donor often took as great a risk as the recipient: in theory the client owed every third or fourth offspring to the patron, and the hind-quarters of every cow that died, but in either case it was not difficult for the client to obfuscate, and the terms were often open to renegotiation; in fact the patron often had to visit the recipient to claim his due—a situation unthinkable in a context of ubuhake relationship. In short, receiving an ubugabire cow—again one of multiple forms of cattle transfer— was seen as a happy circumstance by the recipient, not a source of resentment, as was so often the case of the client in an ubuhake relationship.

Three conclusions follow from such a historical perspective on these forms of personal dependence across class and ethnic lines, clientship ties that in popular works are often presented as the paramount characteristic of Rwandan social organization. Rather than serving as primordial features of Rwandan culture, widespread clientship ties were relatively recent, gaining political significance only with the expansion of the court in the nineteenth century. Second, they altered over time—sometimes quite dramatically. Third, cattle clientship was often rooted in land clientship, and, over time, for many people land clientship became more significant than cattle clientship.

Thus Gahindiro's reign saw the consolidation of court power in three dimensions. The ritual component of kingship was restructured, with more direct control by the dynastic court assumed by (nonhereditary) direct appointees from the court. At the same time, while the power of the aristocratic families challenged the control of the king, this competition was contained within the court. And finally, the foundations were set for new forms of personal dependence, particularly dealing with land access. Each of these trajectories differed quite significantly from Burundi royal history in the nineteenth century.

Kigeri Rwabugiri. The centralization of power was greatly intensified over the last third of the nineteenth century, and especially from ca. 1876, during the personal reign of Kigeri Rwabugiri.[119] Rwabugiri is renowned in Rwanda as the great warrior-king of the late nineteenth century, but his reign was equally as important for structural transformations within Rwanda and for establishing the image of Rwandan society at the time of European arrival; the Rwanda of Rwabugiri's reign is taken by many to represent the model of a static "traditional" Rwanda.

Rwabugiri acceded to power in a complicated set of events that resembled an internal coup, deriving from the intrigue so representative of the court throughout the nineteenth century. In fact, in all but one of the seven successions from Rujugira to Musinga, conflict over the position of queen mother was the critical issue, for in naming the queen mother one indirectly named the king; one also brought the queen mother's kin to the center of power. Therefore, mobilizing matrilateral kin was the essential resource in the struggle for dynastic succession, and the women themselves appear in these traditions as the dominant political actors in these struggles.[120] The intensity of these struggles is clearly illustrated in the record: whereas the dynastic code prescribes an alternating cycle of clans for the position of queen mother, from the reign of Rujugira (himself probably a usurper) seven of the next nine queen mothers came from a single clan, the Abega.[121]

Rwabugiri's ancestry is clouded in the official traditions by a tortuous explanation for how he was the rightful heir. Seeking to consolidate power among her kin, the queen mother of Rwabugiri's predecessor, Rwogera, insisted that the next queen mother be drawn from her own clan, the Abakono; she therefore opposed Rwogera's marriage to women of other clans even though ritual required a queen mother of another clan. Nonetheless, court traditions assure us—with perhaps too great zeal to be credible—that during the absence of Rwogera's brother on extended military exercises, Rwogera secretly courted his brother's wife, a woman of a different clan from that of the queen mother. This woman then gave birth to a son, Sezisoni, claimed in the traditions as the biological son of Rwogera, though legally the son of his brother. Subsequently Rwogera proposed to swap sons with his brother, adopting Sezisoni, later renamed Rwabugiri. So either Rwabugiri was born of adulterous liaison or we are faced with an internal coup, whereby the official traditions seek to explain away succession by the son of the former king's brother. Either way, Sezisoni's succession to the throne brought his mother—the wife of Rwogera's brother—to a position of power as queen mother; but it also initiated a series of plots and machinations that eventually led to her assassination, as well as to the death of Rwabugiri's postadoptive "uncle" (and probably also his biological father), among many others, and to the mutilation of his two brothers (to prevent any later pretensions to power). So Rwabugiri eventually claimed uncontested power likely as both matricide and patricide. And the vicious political machinations that so marked this time were in fact to continue through Rwabugiri's reign and well into the next.[122]

Having acceded by power, Rwabugiri ruled by force: in internal affairs his armies constantly challenged the influence of powerful lineages and of the ritualists; in external affairs he engaged in almost continual military expeditions and campaigns. But even at a time of significant consolidation of power of the central court in Rwanda and of the arbitrary power of the monarch, this was also a time of the consolidation of power by important court personalities, army leaders, and aristocratic lineages.[123] In seeking to outflank the aristocrats, Rwabugiri appointed his own administrative authorities (including Hutu and Twa), men dependent on his own favor, rather than deferring to members of powerful Tutsi families that had increasingly claimed positions of power. To extend his regional power and dissolve institutional alliances by others, he constantly moved his capital—some accounts say at least thirty-six times in a reign of thirty years—not only within the heartland of the kingdom, but frequently visiting those areas outside full dynastic authority; his visits to these regions were used to consolidate central court control over land, political appointments, tribute payments, and especially army recruitment, including Hutu and Twa.[124]

But in song and memory he is best remembered for the extensive and almost perpetual military campaigns that marked his reign, especially but not exclusively to areas west and north of Rwanda. In fact, it was the booty and rewards, in cattle, women, military honor, and political positions to result from those campaigns—and Rwabugiri's to distribute as he saw fit—that made possible the expansion of power at the central court within Rwanda: external war consolidated internal power (but it also intensified internal conflicts). His reign can be seen as one long military campaign (some would say cattle raid) directed both against neighboring societies and regions within Rwanda. Yet it is important to distinguish between three types of campaigns: those resulting in the full incorporation of other regions (that is, resulting in the geographical expansion of Rwanda); those leading to simple a military occupation (often of brief duration); and those consisting of simple raids.[125]

These military campaigns occupied Rwabugiri's entire reign. He attacked Nkore to the northeast, Bushubi to the southeast, Burundi to the south, and the areas around Lake Rweru far to the north—indeed, virtually all the states on his borders except Karagwe to the east. He directed his main attentions, however, to the states to the west, Bushi, Butembo, Buhunde, and Buhavu. In fact, these western domains were among the first and final campaigns of his reign (he died on an expedition to Bushi), and his frequent attacks there involved progressively larger military forces and increasingly sophisticated techniques (including effective espionage).[126] Military assignments, for example, seem to have been used as a frequent tactic for removing court rivals to power. But though this military power intensified court administrative structures in such regions as Kinyaga, Bugoyi, and Gisaka, these constant campaigns were notably unsuccessful in annexing new territory; the lasting legacy of these incessant campaigns was more in tightening court control within Rwanda than in expansion per se. Thus, for all his renown as a great warrior-king, there was a paradox to these policies: they seemed more significant for achieving internal political objectives than for external expansion. Few areas of his attacks survived as Rwandan conquests after his death.

So Rwabugiri's reign was important not simply for his military exploits but also for his considerable administrative innovations and for the simultaneous centralization of royal power and fragmentation of the aristocratic court. Like many of his predecessors—especially those of doubtful legitimacy—he sought to reduce the power of the ritualists. The most famous case of this was in his appointment of Kanjogera as adoptive queen mother of his named successor (discussed below): she had a son of her own and therefore, according to the royal Code, was not eligible to serve as queen mother, for reasons that became abundantly clear in the coup of Rucunshu. But more than his confrontation with the ritualists, it was his constant conflict with the most powerful lineages of the land—the aristocratic elite—that most indicated his attempt to free the kingship from all political constraint. He killed his own mother and father, and he attacked his powerful maternal uncle, who had largely put him on the throne, because, in one way or another, he saw each as threatening his autonomy. (This conflict was reminiscent of Mwezi's conflict with his older brother at about the same time in Burundi—but one that had a different outcome because of the

Rwandan monarch's control of the armies.) He dismissed—or executed—many army leaders, often from politically powerful families, and he had the audacity to name Hutu, or even Twa, to some of these positions.[127] In short, this was clearly an attempt to centralize power in the hands of the king by making delegated authority greater than inherited authority and thus undercutting the autonomous political basis of the power of individual families. Such decisive political tactics differ from the dynastic history of Burundi, for the centralization process in Rwanda and the power of the state had developed far beyond that in Burundi— but at great cost to aristocrat and commoner alike.[128]

Nonetheless, despite these attempts—which distinguish the Rwandan court dramatically from that of Burundi at the same epoch—Rwabugiri was not the omnipotent autocrat that some observers have made him out to be. His struggles with both ritualists and court factions were in part a sign of their power— rather than of his power. His innovations were sometimes stunning but seldom enduring. Similarly his campaigns abroad, while frequent, were often unsuccessful, and his victories often ephemeral. His impulsive character was in part caused by, as well as a cause of, the ongoing power of individuals or factions at the court. He remained credulous of court diviners and fearful of army chiefs, even as he maneuvered around them and fought against them. His reign was hardly illustrative of omnipotent rule, but rather of a shrewd and meteoric—and sometimes desperate—manipulator.[129]

Rwabugiri died in 1895, while he was directing an expedition to Bushi, west of Lake Kivu. It was the end of an era, not only an era of energetic expansion and militarization but also of Rwanda's status as an independent monarchy. Two events symbolize the political transformation following the death of Rwabugiri. Internally, within eighteen months of his death, his named successor, Mibambwe Rutarindwa, was overthrown in an internal coup organized by the woman whom he himself had designated as his successor's queen mother. During his own lifetime, Rwabugiri had taken the unusual (but not unheard of) step of establishing Rutarindwa as "co-ruler" (and therefore designated successor), and on the death of Rutarindwa's mother, Rwabugiri had named another of his wives, a young woman named Kanjogera, as "ritual mother" of the new king. But she also had a young child of her own, and therefore she was theoretically proscribed from serving in this role by the ritual code. With the willing help of her brothers, however, she resolved the dilemma by dispensing entirely with the succession protocol as prescribed by the royal ritual code. On Rwabugiri's death, she and her brothers of the Abakagara lineage of the Abega clan (who had for a century been political rivals to the royal lineage of the Abanyiginya clan) masterminded a coup to bring to power the young son of Kanjogera, named Musinga. In so doing they overthrew Mibambwe Rutarindwa, the publicly designated successor to Rwabugiri and Rwabugiri's co-ruler over the last six years of his reign—and, indeed, brother-in-law of Kabare, Kanjogera's influential brother—in a military confrontation known as "the Coup of Rucunshu," in which Rutarindwa was killed along with many other members of the royal lineage and ritualists and allies who supported him. In the eyes of one astute observer (writing in 1939), it was "a holocaust."[130] Thus Musinga came to power as a young child, with but a tenuous claim to legitimacy; for many years into his reign, effective power was retained by the young queen mother and her formidable brothers, Kabare and Ruhinankiko.

The second harbinger of Rwanda's changing fortunes occurred in external relations. Even while vigorously defending his autonomy, Rwabugiri had cultivated cautious ties with outsiders—with other powerful kingdoms, with traders from the East Coast, and with European travelers. He was, for example, the first Rwandan monarch to meet with Europeans, and he was very interested in developing trade ties to the East Coast commercial networks—including a small trade in slaves, probably seized in his western campaigns (or from areas of recent conquest in western Rwanda). But he was not always successful in establishing full alliance with the new intrusive power that guaranteed or reinforced Rwandan autonomy. The court was clearly undecided on how close such ties should be: the guiding strategy seemed more oriented to preventing powerful outsiders from aiding Rwanda's more proximate state rivals than to becoming too deeply involved; for example, Rwabugiri instituted a ban on direct trade with outsiders.

The fears seemed justified, as the new military resources and unclear goals of these new arrivals seemed to threaten Rwandan sovereignty, especially in areas less than fully incorporated into the Nyiginya domain. Shortly after Rwabugiri's death, the court decided to drive out one such incursion in the southwest of the country. The result was a shock to the court. In two battles with troops of the Congo Free State, several of Rwanda's most celebrated military heroes were killed —some of the elite of the court—along with several hundred troops from esteemed regiments: the warriors so highly trained, nurtured, and honored under Rwabugiri. Their defeat symbolized the demise of the system they represented, for the manifest superiority of the firepower of the intruders convinced the central court that a policy of outright confrontation was doomed. Consequently, collaboration between the central court and the colonial forces (an alliance not without tension and political manipulation on both sides) became the operative *modus vivendi*. Such a policy served the objectives of both the Rwandan elites and the aspirant colonial powers, although it also spelled an end to Rwandan independence—and to the regional domination forged by Rwabugiri. His reign was built on incessant military campaigns externally and constant political maneuvering within; indeed, he fought as often against entrenched power within as he did against societies outside. But the luster of his reign today is also based on what came after, for Rwabugiri's reign served as both the apogee and the terminal point of the long process of building royal absolutist hegemony in the precolonial state structures of Rwanda.

AT THE end of the nineteenth century, the two kingdoms of Burundi and Rwanda faced three serious challenges. One was ecological and epidemiological: drought affected the eastern areas, a smallpox epidemic took a heavy toll, and—particularly important—a disastrous epizootic killed large numbers of cattle; in some areas over 90 percent of the cattle were lost. Because of the role of cattle as a store of wealth and a form of social alliance, those losses had very significant effects. Relations within the kingdom were transformed, for example, as the court expropriated many of the remaining cattle in an attempt to reconstitute the royal herds. Similarly, external relations were affected, as Rwabugiri attacked Nkore, primarily to seize surviving cattle in areas north of Rwanda; commercial relations with neighboring areas were transformed as the prices for cattle rose steeply.

A second challenge came from the attacks of armed African forces, often an indirect result of European penetration. In Burundi, this took the form of attacks in the east by African groups of raiders organized along military lines, sometimes offshoots of *ruga-ruga*–type Ngoni organizations, often armed through the expanding East Coast commercial networks. Other attacks from the east came from troops associated with Mirambo, an African leader benefiting from his position at the conjunction of several such trade routes to the coast (near what is now Tabora, in central Tanzania). For Rwanda, on the other hand, there were attacks from the west, from African troops fleeing the disaster of the "Dhanis column," a misguided attempt to establish King Leopold's claims across southern Sudan to the Nile—and probably beyond. When this expedition disintegrated northwest of Lake Rutanzige (Albert), these poorly equipped and poorly trained troops, with no ties to the local populations, moved south, raiding as they went; in two skirmishes they defeated some of the most illustrious Rwanda armies.

Though these troops then withdrew, in their wake they created a crisis at the central court.

The third challenge came directly from European presence. Some of these outsiders came as state authorities, occasionally providing arms and resources to internal factions against the state (as in the case of Kilima in his struggles against Mwezi). Others came as missionaries of the White Fathers missionary order. But in the eyes of the central court these missionaries simply represented an invading force of their own: they came with African evangelists from Buganda who often acted arrogantly, as if indeed they were minor chiefs for an incipient European/Christian rule. Furthermore, these Catholic missionaries arrived with a set of preconceptions about African states derived from their earlier experiences in the religious wars in Buganda—and with a set of views on African rulers based on their perception of Mwanga, the king of Buganda. Consequently, their behavior in the early years was sometimes less than diplomatic.

But local political crises faced by the two states at the end of the nineteenth century were in some ways even more important than these outside influences. In Burundi Mwezi faced many secessionist movements and pretenders to power —who were reinforced by outside power. Rwanda, on the other hand, had just been wracked by a divisive succession war on the death of Rwabugiri, leading to a coup d'état by a powerful lineage, in opposition to the Nyiginya royal line; they brought to power a young child, Musinga, under the tutelage of his ambitious mother and her two formidable brothers. In both countries, therefore, Europeans arrived in the midst of internal crises that fully preoccupied the state elites.[131] After initial opposition, court elites in both kingdoms came to welcome European power as a potential resource within their own factional disputes, which were more important to them at the time than these quixotic strangers. Thus European establishment was more indicative of the continuity of African action than a sign of discontinuity—more significant for reinforcing the power of the state elite than for the loss of state sovereignty.

But for the local populations the effect was more dramatic. Because there were very few Europeans present, the transformations to affect the lives of the common people did not occur through direct European intervention (though serious fighting took place in Rwanda during World War I). Instead, for both kingdoms, the European presence was transmitted through the reinforcement of the local power of the state elites and in the quite dramatic expansion of court rule to new areas, formerly only informally under dynastic control, if at all: during the first twenty years of European rule both states roughly doubled the areas under their effective administration. And with this shift in power came new demands on the local populations incorporated within these expanding state structures and with fewer alternatives open to them.

THIS SKETCH of precolonial political transformations in Burundi and Rwanda has tried to show both the distinctions and the parallels of political histories within these two political orders. In both cases the transformation of the old regime, however, was gradual, and indeed partial. What was surrendered was external sovereignty, not internal administrative power. In fact, European political objectives in this region privileged two goals compatible with the internal objectives of the local dynastic courts and the aristocratic elites. One was the consolidation of administrative capacities—seen in terms of administrative standardization (reducing the number and variety of chiefly functionaries) and effective penetration (increasing the capacity of the state to impose policy and to extract resources). The other was the expansion of the territorial domain of centralized power. Outlying areas lost their autonomy. Administrative chiefs delegated from the court replaced local authorities. Areas sharing cultural features with the central areas but formerly resistant to central court control were incorporated firmly into the court administrative responsibilities of the dynastic courts, by force if necessary. Still, despite the energetic attempts at rationalization of a complex administrative reality, to advance standardization, centralization, and hierarchy, the legacy at the local levels included a strong component of local identity: the colonial states were not the simple continuation of precolonial kingdoms that some portray. While Burundi and Rwanda today are each constructed on a historical state presence, culturally they are each internally much more diverse, and politically much more differentiated, than the conventional images of either precolonial homogeneity or colonial domination allow for.

But these issues form part of a different story: the interest here has been to sketch out the precolonial configurations, resulting from local factors and regional influences. The range and the nature of influences and resources acting on these areas was to expand dramatically over the next decades. But the way these influences were interpreted into the local cultural idiom, and the way these resources were applied within the internal political pathways, were in large part legacies of the processes that had gone before.

Beyond formal politics, outsiders were to bring their own mental maps of the historical practices and cultural premises of this region. And their legees were often to accept those models as valid representations of lived experiences in the region. In many ways, however, they were not. It has been the purpose here to test out those received models against the empirical record, as best we can decipher it. Like every sketch, this presentation is more suggestive than comprehensive. But drawing critically on the data available to understand the factors behind such processes is a useful step in understanding subsequent events. By laying out the record as far as can at present be constructed from the empirical record, that is what this presentation has tried to do.

NOTES

Oral sources are dated as month/day/year; unless otherwise indicated, all interviews cited were conducted by David Newbury. For complete citations—full name and clan affiliation of the interviewee, as well as date and location of the interview—see my *Kings and Clans: Ijwi Island and the Lake Kivu Rift, 1780–1840* (Madison: University of Wisconsin Press, 1991), 335–49.

Foreword

1. The general results of this research were published in Catharine Newbury, *The Cohesion of Oppression: Clientship and Ethnicity in Rwanda, 1860–1960* (New York: Columbia University Press, 1989), and David Newbury, *Kings and Clans: Ijwi Island and the Lake Kivu Rift, 1780–1840* (Madison: University of Wisconsin Press, 1991).

Chapter 1: Bushi and the Historians

This chapter appeared as an article in History in Africa *5 (1978): 131–51.*

I am grateful to Jean-Luc Vellut for his comments and encouragement on the original article, and to Richard Sigwalt and Elinor Sosne for their comments on the present draft.

1. Jean-Baptiste Cuypers, "Les Bantous interlacustres du Kivu," in *Introduction à l'ethnographie du Congo,* by Jan Vansina (Kinshasa: Éditions universitaires du Congo, 1966), 201–11; Cuypers, *L'alimentation chez les Shi* (Tervuren: MRAC, 1960).

2. A. Moeller de Laddersous, *Les grandes lignes des migrations des Bantous de la Province Orientale du Congo Belge* (Brussels: IRCB, 1936), 29–30.

3. Cuypers, "Les Bantous interlacustres," 204.

4. Ibid.

5. Ibid.

6. Cuypers, *L'alimentation,* 19, based on Moeller, *Les grandes lignes.*

7. Cuypers, *L'alimentation,* 17 (emphasis added).

8. Ibid., 17, citing Jean Hiernaux, *Les caractères physiques des Bashi* (Brussels: IRCB, 1953), and Hiernaux, *Analyse de la variation des caractères physiques humains en une région de l'Afrique centrale: Ruanda-Urundi et Kivu* (Tervuren: MRAC, 1956).

9. Hiernaux, *Les caractères physiques,* 5–6.

10. Ibid., 7, 9.

11. Cited by Cuypers, *L'alimentation,* 17; Hiernaux, *Analyse,* 34.

12. Cuypers, *L'alimentation,* 20, 21.

13. Ibid., 20.

14. Ibid.

15. Ibid., 22.

16. Recent research that should alleviate this lack has been undertaken by Cenyange Lubula, Bishikwabo Chubaka, Njangu Canda-Ciri, Pilipili Kagabo, Elinor Sosne, and Richard Sigwalt.

17. Jean-Claude Willame, *Les provinces du Congo: Structure et fonctionnement: Lomami et Kivu central,* Cahiers économiques et sociaux, Collection d'études politiques 4 (Kinshasa: Université Lovanium, 1964).

18. Ibid., 115.

19. Ibid., 114.

20. Ibid., 156–57.

21. Ibid., 122, 156–57.

22. Ibid., 115.

23. Ibid., 122.

24. Moeller, *Les grandes lignes,* 10, 16–17, 115–16.

25. Ibid., 16n1, 115n1.

26. Moeller's attempt to combine all the traditions into a single "pure" synthesis is reminiscent of the administrative innovations he initiated throughout Orientale Province, which at the time included Kivu. These included the sometimes arbitrary establishment of larger administrative *secteurs* comprising several *chefferies.* It is possible that these administrative preoccupations and the demands of administrative efficiency influenced his interpretation of the historical and sociological data by encouraging him to look for common historical origins even among the peoples for whom the traditions and ethnographic data did not directly support such a hypothesis.

27. Moeller, *Les grandes lignes,* 7–8, 14.

28. Ibid., 108–9, 110.

29. L. Viaene, "La vie domestique des Bahunde (Nord-Est du Kivu)," *Kongo-Overzee* 12, no. 2 (1951): 113; Daniel P. Biebuyck, "De Mumbo-Instelling bij de Banyanga," *Kongo-Overzee* 21, no. 5 (1955): 441; Biebuyck, "L'organisation politique des Nyanga: La chefferie Ihana," *Kongo-Overzee* 22, nos. 4–5 (1956): 304; Cuypers, "Les Bantous interlacustres," 204.

30. Biebuyck, for example, wrote that "leurs traditions historiques remontent au Bunyoro (Uganda)" ("L'organisation politique," 304). This form and the quality of his fieldwork throughout the area would indicate that this was drawn directly from Nyanga oral sources, but it is possible, in the absence of specific citation, that it was a résumé of Moeller's conclusions. Viaene, like (probably) Moeller, worked closely with the "royal" family of Bunyungu (Buhunde) and they probably drew their historical data primarily from similar milieux, though separated by a generation and by the publication of *Les grandes lignes.*

31. Moeller was involved in the administration of Orientale-Kivu Province for seventeen years, the last seven as Vice-Gouverneur-Général, and he had an important impact on administrative theory and practice in the area. Later he trained prospective colonial administrators at the Université Colonial for several years.

32. Moeller, *Les grandes lignes,* 29–30.

33. Ibid., 31–32.

34. Ibid., 116.

35. Paradoxically, Moeller also incorporated a variant of the conquest theory by postulating that part of the Shi migration turned back on itself, roughly retracing its steps

from Lwindi and, according to Moeller, "subjected the autochthones as well as the [mi-grating] clans which had remained behind [in Bushi]" (ibid., 117).

36. P. Colle, "L'organisation politique des Bashi," *Congo* 2, no. 2 (1921): 657–84; Colle, *Essai de monographie des Bashi* (Bukavu: CELA, 1971). References to Colle's *Essaie de monographie* are to the pagination of the mimeographed version issued at Bukavu in 1971, since this is more readily available than the original 1937 edition; hence I will refer to the page number followed by the paragraph number, e.g., 220/141.

37. Colle, "L'organisation politique," 657–58, and *Essai de monographie,* 220/141.

38. In this regard, Cuypers, though distinguishing between central and peripheral Shi culturally, does not specify the grounds for his differentiation (*L'alimentation,* 13 and passim).

39. Colle, "L'organisation politique," 657.

40. Colle, *Essai de monographie,* 220/141.

41. Ibid., 275/187 (emphasis added).

42. Cuypers, *L'alimentation,* 20; Willame, *Les provinces du Congo,* 115.

43. Moeller, *Les grandes lignes,* 17.

44. Colle, "L'organisation politique," 659, and *Essai de monographie,* 221/141.

45. Colle, *Essai de monographie,* 221, 264–66.

46. Cuypers, *L'alimentation,* 22; Willame, *Les provinces du Congo,* 115.

47. Colle, *Essai de monographie,* 256/174.

48. For further discussion, see Richard Sigwalt and Elinor Sosne, "A Note on the Luzi of Bushi," *Études d'Histoire Africaine* 7 (1975): 137–43.

49. Colle, "L'organisation politique," 658, and *Essai de monographie,* 220/141.

50. Colle, *Essai de monographie,* 71–78/94.

51. E.g., Elinor Sosne, "Kinship and Contract in Bushi: A Study of Village-Level Politics" (PhD diss., University of Wisconsin–Madison, 1974), and Richard Sigwalt, "The Early History of Bushi: An Essay in the Historical Use of Genesis Traditions" (PhD diss., University of Wisconsin–Madison, 1975).

Chapter 2: Recent Historical Research in the Area of Lake Kivu

This chapter appeared as an article in History in Africa *7 (1980): 23–45.*

1. Historical research in Burundi has followed a different pattern of evolution from that described here for Rwanda and eastern Kivu. We have therefore omitted Burundi studies from consideration. For a recent assessment, see Jean-Pierre Chrétien, "Le Burundi vu du Burundi," *Journal des Africanistes* 47, no. 2 (1977): 176–98.

2. For recent published accounts on Rwanda in English, see René Lemarchand, *Rwanda and Burundi* (London: Pall Mall, 1970); J. Keith Rennie, "The Precolonial Kingdom of Rwanda: A Reinterpretation," *Transafrican Journal of History* 2, no. 2 (1972): 11–53; Helen Codere, *The Biography of an African Society: Rwanda, 1900–1960* (Tervuren: MRAC, 1973); and Ian Linden and Jane Linden, *Church and Revolution in Rwanda* (Manchester: Manchester University Press, 1977). Recent works in French include Alexis Kagame, *Un abrégé de l'ethnohistoire du Rwanda precolonial,* vol. 1 (Butare: Éditions universitaires du Rwanda, 1972) and vol. 2 (1975); Pierre Smith, *Le récit populaire au Rwanda* (Paris: Armand Colin, 1975); Marcel d'Hertefelt, *Les clans du Rwanda ancien* (Tervuren, 1971).

3. Helen Codere, "Power in Rwanda," *Anthropologica*, n.s., 4, no. 1 (1962): 45–85.

4. Claudine Vidal, "Le Rwanda des anthropologues ou le fétischisme de la vache," *Cahiers d'Études Africaines* 9, no. 3 (1969): 384–401.

5. Rwandan settlement occurs on the hilltops and along the ridges of the numerous hills of the country. In addition to providing the dominant geographical characteristic of the country, therefore, these hills form the basis of the local community as well.

6. These were particularly stressed in J. Vansina, *L'évolution du royaume Rwanda dès origines à 1900* (Brussels: ARSOM, 1962), 70–71; Marcel d'Hertefelt, "Le Rwanda," in *Les anciens royaumes de la zone interlacustre méridionale*, by Marcel d'Hertefelt, Albert A. Trouwborst, and J. H. Scherer (Tervuren: MRAC, 1962). Certain earlier works based on local-level or regional studies were also essential in the formulation of this new perspective. Noteworthy among them were Ivan Reisdorff, *Enquêtes foncières au Rwanda* (Rwanda: INRS, 1952); *Historique et chronologie du Ruanda* (Kabgayi, Rwanda: Vicariat apostolique du Ruanda, 1956); and Marcel Pauwels, "Le Bushiru et son muhinza ou roitelet Hutu," *Annali Lateranensi* 31 (1967): 205–322.

7. Pierre Bettez Gravel, "Life on the Manor in Gisaka (Rwanda)," *Journal of African History* 6, no. 3 (1965): 323–31; Gravel, "The Transfer of Cows in Gisaka (Rwanda): A Mechanism for Recording Social Relationships," *American Anthropologist* 69, nos. 3–4 (1967): 322–31; Gravel, "Diffuse Power as a Commodity: A Case Study from Gisaka (Eastern Rwanda)," *International Journal of Comparative Sociology*, 9, nos. 3–4 (1968): 163–76; Gravel, *Remera: A Community in Eastern Rwanda* (The Hague, 1968), esp. 149–86. Although Gravel's work preceded that of Vidal, it has had less impact on Rwandan studies for several reasons. It was undertaken in the eastern periphery of Rwanda rather than in the center, and his publications were in English. But most important, clientship in Gisaka may have approached more closely to the ideal of the integrationist model because the harshest aspects were mitigated in recent times by the proximity of the border and by the long period within which clientship was a part of the society. Consequently his reassessment, though important, was less radical than that which emerged from other empirical fieldwork and so had less of an impact in transforming the conceptual paradigms with which recent research has explored Rwandan client institutions.

8. For the Ugandan side of this mobility, see Audrey Richards, *Economic Development and Tribal Change: A Study of Immigrant Labour in Buganda* (Cambridge: W. Heffer and Sons, 1956).

9. As of 1980, d'Hertefelt was in the process of compiling a comprehensive Rwandan bibliography, including over thirty-five hundred items. This bibliography was eventually published (with Danielle de Lame) as *Société, culture et histoire du Rwanda: Encyclopédie bibliographique, 1863–1980/87* (Tervuren: MRAC, 1987) and included over fifty-five hundred items.

10. Joseph Rwabukumba and Vincent Mudandagizi, "Les formes historiques de la dépendance personnelle dans l'état rwandais," *Cahiers d'Études Africaines* 14, no. 1 (1974): 6–26.

11. Lydia Meschi, "Évolution des structures foncières au Rwanda: Le cas d'un lignage hutu," *Cahiers d'Études Africaines* 14, no. 1 (1974): 39–51.

12. Gravel, *Remera*, chap. 12.

13. Claudine Vidal, "Économie de la société féodale rwandaise," *Cahiers d'Études Africaines* 14, no. 1 (1974): 52–74. Without entering into a full analysis of this pivotal arti-

cle to our understanding of Rwandan society, it should be mentioned in passing that, despite the enormous value of both the data presented and the questions posed, this approach employs a global concept applied to Rwandan society in general and omits a careful assessment of historical change. For a different approach, see Jean-Pierre Chrétien, "Echanges et hiérarchies dans les royaumes des Grands Lacs de l'Est africain," *Annales: Economies, Sociétés, Civilisations* 29 (1974): 1327–37.

14. The major exception to this generalization is found in the army prestations cited in Alexis Kagame, *Les milices du Rwanda précolonial* (Brussels: ARSOM, 1963). But even in this case, the more recent (late-nineteenth-century) prestations cited are often simply extrapolated back to the time of the original army establishment, and hence the chronology of such prestations is not reliable. For the period since 1900, family traditions are valuable, but in most cases little is retained for the period before that time. On this general subject, see also Philippe Leurquin, *Le niveau de vie des populations rurales du Ruanda-Urundi* (Louvain: Nauwelaerts for the Institut de Recherche Economique et Sociale, 1960).

15. There is much interesting material of this nature to be drawn from Codere, *Biography of an African Society.* This collection of biographies contains many references to individuals working for others during the colonial period. Often these were women working the fields of others.

16. At the time of writing Ferdinand Nahimana was studying pre-Nyiginya state formation in the Rukiga areas of Bugoyi and Ruhengeri in northwestern Rwanda; see his "Les 'bami' ou roitelets Hutu du corridor Nyaborongo-Mukungwa avec ses régions limitrophes," *Études Rwandaises* 12, special issue (March 1979): 1–25. His work was later published as *Le Rwanda: Émergence d'un état* (Paris: L'Harmattan, 1993). See also Rita Vanwalle, "Aspecten van Staatsvorming in West-Rwanda," *Africa-Tervuren* 28, no. 3 (1982): 64–77, on nineteenth-century Rusenyi-Bwishaza in western Rwanda (Kinyaga-Kibuye prefectures).]

17. Jean-François Saucier, "The Patron-Client Relationship in Traditional and Contemporary Southern Rwanda" (PhD diss., Columbia University, 1974).

18. Jacques J. Maquet, *Le système des relations sociales dans le Ruanda ancien* (Tervuren: MRAC, 1954); Maquet, *The Premise of Inequality: A Study of Political Relations in a Central African Kingdom* (London: Oxford University Press for the International African Institute, 1962). The term "political clientship" here is taken from Saucier, "Patron-Client Relationship," 74. In brief, Saucier defines a "political client" as one whose patron held an official position in the central court bureaucracy. However, at a broader level, as Catharine Newbury shows, all clientship was "political."

19. Catharine Newbury, "The Cohesion of Oppression: A Century of Clientship in Kinyaga, Rwanda, 1860–1960" (PhD disss., University of Wisconsin-Madison, 1975) Later revised and published as *The Cohesion of Oppression: Clientship and Ethnicity in Rwanda, 1860–1960* (New York: Columbia University Press, 1988).

20. Catharine Newbury, "Ethnicity in Rwanda: The Case of Kinyaga," *Africa* 48, no. 1 (1978): 17–29.

21. Jim Freedman, "Principles of Relationships in Rwandan Kiga Society" (PhD diss., Princeton University, 1974).

22. In this sense it confirmed the earlier work of d'Hertefelt among the Kiga, a work whose impact among the more recent scholars was limited because it was published in Dutch. See Marcel d'Hertefelt, "Huwelijk, familie, en aanverwantschap bij de Reera (noordwestelijk Rwaanda)," *Zaïre* 13, nos. 2 and 3 (1959): 115–47 and 243–85.

23. Luc de Heusch, *Le Rwanda et la civilisation interlacustre* (Brussels: Université Libre de Bruxelles, 1966).

24. Jim Freedman, "Joking, Affinity, and the Exchange of Ritual Services among the Kiga of Northern Rwanda: An Essay in Joking Relationships," *Man*, n.s., 12, no. 1 (1976): 154–66.

25. E.g., see Jim Freedman, "Ritual and History: The Case of Nyibingi," *Cahiers d'Études Africaines* 14, no. 1 (1974): 170–80.

26. Alison Des Forges, "Defeat Is the Only Bad News: Rwanda under Musiinga, 1896–1931" (PhD diss., Yale University, 1972). Some exceptions to the general neglect of Rwandan colonial history include Jean-Pierre Chrétien, "La révolte de Ndungutse (1912): Forces traditionelles et pression coloniale au Rwanda allemand," *Revue Française d'Histoire d'Outre-Mer* 59, no. 4 (1972): 645–80; Louis de Lacger, *Le Ruanda*, 2nd ed. (Kabgayi, Rwanda: Imprimérie de Kabgayi, 1961), pt. 2; and Kagame, *Un abrégé*, vol. 2.

27. Alison Des Forges, "Kings without Crowns: The White Fathers in Rwanda," in *East African History*, ed. Norman R. Bennett, Daniel F. McCall, and Jeffrey Butler (New York, 1969), 176–202.

28. Nahimana, "Les 'bami' ou roitelets hutu."

29. Bernard Lugan, "Le commerce de traite au Rwanda sous le régime allemand (1896–1916)," *Canadian Journal of African Studies* 11, no. 2 (1977): 235–68; Lugan, "Les pôles commerciaux du Lac Kivu à la fin du XIXe siècle," *Revue Française d'Histoire d'Outre-Mer* 64, no. 235 (1977): 176–202; and Lugan, "Les réseaux commerciaux au Rwanda dans le dernier quart du XIXe siècle," *Études d'Histoire Africaine* 9–10 (1977–78): 183–212. Lugan's doctoral thesis, "L'économie d'échange au Rwanda de 1850 à 1914" (Thèse de doctorat de 3e cycle, Université de Provence, Aix-en-Provence, 1976) was not available to us.

30. Bernard Lugan, "Causes et effets de la famine 'Rumanura' au Rwanda, 1916–1918," *Canadian Journal of African Studies* 10, no. 2 (1976): 347–56.

31. Within the field of religious history, Linden and Linden's *Church and Revolution* is an important contribution, but much remains to be done in terms of religious history "from below," including such subjects as the East African Revival in Rwanda, as well as work on non-Christian religions. See Iris Berger, *Religion and Resistance: East African Kingdoms in the Precolonial Period* (Tervuren: MRAC, 1981); de Heusch, *Le Rwanda;* Claudine Vidal, "Anthropologie et histoire: Le cas du Rwanda," *Cahiers Internationaux de Sociologie* 43, no. 2 (1967): 143–57; Alexis Kagame, "L'historicité de Lyangombe, chef des 'Immandwa,'" in *Lyangombe: Mythe et rites: Actes du 2ème colloque du CERUKI du 10 mai au 14 mai 1976*, ed. CERUKI, UNAZA-ISP (Bukavu: Éditions du CERUKI, 1979), 17–28; Catherine Robins, "Rwanda: A Case Study in Religious Assimilation" (paper presented at the Dar es Salaam Conference on the History of African Religions, 1970); Freedman, "Ritual and History." This brief survey has not considered recent research in other fields of potential interest to historians: Francis van Noten, *Les tombes du roi Cyirima Rujugira et de la reine-mère Nyirayuhi Kanjogera: Description archéologique* (Tervuren: MRAC, 1972); several articles in *Études d'Histoire Africaines* 9–10 (1977–78); several studies of popular literary genres by Pierre Smith: *Le récit populaire;* Smith, "La lance d'une jeune fille," in *Échanges et communications,* vol. 2, *Mélanges offerts à Claude Lévi-Strauss,* ed. Claude Lévi-Strauss, Jean Pouillon, and Pierre Maranda (The Hague: Mouton, 1970), 1381–1409; Smith, "Aspects de l'organisation des rites," in *La fonction symbolique: Essais d'anthropologie,* ed. Michel Izard, Pierre Smith, and Claude Lévi-Strauss (Paris: Gallimard, 1979), 139–70; and the linguistic work of André Coupez et al., whose dictionary of Kinyarwanda

includes a wealth of essential data for students of Rwandan history and society: André Coupez, Thomas Kamanzi, Simon Bizimana, G. Sematama, G. Rwabukumba, and C. Ntazinda et al., *Inkoranya y'íkinyarwaanda mu kinyarwaanda nó mu Gifaraansá: Dictionnaire Rwanda-Rwanda et Rwanda-Français* (Tervuren: MRAC, 2005). Finally, a nutritional study provides interesting insights for studies of the Rwandan past as well as guidelines for the future: see Henri Vis, C. Yourassousky, and Henri van der Borght, *Une enquête de consommation alimentaire en République rwandaise* (Butare, Rwanda: INRS, 1972).

32. An important beginning to this regional approach is found in Richard Sigwalt, "Early Rwanda History: The Contribution of Comparative Ethnography," *History in Africa* 2 (1975): 137–46. This type of analysis is also found in Donald Denoon, ed., *A History of Kigezi in Southwestern Uganda* (Kampala: National Trust, 1972); Freedman, "Principles of Relationships"; Gravel, *Remera;* de Heusch, *Le Rwanda;* C. Newbury, *Cohesion of Oppression;* and Rennie, "Precolonial Kingdom of Rwanda." But such regional considerations are still the exception rather than the norm.

33. General introductions to the area are found in Jan Vansina, introduction to d'Hertefelt, Trouwborst, and Scherer, *Les anciens royaumes,* 3–7; and Jean-Baptiste Cuypers, "Les Bantous interlacustres du Kivu," in *Introduction à l'ethnographie du Congo,* by Jan Vansina (Kinshasa: Éditions universitaires du Congo, 1965), 201–11. But the major ethnographic monograph for Bushi is P. Colle, *Essai de monographie des Bashi* (Bukavu: CELA, 1971). Until the mid-seventies, the major published history on Bushi was Paul Masson, *Trois siècles chez les Bashi* (Tervuren: MRAC, 1962), itself a condensation of Catholic missionary documents collected mostly in the 1930s and 1940s. For other regions the historical work most frequently cited is A. Moeller de Laddersous, *Les grandes lignes des migrations des Bantous de la Province Orientale du Congo belge* (Brussels: IRCB, 1936). Bashizi has correctly pointed out that there is a large bibliography of works that touch on Kivu history; nonetheless, it remains true, as Bashizi's own work illustrates, that most recent historical analysis has been based on an extremely narrow range of sources. For a more complete consideration of sources on the region, for the colonial as well as precolonial periods and including both published and unpublished works, see Bashizi Cirhagahula, "Histoire du Kivu: Sources écrites et perspectives d'avenir," *Likundoli,* ser. B, 4 (1976): 65–114; and Bakwa-Lufu Badibanga, Njangu Canda-Ciri, and Sebigamba Rusibiza, "L'UNAZA-Bukavu et la connaissance du Kivu: Inventaire bibliographique," *Antennes* 5 (1977): 411–32. These provide an overview of the sources available, but such sources are of highly variable quality; to date no work has fully utilized them, and there is as yet no critical analysis of them. Unfortunately, many of the theses and mémoires of UNAZA at Lubumbashi and Bukavu are not available to us.

34. Before 1974, of course, many other publications by Zairean scholars had appeared in numerous journals, but never had an international historical journal combined so many Zairean scholars writing with a common regional focus.

35. As testimony to the nature and quality of the UNAZA research program, the Department of History at Lubumbashi established three journals as outlets for work of various types: *Études d'Histoire Africaine, Likundoli* (ser. A and B), and *Enquêtes et Documents d'Histoire Africaine.* In addition, the multidisciplinary journal *Antennes,* published by the Centre d'Études et de Recherches Universitaires au Kivu (CERUKI), affiliated with the Institut Supérieur Pédagogique (UNAZA) in Bukavu, has included many valuable contributions by historians.

36. Tervuren, 1970.

37. Dikonda wa Lumanyisha, "Les rites chez les Bashi et les Bahavu" (PhD diss., Université Libre de Bruxelles, 1972).

38. Elinor Sosne, "Kinship and Contract in Bushi: A Study of Village-Level Politics" (PhD diss., University of Wisconsin–Madison, 1974).

39. Richard Sigwalt, "The Early History of Bushi: An Essay in the Historical Use of Genesis Traditions" (PhD diss., University of Wisconsin–Madison, 1975), esp. chap. 5. Sigwalt distinguishes between three levels of political conceptualization: the concept of kingship (*ubwami*), the claims of the royal dynasty to represent those concepts, and the legitimacy of a particular descent line within the dynasty; but he concentrates on the first two.

40. Moeller, *Les grandes lignes;* Masson, *Trois siècles.* Both mention a proximate origin of the royal family in Lwindi, just southwest of Bushi, but this is seen as but a stopping point in a longer migration; kingship norms are assumed to be general to the migration from the north. Other works postulate the origins of kingship in Bushi as derived from Rwanda.

41. For an earlier work of this genre, see Bishikwabo Chubaka, "Deux chefs du Bushi sous le régime colonial: Kabare et Ngweshe (1912–1960)," *Études d'Histoire Africaine* 7 (1975): 89–112. Among Bishikabo's other publications on Bushi, see "L'économie d'échange dans les états précoloniaux du Sud-Kivu du XIXe siècle à 1920" (paper presented at the Journées d'Historiens Zaïrois, Lubumbashi 1975); "Les relations extérieures du Kaziba au XIXe siècle" (paper presented at the Journées d'Historiens Zaïrois, 1977); "Le Bushi au XIXe siècle: Un peuple, sept royaumes," *Revue Française d'Histoire d'Outre-Mer* 47, nos. 1–2 (1980): 89–98; "Interprétation du rite du remerciement à Lyangombe," in *Lyangombe: Mythe et rites,* 173–81.

42. For some of the results of this work, see Cenyange Lubula, "L'origine de Lyangombe d'après les Bashi," in *Lyangombe: Mythe et rites,* 129–31; Njangu Canda-Ciri, "Muzungu: L'arrivée des premiers Européens au Bushi," *Enquêtes et Documents d'Histoire Africaine* 1 (1975): 27–45 (a translation of a text of Nyakandolya Cibagula recorded by Abbé Bakarongotane); and text #6 by Nyakandolya in Sigwalt, "Early History of Bushi," 298–314 (from a text provided by Abbé Cenyange).

43. Njangu Canda-Ciri, "La résistance Shi à la pénération européenne (1900–1920)" (Mémoire de license en histoire, UNAZA-Lubumbashi, 1973); Njangu, "Muzungu"; Njangu, "Notes sur les sources orales de la première résistance Shi," *Études d'Histoire Africaine* 7 (1975): 203–6; Njangu, "La secte de Binji-Binji ou la renaissance de la résistance des Bashi (juillet-septembre 1931)," in *Lyangombe: Mythe et rites,* 121–28.

44. Pilipili Kagabo, "Contribution à la connaissance des origines du centre de Bukavu (Kivu) de 1870 à 1935" (Mémoire de licence en histoire, UNAZA-Lubumbashi, 1973).

45. P. van Vracem, "La frontière de la Rusizi-Kivu de 1884 à 1910: Conflit Germano-Congolais et Anglo-Congolais en Afrique orientale" (Thèse de doctorat, Université Officielle du Congo–Elisabethville, 1958); Léon de Saint Moulin, "Les anciens villages des environs de Kinshasa," *Études d'Histoire Africaine* 2 (1971): 83–119.

46. For many other works of this general tendency for the Shi areas, see the entries cited in Bashizi, "Histoire du Kivu," for Bagisha, Babizi, Balolebwami, Biganga, Bifuko, Bimanyu, Bishikwabo B., Bishikwabo C., Bizuru, Bweyamimwe, Balakali, Greindl, Kalemaza, Kashamura, Kashara, Kirhero, Kiwanuka, Maheshe, Mahenge, Muhima, Murizihirwa, Mushagasa, Mushaka, Nkuburi, and Singaye.

47. In one important respect, however, the use of Shi informants apparently skewed the data in such a way as to emphasize Havu differences from Shi practices. Early missionary documents (and largely on that basis, early administrative documents too) present the succession practices of the Havu as based on the institution of the *mumbo,* whereby the king was married to his classificatory sister (or niece) and the legitimate heir resulted from this marriage alone. In fact, this has never been a Havu practice, at least as far back as the early nineteenth century, the time depth for which queen mothers can be traced. However, this custom of the mumbo marriage does exist among the Tembo, to the west of the Mitumba Mountains, and may well have existed in the present areas of Havu kingship before the arrival of the Havu royal line in the mid-nineteenth century. It would appear therefore that a non-Havu informant simply ascribed to the Havu another custom practiced in the area, one particularly bizarre to the Shi. Since Havu are classified as non-Shi, and therefore as people of the forest ("Babembe") to many Shi, it is but a short step to ascribe to them customs of the "forest peoples" (such as the Tembo) that do not in fact apply to the Havu.

48. This work includes Baharanyi Bifuko, "Contribution à l'étude de l'évolution des sociétés humaines: Cas du mode de production des Havu de la région interlacustre" (Mémoire de licence, UNAZA-Lubumbashi, 1973); Kalemaza Kayuha, "Le développement de l'agriculture au Kivu colonial (1903–1940)" (Mémoire de licence, UNAZA-Lubumbashi, 1973); Kashamura K., "Occupation économique du Kivu (1920–1940)" (Mémoire de licence, UNAZA-Lubumbashi, 1973); Nsibula Kirhero, "Evolution politique des localités de Lugendo et Ishungu (1830–1964)" (Mémoire de licence, ISP, UNAZA-Bukavu, 1977); Murhebwa L-K., "Histoire politique d'Idjwi sous les Basibula: Essai de périodisation (début XIXè S. à 1960)" (Travail de fin d'études, ISP, UNAZA-Bukavu, 1976).

49. David Newbury, *Kings and Clans: Ijwi Island and the Lake Kivu Rift, 1780–1840* (Madison: University of Wisconsin Press, 1991).

50. As of now, very little historical research has been carried out for the areas of Buhunde, Bunyanga, or Bwisha.

51. One exception to this is the published work of Lieven Bergmans, especially *L'histoire des Baswaga* (Butembo: Editions A.B.B., 1970); *Les Wanande: Croyances et pratiques traditionelles* (Butembo: Editions A.B.B., 1971); and *Histoire des Bashu* (Butembo: Editions A.B.B., 1974). Among the unpublished documentation on the Banande, see the theses at the Institut Supérieur Pédagogique in Bukavu of M. Butala, "Occupation coloniale Belge au Bunande (1889–1935)" (Mémoire de licence, Institut Supérieur Pédagogique, UNAZA-Bukavu); Kakiranyi K., "Le couronnement du Mwami dans la tradition Nande" (Mémoire de licence, Institut Supérieur Pédagogique, UNAZA-Bukavu); Kaligho E., "Le munande face au Christianisme" (Mémoire de licence, Institut Supérieur Pédagogique, UNAZA-Bukavu); Katembo M., "La resistance passive du Munande face à l'action coloniale en agriculture" (Mémoire de licence, Institut Supérieur Pédagogique, UNAZA-Bukavu); Kifimoja Sh., "Intronisation du chef traditional Nyanga" (Mémoire de licence, Institut Supérieur Pédagogique, UNAZA-Bukavu); Kyakimwa K., "L'évolution de la dot chez les Banande" (Mémoire de licence, Institut Supérieur Pédagogique, UNAZA-Bukavu); Mahindule Nk., "Historique de la cité de Lubero (1924–1974)" (Mémoire de licence, Institut Supérieur Pédagogique, UNAZA-Bukavu); Malikani Nd., "Le Buswaga sous le règne de Mwami Biondi" (Mémoire de licence, Institut Supérieur Pédagogique, UNAZA-Bukavu); Mtoto K., "L'évolution du commerce dans le centre de Butembo

(1928–1958)" (Mémoire de licence, Institut Supérieur Pédagogique, UNAZA-Bukavu); Saruti K., "Histoire du Protestantisme au Bunande (1928–1973)" (Mémoire de licence, Institut Supérieur Pédagogique, UNAZA-Bukavu). Research theses found in Lubumbashi include Lubigho K., "L'impact de la colonisation sur l'organisation politique traditionnelle des Wanande du Nord-Kivu: Cas de la chefferie des Batangi" (Mémoire de licence, UNAZA-Lubumbashi); those at Kinshasa include Paluku D., "Du régime foncier chez les Nande" (Mémoire de licence, UNAZA-Kinshasa); Waruwene R., "Le chef traditionnel chez les Banande du Kivu" (Mémoire de licence, UNAZA-Kinshasa).

52. Randall Packard, *Chiefship and Cosmology* (Bloomington: Indiana University Press, 1981).

53. F. G. Bailey, *Stratagems and Spoils* (New York: Schocken Books, 1969); A. W. Southall, *Alur Society* (Cambridge: East African Institute of Social Research, 1956).

54. Though this problem is not directly addressed in his thesis, Packard has explored a similar aspect of Shu history in a preliminary paper, "Witchcraft: The Historical Dimension" (paper presented at the African Studies Association Annual Meeting, Baltimore, 1978).

55. Other work of this type includes Claude Lévi-Strauss, "The Story of Asdiwal," in *The Structural Study of Myth and Totemism*, ed. E. R. Leach (London: Tavistock, 1967); Lévi-Strauss, *Structural Anthropology* (New York: Basic Books, 1963); Christopher C. Wrigley, "The Story of Rukidi," *Africa* 43, no. 3 (1973): 219–35; Luc de Heusch, *Le roi ivre ou l'origine de l'état* (Paris: Gallimard, 1972); and Steven Feierman, *The Shambaa Kingdom: A History* (Madison: University of Wisconsin Press, 1974), chap. 4.

56. Jacques Depelchin, "From Precapitalism to Imperialism: A History of Social and Economic Formations in Eastern Zaïre (Uvira Zone), c. 1800–1964" (PhD diss., Stanford University, 1974).

57. By this we do not, of course, mean that carefully conducted local research is unimportant, but only that locally determined monographs are not an end in themselves. They can best be carried out when they relate not only to other areas, but to larger historical issues, which themselves both guide research and give meaning to it.

58. Some valuable work has already begun on these topics; e.g., *Lyangombe: Mythes et Rites,* as well as Dikonda wa Lumanyisha, "Les rites chez les Bashi."

59. An excellent discussion of sources, approaches, biases, and opportunities for such studies is Elinor Sosne, "Of Biases and Queens: The Shi Past through an Androgynous Looking Glass," *History in Africa* 6 (1979): 225–52.

Chapter 3: Lake Kivu Regional Trade in the Nineteenth Century

This chapter appeared as an article in Journal des Africanistes 50, no. 2 (1980): 6–30.

I would like to thank Citoyens Ntambuka Barhahakana, Ntambuka Sibula, and Senyambo Gitabaka, among many others, for their assistance during the fieldwork. I am also indebted to Jan Vansina, Bertin Webster, Marcel d'Hertefelt, and Jean-Pierre Chrétien for their helpful comments on earlier drafts.

1. Some of the relevant works are Paul Bohannan and G. Dalton, eds., *Markets in Africa* (Evanston: Northwestern University Press, 1962), introduction, as well as several chapters; Claude Meillassoux, ed., *The Development of Indigenous Trade and Markets* (London: Oxford University Press for the International African Institute, 1971), introduc-

tion; B. W. Hodder, "Some Comments on the Origins of Traditional Markets in Africa South of the Sahara," *Transactions of the Institute of British Geographers* 36 (1965): 97–105. Charles M. Good provides a review of these issues in "Markets in Africa: A Review of Research Themes and the Question of Market Origins," *Cahiers d'Études Africaines* 13, no. 4 (1973): 769–81. Polly Hill provided the challenge by writing that "the general absence of markets in East and Central Africa until very recently and their existence in precolonial times in many parts of West Africa is one of the great geographical dichotomies of Africa." Polly Hill, "Markets in Africa," *Journal of Modern African Studies* 1, no. 4 (1963): 447; see also 444 and 449. (In this she was echoing the sentiment of Melville Herskovits in the preface to Bohannan and Dalton, *Markets in Africa*.) This challenge was taken up by Godfrey N. Uzoigwe, "Precolonial Markets in Bunyoro-Kitara," *Comparative Studies in Society and History* 14, no. 4 (1972): 422–55; E. R. Kamuhangire, "The Economic and Social History of the Southwest Uganda Salt Lakes Region," in *Hadith 5: The Economic and Social History of East Africa,* ed. B. A. Ogot (Nairobi: East African Publishing House, 1974), 66–89; B. Turyahikayo-Rugyema, "Markets in Precolonial East Africa: The Case of the Bakiga," *Current Anthropology* 17, no. 2 (1976): 286–90; Charles M. Good, *Market Development in Traditionally Marketless Societies* (Athens: Ohio University Press, 1971); Bernard Lugan, "Échanges et routes commerciales au Rwanda, 1880–1914," *Africa-Tervuren* 22, nos. 2–4 (1976): 33–39. In addition, many of the contributors to *Pre-colonial African Trade,* ed. Richard Gray and David Birmingham (London: Oxford University Press, 1970) implicitly address this issue.

2. These two positions are fully developed in Hodder, "Some Comments." While accepting the general implications of Hodder's argument, this essay suggests a refinement, on several points, of his conclusion, which reads (in part): "It appears that the bulk of traditional markets in Subsaharan Africa received their initial stimulus from external, long-distance trading contacts . . . two other conditions—a sufficiently high density of population and a political structure powerful enough to secure and maintain market peace —were necessary [for the development of market institutions]."

3. Lake Kivu itself does not provide the major cultural divide, as there are today a series of lacustrine societies just west of the lake as well as east of it. But these do not generally extend west of the Mitumba Mountains, which form the western edge of the Kivu Rift Valley. See Richard Sigwalt, "Early Rwanda History: The Contribution of Comparative Ethnography," *History in Africa* 2 (1975): 137–46 for a discussion of this point. Over the last two hundred years the interface between lacustrine and forest-area cultures has also gradually moved west, from east of the lake to its western shores.

4. The material on Butembo is based on my own fieldwork in Bufumandu, Ziralo, Mubugu, Buloho, Kalima, and Kalonge in 1972 and 1974. No complete ethnographic studies have been undertaken among the Tembo, but references to them are found in Jean-Baptiste Cuypers, "Les Bantous interlacustres du Kivu," in *Introduction à l'ethnographie du Congo,* by Jan Vansina (Kinshasa: Éditions universitaires du Congo, 1965), 201–11; and Daniel P. Biebuyck, *Lega Culture* (Berkeley and Los Angeles: University of California Press, 1973), 20. In many respects, Tembo political and social organization shows similarities to that described for the Nyanga (their neighbors to the northwest) by Biebuyck in several works, including "L'organisation politique des Nyanga: La chefferie Ihana," *Kongo-Overzee* 22, nos. 4–5 (1956): 301–41; 23, nos. 1–2 (1957): 58–98; *Rights in Land and Its Resources among the Nyanga* (Brussels: ARSOM, 1966); *Hero and Chief: Epic Literature from the Banyanga (Zaïre Republic)* (Berkeley: University of California Press, 1978); and Daniel

Biebuyck and Mateene Kahombo, *The Mwindo Epic from the Banyanga (Congo Republic)* (Berkeley and Los Angeles: University of California Press, 1971).

5. D'Hertefelt, "Le Rwanda"; and "The Rwanda of Rwanda," in *The Peoples of Africa,* ed. James L. Gibbs (New York 1965), 403–41.

6. Discussions on the evolution of Rwandan institutions include J. Vansina, *L'évolution du royaume Rwanda dès origines à 1900* (Brussels: ARSOM, 1962), 70–71; Claudine Vidal, "Le Rwanda des anthropologues ou le fétichisme de la vache," *Cahiers d'Études Africaines* 9, no. 3 (1969): 376–77; Joseph Rwabukumba and Vincent Mudandagizi, "Les formes historiques de la dépendance personnelle dans l'état Rwandais," *Cahiers d'Études Africaines* 14, no. 1 (1974): 6–25; Jean-François Saucier, "The Patron-Client Relationship in Traditional and Contemporary Southern Rwanda" (PhD diss., Columbia University, 1974), 19–28.

7. The basic ethnographic work on the Shi is P. Colle, *Essai de monographie des Bashi* (Bukavu: CELA, 1971); Shi material culture is discussed in Jean-Baptiste Cuypers, *L'alimentation chez les Shi* (Tervuren: MRAC, 1960). Two important recent works on the Shi are Elinor Sosne, "Kinship and Contract in Bushi: A Study of Village-Level Politics" (PhD diss., University of Wisconsin–Madison, 1974), and Richard Sigwalt, "The Early History of Bushi: An Essay in the Historical Use of Genesis Traditions" (PhD diss., University of Wisconsin–Madison, 1975). No general ethnography is available for the Havu.

8. Jan Vansina, introduction to *Les anciens royaumes de la zone interlacustre méridionale,* by Marcel d'Hertefelt, Albert A. Trouwborst, and J. H. Scherer (Tervuren: MRAC, 1962), 3–7.

9. Biebuyck, "L'organisation politique," 304–11; L. Viaene, "L'organisation politique des Bahunde," *Kongo-Overzee* 18, no. 1 (1952): 8–34; nos. 2–3 (1952): 111–21.

10. There seems to have been a flourishing trade in iron goods from Kayonza, a small state in present Kigezi, south into Rwanda through Mulera and Bugoyi, probably from the late eighteenth century, or before the Kivu trade extended into Rwanda from the southwest; E. R. Kamuhangire, "The Economic and Social History of the Southwest Uganda Salt Lakes Region" (paper presented to the Historical Society of Kenya, August 1972), 10; Kamuhangire, "Migration, Settlement, and State Formation in the Southwest Uganda Salt Lake Region" (Makerere University Seminar Paper, 1972), 18, 21. (I am indebted to J. Bertin Webster for calling my attention to these valuable papers.) See also Donald Denoon, *A History of Kigezi in Southwestern Uganda* (Kampala: National Trust, 1972); M. R. Rwankwenda, "The History of Kayonza," in Denoon, *History of Kigezi,* 124–33; Lugan, "Échanges et routes commerciales," n4. It may be that the commerce in hoes to Rwanda from the southwest did not assume important dimensions until after the incorporation of Kinyaga into the Rwandan polity, and the increasing intensity of commercial ties between central Rwanda and areas west of the Rusizi. The research of Bishikwabo Chubaka (in Kaziba) and Bernard Lugan (in Rwanda) may help clarify some of these issues.

11. Lugan, "Échanges et routes commerciales"; Félix Dufays and Vincent de Moor, *Au Kinyaga: Les Enchaînés* (Brussels: Éditions universelles, 1938), 15.

12. Personal fieldwork on Ijwi Island by the author.

13. Ivory trumpets were a significant element of royal regalia west of Lake Kivu and ivory bracelets were common. See also A. Pagès, *Au Rwanda: Sur les bords du lac Kivu, Congo belge: Un royaume hamite au centre de l'Afrique* (Brussels: IRCB, 1933), 667. The

memory of the raids of armed bands of slave—and ivory—hunters from Maniema (referred to in much of the colonial literature as "les Arabisés") is still very much alive west of the Mitumba Mountains. For one such example, see Hangi Shamamba, "Note sur Ngyiko Kingumwa," *Antennes* 5 (1977): 348–57.

14. Pagès, *Un royaume hamite*, 163; Jacques Depelchin, "From Precapitalism to Imperialism: A History of Social and Economic Formations in Eastern Zaïre (Uvira Zone), c. 1800–1964" (PhD diss., Stanford University, 1974), 168n31, 170. The number of slaves was "small" relative both to the population of Rwanda and to the numbers exported from other regions. Trade in slaves was a late development in Rwanda.

15. Grammatically, the correct term is *amatega* (plural of *ubutega*), but in the collective sense, as used here, the singular form is invariably used. There are actually many different forms of *butega,* varying in size and in the design of the weave, but these distinctions do not seem to have affected the patterns of trade at the regional level. Pagès, *Un royaume hamite,* plates Ib and XXIa, includes two excellent photographs of these as they were worn at the Rwandan court during the reign of Musinga. Another excellent photograph of *butega* being used as a means of exchange is found as fig. 63 in Thomas Alexander Barns, *Across the Great Craterland to the Congo* (London: Benn, 1923), facing p. 166.

16. Throughout this chapter the term "Butembo" will be used to refer to the land inhabited by the Batembo. They are located west of the Mitumba Mountains, mostly in the present Kalehe Zone, but are dispersed also in other zones: Masisi, Walikale, Kabare, and Shabunda. Butembo, as referred to here, is not to be confused with the important commercial center of the same name located in North Kivu, Beni Zone.

17. In general, population density for the forest areas today can be estimated at 5–10 per km²; in Rwanda [1975] the average figure is over 150/km² and much more in many areas of western Rwanda; Bushi is similar today. Léon de Saint Moulin, *Carte de la densité de la population du Zaïre* (Kinshasa: Institut géographique du Zaïre, 1975); Biebuyck, *Lega Culture,* 16; CINAM, *Étude du développement de la région du Lac Kivu (Rwanda),* vol. 2 (Paris: n.p., 1973), 4. The total Tembo population today can be roughly estimated at less than 1 percent of the Rwandan population; in the past, however, this figure may have been greater because of recent marked differences in the population growth rates in the two areas. It is also probable that demand for butega increased as the Rwandan state expanded during the nineteenth century, thereby increasing the numbers of the elite class and extending central court norms of fashion. A continuing demand was assured as long as butega were culturally prized, since they had to be replaced frequently.

18. For an example, see Joseph C. Miller, "Cokwe Trade and Conquest in the Nineteenth Century," in Gray and Birmingham, *Pre-colonial African Trade,* 175–201. For the colonial period, see Robert Harms, "The End of Red Rubber: A Reassessment," *Journal of African History* 14, no. 1 (1975): 73–88. This and the next several paragraphs are based on fieldwork undertaken among the Tembo in 1972 and 1974. Much historical work remains to be done in this area, including empirical inquiries on the internal role of butega and their significance in relationships between Butembo and areas to the west, as well as aspects of production and accessibility to raphia supplies.

19. References to "bracelets" among the Lega are found in Biebuyck, *Lega Culture,* 32, 33. Some of the many internal uses of butega within Nyanga society, bordering Butembo and Buhunde on the west and northwest, are noted in Biebuyck and Mateene, *Mwindo Epic,* 13, 47n28, 51, 55n59, 109, 127, and 127n242, where *butéa* are associated with royal regalia.

20. The internal circulation of butega within Tembo society, and the cultural preference for increased circulation over increased production in the face of increased demand,
parallels the situation portrayed for raffia cloth by Mary Douglas in "Raffia Cloth Distribution in the Lele Economy," *Africa* 28, no. 2 (1958): 109–22. Although more research is
needed in Butembo, it is possible that Douglas's conclusions would also help to explain
the restraints on overproduction of butega in Butembo. The conclusions presented in
this essay concerning the role of butega as "money" differ from Douglas's conclusions,
however, in part because this article is concerned with the interethnic ("external") role of
butega circulation.

21. Commercial profits in other commodities reported elsewhere in the region are
roughly comparable: Charles M. Good notes profit margins of 200 percent on salt commerce between Kigezi and the interior of Rwanda early in this century; see his *Rural Markets and Trade in East Africa* (Chicago: University of Chicago, Department of Geography
1970), 158n2, citing the Kigezi District Annual Report, 1922, par. 59.

22. I have no figures on the changes in these exchange values in the nineteenth century.
These prices might well reflect inflated values relative to mid-nineteenth century prices,
as a result of the disastrous rinderpest epidemic in Rwanda in 1893 and the drastic losses
in cattle which accompanied the arrival of the Europeans with their African forces. For
a discussion of some of the social and commercial repercussions within Rwanda, see
Catharine Newbury, *The Cohesion of Oppression: Clientship and Ethnicity in Rwanda,
1860–1960* (New York: Columbia University Press, 1988), 2.

23. See, for example, Andrew D. Roberts, "The Nyamwezi," in *Tanzania Before 1900,*
ed. Andrew D. Roberts (Nairobi: East African Publishing House, 1968), 128–40; Miller,
"Cokwe Trade and Conquest"; E. A. Alpers, "Trade, State, and Society among the Yao in
the Nineteenth Century," *Journal of African History* 10, no. 3 (1969): 405–20; Alpers, *Ivory
and Slaves in East Central Africa* (London: Heinemann 1975), 22. The circulation of butega
with people to the west (Kano, Lega, Nyanga) through both social and commercial channels may have reached considerable proportions, but is not considered here.

24. A potentially fruitful line of inquiry in Rwanda would be the examination of the
role of the Rwandan broker along lines suggested by Alpers, *Ivory and Slaves,* 202, and
more fully explored in the references noted at 208n84. Elsewhere, too, putative kin-ties facilitated travel over great distances in the absence of blood-pact ties; see John Middleton,
The Lugbara of Uganda (New York: Holt, Rinehart and Winston, 1965), 7.

25. Pagès, *Un royaume hamite,* 637; d'Hertefelt, "Le Rwanda," 36; d'Hertefelt, "The
Rwanda of Rwanda," 414; Alexis Kagame, *Les milices du Rwanda précolonial* (Brussels:
ARSOM, 1963), 65, 131, 160; Claudine Vidal, "Économie de la société féodale," *Cahiers
d'Études Africaines* 14, no. 1 (1974): 56n1. The research of Lugan highlights the importance
both of internal trade and especially of trade with the west. Lugan, "Échanges et routes
commerciales" and "Causes et effets de la famine 'Rumanura' au Rwanda, 1916–1918,"
Canadian Journal of African Studies 10, no. 2 (1976): 347–56.

26. While earlier references had noted the existence of markets only in western and
northwestern Rwanda in the late nineteenth century (d'Hertefelt, "Le Rwanda," 35–36),
recent research by Lugan has reexamined commercial developments in central Rwanda as
well: Lugan, "Échanges et routes commerciales." While further research should help to
clarify the role of markets within a wider commercial regional network and their development and evolution through time, it can tentatively be concluded that while precolo-

nial markets were present, even numerous, in Rwanda, they were preceded by trade in butega and other goods on an important scale, through other mechanisms. In the East African area more generally, early markets have been noted in Good, *Market Development;* Turyahikayo-Rugyema, "The Case of the Bakiga"; and Uzoigwe, "Precolonial Markets in Bunyoro-Kitara."

27. Pagès, *Un royaume hamite,* 636–37; Vidal, "Économie de la société féodale," 56n1; interviews conducted by Catharine Newbury.

28. Sigwalt, "Early Rwanda History."

29. Many early groups on Ijwi Island, for example, and among the Havu west of the lake, claim that cattle "came" from Rwanda.

30. While the absence of earlier data on this point does not prove that there was no earlier trade in butega, it is nevertheless likely that a growing demand for butega and similar prestige items in the Lake Kivu area was related to the development of social stratification in Rwanda and specifically, to the extension of Rwandan court influence toward the west. This is viewed as an historical correlation specific to the Lake Kivu trade in butega bracelets, not a necessary correlation: many non-stratified societies use such ornamentation, as indeed do Hutu in Rwanda and agriculturalists west of Rwanda. But during the early colonial period, at least, and probably before, Hutu used only relatively small amounts; thus the major demand stimulus of the Kivu regional trade in butega seems to have been related to the presence of Tutsi hegemony west of the mountainous Nile-Zaire divide in Rwanda. Where the demand for butega was modest, this could more readily be contained within politically determined channels of transaction as discussed above.

31. One earlier reference in Alexis Kagame, *Inganji Karinga,* 2nd ed. (Kabgayi, Rwanda: n.p., 1959), asserts that Sibula Nyebunga (a putative contemporary of the Rwandan king Ruganzu Ndoori) fled Bugesera (in the east) disguised as a *butega* trader from Kinyaga, but this reference is clearly an anachronism for reasons I shall discuss in a forthcoming work. See chapter 11, this volume.

32. Pagès, *Un royaume hamite,* 638: "Les Bagoyi . . . sont presque tous originaires du Nord-Ouest du Lac Kivu. Les régions qui fournirent le plus fort contingent d'émigres sont le Kameronsa, le Bunyungu, le Gishari, le Masisi, et le Bwito, pays divers dont les habitants portent le nom générique de Bahunde. L'arrivée des premiers immigrants . . . ne remonte pas au déla de deux cent ans." Further references to the cultural ties between Bugoyi and Buhunde are found on 661–62, 667, 676, 682. Pagès also gives a list of "clans et sous-clans" of Bugoyi in which he attributes western origins to almost half of the groups cited (27 out of 57) (ibid., 644–45). Linguistically, the inhabitants of Bugoyi formerly spoke a language similar to Kihunde; dialects of "Kihunde" are apparently still spoken in some small pockets within Bugoyi. (I am indebted to André Coupez for his communication on this point.)

33. Ibid., 636–37. To the west of Buhunde, the Nyanga peoples were also known for making "plaited bangles" which "they sell in large quantities to the Watusi and Wahutu women who encase their legs with thousands of them from knee to ankle in some cases" (Barns, *Across the Great Craterland,* 115–16). Although these passages both refer to the early twentieth century, it is likely that Bugoyi had long before served as an important center of butega trade because of the cultural ties of the Bagoyi with the Bahunde-Batembo, and their longstanding commercial contact with central Rwanda. Other references, cited below, confirm this.

34. Kagame, *Les milices*, 159–60. This army also had sections based in Bufumbira and hence may have drawn on sources of butega among the Nande peoples who also share certain cultural affinities with the Hunde and Tembo, including the fabrication of butega (personal communication from Randall Packard). The fact that butega production is more widely spread around the northern commercial contact point with Rwanda than the southern may indicate, again, the likelihood of more longstanding butega commerce in that region.

35. Vansina, *L'évolution du royaume Rwanda*, 88; Pagès, *Un royaume hamite*, 634, 641, 652. In a limited sample, Ivan Reisdorff, *Enquêtes foncières au Rwanda* (Butare, Rwanda: INRS, 1952), also notes both considerable immigration from the west and early political links with central Rwanda during the reign of Cyilima Rujugira (Enquête 31). The earliest evidence of prestations in "bracelets" is under Rwabugiri, but the quantities demanded (up to 6,000 per year for one family) would indicate the presence of substantial movements of butega from long before.

36. C. Newbury, *Cohesion of Oppression*, passim.

37. Kagame, *Les milices*, 63–65, 129–31.

38. Among the numerous references to butega noted in the interviews conducted by Catharine Newbury in Kinyaga, Rwanda, in 1970–71, the locales, exchange values, and associated commodities are best described by Bucuti (Nyamavugo, Gafunzo) 9/28/70, 8–9; Habarugira, Hambimaana, and Gahima (Cyibumba, Kamembe) 8/25/70, 2; Kanyaanziga (Mutango, Cyimbogo) 11/28/70, 4; Rwagasore (Nkanka, Kamembe) 8/13/70, 12; Mukiindangiga (Winteko, Cyimbogo) 12/7/70, 2; and Rutuungwa and Rubaanza (Gitanga, Kirambo) 2/17/71, 4. The relatively recent flowering of butega trade in Kinyaga and its association with different types of prestations is mentioned in Ndaziimanye (Nyakarenzo, Cyimbogo) 12/22/70, 9; and Shabani (Bugarama, Bugarama) 1/14/71, 7.

39. By the end of the nineteenth century, butega had clearly achieved significant commercial importance in Kinyaga. What remains at issue is how long this situation had existed. The evidence and analysis presented here indicate that early nineteenth century trade was stronger in Bugoyi than in Kinyaga. In the absence of more empirical data this conclusion remains tentative.

40. For example, Barns notes that at the Cyangugu market "plaited bracelets took the place of currency" (*Across the Great Craterland*, 163). His photograph of butega being exchanged in the market is captioned, "The *bureau de change* at Cyangugu market" (opposite p. 166).

41. These movements will be considered more fully in a forthcoming study based on my fieldwork among the Havu. It might be noted that butega never held an important place in Burundi, either for commerce or dress; personal communication from Jean-Pierre Chrétien. Entries from the Nyangezi Mission diary (Congo) also indicate that butega were not known south of the Shi plateau, at least in the early twentieth century; personal communication from Richard Sigwalt. This would also indicate that butega came into use at the southern end of the lake only relatively recently; compare with note 34 above.

42. In "Migration, Settlement, and State Formation," Kamuhangire attributes the origins of the salt trade from Lake Katwe to immigration from the south in the mid-eighteenth century (12), but notes that the establishment of an important network of trade relations around the shores of Lake Edward took place only during the second quarter of the nineteenth century (App. 3, 3). Kamuhangire refers to the emergence of a widespread salt and

iron trade network by the mid-nineteenth century, noting also that this trade was a vast expansion of previous trade patterns ("Economic and Social History," 74–76, 85–86). Some of the new immigrants associated with this commercial expansion were of Rwandan origin, which may serve to emphasize the southern orientation of this new trade. Other references to dating the evolution of the salt trade network are found in Good, *Rural Markets and Trade,* chap. 5, and "Salt, Trade, and Disease: Aspects of Development in Africa's Northern Great Lakes Region," *International Journal of African Historical Studies* 5, no. 4 (1972): 543–87, where he concludes that "the data suggest that Katwe salt was probably circulated more extensively [in the mid- and late-nineteenth century] than any other commodity in this part of east-central Africa" (555). See also Good, *Rural Markets,* 154. Both the extent and organization of this salt trade, and the quantities traded, testify that this network was not a recent development. Commerce in Katwe salt with Rwanda into the twentieth century is mentioned in many contemporary sources, among them Evan M. Jack, *On the Congo Frontier* (London: T. F. Unwin, 1914), 110–11, and Patrick Millington Synge, *Mountains of the Moon: An Expedition to the Equatorial Mountains of Africa* (New York: E. P. Dutton, 1938), 11–12; a photograph of salt porters is opposite p. 12. Commerce in mineral salt is also mentioned in both Tembo and Havu oral traditions relating to the nineteenth and early twentieth centuries.

43. H. F. Morris, *A History of Ankole* (Nairobi: East African Literature Bureau, 1962): 12–13; Samwiri R. Karugire, *A History of the Kingdom of Nkore in Western Uganda to 1896* (Oxford: Clarendon Press, 1971), 218.

44. The best account available on this is Kenneth Ingham, *The Kingdom of Toro in Uganda* (London: Methuen, 1975), 28–30, 43–47, 51, 57–58, 66–67, 78–80, 98–99. From Ingham's presentation it would appear that northern political influence was present in Busongora from the mid-nineteenth century, and dominant from the late 1870's, diverting most of the trade from its previous southern orientation. Incursions to Busongora from mid-century on the part of Ganda, Toro, Nkore, and Nyoro are also noted in Kamuhangire, "Migration, Settlement, and State Formation," App. 3, 3. Rwandan sources cite a campaign of Rwabugiri against "Bunyampaka" toward the end of the nineteenth century. (See chapter 5, this volume.) The Banyampaka states included the precise region of Lake Katwe and were subject to the rulers of Busongora; Kamuhangire, "Migration, Settlement, and State Formation," 21; also note 91 and map I. Consequently, although Rwandan sources emphasize the booty in cattle, it is entirely possible that this raid was encouraged by the attraction of the salt lakes, and more particularly, perhaps, by the objective of reestablishing the southern orientation of the salt trade disrupted by northern incursions. A summary of foreign involvement with Katwe is found in John Tosh, "The Northern Lacustrine Region," in Gray and Birmingham, *Pre-colonial African Trade,* 105. Marie de Kiewet Hemphill, "The British Sphere, 1884-1894," in *History of East Africa,* vol. 1, ed. Roland Oliver and Gervase Mathew (Oxford: Clarendon Press, 1963), 403–7, 425–26, refers to raids on the salt lake from the west. This apparently refers to army mutineers from the Congo Free State passing through the area in 1897–98. See F. Flamant et al., *La force publique de sa naissance à 1914* (Brussels: IRCB, 1952), 406–19; an indirect reference to Katwe, for May 1897, is noted at 410. These and earlier raids are mentioned also in Ingham, *Kingdom of Toro,* 98–99, and frequently in the many primary sources.

45. Apollo Kagwa, *The Kings of Buganda,* ed. M. S. M. Kiwanuka (Nairobi: East African Publishing House, 1971), 160.

46. Gaetano Casati, J. Randolph Clay, I. Walter Savage, and Emin Pasha, *Ten Years in Equatoria* (London: F. Warne and Co., 1898), 323; cited in Good, "Salt, Trade, and Disease," 566.

47. Karugire refers to local African leaders playing off Belgian and British administrators (*History of Nkore,* 124n51). According to British sources, Belgian authorities made demands for salt on the local leaders (Ingham, *Kingdom of Toro,* 99). European involvement is summarized in Tosh, "Northern Lacustrine Region," 105, and detailed in Ingham, *Kingdom of Toro* (see note 44 above). Foreign involvement under colonial rule is also considered in Good, *Rural Markets,* chap. 6.

48. Good, "Salt, Trade, and Disease," 571–77; Kamuhangire, "Migration, Settlement, and State Formation," 10; John Ford, *The Role of the Trypanosomiases in African Ecology* (Oxford: Clarendon Press, 1971), chaps. 8, 10. Elsewhere, Good notes that Katwe salt production may have been subject to seasonal fluctuations("Salt, Trade, and Disease," 548–50). Uvinza salt production apparently experienced even more pronounced fluctuations, being curtailed for most of the year, but production was apparently greater; Andrew D. Roberts, "The Nyamwezi Trade," in Gray and Birmingham, *Pre-colonial African Trade,* 46–47.

49. On the Uvinza salt workings, see J. E. G. Sutton and Andrew D. Roberts, "Uvinza and Its Salt Industry," *Azania* 3 (1968): 45–86.

50. Roberts, "Nyamwezi Trade," 47n2. This dating roughly correlates with other estimates for the penetration of Lake Tanganyika trade into the hinterland north of the lake; Roberts, "Nyamwezi," 123–26; and note 51 below.

51. For the trade at the northern end of Lake Tanganyika, see Richard Francis Burton, *The Lake Regions of Central Africa,* vol. 2 (London: Longman, Green, Longman and Roberts, 1861), 147; Depelchin, "From Precapitalism to Imperialism," 34, 36, 37, 74, 89, 166–79, esp. 172; Christopher St. John, "Kazembe and the Tanganyika-Nyasa Corridor, 1800–1890," in Gray and Birmingham, *Pre-colonial African Trade,* 217, 223–24. Stanley also notes iron, wire, bracelets, and anklets being traded in Ujiji in 1876. Henry Morton Stanley, *Through the Dark Continent,* vol. 2 (New York: Harper, 1878), 4.

52. Commercial concentration in the peripheral Shi states is stressed in Bishikwabo Cubaka, "L'économie d'échange dans les états précoloniaux du Sud-Kivu du XIXe siècle à 1920" (paper presented at the Journées d'Historiens Zaïrois, Lubumbashi, 1975). I am grateful to Dr. Bishikwabo for providing me access to this valuable paper based on original fieldwork; his present research may well force a revision of our present understanding of Shi participation in this trade.

53. The area of Cishoke (Bujombo) and Luhihi is today administratively a part of Bushi. However, these populations continue to share many linguistic, social and cultural elements with the Havu, whose centers have since been displaced north, and with the populations across the narrow straits of Lake Kivu (in present-day Rwanda).

54. Most Havu and Tembo traditions refer to Kaziba as the major southern center of exchange in the late nineteenth century. This implies intensive contacts of the Shi peoples with others to their north. Bishikwabo, "L'économie d'échange," emphasizes the importance of the multiplicity of trade goods between Lakes Kivu and Tanganyika, focusing on Kaziba, during the late nineteenth century especially. See also note 52 above.

55. Norman Bennett mentions that Arab traders may have begun trading on the lake as early as the 1840s, but that they did not themselves penetrate the hinterland. Bennett, *Leadership in Eastern Africa* (Boston: Boston University Press, 1968, 148. Depelchin cites 1840 for the earliest Arab presence at the north end of Lake Tanganyika ("From Precapi-

talism to Imperialism," 166). Lake Tanganyika trade of course long preceded the Arab arrival, but many of the Tanganyika goods that were most determinant for the Kivu trade
seem to be those associated with the coastal trade.

56. For examples, see James Augustus Grant, *A Walk across Africa, or, Domestic Scenes
from My Nile Journal* (London: W. Blackwood and Sons, 1864), 161; Stanley, *Through the
Dark Continent,* vol. 1, 454–55, 464, 480; Stanley, *In Darkest Africa* (New York: Charles
Scribner's 1891), 11, 359–60. Certain coastal goods had apparently been present in Rwanda
long before the nineteenth century, but their presence could be accounted for by informal
contacts rather than direct participation. See Alexis Kagame, *Un abrégé de l'ethno-histoire
du Rwanda précolonial,* vol. 1 (Butare: Éditions universitaires du Rwanda, 1972), 131–32;
Kagame, "Le premier Européen au Rwanda" (paper presented at the Institut Pédagogique
National, Butare, Rwanda, February 1970); Francis van Noten, *Les tombes du roi Cyirima
Rujugira et de la reine-mère Nyirayuhi Kanjogera: Description archéologique* (Tervuren:
MRAC, 1972), 43–62.

57. Pagès, *Un royaume hamite,* 160–64; Kagame, *Les milices,* 161–62; Kagame, *Un abrégé
de l'histoire du Rwanda de 1853 à 1972,* vol. 2 (Butare: Éditions universitaires du Rwanda,
1975), 91–94.

58. This characteristic of separate transactional spheres is discussed in Bohannan
and Dalton, *Markets in Africa,* 6–7. Douglas also stresses that within the Lele economy
raffia cloth circulated almost exclusively through social channels; see note 21 above.

59. The intense commercial aspect of the trade is confirmed by the fact that the
economic functions of butega came increasingly to dominate the social. Despite their important social role within Butembo, butega appear to have become increasingly mone-
tized and hence were readily replaced by new exchange units. The second quarter of the
twentieth century saw a decline in the regional role of butega both as items of consumption and units of value: copper bracelets of various kinds replaced the ornamental role of
butega; beads and coins replaced their role as currency. The decline in their regional economic roles was accompanied by a reduction in their social role within Butembo: today
butega are seldom used and rarely required for bridewealth; they are anachronisms of a
purely antiquarian value.

60. Other examples of this are Marvin Miracle, "Plateau Tonga Entrepreneurs in
Historical Inter-regional Trade," *Rhodes-Livingstone Journal* 26 (1960): 39–40; and Kamuhangire, "Economic and Social History."

61. Claude Meillassoux, "L'économie des échanges précoloniaux en pays Gouro,"
Cahiers d'Études Africaines 3, no. 4 (1963): 551–76; Meillassoux, "Social and Economic
Factors Affecting Markets in Guro Land," in Bohannan and Dalton, *Markets,* 297–98:
"Markets are primarily induced by external exchange of complementary products with
an alien population," and therefore tend first to be localized at the contact area between
different zones.

62. Jan Vansina, "Trade and Markets among the Kuba," in Bohannan and Dalton,
Markets in Africa, 194: "Markets were important only in strategic places along the trade
routes on the borders of areas with different products."

63. M. G. Smith, "Exchange and Marketing among the Hausa," in Bohannan and
Dalton, *Markets,* 301–5, esp. 304: "The growth of important city markets is clearly linked
with the spread of foreign contacts."

64. Ibid.: "Exchange by gift and barter among occupationally specialized clans preceded markets." The pattern identified by Smith for the Hausa may also be applicable to

Rwanda, especially central Rwanda, where internal cultural heterogeneity associated with differential economic production was more marked. Recent research should do much to clarify these points for central Rwanda. See Lugan, "Échanges et routes commerciales," 33.

65. This hypothesis draws heavily on Claude Meillassoux, *The Development of Indigenous Trade and Markets in West Africa* (London: Oxford University Press for the International African Institute, 1971), 82: "Between neighbouring communities, transactions tend to take on the form of gift and counter-gift rather than of commercial exchange;" therefore, commerce results "only from contacts between societies who can offer scarce goods to each other, and between agents who are in a social position which frees them from involvement in prestations and gift exchange." Both forms of transfer took place in relations between Ijwi and Rwanda; sometimes the same individual engaged in both. Sometimes the question of gift/counter-gift or commercial transfer would not be seen identically by the two agents: what was clearly seen as a commercial transaction (with no ulterior social or personal responsibilities) by an Ijwi trader who did not accept a hierarchical perception of relations with foreigners, would probably not infrequently have been seen as a gift/counter-gift by his Rwandan counterpart.

66. Kaziba may be an example of the former; Kinyaga of the latter.

67. In Bushi, trade was particularly intense in Kaziba and Kalonge, two small states peripheral to major centers of political power, and near the lines of ethnic and ecological frontiers; in the case of Kaziba, trade influences from Lake Tanganyika may have played a part as well. Bugoyi and Kinyaga were only imperfectly integrated to the Rwandan polity before the colonial period. In the Katwe salt area, political intrusion reduced total production as well as redirected trade. Thus while the major centers may provide security for state officials, they may also inhibit larger trans-state patterns of informal commerce, and impede its emergence in an area.

68. D'Hertefelt, *Les anciens royaumes*, 36, and Bishikwabo, "L'économie d'échange" both mention the personal dangers associated with marketplaces; the latter notes that in Bushi, early markets were considered outside the juridical domain of the local political authorities.

69. A. Pagès, "Au Rwanda: Droits et pouvoirs des chefs sous la suzeraineté du roi hamite: Quelques abus du système," *Zaïre* 3, no. 4 (1949): 359–77; Pagès, *Un royaume hamite*, 642n1, 684–48; C. Newbury, *Cohesion of Oppression*.

70. Hodder, "Some Comments," 97–105; Hill, "Markets in Africa," 448; and Uzoigwe, "Precolonial Markets in Bunyoro-Kitara," make the same point. See also Charles M. Good, "Markets in Africa: A Review of Research Themes and the Question of Market Origins," *Cahiers d'Études Africaines* 13, no. 4 (1973): 769–81.

71. For example, the conclusions reached here do not exclude economic influences from a Lake Tanganyika trade network as potential contributing factors to Shi consolidation during the late eighteenth and early nineteenth centuries.

Chapter 4: Kamo and Lubambo

This chapter appeared in Les Cahiers du CEDAF 5 *(1979): 1–47.*

1. Luc de Heusch, *Le roi ivre ou l'origine de l'état* (Paris: Gallimard, 1972), and Christopher C. Wrigley, "The Story of Rukidi," *Africa* 43, no. 3 (1973): 219–35, are examples of these initiatives applied to African genesis traditions.

2. Andrew D. Roberts, *A History of the Bemba* (London: Longman, 1973); Feierman, *The Shambaa Kingdom* (Madison: University of Wisconsin Press, 1974); Joseph C. Miller, *Kings and Kinsmen: Early Mbundu States in Angola* (Oxford: Clarendon Press, 1975).

3. Roy G. Willis, "The Fipa," in *Tanzania before 1900*, ed. Andrew D. Roberts (Nairobi: East African Publishing House, 1968), 82–96; Willis, "Traditional History and Social Structure in Ufipa," *Africa* 34, no. 4 (1964): 340–52.

4. By "form," I mean the nature of reference to individuals and events, the kinds of idioms and allusions that appear in the traditions, and the way in which each tradition is narrated.

5. There is considerable variation among social groups on Ijwi in terms of composition, corporate identity, and genealogical depth. In some cases these components of social identification have altered significantly over the last two hundred years. Because these distinctions are not important to the argument here, I will refer to all such social identity groups, regardless of their composition and internal structure, as "clans," for simplicity.

6. This essay is based on ten months of fieldwork carried out on Ijwi Island at various intervals from 1972 to 1975. In addition, shorter periods of fieldwork were conducted on the mainland, both in Zaire (Buhavu, Bushi, and Butembo), and in lakeshore areas of present-day Rwanda. On Ijwi interviews were conducted primarily with older men; an attempt was made to include all clans, regions, and occupational differences in the interviews, which included roughly 20 percent of the male population over about fifty years of age. I gratefully acknowledge the kind assistance and encouragement of Ntambuka Barhahakana, the mwami of Ijwi, and of his son Ntambuka Sibula, as well as the friendship, patience, and kindness of many other Bany'Iju, too numerous to cite individually here. In the preparation of this work I have also benefited from the advice and comments of many people, but the critique and encouragement of Jan Vansina, Joseph Miller, and Richard Sigwalt have been especially useful.

7. Examples of these traditions are found in the appendices to my "Kamo and Lubambo" (MA thesis, University of Wisconsin–Madison, 1977).

8. The most complete accounts are: Nyamuheshera 5/17/72; Kalwiira 6/10/72; Bakengamwami 6/24/72; and Musengo 1/24/75. Among other accounts are Mulengezi 5/18/72; Myavu 6/2/72; Kalwiira 6/5/72; Ngenyozi 6/5/72; Rusingiza 6/10/72; Buraho 8/7/72; Bwayu 8/8/72, 8/9/72; Ruhamanya 8/8/72; and Muregera 8/11/72.

9. The Lubambo mentioned here is not to be confused with the title of "Lubambo," associated with the Rwandan annual First Fruits rituals. See Marcel d'Hertefelt and André Coupez, *La royauté sacrée de l'ancien Rwanda* (Tervuren: MRAC, 1964), 493; Alexis Kagame, *Inganji Karinga*, 2nd ed. (Kabgayi, Rwanda: n.p., 1959), sec. V, par. 31.

10. Certain fishing styles in this area use an *omugera*, a thin metal rod, to spear the fish; the accident occurred as part of this process; all sources note that Kabwiika's death resulted from an accident.

11. See Otto Rank, *The Myth of the Birth of the Hero and Other Writings,* ed. Philip Freund (New York: Vintage, 1964), 14–64. Two well-known Interlacustrine examples are those of Bunyoro and Rwanda. On the former, see John Beattie, *The Nyoro State* (Oxford: Clarendon Press, 1971), 46–47; and Iris Berger, "The *Kubandwa* Religious Complex of Interlacustrine East Africa: An Historical Study, c. 1500–1900" (PhD diss., University of Wisconsin–Madison, 1973). For Rwanda, see Vansina, *L'évolution du royaume Rwanda,* 50–51; A. Pagès, *Au Rwanda: Sur les bords du Lac Kivu, Congo belge: Un royaume hamite au centre de l'Afrique* (Brussels: IRCB, 1933), 232–76; Kagame, *Un abrégé de l'ethno-histoire du*

Rwanda précolonial, vol. 1 (Butare: Éditions universitaires du Rwanda, 1972), 96–101. The Ijwi case differs from the former in that while other versions go to great lengths to prove the legitimacy of the new pretender to royal status and descent, the Ijwi version implies descent but not status, since most versions accept that Nkobwa and Kabwiika were not married. This reflects the fact that all Bany'Iju, all Havu in fact (including those on the mainland), accept the Ijwi line as the junior descent line of the Havu royal dynasty, and hence it represents a hiatus in the "legitimacy of royal status."

12. Testimony is not clear on the residences of Mwendanga on Ijwi, and it seems that even after his arrival on Ijwi, Mwendanga's primary residences were on the mainland, where, in fact, he died.

13. Marcel d'Hertefelt, "Mythes et idéologies dans le Rwanda ancien et contemporain," in *The Historian in Tropical Africa,* ed. Jan Vansina, Raymond Mauny, and L. V. Thomas (London: Oxford University Press for the International African Institute, 1964), 219–38; Alexis Kagame, *Le code des institutions politiques du Rwanda précolonial* (Brussels: IRCB, 1952), 20 (#12), 41 (#79 and note 15); Jacques J. Maquet, *Le système des relations sociales dans le Ruanda ancien* (Tervuren: MRAC, 1954), 146–47; d'Hertefelt, "Le Rwanda," 69–70: "[Le roi] était complètement soustrait à la sphere des profanes. Il était considéré aussi comme étant d'origine céleste. L'idéologie l'élévait par conséquent au-dessus de la hiérarchie des castes: il n'était ni Tuutsi, ni Hutu, ni Twa."

14. Martin Southwold, "Succession to the Throne in Buganda," in *Succession to High Office,* ed. Jack Goody (Cambridge: Cambridge University Press, 1966), 86–89 and note 8: "The Kabaka belonged to his mother's clan."

15. It is interesting that this fish is caught and presented at the ceremony by a member of the Babambo clan, thus reversing the roles portayed in this tradition of the Babambo as passive onlookers to Kabwiika's death, but also as protectors of Kabwiika, who were to benefit from his death. While the royal rituals of the Havu senior line (at Mpinga) also included the presentation of a fish, this was not done by a member of the Babambo clan.

16. See, for example, J. S. Boston, "The Hunter in Igala Legends of Origin," *Africa* 34, no. 2 (1964): 116–26; de Heusch, *Le roi ivre;* Feierman, *Shambaa Kingdom,* 40–70.

17. Connected to this episode is another aspect of the narration: the words "Bene Shando" are sometimes pronounced in a way close to "Bene Shamvu," a play on words, since the keepers of the royal drum on Ijwi are sometimes referred to as the "Abashamvu" and the royal drum in Mpinga is named "Shamvu." In this case, then, the story refers back to the conflict over royalty, represented by the drums, since the fishermen refuse to give fish to Kabwiika (or alternatively are far out in the lake).

18. Interviews with Babambo informants were carried out in Kinyaga (Rwanda) in April 1975. There is a possible confusion of "Gahindiro" here, since every *mwami* named Mibambwe is said to have had a son named Gahindiro, but the fact that he is identified as a king, and that all genealogical data coincide on this point, would identify the Gahindiro of the Babambo traditions with the mwami Yuhi IV Gahindiro (1801–ca. 1830, according to Vansina's revised dating). Jan Vansina, *La légende du passé: Traditions orales du Burundi* (Tervuren: MRAC, 1972), 133, 133n2, where he corrects the dates previously put forth in *L'évolution du royaume Rwanda,* 52–56.

19. Interviews from Luhihi, February 1975.

20. Kagame, *Un abrégé,* vol. 1, 190.

21. Ibid., 168–69. Furthermore, it appears that the Babambo were recent immigrants to the area, perhaps coming from the south. In Burundi the Babambo are a major clan, whose center is now in the south of the country (in Bututsi), but who claim to have come from the north of Burundi (personal communication from Jan Vansina). That the Rundi references in the royal traditions of smallpox coincide with possible Rundi ties for the Babambo, in independent traditions, only reinforces—but does not in itself establish—the claim of Lubambo's expertise in healing the disease. I am not aware of the symbolism of smallpox in Rwandan and Rundi traditions, but it is possible that these references are not literal "reports" (in the narrow sense of the term), and hence the convergence of the two traditions in this respect would lose its significance. It should only be noted here the potential for symbolic conflict in the traditions at this point: Sentabyo died after a reign of only five years; Gahindiro, very young at the time of Sentabyo's death, was the son of an unmarried servant (*umuja*) in Sentabyo's court, rather than one of his wives (compare with the Nkobwa-Kabwiika story), and Gahindiro is said to have told Lubambo later: "I like you but I do not like your sons," a statement that also reappears in Rwandan traditions as a cliché for potential conflict.

22. Kagame, *Un abrégé*, vol. 1, 209; Kagame, *La poésie dynastique du Rwanda* (Brussels: IRCB, 1951), 9n1.

23. In general terms, the regalia and concept of royalty are similar in the two Havu kingdoms, Mpinga (Kalehe) and Ijwi, but the individuals fulfilling these ritual functions and the details of certain ceremonies (e.g., the First Fruits ceremony, which itself is reflective of the enthronement rituals) are quite different in the two kingdoms. On Ijwi these are clearly a product of the historical integration of Sibula royal drum forms to the Ijwi social context of the mid-nineteenth century; so strong is the mark of this Ijwi context as to make it seem extremely doubtful that Mwendanga arrived with a previously functioning royal tradition. The influence of the Ijwi population on present royal practices, related to the evident lack of social cohesion and common identity on Ijwi in the pre-Sibula period, would indicate that he did not.

24. Informants of the Banyakabwa clan state that Mwendanga was "summoned" to Ijwi by people already on the island. The "summons," too, is obviously a cliché, but it seems clear that there was an internal rift within the most prominent family on Ijwi at the time (the Banyakabwa), and that this rift facilitated Mwendanga's arrival, even to the extent that one faction did seek an outside ally in Mwendanga. This episode, as with all other references to internal Ijwi history, is totally neglected in most Babambo traditions.

25. Widespread traditions on the mainland, but notably testimony of Ciringwe, Luhihi, February 1975.

26. The Babambo traditions assert that Lubambo was invited to the court because of his skill (and reputation) as a healer. For Lubambo to have built up a reputation respected at the court, even from an area so distant from central Rwanda, he was likely already to have been an older man at the time, probably over fifty, and possibly considerably older. It is therefore possible that Nkobwa was at least thirty years old in 1797, at the time of the "smallpox epidemic" at the Rwandan court and Sentabyo's death. Since Kabwiika, contending the throne, was young enough to be single and without other children at Mwendanga's birth, it seems likely that she would have been roughly eighteen to twenty years old at the time of Mwendanga's birth—perhaps younger, since women in this area are

said to have often married younger in the past than at present. Therefore Mwendanga's birth can be suggested as falling roughly around 1785, recognizing that we are dealing with very broad generalizations and hence with a very wide estimate range. If this is so, then it is plausible to date Mwendanga's arrival on Ijwi, at roughly the age of twenty-five to thirty-five, to the period 1810–20. Other Ijwi data would be consistent with this.

27. These events and the associated chronology will be discussed in greater detail in a later work based on a broader analysis of the Ijwi oral data.

28. Among the accounts that deal with this are Mushayma 2/5/72; Ndwanyi 2/29/72; Ciruza 3/6/72; Mahenga 3/9/72; Nyamienda 3/17/72; Rubambiza 3/18/72; Luganwa 3/22/72; Gaseserwa 3/23/72; Batindi 3/24/72; Mbaraga 3/28/72; Magendo 5/2/72; Ngwasi 5/5/72. By far the most complete are Rubambiza 6/17/74, 6/23/74, 3/20/75; Rugo 6/14/74, 3/20/75; and Ngwasi 10/12/74. The more elaborate recitations include references to hunting, forest plants, and Barhwa (pygmies) associated with the forest.

29. Research was carried out in the six Tembo kingdoms to the west of the Mitumba Mountains at various times during 1972–74.

30. There is little precise historical background material relating to Kamo. What vague references we have are drawn from genealogies and cultural allusions in the traditions relating to him. Though vague, such information is still internally consistent, and conforms to the external cultural indications noted in the text, relating to probable forest culture origins. Munazi 2/10/72; Rwankuba 3/8/72; Luganwa 3/22/72; Gaseserwa 3/23/72; Batindi 3/24/72; Mbaraga 3/23/72; Malekera 5/1/72; and especially Ngwasi 3/3/72 and Rubambiza 3/1/72, 6/23/74.

31. The Banyakabwa tradition is the only other tradition that could be said to deal with these matters. But that tradition is almost solely concerned with events on Ijwi, and especially among the Banyakabwa themselves. No information is given on Mwendanga's background, or that of the royal family. According to the Banyakabwa narrative, Mwendanga simply arrives on the island during their internal dispute; his presence is almost that of a *deus ex machina* to account for the demise of the Banyakabwa on Ijwi.

32. The conclusion is supported by traditions by all parties, traditions that state that Mwendanga lived his last years with Vuningoma on the mainland, and in fact died there. The Babambo cite this as support for Vuningoma's status as "favorite son," while descendants of Kawiika imply, instead, that in fact Vuningoma "starved" Mwendanga, and thus caused his death. Food is, of course, here as elsewhere, a common metaphor for well-being; the concept of eating is closely tied to that of dominance, and hence, more specifically, of governing. Hence when, in the narrative, Kamo places food in the sack, explaining that the sack "eats," this is also a direct play on words, referring to Mwendanga's future status as ruler. (The verb *okulya* means both to eat and to govern, as well as to have sex, among other meanings.) At any rate, all parties agree that Mwendanga died on the mainland.

33. This is the conclusion to be drawn from such traditions as Musengo 1/24/75.

34. This includes the area south of the mountainous forest belt along the eastern shore of Ijwi, a rugged highland area quite distinct historically and socially from other parts of the southern half of the island. Though the Baloho are concentrated in the locale of Mugote, the general area of their influence includes the present administrative "villages" of Musama-Buholo II, Bwando, Lubuye, Mugote, Bukere, Bwiiru, Butyangali, Bushovu, Nyakibamba, Bushake, Nkuvu, and Bulegeyi.

35. West of the Mitumba Mountains in this area live the Tembo peoples, among whom one kingdom today is known as Buloho; in terms of population, it is the largest of the Tembo kingdoms, and clearly has experienced intensive ties with Shi and Havu east of the mountains over the recent past. However, the people in this area do not know anything of the name of "Kamo." (Fieldwork was carried out in Buloho in July and August 1974.)

36. House construction, language differences, and occupational differences are apparent among those cultural distinctions of the East. In some parts of the East, houses are round and the walls are of mud (and sand), rather than the semispherical thatched "beehive" houses of other parts of Ijwi. Linguistically, some of the words differ: "Bwacere," for example, is used as a greeting during the day—the same word as used in the forest areas west of the Mitumba Mountains where Kitembo is the language spoken. Finally, until recently hunting was a relatively common activity in this area, as it is still in the forest area on the mainland. That alone is not sufficient to draw firm conclusions, of course, but the conjunction of many (sometimes precise) cultural traits so similar to the Tembo areas—including language, material culture and economic preferences—is nonetheless noteworthy.

37. These marriages went both ways; they represented, in effect, an "exchange" of wives; but in general, women from the royal family more frequently married Baloho men than vice versa. (Of course, too, there were more Baloho men seeking wives from the royal family.) Also, in general, the marriage of royal women out was a more significant political indicator than the marriage of commoner women to the king.

38. A fuller analysis of these traditions formed a part of my doctoral dissertation on the impact of the Basibula royal line on the social organization of the island, later published as *Kings and Clans: Ijwi Island and the Lake Kivu Rift, 1780–1840* (Madison: University of Wisconsin Press, 1991). It might be pointed out, however, that these areas provide the highest degrees of clan localization on the island still today (1975).

39. The term "ties to ritual" is deliberately vague because the traditions are not very precise. Suffice it to say that there are several forms of data that indicate the probability of some form of historical relationship to the areas and descent groups important to Rwandan royal ritual. It is significant also that these groups on Ijwi were later incorporated into Ijwi royal rituals, which in these respects are closer to Rwandan rituals than to Mpinga-Havu rituals. For a more developed analysis of these ties, see D. Newbury, *Kings and Clans*, chaps. 5–7.

40. This area is still viewed today as "remote" and "difficult" to govern by the central court and present-day Zaïrian administration alike. On at least two occasions in the postcolonial period, there have been administrative "difficulties" in this area that have been interpreted as no less than "rebellion" by the royal court. One of these involved the transfer of authority from a Muloho authority to another man. In the other case, the population of the rest of the south was mobilized and sent to "punish" a village, whose members were dispersed into the forested areas. Only after several weeks were they allowed to return, when the mwami had to perform certain rituals of reintegration.

41. At the time of the research the Baloho numbered 77 married males on the island out of a total of 6,583 married males in the villages for which figures are available. (Clan statistics for some villages are unavailable. Extrapolating from comparative population figures, these missing statistics would account for about 1,000 additional married men

total. But all these villages were in areas where no other Baloho lived in neighboring villages; they were unlikely to have added significantly to Baloho numbers.) Yet the Baloho held three (and "traditionally" had held four) of seventy-six positions as village capitas—far out of proportion to their representation among the population at large.

42. This is one of the most widely known stories on Ijwi and has achieved almost symbolic status as representative of the treachery of the early Europeans in their dealings with the people on Ijwi. Camukenge, the trusted spokesman of the king, came forward to represent the king, Ndogosa, who at that time had withdrawn into the forest to flee European brutality. When Camukenge would not divulge the whereabouts of his king, he was seized and buried up to his neck. On still refusing to betray Ndogosa, his tongue was cut out and he was then buried alive. There are many stories of other Bany'Iju being buried alive by Europeans (or their soldiers), usually for refusing to report for forced labor.

43. Multiple testimonies from Ngwasi and Rugo. Some of these testimonies, however, and particularly from the latter, show signs of having been embellished. It is inconceivable that there be two sets of royal rituals in the same "kingdom," since these royal rituals were the essence of legitimacy and sovereignty. Hence this assertion, if taken literally, can only be read as rebellion: claiming a counter-dynasty in opposition to (or at least separate from, autonomous to) that of the Basibula. However, there are no indications that the Basibula ever viewed the Baloho as "rebels"—until very recent times, when one of the principal actors involved in these accusations was Rugo himself; it may be this which motivates his rather extreme account of the Baloho possessing rituals of their own. Therefore, this seems to be more a metaphorical statement of Baloho "power" (or status and influence) in their eastern strongholds than a simple statement of historical fact. Most informants will stare in amazement and shake their heads in wonder, or simply laugh, when queried directly about this aspect of the Baloho past—the claim by some Baloho to royal rituals of their own. It is nonetheless an interesting commentary on Baloho political authority—if not ritual legitimacy—within this "remote" region.

44. This area was particularly affected during the period 1928–36, when the kings were deposed (Ndogosa died in exile and his successor was not permitted to reign), and the island was administered by a chief from the north, also a member of the royal family. He placed many of his favorites from the north as capitas in the villages in the south—often these were men with previous contacts with Europeans (former plantation capitas or mission workers, sometimes literate). For more on these points, see chapter 7, this volume.

45. It is nowhere apparent what prevented a secession that would have resulted in the establishment of two royal lines—Ijwi and the mainland, one under Kabego, one under Vuningoma. Two possible explanations appear in the traditions, however. The first is that Kabego so smashed Babambo strength as to assure his own preeminence in the mainland area, even though his major center remained on Ijwi. This is indicated by the fact that the islands and peninsulas remained under Kabego's domain in the nineteenth century. However, there is little evidence to show that the battle was of that scale, either from Ijwi traditions, where the conflict is portrayed as a succession struggle within the royal family, which did not mobilize large segments of the Ijwi population, or on the mainland, where it is hardly known at all. The second possibility suggested in these testimonies is that Vuningoma was inextricably tied to Babambo support, and that the Babambo themselves were so "arrogant" (as implied in the Ijwi traditions) and contentious as to preclude a broadening of their support to incorporate a following large enough to generate a "king-

dom." A third possible explanation is that of the political context of the mainland area at the time—the Rwanda, the Shi, and the senior Havu lines all potentially wielded some sort of indirect influence in the area; only Ijwi was remote enough for the royal pretenders to succeed in setting up a new political order, separate from earlier established dynastic lines.

46. By "explanation" here I mean essentially a response to the question: "Why the alliance of Baloho with Basibula on Ijwi?" or "Why the alliance of the Babambo with Vuningoma on the mainland against Kabego on Ijwi?" This criterion, of course, could also apply to etiological explanations, or explanations of the past that were etiological in origin. This section will try to consider this possibility; it will show why these genesis traditions can be seen as historical, rather than etiological, although in some respects the distinctions between the two genres may not be very clearly defined.

47. See Jan Vansina, *Oral Tradition: A Study in Historical Methodology* (Chicago: Aldine, 1965), 158–59.

48. Recent examples of such a single legitimizing tradition are found in Feierman, *Shambaa Kingdom;* Roberts, *History of the Bemba;* and Miller, *Kings and Kinsmen,* among others. For a different type of example drawn from the immediate area under consideration, see Richard Sigwalt, "The Early History of Bushi: An Essay in the Historical Use of Genesis Traditions" (PhD diss., University of Wisconsin–Madison, 1975). From a detailed analysis of nine variant traditions and their historical transformations, Sigwalt explores the origin of kingship itself in the area, as well as tracing the legitimacy of specific individuals to wield the power of kingship.

49. We have already noted the likelihood that Mwendanga arrived as an adult because of the need for him to have formed alliances prior to his arrival on Ijwi. In addition, the traditions on Ijwi refer to little else that occurred during Mwendanga's reign. This is a general feature of oral tradition: Pocock refers to it as "Eventual Time" because this type of historical narrative deals with discrete events separately, without filling in the intervening time spans. See David F. Pocock, "The Anthropology of Time Reckoning," in *Myth and Cosmos,* ed. John Middleton (Garden City, NY: Natural History Press, 1967), 303–14. Many others, too, note that in general oral traditions do not form a running narrative through time as measured along a continuous scale. The absence in Ijwi traditions of any reference to Mwendanga's reign between his arrival and his death does not itself "prove" they occurred close in time. But it does conform to the other indications that Mwendanga's reign on Ijwi was not particularly long.

50. It is conceivable that the "sack" theme, which figures so strongly in the Baloho tradition associated with protecting Mwendanga from his enemies, refers to the protection of Mwendanga from the Babambo rather than from the Havu royal line. But this does not accord well with either the Baloho data or other independent data: direct conflict between Baloho and Babambo is absent from the traditions, and the Babambo appear to have continued their relations with the royal line, even if these relations may have been strained.

51. Vansina, *Oral Tradition.*

52. Cf. Rugo 6/14/74; Rubambiza 6/23/74; Ngwasi 10/12/74.

53. See chapter 5, this volume.

54. This term is a play on words, as it is said to be an elision of the term "akalyo omu mvumba": *kalyo*—food; *omu*—within; I am unaware of the meaning of the term *mvumba*.

Akalyo also derives from the verb *okulya,* which in this area (as elsewhere) is connected not only with eating but with "dominance"—specifically in this context, "to govern." Hence when food was placed in the sack with the imperative "Eat, sack!" or the declarative "The sack eats," this phrase had the dual meaning of "Govern!" or "The sack governs," a reference to Mwendanga's claimed royal status.

55. See pages 89 and 95, above.

56. See section 2 above in this chapter, "The Social and Historical Characteristics of the Two Clans on Ijwi." One principal informant, Rugo, had worked at Kalehe. But he does not seem to have been the source of the Ngwasi variant. This and the exclusive application of Rugo's account to Kamo indicate that he did not pick up the tradition at Kalehe and simply graft it onto the Kamo story. Besides, were he (or any other person) the single source for the present Ijwi version, this would not account for the fragmentary bits (found among other informants elsewhere on Ijwi) that conform to Rugo's variant and refer only to Kamo.

57. Vansina, *La légende du passé,* 155–59. Like the Mpinga tale, this deals with royal conflict which occurred in the latter part of the nineteenth century. Unlike the versions elsewhere, however, in the Rundi case it is the regent who is placed in a mat, thus representing burial and removal, rather than protection and continuity.

58. Pierre Smith, *Le récit populaire au Rwanda* (Paris: Armand Colin, 1975), 360–66.

59. Among such elements are the form of clan organization and the associated terminology—*ishanja* ("subclan") is virtually the same word in Kihavu and Kitembo, and on Ijwi the clan (*ishanja*) has almost identical meaning to that of "subclan" in Rwanda's northwest. For a historical application of these terminological comparisons, see chapter 8, this volume. Joking relations among clans in Bugoyi and on Ijwi are also structured similarly (but not identically)—and differently from those of central Rwanda. Linguistically, there are also very close morphological similarities between the langue of Bugoyi and Kihunde, spoken to the west (and similar to Kitembo). (Personal communication from André Coupez of the Musée Royal de l'Afrique Centrale in Tervuren, Belgium.) Finally, Bugoyi has shared close historical ties with Buhunde into the very recent past, but dating from several centuries ago at least, to judge by population movements into Bugoyi; see Pagès, *Un royaume hamite,* 638, 644–45, 661–62, 667, 676, 682; also Ivan Reisdorff, *Enquêtes foncières au Rwanda* (Butare, Rwanda: INRS, 1952), Enquête 36. Many aspects of Hunde domestic culture are similar to, if not indistinguishable from, Tembo culture.

60. Alexis Kagame, *Introduction aux grands genres lyriques de l'ancien Rwanda* (Butare, Rwanda: Éditions universitaires du Rwanda, 1969); Vansina, *Oral Tradition,* 165; Vansina, *L'évolution du royaume Rwanda,* 17–38; Smith, *Le récit populaire,* 15–17, 79–94.

61. See section 2 above, esp. text at note 35, above.

62. This aspect of culture history is considered in greater detail in my dissertation, later published as *Kings and Clans.*

63. Ntale's grandfather lived at Lushasha in Irhambi, south of Mpinga, near present-day Katana.

64. Vansina, *Oral Tradition,* 165, table IV, for a classification of this literary tradition; also Vansina, *L'évolution du royaume Rwanda,* 17–38; André Coupez and Thomas Kamanzi, *La littérature de la cour du Rwanda* (Oxford: Clarendon Press, 1974); Alexis Kagame, *Introduction aux grands genres lyriques;* Kagame, *La poésie dynastique;* Smith, *Le récit populaire,* among many other collections. For an extensive sample of historical traditions, see

Jan Vansina, "Ibiteekerezo: Historical Narratives from Rwanda" (CAMP Microfilms, MF-2739) for the most complete collection, and André Coupez and Thomas Kamanzi, eds., *Récits historiques Rwanda, dans la version de C. Gakaniisha* (Tervuren: MRAC, 1962).

65. This tendency is especially apparent in the work of Anicet Kashamura, *Famille, sexualité, et culture* (Paris: Payot, 1973). Although he himself spent his early youth on Ijwi (prior to 1954), and his father held an important administrative position in the southwestern part of the island, the section of his book on Ijwi culture is very strongly reminiscent of Rwandan norms. Many people on Ijwi themselves remarked on this aspect of the book. Indeed, he himself told me this was not intended as an ethnographic study of Ijwi.

66. Philip D. Curtin, "The Uses of Oral Tradition in Senegambia: Maalik Sii and the Foundation of Bundu," *Cahiers d'Études Africaines* 15, no. 2 (1975): 189–207; Phillips Stevens, "The Kisra Legend and the Distortion of Historical Tradition," *Journal of African History* 14, no. 2 (1965): 185–200; Wyatt MacGaffey, "Oral Tradition in Central Africa," *International Journal of African Historical Studies* 7, no. 3 (1975): 417–26; T. O. Beidelman, "Myth, Legend, and Oral History: A Kaguru Traditional Text," *Anthropos* 65 (1970): 74–97; de Heusch, *Le roi ivre*. For a slightly different sort of analysis, see Claude-Hélène Perrot, "Ano Asemã: Mythe et histoire," *Journal of African History* 15, no. 2 (1974): 199–222.

67. The new analytic perspectives of Harold Scheub on the form and dynamics of oral literature, composed of a series of "core images," are an important breakthrough in this regard. Harold Scheub, *The Xhosa Ntsomi* (Oxford: Clarendon Press, 1975).

Chapter 5: The Campaigns of Rwabugiri

This chapter appeared (in French) as an article in
Cahiers d'Études Africaines *14, no. 1 (1974): 181–91.*

1. Rwabugiri is said to have celebrated the annual First Fruits ceremony in thirty-two different locales in the course of his reign. Alexis Kagame, *La notion de génération appliquée à la généalogie dynastique et à l'histoire du Rwanda dès Xe–XIe siècles à nos jours* (Brussels: ARSOM, 1959), 65–67.

2. This is noted in A. Pagès, *Au Rwanda: Sur les bords du Lac Kivu, Congo belge: Un royaume hamite au centre de l'Afrique* (Brussels: IRCB, 1933), 160. Many other sources concur with this conclusion.

3. Among many states that showed significant changes in their military organization during the nineteenth century in Africa, perhaps Buganda is the most notable for this region. Although the intensity of social stratification in Rwanda dampened this process somewhat, the basic processes were similar in Rwanda and Buganda. Among the most valuable sources on this issue for Buganda, see Lloyd Fallers, "Despotism, Status Culture, and Social Mobility in an African Kingdom," *Comparative Studies in Society and History* 2, no. 1 (1959): 11–32; Fallers, ed., *The King's Men: Leadership and Status in Buganda on the Eve of Independence* (London: Oxford University Press for the East African Institute of Social Research, 1964); Marie de Kiewet Hemphill, "The British Sphere, 1884–1894," in *History of East Africa*, vol. 1, ed. Roland Oliver and Gervase Mathew (Oxford: Clarendon Press, 1963), 399–403; M. S. M. Kiwanuka, *A History of Buganda* (London: Longman, 1971); D. A. Low, "The Northern Interior, 1840–1884," in R. Oliver and G. Mathew, eds., *History of East Africa*, vol. 1, ed. Roland Oliver and Gervase Mathew (Oxford: Clarendon

Press, 1963), 331–37; Low, "The Advent of Populism in Buganda," *Comparative Studies in Society and History* 7, no. 4 (1964): 424–44; Low, *Buganda in Modern History* (London: Weidenfeld and Nicolson, 1971); and Michael Wright, *Buganda in the Heroic Age* (London: Oxford University Press, 1971) (who does not accept all the conclusions of the authors previously cited). Low ("Northern Interior," 331) refers to Rwabugiri's "belligerent career" and writes of "the reorganization of the military potential" of his state. He also notes that the most important battles of Rwabugiri were those directed to the north of Rwanda (to Nkore, a part of present-day Uganda). But he bases this conclusion on references in Pagès (*Un royaume hamite*), who is quite imprecise on the wars of Rwabugiri. It is possible that this might only be a question of perspective, but the evidence on which the present analysis is based clearly shows that the principal preoccupations of Rwabugiri were directed toward the regions west of Rwanda; the occasional expeditions directed to the north were not followed up with any consistency.

4. Kagame, *La poésie dynastique du Rwanda* (Brussels: IRCB, 1951); see also Kagame, *La notion de génération;* and Kagame, *Les milices du Rwanda précolonial* (Brussels: ARSOM, 1963).

5. For European sources, that of Pagès is especially relevant (*Un royaume hamite,* 152–71). At the time of the original publication of this article (1974), no thorough study had been made of Rwabugiri's reign in its entirety. However, since that time the work of Kagame, *Un abrégé de l'ethno-histoire du Rwanda précolonial,* vol. 2 (Butare: Éditions universitaires du Rwanda, 1975), 13–103, and Jan Vansina, *Antecedents to Modern Rwanda: The Nyiginya Kingdom* (Madison: University of Wisconsin Press, 2004), 164–95, have filled that gap.

6. Kagame, *La poésie dynastique,* 195, 197, gives the impression that Rwanda governed Ijwi Island immediately after the death of the king Kabego. However, widespread independent testimony from Ijwi is unanimous that after the death of Kabego, only very few Rwandans remained on Ijwi. Political power on the island was turned over to Nkundiye, the son of Kabego, who was the direct subordinate of Rwabugiri; the events around the battle of Kanywilili (discussed below) show that Nkundiye was indeed a favorite at the Rwandan court. Such corroboration lends credibility to the Ijwi accounts on other points as well. (For more detail see the following chapter.)

7. Kagame, *Les milices;* for the interesting events surrounding the succession of Rwabugiri to power, see 153–56, and especially 156n2.

8. Kagame, *La poésie dynastique,* 189; Kagame, *L'histoire des armées bovines dans l'ancien Rwanda* (Brussels: ARSOM, 1961), 38; Kagame, *Les milices,* 85.

9. Poem 125 (in Kagame, *La poésie dynastique,* 190) recounts the expedition against Ijwi as a "triumph": the Rwandans had "mis le feu à Ijwi" (set Ijwi aflame). According to multiple Ijwi sources, however, this poem could refer only to the second campaign against the island for in these local accounts the Rwandans were repelled before even arriving. (See chapter 6, this volume.) Kagame dates this poem to the first campaign because he mentions also the queen mother, who had died before the second campaign took place. Thus we are led to the conclusion that either the poem describes a fictive outcome or it confuses the conditions of the first attack with the result of the second.

10. Pagès, *Un royaume hamite,* 154ff.

11. Kagame, *Les milices,* 46. The queen mother died very early in the reign of Rwabugiri.

12. Kagame, *La poésie dynastique*, 190.

13. Kagame, *Les milices*, 46.

14. Kagame, *La poésie dynastique*, 190.

15. Pagès, *Un royaume hamite*, 195, adds the name *Bushengere* to this campaign.

16. Again, it is difficult to be precise on the dates. See the reference in Kagame, *La notion de génération*, 68, where he notes that "it has been impossible to establish with certitude the chronological order of these events" during the period that includes the probable date of the Bumpaka expedition.

17. Pagès, *Un royaume hamite*, 195; Kagame, *La poésie dynastique*, 129–33, 191–92; Kagame, *L'histoire des armées bovines*, 109; Kagame, *Les milices*, 46, 116.

18. A military herd—"une armée bovine"—was a herd of cattle given a particular name and assigned by the king to a particular social army; the herder was directly designated by the king (although in fact this position might often become quasi-hereditary through several generations). Such a herdsman often had responsibilities to the king; Kagame, *L'histoire des armées bovines*, esp. 5–11.

19. Kagame, *L'histoire des armées bovines*, 102–12.

20. Kagame, *La poésie dynastique*, 191, where the summary of poem 129 refers to the "insolence" of an unspecified "king"—again a reference to personal vengeance. Also Kagame, *Les milices*, 139.

21. Léon Delmas, *Les généalogies de la noblesse (les Batutsi) du Ruanda* (Kabgayi, Rwanda: Vicariat apostolique du Rwanda, 1950), 355; Kagame, *La poésie dynastique*, 192–93; Kagame, *Les milices*, 134, 141, 152–53.

22. Kagame, *Les milices*, 153, 157. Other motives also seem possible for such a policy against Nkoronko; cf. Kagame, *Les milices*, 156n, and Kagame, *La poésie dynastique*, 192, where it is implied that Nkoronko supported a competitor to the throne, Nyamwesa. Kagame, *Les milices*, 157 leaves the impression that the great popularity of Nkoronko could be considered as a threat by Rwabugiri, and that his death could therefore be an example of the increasing campaign to reduce any centers of political opposition that did not depend directly on the king.

23. On the basic facts surrounding the execution of Nkoronko, see Kagame, *La poésie dynastique*, 193; Kagame, *L'histoire des armées bovines*, 98, 102; Kagame, *Les milices*, 157, 134, 152–53, 163. Pagès, *Un royaume hamite* 191; 165–66, cites another version of the history of Nkoronko. This is repeated in Louis de Lacger, *Le Ruanda*, 2nd ed. (Kabgayi, Rwanda: Imprimérie de Kabgayi, 1961), 355.

24. In fact, it seems that Rwabugiri never arrived all the way to Butembo, a region well to the west of Lake Kivu, beyond the Mitumba mountain chain. These attacks were instead directed against the Hunde states, north of Lake Kivu, and especially against Bunyungu, one of those kingdoms. Nonetheless, all Rwandan sources refer to this expedition as that directed against Butembo; to avoid confusion, this essay will retain that term. The best description of this campaign in the Rwandan sources is that of Kagame, *Les milices*, 139. The manner by which Kagame arrives at the date of 1874 for this expedition is found in Kagame, *La poésie dynastique*, 163n227, and Kagame, *La notion de génération*, 68.

25. Kagame, *La poésie dynastique*, 193; Kagame, *La notion de génération*, 67; Kagame, *L'histoire des armées bovines*, 38, 87; Kagame, *Les milices*, 139, 157.

26. Kagame, *Les milices*, 47, 79.

27. Kagame, *La poésie dynastique*, 196, poem 143, and poem 144.

28. Pagès, *Un royaume hamite*, 154; Kagame, *La poésie dynastique*, 195; Kagame, *Les milices*, 166. Moreover, a note in Kagame, *La poésie dynastique*, 195, mentions another disastrous defeat at Murago, which does not appear in any other source.

29. Kagame, *La poésie dynastique*, 195; for a full recitation on the death of Rwanyonga, see Coupez and Kamanzi, *Récits historiques Rwanda*, 318–27.

30. Pagès, *Un royaume hamite*, 154; Kagame, *La poésie dynastique*, 198; Kagame, *L'histoire des armées bovines*, 87; Kagame, *Les milices*, 141, 147.

31. Kagame, *Les milices*, 147.

32. Nyamushanja (of the Abega clan, Abakagara lineage) was the grandson of the brother of the mother of Rwogera, the predecessor of Rwabugiri. He was married to the consanguineal sister of Rwabugiri (a woman of the same mother and same father as Rwabugiri); he was the half-brother of Kabare, the most influential person in Rwabugiri's succession and the power behind the throne during the early years in the court of Musinga, the successor to Rwabugiri; he was the half-brother of Sharibabaza, a wife of Rwogera, and of Kanjogera, a wife of Rwabugiri and later the queen mother of Rutarindwa and of Musinga (her biological son), the two successors to Rwabugiri (Kagame, *L'histoire des armées bovines*, 87, 89; Delmas, *Les généalogies*, 116 ff., esp. 125). It was this family that took power during the coup d'état of Rucunshu in 1896, following Rwabugiri's death.

33. Kagame, *Les milices*, 139. For another version of the fall of Giharamagara, see Pagès, *Un royaume hamite*, 165–66, 191.

34. Kagame, *Les milices*, 141.

35. There is no doubt that much mutual jealousy existed at this time both between armies and among individual soldiers. Kagame cites at least two examples of open conflict between two Rwandan armies (*Les milices*, 46, 95–96, 124, 137, 146, 155, 157, 172). Ijwi accounts affirm that Nkundiye (the son of Kabego) participated in the battle of Kanywilili, and that it was only after Kanywilili that Nkundiye lost favor at the Rwandan court. Ijwi informants cite two reasons for that: first, that Nkundiye's success as a fighter elicited the jealousy of others; and second, that he had in fact "killed" (or was accused of killing) certain important Rwandan leaders at Kanywilili. Rwandan and Ijwi sources agree that Nkundiye had been the head of a regiment from Ijwi that had been incorporated in the "Nyange" army; Nyamushanja's army was "Uruyange" (sometimes cited as "Utuyange").

36. Kagame, *La poésie dynastique*, 145, 197; Kagame, *L'histoire des armées bovines*, 104. The attacks against Mpinga and Irhambi are nowhere mentioned in the sources currently available.

37. This date is based on the fact that Kabare participated in this campaign; yet he was promoted to lead his army only after the enthronement of Rutarindwa as "co-régent" of Rwabugiri, an event that occurred in 1889, according to Kagame, *La notion de génération*, 66, 67; and Kagame, *Les milices*, 141, 169.

38. Kagame, *La poésie dynastique*, 195–96, 200; Kagame, *Les milices*, 141, 164; Pagès, *Un royaume hamite*, 164; Paul Masson, *Trois siècles chez les Bashi* (Tervuren: MRAC, 1962), 87–88. Kagame dates this battle as occurring at the same time as Kanywilili; *La poésie dynastique*, 196.

39. Kagame, *L'histoire des armées bovines*, 112.

40. Kagame, *Les milices*, 161. Many sources give the impression that Rwabugiri was very interested in the development of commerce; Pagès, *Un royaume hamite*, 160–63; de Lacger, *Le Ruanda*, 344–45; Kagame, *Les milices*, 161–62, all show Rwabugiri appearing favorable to commercial ties with the East African coast.

41. Kagame, *Les milices*, 59, 59n, 91, 151–52; it is also possible that another reference to this incident is found in Pagès, *Un royaume hamite*, 172.

42. Other unpublished sources indicate that the occupation could have been part of another attack against Bushi, without result, in which Rwabugiri would have crossed the Rusizi; instead of having deserted their post, these men could have been defeated by Shi forces. I am grateful to Richard Sigwalt for having made me aware of these unpublished sources.

43. Pagès, *Un royaume hamite*, 195: "the expedition could not have lasted more than two months."

44. Ibid., 176–77: "Although defeated, the inhabitants of Nkore [*sic*] were only apparently conquered"; Kagame, *Les milices*, 48, 74, 129, 141; Donald Denoon, *A History of Kigezi in Southwestern Uganda* (Kampala: National Trust, 1972), 15; D. Z. Rwabihigi gives the impression that Rwabugiri's attack was only very short, without meaningful effect on the politics of Nkore: "Chief Katuregye: The Man and His Times," in Denoon, *History of Kigezi*, 141, 143.

45. Kagame, *Les milices*, 119, 129.

46. Samwiri R. Karugire, *A History of the Kingdom of Nkore in Western Uganda to 1896* (Oxford: Clarendon Press, 1971), 229–30; Low 1963, 331. Although it was clear that Rwabugiri pursued a policy against Nkore throughout his reign (Denoon, *History of Kigezi*, 14), the goals of this policy were limited to seizing pasture for cattle; it was only at the end of his reign that Rwabugiri aimed for a true conquest of Nkore, including the occupation and administration of the conquered terrain. If this were his objective, he failed because of the arrival of Europeans in Nkore.

Chapter 6: Rwabugiri and Ijwi

This chapter appeared as an article in Études d'Histoire Africaine *7 (1975): 155–73.*

1. This chapter is intended as a case study of the broader external wars of Rwabugiri, as discussed in the preceding chapter. I am indebted to Mwami Ntambuka Barhahakana of Ijwi, his son, Citoyen Ntambuka Nsibula, and to the many informants who so willingly contributed to this study. The author expresses his gratitude also to Dr. Ntika-Nkumu, Directeur-General of the Institut de Recherche Scientifique en Afrique Centrale, for support with the research. Richard Sigwalt, Keith Rennie, and Jan Vansina contributed valuable comments on an earlier draft of this chapter.

2. For these larger campaigns see chapter 5, this volume.

3. Albert A. Trouwborst refers to this aspect of *bugabire* in a small number of cases in Burundi, occurring principally between two important men; but he also refers to the inequality of the relationship under other circumstances. This last aspect of bugabire is rarely found on Ijwi. Trouwborst, "Le Burundi," in *Les anciens royaumes de la zone interlacustre méridionale*, ed. M. d'Hertefelt, Albert A. Trouwborst, and J. H. Scherer (Tervuren: MRAC, 1962), 151–52. See also Roger Botte, "Burundi: La relation *ubugabire* dans la tête de ceux qui la décrivent," *Cahiers d'Études Africaines* 9, no. 3 (1969): 363–71.

4. For the unresolved discussion of cattle relations in Rwanda, see Pierre Bettez Gravel, "The Transfer of Cows in Gisaka (Rwanda): A Mechanism for the Recording of Social Relationships," *American Anthropologist* 69, nos. 3–4 (1967): 322–31; Gravel, *Remera: A Community in Eastern Rwanda* (The Hague: Mouton, 1968), 24–25 and 157–69; Claudine

Vidal, "Le Rwanda des anthropologues ou le fétischisme de la vache," *Cahiers d'Études Africaines* 9, no. 3 (1969): 384–401; Jacques J. Maquet, "Institutionalisation féodale des relations de dependence," *Cahiers d'Études Africaines* 9, no. 3 (1969): 402–14, and the sources cited in these works. See also Catharine Newbury, *The Cohesion of Oppression: Clientship and Ethnicity in Rwanda, 1860–1960* (New York: Columbia University Press, 1988).

5. For an example of how clientship served as an instrument of central court control in Rwanda, see Catharine Newbury, "Deux lignages au Kinyaga," *Cahiers d'Études Africaines* 14, no. 1 (1974): 26–39.

6. These attitudes are expressed often in the Rwandan literature. See, for example, the following works by Kagame: *La poésie dynastique du Rwanda* (Brussels: IRCB, 1951), 9, 9n1; *L'histoire des armées bovines dans l'ancien Rwanda* (Brussels: ARSOM, 1961), 115; *Un abrégé de l'ethno-histoire du Rwanda précolonial*, vol. 1 (Butare: Éditions universitaires du Rwanda, 1972), 209.

7. In *La poésie dynastique*, 9n1, Kagame states that Kabego himself spent his youth at the court of Gahindiro, although this is not confirmed on Ijwi. It might be noted that on Ijwi a man is often referred to by the name of his father; thus (although in Rwanda such practice is much less frequent) Kagame's statement may be a reference to Kabego's sons, on whom Ijwi traditions are clear.

8. The Rwandan sources confirm the broad outline of these events but add some detail and assign them slightly different causes. Kagame remarks that "Kabego se révolta à la mort de Mutara II Rwogera, successeur de Yuhi IV, à la suite du refus de la Cour d'accepter les présents que le souverain vassal avait envoyés à son maître durant les derniers jours de sa maladie" *(La poésie dynastique,* 10n1). He enlarges on this in a later work (*Un abrégé,* vol. 1, 209), saying that Kabego had sent a large caravan of "redevances traditionnelles" by which Kabego is said to have recognized the suzerainty of the king of Rwanda (it has been pointed out above that the Bany'Iju view the relationship as one of alliance, not of suzerainty). But Rwogera, the king of Rwanda at that time, was on his deathbed; the court councilors refused to accept the gift, which was returned to Ijwi. From this time, continues Kagame, Kabego refused to send further "tribute" to Rwanda, and "ne voulut rien avoir de commun avec le roi du Rwanda."

9. For a full account of these attacks from the Rwandan perspective, see R. Bourgeois, *Ethnographie,* vol. 1 of *Banyarwanda et Barundi* (Brussels: ARSOM, 1957), 153–60. In this account, the general facts are similar but the details differ slightly from the Ijwi accounts; in particular, Bourgeois seems to have telescoped data from different battles into a single campaign, if the Ijwi reports are believed.

10. Chapter 5, this volume, pp. 136–137.

11. On Ijwi there is little precise knowledge of this attack, except for the fact that Rwabugiri succeeded in penetrating the island in the north, while he had failed in his more direct frontal assault on the south. Circumstantial evidence would imply that Tabaro had reached some sort of entente with Rwabugiri, either before the attack or later, as a result of assistance given to Rwabugiri at the time of the attacks. After Kabego's death, Tabaro maintained and in fact strengthened his position in the north. On Tabaro's death, his children fled from Nkundiye to Rwanda (i.e., to Rwabugiri's protection); finally, testimony from the south implies that during the occupation that followed, Rwandan rule was milder in the north.

12. This reference in the traditions is undoubtedly to the Kanywilili affair, where Rwandan armies (including a regiment assembled by Nkundiye) were defeated on the mainland, not on Ijwi. After the defeat, Nkundiye's army was accused of abandoning their Rwandan commander, a favorite of Rwabugiri. Many on Ijwi explicitly associate Nkundiye's downfall with the Rwandan defeat at Kanywilili, saying that Nkundiye excelled in this battle, notwithstanding the Rwandan defeat. It was this excellence—and the search for a vulnerable scapegoat—they continue, that attracted the jealousy of other Rwandan soldiers and resulted in Nkundiye's eventual fall from favor.

13. Pagès also reports that Katobera was killed by Rwabugiri in Rwanda (*Un royaume hamite*, 192).

14. For a more complete discussion of these issues, see my *Kings and Clans: Ijwi Island and the Lake Kivu Rift, 1780–1840* (Madison: University of Wisconsin Press, 1991), chaps. 5–7.

15. Some accounts deny there were Rwandan chiefs on Ijwi until after Nkundiye's death. The references to Nkundiye's conflicts with Rwandan chiefs and the confiscation of their cattle would refute this; however it is still possible that these refer to conflicts at the Rwandan court and not on the island.

16. Kagame refers to this bull as "Nkurumugoyo" (*L'histoire des armées bovines*, 115).

17. Anicet Kashamura, *Famille, sexualité, et culture* (Paris: Payot, 1973).

18. See chapter 5, this volume.

Chapter 7: King and Chief on Ijwi Island

This chapter appeared as an article in International Journal
of African Historical Studies *15, no. 2 (1982): 221–46.*

1. Recently, of course, this problem has received much greater attention; for examples from the Kivu area, see Elinor Sosne, "Colonial Peasantization and Contemporary Underdevelopment: A View from a Kivu Village," in *Zaïre: The Political Economy of Underdevelopment*, ed. Guy Gran (New York: Praeger, 1979), 189–210; and Catharine Newbury, *The Cohesion of Oppression: Clientship and Ethnicity in Rwanda, 1860–1960* (New York: Columbia University Press, 1988).

2. Joan Vincent, "Colonial Chiefs and the Making of Class: A Case Study from Teso, Eastern Uganda," *Africa* 47, no. 2 (1977): 155–56.

3. On the arrival of the Basibula dynasty on Ijwi, see chapter 4, this volume. The cleavages within the royal family on Ijwi during the late nineteenth century are explored in chapter 6, this volume.

4. Early settlement on Ijwi is considered more fully in David Newbury, *Kings and Clans: Ijwi Island and the Lake Kivu Rift, 1780–1840* (Madison: University of Wisconsin Press, 1991), chaps. 5–7.

5. Rwabugiri's military campaigns are explored in chapter 5, this volume; for their impact on Ijwi politics, see chapter 6, this volume.

6. From 1899 to 1905 German and Belgian officers (serving in the Congo Free State army) alternated in raising their respective flags over Ijwi. Some years later, in 1910, representatives of Germany, Belgium, and Britain agreed to colonial boundaries in the Kivu

area that left Ijwi Island within the Belgian sphere. (Germany had been reluctant to relinquish claims over Ijwi, in part because there was by then a German missionary presence on the island). For a more complete consideration of these competing imperial claims, see William Roger Louis, *Ruanda-Urundi, 1884–1919* (Oxford: Clarendon Press, 1963), 58–59, 86–87, 90–91.

7. The post was located at the very southern tip of Ijwi at Kagi (in the Nyakalengwa area of the island), facing across the lake toward Shangi (Rwanda), where the major German post of southwestern Rwanda was located.

8. Ndogosa was recognized as chief of Ijwi Island and of the surrounding islands by Procès Verbale No. 49 of April 30, 1913.

9. Many people mentioned men killed by Europeans "whose only friends were the planks in the forest." Bany'Iju often had to drag huge logs from the forest and saw them into planks for the Europeans. No pay was offered for such requisitioned labor; some accounts go so far as to claim the workers were chained together. The context of the times is illustrated in the Ijwi sobriquet given to A. Verdonck, the best-known administrator on the south of the island. He was called "Funga-Funga" (Swahili for "to close" or "to lock up"), a name referring to his predilection for imprisoning people for the most trivial reasons. Verdonck is associated with exceptionally cruel policies. It is widely recounted that when people pronounced the colloquialism "nafire na njala" (I am dead with hunger) or "nafire na ndwala" (I am dead with illness), Funga-Funga would sometimes bury the man alive, saying that if he were dead, then he must be buried.

10. Among the testimonies that emphasize raiding cattle and killing men as two characteristics of European arrival are Bakengamwami 6/24/72; Bashwira 4/27/72; Bikenyere 1/31/73; Bugabanda 8/7/72; Gahungura 6/6/72; Kamaka 6/34/72; Kamusinzi 3/28/72; Mafundo 3/22/72; Magamba 3/7/72; Makanira 5/30/72; Bukatara 4/29/72; Munyankiko 5/28/72; Ngwije 6/33/72; Nyamukaza 2/7/73; Rubaka 2/9/73; Rwankuba 3/8/72; Shamavu 2/9/73.

11. This is the version noted in "Histoire de l'Île Idjwi" (typescript, n.p., n.d. [early 1960s]; hereafter "Histoire Idjwi"), a narrative based on official documents and oral accounts compiled in the 1960s by several members of the modern Ijwi elite. The incident of the fish, based on reports of a German missionary on Ijwi at the time, is also noted in Louis, *Ruanda-Urundi*, 190–91; Bweshe 6/13/72; Gahangaza 6/9/72.

12. "Rapport d'enquête préalable à la construction de la Chefferie, et résumé de l'Histoire du Buhavu (Contribution Verdonck ou R. P. Feys)" (White Fathers Archives, Bukavu); hereafter cited as "Rapport d'enquête . . . [sur] l'Histoire du Buhavu." For testimony from Ijwi, see also Kilumera 2/1/73; Munyantole 5/21/74; Murhanyi 5/30/72; Mwanganya 5/30/72; Nyamulisa 5/31/72; Ruzigamanzi 5/31/72.

13. Accounts from Ijwi confirm that there was Bany'Iju involvement, but versions differ as to the extent of that involvement. One version states that Mugenzi, after having obtained permission from his father, went to Gisenyi in Rwanda and asked the Germans to come and expel the Belgians. The German forces set out in canoes, accompanied by Rwagataraka, a powerful Tutsi chief who commanded a large portion of southwest Rwanda. They were able to take positions on the hill behind Kagi without the Belgians being aware of their presence ("Histoire Idjwi"). Mugenzi's own account does not mention such direct collaboration; he does, however, note that "he worked with" the Germans

during their occupation of Ijwi (1914–16). It was common knowledge on Ijwi that Mugenzi had been a partisan of the Germans; Mugenzi learned how to use a gun from them, and two Germans accompanied him on a raid against Lugendo, an area on the western shore of the lake. Mugenzi 6/5/72; Caruhinga 6/9/72; Gahagaza 6/9/72; Bweshe 6/13/72.

14. For analyses of the development of German colonial structures in Rwanda, see Alison Des Forges, "Defeat Is the Only Bad News: Rwanda under Musiinga" (PhD diss., Yale University, 1972); Ian Linden and Jane Linden, *Church and Revolution in Rwanda* (Manchester: Manchester University Press, 1977); C. Newbury, *Cohesion of Oppression.*

15. Political sovereignty and popular support were but the external reflections of deeper concepts of legitimacy tied to ritual autonomy and authority—and the royal rituals could only be properly performed by the joint participation of many recognized ritualists drawn from diverse social groups on the island. During colonial rule the effectiveness of colonially imposed authorities—following the exile of the ritually enthroned king—was severely compromised because they could not assemble the ritualists to perform the required rites. Lacking consecration as king through the performance of prescribed rituals, these pretenders never succeeded in gaining the compliance of the population at large. For a consideration of the changing concepts of political legitimacy on Ijwi during the nineteenth century, see my *Kings and Clans.* For a more general discussion of the conceptual framework related to royal legitimacy, see chapter 10, this volume.

16. Throughout the Congo, withdrawal of this type was a common response to the European superiority in weapons. See Allen Isaacman and Jan Vansina, "African Initiatives and Resistance in Central Africa, 1880–1914," in *Africa under Colonial Domination, 1880–1935,* ed. A. Adu Boahen (Berkeley and Los Angeles: University of California Press, 1985), 169–93. For a consideration of this behavior as one among many forms of resistance, see Allen Isaacman and Barbara Isaacman, "Resistance and Collaboration in Southern and Central Africa, c. 1850–1920," *International Journal of African Historical Studies* 10, no. 1 (1977): 31–62.

17. The Belgians believed that Ndogosa remained in hiding because he was implicated in the death of two Congolese soldiers who had become separated from their fellows during the German invasion of the island in 1914. In their efforts to reach the mainland, they had shot and killed a number of Ndogosa's subjects, including two important members of the royal family. To avenge these deaths, emissaries of Ndogosa's nephew offered to lead the soldiers to the Catholic mission at Mwanda, on the mainland near Katana. Instead, the soldiers were taken in a canoe to Iko Island, where they were killed with spears. This is the account cited in "Rapport d'enquête . . . [sur] l'Histoire du Buhavu" and "Histoire Idjwi." But Ijwi oral accounts elaborate on this, explaining that on Iko the soldiers requisitioned a canoe with oarsmen who selected a leaky canoe caulked only with grass; far out into the lake they pulled the caulking, jumped overboard, and swam ashore. Burdened by their heavy boots and clothes, the soldiers drowned in the lake.

18. The most famous example of this is the execution of Camukenge, one of Ndogosa's most important advisors. When the Belgians summoned Ndogosa, Camukenge presented himself as Ndogosa's representative but refused to divulge the whereabouts of his patron. Consequently he was, as the traditions relate in detail, buried alive up to his neck. When he still refused to talk, his tongue was cut out; many add that he was then shot. This story is widely known on southern Ijwi, often used as a metaphor both of Belgian brutality in

this period and of Ijwi resistance and honor. Among such references are Batindi 3/24/2; Bikere 3/21/72; Burhola 3/20/72; Gaherwa 3/20/72; Kamusinzi 3/28/72; Malekera 5/1/72; Mutanyerera 5/11/72; Ngonyosi 5/7/4; Ruginyambuga 3/28/72; Rugo 6/14/74.

19. The official portraits of administrative effectiveness stand in stark contrast to the reality on Ijwi. At a slightly later period, the colonial authorities noted that "the military occupation continues on the south [of Ijwi]. . . . All is calm there and the results from tax collection and various work schemes [e.g., forced labor] are most satisfactory" ("Rapport d'enquête . . . [sur] l'Histoire du Buhavu"). A more eloquent expression of the guiding principles of the day is found in the words of the Prince de Ligne, who established a plantation on Ijwi shortly before Ndogosa's death: "Au Kivu, l'administration, les missions, et quelques colons formaient la charpente d'une civilisation naissante." Eugène Prince de Ligne, *Africa: L'évolution d'un continent vue des volcans du Kivu* (Brussels: Librarie Générale, 1961), 98.

20. The early raids are remembered in Gahengera 6/6/72; Kamusinzi 3/28/72; Kanywesi 5/16/74; Magamba 3/7/72; Munyankiko 5/18/72; Musahura 3/17/72; Ndengeyi 6/2/72. Of the later raids those of Lushombo, the mainland Havu king of Mpinga, are especially remembered; Gacuka 5/16/74; Gihire 3/31/73; Kadusi 1/26/73; Kohonze Shabuli 3/23/72; Mulahuko 5/13/74; Rubaka 2/9/73; Shamavu 2/9/73. The mood on Ijwi was duly noted in the European documents relating to this period (1920): "Lushombo [the king of Buhavu, and a colonial ally] dared to go [to Ijwi] only when accompanied by a European" ("Rapport d'enquête . . . [sur] l'Histoire du Buhavu").

21. "Rapport d'enquête . . . [sur] l'Histoire du Buhavu" noted for the period 1918–20 that "famine reigned. . . . The entire area was impoverished by the war, especially Ijwi Island, which was submitted to German military occupation, followed by a [Belgian] military operation on the German withdrawal. The cattle herds were severely reduced. . . . Several epidemics (cerebro-spinal meningitis, smallpox, dysentery) seriously affected the population. Many thousands of deaths followed." Subsequent cattle and human epidemics were also noted in the reports for the years 1922 and 1926.

22. The decline of the herds is mentioned by many: Gacuka 5/16/74; Kamusinzi 3/28/72; Kihonzi 3/23/72; Magamba 3/7/72; Makanda 3/27/72; Ndengeyi 6/2/72; Ntayira 5/15/72; Rubasha 3/24/72; Ruginyambuga 3/28/72; Rukomera 3/21/72; Rulinda 4/17/72; Rwantunda 3/30/72. In addition to those jailed or exiled, many people either withdrew into the forest areas or fled Ijwi completely. The government documents, sketchy as they are, make this abundantly clear: 1917: "une grande partie de la population fuiaient devant les blancs;" 1922 (on the exile of Mugenzi): "la plupart de ses partisans [those of Mugenzi] se refugiaient au Ruanda, emportant avec eux une grande partie du bétail de l'île;" 1926: "nous ayons à y déplorer [à Ijwi] l'exode en masse vers le Ruanda et l'Unya-Bongo [Bushi] des anciens sujets de Mihigo [Ndogosa]" ("Rapport d'enquête . . . [sur] l'Histoire du Buhavu").

23. The administrative accounts for 1928 note that: "L'Administrateur Territorial du Buhavu s'est rendu à Ishara (Ruanda) où il a rencontré le délégué du Résident de Shangugu. Il est parti le lendemain à Kibimbi (Ruanda) où il a rencontré le délégué du Résident de Lubengera. But: remise de tranfuges; 109 hommes, 100 femmes, et 123 enfants originaires de l'Ile Idjwi on été renvoyés dans leur chefferie d'origine. . . . En décembre 1928 l'Administrateur Territorial de l'Unya-Bongo [Bushi] est venu et a été entretenu à vive voix de la question de tranfuges. Banya-Idjwi toujours nombreux dans l'Unya-

Bongo." ("Rapport d'enquête . . . [sur] l'Histoire du Buhavu"; the numbers cited, of course, apply only to a small fraction of those affected.)

24. Ibid.

25. The chiefdoms were those headed by Nakalonge (Kalonge), Bigilimani (Boban-dana), Mihigo (Ijwi), Mukuku (Mpinga Nord), and Kitchwa-Molefu (Buzi). Later, other such groupements were those under Musikami (Kalima) and Ndalemwa (Mubugu), while Buzi and Bobandana were fused into a single chiefdom under Bigilimana.

26. "Rapport d'enquête . . . [sur] l'Histoire du Buhavu."

27. Bweshe 6/13/72; Caruhinga 6/9/72; Gatumwa 6/10/72; Mbaraga 3/21/75; Ruboneza 6/10/72; Rwangayo 6/14/72; Rwankuba 3/8/72. There was obviously a conflict between Ndogosa and Mugenzi, but the source of the conflict is not clear. A standard Ijwi version suggests that Ndogosa was displeased at the way Mugenzi was treating the population in general, and especially Ndogosa's personal clients. To increase his standing before those who had put him in office, Mugenzi threatened and tortured even the most beloved of his father's *bashamuka* (local family heads). "What Migho [Ndogosa] expected from his son was no longer being accomplished; instead, any positive effects were being counteracted by a deception which even the greatest enemies of Mihigo were criticizing. . . . Ndogosa then decided: 'I will come out of hiding; better that I die rather than wait while my men are mistreated by a son whom I myself sent.'" This is the account given in "Histoire Idjwi." The Belgian account in "Rapport d'enquête . . . [sur] l'Histoire du Buhavu" notes only that in 1922 conflicts were emerging between supporters of Mugenzi and supporters of Ndogosa. The oral accounts cited above corroborate the "Histoire Idjwi" version, men-tioning especially Mugenzi's treatment of Nkingi, one of Ndogosa's closest advisors.

28. This conversation is cited in "Histoire Idjwi."

29. The Belgians had excised from the Ijwi kingdom several islands (which were placed under the authority of Lushombo) and the peninsula of Ishungu (which was in-corporated into the Territoire de l'Unya-Bongo [Bushi]). Kacuka 8/14/72; Mayange 6/18/74; Mushayuma 8/14/72; Ndengeyi 6/2/72; Nangurane 5/24/72; Rukanika 4/27/72; Rusingiza 6/10/72. The general thrust of these testimonies (and others) is illustrated by Kinyonya 3/20/72: "Mwendanga held Iko, Ibinja, Ishungu, Rambira, Nyamisi [all islands and peninsulas south and west of Ijwi]—all the islands were formerly part of Mwen-danga's domain. They were lost at the time of Ndogosa. The Belgians took them. . . . There was no fight over them. Other bami made trouble for Ndogosa at the time of the Belgians. He became like a conquered king (*muhunyi*) because all of Ijwi was taken by Bera. First, all of Ijwi was claimed by Lushombo; the Belgians gave it to him. Then, Lushombo di-rected Bera to take over the administration of Ijwi." The arbitrary nature of such trans-fers is evident in "Rapport d'enquête . . . [sur] l'Histoire du Buhavu," where the Belgian administrators show they were aware of the domain of the Ijwi kings, as it notes that Iko (one of the islands) was transferred to the administrative domain of Kamerogosa "pour donner à Lushombo un témoignage de notre satisfaction. . . . Cette île [Iko], qui jadis avait été (comme toutes les îles du Lac Kivu) occupée par les Bahavu, était administrée avant la guerre [1914–18] par Mihigo [Ndogosa]."

30. District du Kivu, Décision No. 4, du 2 avril 1926.

31. Arrêté No. 14, du 14 mai 1926.

32. "Histoire Idjwi"; "Rapport d'enquête . . . [sur] l'Histoire du Buhavu."

33. Arrêté No. 141, du 30 octobre 1928.

34. The Belgians tried several approaches unsuccessfully. Earlier they had appointed Ciraba (son of Ciriba, son of Mwendanga, and therefore a first cousin to Ndogosa) to rule, but he held no influence over the population. They then appointed Nyanguranye as a delegated authority on Ijwi. It was a poor choice. Nyanguranye was the soldier who had guarded Ndogosa at Kalehe following his arrest. It was Nyanguranye who had imposed the harsh conditions and required that Ndogosa perform demeaning physical labor. At one point, Nyanguranye apparently struck Ndogosa and knocked out his two incisors— the teeth essential for ritual ceremonies of burial. The act prompted Ndogosa to curse Nyanguranye publicly. But by his firm treatment of Ndogosa, Nyanguranye came to the notice of the Belgians as a strict disciplinarian, and it was this status that led them to appoint him as the colonial administrative delegate on Ijwi. Within a few months he was assassinated by Rutwaza and his "band" of fifty men—a deed which was later, in turn, to lead to Rutwaza's exile. Thus ironically, it was Nyanguranye's elevation in the colonial ranks (through his treatment of Ndogosa) that led directly to his death ("Histoire Idjwi"; among the Ijwi accounts of this, see especially Rutaguramura 6/2/72).

35. Among others, see Bendera 2/16/73; Camboko 2/16/73; Garhwanywa 2/14/73; Gihire 1/31/73; Rubambura 2/16/73.

36. "Rapport d'enquête . . . [sur] l'Histoire du Buhavu."

37. Ibid.

38. Ibid.

39. Ibid.; the fifty men were those implicated in the assassination of Nyanguranye (see note 35.)

40. Ibid.

41. Ibid.

42. Ibid.

43. "Histoire Idjwi" cites several of these abuses, and notes that evidence on Rutishereka's abuses had been brought to the attention of the Belgian administration by Catholic missionaries. (A Catholic mission was established on Ijwi in 1936; before that, the island had been regularly visited by Catholic missionaries from the Congolese mainland, and they were well informed on events of the island—see, e.g., the diary of the Mission of Liège St. Lambert, Mwanda [Katana].) But the real causal factors, in the eyes of both the government reports and the Ijwi population, were related to the Mugote tax revolt on eastern Ijwi.

44. In explaining the eventual recall of Ntambuka, the "Rapport d'enquête . . . [sur] l'Histoire du Buhavu" summarizes the situation thus: "Des incidents se produisèrent au début de janvier 1937 dans quelques villages de la région de Mugote à l'occasion de la perception de l'impôt. En résumé, le situation politique avait provoqué un malaise général; la perception de l'impôt était pénible, les villages étaient désertés à l'approche de l'européen et la population opposait l'inertie à tous les orders de l'authorité. Un Agent Territorial fut envoyé sur place avec une escorte renforcée de 18 soldats, afin d'intimider les indigènes et de ramener plus promptement le calme dans la population. Les travaux [forced labor] reprirent mais la nombre de transfuges ne diminua pas. La grande majorité de la population souhaitait le retour de Ntambuka, fils de Mihigo, relégué à Lubero."

45. "Histoire Idjwi"; "Rapport d'enquête . . . [sur] l'Histoire du Buhavu."

46. Gashina 5/6/74; Nadorho 2/9/73; Shanzige 2/8/73.

47. This point is illustrated by an incident that occurred soon after Ntambuka returned to Ijwi. A Belgian administrative officer was sent to the island to delimit the boundaries between the north and south. Upon his arrival at Ijwi-Sud, accompanied by his wife, he found the beach deserted. He viewed this as a great insult; it was apparently expected that a visiting Belgian official would be greeted with an escort of people and a litter with bearers. Upon hearing of the official's arrival, Ntambuka and his men had set out from the *bwami* to meet him. But by that time, the Belgian and his wife had already climbed halfway up the hill and they were furious. The subsequent meeting went badly: with the Belgian official ultimately prohibited Ntambuka from accompanying him on his boundary delimitation mission. By contrast, when the Belgian arrived in the north, Rubenga and a large crowd of people were waiting to "acclaim" him and give him a warm welcome ("Histoire Idjwi").

48. Ntambuka was deported because of taxation irregularities in which one of his sons was implicated. (This son was later virtually disinherited by the king; he permanently lost status at the court, which he rarely visited; and he played no influential role in more recent Ijwi politics.) It is significant that the tax irregularities were brought to the attention of the colonial authorities by Rubenga—Ntambuka's antagonist and rival, who had clearly hoped to gain from Ntambuka's exile—rather than by action of the population, as occurred under Bera.

49. One of Muhamiriza's daughters was Kamerogosa's senior wife (Mwanyundo).

50. Procès verbale de la réunion du Conseil du Territoire Kalehe, 18–20 novembre 1954; Ntambuka Barhahakana to Gouverneur de la Province du Kivu, Fizi, 12 juillet 1956; Administrateur Territorial Kalehe to CommDistrict s/Kivu, 14 mars 1958.

51. "Histoire Idjwi."

52. This was one typical statement to this effect: "The Europeans came and took my cows. During the time of Bera they came with soldiers to look for cows; Bera was required to produce cows every month. I also worked at Kalehe for no pay; I had to do it so they wouldn't seize my banana trees. And I worked for the *mwami* a lot! At Bugarula [Bera's administrative seat] I used to fetch water, cut wood, pay court. I received nothing for this work; not a franc! I did it to avoid being beaten; if I hadn't gone to work when Rubenga commanded me to, he would have seized my banana grove. Normally a *mwami* could not take back land once given, but during the European period if one didn't go to Kalehe when commanded, they could take back your land, and there was nothing to be done about it."

53. On Bera's marriage ties, see, among others, Gacuka 5/16/74; Gahala 1/30/73; Kuzanwa 1/29/73; Masasa 2/14/74; Mbogobogo 4/26/74; Miringa 4/30/74; Nadorho 2/9/73; Rubaka 2/9/73; Rukanika 5/21/74.

54. Ntambuka 4/20/72, 4/21/72, 3/9/73, 3/19/75.

55. Kabango 6/7/72; Malekera 5/22/74; Mesobukina 5/3/72; Ngoyozi Bifuko 5/10/74; Ngonyozi Ruticambuka 5/7/74; Ngwasi 6/13/72; Rugwira 6/26/72; Ruziraboba 6/14/72; Sebisaho 5/7/74.

56. The Banyakabwa of Kirhanga in the far north of Ijwi provide an example of this; see D. Newbury, *Kings and Clans,* chap. 5.

57. This resulted partly from the fact that multiple marriages with a single lineage were more common in the south. See ibid., chap. 10, for an example.

58. On this point see James Scott, "Hegemony and the Peasantry," *Politics and Society* 7, no. 3 (1977): 280n36.

59. As independence approached, the Belgian administration organized a referendum between the sons of Ntambuka and Muhamiriza as surrogate candidates, with each standing for his father. Ntambuka's son won overwhelmingly. Muhamiriza retired to Mpene, his only area of strong popular support in the south, and later withdrew from Karhongo (the south) entirely, to settle in Malambo (the north).

60. These policies are discussed in René Lemarchand, "The Politics of Penury in Rural Zaïre: The View from Bandundu," in Gran, *Zaïre,* 237–60; and Sosne, "Colonial Peasantization."

61. Ntambuka Pascal to Basiraboba François (Rambo, 13 avril 1960), cited in "Histoire Idjwi"; Delegation Bany'Idjwi au CommDistrict s/Kivu (Idjwi, 24 avril 1960).

62. "Rapport d'enquête . . . [sur] l'Histoire du Buhavu."

Chapter 8: The Clans of Rwanda

This chapter appeared as an article in Africa 50, no. 4 (1980): 389–403.

This chapter was originally presented to the conference on "La civilisation ancienne des peuples des Grands Lacs" organized by the Centre de Civilisation Burundaise, September 1979, Bujumbura, Burundi. I am grateful to the organizers of this conference and to David Henige for his comments on the original draft.

1. Examples from the Interlacustrine area include Carole Ann Buchanan, "The Kitara Complex: The Historical Tradition of Western Uganda to the Sixteenth Century" (PhD diss., Indiana University, 1974); D. W. Cohen, *The Historical Tradition of Busoga: Mukama and Kintu* (Oxford: Clarendon Press, 1972); Gerald Hartwig, *The Art of Survival in East Africa: The Kerebe and Long Distance Trade, 1800–1875* (New York: Africana, 1976); J. Keith Rennie, "The Precolonial Kingdom of Rwanda: A Reinterpretation," *Transafrican Journal of History* 2, no. 2 (1972): 11–53; and several of the contributions included in Donald Denoon, *A History of Kigezi in Southwestern Uganda* (Kampala: National Trust, 1972). The subtle analysis found in John Tosh, *Clan Leaders and Colonial Chiefs in Lango: The Political History of an East African Stateless Society, 1800–1939* (Oxford: Clarendon Press, 1978) is particularly noteworthy in this regard.

2. The early published material dealing with clan composition in Rwanda is admirably reviewed in d'Hertefelt, *Les clans du Rwanda ancien* (Tervuren: MRAC, 1962).

3. Although clientship is often seen as the most characteristic form of integration within the "traditional" Rwandan state, this is only one of several mechanisms accounting for ethnic diversity within Rwandan clans, as discussed in d'Hertefelt, *Les clans,* 56–62, and elaborated on in Émile Mworoha, *Peuples et rois de l'Afrique des Lacs: Le Burundi et les royaumes voisins au XIXe siècle* (Dakar: Nouvelles éditions africaines, 1977), 30–40. All these mechanisms explaining the multiethnic character of Rwandan clans are based on the concept of individuals moving into (or out of) predetermined social groups, groups that themselves remain within a more or less unchanging framework of social structures. In general, Mworoha adopts this line of reasoning, but the subtlety of his general discussion demonstrates that he is aware of the structural problems discussed here, as well as the problem of individual mechanisms of clan alteration (36, 40).

4. Claudine Vidal, "Le Rwanda des anthropologues ou le fétischisme de la vache," *Cahiers d'Études Africaines* 9, no. 3 (1969): 384–401.

5. Ibid.; Joseph Rwabukumba and Vincent Mudandagizi, "Les formes historiques de la dépendance personnelle dans l'état rwandais," *Cahiers d'Études Africaines* 14, no. 1 (1974): 6–25; Jean-François Saucier, "The Patron-Client Relationship in Traditional and Contemporary Southern Rwanda" (PhD diss., Columbia University, 1974); Catharine Newbury, *The Cohesion of Oppression: Clientship and Ethnicity in Rwanda, 1860–1960* (New York: Columbia University Press, 1988); on the concept of "caste" see d'Hertefelt, *Les clans*, 75n1; and Jean-Pierre Chrétien, "Échanges et hiérarchies dans les royaumes des Grands Lacs de l'Est africain," *Annales* 29, no. 6 (1974): 1327–37.

6. In admirably succinct terms, d'Hertefelt has spelled out the problems associated with the term "caste" as applied to Rwandan ethnic categories (*Les clans*, 75n1); see also Chrétien "Échanges et hiérarchies." Subsequently, in "Ethnicity in Rwanda," *Africa* 48, no. 1 (1978), 17–30, Catharine Newbury suggested that at least in the western areas of Rwanda the concept of a broad "Hutu" identification was relatively recent. She thus argued for the need to consider the historicity of the ethnic classifications themselves and the evolution of the very concepts of ethnic categories, as well as the changes in membership at the margins.

7. For an excellent summary of present clan characteristics in Rwanda see d'Hertefelt, *Les clans*, 3–7.

8. De Heusch notes that whereas in Bunyoro there were about 150 clans for ca. 110,000 people (1957 figures), and in Buhaya 124 clans for 325,000 people, Rwanda counted 13 clans for a population of more than 2,000,000 and Nkore four clans (at one level of interpretation) for 500,000. (The number of Rwandan clans and the different identification of clans by different authors is discussed in d'Hertefelt, *Les clans*, 11–20 and table I; d'Hertefelt settles on 18 principal clans.) De Heusch, assuming that the number of clans in Rwanda has remained constant over a very long period, attributes the relatively low number of clans in Rwanda to an absence of political "functions" of clans within a "caste society." Luc de Heusch, *Le Rwanda et la civilisation interlacustre* (Brussels: Université Libre de Bruxelles, 1966), 151.

9. John Roscoe, *The Banyankore* (Cambridge: Cambridge University Press, 1923), 4–11; Samwiri R. Karugire, *A History of the Kingdom of Nkore in Western Uganda to 1896* (Oxford: Clarendon Press, 1971), 72.

10. This problem is discussed at length in d'Hertefelt, *Les clans*, 25–47, 56–62. However, given the variations in both the concepts of ethnicity (noted above) and the changing nature of clan identities (proposed here), such attempts to classify clans by their ethnic origins may no longer be such a central issue in understanding Rwandan history.

11. d'Hertefelt, *Les clans*, 3 and 76n2.

12. Alexis Kagame, "La structure des quinze clans au Rwanda," *Annali Lateranensi* 18 (1954): 103–17.

13. "Alors que le lignage, aux deux niveaux de profondeur est strictement exogame, le clan est agame. L'exogamie normative des clans soulignée par certains auteurs . . . est manifestement une régie datant d'une époque assez éloignée" (d'Hertefelt, *Les clans*, 3; see also 5).

14. In doing so, and despite the enormous breadth of knowledge and many valuable insights contained in this work, he appears to overlook the role of models in our

conceptualization of the past, instead taking normative rules as valid empirical data for the past. But where models are used for present clan conceptualizations it is likely that they will also be used for historical conceptualization, since all our data of the past are filtered through the conceptual models. (The same is true for literate societies.) Therefore, is it not likely that the "normative exogamy" of clans of the past is also a product of the lineage model, rather than some empirical "survival"? If this is true, then the problem of multiethnic clans dissolves—or at least becomes transposed into a new problem, that of the meaning of clan classification in the past. From this perspective the multiethnic character of clans becomes part of the problem to be explained: we are asking what this tells us of the character of clans in the past, not how to explain this phenomenon within the constraints of rigid "ethnic" and "clan" categories.

15. I do not intend to go into the question of the evolution of conceptual models of clans here. To my knowledge, models of clanship in Africa have never been explored in the way that models of kinship have been investigated: Meyer Fortes, "The Structure of Unilineal Descent Groups," *American Anthropologist* 55 (1953): 17–41; Fortes, "Descent, Affiliation, and Affinity," *Man* 59 (1959): 193–97, 206–12; M. G. Smith, "On Segmentary Lineage Systems," *Journal of the Royal Anthropological Institute* 86 (1956): 39–80; Morton Fried, "The Classification of Corporate Unilineal Descent Groups," *Journal of the Royal Anthropological Institute* 87, no. 1 (1957): 1–29; Edmund R. Leach, *Rethinking Anthropology* (Cambridge: Cambridge University Press, 1961); J. A. Barnes, "African Models in the New Guinea Highlands," *Man* 62 (1962), 5–9; Barnes, *Three Styles in the Study of Kinship* (Berkeley and Los Angeles: University of California Press, 1971); Philip H. Gulliver, *Neighbours and Networks: The Idiom of Kinship in Social Action among the Ndendeuli of Tanzania* (Berkeley and Los Angeles: University of California Press, 1971); Jack Goody, *The Character of Kinship* (Cambridge: Cambridge University Press, 1973); Maurice Bloch, "Property and the End of Affinity," in *Marxist Analyses and Social Anthropology,* ed. Maurice Bloch (London: Malaby Press, 1975), 203–28; Claude Meillassoux, *Femmes, Greniers, Capitaux* (Paris: Maspero, 1975).

16. Vansina, *L'évolution du royaume Rwanda.*

17. David Newbury, *Kings and Clans: Ijwi Island and the Lake Kivu Rift, 1780–1840* (Madison: University of Wisconsin Press, 1991), chaps. 4–6.

18. See chapter 6, this volume.

19. See, for example, Lubaye 3/9/72 among the many other such references from among field data drawn from Ijwi over the period 1972–75; the early history of the Mbiriri on Ijwi is discussed in D. Newbury, *Kings and Clans,* chap. 6.

20. Of seven communes in this area for which figures are available, Singa accounted for about one-third of the population in three communes, and over one-quarter in two others, averaging 31.65 percent of the population in these five communes (1960 boundaries). Overall for the seven communes, Singa accounted for 27 percent—almost twice their average for Rwanda as a whole. I am grateful to Marcel d'Hertefelt for providing me with these statistics based on as yet unpublished data. It should be mentioned that the commune boundaries do not coincide precisely with the area of Bunyambiriri.

21. Kagame, *Inganji Karinga,* 2nd ed. (Kabgayi, Rwanda: n.p., 1959), sec. II, pars. 9–12, and sec. V, pars. 6ff., 30; Kagame refers to the Singa as "Tuutsi." For a different view see Rennie, "Precolonial Kingdom," 17–19; on the basis of clan composition, ritual function, and historical traditions, Rennie claims the Singa were "agriculturalist."

22. D'Hertefelt, *Les clans,* table II.

23. Ijwi interviews: Bahoye 2/10/72; Bakaza 2/12/72; Kavura Kabambare 3/27/72; Mbaraga 3/28/72; Kizinduka 3/28/72; Mukatare 4/19/72.

24. De Heusch, *Le Rwanda,* 51–66 and passim, argues that such a tie can either re-affirm a former common status or represent an independent origin for clans in the process of coalescing. In this case the evidence is strongly in favor of the latter. For a further discussion of *bukumbi* roles on Ijwi, see D. Newbury, *Kings and Clans,* 121–25.

25. C. Newbury, *Cohesion of Oppression,* chap. 2.

26. The interpretation proposed here does not exclude the processes noted by d'Hertefelt in *Les clans,* and Mworoha, *Peuples et rois,* but it places less emphasis on these individual mechanisms.

27. D'Hertefelt, *Les clans,* table II.

28. Ibid., 9–20, 63–71.

29. The smallest clan noted in d'Hertefelt's list, the Abeneengwe, accounts for only 0.004 percent of the sample, or 4 individuals of a total sample of over 92,000; it is likely that the Abeneengwe have been included in the tabulations because of their historical significance and their concentration in only two prefectures, rather than because of their size alone. Other small groups in the table account for about 100 and 130 individuals in the sample. I am assuming that the groups included in the category of "others" are smaller than that; otherwise they would likely have deserved separate entries of their own. But they need not, in these tabulations, have been smaller than the Abeneengwe.

30. d'Hertefelt (*Les clans,* 13) also notices this, attributing the preponderance of small clans to the presence of many recent immigrants from the west. While this may well be true for Bugoyi (and less so for Kinyaga), it provides a less convincing explanation for Kibuye and Ruhengeri Prefectures. Furthermore, simply attributing it to "recent" immigrants does not explain why immigrant groups eventually adopted "Rwandan" clan identities. I prefer to see this situation within the context of the extension of Rwandan culture norms. See also Kagame, "La structure des quinze clans," 104.

31. The exact ages of the different clan identities are of course impossible to determine. The relative age of these three clan identities, however, is indicated by their ritual status as *abasangwabutaka* (owners of the soil), whose members perform certain clearly defined ritual duties for members of all other Rwandan clan identities. See Alexis Kagame, *Les organisations socio-familiales de l'ancien Rwanda* (Brussels: ARSOM, 1954), 209–13; d'Hertefelt, "Le Rwanda," 42; d'Hertefelt and Coupez, *La royauté sacrée,* 310. For a comparison with similar duties in other regions see Jim Freedman, "Principles of Relationships in Rwandan Kiga Society" (PhD diss., Princeton University, 1974); D. Newbury, *Kings and Clans,* chaps. 5–7.

32. This process was probably common in the region, with new identities replacing former categorizations. For other examples of this process, see J. Jensen, "Die Erweiterung des Lungenfisch-Clans in Buganda (Uganda) durch den Anschluss von Bavuma-Gruppen," *Sociologus* 19, no. 2 (1962): 153–66, esp. 156–57; D. Newbury, *Kings and Clans,* chap. 3. Also de Heusch, *Le Rwanda,* includes many examples of clan alterations of this general type, as do Buchanan, "Kitara Complex" and Rennie, "Precolonial Kingdom," 22–23 (on Busigi) and 17 (for a caveat on current clan identities).

33. Kagame, *Inganji Karinga,* sec. II, pars. 9–12; Kagame, *Un abrégé de l'ethno-histoire du Rwanda précolonial,* vol. 1 (Butare: Éditions universitaires du Rwanda, 1972), 27–28;

d'Hertefelt, *Les clans,* 24, 27; Jean Hiernaux, "Note sur une ancienne population du Ruanda-Urundi: Les Renge," *Zaïre* 10, no. 4 (1956): 353, 355, 358.

34. D'Hertefelt, *Les clans,* 77n12.

35. For references to the Renge in areas southwest of Lake Kivu see Daniel P. Biebuyck, *Lega Culture: Art, Initiation and Moral Philosophy among a Central African People,* 7; and Jacques Depelchin, "From Precapitalism to Imperialism: A History of Social and Economic Formations in Eastern Zaïre (Uvira Zone), c. 1800–1964" (PhD diss., Stanford University, 1974), 42, 44. For areas north of Rwanda, see M. R. Rwankwenda, "The History of Kayonza," in Denoon, *History of Kigezi,* 124–33; Kamuhangire, "The Economic and Social History of the Southwest Uganda Salt Lakes Region"; and Randall Packard, "The Politics of Ritual Control among the Bashu of Eastern Zaïre during the Nineteenth Century" (PhD diss., University of Wisconsin–Madison, 1976), 132–34. From a spatial point of view it is interesting that in both Kayonza (in Kigezi, Uganda) and Buvira (north of Lake Tanganyika) the ruling family is said to be of the Barenge clan.

36. Hiernaux, "Note sur une ancienne population," 353; d'Hertefelt, *Les clans,* 13.

37. Kagame, *Inganji Karinga,* sec. II, pars. 1–26; Kagame, *Les organisations socio-familiales,* 39–60; Kagame, "La structure des quinze clans"; d'Hertefelt, *Les clans,* 27–37.

38. Kagame, "La structure des quinze clans," 106–7, but see also 112.

39. D'Hertefelt, *Les clans,* 56–62 and "Postulate #4."

40. D'Hertefelt correctly argues that it is foolish to explain individual absorption on the basis of a unique mechanism. But if the present clan structures are a product of the expansion of "Tutsi" (in this case read "central court") power, then it stands to reason that the multiethnic character of these clan structures is also a product of this new political context. I do not accept that clientship was the only mechanism for achieving this, as some authors imply; instead, I employ the reference to "clientship" in the previous sentence as a metaphorical allusion to less concrete forms of central court power.

41. Vidal, "Le Rwanda des anthropologues," first unveiled the mistaken centrality of cattle clientship in Rwandan studies: many other empirical works have since confirmed her observation on this point.

Chapter 9: Bunyabungo

This chapter appeared in The African Frontier, *ed. I. Kopytoff*
(Bloomington: Indiana University Press, 1986), 162–92.

I am grateful to Elizabeth Traube for her comments on this chapter.

1. There is disagreement on the precise chronology of Rwandan kings. The two major chronological schema are Alexis Kagame, *La notion de génération appliquée à la généalogie dynastique et à l'histoire du Rwanda dès Xe–XIe siècles à nos jours* (Brussels: ARSOM, 1959); and Jan Vansina, *L'évolution du royaume Rwanda dès origines à 1900* (Brussels: ARSOM, 1962), 42–57. I have followed the general analysis proposed in the latter, although institutions of Rwanda are described in Marcel d'Hertefelt, "Le Rwanda," in *Les anciens royaumes de la zone interlacustre méridionale,* by Marcel d'Hertefelt, Albert A. Trouwborst, and J. H. Scherer (Tervuren: MRAC, 1962). For reviews of recent research and how this has altered earlier portrayals of Rwandan social structures and history, see chapters 2 and 8, this volume.

2. Of course, a "Hutu" who held such a position of power for any length of time (especially if he also adopted Tutsi social norms) would most likely gradually come to be seen as sharing Tutsi status. The literature on ethnicity in Rwanda is as diverse as it is vast. Most analyses, however, neglect the dynamics of the Rwandan system and fail to account for changes in the patterns associated with the terms "Hutu" and "Tutsi." For a consideration of this question for western Rwanda, see Catharine Newbury, "Ethnicity in Rwanda: The Case of Kinyaga," *Africa* 48, no. l (1978): 17–29.

3. The period of time involved may in fact have been longer than that implied by reference to a single king. Rujugira himself may have usurped the throne from his predecessor (and brother) Rwaka: Vansina, *L'évolution du royaume Rwanda*, 51–52. Kagame reverses this relationship, stating that Rwaka preempted the rightful heir, Rujugira, and was therefore the usurper, though Rujugira later attained the throne: Kagame, *Un abrégé de l'ethno-histoire du Rwanda précolonial*, vol. 1 (Butare: Éditions universitaires du Rwanda, 1972), 129–31. All sources, however, agree that they were brothers, that Rujugira removed Rwaka from power and that subsequently Rujugira has been recognized as the only legitimate king of this generation (corresponding to the ideal of one king per generation). Consequently, these two kings are considered as part of a single reign in the dynastic chronicles and are so considered here; the "reign" of Rujugira refers in fact to the rule of two persons.

4. Raiding outside the core areas and especially into the agricultural areas of high population clearly had an important role to play in the internal transformations summarized below; it provided (in the form of booty), prestige in raids, important new political functions for the central court (spoils to distribute and positions to dispense), and a new purpose to the state (expansion). Therefore, the alterations discussed here were not simply internal transformations in response to an external threat; they were a product of the changing relations with Rwanda's neighbors, especially those to the west. Such raids made the internal changes possible as well as desirable. To neglect the external interactions—so important in understanding the accumulation of political resources (material and prestigious)—is to seriously distort the nature of change within Rwanda.

5. Kagame, *Les milices du Rwanda précolonial* (Brussels: ARSOM, 1963), 72–125 and passim; Kagame, *Un abrégé*, vol. 1, 135–53; *Historique et chronologie du Ruanda* (Kabgayi, Rwanda: Vicariat apostolique du Ruanda, 1956), 114–15, 159–61. Although it is not used as a nominal in Kinyarwanda for these "social armies" the term *umuheto* (pl. *imiheto*; literal translation: "bow" or "arc") is constantly associated with army functions: an army chief is *umutware w'umuheto* (sometimes *umutware w'ingabo*) and army prestations are *amakoro y'umuheto*. I have therefore adopted the nominal *umuheto* from time to time to refer to the corporate army group.

6. Kagame, *Les milices*, 10 and passim.

7. *Historique et chronologie*, 159–61.

8. Kagame, *Les milices*, 77, 79, 102, 103; *Historique et chronologie*, 114–15, 121–25, 149–52, 161–62.

9. Catharine Newbury, "Deux lignages au Kinyaga," *Cahiers d'Études Africaines* 14, no. 1 (1974): 26–39; Catharine Newbury, *The Cohesion of Oppression: Clientship and Ethnicity in Rwanda, 1860–1960* (New York: Columbia University Press, 1988); A. Pagès, *Au Rwanda: Sur les bords du Lac Kivu, Congo belge: Un royaume hamite au centre de l'Afrique* (Brussels: IRCB, 1933), 634–700.

10. R. Spitaels, "Transplantation des Banyaruanda dans le Nord Kivu," *Problèmes d'Afrique Centrale* 6, no. 2 (1953), 110–16; Jacques J. Maquet, "Les pasteurs de l'Itombwe," *Science et Nature* 8 (1955): 3–12; J. Kajiga, "Cette immigration séculaire des Ruandais au Congo," *Bulletin Trimestriel du Centre d'Études des Problèmes Sociaux Indigènes* 32 (1956): 5–65.

11. Marcel Pauwels, "Le Bushiru et son muhinza ou roitelet Hutu," *Annali Lateranensi* 31 (1967): 205–322; Louis de Lacger, *Le Ruanda*, 2nd ed. (Kabgayi, Rwanda: Imprimérie de Kabgayi, 1961), 82–89; Ferdinand Nahimana, "Les 'bami' ou roitelets hutu du corridor Nyaborongo-Mukungwa avec ses régions limitrophes," *Études Rwandaises* 12, special issue (March 1979): 8–11; Pagès, *Un royaume hamite*, 328–45; *Historique et chronologie*, 94–169.

12. Vansina, *L'évolution du royaume Rwanda*, 88–89; *Historique et chronologie*, 96–97.

13. Kagame for example, notes Rwandan presence in the Bwishaza-Nyantango-Budaha area (the central corridor from the Rwandan heartland west to Lake Kivu) from the reign of Yuhi II (eight named kings before Rujugira) and even earlier for raids. But such references are to be treated with caution.

14. *Historique et chronologie;* Kagame, *L'histoire des armées bovines dans l'ancien Rwanda* (Brussels: ARSOM, 1961); Kagame, *Les milices;* army placement during the reigns of Mazimpaka, Rujugira, and Ndabarasa are considered in greater detail in David Newbury, *Kings and Clans: Ijwi Island and the Lake Kivu Rift, 1780–1840* (Madison: University of Wisconsin Press, 1991), chap. 4.

15. Vansina, *L'évolution du royaume Rwanda*, 79–80, 86–90; C. Newbury, *Cohesion of Oppression*, chaps. 2 and 3.

16. Pagès, *Un royaume hamite*, 141–43, 598–652; Ivan Reisdorff, *Enquêtes foncières au Rwanda* (Butare, Rwanda: INRS, 1952), Enquête 31; Vansina, *L'évolution du royaume Rwanda*, 88; de Lacger, *Le Ruanda*, 111; *Historique et chronologie*, 121–23.

17. This is clear in many of the interviews conducted in Kinyaga by Catharine Newbury; among others, see Bakomoza 7/27/70; Bagaruka 2/11/71; Gihura 7/10/70; Nyiramandwa 7/11/70; Rwaambikwa 2/18/71.

18. Here I use the term "Tutsi" to refer to those who shared Rwandan state norms, though perhaps not originally tied to the Rwandan central court.

19. The standard orthography of Kinyarwanda has been retained here; *icyivugo* is pronounced *ichyivugo* in English phonetics. These poems are not usually passed down from generation to generation. Therefore, it is impossible to assign specific *ibyivugo* to specific time periods, or to trace the evolution of the genre. Two examples illustrating these Rwandan praise poems as they portray western peoples are found in Alexis Kagame, *Introduction aux grands genres lyriques de l'ancien Rwanda* (Butare, Rwanda: Éditions universitaires du Rwanda, 1969), 16–19.

20. Kagame, *Introduction aux grands genres lyriques*, 15–55; André Coupez and Thomas Kamanzi, *Récits historiques Rwanda, dans la version de C. Gakaniisha* (Tervuren: MRAC, 2005), 96–112.

21. Alexis Kagame, *Les organisations socio-familiales de l'ancien Rwanda* (Brussels: ARSOM, 1954); Kagame, *Introduction aux grands genres lyriques*, 151–245; Coupez and Kamanzi, *Récits historiques Rwanda*, 159–97.

22. While it is not surprising that more poems are retained from more recent reigns, the pattern of these retentions, even if only suggestive, is still significant in terms of the timing of the processes proposed here, with a marked concentration around the reign of

Rujugira; this indicates that changes in the ideology were directly associated with political changes. The figures are: Ruganzu, 2; Semugeshi, 0; Nyamuheshera, 3; Gisanura, 6; Mazimpaka, 11; Rujugira, 30; Ndabarasa, 4; Seentabyo, 21; Gahindiro, 12; Rwogera, 30; Rwabugiri, 41. (Kagame 1954, passim; Kagame also mentions the importance of Rujugira's reign in the emergence of this type of poetry: *Introduction,* 16.)

23. Pagès, *Un royaume hamite,* 128–29, 228–345; Vansina, *L'évolution du royaume Rwanda,* 86–87; Kagame, *Un abrégé,* vol. 1, 93–109; de Lacger, *Le Ruanda,* 107–8; Coupez and Kamanzi, *Récits historiques Rwanda,* nos. 12–14, 16.

24. The fullest version available to me, and the one followed here, is that which appears in A. Bigirumwami, *Ibitekerezo, indilimbo, imbyino, ibihozo, inanga, ibyivugo, ibigwi, imato, amahamba n'amazina y'inka, ibiganiro,* mimeo (Nyundo, Rwanda: n.p., 1971), no. 23: 68–75. Other versions are found in Vansina, "Ibitéekerezo: Historical Narratives from Rwanda" (CAMP) (Chicago: Center for Research Libraries); and Vansina, "Ibitéekerezo: Historical Narratives of Rwanda" (MRAC) (on file at the Musée Royal de l'Afrique Centrale at Tervuren, Belgium); E. Johanssen, *Ruanda. Kleine Anfänge—Grosse Aufgaben der Evangelischen mission im Zwischenseengbeit Deutsch-Ostafrikas* (Bethel bei Bielefeld: Verlagshandlung der Anstalt Bethel, 1912), 141–45; Pagès, *Un royaume hamite,* 298–311, and my interview in Kinyaga of Bagaruka 2/11/71. Rutungwa 2/17/71 and Rubanza 2/17/71 both apply this tale to nineteenth-century Rwandan campaigns to the west. Bagaruka notes that Gatabirora was a "Shi" from "Buhunde"; and in his icyivugo, Ruganzu notes, "I am Ruganzu, he who constantly seeks to attack the Bahunde."

25. Pagès, *Un royaume hamite,* 298, notes that it is "Un de ceux [des récits] qui sont les plus goutés des Banyarwanda." Partial confirmation is given by the number of times is reappears in the published collections.

26. "Kabibi" may be a reference to "Mbeba"—"Ka-" being the diminutive (or generic) prefix. "Mbeba" is the name of a legendary culture hero commonly associated with the Havu areas, but more directly associated with the forest-culture Tembo peoples who preceded the Havu in these areas west of the lake.

27. This theme also reflects a common image found among the western forest cultures that form the object of the parody here. See, for example, Daniel P. Biebuyck and Mateene Kahombo, *The Mwindo Epic from the Banyanga (Congo Republic)* (Berkeley and Los Angeles: University of California Press, 1969), where Mwindo, the epic hero of the Nyanga, communicates with his aunt by means of a rope: 27, 28, 99–100, 102, 106, 110, 114. See also 94, where Mwindo sets out on one of his adventures; he carries with him a rope, but leaves one end with his aunt, telling her: "You, my aunt, you stay here in the village of your birth . . . . [H]ere is the rope. Remain with one end, holding it in your hand . . . . [I]f one day you feel that this rope has become still, if it does not move any more, then pay no more attention to where I have gone. Lo! The fire has dwindled—I am dead then." The repetition of this theme, a literary technique well illustrated in the various versions of this text, both relates the narrative to a larger corpus of Rwandan oral literature and demonstrates the way in which these stories are constructed, by reformulating certain "core images" to fit different narrative contexts. This literary device is considered in Harold Scheub, *The Xhosa Ntsomi* (Oxford: Clarendon Press, 1975); he summarizes the use of these core images: "The core cliché is the remembered element of the *ntsomi* tradition, the stable element; it is recalled during the production by means of a complex process of cuing and scanning whereby an artist dips into her rich repertory of *ntsomi* images and

brings into performance appropriate images and image-segments which combine to create the finished work" (3). In their literary style, the *ibiteekerezo* also constantly remind the reader of the central role of the dramatic performance in their creation and retelling, another element stressed by Scheub in his analysis of the *ntsomi* form.

28. Daniel P. Biebuyck, "Die Mumbo Instelling bij de Banyanga," *Kongo-Overzee* 21, no. 5 (1955): 441–48; Biebuyck, "L'organisation politique des Nyanga: La chefferie Ihana," *Kongo Overzee* 22, nos. 4–5 (1956): 301–41; 23, nos. 1–2 (1957): 59–98.

29. Seven is also the perfect number in the cosmology of the western cultures, as indicated in both the content and stylistic features of their oral literature: Biebuyck and Mateene, *Mwindo Epic*, 42n4 and passim; D. Biebuyck, "Stylistic Techniques and Formulating Devices in the Mwindo Epic from the Banyanga," *Cultures et Développement* 11, no. 4 (1979): 551–600. This reference in the Rwandan text is therefore an accurate reflection of western cosmological patterns.

30. In fact the "Rw-" of the term "Rwanda" is pronounced so that it sounds somewhat like "Gw-," but the "Rw-"of Kinyarwanda is regarded as much more refined than the simple "Gw-." To pronounce the word in this way would be the equivalent of speaking "pidgin" in this language.

31. Vansina, "Ibitéekerezo" (MRAC).

32. This tradition therefore reflects the widespread perception that the "cultural order" (in this case represented by the Court milieu) is signified by a proliferation of distinctions. The "chaos" of the forest, on the other hand, is shown in the abolition or ignorance of such distinctions, the essence of culture. The same discrepancy is shown in the culinary code noted below, where the forest peoples are associated with rotten food and its decay.

33. Published versions of the Nzira tale are found in Bigirumwami, *Ibitekerezo,* nos. 14: 35, 21:49; Pagès, *Un royaume hamite,* 178–81; Coupez and Kamanzi, *Récits historiques Rwanda,* 222–54; see also Vansina, "Ibiteekerezo" (CAMP).

34. Pagès, *Un royaume hamite,* 238–43, 251–53; Vansina, "Ibitéekerezo" (CAMP) and "Ibitéekerezo" (MRAC); Bigirumwami, *Ibitekerezo,* 100ff.; Pierre Smith, *Le récit populaire au Rwanda* (Paris: Armand Colin, 1975), 313–19.

35. The relativity of ethnic terms has been argued in many other contexts. For one noteworthy example, see Wendy James, "The Funj Mystique: Approaches to a Problem of Sudan History," in *Text and Context: The Social Anthropology of Tradition,* ed. R. K. Jain (Philadelphia: ISHI, 1977).

36. Bernard Lugan, "Les réseaux commerciaux au Rwanda dans le dernier quart du XIXe siècle," *Études d'Histoire Africaine* 9–10 (1977–78): 183–212; Lugan, "Les pôles commerciaux du Lac Kivu à la fin du XIXe siècle," *Revue Française d'Histoire d'Outre-Mer* 64, no. 235 (1977): 176–202; chapter 3, this volume.

37. The quotations, in order, are from my interviews with the following interviewees and on the following dates: Ntamati 2/6/73; Gahangamira 2/17/73; Rubanganjura 4/28/72; and a summary of Rubenga 5/4/72. For additional Ijwi accounts similar to those cited below, see Shabalikwa 3/3/72; Kasi 4/27/72; Kayirara 5/24/72; Gahangamire 2/17/73; Musemakweri 2/19/73; Rwanga 2/20/73; Gashoku 4/29/74; Gashina 5/6/74; Binombe 5/13/74; Kanyeju Kahise 5/18/74; Ntamusige 5/25/75. European observation concurs: "Kwidjwi est pour ainsi dire le grenier du lac. D'énormes quantités de produits agricoles sont exportées chaque année." Richard Kandt, *Caput Nili: Eine empfindsame Reise zu den Quellen des Nils* (Berlin: D. Reimer, 1904), II 587 (cited in Lugan, "Les pôles," 185).

38. I have argued elsewhere that one determinant of demand for ornamental commodities such as *ubutega* (discussed below) was the nature of the social hierarchy and social stratification associated with the internal evolution of royal court structures in Rwanda (see chapter 3, this volume). But while the demand for prestations for the royal court appears to have been effectively enforced in northwestern and southwestern Rwanda (Bugoyi and Kinyaga) only during the nineteenth century, local patterns of trade east and west across Lake Kivu (particularly at the northern end of the lake) are clearly much older, especially local trade in foodstuffs. The court traditions sometimes distort these trade patterns in two ways. One is to portray all trade in goods ultimately destined for the royal court as "prestations," whereas in fact they were traded through many hands; not all links in this chain of transfer were prestation payers to the Rwandan court. The other distortion in the Rwandan representations is the common assumption that court influence existed in the region for as long as the trade in such items existed—as proved (in the eyes of court officials) by the fact that these items were "prestations." Data from recent research in the west and in Kinyaga demonstrate that such blanket claims are extravagant.

39. For illustrations of these, see Pagès, *Un royaume hamite*, plates Ib, XXIa; for references in the written sources, see ibid., 22–23 and 636–37. Other references to ubutega and their trade are found in chapter 3, this volume.

40. Biebuyck and Kahombo, *Mwindo Epic*, 13, 47, 51, 55, 127; Thomas Alexander Barns, *Across the Great Craterland to the Congo* (London: Benn, 1923), 115, 116; Pagès, *Un royaume hamite*, 22–23, 636–37, plates Ib, XXIa.

41. Early Tutsi immigrants from the east appear to have married into local families, often those of higher social standing in the area. For examples of this in Kinyaga see C. Newbury, *Cohesion of Oppression*, chap. 2.

42. These rulers are invariably referred to in the Rwandan Court literature as *abahinza*, a term apparently retroactively bestowed (after conquest). The abahinza of at least two of these conquered "principalities," Busozo and Bukunzi (both in southwestern Rwanda as defined by its present boundaries) were always referred to locally as *bami*. Nahimana argues similarly for the northern pre-Tutsi kingdoms: "Les 'bami' ou roitelets hutu." For other sources on these polities see Pagès, *Un royaume hamite*, 335–45 (including genealogies of the ruling families of sixteen of these Hutu "toparchies"); de Lacger, *Le Ruanda*, 82–89; J. Keith Rennie, "The Precolonial Kingdom of Rwanda: A Reinterpretation," *Transafrican Journal of History* 2, no. 2 (1972): 15–25; and especially Pauwels, "Le Bushiru."

43. My interviews on Ijwi with Nkuruziza Kabulibuli 5/26/72; Gasarahinga 3/30/72; Ndengeyi 6/2/72. "Rugaba" was the last of the Mpembe *abami;* however, the use of the term here may well be anachronistic, since "Rugaba" is often used to refer to all such abami. Marriage ties between Mpembe and Bukunzi are also mentioned frequently in Kinyaga interviews conducted by Catharine Newbury.

44. Pagès, *Un royaume hamite*, 296–98, 465.

45. De Lacger, *Le Ruanda*, 103.

46. Interviews with Migayo Shamahanga, 2/12/73; Kakomera, 6/21/74. For the people of Ijwi and the west, adequate food, of course, is a metaphor for general well-being. When a woman from Ijwi, married in Rwanda, divorces and returns to Ijwi, the divorce is invariably attributed to a "lack of food over there."

47. Rwandans also "explain" the westward movement of women in terms of their own ideology: only unmarried women who become pregnant were sent west, they say,

onto the islands in Lake Kivu; Pagès, *Un royaume hamite,* 52; R. Bourgeois, *Ethnographie,* vol. 1 of *Banyarwanda et Barundi* (Brussels: ARSOM, 1954), 424; A. Lestrade, *Notes d'ethnographie du Rwanda* (Tervuren: MRAC, 1972), 3–4. Sometimes this is said to be Ijwi itself, but people from Ijwi indicated yet another small island, Cihaya, south of Nkombo. When Rwandans placed their pregnant unmarried women on the islands in this fashion, the Bany'Iju explain, they would go and save these women and marry them into their own families. Despite the disparaging tone in such Rwandan traditions—a reflection of literary themes—associated with sending women west, it is notable that the phenomenon apparently occurred frequently enough to require an explanation.

48. Pagès, *Un royaume hamite,* 636; further references to the close cultural ties binding the populations of Bugoyi with those west of Lake Kivu are found in ibid., 661–62, 667, 676, 682. For Kinyaga, see C. Newbury, *Cohesion of Oppression,* 34–35.

49. Pagès, *Un royaume hamite,* 644–45.

50. Ibid., 653–59, 666, 668, 671, 676, 682.

51. Kajiga, "Cette immigration"; Spitaels, "Transplantation des Banyaruanda."

52. D. Newbury, *Kings and Clans,* chaps. 5–7.

53. Chapter 6, this volume.

54. Chapter 8, this volume.

55. In regions west of Rwanda, the polarizations between metropole and frontier were nowhere as strong as they were on the Rwandan frontier, as central court institutions penetrated the western areas. The people on Ijwi, for example, refer to those who live in the mountains west of Lake Kivu as "Babindi," a term of opprobrium. (The same term is sometimes applied to people living on remote mountainous areas of Ijwi itself.) The presence of such stereotypes, however, meant that there existed the potential for constantly expanding the frontier west—not by extending the definition of barbarian to yet new peoples farther west so much as by creating a polarized context in which those on the immediate border were continually seeking to identify themselves as "Rwandan," adopting an identity opposed to those farther west.

56. Vladimir Propp, *Morphology of the Folktale* (Austin: University of Texas Press, 1968).

Chapter 10: What Role Has Kingship?

This chapter appeared as an article in Africa-Tervuren *27, no. 4 (1981): 89–101.*

I am most grateful to Marcel d'Hertefelt, Pierre Smith, and Jan Vansina for their comments on an earlier draft of this paper. They, of course, are not responsible for errors of fact or interpretation that remain.

1. Claude Lévi-Strauss, "Four Winnebago Myths," in *The Structuralists: From Marx to Lévi-Strauss,* ed. Richard T. De George and Fernande M. De George (New York, 1972), 201. The fuller context of this statement is worth citing here: "There must be, and there is, a correspondence between the unconscious meaning of myth—the problem it is trying to solve—and the conscious content it makes use of to reach that end, ie, the plot."

2. Claude Lévi-Strauss, "The Effectiveness of Symbols," in *Structural Anthropology* (New York: Basic Books, 1963), 186–205.

3. In addition to the published ritual code discussed below, this ritual is also described in R. Bourgeois, *Ethnographie,* vol. 1 of *Banyarwanda et Barundi* (Brussels: ARSOM, 1957), 418–28; A. Pagès, *Au Rwanda: Sur les bords du Lac Kivu, Congo belge: Un royaume hamite*

au centre de l'Afrique (Brussels: IRCB, 1933), 498–503; Louis de Lacger, *Le Ruanda,* 2nd ed. (Kabgayi, Rwanda: Imprimérie de Kabgayi, 1961), 97–98, 128; Léon Delmas, *Les généalogies de la noblesse (Batutsi) du Ruanda* (Kabgayi, Rwanda: Vicariat apostolique du Ruanda, 1950), 107; A. Kagame, "Le code ésotérique de la dynastie du Rwanda," *Zaïre* 1, no. 4 (1947): 363–86; Lestrade, *Notes d'ethnographie,* 349–62. Kagame presents a list of places where the *Umuganura* rites were said to have been celebrated under Kigeri Rwabugiri (d. 1895), in *La notion de génération appliquée à la généalogie dynastique et à l'histoire du Rwanda dès Xe–XIe siècles à nos jours* (Brussels: ARSOM, 1959), 64n1; the list is reproduced in his *Un abrégé de l'ethno-histoire du Rwanda précolonial,* vol. 2 (Butare: Éditions universitaires du Rwanda, 1975), 15–21. I should stress again that the present exploration is intended as an analysis of the official "esoteric code" of Rwanda, as presented in d'Hertefelt and Coupez, *La royauté sacrée.* It is not intended as an analysis of the ceremony itself, for which the few eyewitness accounts available in the published sources are incomplete and sometimes misleading, though in some cases (notably in Bourgeois, *Ethnographie*) such accounts provide useful additions to the material presented in the *Ubwiiru,* the formal text of the performed esoteric code. The code was published in its near entirety in 1964: d'Hertefelt and Coupez, *La royauté sacrée.* For a statement on the troubled history of its publication, see Marcel d'Hertefelt, André Coupez, and Alexis Kagame, "À propos du code ésotérique de l'ancien Rwanda," *Africa-Tervuren* 14, no. 4 (1968): 117.

4. Jan Czekanowski, *Ethnographie: Zwischenseengebiet Mpororo, Ruanda,* vol. 1 of *Forschungen im Nil-Congo Zwischengebeit* (Berlin: Klinkhardt and Biermann, 1917), 109–15.

5. D'Hertefelt and Coupez, *La royauté sacrée.*

6. Kagame, *La notion de génération,* 61–70, and Kagame, *Un abrégé,* vol. 2, 17, notes that the first part of the ceremony took place during the moon of *werurwe* (March–April) instead of *mutarama* as noted in the published text, and that the height of the ritual sequence occurred during the moon of *kamena* (roughly corresponding to June) rather than *gashyantare;* Bourgeois, *Ethnographie,* 423, also notes that the initial ceremony took place during the moon of *werewe,* but he does not cite the moon of kamena as the ritual culmination.

7. Bourgeois, *Ethnographie,* 414, also notes that in an analogous commoner ceremony, the wife precedes the husband on returning home from the field, "contrairement à la règle habituelle."

8. The ritual importance of these hoes is underscored by the fact that the package containing these hoes is bound by the same type of cords used to secure the ritual drum of the kingdom (*Kalinga*) to one of the pillars of the hut where it is housed. Bourgeois, *Ethnographie,* 421.

9. Ibid., 418–23, notes that these *bami* Baswere also claimed ritualists of their own (of the Zigaaba clan), and that the new seeds are sowed jointly by Muswere and his ritualist.

10. Of course in Rwandan cosmology the king is outside of society, being neither Tutsi nor Hutu nor Twa; his enthronement elevates him from Tutsi status: d'Hertefelt, "Le Rwanda," 69–70. Also d'Hertefelt, "Mythes et idéologies"; Kagame, *Le code des institutions politiques du Rwanda précolonial* (Brussels: IRCB, 1952), 20, 41, 41n15; Maquet, *Le système des relations sociales dans le Ruanda ancien* (Tervuren: MRAC, 1954), 146–47.

11. D'Hertefelt and Coupez, *La royauté sacrée,* Ritual VI, "Nzira y Umuriru."

12. Bourgeois, *Ethnographie,* 422–23.

13. Kagame, *La notion de génération,* 64n1. On Ijwi Island millet is the principal ritual grain of the analogous muganuro ceremony; David Newbury, *Kings and Clans: Ijwi Island*

and the Lake Kivu Rift, 1780–1840 (Madison: University of Wisconsin Press, 1991), chap. 12. In Burundi also, millet provides the focus for important harvest rituals, though not the royal ritual of umuganuro. More generally, see J. M. J. de Wet, "Domestication of African Cereals," *African Economic History* 3 (1977): 20, 22; Roland Portères, "Berceaux agricoles primaires sur le continent africain," *Journal of African History* 3, no. 2 (1962), 195–210; J. W. Purseglove, "The Origins and Migrations of Crops in Tropical Africa," in *The Origins of African Plant Domestication*, ed. J. Harlan, J. M. J. de Wet, and A. B. L. Stempler, 191–309 (The Hague: Mouton, 1976); and Roland Portères, "African Cereals: *Eleusine*, Fonio, Black Fonio, Teff, *Brachiaria, Paspalum, Pennisetum* and African Rice," in Harlan, de Wet, and Stempler, *Origins of African Plant Domestication*, 409–52.

14. D'Hertefelt and Coupez, *La royauté sacrée*, 308n65.

15. Bourgeois, *Ethnographie*, 426; d'Hertefelt and Coupez, *La royauté sacrée*, 312n206.

16. D'Hertefelt and Coupez, *La royauté sacrée*, 302n244, 309n85 and sources cited therein.

17. Bourgeois (*Ethnographie*, 426) cites a prescribed crossing of the Nyabarongo.

18. Ibid.

19. D'Hertefelt and Coupez, *La royauté sacrée*, 309–310nn126–36.

20. Ibid., 309n125. Bourgeois (*Ethnographie*, 426) notes specifically that the basket was indeed emptied before transport, and that the contents were carried in smaller baskets.

21. D'Hertefelt and Coupez, *La royauté sacrée*, 312n194; this plant is also used in other (nonroyal) rituals, such as the celebration of Ryangombe rites.

22. D'Hertefelt and Coupez, ibid., note that these stalks give the appearance of a distinctive hair style, most closely associated with the high fashion of the royal court. I would suggest that this was more a metaphorical explanation on the part of secondary informants than a prescription required by or a symbol related to the Code.

23. Compare ibid., VIII, lines 199–207, and lines 287–314.

24. Ibid., 313nn213–14.

25. Bourgeois, *Ethnographie*, 418.

26. This phrase is used in E. E. Evans-Pritchard, *Essays in Social Anthropology* (London: Faber and Faber, 1962), 79, and in Jean-Pierre Chrétien, "La royauté capture les rois," appendix to *L'intronisation d'un Mwami*, by Pascal Ndayishinguje (Nanterre: Laboratoire d'ethnologie et de sociologie comparative, 1977). Evans-Pritchard also notes, "In my view kingship everywhere and at all times has been in some degree a sacred office. . . . This is because a king symbolizes a whole society and must not be identified with any part of it, and this is only possible if his office is raised to a mystical plane. It is the kingship and not the king who is divine" (*Essays in Social Anthropology,* 36). In this essay I have argued that it is not kingship alone that is divine, but its relationship to the larger symbolic universe that makes it so.

Chapter 11: Trick Cyclists

This chapter appeared as an article in History in Africa *21 (1994): 191–217.*

1. For the area of Interlacustrine Africa, see, e.g., David W. Cohen, "A Survey of Interlacustrine Chronology," *Journal of African History* 11, no. 2 (1970): 111–201; J. Bertin Webster, ed., *Chronology, Migration, and Drought in Interlacustrine Africa* (New York:

Africana, 1979); David Henige, *The Chronology of Oral Tradition: The Quest for a Chimera* (Oxford: Clarendon Press, 1974); Henige, "Oral Tradition and Chronology," *Journal of African History* 12, no. 3 (1971): 371–89; Henige, "Reflections on Early Interlacustrine Chronology: An Essay in Source Criticism," *Journal of African History* 15, no. 1 (1974): 27–46. The comprehensive bibliography on method formerly produced annually in *History in Africa* includes discussions on issues relating to comparative chronology.

2. The starting point for the chronology of Rwandan dynastic history is Alexis Kagame, *La notion de génération appliquée à la généalogie dynastique et à l'histoire du Rwanda dès Xe–XIe siècles à nos jours* (Brussels: ARSOM, 1959). For elaboration, see Kagame, *Inganji Karinga*, 2nd ed. (Kabgayi, Rwanda: n.p., 1959); Kagame, *Un abrégé de l'ethno-histoire du Rwanda précolonial*, vol. 1 (Butare: Éditions universitaires du Rwanda, 1972), 35–39; Kagame, "La chronologie du Burundi dans les genres littéraires de l'ancien Rwanda," *Études Rwandaises* 12 (1979): 1–30. The most important reassessments of Kagame's proposals are Vansina, *L'évolution du royaume Rwanda*; J. Keith Rennie, "The Precolonial Kingdom of Rwanda: A Reinterpretation," *Transafrican Journal of History* 2, no. 2 (1972): 11–53 ; and Jean-Népomucène Nkurikiyimfura, "La revision d'une chronologie: Le cas du royaume du Rwanda," in *Sources orales de l'histoire de l'Afrique*, ed. Claude-Hélène Perrot (Paris, 1989), 149–80. See also Francis van Noten, *Les tombes du roi Cyirima-Rujugira et de la reine-mère Nyirayuhi Kanjogera: Description archéologique* (Tervuren: MRAC, 1972), and the review of this work by Jan Vansina in *International Journal of African Historical Studies* 7, no. 4 (1975): 528–31.

3. The best known of these was Pagès, *Un royaume hamite*. But such observers were not in a position to have access to deep knowledge of Rwandan historical sources, and this seems to be the thrust of Kagame's implicit critique of such work. In fact, Kagame seldom referred explicitly to the earlier works on Rwandan history by Europeans; the two exceptions are *La notion de génération*, 92–112; and "La documentation du Rwanda sur l'Afrique interlacustre des temps anciens," in *La civilisation ancienne des peuples des Grands Lacs*, ed. Centre de Civilisation Burundaise (Paris: Karthala, 1981), 300–330. Nonetheless, his own proposals leave certain questions unresolved, partly because his technique also obviated the analysis of his primary sources—their divergence and ambiguities, their social provenance, and the conditions of their recording. His approach was often to give a short extract from the data, and promise a subsequent, and more complete, presentation of these data. Lacking such elements, we will probably never entirely resolve these issues. But that does not mean the debate is closed; this inquiry touches on a few of these issues.

4. On Kagame see Claudine Vidal, "Alexis Kagame entre mémoire et histoire," *History in Africa* 15 (1988): 493–504; and Jean-Pierre Chrétien, "Confronting the Unequal Exchange between the Oral and the Written," in *African Historiographies*, ed. Bogumil Jewsiewicki and David Newbury (Beverly Hills: Sage, 1986), 84–87.

5. Pagès, *Un royaume hamite*, and an unnamed official writing in the Territorial Archives of Kibungu, both cited in A. d'Arianoff, *L'histoire des Bagesera: Souverains du Gisaka* (Brussels: IRCB, 1952), 38. The Territorial Archives were transferred to Kigali in 1956, and apparently never returned to Kibungu; at any rate, they are not accessible at present. Luc de Heusch accepts d'Arianoff's king list, but notes the chronological incompatibility with Rwandan claims to contemporaneous status with Gisaka kings, as asserted by Kagame and d'Arianoff. Luc de Heusch, *Le Rwanda et la civilisation interlacustre* (Brussels: Université Libre de Bruxelles, 1966), 46; see also 100–101, 111–12.

6. D'Arianoff, *L'histoire des Bagesera*, 36–37: "Les notables Banyagisaka [donnent] libre cours à leur fantaisie, se contredire les uns les autres, et se contredire eux-mêmes.... Si nous gardons quelque espoir ... c'est surtout grace aux précieux moyens de contrôle qui nous a été fournis par la récente mis à jour de la chronologie dynastique rwandaise." This assumption was restated in Kagame, *La notion de génération*, 98.

7. D'Arianoff, *L'histoire des Bagesera*, 38.

8. Ibid., 36 (emphasis added).

9. The most elaborate exegeses on this episode are Kagame, *Inganji Karinga*, sec. II, par. 6; and Kagame, *Un abrégé*, vol. 1, 57–61. Other versions appear in Pagès, *Un royaume hamite*, 114–20, and d'Arianoff, *L'histoire des Bagesera*, 50–53.

10. D'Arianoff, *L'histoire des Bagesera*, 54–56. It is worth pointing out that both are suspect: the tie-in to Mutabazi would correspond to the original Kimenyi were Kagame's two additions to be deleted; the second tie-in (that of Kigeri Nyamuheshera), also to a Kimenyi, is suspect on internal grounds, to be discussed below.

11. On the importance of Kagame's influence, see Vidal, "Alexis Kagame," and Chrétien, "Confronting the Unequal Exchange," 84–87.

12. D'Arianoff, *L'histoire des Bagesera*, 15.

13. Ibid., 16.

14. Jim Freedman, "Ritual and History: The Case of Nyabingi," *Cahiers d'Études Africaines* 14, no. 1 (1974): 174; note that of the cases cited, only Rwanda had a "repeating cycle" of names. Freedman, "Three Muraris, Three Gahayas, and the Four Phases of Nyabingi," in Webster, *Chronology, Migration, and Drought*, 175–85, develops new dimensions to this theme, but adds little to the interests that engage us here.

15. Freedman, "Ritual and History," 174. But note two aspects to this argument: that names are assumed to occur in all ("the," not "some") Interlacustrine kingdoms; and that this feature of repeating dynastic names becomes transformed to a "cycle" of kingship names; in fact, very few kingdoms adhered rigidly to such a cyclic pattern.

16. Ibid.

17. Ibid. And in most cases, where there are gaps in chronology or content, these are filled in by reference to Kagame's king list (ibid., 175–78), even to the point of denying local traditions to the contrary.

18. Jan Vansina, "Note sur la chronologie du Burundi," *Bulletin d'ARSOM* 38 (1967): 431. This pattern and its emergence is also considered in Jean-Pierre Chrétien, "Du hirsute au hamite: Les variations du cycle de Ntare Rushatsi, fondateur du royaume du Burundi," *History in Africa* 8 (1981): 3–41; Chrétien, "Les traditionnistes lettrés du Burundi à l'école des bibliothèques missionnaires (1940–1960)," *History in Africa* 15 (1988): 407–30.

19. Kagame, *La notion de génération*; Kagame, *Un abrégé*, vol. 1; and Kagame, *La poésie dynastique du Rwanda* (Brussels: IRCB, 1951), are the most relevant sources.

20. Kagame, "La chronologie"; Jan Vansina, *La légende du passé: Traditions orales du Burundi* (Tervuren: MRAC, 1972), 192. On tie-ins see Émile Mworoha et al., eds., *L'histoire du Burundi des origines à la fin du XIXe siècle* (Paris: Hatier, 1987), 131–34; Vansina, "Notes sur la chronologie," 432, 434; Kagame, *La notion de génération*, 46n2.

21. On Baranyanka see Chrétien, "Du hirsute au hamite," 16–18; Chrétien, "Confronting the Unequal Exchange," 83–84; Chrétien, "Nouvelles hypothèses sur les origines du Burundi: Les traditions du nord," in *L'arbre-mémoire: Traditions orales du Burundi*, ed. Léonidas Ndoricimpa and Claude Guillet (Paris: Karthala, 1984), 12–15; and Chrétien, "Les traditionnistes lettrés," 410, 416, 421, 424.

22. The best examples of this are found in Vansina, *La légende du passé;* Chrétien, "Du hirsute au hamite" and "Nouvelles hypothèses."

23. Vansina, *La légende du passé*, 192; Chrétien, "Les traditionnistes lettrés."

24. Kagame, "Chronologie du Burundi," 24–25, also notes that one of the most influential of the early accounts on the Rundi royal dynasty—that of Mgr. Julien Gorju, *Face au royaume hamite du Ruanda: Le royaume frère de l'Urundi* (Brussels: IRCB, 1938)—was premised on the assumption that the line descended from the Bacwezi, the rulers of an extensive domain some two hundred years ago; this excluded a four-cycle regional history. I concur that Gorju's assumptions were erroneous, but this in itself does not invalidate the possibility of eight reigns in this dynasty. Ironically, Kagame adopts a similar logic—that external tie-ins set the framework for internal analysis, and that "fit" becomes the most essential criterion in historical reconstruction; he just uses a different, though no less dogmatic, criterion for setting up an external grid within which Rundi history is assumed to have operated. For a wider view of regional chronology, see Kagame, "Documentation du Rwanda"; and J. Bertin Webster, "Noi! Noi! Famines as an Aid to Interlacustrine Chronology," in Webster, *Chronology, Migration, and Drought*, 1–37.

25. Kagame, "Chronologie du Burundi," 19.

26. Curiously, Kagame justifies this silence in the Rundi king list by reference to a Rwandan tradition, by which he maintains that genealogical data before Cyilima Rujugira (whom he cites as the contemporary of the two successors to the third Ntare) were no longer retained: ibid., 22; Kagame, "Le code ésotérique de la dynastie du Rwanda," *Zaïre* 1, no. 4 (1947): 377–78; d'Hertefelt and Coupez, *La royauté sacrée*, 94–154.

27. Kagame, *La notion de génération*, 46n1 (emphasis added).

28. Kagame, "Documentation du Rwanda."

29. Here Kagame seems to overlook his own argument that the recent cyclic pattern in Rwanda was set in place by a personal decision of Mutara Semugeshi, a king who arbitrarily abolished three dynastic names: that of his grandfather (Ndahiro), that of his father (Ruganzu, the epic hero of the Rwandan dynasty), and even his own dynastic name (Nsoro). It seems curious that he would thus cast doubt on his own legitimacy by removing the names of his two predecessors—not to mention his own royal persona—from the pool of dynastic names. Kagame, "Le code ésotérique," 377, 377 nn23, 24. Also Kagame, *La notion de génération*, 1n2; Kagame, "Chronologie du Burundi," 18; Kagame, *Un abrégé*, vol. 1, 113–14; Vansina, *L'évolution du royaume Rwanda*, 69–70, attributes this to the reign of Rujugira. The principle is summarized in d'Hertefelt and Coupez, *La royauté sacrée*, 478 ("Noms Dynastiques"). Curiously, by 1900 the Rwanda king list recorded only a maximum of three cycles of dynastic names (and one of those is less than certain); yet Kagame insists on four cycles—invariably—for Burundi. But if Rujugira was a usurper, as Vansina maintains, there remain, ironically, only two complete cycles for Rwanda back from 1900: the very number Kagame rejects for Burundi by reference to Rwanda!

30. Vansina, "Notes sur la chronologie"; Mworoha et al., *L'histoire du Burundi*, 131–33; Chrétien, "Du hirsute au hamite," "Nouvelles hypothèses," and "Les traditionnistes lettrés."

31. Kagame, *La notion de génération*, 98n1.

32. Such transformations bear close parallels with those portrayed elsewhere in the region: in Bunyoro, Sir Tito Winyi, hitherto known by the dynastic name of Winyi II, in 1934 suddenly became transformed, "in a trice," to Winyi IV (Henige, *Chronology*, 105–14). See also Henige, "Reflections."

33. For further discussion of this prevalent assumption see chapter 1, this volume.

34. Kagame, *Inganji Karinga,* sec. VII, pars. 61–68; Kagame, *La poésie dynastique,* 37–38; Kagame, *Les milices du Rwanda précolonial* (Brussels: ARSOM, 1963), 24; Kagame, *Un abrégé,* vol. 1, 87–91; Vansina, *L'évolution du royaume Rwanda,* 86–87.

35. Vansina, *L'évolution du royaume Rwanda,* 87.

36. For an analysis of these traditions, see David Newbury, *Kings and Clans: Ijwi Island and the Lake Kivu Rift, 1780–1840* (Madison: University of Wisconsin Press, 1991), 126–42.

37. Kagame, *Inganji Karinga,* sec. II, par. 68; Delmas, *Les généalogies,* 28–29; Kagame, *Les milices,* 23–24; Kagame, *Un abrégé,* vol. 1, 91; Kagame, *La poésie dynastique,* 37–38.

38. Delmas, *Les généalogies,* 47–49; there are may other instances in Delmas that could be drawn on to make the same point—that commoner genealogies are almost invariably shorter than the royal genealogy.

39. L. Viaene, "Historique des Bahunde" (Bukavu, n.d.). To be sure, the Bunyungu king list is suspect. But what is significant here is that even were the list fabricated by reference to other king lists as then available, it speaks to a shorter Rwandan list at the time of its creation, since the tie-in to Rwanda is precise.

40. Kagame explains the discrepancy of commoner to royal genealogies by reference to the mechanism noted above (note 29 and "Le code ésotérique," 386), by which commoner ancestors before Rujugira were no longer remembered because their spirits could no longer harm those descendants who failed to honor their memory. But it is important to note that this practice was effective only by the decree of a Rwandan monarch. Therefore, while an interesting argument for those families close to the royal line, it is unlikely to apply to those areas incorporated into Rwandan state structures only after the time of Rujugira. It certainly does not apply to areas outside Rwanda, such as Buhavu and Buhunde.

41. "Rapport d'enquête préalable à la construction de la Chefferie, et résumé de l'Histoire du Buhavu (Contribution Verdonck ou R. P. Feys)" (White Fathers Archives, Bukavu).

42. The nearest mission to Buhavu was at Mwanda, near Karhana [Katana], south of Buhavu. From this mission the priests visited Mpinga, the heartland of the Buhavu kingdom.

43. On the Ijwi kings see D. Newbury, *Kings and Clans,* esp. 178–99; and chapter 4, this volume.

44. D. Newbury, *Kings and Clans,* 166–77; Feys, "Histoire des Bahavu."

45. Catharine Newbury, *The Cohesion of Oppression: Clientship and Ethnicity in Rwanda, 1860–1960* (New York: Columbia University Press, 1988) was based on this research, although the interview data cover greater historical breadth than what appears in the published work.

46. I consider this unlikely since none of these names are remembered as former Havu kings in the oral sources extant in the 1970s on Ijwi or in Mpinga, the center of the senior Havu line. It remains possible that these names are drawn from the dynastic line of one of the other small polities west of the Nile-Zaire divide, a social formation no longer extant in the published sources.

47. Vansina, Rennie, and Nkurikiyimfura would date this to a seventeenth-eighteenth century cycle. Their dates are as follows: Kagame: Ruganzu (1510–1543), Rujugira

(1675–1708); Vansina: Ruganzu (1600–1624), Rujugira (1744–1768); Rennie: Ruganzu (1603–1630), Rujugira (1756–1765); Nkurikiyimfura: Ruganzu (1600–1623), Rujugira (1731–1769).

48. Kagame, *La poésie dynastique;* Kagame, *Un abrégé,* vol. 1, 118–22; Kagame, *Les milices.*

49. Vansina, *L'évolution du royaume Rwanda,* 87.

50. Emmanuel Ntezimana, "Coutumes et traditions des royaumes Hutu du Bukunzi et du Busozo," *Études Rwandaises* 13, no. 2 (1980), 15–39; Ntezimana, "L'arrivée des Européens au Kinyaga et la fin des royaumes Hutu du Bukunzi et du Busozo," *Études Rwandaises* 13, no. 3 (1980): 1–29; Louis de Lacger, *Le Ruanda,* 2nd ed. (Kabgayi, Rwanda: Imprimérie de Kabgayi, 1961), 82–89; C. Newbury, *Cohesion of Oppression,* 214–15 and 291n14. The ritual autonomy of Bukunzi—including a ritual attack by the Rwandan court —is discussed in d'Hertefelt and Coupez, *La royauté sacrée,* 151, 277–79, 449–50.

51. De Lacger, *Le Ruanda,* 109; Kagame, *La poésie dynastique,* 41, 121.

52. Sigwalt suggests that instead of direct Rwandan involvement, Shi pretenders usurped the throne of Ngweshe, perhaps with tacit Rwandan support. Richard Sigwalt, "The Early History of Bushi: An Essay in the Historical Use of Genesis Traditions" (PhD diss., University of Wisconsin–Madison, 1975), 65–66. But this interpretation differs from Rwandan conquest, as claimed in the Rwanda royal sources: Kagame, *La poésie dynastique,* 41. Furthermore, claims in Rwanda sources to Nyamuheshera's attacks on the kings on Ijwi are clearly specious: see D. Newbury, *Kings and Clans,* 126–42. This casts doubt on the validity of similar claims to Nyamuheshera's exploits elsewhere in the region. By contrast, Sigwalt suggests considerable Rwandan influence in this area during Gahindiro's reign ("Early History of Bushi," 12). See also Paul Masson, *Trois siècles chez les Bashi* (Tervuren: MRAC, 1962).

53. Kagame, *La poésie dynastique,* 41, 121.

54. D. Newbury, *Kings and Clans,* 65–80, 156–65. The anachronistic nature of this claim is shown by the fact that it reappears as a rationale for Rwabugiri's attack of the late nineteenth century; for a discussion of this episode see chapter 6, this volume.

55. Kagame, *La poésie dynastique,* 129–30; 92 and 121 add little; 102 refers to his western conquests, but Kagame's reference to Nyamizi is clearly an anachronism which applies to Kigeri Rwabugiri. On Rwabugiri's campaigns in this area see chapters 5 and 6, this volume.

56. For an account of Rwabugiri's battles on Ijwi, see chapter 6, this volume. On the Rwandan traditions of Nyamuheshera, see Kagame, *La poésie dynastique,* 41, 121; Nyamuheshera's attacks on Ijwi are not mentioned in Kagame, *Un abrégé,* vol. 1. For fuller consideration of these traditions, see D. Newbury, *Kings and Clans,* 126–42.

57. For another example of this see Kagame, *Le code des institutions politiques.*

58. Kagame, *Un abrégé,* vol. 1, 121, where he notes that Bwanacyambwe was retained by Rwanda from these wars. Vansina, suggesting that this area was seized during a war between Gisaka and Ndorwa rather than as a result of a specific Rwandan campaign, uses this as an example of the general tendency to inflate military claims in Rwandan official dynastic traditions, and he refers specifically to the Ndorwa "wars" of Kigeri Nyamuheshera as illustrative of this tendency; Vansina, *L'évolution du royaume Rwanda,* 75–76, 87.

59. Kagame, *Les milices,* 66. Similarly, Pagès includes no information on Nyamuheshera or his successor, Mibambwe Gisanura, though he includes them both on his

king list (*Un royaume hamite*,136). Nonetheless, it is interesting that Pagès notes Kigeri Ndabarasa, four reigns later, as Kigeri II, not, as Kagame asserts, Kigeri III (ibid., 143).

60. Kagame, *Les milices,* 66.

61. Kagame, *Un abrégé,* vol. 1, 122.

62. Ibid., 121.

63. Delmas, *Les généalogies,* 54–56.

64. Ibid., 55–56.

65. In *La poésie dynastique,* 40, Kagame does mention some minor campaigns, however.

66. Delmas, *Les généalogies,* 55–56. This is not impossible; after all, Nzuki did descend from Ruganzu according to this genealogy. But this group also descends from a more recent king, Semugeshi. The implication here is that Nzuki was not a lineal descendant, but a junior brother of Semugeshi—and that the same process, counting intragenerational seniority as intergenerational lineality, could be extended to others. In addition to its chronological implications, this reference of course also brings into question the claim of Semugeshi to the status of king. Rather, he may have been an eminent authority associated with kingship over a long period and only later elevated to that status to complete the cycle. We have already mentioned the bizarre assertion that Semugeshi abolished the royal names of Ruganzu, Ndahiro, and his own reign from the cycle of dynastic names.

67. Kagame, *Un abrégé,* vol. 1, 111, 118; Kagame, *Les milices,* 61ff. Others note that this position was most likely first introduced under Cyilima Rujugira: Delmas, *Les généalogies,* 67, 93; Vansina, *L'évolution du royaume Rwanda,* 70.

68. Kagame, *Un abrégé,* vol. 1, 106. 117; de Heusch, *Le Rwanda.*

69. Kagame, *Les milices,* 62.

70. The concept of the *umutabazi,* or liberator-hero, is an institution in the Rwandan traditions, designating a warrior who is martyred for the cause of Rwanda; his death, according to the augurs, assures the victory of Rwanda in war: Kagame, "Le code ésotérique," 368n8.

71. Delmas, *Les généalogies,* 108.

72. Kagame, *La poésie dynastique,* 157, 158; Kagame informs us that Poem 49 "*fait allusion à* un retour en armes" (emphasis added).

73. Kagame, *Les milices;* the histories of those armies formed under Ruganzu are found on 54–60.

74. Delmas, *Les généalogies,* 185.

75. Kagame, *Les milices,* 56.

76. Kagame, *La notion de génération,* 47: "L'air des monarchies situées dans le Nord-Est [du Rwanda] (Nkole, Buganda, etc.) admettent l'intronisation des frères, des oncles et des cousins du monarque décédé. . . . Les dispositions du 'Code ésotérique' nous ont épargné cette éventualité en ce qui concerne le Rwanda. Nos monarques ont regné de père en fils, d'une manière ininterrompues." On Rwaka Karemera, compare Kagame, *Un abrégé,* vol. 1, 133–34, with Vansina, *L'évolution du royaume Rwanda,* 51. This situation recalls the manner in which Rutarindwa was removed from the royal genealogy when overthrown by his uncles, who then invested his half-brother, Yuhi Musinga, in the succession struggle to follow Rwabugiri's death in 1895. Rutarindwa does not appear on Kagame's list of kings, even though he was enthroned before the death of Rwabugiri as co-ruler; Kagame, *Les milices,* 87, 89.

77. See Jan Vansina, "The Power of Systematic Doubt in Historical Enquiry," *History in Africa* 1 (1974): 109–27. Since the original publication of this essay (in 1994), Jan Vansina has published an entirely new royal chronology, dating Ruganzu Ndori to the mid-seventeenth century and Rujugira's accession to about 1770. J. Vansina, *Antecedents to Modern Rwanda: The Nyiginya Kingdom* (Madison: University of Wisconsin Press, 2004), 207–16.

78. It has been argued—most forcefully in Jan Vansina, *De la tradition orale* (Tervuren: MRAC, 1961) and in many works by Kagame—that the controlled transmission of Rwandan royal traditions made them more reliable than other oral sources. However, with growing awareness of the powerful role of cultural hegemony and the role of ideology in historical understanding, and with greater sensitivity to how the power of knowledge accompanies the knowledge of power, these assumptions have been increasingly challenged. Greater control over the transmission of esoteric traditions may serve to reinforce ideological assertions of the past rather than to conserve the "facts" in some pure positivistic form. In fact, removing such historical debates from the public realm may be one of the essential techniques of defining history according to the perspectives of the ruling elite. This appears to be less frequent in societies without a written tradition—or that abjure the use of writing in political contexts; see Janet Ewald, "Speaking, Writing, and Authority: Explorations in and from the Kingdom of Taqali," *Comparative Studies in Society and History* 30 (1988): 199–227. But it is not unknown: Rwanda provides an excellent example of how esoteric—ideological—history is captured through the use of esoteric traditions. The claim that controlled transmission assures historical fidelity is manifestly false; it only makes for easier manipulation of sources, whether through deliberate distortion or (more likely) unconscious alteration in the name of ideological/hegemonic coherence. The cases of Gisaka, Ndorwa, and Burundi, discussed above, provide sufficient illustration of the rationalizations for manipulation.

Chapter 12: Precolonial Rwanda and Burundi

This chapter appeared as an article in International Journal of African Historical Studies *34, no. 2 (2001): 255–314.*

1. For example, Donald Denoon and Adam Kuper, "Nationalist Historians in Search of a Nation: The 'New Historiography' in Dar es Salaam," *African Affairs* 69, no. 277 (1970): 329–49. Moving rapidly beyond a nationalist historiography was expedited by the fact that many of these historians were not nationals themselves. However, among those historians who were citizens of Burundi and Rwanda a nationalist orientation was prominent: Émile Mworoha et al., *L'histoire du Burundi des origines à la fin du XIXe siècle* (Paris: Hatier, 1987); Joseph Gahama, *Le Burundi sous administration belge* (Paris: Karthala, 1983); Kagame, *Un abrégé de l'ethno-histoire du Rwanda précolonial*, vol. 1 (Butare: Éditions universitaires du Rwanda, 1972) and vol. 2 (1975); Jean Rumiya, *Le Rwanda sous le régime du mandat Belge* (Paris: L'Harmattan, 1992); Jean-Néopomucène Nkurikiyimfura, *Le gros bétail et la société rwandaise: Évolution historique dès XIIe–XIVe siècles à 1958* (Paris: L'Harmattan, 1994).

2. For precolonial history there were a few notable exceptions: Émile Mworoha, *Peuples et rois de l'Afrique des lacs: Le Burundi et les royaumes voisins au XIXe siècle* (Dakar: Nouvelles éditions africaines, 1977); René Lemarchand, *Rwanda and Burundi* (London:

Pall Mall, 1970); Jean-Pierre Chrétien, *L'Afrique des Grands Lacs: Deux milles ans de l'histoire* (Paris: Aubier, 2000); Bernard Lugan, *Histoire du Rwanda: De la préhistoire à nos jours* (Paris: Bartillat, 1997); and especially Jan Vansina, *Le Rwanda ancien: Le royaume Nyiginya* (Paris: Karthala, 2001). A recent assessment of the thematic developments of the field is found in David Newbury and Catharine Newbury, "Bringing the Peasants Back In: Agrarian Themes in the Construction and Corrosion of a State Historiography in Rwanda," *American Historical Review* 105, no. 3 (2000): 832–77.

3. For works exploring these debates over history, see Catharine Newbury, "Ethnicity and the Politics of History in Rwanda," *Africa Today* 45, no. 1 (1998): 7–25; Lisa Malkki, "Context and Consciousness: Local Conditions for the Production of Historical and National Thought among Hutu Refugees in Tanzania," in *Nationalist Ideology and the Production of National Cultures,* ed. Richard G. Fox (Washington, DC: American Ethnological Society, 1990), 32–62; Danielle de Lame, "Instants retrouvés: Rwanda, regards neufs au fil du temps," in *Liber Amicorum Marcel d'Hertefelt,* ed. P. Wymeersch (Brussels: Institut Africain, 1993), 115–33; Claudine Vidal, "La désinformation en histoire: Données historiques sur les relations entre Hutu, Tutsi et Twa durant la période précolonial," *Dialogue,* no. 200 (1997): 11–20; Vidal, "Questions sur le rôle des paysans durant le génocide des Rwandais tutsi," *Cahiers d'Études Africaines* 38, nos. 2–4 (1998): 331–45; René Lemarchand, "Genocide in the Great Lakes: Which Genocide? Whose Genocide?" *African Studies Review* 41, no. 1 (1998): 3–16.

4. Works on this region in French have been less neglectful of these broader historical frameworks: Mworoha, *Peuples et rois;* Mworoha et al., *L'histoire du Burundi;* Gahama, *Le Burundi;* Rumiya, *Le Rwanda sous le régime Belge;* Antoine Nyagahene, "Histoire et peuplement: Ethnies, clans, et lignages dans le Rwanda ancien et contemporain" (PhD diss., Université de Paris-VII, Septentrion, 1997); Ferdinand Nahimana, *Le Blanc est arrivé; le roi est parti: Une facette de l'histoire du Rwanda contemporain, 1894–1931* (Kigali: Éditions Printer Set, 1987); Lugan, *Histoire du Rwanda;* Chrétien, *L'Afrique des Grands Lacs.* A particularly useful, if unconventional, contribution is Roger Botte, "Rwanda and Burundi, 1899–1930: Chronology of a Slow Assassination," *International Journal of African Historical Studies* 18, no. 1 (1985): 53–91; 18, no. 2 (1985): 289–314.

5. For consideration of some of those themes for Rwanda, see chapter 2, this volume; also Newbury and Newbury, "Bringing the Peasants Back In."

6. Each country is about the size of Belgium, or the state of Vermont. But whereas the population of Vermont was 500,000 in the early 1990s, Rwanda and Burundi, with population densities similar to those in Bangladesh, each had 7–8 million—fifteen times that of Vermont.

7. For the range of materials published on Rwanda in the social sciences and humanities up to 1980 (1987 for books), see d'Hertefelt and de Lame, *Société, Culture, et Histoire du Rwanda.*

8. For a discussion of these issues, see Mworoha et al., *L'histoire du Burundi,* 35–56; Joseph Gahama and Christian Thibon, eds., *Les régions orientales du Burundi: Une périphérie à l'épreuve du développement* (Paris: Karthala, 1994).

9. Of course, there were many other distinct subregions, whose salience varied over time. Consequently, those discussed here are in a sense arbitrary (as well as self-defined) regions, since at the periphery most shaded into the other, and with yet more local loyalties also in play, at any given moment the level of identity was always determined by con-

text, not by culture alone. Regional histories are not available for all areas, but for a broad survey, see *Historique et chronologie du Ruanda* (Kabgayi, Rwanda: Vicariat apostolique du Ruanda, 1956). In addition, for Kinyaga, see Catharine Newbury, *The Cohesion of Oppression: Clientship and Ethnicity in Rwanda, 1860–1960* (New York: Columbia University Press, 1988); and Antoine Nyagahene, "Les activités économiques et commerciales au Kinyaga dans la séconde partie du XIXe S." (Mémoire de licence, Université Nationale du Rwanda-Butare, 1979). For Bwishaza, see R. Vanwalle, "Aspecten van Staatsvorming in West-Rwanda," *Africa-Tervuren* 28, no. 3 (1982): 64–77; and Danielle de Lame, *Une colline entre mille, ou, le calme avant la tempête: Transformations et blocages du Rwanda rural* (Tervuren: MRAC, 1996). For Bugoyi, see A. Pagès, *Au Rwanda: Sur les bords du Lac Kivu, Congo belge: Un royaume hamite au centre de l'Afrique* (Brussels: IRCB, 1933), 634–701; and chapter 3, this volume. On Mulera: Marcel d'Hertefelt, "Huwelijk, familie en aanverwantschap bij de Reera," *Zaire* 13 (1959): 115–48, 243–85; May Edel, *The Chiga of Uganda* (London: Oxford University Press for the International African Institute, 1957). For Ndorwa: Jim Freedman, "Principles of Relationships in Rwandan Kiga Society" (PhD diss., Princeton University, 1974); Freedman, *Nyabingi: The Social History of an African Divinity* (Tervuren: MRAC, 1984); Alison Des Forges, "The Drum Is Greater Than the Shout: The 1912 Rebellion in Northern Rwanda," in *Banditry, Rebellion, and Social Protest in Africa,* ed. Donald Crummey (Portsmouth, NH: Heinemann, 1986), 311–31. For Gisaka, see d'Arianoff, *L'histoire des Bagesera*. Regional autonomy is reflected also in the recent publications from this area, Justin Kalibwami, *Le Catholicisme et la société rwandaise* (Paris: Présence Africaine, 1991); and Emmanuel Nkunzumwami, *La tragédie rwandaise: Historique et perspectives* (Paris: L'Harmattan, 1996).

10. For Buyogoma, see Gahama and Thibon, *Les régions orientales du Burundi.* For Buragane, see Michele D. Wagner, "Whose History Is History? A History of the Baragane People of Buragane, Southern Burundi, 1850–1932" (PhD diss., University of Wisconsin–Madison, 1991). For the Imbo, see Jean-Pierre Chrétien, "La crise écologique de l'Afrique orientale du début du XIXe siècle: Le cas de l'Imbo au Burundi, 1890–1916," in *Questions sur la paysannerie au Burundi: Actes de la table ronde sur "Sciences sociales, humaines et développement rural,"* organisé par la Faculté des Lettres et Sciences Humaines (Bujumbura: Université de Bujumbura, 1987), 55–93; Jacques Depelchin, "From Precapitalism to Imperialism: A History of Social and Economic Formations in Eastern Zaïre (Uvira Zone), c. 1800–1964" (PhD diss., Stanford University, 1974); David Newbury, *Kings and Clans: Ijwi Island and the Lake Kivu Rift, 1780–1840* (Madison: University of Wisconsin Press, 1991), 146–52.

11. Among an extensive literature, see Marie-Claude van Grunderbeek, Émile Roche, and Hugues Doutrelepont, "L'âge du fer ancien au Rwanda et au Burundi: Archéologie et environnement," *Journal des Africanistes* 52, nos. 1–2 (1982): 5–58, esp. 17; see also Van Grunderbeek, Roche, and Doutrelepont, *Le premier âge du fer au Rwanda et au Burundi* (Brussels: Université Libre de Bruxelles, 1983); Peter Schmidt, "A New Look at Interpretations of the Early Iron Age in East Africa," *History in Africa* 2 (1975): 137–47; Schmidt, *Historical Archaeology* (Westport, CT: Greenwood Press, 1978). David L. Schoenbrun, *A Green Place, a Good Place: Agrarian Change, Gender, and Social Identity in the Great Lakes Region to the Fifteenth Century* (Portsmouth, NH: Heinemann, 1998), chap. 1; Peter Robertshaw and David Taylor, "Climate Change and the Rise of Political Complexity in Western Uganda," *Journal of African History* 41, no. 1 (2000): 1–28; Vansina, *Le Rwanda ancien,* 20–27.

12. Van Grunderbeek, Roche, and Doutrelepont, *Le premier âge du fer.* Also, Francis van Noten, *Histoire archéologique du Rwanda* (Tervuren: MRAC, 1983). However, in separate commentaries Jan Vansina and Robert Soper suggest that these works be used with some caution; see Jan Vansina's review in *Azania* 19 (1984): 145–47, and Robert Soper's review in *Azania* 19 (1984): 148–51.

13. Francis van Noten, "The Early Iron Age in the Interlacustrine Region: The Diffusion of Iron Technology," *Azania* 14 (1979): 61–81; see esp. 76, where Van Noten makes several associations among different sites, but these classifications combine sites either west of the divide or east of the divide, never across the divide: "There is a clear distinction between the sites along the Lake Kivu axis [i.e., those west of the divide] from those situated to the east. . . . These sites very often have a series of decorative patterns quite different from one another and also different from the decorative patterns of the 'inland' sites to the east." But with such a thin base of archaeological remains in the region, it should be noted that Van Grunderbeek, Roche, and Doutrelepont disagree with Van Noten's interpretation on some particulars: "L'âge de fer ancien au Rwanda et au Burundi," 25. For cultural elaboration on this point, see D. Newbury, *Kings and Clans,* chap. 2.

14. A similarly fundamental reinterpretation has been proposed for western Uganda, drawing on the work of Peter Robertshaw, "Archaeological Survey, Ceramic Analysis, and State Formation in Western Uganda," *African Archaeological Review* 12 (1994): 105–31; D. A. M. Reid, "The Role of Cattle in the Later Iron Age Communities of Southern Uganda (PhD diss., Cambridge University, 1991); and Renée Louise Tantala, "The Early History of Kitara in Western Uganda: Process Models of Religious and Political Change" (PhD diss., University of Wisconsin–Madison, 1989); and others: see Robertshaw and Taylor, "Climate Change."

15. The work of David Schoenbrun has been particularly important in transforming our understanding of this deep history: "We Are What We Eat: Ancient Agriculture between the Great Lakes," *Journal of African History* 34, no. 1 (1993): 1–31; Schoenbrun, *Green Place,* chaps. 1–2.

16. David L. Schoenbrun, "Cattle Herds and Banana Gardens: The Historical Geography of the Western Great Lakes Region," *African Archaeological Review* 11 (1993): 39–72, esp. 45–47. An important source on the archaeology of such early cattle histories in western Uganda is Reid, "Role of Cattle."

17. Schoenbrun, "We Are What We Eat." For this area, the work of Peter Schmidt is particularly important on such issues: Schmidt, "Early Iron Age Settlements and Industrial Locales in West Lake," *Tanzania Notes and Records* 84–85 (1980): 77–94; Schmidt, "New Look;" Schmidt, *Historical Archaeology;* Schmidt, "Archaeological Views on a History of Landscape Change in East Africa," *Journal of African History* 38, no. 3 (1997): 393–421.

18. Schoenbrun, "Cattle Herds," 54–64.

19. Chrétien, "Les années de l'eleusine, du sorgho, et des haricots dans l'ancien Burundi: Ecologie et idéologie," *African Economic History* 7 (1982): 75–92. For descriptions of the First Fruits ceremonies elsewhere in the region, see d'Hertefelt and Coupez, *La royauté sacrée,* 73–96; chapter 10, this volume; D. Newbury, *Kings and Clans,* chap. 12.

20. Jean-Pierre Chrétien, "Le sorgho dans l'agriculture, la culture, et l'histoire du Burundi," *Journal des Africanistes* 52, nos. 1–2 (1982): 145–62.

21. Jennifer M. Olson, "Farmer Responses to Land Degradation in Gikongoro, Rwanda" (PhD diss., Michigan State University, 1994). On the general agrarian processes

common in this region, see Priscilla Reining, "Social Factors in Food Production in an East African Peasant Society: The Haya," in *African Food Production Systems*, ed. Peter F. M. McLoughlin (Baltimore: Johns Hopkins University Press, 1970), 41–89.

22. For an exploration of these historical processes, see David Newbury, "The Invention of Rwanda: The Alchemy of Ethnicity" (paper presented at the African Studies Association Annual Meeting, Orlando, 1995).

23. Jan Czekanowski, *Ethnographie: Zwischenseengebiet Mpororo, Ruanda*, vol. 1 of *Forschungen im Nil-Congo Zwischengebeit* (Berlin: Klinkhardt and Biermann, 1917), 262. On the historical development of ethnic identity, varying for different ethnic categories as well as for regions, see Catharine Newbury: "Ethnicity in Rwanda: The Case of Kinyaga," *Africa* 48, no. l (1978): 17–29. For commentaries on the common perceptions of ethnicity in this region, see chapter 1, this volume; Jean-Pierre Chrétien, "Les deux visages de Cham: Points de vue français du XIXème siècle sur les races africaines d'après l'exemple de l'Afrique Orientale," in *L'idée de race dans la pensée politique française contemporaine*, ed. Pierre Guiral and Emile Temime (Paris: Éditions du Centre national de la recherche scientifique, 1977), 171–99; Claudine Vidal, "Situations ethniques au Rwanda," in *Au coeur de l'ethnie: Ethnies, tribalisme et état en Afrique*, ed. Jean-Loup Amselle et Elikia M'Bokolo (Paris: La Découverte, 1985), 167–84.

24. Jean-Claude Desmarais, "Le Rwanda des anthropologues: L'archéologie de l'idéologie raciale," *Anthropologie et Sociétés* 2, no. 1 (1978): 71–92; Vidal, "Situations ethniques"; Jean-Pierre Chrétien, "Hutu et Tutsi au Rwanda et au Burundi," in *Au coeur de l'ethnie*, ed. Jean-Loup Amselle and Elikia M'Bokolo (Paris: La Découverte, 1985), 129–65.

25. For an example of the divergence within a classification see Helen Codere, *The Biography of an African Society: Rwanda, 1900–1960* (Tervuren: MRAC, 1973), 20. Codere argues that by the late nineteenth century in Rwanda less than 10 percent of Tutsi could be considered to be in the "political" class—that is, holding positions of state power. But compare this to Burundi, where positions of "state power" were less clearly defined and more numerous, and where there was almost certainly less difference in life styles between the political class and other classes. Both the narrow class stratification among Tutsi in Rwanda and the fact of significant differences between the two societies refute the concept of corporate homogeneity commonly attributed to ethnic labels—and therefore undercut any assumptions of some essentialist historical significance to ethnicity. Again, ethnicity is important, but not in the deterministic fashion often portrayed in popular accounts.

26. John Hanning Speke, *Journal of the Discovery of the Source of the Nile* (Edinburgh: William Blackwood, 1863), esp. chap. 9.

27. C. Newbury, "Ethnicity in Rwanda"; chapter 8, this volume. In areas of close association with the royal court, the nature of the term differed: Vansina, *Le Rwanda ancien*, 45, 164–70; but caution should be exercised in extrapolating this model to all of Rwanda.

28. Lemarchand, *Rwanda and Burundi*, 23–25; Lemarchand, *Burundi: Ethnocide as Discourse and Practice* (New York: Cambridge University Press, 1994), 6–11, 34–57; Albert A. Trouwborst, "Le Burundi," in *Les anciens royaumes de la zone interlacustre méridionale*, edited by M. d'Hertefelt, Albert A. Trouwborst, and J. H. Scherer (Tervuren: MRAC, 1962).

29. Pascal Ndayishinguje, *L'intronisation d'un Mwami* (Nanterre: Laboratoire d'ethnologie et de sociologie comparative, 1977); Claude Guillet, "Higiro et Banga: Deux domaines de tambourinaires," in *L'arbre-mémoire: Traditions orales du Burundi*, ed. Léonidas Ndoricimpa and Claude Guillet (Paris: Karthala, 1984), 95–146; Émile Mworoha,

"La cour du roi Mwezi Gisabo du Burundi à la fin du XIXe siècle," *Études d'Histoire Africaine* 7 (1975): 39–58.

30. Trouwborst, "Le Burundi," 147–48; Lemarchand, *Rwanda and Burundi*, 28–29, 76; Lemarchand, *Burundi*, 39, 167.

31. These concepts are developed at length in C. Newbury, *Cohesion of Oppression;* C. Newbury, "Ethnicity in Rwanda"; chap. 1, this volume; D. Newbury, "Alchemy of Ethnicity"; Vidal, "Situations ethniques"; and Chrétien, "Hutu et Tutsi au Rwanda et au Burundi."

32. Versions of these genesis traditions are found in P. Loupias, "Tradition et légende des Batutsi sur la création du monde et leur établissement au Ruanda," *Anthropos* 3, no. 1 (1908): 1–13; Kagame, *Inganji Karinga*, 2nd ed. (Kabgayi, Rwanda: n.p., 1959); Luc de Heusch, *Rois nés d'un coeur de vache* (Paris: Gallimard, 1982); and Pierre Smith, "La lance d'une jeune fille," in *Échanges et Communications*, vol. 2, *Mélanges offerts à Claude Lévi-Strauss*, ed. Claude Lévi-Straus, Jean Pouillon, and Pierre Maranda (The Hague: Mouton, 1970), 1381–1409. For a summary, see D. Newbury, *Kings and Clans*, 82–85. For wider regional considerations, see Christopher C. Wrigley, *Kingship and State: The Buganda Dynasty* (Cambridge: Cambridge University Press, 1996); Mworoha, *Peuples et rois;* and Tantala, "Early History of Kitara."

33. On the use of the concept of "clan" as a corporate group, see d'Hertefelt, *Les clans;* chapter 8, this volume; D. Newbury, *Kings and Clans*, passim.

34. For reasons we shall explore below, Vansina dates the creation of this tradition to the reign of Mazimpaka, near the beginning of the eighteenth century (*Le Rwanda ancien*, 115ff.).

35. Kagame, *Un abrégé*, vol. 1, 39–47; Vansina, *L'évolution du royaume Rwanda*, 9–10; André Coupez and Thomas Kamanzi, *Récits historiques Rwanda, dans la version de C. Gakaniisha* (Tervuren: MRAC, 1962), 71–87. For a summary of some of these sources, and an alternative analysis, see Ferdinand Nahimana, *Le Rwanda: Emergence d'un état* (Paris: L'Harmattan, 1993), esp. chap. 4. For broader commentary, see D. Newbury, *Kings and Clans*, 82–87 and chaps. 6–7.

36. Structuralist explorations of such traditions are found in de Heusch, *Rois nés;* Smith, "La lance d'une jeune fille"; Smith, "La forge de l'intelligence," *L'Homme* 10, no. 2 (1970): 5–21; Christopher C. Wrigley, "The Story of Rukidi," *Africa* 43, no. 3 (1973): 219–35; Wrigley, *Kingship and State.*

37. Nahimana, *Le Rwanda;* Marcel Pauwels, "Le Bushiru et son muhinza ou roitelet Hutu," *Annali Lateranensi* 31 (1967): 205–322; *Historique et chronologie;* Jim Freedman, "Ritual and History: The Case of Nyibingi," *Cahiers d'Études Africaines* 14, no. 1 (1974): 170–80; Vansina, *Le Rwanda ancien*, chap. 2.

38. D. Newbury, *Kings and Clans*, 133–35. According to the official king list, Ruganzu was the fourteenth king before the nineteenth century. Kagame dates Ruganzu to 1510–43; Vansina's reconsideration places Ruganzu in the mid-seventeenth century; *Le Rwanda ancien*, 246–58. I date Ruganzu's reign to the late seventeenth century or early eighteenth centuries; see chapter 11, this volume. A selection of traditions on Ruganzu appears in Pagès, *Un royaume hamite*, 238–354.

39. Vansina, *L'évolution du royaume Rwanda*, 46–47; de Heusch, *Rois nés*, chap. 4; but see also d'Hertefelt, *Les clans*, 24.

40. For an important statement on this approach, see Richard Sigwalt, "Early Rwandan History: The Contribution of Comparative Ethnography," *History in Africa* 2 (1975): 137–46. See also D. Newbury, *Kings and Clans;* and d'Hertefelt and Coupez, *La royauté sacrée.*

41. Rundi genesis traditions are discussed in Vansina, *La légende du passé: Traditions orales du Burundi* (Tervuren: MRAC, 1972), 69–117; Jean-Pierre Chrétien, "Du hirsute au hamite: Les variations du cycle de Ntare Rushatsi, fondateur du royaume du Burundi," *History in Africa* 8 (1981): 3–41; and Chrétien, "Nouvelles hypothèses sur les origines du Burundi: Les traditions du nord," in Ndoricimpa and Guillet, *L'arbre-mémoire,* 11–52. For a summary, see Mworoha et al., *L'histoire du Burundi,* 105–20.

42. In addition to the sources noted above, see Jan Vansina, "Notes sur l'histoire du Burundi," *Aequatoria* 24, no. 1 (1961): 1–10; Jan Vansina, "Note sur la chronologie du Burundi ancien," *Bulletin de l'ARSOM* 38 (1967): 429–44. For a contrasting interpretation, see Alexis Kagame, "La chronologie du Burundi dans les genres littéraires de l'ancien Rwanda," *Études Rwandaises* 12 (1979): 1–30.

43. Chrétien, "Nouvelles hypotheses," 26.

44. This process is described in Gahama, *Le Burundi,* 37–134.

45. An influential informant in this process was Pierre Baranyanka. However, on closer examination his role in this process has become an object lesson in the dangers of naïve oral methodology: Lemarchand, *Burundi,* 47–51; chapter 11, this volume; Chretien, "Nouvelles hypothèses," 12–13; Vansina, *Le Rwanda ancien,* 11–13.

46. On Buragane, see Wagner, "Whose History?"; on the Imbo, see D. Newbury, *Kings and Clans,* chap. 8.

47. Vansina, "Note sur la chronologie"; Vansina, *La légende du passé,* 133–65, 205–16; Mworoha, *Peuples et rois,* 116–209; Chrétien, *L'Afrique des Grands Lacs,* 134–72.

48. Elements of court organization, ritual celebration, and administrative ideology for the reign of Mwezi Gisabo in the late nineteenth century are presented in Mworoha, *Peuples et rois,* 116–210; Mworoha, "Mwezi Gisabo"; Ndayishinguje, *Intronisation;* and Augustin Nsanze, *Un domaine royal au Burundi: Mbuye, 1850–1945* (Paris: Société Française d'Histoire d'Outre Mer, 1980).

49. On early commerce, see Jean-Pierre Chrétien, "Le commerce du sel de l'Uvinza au XIXe siècle: De la cueillette au monopole capitaliste," *Revue Française d'Histoire d'Outre-Mer* 65 (1978): 401–22.

50. Vansina, "Notes sur l'histoire du Burundi," 4–5; Vansina, *La légende du passé,* 74–81.

51. Adrien Ndikuriyo, "Contrats de bétail, contrats de clientèle, et pouvoir politique dans le Bututsi du XIXè S.," *Études d'Histoire Africaine* 7 (1975): 60–65; Depelchin, "From Precapitalism to Imperialism."

52. J. Rugomana, "Inkuru y'Imuganuro uko wagira kera," trans. and annotated F. Rodegem as "La Fête des Prémices au Burundi," *Africana Linguistica* 5 (1971): 205–54; E. Simons, "Coutumes et institutions des Barundi," *Bulletin des Juridictions Indigènes et du Droit Coutumier Congolaise* 12, no. 11 (1944): 248–54; Joseph Gahama, "La disparition du Muganuro," in Ndoricimpa and Guillet, *L'arbre-mémoire,* 169–94; Mworoha, *Peuples et rois,* 254–62; D. Newbury, *Kings and Clans,* chap. 12.

53. Iris Berger, *Religion and Resistance: East African Kingdoms in the Precolonial Period* (Tervuren: MRAC, 1981); Berger, "Spirit Mediums, Priestesses and the Precolonial State in

Interlacustrine East Africa," in *Revealing Prophets,* ed. David Anderson and Douglas H. Johnson (London: James Currey, 1995), 65–82; Luc de Heusch, *Le Rwanda et la civilisation interlacustre* (Brussels: Université Libre de Bruxelles, 1964); Schoenbrun, *Green Place.*

54. Chapter 11, this volume; Chrétien, "Du hirsute au hamite"; J. Vansina, "Notes sur la chronologie du Burundi," *Bulletin de l'ARSOM* 38, no. 7 (1967): 429–44.

55. For an example of court claims refuted by local histories, see Wagner, "Whose History?" 11 and chap. 5; D. Newbury, *Kings and Clans,* 150–53.

56. For case studies, see Roger Botte, "La guerre interne au Burundi," in *Guerres de lignages et guerres d'états en Afrique,* ed. Jean Bazin and Emmanuel Terray (Paris: Éditions des archives contemporaines, 1982), 309–13; and Wagner, "Whose History?" esp. chap. 5.

57. For a comprehensive interpretation of these conflicts, see Botte, "La guerre interne."

58. On Kilima, see D. Newbury, *Kings and Clans,* 151–52; Vansina, *La légende du passé,* 216; Léonidas Ndoricimpa, "Du roi fondateur au roi rebelle: Le récit du rebelle dans les traditions orales du Burundi," in Ndoricimpa and Guillet, *L'arbre-mémoire,* 56–57; Botte, "La guerre interne," 273.

59. On Maconco, see Vansina, *La légende du passé,* 32–55; Jean-Pierre Chrétien, "Le cycle d'histoire de Maconco," in *Burundi: Histoire retrouvée: Vingt-cinq ans de métier d'historien en Afrique* (Paris: Aubier, 1993), 107–19. Ndoricimpa ("Du roi fondateur au roi rebelle," 53–93) considers the larger genre of resistance traditions, illustrating both regional and cultural diversity and the dichotomy between the powerful ideology and weak reality of royal rule.

60. John Iliffe, *Tanganyika under German Rule, 1905–1912* (Cambridge: Cambridge University Press, 1969); William Roger Louis, *Ruanda-Urundi, 1884–1919* (Oxford: Clarendon Press 1963); Hans Meyer, *Les Barundi: Une étude ethnologique en Afrique orientale,* trans. Françoise Willmann, ed. Jean-Pierre Chrétien (Paris: Société Française d'Histoire d'Outre Mer, 1984); Pierre Ryckmans, *Une page d'histoire coloniale: L'occupation allemande dans l'Urundi* (Brussels: ARSC, 1953).

61. Gahama, *Le Burundi;* Chrétien, "Nouvelles hypothèses," 52, and "Du hirsute au hamite."

62. Gahama, "La disparition du Muganuro."

63. Gahama, *Le Burundi,* 61–135.

64. Ibid., 104. The proportion of Bezi chiefs went from 26 to 48 percent over that time.

65. Lemarchand, *Rwanda and Burundi,* 314–15; and Lemarchand, *Burundi,* 47–51.

66. Chapter 11, this volume.

67. While they had different histories, it is worth noting that in postcolonial times, the recent political histories of Burundi and Rwanda have affected each other in what might be referred to as a "mirror" effect: Filip Reyntjens, *L'Afrique des Grands Lacs en crise* (Paris: Karthala, 1994); R. Lemarchand, "Genocide in the Great Lakes: Which Genocide? Whose Genocide?" *African Studies Review* 41, no. 1 (1998): 3–16; Lemarchand, *Burundi,* 29–30, 175–76.

68. For an assessment of these historiographical trends, see Newbury and Newbury, "Bringing the Peasants Back In."

69. This presentation of Rwandan dynastic history will be more complete than for Burundi, as a reflection of the sources, which are much richer on dynastic history for Rwanda than for Burundi. Because of the imbalance in the sources, some authors are

tempted to extrapolate events and structures from one state (Rwanda) to the other (northern Burundi). There is a history to this historiography, which can be related to European objectives of standardizing colonial structures in the two colonial territories—even including them in a single colonial administrative unit under a single "vice gouverneur." Pierre Baranyanka, a chief in Ngozi, bordering Rwanda (and a collaborator with Alexis Kagame in his interest in the reconstruction of the history of these histories), was a willing accomplice to this process of homogenizing the histories of the two kingdoms. Many recent commentators have accepted this fiction. However, despite their apparent similarities and recent interaction, it cannot be stressed enough that these two kingdoms were distinct political units, with independent dynastic origins, different precolonial political structures, and their own paths of historical development.

70. D'Hertefelt, "Le Rwanda," 36–37; d'Hertefelt, "Huwelijk, familie, en aanverwantschap"; Freedman, "Principles of Relationships"; Edel, *Chiga of Uganda*. For a summary of these land practices, see Catherine André, "Terre Rwandaise, accès politique et reforme foncières," in *L'Afrique des Grands Lacs: Annuaire 1997–98,* ed. Filip Reyntjens and Stefan Marysse (Paris: L'Harmattan, 1998), 141–73.

71. D. Newbury, *Kings and Clans,* chap. 3; Pauwels, "Le Bushiru"; Ferdinand Nahimana, "Les principautés Hutu du Rwanda septentrional," in *La civilisation ancienne des peuples des Grands Lacs: Colloque de Bujumbura (4–10 septembre 1979),* ed. Centre de Civilisation Burundaise (Paris: Karthala, 1981), 115–37; Nahimana, *Le Rwanda;* Emmanuel Ntezimana, "Coutumes et traditions des royaumes Hutu du Bukunzi et du Busozo," *Études Rwandaises* 13, no. 2 (1980): 15–39.

72. For a discussion of such ritual foundations to political power, see Randall Packard, *Chiefship and Cosmology* (Bloomington: Indiana University Press, 1981), a study that examines the ontology of power among the Bashu, a people living to the northwest of Rwanda. The ritual authority (*umuhinza*) of Bukunzi was renowned on both sides of the Kivu Rift as a rainmaker, so much so that he was respected at the royal court of Rwanda, as well as other kingdoms. The political authority on Mpembe, a large peninsula on the western shore of Lake Kivu (near Kibuye) was also a rainmaker, as was also the *mwami* of Suti, in Bunyambiriri; D. Newbury, *Kings and Clans,* 105–6 and 285–86n23, 119, Pagès, *Un royaume hamite,* 441; Louis de Lacger, *Le Ruanda,* 2nd ed. (Kabgayi, Rwanda: Imprimérie de Kabgayi, 1961), 82–89, 103–4.

73. For consideration of these forms and their extent, see D. Newbury, *Kings and Clans,* chap. 2; Packard, *Chiefship and Cosmology.*

74. Nahimana, "Les principautés Hutu"; Nahimana, *Le Rwanda.*

75. Commerce with the forest cultures west of the Kivu Rift was also important for these regions, especially the trade in luxury goods such as ornamental *ubutega* anklets made of special forest fibers, tobacco, and iron products. Chapter 3, this volume; M. R. Rwankwenda, "The History of Kayonza," in *A History of Kigezi in Southwestern Uganda,* ed. Donald Denoon (Kampala: National Trust, 1972), 124–33; Bishikwabo Chubaka, "L'économie d'échange dans les états précoloniaux du Sud-Kivu du XIXe siècle à 1920" (paper presented at the Journées d'Historiens Zaïrois, Lubumbashi, 1975); Birhakaheka Njiga and Kirhero Nsibula, "Nyangezi dans ces relations commerciales avec le Rwanda, le Burundi, et le Bufulero," *Études Rwandaises* 14, no. 1 (1981): 36–51.

76. One exception is that of Mashira: Coupez and Kamanzi, *Récits historiques Rwanda,* 143–49; another is found in the accounts of Jabwe and Nsoro, noted above, for Burundi.

77. See chapter 10, this volume; for an analogous case: D. Newbury, *Kings and Clans,* chap. 12 and passim; also see Sigwalt, "Early Rwanda History."

78. For case studies of particular rituals see D. Newbury, "What Role Has Kingship?"; Smith, "La forge de l'intelligence"; and (for the First Fruits Ceremonies) the sources cited in note 52 above. The range of royal rituals are discussed briefly in Kagame, "Le code ésotérique de la dynastie du Rwanda," *Zaïre* 1, no. 4 (1947), 363–86. The Rwandan royal rituals are presented in more complete form in the magnificent volume edited by d'Hertefelt and Coupez, *La royauté sacrée.*

79. These conclusions are elaborated in D. Newbury, "What Role Has Kingship?"

80. D'Hertefelt and Coupez, *La royauté sacrée;* Sigwalt, "Early Rwanda History."

81. D. Newbury, "What Role Has Kingship?" For Burundi, see Jean-Pierre Chrétien, "La royauté capture les rois," appendix to Ndayishinguje, *L'intronisation,* 61–70. For a broader regional analysis, see D. Newbury, *Kings and Clans,* chap. 12; A. Pagès, "Note sur le régime des biens dans la région du Bugoyi," *Congo* 19, no. 4 (1938): 392–433.

82. Chapter 9, this volume.

83. Two prominent examples illustrate this cultural autonomy of the north. Ferdinand Nahimana was a historian who wrote on the western polities and their conquest and absorption within the Nyiginya dynastic expansion; see his *Le Rwanda.* He was also deeply implicated in the organization of the 1994 genocide, as a highly placed administrator responsible for the notorious Radio Libre de Mille Collines, one of the mechanisms for mobilizing militias in the genocide. President Habyarimana's wife was also of a family influential in Bushiru, one of the last of the autonomous western polities to be absorbed into the Rwanda state during colonial rule.

84. Even at the height of dynastic consolidation under colonial rule, the Belgians seriously considered dividing the state, roughly along the lines of earlier cultural traditions (east and west)—but, in conformity with the racial-ethnic strictures of the day, with both segments under Tutsi aristocratic control.

85. The most complete discussion of this is in Vansina, *Le Rwanda ancien,* where he associates the construction of tradition itself to the reign of Mazampaka (in the early eighteenth century), and the claims to Nyiginya presence in Buganza as instrumental, part of a process legitimating Rwandan military campaigns in this rich pastoral area. But in addition to being pastoral land par excellence, Buganza was also contested terrain between Rwanda and Gisaka, and claimed by the latter; therefore, such a reading as proposed by Vansina would also help explain the subsequent conflicts between Gisaka and Rwanda during the successions of Rujugira, Ndabarasa, Sentabyo, and Gahindiro.

86. Various dates have been proposed for the emergence of the Nyiginya dynastic line, but these estimates all seem unreliable because based on two premises which are suspect. First, structurally, the official genealogy posits an unbroken father-to-son succession over close to a thousand years: Kagame, *Un abrégé,* vol. 1, 37–38. Second, in content, it is not clear that every name cited in the king list—even for the recent years—was a ruling monarch, or that each reign length extended over the time period attributed to it. For the debates, see Kagame, *La notion de génération appliquée à la généalogie dynastique et à l'histoire du Rwanda dès Xe–XIe siècles à nos jours* (Brussels: ARSOM, 1959); Vansina, *L'évolution du royaume Rwanda* and the "Supplément" to the second edition (Brussels, 2000), especially 89–91; J. Keith Rennie, "The Precolonial Kingdom of Rwanda: A Reinterpretation," *Transafrican Journal of History* 2, no. 2 (1972): 11–53 ; Jean-Népomucène Nkurikiyimfura, "La révision d'une chronologie: Le cas du royaume du Rwanda," in

Sources orales de l'histoire de l'Afrique, ed. Claude-Hélène Perrot (Paris: Éditions du Centre national de la recherche scientifique, 1989), 149–80; and chapter 11, this volume. It is also useful to recall that the Nyiginya were not a ruling clan, but the clan from which the rulers were chosen; not all Nyiginya held royal authority, just as not all Tutsi were among the political elite; though the kings were Tutsi, this was not "Tutsi rule." However, our understanding of the early history of the Nyiginya dynasty, including its chronology, has been completely revised with the publication of Vansina, *Le Rwanda ancien;* on the chronology, see Appendix I, 245–58.

87. On Ruganzu, see Pagès, *Un royaume hamite,* 228–353; de Lacger, *Le Ruanda,* 107–9; Coupez and Kamanzi, *Récits historiques Rwanda,* 205–55; Kagame, *Un abrégé,* vol. 1, 93–108; Kagame, *Grands genres lyriques,* 277–78; de Heusch, *Rois nés,* 54–112 (and frequently thereafter to 243) illustrates the structural contours of these traditions within the larger corpus.

88. Kagame dates Ruganzu to the early sixteenth century: *La notion de génération,* 87; *Un abrégé,* vol. 1, 35–38. Vansina (*L'évolution du royaume Rwanda,* 56) places him early seventeenth century, a figure accepted by most others. But the chronology is not sure, for that presumes the acceptance of all others in the king list; for a discussion, see chapter 11, this volume. Vansina's more recent, revised chronology dates Ruganzu to near the turn of the eighteenth century (*Le Rwanda ancien,* 55).

89. Vansina, *L'évolution du royaume Rwanda,* 51. It is worth noting that, from the time of Rujugira (in the mid-eighteenth century) through the accession of Rudahigwa (1931), 7 of 9 royal successions can be seen as of questionable legitimacy by reference to the formal rules of succession; this in a state in which succession to kingship was assumed to be strictly governed by rigidly prescribed ritual protocol. Kagame, *La notion de génération,* passim; Kagame, *Un abrégé,* vol. 1, 11–12, 35–38.

90. For an analysis, see D. Newbury, *Kings and Clans,* 135 and 295–96nn 38–40.

91. While we lack ecological precisions for the precolonial period, colonial indications are suggestive: C. de l'Epine, "Historique des famines et disettes dans l'Urundi," *Bulletin Agricole du Congo Belge* 20, no. 3 (1929): 440–42; Henri Jaspar, "Le Ruanda-Urundi, pays à disettes périodiques," *Congo* 2, no. 1 (1929): 1–22; Henri Scaëtta, *Les famines périodiques dans le Ruanda* (Brussels: IRCB, 1932). For the wider region (though the dates need be taken with caution), see the suggestive essay by J. Bertin Webster, "Noi! Noi! Famines as an Aid to Interlacustrine Chronology," in *Chronology, Migration, and Drought in Interlacustrine Africa,* ed. J. Bertin Webster (New York: Africana, 1979), 1–37.

92. On Rujugira, see Coupez and Kamanzi, *Récits historiques Rwanda,* 282–91; Kagame, *Un abrégé,* vol. 1, 135–53; Léon Delmas, *Les généalogies de la noblesse (Batutsi) du Rwanda* (Kabgayi, Rwanda: Vicariat apostolique du Rwanda, 1950), 187–88; D. Newbury, *Kings and Clans,* chap. 4; Vansina *L'évolution du royaume Rwanda,* 69–70; Vansina, *Le Rwanda ancien,* 111–19, 127–32, 141–51.

93. For a description, see d'Hertefelt and Coupez, *La royauté sacrée,* 73–96; chapter 10, this volume; and D. Newbury, *Kings and Clans,* chap. 12.

94. Rujugira's principal wife, the mother of Ndabarasa, Rujugira's putative successor, is the only queen mother of Rwanda of the Bagesera clan, the clan of the rulers of Gisaka. Kagame, *La notion de génération,* 22.

95. On the development of a class-based court etiquette distinct from common culture, see chapter 9, this volume. On the dynastic poetry, see Alexis Kagame, *La poésie dynastique du Rwanda* (Brussels: IRCB, 1951), and D. Newbury, *Kings and Clans,* 277–78n25.

While it is not surprising that more poems have been retained from recent reigns, still, the pattern of poetry associated with each reign and extant in the current sources is significant: Ruganzu, 2; Semugeshi, 0; Nyamuheshera, 3; Gisanura, 6; Mazimpaka, 11; Rujugira, 30; Ndabarasa, 4; Sentabyo, 21; Gahindiro, 12, Rwogera, 30; Rwabugiri, 41.

96. David Newbury, "Augustinian Models in Rwanda: Religious Movements and Political Transformation," *Svensk Missionstidskrift* 3 (1995): 16–35, traces out the religious history. Claudine Vidal, "De la contradiction sauvage," *L'Homme* 14 (1974): 5–58, and Luc de Heusch, "Mythe et société féodale: Le culte du Kubandwa dans le Rwanda traditionnelle," *Archives de Sociologie des Religions* 9 (1964): 133–46, engage in an interesting exchange on the relationship of Ryangombe to the court: Was it a movement of protest, reversing ethnic statuses, as de Heusch argues? Or was it a form of cultural integration by the fact that the rituals of Ryangombe reflected the rituals of kingship, and therefore at a deep level validated them, as Vidal suggests? In this debate, each party sought to establish an essentialist nature of the relationship of Ryangombe to the court, without accounting for historical particularity and changing circumstances. In fact, of course, both interpretations could have been valid: what we observe today and what has been retained in testimony may result from the condensation of various historical periods or social classes; rather than denying change, the contradictions within the traditions may in fact retain history. See also Berger, *Religion and Resistance,* and de Heusch, *Le Rwanda,* for differing views on Ryangombe seen within the religious history of the wider Great Lakes region of Africa. Some traditions claim Ryangombe's introduction at the royal court is associated with an earlier king, Mukobanya (in the late seventeenth century). But no extant traditions trace the Ryangombe authority at the court from the time of Mukobanya (though they do from Rujugira), and there is no other evidence to indicate the court's incorporation of Ryangombe at that earlier time. I am of the opinion that these earlier references to Ryangombe in the official court traditions reflect either the introduction (or growth) of Ryangombe practices within Rwandan society generally (and thus indicate an attempt to co-opt popular practices within official court traditions), or they represent a failed earlier attempt by the court to incorporate Ryangombe. At any rate, it seems clear that only from the time of Rujugira's reign (in the late eighteenth century) is there a continuous formal presence of Ryangombe at the court. It thus represents yet another initiative of the court at this time to incorporate a popular movement which might pose a political threat; it thus also represents an attempt to reinforce claims of the court's (and Rujugira's) legitimacy. Such a wide range of endeavors to solidify the court's legitimacy suggest that it was weak, either because of its incorporation of new regions (and subjects) to the dynastic domain, or because of questions on Rujugira's legitimate claims to succession (or both).

97. Though the Rwandan court sources claim the three states of Ndorwa, Gisaka and Burundi formed a single alliance against Rwanda, in fact this seems unlikely; the data suggest instead that these wars were separate and sequential—and may indeed have been provoked by Rwandan dynastic expansion. In other words, rather than fighting defensively against the unlikely alliance of three widely separate states, the indications are that under Rujugira and his successors, the Nyiginya dynasty was in an expansionist mode. On the Rwandan hegemony in the western areas, differing from outright conquest of the east, see D. Newbury, *Kings and Clans,* for a parallel case in the consolidation of power in a neighboring kingdom. This was, for example, a time when many refugees, both Hutu and Tutsi, fled west, from Ndorwa and Gisaka, to Budaha, Bunyambiriri, Kinyaga, Ijwi

Island, and (a few) further still, to the crest of the Mitumba Mountains on the western side of the Kivu Rift Valley. Some of the descendants of the latter have recently taken on the identity of "Banyamulenge"; see David Newbury, "Irredentist Rwanda: Ethnic and Territorial Frontiers in Central Africa," *Africa Today* 42, no. 2 (1997): 211–23; David Newbury, "Returning Refugees: Four Historical Patterns of 'Coming Home' to Rwanda," *Comparative Studies in Society and History* 47, no. 2 (2005): 252–85.

98. D. Newbury, *Kings and Clans*, 88–89.

99 On the histories of Rwandan dynastic armies: A. Kagame, *Les milices du Rwanda précolonial* (Brussels: ARSOM, 1962); and Alison Des Forges, "Court and Corporation in the Development of the Rwandan State" (1984).

100. C. Newbury, *Cohesion of Oppression*, documents this process in detail for the southwest. Many other examples are found in Ivan Reisdorff, *Enquêtes foncières au Rwanda* (Butare, Rwanda: INRS, 1952), and *Historique et chronologie*. Ironically, some of those co-opted individuals were from the families who had previously fled—as refugees—from the areas attacked during the reigns of Rujugira and his successor Ndabarasa.

101. On the changes in *ibikingi* relations from alliance to clientship, see Joseph Rwabukumba and Vincent Mudandagizi, "Les formes historiques de la dépendance personnelle dans l'état rwandais," *Cahiers d'Études Africaines* 14, no. 1 (1974): 6–25.

102. Reisdorff, *Enquêtes foncières*, Enquête 31; Pagès, *Un royaume hamite*, 578–612; Czekanowski, *Ethnographie*, 250–51, 265, 273. For more detail on this process and full references see D. Newbury, *Kings and Clans*, 91–95, 279–82nn 30–47. For an example of court attitudes involved in this process, see chapter 9, this volume.

103. Czekanowski, *Ethnographie*, 265; Reisdorff, *Enquêtes foncières*, 81, 85, 86, 88, 89; *Historique et chronologie*, 124.

104. D. Newbury, *Kings and Clans*, 276n19. For a more complete exposition of these traditions, see. Kagame, *Les milices*.

105. D. Newbury, "Irredentist Rwanda."

106. Within the history of dynastic successions, it is interesting that Gatarabuhura came from Gisaka; so too did Rujugira in succeeding to Rwaka. Rujugira was succeeded by Ndabarasa, a favored army general whom the official traditions claimed to be Rujugira's son. Nonetheless, on his death the major challenge to the legitimate succession claims of Ndabarasa's son Sentabyo was that of Gatarabuhura, also from Gisaka. It seems possible that Ndabarasa (and Sentabyo) were seen as illegitimate successors to Rujugira, and Gatarabuhura sought to re-establish the Gisaka line, introduced by Rujugira.

107. Kagame, *Un abrégé*, vol. 1; Kagame, *Les milices*, 103.

108. David Newbury, "Rex and Regina: Women in Court Politics in the Western Rift Kingdoms" (paper presented at the IRSAC Seminar Series, Lwiro, Zaïre, 1972). It is worth noting that from Rujugira, the mothers of six of the next eight kings were members of the Bega clan (including Nyiratunga).

109. In addition to the widespread traditions claiming Sentabyo died from smallpox, local traditions drawn from the southern Lake Kivu area, a cultural milieu very different from the court and unlikely to have been influenced by Rwandan dynastic traditions on this point, confirm that there was a serious smallpox epidemic early in the reign of Gahindiro (see chapter 4, this volume). There was also a serious famine at the time of Sentabyo's death (Kagame, *Les milices*, 145). Many family histories on Ijwi Island and in western Rwanda note this as a time of significant population movement: C. Newbury,

Cohesion of Oppression, chap. 2; D. Newbury, *Kings and Clans,* 86, 92–93, 100–101; Reisdorff, *Enquêtes foncières; Historique et chronologie,* 12.

110. Kagame, "Le code ésoterique," 36; d'Hertefelt and Coupez, *La royauté sacrée,* 5–6; Vansina, *L'évolution du royaume Rwanda,* 70.

111. One of the newly appointed ritualists was a woman, whose origins lay outside the kingdom. Vansina *Le Rwanda ancien,* 175–76.

112. Des Forges, "Court and Corporation," 51; see also 37–38.

113. Rwabukumba and Mudandagizi, "Les formes historiques"; Lydia Meschi, "Évolution des structures foncières au Rwanda: Le cas d'un lignage hutu," *Cahiers d'Études Africaines* 14, no. 1 (1974): 39–51; Catharine Newbury, "Deux lignages au Kinyaga," *Cahiers d'Études Africaines* 14, no. 1 (1974): 26–39.

114. Maquet's position is represented in Maquet, *The Premise of Inequality in Ruanda: A Study of Political Relations in a Central African Kingdom* (London: Oxford University Press for the International African Institute, 1962), 138, 150; "Rwanda Castes," in *Social Stratification in Africa,* ed. Arthur Tuden and Leonard Plotnikov (New York: Free Press, 1970), esp. 117–20. The more recent work, on which the following paragraphs are based, includes Helen Codere, "Power in Rwanda," *Anthropologica,* n.s., 4, no. 1 (1962): 45–85; Pierre Bettez Gravel, "The Transfer of Cows in Gisaka (Rwanda): A Mechanism for Recording Social Relationships," *American Anthropologist* 69, nos. 3–4 (1967): 322–31; Claudine Vidal, "Le Rwanda des Anthropologues ou le fétischisme de la vache," *Cahiers d'Études Africaines* 9, no. 3 (1969): 384–401; Vidal, "Économie de la société féodale rwandaise," *Cahiers d'Études Africaines* 14, no. 1 (1974): 52–74; Jean-François Saucier, "The Patron-Client Relationship in Traditional and Contemporary Southern Rwanda" (PhD diss., Columbia University, 1974); C. Newbury, *Cohesion of Oppression,* 73–147; Catharine Newbury, "Ubureetwa and Thangata: Catalysts to Peasant Political Consciousness in Rwanda and Malawi," *Canadian Journal of African Studies* 14, no. 1 (1980): 97–112; de Lame, *Une colline,* 48, 220. For further commentary on Maquet, see C. Newbury, *Cohesion of Oppression,* chap. 1; and Newbury and Newbury, "Bringing the Peasants Back In," 837n12.

115. Saucier, "Patron-Client Relationship." Saucier's interviews were conducted with men born around the first decade of the century; the two previous generations would have represented the early colonial years and the end of the precolonial period.

116. C. Newbury, *Cohesion of Oppression,* 73–151.

117. Rwabukumba and Mudandagizi, "Les formes historiques"; Vidal, "Économie de la société féodale"; Vidal, "Le Rwanda des anthropologues."

118. Ndikuriyo, "Contrats de bétail"; Albert A. Trouwborst, "L'organisation politique en tant que système d'échanges au Burundi," *Anthropologica* 3, no. 1 (1961): 65–81; Trouwborst, "L'organisation politique et l'accorde de clientèle au Burundi," *Anthropologica* 4, no. 1 (1962): 9–43; Roger Botte, "Burundi: La relation *ubugabire* dans la tête de ceux qui la décrivent," *Cahiers d'Études Africaines* 9, no. 35 (1969): 363–71; Simons, "Coutumes et institutions des Barundi."

119. Vansina, *Le Rwanda ancien.* Rwabugiri acceded to power as a youth in a contested succession; it was only from 1876, with the death of his mother and his biological father (the brother of the former king), that power devolved fully into his hands.

120. D. Newbury, "Rex and Regina."

121. A. Kagame, *La notion de génération,* 22. The prescriptions for queen mother were much more complex than this rule of alternation alone. In fact, such normative rules were seldom a clear guide to the actual procedures; yet they were often useful for different factions in advancing their competing claims.

122. On the intrigues surrounding Rwabugiri's accession and their legacy well into Rwabugiri's reign, see, inter alia, Kagame, *Un abrégé,* vol. 1, 210–14, and vol. 2, 13–15 and 22–47; d'Hertefelt and Coupez, *La royauté sacrée,* 333–34.

123. The Abakagara lineage mentioned below illustrates this process. See Alison Des Forges, "Defeat Is the Only Bad News: Rwanda under Musiinga, 1896–1931" (PhD diss., Yale University, 1972), 1; C. Newbury, *Cohesion of Oppression,* chaps. 3–4; de Lacger, *Le Ruanda,* 360–69; Vansina, *Le Rwanda ancien,* chaps. 6–7.

124. Kagame, *Un abrégé,* vol. 2, 13–103; Des Forges, "Court and Corporation"; C. Newbury, *Cohesion of Oppression,* chap. 3; Czekanowski notes that people told him that the population got tired of Rwabugiri's campaigns, because they had to provide food to the royal residences located in their area (*Ethnographie,* 267). Vansina confirms this: the visits of the king's entourage was a disaster for the local population (*Le Rwanda ancien,* 229–30).

125. On the wars of Rwabugiri, among many other sources, see chapter 5, this volume; Kagame, *Un abrégé,* vol. 2, 26–103; chapter 6, this volume. Vansina first proposed the historical importance of distinguishing between annexation, occupation, and raid; *L'évolution du royaume Rwanda.*

126. For a detailed account of the tactics he used and the effects of his campaigns, see chapter 6, this volume.

127. Kagame, *Les milices,* 153–54; and 66, noting an incident in which an aristocratic army chief was dismissed because he refused to drink from the same straw as a Twa appointed by Rwabugiri to a position as chief.

128. Kagame, *Un abrégé,* vol. 2, 13–113. Many examples of his army replacements are found in Kagame, *Les milices.* On the administrative structures, see Newbury, *The Cohesion of Oppression,* chap. 3; and Catharine Newbury and Joseph Rwabukumba, "Political Evolution in a Rwandan Frontier District: A Case Study of Kinyaga," in *Rapport annual pour les années 1965–70,* ed. Institut National de Recherche Scientifique (Butare, Rwanda: INRS, 1971): 93–119. Also Czekanowski, *Ethnographie,* 267: "Kigeri is reputed to have centralized the state and partitioned, scattered, and interwoven the holdings of the chiefs in order to destroy the centrifugal tendencies of the feudal lords."

129. Such image of Rwabugiri—in such contrast to Kagame's account—is apparent in the detailed and insightful account of Vansina, *Le Rwanda ancien,* chap. 7.

130. De Lacger, *Le Ruanda,* 367–71. Among many other sources, see also Kagame, *Un abrégé,* vol. 2, 105–28; and E. Ruhashya, *Rucunshu* (Kigali, 1984), a long epic poem on the episode. This struggle essentially opposed the powerful members of the Abakagara lineage of the Ega clan to the royal Abahindiro lineage of the Nyiginya clan. These families were tightly intertwined, Rwabugiri having married Kabare's sister, and having in turn married his daughter to Kabare—and then had Kabare castrated (de Lacger, *Le Ruanda,* 357). In 1896, Kabare appeared to gain some revenge in the climatic battle at Rucunshu, where Rutarindwa, the heir to Rwabugiri, was killed, along with many of his supporters, by the armies associated with Kabare and Ruhinankiko, brothers of Kanjogera, the mother

of the Musinga. But the power struggle continued long after that. In 1899, the factions supporting Kabare and Ruhinankiko fought each other. In 1905 there was another major purge of Abahindiro chiefs—members of the official royal lineage. And after the deposition of Musinga in 1931, his replacement, Rudahigwa, reinstated Nyiginya chiefs at the expense of Ega authorities.

131. For Burundi: Gahama, *Le Burundi;* for Rwanda, see Rumiya, *Le Rwanda sous le régime;* Des Forges, "Defeat"; Ferdinand Nahimana, *Le Blanc est arrivée; le Roi est parti: Une facette de l'histoire du Rwanda contemporain, 1894–1931* (Kigali: Éditions Printer Set, 1987). Indeed, two eminent historians of Rwanda note that "both oral and written sources openly question whether the Nyiginya dynastic lineage would have been exterminated if the Europeans had not arrived [when they did]." Roger Heremans and Emmanuel Ntezimana, eds., introduction to *Journal de la Mission de Save, 1899–1905* (Ruhengeri, Rwanda: Éditions universitaires du Rwanda, 1987), 15.

BIBLIOGRAPHY

Abbreviations

ARSOM: Académie Royale des Sciences d'Outre-Mer, Brussels, Belgium
ASA: African Studies Association (U.S.)
CEDAF: Centre d'Études et de Documentation Africaines, Brussels, Belgium
CELA: Centre d'Études des Langues Africaines, Bukavu, Zaïre/Congo
CERUKI: Centre d'Études de Recherche Universitaire du Kivu, Zaïre/Congo
INRS: Institut National de Recherche Scientifique, Butare, Rwanda
IRCB: Institut Royal Colonial Belge
IRSAC: Institut de Recherche Scientifique en Afrique Centrale
IRST: Institut de Recherche Scientifique et Technologique, Butare, Rwanda
ISP: Institut Supérieur Pédagogique, Bukavu, Zaïre/Congo
MRAC: Musée Royal de l'Afrique Centrale, Tervuren, Belgium
UNAZA: Université Nationale du Zaïre

Alpers, Edward A. *Ivory and Slaves in East Central Africa.* London: Heinemann, 1975.
———. "Trade, State, and Society among the Yao in the Nineteenth Century." *Journal of African History* 10, no. 3 (1969): 405–20.
André, Catherine. "Terre Rwandaise, accès politique et reformes foncières." In *L'Afrique des Grands Lacs: Annuaire 1997–1998,* edited by Filip Reyntjens and Stefaan Marysse, 141–73. Paris: L'Harmattan, 1998.
Baharanyi, Bifuko. "Contribution à l'étude de l'évolution des sociétés humaines: Cas du mode de production des Havu de la région interlacustre." Mémoire de licence, UNAZA-Lubumbashi, 1973.
Bailey, F. G. *Stratagems and Spoils.* New York: Schocken Books, 1969.
Bakwa-Lufu Badibanga, Njangu Canda-Ciri, and Sebigamba Rusibiza. "L'UNAZA-Bukavu et la connaissance du Kivu: Inventaire bibliographique." *Antennes* 5 (1977): 411–32.
Barnes, J. A. "African Models in the New Guinea Highlands." *Man* 62 (1962): 5–9.
———. *Three Styles in the Study of Kinship.* Berkeley and Los Angeles: University of California Press, 1971.
Barns, Thomas Alexander. *Across the Great Craterland to the Congo.* London: Benn, 1923.
Bashizi Cirhagahula. "Histoire du Kivu: Sources écrites et perspectives d'avenir." *Likundoli,* ser. B, 4 (1976): 65–114.
Beattie, John. *The Nyoro State.* Oxford: Clarendon Press, 1971.
Beidelman, T. O. "Myth, Legend, and Oral History: A Kaguru Traditional Text." *Anthropos* 65 (1970): 74–97.
Bennett, Norman. *Leadership in Eastern Africa.* Boston: Boston University Press, 1968.
Berger, Iris. "The *Kubandwa* Religious Complex of Interlacustrine East Africa: An Historical Study, c. 1500–1900." PhD diss., University of Wisconsin–Madison, 1973.

————. *Religion and Resistance: East African Kingdoms in the Precolonial Period.* Tervuren: MRAC, 1981.

————. "Spirit Mediums, Priestesses and the Precolonial State in Interlacustrine East Africa." In *Revealing Prophets: Prophecy in Eastern African History,* edited by David Anderson and Douglas H. Johnson, 65–82. London: James Currey, 1995.

Bergmans, Lieven. *Histoire des Bashu.* Butembo: Editions A.B.B., 1974.

————. *L'histoire des Baswaga.* Butembo: Editions A.B.B., 1970.

————. *Les Wanande: Croyances et practiques traditionelles.* Butembo: Editions A.B.B., 1971.

Biebuyck, Daniel P. *Hero and Chief: Epic Literature from the Banyanga (Zaïre Republic).* Berkeley and Los Angeles: University of California Press, 1978.

————. *Lega Culture: Art, Initiation and Moral Philosophy among a Central African People.* Berkeley: University of California Press, 1973.

————. "De Mumbo-Instelling bij de Banyanga." *Kongo-Overzee* 21, no. 5 (1955): 441–48.

————. "L'organisation politique des Nyanga: La chefferie Ihana." *Kongo-Overzee* 22, nos. 4–5 (1956): 301–41; 23, nos. 1–2 (1957): 59–98.

————. *Rights in Land and Its Resources among the Nyanga.* Brussels: ARSOM, 1966.

————. "Stylistic Techniques and Formulating Devices in the Mwindo Epic from the Banyanga." *Cultures et Développement* 11, no. 4 (1979): 551–600.

Biebuyck, Daniel P., and Mateene Kahombo. *The Mwindo Epic from the Banyanga (Congo Republic).* Berkeley and Los Angeles: University of California Press, 1969.

Bigirumwami, A. *Ibitekerezo, indilimbo, imbyino, ibihozo, inanga, ibyivugo, ibigwi, imato, amahamba n'amazina y'inka, ibiganiro* [Récits historiques, chansons, chansons dansées, berceuses, chansons pour harpe, poèmes guerriers, chants pastoraux, poèmes pastoraux, jeux de mots, humor]. Mimeo. Nyundo, Rwanda: n.p., 1971.

Birhakaheka Njiga and Kirhero Nsibula. "Nyangezi dans ces relations commerciales avec le Rwanda, le Burundi, et le Bufulero." *Études Rwandaises* 14, no. 1 (1981): 36–51.

Bishikwabo Chubaka. "Le Bushi au XIXe siècle: Un peuple, sept royaumes." *Revue Française d'Histoire d'Outre-Mer* 47, nos. 1–2 (1980): 89–98.

————. "Deux chefs du Bushi sous le régime colonial: Kabare et Ngweshe (1912–1960)." *Études d'Histoire Africaine* 7 (1975): 89–112.

————. "L'économie d'échange dans les états précoloniaux du Sud-Kivu du XIXe siècle à 1920." Paper presented at the Journées d'Historiens Zaïrois, Lubumbashi, 1975.

————. "Interprétation du rite du remerciement à Lyangombe." In *Lyangombe: Mythe et rites: Actes du 2ème colloque du CERUKI du 10 mai au 14 mai 1976,* edited by CERUKI, UNAZA-ISP, 173–81. Bukavu: Éditions du CERUKI, 1979.

————. "Les relations extérieures du Kaziba au XIXe siècle." Paper presented at the Journées d'Historiens Zairois, Lubumbashi, 1977.

Bishikwabo Chubaka and David Newbury. "Recent Research in the Area of Lake Kivu: Rwanda and Zaïre." *History in Africa* 8 (1980): 23–45.

Bloch, Maurice. "Property and the End of Affinity." In *Marxist Analyses and Social Anthropology,* edited by Maurice Bloch, 203–28. London: Malaby Press, 1975.

Bohannan, Paul, and George Dalton, eds. *Markets in Africa.* Evanston: Northwestern University Press, 1962.

Boston, J. S. "The Hunter in Igala Legends of Origin." *Africa* 34, no. 2 (1964): 116–26.

Botte, Roger. "Burundi: La relation *ubugabire* dans la tête de ceux qui la décrivent." *Cahiers d'Études Africaines* 9, no. 35 (1969): 363–71.

———. "La guerre interne au Burundi." In *Guerres de lignages et guerres d'états en Afrique,* edited by Jean Bazin and Emmanuel Terray, 271–317. Paris: Éditions des archives contemporaines, 1982.

———. "Rwanda and Burundi, 1899–1930: Chronology of a Slow Assassination." *International Journal of African Historical Studies* 18, no. 1 (1985): 53–91; 18, no. 2 (1985): 289–314.

Bourgeois, R. *Banyarwanda et Barundi.* Vol. 1, *La Coutume.* Brussels: ARSOM, 1957.

———. *Banyarwanda et Barundi.* Vol. 2, *Ethnographie.* Brussels: ARSOM, 1954.

Buchanan, Carole Ann. "The Kitara Complex: The Historical Tradition of Western Uganda to the Sixteenth Century." PhD diss., Indiana University, 1974.

Burton, Richard Francis. *The Lake Regions of Central Africa.* Vol. 2. London: Longman, Green, Longman and Roberts, 1860.

Butala, M. "Occupation coloniale belge au Bunande (1889–1935)." Mémoire de licence, Institut Supérieur Pédagogique, UNAZA-Bukavu.

Casati, Gaetano, J. Randolph Clay, I. Walter Savage, and Emin Pasha. *Ten Years in Equatoria.* London: F. Warne and Co., 1898.

Cenyange Lubula. "L'origine de Lyangombe d'après les Bashi." In *Lyangombe: Mythe et rites: Actes du 2ème colloque du CERUKI du 10 mai au 14 mai 1976,* edited by CERUKI, UNAZA-ISP, 129-31. Bukavu: Éditions du CERUKI, 1979.

Chrétien, Jean-Pierre. *L'Afrique des Grands Lacs: Deux milles ans d'histoire.* Paris: Aubier, 2000.

———. "Les années de l'eleusine, du sorgho, et des haricots dans l'ancien Burundi: Ecologie et idéologie." *African Economic History* 7 (1982): 75–92.

———. "Le Burundi vu du Burundi." *Journal des Africanistes* 47, no. 2 (1977): 176–98.

———. "Le commerce du sel de l'Uvinza au XIXe siècle: De la cueillette au monopole capitaliste." *Revue Français d'Histoire d'Outre-Mer* 65 (1978): 401–22.

———"Confronting the Unequal Exchange between the Oral and the Written." In *African Historiographies,* edited by Bogumil Jewsiewicki and David Newbury, 75–90. Beverly Hills: Sage, 1986.

———. "La crise écologique de l'Afrique orientale du début du XIXe siècle: Le cas de l'Imbo au Burundi, 1890–1916." In *Questions sur la paysannerie au Burundi: Actes de la table ronde sur "Sciences sociales, humaines et développement rural,"* organisé par la Faculté des Lettres et Sciences Humaines, 55–93. Bujumbura: Université de Bujumbura, 1987.

———. "Le cycle d'histoire de Maconco." In *Burundi: Histoire retrouvée: Vingt-cinq ans de métier d'historien en Afrique,* 107–19. Paris: Aubier, 1993.

———. "Les deux visages de Cham: Points de vue français du XIXème siècle sur les races africaines d'après l'exemple de l'Afrique Orientale." In *L'idée de race dans la pensée politique française contemporaine,* edited by Pierre Guiral and Emile Temime, 171–99. Paris: Éditions du Centre national de la recherche scientifique, 1977.

———. "Échanges et hiérarchies dans les royaumes des Grands Lacs de l'Est africain." *Annales* 29, no. 6 (1974): 1327–37.

———. "Du hirsute au hamite: Les variations du cycle de Ntare Rushatsi, fondateur du royaume du Burundi." *History in Africa* 8 (1981): 3–41.

———. "Hutu et Tutsi au Rwanda et au Burundi." In *Au coeur de l'ethnie: Ethnies, tribalisme, et état en Afrique,* edited by Jean-Loup Amselle and Elikia M'Bokolo, 129–65. Paris: La Découverte, 1985.

————. "Nouvelles hypothèses sur les origines du Burundi: Les traditions du nord." In *L'arbre-mémoire: Traditions orales du Burundi*, edited by Léonidas Ndoricimpa and Claude Guillet, 11–52. Paris: Karthala, 1984.

————. "La révolte de Ndungutse (1912): Forces traditionelles et pression coloniale au Rwanda allemand." *Revue Française d'Histoire d'Outre-Mer* 59, no. 4 (1972): 645–80.

————. "La royauté capture les rois." Appendix to *L'intronisation d'un Mwami*, by Pascal Ndayishinguje, 61–70. Nanterre: Laboratoire d'ethnologie et de sociologie comparative, 1977.

————. "Le sorgho dans l'agriculture, la culture, et l'histoire du Burundi." *Journal des Africanistes* 52, nos. 1–2 (1982): 145–62.

————. "Les traditionnistes lettrés du Burundi à l'école des bibliothèques missionnaires (1940–1960)." *History in Africa* 15 (1988): 407–30.

CINAM. *Étude du développement de la région du Lac Kivu (Rwanda)*. Vol. 2. Paris: n.p., 1973.

Codere, Helen. *The Biography of an African Society: Rwanda, 1900–1960*. Tervuren: MRAC, 1973.

————. "Power in Rwanda." *Anthropologica*, n.s., 4, no. 1 (1962): 45–85.

Cohen, David W. *The Historical Tradition of Busoga: Mukama and Kintu*. Oxford: Clarendon Press, 1972.

————. "A Survey of Interlacustrine Chronology." *Journal of African History* 11, no. 2 (1970): 111–201.

Colle, P. *Essai de monographie des Bashi*. 1937. Bukavu: CELA, 1971.

————. "L'organisation politique des Bashi." *Congo* 2, no. 2 (1921): 657–84.

Coupez, André, and Thomas Kamanzi. *La littérature de cour au Rwanda*. Oxford: Clarendon Press, 1970.

————, eds. *Récits historiques Rwanda, dans la version de C. Gakanîisha*. Tervuren: MRAC, 1962.

Coupez, André, Thomas Kamanzi, Simon Bizimana, G. Sematama, G. Rwabukumba, and C. Ntazinda et al. *Inkoranya y'íkinyarwaanda mu kinyarwaanda nó mu Gifaraansá: Dictionnaire Rwanda-Rwanda et Rwanda-Français*. Tervuren: MRAC, 2005.

Curtin, Philip D. "The Uses of Oral Traditon in Senegambia: Maalik Sii and the Foundation of Bundu." *Cahiers d'Études Africaines* 58, no. 2 (1975): 189–207.

Cuypers, Jean-Baptiste. *L'alimentation chez les Shi*. Tervuren: MRAC, 1960.

————. "Les Bantous interlacustres du Kivu." In *Introduction à l'ethnographie du Congo*, by Jan Vansina, 201–11. Kinshasa: Éditions Universitaires du Congo, 1965.

Czekanowski, Jan. *Ethnographie: Zwischenseengebiet Mpororo, Ruanda*. Vol. 1 of *Forschungen im Nil-Congo-Zwischengebiet*. Berlin: Klinkhardt and Biermann, 1917.

d'Arianoff, A. *L'histoire des Bagesera, Souverains du Gisaka*. Brussels: IRCB, 1952.

de Heusch, Luc. "Mythe et société féodale: Le culte du Kubandwa dans le Rwanda traditionnelle." *Archives de Sociologie des Religions* 18 (1964): 133–46.

————. *Le roi ivre ou l'origine de l'état*. Paris: Gallimard, 1972.

————. *Rois nés d'un coeur de vache*. Paris: Gallimard, 1982.

————. *Le Rwanda et la civilisation interlacustre*. Brussels: Université Libre de Bruxelles, 1966.

de Lacger, Louis. *Le Ruanda*. 2nd ed. Kabgayi, Rwanda: Imprimérie de Kabgayi, 1961.

de Lame, Danielle. *Une colline entre mille, ou, Le calme avant la tempête: Transformations et blocages du Rwanda rural*. Tervuren: MRAC, 1996.

————. "Instants retrouvés: Rwanda, regards neufs au fil du temps." In *Liber Amicorum Marcel d'Hertefelt*, edited by Patrick Wymeersch, 115–33. Brussels: Institut Africain, 1993.

de l'Epine, C. "Historique des famines et disettes dans l'Urundi." *Bulletin Agricole du Congo Belge* 20, no. 3 (1929): 440–42.

Delmas, Léon. *Les généalogies de la noblesse (Batutsi) du Rwanda*. Kabgayi, Rwanda: Vicariat apostolique du Rwanda, 1950.

Denoon, Donald, "The Allocation of Official Posts in Kigezi, 1908–1930." In Denoon, *History of Kigezi*, 211–30.

————, ed. *A History of Kigezi in Southwestern Uganda*. Kampala: National Trust, 1972.

Denoon, Donald, and Adam Kuper. "Nationalist Historians in Search of a Nation: The 'New Historiography' in Dar es Salaam." *African Affairs* 69, no. 277 (1970): 329–49.

Depelchin, Jacques. "From Precapitalism to Imperialism: A History of Social and Economic Formations in Eastern Zaïre (Uvira Zone), c. 1800–1964." PhD diss., Stanford University, 1974.

de Saint Moulin, Léon. "Les anciens villages des environs de Kinshasa." *Études d'Histoire Africaine* 2 (1971): 83–119.

————. *Carte de la densité de la population du Zaïre*. Kinshasa: Institut géographique du Zaïre, 1975.

Des Forges, Alison. "Court and Corporation in the Development of the Rwandan State." N.p.: n.p., 1984.

————. "Defeat Is the Only Bad News: Rwanda under Musiinga, 1896–1931." PhD diss., Yale University, 1972.

————. "The Drum Is Greater Than the Shout: The 1912 Rebellion in Northern Rwanda." In *Banditry, Rebellion, and Social Protest in Africa*, edited by Donald Crummey, 311–31. Portsmouth, NH: Heinemann, 1986.

————. "Kings without Crowns: The White Fathers in Rwanda." In *East African History*, edited by Norman R. Bennett, Daniel F. McCall, and Jeffrey Butler, 176–202. New York: Praeger, 1969.

Desmarais, Jean-Claude. "Le Rwanda des anthropologues: L'archéologie de l'idéologie raciale." *Anthropologie et Sociétés* 2, no. 1 (1978): 71–92.

de Wet, J. M. J. "Domestication of African Cereals." *African Economic History* 3 (1977): 15–33.

d'Hertefelt, Marcel. *Les clans du Rwanda ancien: Éléments d'ethno-sociologie et d'ethno-histoire*. Tervuren: MRAC, 1971.

————. "Huwelijk, familie, en aanverwantschap bij de Reera (Noordwestelijk Rwaanda)." *Zaïre* 13, No. 2 (1959): 115–47; no. 3: 243–85.

————. "Mythes et idéologies dans le Rwanda ancien et contemporain." In *The Historian in Tropical Africa*, edited by Jan Vansina, Raymond Mauny, and L. V. Thomas, 219–38. London: Oxford University Press for the International African Institute, 1964.

————. "Le Rwanda." In *Les anciens royaumes de la zone interlacustre méridionale*, edited by Marcel d'Hertefelt, Abert. A. Trouwborst, and J. H. Scherer, 9–112. Tervuren: MRAC, 1962.

————. "The Rwanda of Rwanda." In *The Peoples of Africa*, edited by James L. Gibbs, 403–41. New York: Holt, Rinehart, and Winston, 1965.

d'Hertefelt, Marcel, and André Coupez, eds. *La royauté sacrée de l'ancien Rwanda*. Tervuren: MRAC, 1964.

d'Hertefelt, Marcel, André Coupez, and Alexis Kagame. "À propos du code ésotérique de l'ancien Rwanda," *Africa-Tervuren* 14, no. 4, (1968): 117.

d'Hertefelt, Marcel, and Danielle de Lame. *Société, culture, et histoire du Rwanda. Encyclopédie bibliographique, 1863–1980/87.* Tervuren: MRAC, 1987.Dikonda wa Lumanyisha. "Les rites chez les Bashi et les Bahavu." PhD diss., Université Libre de Bruxelles, 1972.

Douglas, Mary. "Raffia Cloth Distribution in the Lele Economy." *Africa* 28, no. 2 (1958): 109–22.

Dufays, Félix, and Vincent de Moor. *Au Kinyaga: Les Enchaînés.* Brussels: Éditions universelles, 1938.

Edel, May. *The Chiga of Uganda.* London: Oxford University Press for the International African Institute, 1957.

Evans-Pritchard, E. E. *Essays in Social Anthropology.* London: Faber and Faber, 1962.

Ewald, Janet. "Speaking, Writing, and Authority: Explorations in and from the Kingdom of Taqali." *Comparative Studies in Society and History* 30 (1988): 199–227.

Fallers, Lloyd. "Despotism, Status Culture, and Social Mobility in an African Kingdom." *Comparative Studies in Society and History* 2, no. 1 (1959): 11–32.

———. ed. *The King's Men: Leadership and Status in Buganda on the Eve of Independence.* London: Oxford University Press for the East African Institute of Social Research, 1964.

Feierman, Steven. *The Shambaa Kingdom: A History.* Madison: University of Wisconsin Press, 1974.

Feys, R. "Histoire des Bahavu." White Fathers Archives, Bukavu, n.d.

Flamant, F., et al. *La force publique de sa naissance à 1914.* Brussels: IRCB, 1952.

Ford, John. *The Role of the Trypanosomiases in African Ecology.* Oxford: Clarendon Press, 1971.

Fortes, Meyer. "Descent, Affiliation, and Affinity." *Man* 59 (1959): 193–97, 206–12.

———. "The Structure of Unilineal Descent Groups." *American Anthropologist* 55 (1953): 17–41.

Freedman, Jim. "Joking, Affinity, and the Exchange of Ritual Services among the Kiga of Northern Rwanda: An Essay in Joking Relationships." *Man,* n.s., 12, no. 1 (1976): 154–66.

———. *Nyabingi: The Social History of an African Divinity.* Tervuren: MRAC, 1984.

———. "Principles of Relationships in Rwandan Kiga Society." PhD diss., Princeton University, 1974.

———. "Ritual and History: The Case of Nyibingi." *Cahiers d'Études Africaines* 14, no. 1 (1974): 170–80.

———. "Three Muraris, Three Gahayas, and the Four Phases of Nyabingi." In *Chronology, Migration, and Drought in Interlacustrine Africa,* edited by J. B. Webster, 175–87. New York: Africana, 1979.

Fried, Morton. "The Classification of Corporate Unilineal Descent Groups." *Journal of the Royal Anthropological Institute* 87, no. 1 (1957): 1–29.

Gahama, Joseph. *Le Burundi sous administration belge.* Paris: Karthala, 1983.

———. "La disparition du Muganuro." In *L'arbre-mémoire: Traditions orales du Burundi,* edited by Léonidas Ndoricimpa and Claude Guillet, 169–94. Paris: Karthala, 1984.

Gahama, Joseph, and Christian Thibon, eds. *Les régions orientales du Burundi: Une périphérie à l'épreuve du développement.* Paris: Karthala, 1994.

Good, Charles M. *Market Development in Traditionally Marketless Societies.* Athens: Ohio University Press, 1971.

———. "Markets in Africa: A Review of Research Themes and the Question of Market Origins." *Cahiers d'Études Africaines* 13, no. 4 (1973): 769–81.

———. *Rural Markets and Trade in East Africa: A Study of the Functions and Development of Exchange Institutions in Ankole, Uganda.* Chicago: University of Chicago, Department of Geography, 1970.

———. "Salt, Trade, and Disease: Aspects of Development in Africa's Northern Great Lakes Region." *International Journal of African Historical Studies* 5, no. 4 (1972): 543–87.

Goody, Jack. *The Character of Kinship.* Cambridge: Cambridge University Press, 1973.

Gorju, J. *Face au royaume hamite du Ruanda: Le royaume frère de l'Urundi.* Brussels: IRCB, 1938.

Grant, James Augustus. *A Walk across Africa, or, Domestic Scenes from My Nile Journal.* London: W. Blackwood and Sons, 1864.

Gravel, Pierre Bettez. "Diffuse Power as a Commodity: A Case Study from Gisaka (Eastern Rwanda)." *International Journal of Comparative Sociology* 9, nos. 3–4 (1968): 163–76.

———. "Life on the Manor in Gisaka (Rwanda)." *Journal of African History* 6, no. 3 (1965): 323–31.

———. *Remera: A Community in Eastern Rwanda.* The Hague: Mouton, 1968.

———. "The Transfer of Cows in Gisaka (Rwanda): A Mechanism for Recording Social Relationships." *American Anthropologist* 69, nos. 3–4 (1967): 322–31.

Gray, Richard, and David Birmingham, eds. *Pre-colonial African Trade: Essays on Trade in Central and Eastern Africa before 1900.* London: Oxford University Press, 1970.

Guillet, Claude. "Higiro et Banga: Deux domaines de tambourinaires." In *L'arbre-mémoire: Traditions orales du Burundi,* edited by Léonidas Ndoricimpa and Claude Guillet, 95–146. Paris: Karthala, 1984.

Gulliver, Philip H. *Neighbours and Networks: The Idiom of Kinship in Social Action among the Ndendeuli of Tanzania.* Berkeley and Los Angeles: University of California Press, 1971.

Hangi Shamamba. "Note sur Ngyiko Kingumwa." *Antennes* 5 (1977): 348–57.

Harms, Robert. "The End of Red Rubber: A Reassessment." *Journal of African History* 14, no. 1 (1975): 73–88.

Hartwig, Gerald. *The Art of Survival in East Africa: The Kerebe and Long Distance Trade, 1800–1875.* New York: Africana, 1976.

Hemphill, Marie de Kiewit. "The British Sphere, 1884–1894." In *History of East Africa,* vol. 1, edited by Roland Oliver and Gervase Mathew, 391–432. Oxford: Clarendon Press, 1963.

Henige, David. *The Chronology of Oral Tradition: The Quest for a Chimera.* Oxford: Clarendon Press, 1974.

———. "Oral Tradition and Chronology." *Journal of African History* 12, no. 3 (1971): 371–89.

———. "Reflections on Early Interlacustrine Chronology: An Essay in Source Criticism." *Journal of African History* 15, no. 1 (1974): 27–46.

Heremans, Roger, and Emmanuel Ntezimana, eds. *Journal de la Mission de Save, 1899–1905.* Ruhengeri, Rwanda: Éditions Universitaires du Rwanda, 1987.

Herskovits, Melville. Preface to *Markets in Africa,* edited by Paul Bohannan and George Dalton, vii–xvi. Evanston: Northwestern University Press, 1962.

Hiernaux, Jean. *Analyse de la variation des caractères physiques humains en une région de l'Afrique centrale: Ruanda-Urundi et Kivu.* Tervuren: MRAC, 1956.

———. *Les caractères physiques des Bashi.* Brussels: IRCB, 1953.

———. "Note sur une ancienne population du Ruanda-Urundi: Les Renge." *Zaïre* 10, no. 4 (1956): 351–60.

Hill, Polly. "Markets in Africa." *Journal of Modern African Studies* 1, no. 4 (1963): 441–53.

"Histoire de l'Île Idjwi." Typescript, n.p., n.d. (early 1960s).

Historique et chronologie du Ruanda. Kabgayi, Rwanda: Vicariat apostolique du Ruanda, 1956.

Hodder, B. W. "Some Comments on the Origins of Traditional Markets in Africa South of the Sahara." *Transactions of the Institute of British Geographers* 36 (1965): 97–105.

Iliffe, J. *Tanganyika under German Rule, 1905–1912.* Cambridge: Cambridge University Press, 1969.

Ingham, Kenneth. *The Kingdom of Toro in Uganda.* London: Methuen, 1975.

Isaacman, Allen, and Barbara Isaacman. "Resistance and Collaboration in Southern and Central Africa, c. 1850–1920." *International Journal of African Historical Studies* 10, no. 1 (1977): 31–62.

Isaacman, Allen, and Jan Vansina. "African Initiatives and Resistance in Central Africa, 1880–1914." In *Africa under Colonial Domination, 1880–1935,* edited by A. Adu Boahen, 169–93. UNESCO General History of Africa 7. Berkeley: University of California Press, 1985.

Jack, Evan M. *On the Congo Frontier.* London: T. F. Unwin, 1914.

James, Wendy. "The Funj Mystique: Approaches to a Problem of Sudan History." In *Text and Context: The Social Anthropology of Tradition,* edited by Ravindra K. Jain. Philadelphia: ISHI, 1977.

Jaspar, Henri. "Le Ruanda-Urundi, pays à disettes périodiques." *Congo* 2, no. 1 (1929): 1–22.

Jensen, J. "Die Erweiterung des Lungenfisch-Clans in Buganda (Uganda) durch den Anschluss von Bavuma-Gruppen." *Sociologus* 19, no. 2 (1962): 153–66.

Johanssen, E. *Ruanda: Kleine Anfänge—Grosse Aufgaben der Evangelischen Mission im Zwischenseengebiet Deutsch-Ostafrikas.* Bethel bei Bielefeld: Verlagshandlung der Anstalt Bethel, 1912.

Kagame, Alexis. *Un abrégé de l'ethno-histoire du Rwanda précolonial.* Vol. 1. Butare: Éditions Universitaires du Rwanda, 1972.

———. *Un abrégé de l'histoire du Rwanda de 1853 à 1972.* Vol. 2. Butare: Éditions Universitaires du Rwanda, 1975.

———. "La chronologie du Burundi dans les genres littéraires de l'ancien Rwanda." *Études Rwandaises* 12 (1979): 1–30.

———. *Le code des institutions politiques du Rwanda précolonial.* Brussels: IRCB, 1952.

———. "Le code ésotérique de la dynastie du Rwanda." *Zaïre* 1, no. 4 (1947): 363–86.

———. "La documentation du Rwanda sur l'Afrique interlacustre des temps anciens." In *La civilisation ancienne des peuples des Grands Lacs: Colloque de Bujumbura (4–10 septembre 1979),* edited by the Centre de Civilisation Burundaise, 300–330. Paris: Karthala, 1981.

———. *L'histoire des armées bovines dans l'ancien Rwanda.* Brussels: ARSOM, 1961.

————. "L'historicité de Lyangombe, chef des 'Immandwa.'" In *Lyangombe: Mythe et rites: Actes du 2ème colloque du CERUKI du 10 mai au 14 mai 1976*, edited by CERUKI, UNAZA-ISP, 17–28. Bukavu: Éditions du CERUKI, 1979.

————. *Inganji Karinga*. 2nd ed. Kabgayi, Rwanda: n.p., 1959.

————. *Introduction aux grands genres lyriques de l'ancien Rwanda*. Butare, Rwanda: Éditions Universitaires du Rwanda, 1969.

————. *Les milices du Rwanda précolonial*. Brussels: ARSOM, 1963.

————. *La notion de génération appliquée à la généalogie dynastique et à l'histoire du Rwanda dès Xe–XIe siècles à nos jours*. Brussels: ARSOM, 1959.

————. *Les organisations socio-familiales de l'ancien Rwanda*. Brussels: ARSOM, 1954.

————. *La poésie dynastique du Rwanda*. Brussels: IRCB, 1951.

————. "Le premier Européen au Rwanda." Paper presented at the Institut Pédagogique National, Butare, Rwanda, February 1970.

————. "La structure des quinze clans au Rwanda." *Annali Lateranensi* 18 (1954): 103–17.

Kagwa, Apollo. *The Kings of Buganda*. Edited by M. S. M. Kiwanuka. Nairobi: East African Publishing House, 1971.

Kajiga, J. "Cette immigration séculaire des Ruandais au Congo." *Bulletin Trimestriel du Centre d'Études des Problèmes Sociaux Indigènes* 32 (1956): 5–65.

Kakiranyi K. "Le couronnement du Mwami dans la tradition Nande." Mémoire de licence, Institut Supérieur Pédagogique, UNAZA-Bukavu.

Kalemaza Kavuha. "Le développement de l'agriculture au Kivu colonial (1903–1940)." Mémoire de licence, UNAZA-Lubumbashi, 1973.

Kalibwami, Justin. *Le Catholicisme et la société rwandaise*. Paris: Présence Africaine, 1991.

Kaligho E. "Le munande face au Christianisme." Mémoire de licence, Institut Supérieur Pédagogique, UNAZA-Bukavu.

Kamuhangire, E. R. "The Economic and Social History of the Southwest Uganda Salt Lakes Region." In *Hadith 5: The Economic and Social History of East Africa*, edited by B. A. Ogot, 66–89. Nairobi: East African Publishing House, 1974.

————. "Migration, Settlement, and State Formation in the Southwest Uganda Salt Lake Region." Makerere University Seminar Paper, 1972.

Kandt, Richard. *Caput Nili: Eine empfindsame Reise zu den Quellen des Nils*. 2 vols. Berlin: D. Reimer, 1919.

Karugire, Samwiri R. *A History of the Kingdom of Nkore in Western Uganda to 1896*. Oxford: Clarendon Press, 1971.

Kashamura, Anicet. *Famille, sexualité, et culture*. Paris: Payot, 1973.

Kashamura, K. "Occupation économique du Kivu (1920–1940)." Mémoire de licence, UNAZALubumbashi, 1973.

Katembo M. "La résistance passive du Munande face à l'action coloniale en agriculture." Mémoire de licence, Institut Supérieur Pédagogique, UNAZA-Bukavu.

Kifimoja Sh. "Intronisation du chef traditional Nyanga." Mémoire de licence, Institut Supérieur Pédagogique, UNAZA-Bukavu.

Kirhero Nsibula. "Évolution politique des localités de Lugendo et Ishungu (1830–1964)." Mémoire de licence, Institut Supérieur Pédagogique, UNAZA-Bukavu, 1977.

Kiwanuka, M. S. M. *A History of Buganda*. London: Longman, 1971.

Kyakimwa K. "L'évolution de la dot chez les Banande." Mémoire de licence, Institut Supérieur Pédagogique, UNAZA-Bukavu.

Leach, Edmund. R. *Rethinking Anthropology.* Cambridge: Cambridge University Press, 1961.

Lemarchand, René. *Burundi: Ethnocide as Discourse and Practice.* New York: Cambridge University Press, 1994.

———. "Genocide in the Great Lakes: Which Genocide? Whose Genocide?" *African Studies Review* 41, no. 1 (1998): 3–16.

———. "The Politics of Penury in Rural Zaïre: The View from Bandundu." In *Zaïre: The Political Economy of Underdevelopment,* edited by Guy Gran, 237–60. New York: Praeger, 1979.

———. *Rwanda and Burundi.* London: Pall Mall, 1970.

Lestrade, A. *Notes d'ethnographie du Rwanda.* Tervuren: MRAC, 1972.

Leurquin, Philippe. *Le niveau de vie des populations rurales du Ruanda-Urundi.* Louvain: Nauwelaerts for the Institut de Recherche Economique et Sociale, 1960.

Lévi-Strauss, Claude. "The Effectiveness of Symbols." In *Structural Anthropology,* 186–205. New York: Basic Books, 1963.

———. "Four Winnebago Myths." In *The Structuralists: From Marx to Lévi-Strauss,* edited by Richard T. De George and Fernande M. De George, 195–208. New York: Doubleday Anchor, 1972.

———. "The Story of Asdiwal." In *The Structural Study of Myth and Totemism,* edited by Edmund R. Leach, 1–47. London: Tavistock, 1967.

———. *Structural Anthropology.* New York: Basic Books, 1963.

Linden, Ian, and Jane Linden. *Church and Revolution in Rwanda.* Manchester: Manchester University Press, 1977.

Louis, William Roger. *Ruanda-Urundi, 1884–1919.* Oxford: Clarendon Press, 1963.

Loupias, P. "Tradition et légende des Batutsi sur la création du monde et leur établissement au Ruanda." *Anthropos* 3, no. 1 (1908): 1–13.

Low, D. A. "The Advent of Populism in Buganda." *Comparative Studies in Society and History* 6 (1963–64): 424–44.

———. *Buganda in Modern History.* London: Weidenfeld and Nicolson, 1971.

———. "The Northern Interior, 1840–1884." In *History of East Africa,* vol. 1, edited by Roland A. Oliver and Gervase Mathew, 297–351. Oxford: Clarendon Press, 1963.

Lubigho K. "L'impact de la colonisation sur l'organisation politique traditionnelle des Wanande du Nord-Kivu: Cas de la chefferie des Batangi." Mémoire de licence, UNAZA-Lubumbashi.

Lugan, Bernard. "Causes et effets de la famine 'Rumanura' au Rwanda, 1916–1918." *Canadian Journal of African Studies* 10, no. 2 (1976): 347–56.

———. "Le commerce de traite au Rwanda sous le régime allemand (1896–1916)." *Canadian Journal of African Studies* 11, no. 2 (1977): 235–68.

———. "Échanges et routes commerciales au Rwanda, 1880–1914." *Africa-Tervuren* 22, nos. 2–4 (1976): 33–39.

———. "L'économie d'échange au Rwanda de 1850 à 1914." Thèse de doctorat de 3e cycle, Université de Provence, Aix-en-Provence, 1976.

———. *Histoire du Rwanda: De la préhistoire à nos jours.* Paris: Bartillat, 1997.

———. "Les pôles commerciaux du Lac Kivu à la fin du XIXe siècle." *Revue Française d'Histoire d'Outre-Mer* 64, no. 235 (1977): 176–202.

———. "Les réseaux commerciaux au Rwanda dans le dernier quart du XIXe siècle." *Études d'Histoire Africaine* 9–10 (1977–78): 183–212.

MacGaffey, Wyatt. "Oral Tradition in Central Africa." *International Journal of African Historical Studies* 7, no. 3 (1975): 417–26.

Mahindule Nk. "Historique de la cité de Lubero (1924–1974)." Mémoire de licence, Institut Supérieur Pédagogique, UNAZA-Bukavu.

Malikani Nd. "Le Buswaga sous le règne de Mwami Biondi." Mémoire de licence, Institut Supérieur Pédagogique, UNAZA-Bukavu.

Malkki, Lisa. "Context and Consciousness: Local Conditions for the Production of Historical and National Thought among Hutu Refugees in Tanzania." In *Nationalist Ideology and the Production of National Cultures,* edited by Richard G. Fox, 32–62. Washington, DC: American Ethnological Society, 1990.

Maquet, Jacques J. "Institutionalisation féodale des relations de dépendance." *Cahiers d'Études Africaines* 9, no. 3 (1969): 402–14.

———. "Les pasteurs de l'Itombwe." *Science et Nature* 8 (1955): 3–12.

———. *The Premise of Inequality in Ruanda: A Study of Political Relations in a Central African Kingdom.* London: Oxford University Press for the International African Institute, 1962.

———. "Rwanda Castes." In *Social Stratification in Africa,* edited by Arthur Tuden and Leonard Plotnikov, 93–124. New York: Free Press, 1970.

———. *Le système des relations sociales dans le Ruanda ancien.* Tervuren: MRAC, 1954.

Masson, Paul. *Trois siècles chez les Bashi.* Tervuren: MRAC, 1962.

Meillassoux, Claude, ed. *The Development of Indigenous Trade and Markets in West Africa.* London: Oxford University Press for the International African Institute, 1971.

———. "L'économie des échanges précoloniaux en pays Gouro." *Cahiers d'Études Africaines* 3, no. 4 (1963): 551–76.

———. *Femmes, Greniers, Capitaux.* Paris: Maspero, 1975.

———. "Social and Economic Factors Affecting Markets in Guro Land." In *Markets in Africa,* edited by Paul Bohannan and George Dalton, 279–98. Evanston: Northwestern University Press, 1962.

Meschi, Lydia [Lidia Meschy]. "Évolution des structures foncières au Rwanda: Le cas d'un lignage hutu." *Cahiers d'Études Africaines* 14, no. 1 (1974): 39–51.

Meyer, Hans. *Les Barundi: Une étude ethnologique en Afrique orientale.* Translated by Françoise Willmann. Edited by Jean-Pierre Chrétien. Paris: Société Française d'Histoire d'Outre Mer, 1984.

Middleton, John. *The Lugbara of Uganda.* New York: Holt, Rinehart and Winston, 1965.

Miller, Joseph C. "Cokwe Trade and Conquest in the Nineteenth Century." In Gray and Birmingham, *Pre-colonial African Trade,* 175–201.

———. *Kings and Kinsmen: Early Mbundu States in Angola.* Oxford: Clarendon Press, 1976.

Miracle, Marvin. "Plateau Tonga Entrepreneurs in Historical Inter-regional Trade," *Rhodes-Livingstone Journal* 26 (1960): 34–50.

Moeller de Laddersous, A. *Les grandes lignes des migrations des Bantous de la Province Orientale du Congo belge.* Brussels: IRCB, 1936.

Morris, H. F. *A History of Ankole.* Nairobi: East African Literature Bureau, 1962.

Mtoto K. "L'évolution du commerce dans le centre de Butembo (1928–1958)." Mémoire de licence, Institut Supérieur Pédagogique, UNAZA-Bukavu.

Murhebwa, L-K. "Histoire politique d'Idjwi sous les Basibula: Essai de périodisation (début XIXe S. à 1960)." Travail de fin d'études, Institut Supérieur Pédagogique, UNAZA-Bukavu, 1976.

Mworoha, Émile. "La cour du roi Mwezi Gisabo du Burundi à la fin du XIXe siècle." *Études d'Histoire Africaine* 7 (1975): 39–58.

———. *Peuples et rois de l'Afrique des lacs: Le Burundi et les royaumes voisins au XIXe siècle.* Dakar: Nouvelles éditions africaines, 1977.

Mworoha, Émile, et al., eds. *L'histoire du Burundi des origines à la fin du XIXe siècle.* Paris: Hatier, 1987.

Nahimana, Ferdinand. "Les 'bami' ou roitelets hutu du corridor Nyaborongo-Mukungwa avec ses régions limitrophes." *Études Rwandaises* 12, special issue (March 1979): 1–25.

———. *Le Blanc est arrivé; le Roi est parti: Une facette de l'histoire du Rwanda contemporain, 1894–1931.* Kigali: Éditions Printer Set, 1987.

———. "Les principautés Hutu du Rwanda septentrional." In *La civilisation ancienne des peuples des Grands Lacs: Colloque de Bujumbura (4–10 septembre 1979)*, edited by the Centre de Civilisation Burundaise, 115–37. Paris: Karthala, 1981.

———. *Le Rwanda: Émergence d'un état.* Paris: L'Harmattan, 1993.

Ndayishinguje, Pascal. *L'intronisation d'un mwami.* Nanterre: Laboratoire d'ethnologie et de sociologie comparative, 1977.

Ndikuriyo, Adrien. "Contrats de bétail, contrats de clientèle, et pouvoir politique dans le Bututsi du XIXe S." *Études d'Histoire Africaine* 7 (1975): 59–76.

Ndoricimpa, Léonidas. "Du roi fondateur au roi rebelle: Le récit du rebelle dans les traditions orales du Burundi." In *L'arbre-mémoire. Traditions orales du Burundi*, edited by Léonidas Ndoricimpa and Claude Guillet, 53–93. Paris: Karthala, 1984.

Newbury, Catharine. "The Cohesion of Oppression: A Century of Clientship in Kinyaga, Rwanda, 1860–1960." PhD diss., University of Wisconsin–Madison, 1975.

———. *The Cohesion of Oppression: Clientship and Ethnicity in Rwanda, 1860–1960.* New York: Columbia University Press, 1988.

———. "Deux lignages au Kinyaga." *Cahiers d'Études Africaines* 14, no. 1 (1974): 26–39.

———. "Ethnicity and the Politics of History in Rwanda." *Africa Today*, 45, no. 1 (1998): 7–25.

———. "Ethnicity in Rwanda: The Case of Kinyaga." *Africa* 48, no. l (1978): 17–29.

———. "Ubureetwa and Thangata: Catalysts to Peasant Political Consciousness in Rwanda and Malawi." *Canadian Journal of African Studies* 14, no. 1 (1980): 91–112.

Newbury, Catharine, and Joseph Rwabukumba. "Political Evolution in a Rwandan Frontier District: A Case Study of Kinyaga." In *Rapport annuel pour les années 1965–70*, edited by the Institut National de Recherche Scientifique, 93–119. Butare, Rwanda: INRS, 1971.

Newbury, David. "Augustinian Models in Rwanda: Religious Movements and Political Transformation." *Svensk Missionstidskrift* 3 (1995): 16–35.

———. "'Bunyabungo': The Western Frontier in Rwanda, c. 1750–1850." In *The African Frontier: The Reproduction of Traditional African Societies*, edited by Igor Kopytoff, 162–92. Bloomington: Indiana University Press, 1987.

———. "Bushi and the Historians." *History in Africa* 5 (1978): 131–51.

———. "Les campagnes de Rwabugiri: Chronologie et bibliographie." *Cahiers d'Études Africaines* 14, no. 1 (1974): 181–91.

———. "The Clans of Rwanda: An Historical Hypothesis." *Africa* 50, no. 4 (1980): 389–403.

———. "The Invention of Rwanda: The Alchemy of Ethnicity." Paper presented at the African Studies Association Annual Meeting, Orlando, 1995.

———. "Irredentist Rwanda: Ethnic and Territorial Frontiers in Central Africa." *Africa Today* 42, no. 2 (1997): 211–23.

———. "Kamo and Lubambo." MA thesis, University of Wisconsin–Madison, 1977.

———. "Kamo and Lubambo: Dual Genesis Traditions on Ijwi Island, Zaïre." *Les Cahiers du CEDAF* 5 (1979): 1–47.

———. "Kings and Clans: Ijwi Island, c. 1780–c. 1840." PhD diss., University of Wisconsin–Madison, 1979.

———. *Kings and Clans: Ijwi Island and the Lake Kivu Rift, 1780–1840.* Madison: University of Wisconsin Press, 1991.

———. "Lake Kivu Regional Trade in the Nineteenth Century." *Journal des Africanistes* 50, no. 1 (1980): 6–30.

———. "Returning Refugees: Four Historical Patterns of 'Coming Home' to Rwanda." *Comparative Studies in Society and History* 47, no. 2 (2005): 252–85.

———. "Rex and Regina: Women in Court Politics in the Western Rift Kingdoms." Paper presented to the IRSAC Seminar Series, Lwiro, Zaïre, 1972.

———. "Rwabugiri and Ijwi." *Études d'Histoire Africaine* 7 (1975): 155–73.

———. "Trick Cyclists? Recontextualising Rwandan Dynastic Chronology." *History in Africa* 21 (1994): 191–217.

Newbury, David, and Catharine Newbury. "Bringing the Peasants Back In: Agrarian Themes in the Construction and Corrosion of a Statist Historiography in Rwanda." *American Historical Review* 105, no. 3 (2000): 832–77.

———. "King and Chief: Colonial Politics on Ijwi Island (Zaïre)." *International Journal of African Historical Studies* 15, no. 2 (1982): 221–46.

Njangu Canda-Ciri. "Muzungu: L'arrivée des premiers Européens au Bushi." *Enquêtes et Documents d'Histoire Africaine* 1 (1975): 27–45.

———. "Notes sur les sources orales de la première résistance Shi." *Études d'Histoire Africaine* 7 (1975): 203–6.

———. "La résistance Shi à la pénétration européenne (1900–1920)." Mémoire de licence en histoire, UNAZA-Lubumbashi, 1973.

———. "La secte de Binji-Binji ou la renaissance de la résistance des Bashi (juillet-septembre 1931)." In *Lyangombe: Mythe et rites: Actes du 2ème colloque du CERUKI du 10 mai au 14 mai 1976,* edited by CERUKI, UNAZA-ISP, 121–28. Bukavu: Éditions du CERUKI, 1979.

Nkunzumwami, Emmanuel. *La tragédie rwandaise: Historique et perspectives.* Paris: L'Harmattan, 1996.

Nkurikiyimfura, Jean-Népomucène. *Le gros bétail et la société rwandaise: Évolution historique dès XIIe–XIVe siècles à 1958.* Paris: L'Harmattan, 1994.

———. "La révision d'une chronologie: Le cas du royaume du Rwanda." In *Sources orales de l'histoire de l'Afrique,* edited by Claude-Hélène Perrot, 149–80. Paris: Éditions du Centre national de la recherche scientifique, 1989.

Nsanze, Augustin. *Un domaine royal au Burundi: Mbuye, 1850–1945.* Paris: Société Française d'Histoire d'Outre Mer, 1980.

Ntezimana, Emmanuel. "L'arrivée des Européens au Kinyaga et la fin des royaumes Hutu du Bukunzi et du Busozo." *Études Rwandaises* 13, no. 3 (1980): 1–29.

———. "Coutumes et traditions des royaumes Hutu du Bukunzi et du Busozo." *Études Rwandaises* 13, no. 2 (1980): 15–39.

Nyagahene, Antoine. "Les activités économiques et commerciales au Kinyaga dans la séconde partie du XIXe S." Mémoire de licence, Université Nationale du Rwanda, 1979.

———. "Histoire et peuplement: Ethnies, clans, et lignages dans le Rwanda ancien et contemporain." PhD diss., Université de Paris-VII, Septentrion, 1997.

Oliver, Roland, and Gervase Mathew, eds. *History of East Africa.* London: Oxford University Press, 1963.

Olson, Jennifer M. "Farmer Responses to Land Degradation in Gikongoro, Rwanda." PhD diss., Michigan State University, 1994.

Packard, Randall. *Chiefship and Cosmology.* Bloomington: Indiana University Press, 1981.

———. "The Politics of Ritual Control among the Bashu of Eastern Zaïre during the Nineteenth Century." PhD diss., University of Wisconsin–Madison, 1976.

———. "Witchcraft: The Historical Dimension." Paper presented at the African Studies Association Annual Meeting, Baltimore, 1978.

Pagès, A. "Au Rwanda: Droits et pouvoirs des chefs sous la suzeraineté du roi hamite: Quelques abus du système." *Zaïre* 3, no. 4 (1949): 359–77.

———. *Au Rwanda: Sur les bords du Lac Kivu, Congo belge: Un royaume hamite au centre de l'Afrique.* Brussels: IRCB, 1933.

———. "Note sur le régime des biens dans la région du Bugoyi." *Congo* 19, no. 4 (1938): 392–433.

Paluku D. "Du régime foncier chez les Nande." Mémoire de licence, UNAZA-Kinshasa.

Pauwels, Marcel. "Le Bushiru et son muhinza ou roitelet Hutu." *Annali Lateranensi* 31 (1967): 205–322.

Perrot, Claude-Hélène. "Ano Asemā: Mythe et histoire." *Journal of African History* 15, no. 2 (1974): 199–222.

Pilipili Kagabo. "Contribution à la connaissance des origines du centre de Bukavu (Kivu) de 1870 à 1935." Mémoire de licence en histoire, UNAZA-Lubumbashi, 1973.

Pocock, David F. "The Anthropology of Time Reckoning." In *Myth and Cosmos,* edited by John Middleton, 303–14. Garden City, NY: Natural History Press, 1967.

Portères, Roland. "African Cereals: *Eleusine,* Fonio, Black Fonio, Teff, *Brachiaria, Paspalum, Pennisetum* and African Rice." In *The Origins of African Plant Domestication,* edited by J. Harlan, J. M. J. de Wet, and A. B. L. Stempler, 409–52. The Hague: Mouton, 1976.

———. "Berceaux agricoles primaires sur le continent africain." *Journal of African History* 3, no. 2 (1962): 195–210.

Prince de Ligne, Eugène. *Africa: L'évolution d'un continent vue des volcans du Kivu.* Brussels: Librarie Générale, 1961.

Propp, Vladimir. *Morphology of the Folktale.* Austin: University of Texas Press, 1968.

Purseglove, J. W. "The Origins and Migrations of Crops in Tropical Africa." In *Origins of African Plant Domestication,* edited by Jack R. Harlan, J. M. J. de Wet, and A. B. L. Stemler, 291–309. The Hague: Mouton, 1976.

Rank, Otto. *The Myth of the Birth of the Hero; and other Writings.* Edited by Philip Freund. New York: Vintage, 1964.

"Rapport d'enquête préalable à la construction de la Chefferie, et résumé de l'Histoire du Buhavu (Contribution Verdonck ou R. P. Feys)." White Fathers Archives, Bukavu. n.d.

Reid, D. A. M. "The Role of Cattle in the Later Iron Age Communities of Southern Uganda." PhD diss., Cambridge University, 1991.

Reining, Priscilla. "Social Factors in Food Production in an East African Peasant Society: The Haya." In *African Food Production Systems,* edited by Peter F. M. McLoughlin, 41–89. Baltimore: Johns Hopkins University Press, 1970.

Reisdorff, Ivan. *Enquêtes foncières au Rwanda.* Butare, Rwanda: INRS, 1952.

Rennie, J. Keith. "The Precolonial Kingdom of Rwanda: A Reinterpretation." *Transafrican Journal of History* 2, no. 2 (1972): 11–53.

Reyntjens, Filip. *L'Afrique des Grands Lacs en crise.* Paris: Karthala, 1994.

Richards, Audrey. *Economic Development and Tribal Change: A Study of Immigrant Labour in Buganda.* Cambridge: W. Heffer and Sons, 1956.

Roberts, Andrew D. *A History of the Bemba.* London: Longman, 1973.

———. "The Nyamwezi." In *Tanzania Before 1900,* edited by Andrew D. Roberts, 117–50. Nairobi: East African Publishing House, 1968.

———. "The Nyamwezi Trade." In Gray and Birmingham, *Pre-colonial African Trade.*

Robertshaw, Peter. "Archaeological Survey, Ceramic Analysis, and State Formation in Western Uganda." *African Archaeological Review* 12 (1994): 105–31.

Robertshaw, Peter, and David Taylor. "Climate Change and the Rise of Political Complexity in Western Uganda." *Journal of African History* 41, no. 1 (2000): 1–28.

Robins, Catherine. "Rwanda: A Case Study in Religious Assimilation." Paper presented at the Dar es Salaam Conference on the History of African Religions, 1970.

Roscoe, John. *The Banyankore.* Cambridge: Cambridge University Press, 1923.

Rugomana, J. "Inkuru y'Imuganuro uko wagira kera." Translated and annotated by F. Rodegem as "La Fête des Prémices au Burundi." *Africana Linguistica* 5 (1971): 205–54.

Ruhashya, E. *Rucunshu.* Kigali: n.p., 1984.

Rumiya, Jean. *Le Rwanda sous le régime du mandat belge.* Paris: L'Harmattan, 1992.

Rwabihigi, D. Z. "Chief Katuregye: The Man and His Times." In *A History of Kigezi,* edited by Donald Denoon, 134–56. Kampala: National Trust, 1972.

Rwabukumba, Joseph, and Vincent Mudandagizi. "Les formes historiques de la dépendance personnelle dans l'état rwandaise." *Cahiers d'Études Africaines* 14, no. 1 (1974): 6–25.

Rwankwenda, M. R. "The History of Kayonza." In *A History of Kigezi in Southwestern Uganda,* edited by Donald Denoon, 124–33. Kampala: National Trust, 1972.

Ryckmans, Pierre. *Une page d'histoire colonial: L'occupation allemande dans l'Urundi.* Brussels: ARSC, 1953.

Saruti K. "Histoire du Protestantisme au Bunande (1928–1973)." Mémoire de licence, Institut Supérieur Pédagogique, UNAZA-Bukavu.

Saucier, Jean-François. "The Patron-Client Relationship in Traditional and Contemporary Southern Rwanda." PhD diss., Columbia University, 1974.

Scaëtta, Henri. *Les famines périodiques dans le Ruanda: Contribution à l'étude des aspects biologiques du phenomène (note préliminaire).* Brussels: IRCB, 1932.

Scheub, Harold. *The Xhosa Ntsomi.* Oxford: Clarendon Press, 1975.

Schmidt, Peter. "Archaeological Views on a History of Landscape Change in East Africa." *Journal of African History* 38, no. 3 (1997): 393–421.

———. "Early Iron Age Settlements and Industrial Locales in West Lake." *Tanzania Notes and Records* 84–85 (1980): 77–94.

———. *Historical Archaeology*. Westport, CT: Greenwood Press, 1978.

———. "A New Look at Interpretations of the Early Iron Age in East Africa." *History in Africa* 2 (1975): 137–47.

Schoenbrun, David L. "Cattle Herds and Banana Gardens: The Historical Geography of the Western Great Lakes Region." *African Archaeological Review* 11 (1993): 39–72.

———. *A Green Place, a Good Place: Agrarian Change, Gender, and Social Identity in the Great Lakes Region to the Fifteenth Century*. Portsmouth, NH: Heinemann, 1998.

———. "We Are What We Eat: Ancient Agriculture between the Great Lakes." *Journal of African History* 34, no. 1 (1993): 1–31.

Scott, James. "Hegemony and the Peasantry." *Politics and Society* 7, no. 3 (1977): 267–96.

Sigwalt, Richard. "The Early History of Bushi: An Essay in the Historical Use of Genesis Traditions." PhD diss., University of Wisconsin–Madison, 1975.

———. "Early Rwanda History: The Contribution of Comparative Ethnography." *History in Africa* 2 (1975): 137–46.

Sigwalt, Richard, and Elinor Sosne. "A Note on the Luzi of Bushi." *Études d'Histoire Africaine* 7 (1975): 137–43.

Simons, E. "Coutumes et institutions des Barundi." *Bulletin des Juridictions Indigènes et du Droit Coutumier Congolais* 12, no. 7 (1944): 137–60; no. 8: 165–79; no. 9: 181–204; no. 10: 205–27; no. 11: 237–65; no. 12: 269–82.

Smith, M. G. "Exchange and Marketing among the Hausa." In *Markets in Africa*, edited by Paul Bohannan and George Dalton, 299–334. Evanston: Northwestern University Press, 1962.

———. "On Segmentary Lineage Systems." *Journal of the Royal Anthropological Institute* 86 (1956): 39–80.

Smith, Pierre. "Aspects de l'organisation des rites." In *La fonction symbolique: Essais d'anthropologie*, edited by Michel Izard, Pierre Smith, and Claude Lévi-Strauss, 139–70. Paris: Gallimard, 1979.

———. "La forge de l'intelligence." *L'Homme* 10, no. 2 (1970): 5–21.

———. "La lance d'une jeune fille." In *Échanges et communications*, vol. 2, *Mélanges offerts à Claude Lévi-Strauss*, edited by Claude Lévi-Straus, Jean Pouillon, and Pierre Maranda, 1381–1409. The Hague: Mouton, 1970.

———. *Le récit populaire au Rwanda*. Paris: Armand Colin, 1975.

Soper, Robert. Review of Francis van Noten, *Histoire archéologique du Ruanda* (Tervuren: MRAC, 1983) and Marie-Claude van Grunderbeek, Emile Roche, and Hugues Doutrelepont, *Le premier age du fer au Rwanda et au Burundi: Archéologie et environnement* (Brussels: Université Libre de Bruxelles, Center of Quaternary Stratigraphy, 1983), *Azania* 19 (1984): 148–51.

Sosne, Elinor. "Colonial Peasantization and Contemporary Underdevelopment: A View from a Kivu Village." In *Zaïre: The Political Economy of Underdevelopment*, edited by Guy Gran, 189–210. New York: Praeger, 1979.

———. "Kinship and Contract in Bushi: A Study of Village-Level Politics." PhD diss., University of Wisconsin–Madison, 1974.

———. "Of Biases and Queens: The Shi Past through an Androgynous Looking Glass." *History in Africa* 6 (1979): 225–52.

Southall, A. W. *Alur Society.* Cambridge: East African Institute of Social Research, 1956.

Southwold, Martin. "Succession to the Throne in Buganda." In *Succession to High Office,* edited by Jack Goody, 82–126. Cambridge: Cambridge University Press, 1966.

Speke, John Hanning. *Journal of the Discovery of the Source of the Nile.* Edinburgh: William Blackwood, 1863.

Spitaels, R. "Transplantation des Banyaruanda dans le Nord Kivu." *Problèmes d'Afrique Centrale* no. 20 (1953): 110–16.

Stanley, Henry Morton. *In Darkest Africa.* 2 vols. New York: Charles Scribner's Sons, 1891.

———. *Through the Dark Continent,* vol. 2. New York: Harper, 1878.

Stevens, Phillips. "The Kisra Legend and the Distortion of Historical Tradition." *Journal of African History* 14, no. 2 (1965): 185–200.

St. John, Christopher. "Kazembe and the Tanganyika-Nyasa Corridor, 1800–1890." In Gray and Birmingham, *Pre-colonial African Trade,* 202–30.

Sutton, J. E. G., and Andrew D. Roberts. "Uvinza and Its Salt Industry." *Azania* 3 (1968): 45–86.

Synge, Patrick Millington. *Mountains of the Moon: An Expedition to the Equatorial Mountains of Africa.* New York: E. P. Dutton, 1938.

Tantala, Renée Louise. "The Early History of Kitara in Western Uganda: Process Models of Religious and Political Change." PhD diss., University of Wisconsin–Madison, 1989.

Tosh, John. *Clan Leaders and Colonial Chiefs in Lango: The Political History of an East African Stateless Society, 1800–1939.* Oxford: Clarendon Press, 1978.

———. "The Northern Lacustrine Region." In Gray and Birmingham, *Pre-colonial African Trade,* 103–18.

Trouwborst, Albert A. "Le Burundi." In *Les anciens royaumes de la zone interlacustre méridionale,* edited by M. d'Hertefelt, Albert A. Trouwborst, and J. H. Scherer. Tervuren: MRAC, 1962.

———. "L'organisation politique en tant que système d'échanges au Burundi." *Anthropologica* 3, no. 1 (1961): 65–81.

———. "L'organisation politique et l'accorde de clientèle au Burundi." *Anthropologica* 4, no. 1 (1962): 9–43.

Turyahikayo-Rugyema, B. "Markets in Precolonial East Africa: The Case of the Bakiga." *Current Anthropology* 17, no. 2 (1976): 286–90.

Uzoigwe, Godfrey N. "Precolonial Markets in Bunyoro-Kitara." *Comparative Studies in Society and History* 14, no. 4 (1972): 422–55.

van Grunderbeek, Marie-Claude, Émile Roche, and Hugues Doutrelepont. "L'âge du fer ancien au Rwanda et au Burundi: Archéologie et environnement." *Journal des Africanistes* 52, nos. 1–2 (1982): 5–58.

———. *Le premier âge du fer au Rwanda et au Burundi.* Brussels: Université Libre de Bruxelles, 1983.

van Noten, Francis. "The Early Iron Age in the Interlacustrine Region: The Diffusion of Iron Technology." *Azania* 14 (1979): 61–81.

———. *Histoire archéologique du Rwanda.* Tervuren: MRAC, 1983.

———. *Les tombes du roi Cyirima Rujugira et de la reine-mère Nyirayuhi Kanjogera. Description archéologique.* Tervuren: MRAC, 1972.

Vansina, Jan. *Antecedents to Modern Rwanda: The Nyiginya Kingdom*. Madison: University of Wisconsin Press, 2004.

———. *De la tradition orale*. Tervuren: MRAC, 1961.

———. *L'évolution du royaume Rwanda dès origines à 1900*. Brussels: ARSOM, 1962.

———. "Ibitéekerezo: Historical Narratives from Rwanda" (CAMP). Center for Research Libraries, Chicago.

———. "Ibitéekerezo: Historical Narratives of Rwanda" (MRAC). On file at the Musée Royal de l'Afrique Centrale at Tervuren, Belgium. (These texts differ from those deposited at the Center for Research Libraries.)

———. *Introduction à l'ethnographie du Congo*. Kinshasa: Éditions universitaires du Congo, 1966.

———. Introduction to *Les anciens royaumes de la zone interlacustre méridionale*, by Marcel d'Hertefelt, Albert A. Trouwborst, and J. H. Scherer, 3–7. Tervuren: MRAC, 1962.

———. *La légende du passé: Traditions orales du Burundi*. Tervuren: MRAC, 1972.

———. "Notes sur l'histoire du Burundi." *Aequatoria* 24, no. 1 (1961): 1–10.

———. "Note sur la chronologie du Burundi ancien." *Bulletin de l'ARSOM* 38 (1967): 429–44.

———. *Oral Tradition: A Study in Historical Methodology*. Chicago: Aldine, 1965.

———. "The Power of Systematic Doubt in Historical Enquiry." *History in Africa* 1 (1974): 109–27.

———. *Le Rwanda ancien: Le royaume Nyiginya*. Paris: Karthala, 2001.

———. "Trade and Markets among the Kuba." In *Markets in Africa,* edited by Paul Bohannan and George Dalton, 190–210. Evanston: Northwestern University Press, 1962.

———. Review of Francis van Noten, *Histoire archéologique du Ruanda* (Tervuren: MRAC, 1983) and Marie-Claude van Grunderbeek, Emile Roche, and Hugues Doutrelepont, *Le premier age du fer au Rwanda et au Burundi. Archéologie et environnement* (Brussels: Unversité Libre de Bruxelles, Center of Quaternary Stratigraphy, 1983), *Azania* 19 (1984): 145–47.

———. Review of Francis van Noten, *Les tombes du roi Cyirima Rujugira et de la reine-mère Nyirayuhi Kanjogera* (Tervuren: MRAC, 1972) in *International Journal of African Historical Studies* 7 (1975): 528–31.

van Vracem, P. "La frontière de la Rusizi-Kivu de 1884 à 1910: Conflit Germano-Congolais et Anglo-Congolais en Afrique orientale." Thèse de doctorat, Université Officielle du Congo-Elisabethville, 1958.

Vanwalle, Rita. "Aspecten van Staatsvorming in West-Rwanda." *Africa-Tervuren* 28, no. 3 (1982): 64–77.

Viaene, L. "Historique des Bahunde." Bukavu, n.d.

———. "L'organisation politique des Bahunde." *Kongo-Overzee* 18, no. 1 (1952), 8–34; nos. 2–3, 111–21.

———. "La vie domestique des Bahunde (Nord-Est du Kivu)." *Kongo-Overzee* 12, no. 2 (1951): 111–56.

Vidal, Claudine. "Alexis Kagame entre mémoire et histoire." *History in Africa* 15 (1988): 493–504.

———. "Anthropologie et histoire: Le cas du Rwanda," *Cahiers Internationaux de Sociologie* 43, no. 2 (1967): 143–57.

————. "De la contradiction sauvage." *L'Homme* 14 (1974): 5–58.

————. "La désinformation en histoire: Données historiques sur les relations entre Hutu, Tutsi et Twa durant la période précolonial." *Dialogue,* no. 200 (September–October 1997): 11–20.

————. "Économie de la société féodale rwandaise." *Cahiers d'Études Africaines* 14, no. 1 (1974): 52–74.

————. "Questions sur le rôle des paysans durant le génocide des Rwandais Tutsi." *Cahiers d'Études Africaines* 38, nos. 2–4 (1998): 331–45.

————. "Le Rwanda des anthropologues ou le fétischisme de la vache." *Cahiers d'Études Africaines* 9, no. 3 (1969): 384–401.

————. "Situations ethniques au Rwanda." In *Au coeur de l'ethnie: Ethnies, tribalisme et état en Afrique,* edited by Jean-Loup Amselle and Elikia M'Bokolo, 167–84. Paris: La Découverte, 1985.

Vincent, Joan. "Colonial Chiefs and the Making of Class: A Case Study from Teso, Eastern Uganda." *Africa* 47, no. 2 (1977): 155–56.

Vis, Henri L., C. Yourassousky, and Henri van der Borght. *Une enquête de consommation alimentaire en République rwandaise.* Butare, Rwanda: INRS, 1972.

Wagner, Michele D. "Whose History is Is History? A History of the Baragane People of Southern Burundi, 1850–1932." PhD diss., University of Wisconsin–Madison, 1991.

Waruwene R. "Le chef traditionnel chez les Banande du Kivu." Mémoire de licence, UNAZA-Kinshasa.

Webster, J. Bertin, ed. *Chronology, Migration, and Drought in Interlacustrine Africa.* New York: Africana, 1979.

————. "Noi! Noi! Famines as an Aid to Interlacustrine Chronology." In *Chronology, Migration, and Drought in Interlacustrine Africa,* edited by J. B. Webster, 1–37. New York: Africana, 1979.

Willame, Jean-Claude. *Les provinces du Congo: Structure et fonctionnement: Lomami et Kivu central.* Cahiers économiques et sociaux, Collection d'études politiques 4. Kinshasa: Université Lovanium, 1964.

Willis, Roy G. "The Fipa." In *Tanzania before 1900,* edited by Andrew D. Roberts, 82–95. Nairobi: East African Publishing House, 1968.

————. "Traditional History and Social Structure in Ufipa." *Africa* 34, no. 4 (1964): 340–52.

Wright, Michael. *Buganda in the Heroic Age.* London: Oxford University Press, 1971.

Wrigley, Christopher C. *Kingship and State: The Buganda Dynasty.* Cambridge: Cambridge University Press, 1996.

————. "The Story of Rukidi." *Africa* 43, no. 3 (1973): 219–35.

Wymeersch, P., ed. *Liber amicorum de Marcel d'Hertefelt.* Brussels: Institut Africain, 1993.

INDEX

Page numbers in italics refer to figures, maps, or tables.